# Modern Cryptography
## Theory and Practice

# Hewlett-Packard® Professional Books

**HP-UX**

| | |
|---|---|
| Fernandez | Configuring CDE |
| Madell | Disk and File Management Tasks on HP-UX |
| Olker | Optimizing NFS Performance |
| Poniatowski | HP-UX 11i Virtual Partitions |
| Poniatowski | HP-UX 11i System Administration Handbook and Toolkit, Second Edition |
| Poniatowski | The HP-UX 11.x System Administration Handbook and Toolkit |
| Poniatowski | HP-UX 11.x System Administration "How To" Book |
| Poniatowski | HP-UX 10.x System Administration "How To" Book |
| Poniatowski | HP-UX System Administration Handbook and Toolkit |
| Poniatowski | Learning the HP-UX Operating System |
| Rehman | HP Certified: HP-UX System Administration |
| Sauers/Weygant | HP-UX Tuning and Performance |
| Weygant | Clusters for High Availability, Second Edition |
| Wong | HP-UX 11i Security |

**UNIX, LINUX, WINDOWS, AND MPE I/X**

| | |
|---|---|
| Mosberger/Eranian | IA-64 Linux Kernel |
| Poniatowski | UNIX User's Handbook, Second Edition |
| Stone/Symons | UNIX Fault Management |

**COMPUTER ARCHITECTURE**

| | |
|---|---|
| Evans/Trimper | Itanium Architecture for Programmers |
| Kane | PA-RISC 2.0 Architecture |
| Markstein | IA-64 and Elementary Functions |

**NETWORKING/COMMUNICATIONS**

| | |
|---|---|
| Blommers | Architecting Enterprise Solutions with UNIX Networking |
| Blommers | OpenView Network Node Manager |
| Blommers | Practical Planning for Network Growth |
| Brans | Mobilize Your Enterprise |
| Cook | Building Enterprise Information Architecture |
| Lucke | Designing and Implementing Computer Workgroups |
| Lund | Integrating UNIX and PC Network Operating Systems |

**SECURITY**

| | |
|---|---|
| Bruce | Security in Distributed Computing |
| Mao | Modern Cryptography: Theory and Practice |
| Pearson et al. | Trusted Computing Platforms |
| Pipkin | Halting the Hacker, Second Edition |
| Pipkin | Information Security |

**WEB/INTERNET CONCEPTS AND PROGRAMMING**

| | |
|---|---|
| Amor | E-business (R)evolution, Second Edition |
| Apte/Mehta | UDDI |
| Mowbrey/Werry | Online Communities |
| Tapadiya | .NET Programming |

## OTHER PROGRAMMING

| | |
|---|---|
| **Blinn** | Portable Shell Programming |
| **Caruso** | Power Programming in HP OpenView |
| **Chaudhri** | Object Databases in Practice |
| **Chew** | The Java/C++ Cross Reference Handbook |
| **Grady** | Practical Software Metrics for Project Management and Process Improvement |
| **Grady** | Software Metrics |
| **Grady** | Successful Software Process Improvement |
| **Lewis** | The Art and Science of Smalltalk |
| **Lichtenbelt** | Introduction to Volume Rendering |
| **Mellquist** | SNMP++ |
| **Mikkelsen** | Practical Software Configuration Management |
| **Norton** | Thread Time |
| **Tapadiya** | COM+ Programming |
| **Yuan** | Windows 2000 GDI Programming |

## STORAGE

| | |
|---|---|
| **Thornburgh** | Fibre Channel for Mass Storage |
| **Thornburgh/Schoenborn** | Storage Area Networks |
| **Todman** | Designing Data Warehouses |

## IT/IS

| | |
|---|---|
| **Missbach/Hoffman** | SAP Hardware Solutions |

## IMAGE PROCESSING

| | |
|---|---|
| **Crane** | A Simplified Approach to Image Processing |
| **Gann** | Desktop Scanners |

# Modern Cryptography
## Theory and Practice

### *Wenbo Mao*

Hewlett-Packard Company

www.hp.com/hpbooks

**PEARSON EDUCATION**
**PRENTICE HALL PROFESSIONAL TECHNICAL REFERENCE**
**UPPER SADDLE RIVER, NJ 07458**
**WWW.PHPTR.COM**

**Library of Congress Cataloging-in-Publication Data**

A CIP catalog record for this book can be obtained from the Library of Congress.

Editorial/production supervision: *Mary Sudul*
Cover design director: *Jerry Votta*
Cover design: *Talar Boorujy*
Manufacturing manager: *Maura Zaldivar*
Acquisitions editor: *Jill Harry*
Marketing manager: *Dan DePasquale*

Publisher, HP Books: *Mark Stouse*
Manager and Associate Publisher, HP Books: *Victoria Brandow*

© 2004 by Hewlett-Packard Company

PRENTICE
HALL
PTR

Published by Prentice Hall PTR
Prentice-Hall, Inc.
Upper Saddle River, New Jersey 07458

Prentice Hall books are widely used by corporations and government agencies for training, marketing, and resale.
The publisher offers discounts on this book when ordered in bulk quantities. For more information, contact Corporate Sales Department, Phone: 800-382-3419; FAX: 201-236-7141;
E-mail: corpsales@prenhall.com
Or write: Prentice Hall PTR, Corporate Sales Dept., One Lake Street, Upper Saddle River, NJ 07458.

Other product or company names mentioned herein are the trademarks or registered trademarks of their respective owners.

Printed in the United States of America

Sixth Printing

ISBN 0-13-066943-1

Pearson Education LTD.
Pearson Education Australia PTY, Limited
Pearson Education Singapore, Pte. Ltd.
Pearson Education North Asia Ltd.
Pearson Education Canada, Ltd.
Pearson Educación de Mexico, S.A. de C.V.
Pearson Education — Japan
Pearson Education Malaysia, Pte. Ltd.

To

Ronghui ∥ Yiwei ∥ Yifan

$$= (榮卉 \parallel 弋桅 \parallel 依帆) \oplus 101101110 \cdots$$

# A SHORT DESCRIPTION OF THE BOOK

Many cryptographic schemes and protocols, especially those based on public-key cryptography, have basic or so-called "textbook crypto" versions, as these versions are usually the subjects for many textbooks on cryptography. This book takes a different approach to introducing cryptography: it pays much more attention to *fit-for-application* aspects of cryptography. It explains why "textbook crypto" is only good in an ideal world where data are random and bad guys behave nicely. It reveals the general unfitness of "textbook crypto" for the real world by demonstrating numerous attacks on such schemes, protocols and systems under various real-world application scenarios. This book chooses to introduce a set of practical cryptographic schemes, protocols and systems, many of them standards or de facto ones, studies them closely, explains their working principles, discusses their practical usages, and examines their strong (i.e., fit-for-application) security properties, often with security evidence formally established. The book also includes self-contained theoretical background material that is the foundation for modern cryptography.

# PREFACE

Our society has entered an era where commerce activities, business transactions and government services have been, and more and more of them will be, conducted and offered over open computer and communications networks such as the Internet, in particular, via WorldWideWeb-based tools. Doing things online has a great advantage of an always-on availability to people in any corner of the world. Here are a few examples of things that have been, can or will be done online:

> Banking, bill payment, home shopping, stock trading, auctions, taxation, gambling, micro-payment (e.g., pay-per-downloading), electronic identity, online access to medical records, virtual private networking, secure data archival and retrieval, certified delivery of documents, fair exchange of sensitive documents, fair signing of contracts, time-stamping, notarization, voting, advertising, licensing, ticket booking, interactive games, digital libraries, digital rights management, pirate tracing, . . .

And more can be imagined.

Fascinating commerce activities, transactions and services like these are only possible if communications over open networks can be conducted in a secure manner. An effective solution to securing communications over open networks is to apply cryptography. Encryption, digital signatures, password-based user authentication, are some of the most basic cryptographic techniques for securing communications. However, as we shall witness many times in this book, there are surprising subtleties and serious security consequences in the applications of even the most basic cryptographic techniques. Moreover, for many "fancier" applications, such as many listed in the preceding paragraph, the basic cryptographic techniques are no longer adequate.

With an increasingly large demand for safeguarding communications over open networks for more and more sophisticated forms of electronic commerce, business and services[a], an increasingly large number of information security professionals

---

[a]Gartner Group forecasts that total electronic business revenues for business to business (B2B) and business to consumer (B2C) in the European Union will reach a projected US $2.6 trillion in

will be needed for designing, developing, analyzing and maintaining information security systems and cryptographic protocols. These professionals may range from IT systems administrators, information security engineers and software/hardware systems developers whose products have security requirements, to cryptographers.

In the past few years, the author, a technical consultant on information security and cryptographic systems at Hewlett-Packard Laboratories in Bristol, has witnessed the phenomenon of a progressively increased demand for information security professionals unmatched by an evident shortage of them. As a result, many engineers, who are oriented to application problems and may have little proper training in cryptography and information security have become "roll-up-sleeves" designers and developers for information security systems or cryptographic protocols. This is in spite of the fact that designing cryptographic systems and protocols is a difficult job even for an expert cryptographer.

The author's job has granted him privileged opportunities to review many information security systems and cryptographic protocols, some of them proposed and designed by "roll-up-sleeves" engineers and are for uses in serious applications. In several occasions, the author observed so-called "textbook crypto" features in such systems, which are the result of applications of cryptographic algorithms and schemes in ways they are usually introduced in many cryptographic textbooks. Direct encryption of a password (a secret number of a small magnitude) under a basic public-key encryption algorithm (e.g., "RSA") is a typical example of textbook crypto. The appearances of textbook crypto in serious applications with a "non-negligible probability" have caused a concern for the author to realize that the general danger of textbook crypto is not widely known to many people who design and develop information security systems for serious real-world applications.

Motivated by an increasing demand for information security professionals and a belief that their knowledge in cryptography should not be limited to textbook crypto, the author has written this book as a *textbook on non-textbook cryptography*. This book endeavors to:

- Introduce a wide range of cryptographic algorithms, schemes and protocols with a particular emphasis on their *non-textbook* versions.

- Reveal general insecurity of textbook crypto by demonstrating a large number of attacks on and summarizing typical attacking techniques for such systems.

- Provide principles and guidelines for the design, analysis and implementation of cryptographic systems and protocols with a focus on standards.

- Study formalism techniques and methodologies for a rigorous establishment of

---

2004 (with probability 0.7) which is a 28-fold increase from the level of 2000 [5]. Also, eMarketer (page 41 of [105]) reports that the cost to financial institutions (in USA) due to electronic identity theft was US $1.4 billion in 2002, and forecasts to grow by a compound annual growth rate of 29%.

strong and fit-for-application security notions for cryptographic systems and protocols.

- Include self-contained and elaborated material as theoretical foundations of modern cryptography for readers who desire a systematic understanding of the subject.

## Scope

Modern cryptography is a vast area of study as a result of fast advances made in the past thirty years. This book focuses on one aspect: introducing fit-for-application cryptographic schemes and protocols with their strong security properties evidently established.

The book is organized into the following six parts:

**Part I** This part contains two chapters (1—2) and serves an elementary-level introduction for the book and the areas of cryptography and information security. Chapter 1 begins with a demonstration on the effectiveness of cryptography in solving a subtle communication problem. A simple cryptographic protocol (first protocol of the book) for achieving "fair coin tossing over telephone" will be presented and discussed. This chapter then carries on to conduct a cultural and "trade" introduction to the areas of study. Chapter 2 uses a series of simple authentication protocols to manifest an unfortunate fact in the areas: pitfalls are everywhere.

As an elementary-level introduction, this part is intended for newcomers to the areas.

**Part II** This part contains four chapters (3—6) as a set of mathematical background knowledge, facts and basis to serve as a self-contained mathematical reference guide for the book. Readers who only intend to "knowhow," i.e., know how to use the fit-for-application crypto schemes and protocols, may skip this part yet still be able to follow most contents of the rest of the book. Readers who also want to "know-why," i.e., know why these schemes and protocols have strong security properties, may find that this self-contained mathematical part is a sufficient reference material. When we present working principles of cryptographic schemes and protocols, reveal insecurity for some of them and reason about security for the rest, it will always be possible for us to refer to a precise point in this part of the book for supporting mathematical foundations.

This part can also be used to conduct a systematic background study of the theoretical foundations for modern cryptography.

**Part III** This part contains four chapters (7—10) introducing the most basic cryptographic algorithms and techniques for providing privacy and data integrity protections. Chapter 7 is for symmetric encryption schemes, Chapter 8, asymmetric techniques. Chapter 9 considers an important security quality possessed by the basic and popular asymmetric cryptographic functions when they are used in an ideal world in which data are random. Finally, Chapter 10 covers data integrity techniques.

Since the schemes and techniques introduced here are the most basic ones, many of them are in fact in the textbook crypto category and are consequently *insecure*. While the schemes are introduced, abundant attacks on many schemes will be demonstrated with warning remarks explicitly stated. For practitioners who do not plan to proceed with an in-depth study of fit-for-application crypto and their strong security notions, this textbook crypto part will still provide these readers with explicit early warning signals on the general insecurity of textbook crypto.

**Part IV** This part contains three chapters (11—13) introducing an important notion in applied cryptography and information security: authentication. These chapters provide a wide coverage of the topic. Chapter 11 includes technical background, principles, a series of basic protocols and standards, common attacking tricks and prevention measures. Chapter 12 is a case study for four well-known authentication protocol systems for real world applications. Chapter 13 introduces techniques which are particularly suitable for open systems which cover up-to-date and novel techniques.

Practitioners, such as information security systems administration staff in an enterprise and software/hardware developers whose products have security consequences may find this part helpful.

**Part V** This part contains four chapters (14—17) which provide formalism and rigorous treatments for strong (i.e., fit-for-application) security notions for public-key cryptographic techniques (encryption, signature and signcryption) and formal methodologies for the analysis of authentication protocols. Chapter 14 introduces formal definitions of strong security notions. The next two chapters are fit-for-application counterparts to textbook crypto schemes introduced in Part III, with strong security properties formally established (i.e., evidently reasoned). Finally, Chapter 17 introduces formal analysis methodologies and techniques for the analysis of authentication protocols, which we have not been able to deal with in Part IV.

**Part VI** This is the final part of the book. It contains two technical chapters (18—19) and a short final remark (Chapter 20). The main technical content of this part, Chapter 18, introduces a class of cryptographic protocols called zero-knowledge protocols. These protocols provide an important security service which is needed in various "fancy" electronic commerce and business applications: verification of a claimed property of secret data (e.g., in conforming with a business requirement) while preserving a strict privacy quality for the claimant. Zero-knowledge protocols to be introduced in this part exemplify the diversity of special security needs in various real world applications, which are beyond confidentiality, integrity, authentication and non-repudiation. In the final technical chapter of the book (Chapter 19) we will complete our job which has been left over from the first protocol of the book: to realize "fair coin tossing over telephone." That final realization will achieve a protocol which has evidently-established strong security properties yet with an efficiency suitable for practical applications.

Needless to say, a description for each fit-for-application crypto scheme or protocol has to begin with a reason why the textbook crypto counterpart is unfit for application. Invariably, these reasons are demonstrated by attacks on these schemes or protocols, which, by the nature of attacks, often contain a certain degree of subtleties. In addition, a description of a fit-for-application scheme or protocol must also end at an analysis that the strong (i.e., fit-for-application) security properties do hold as claimed. Consequently, some parts of this book inevitably contain mathematical and logical reasonings, deductions and transformations in order to manifest attacks and fixes.

While admittedly fit-for-application cryptography is not a topic for quick mastery or that can be mastered via light reading, this book, nonetheless, is not one for in-depth research topics which will only be of interest to specialist cryptographers. The things reported and explained in it are well-known and quite elementary to cryptographers. The author believes that they can also be comprehended by nonspecialists if the introduction to the subject is provided with plenty of explanations and examples and is supported by self-contained mathematical background and reference material.

The book is aimed at the following readers.

- Students who have completed, or are near to completion of, first degree courses in computer, information science or applied mathematics, and plan to pursue a career in information security. For them, this book may serve as an advanced course in applied cryptography.

- Security engineers in high-tech companies who are responsible for the design and development of information security systems. If we say that the consequence of textbook crypto appearing in an academic research proposal may not be too harmful since the worst case of the consequence would be an embarrassment, then the use of textbook crypto in an information security product may lead to a serious loss. Therefore, knowing the unfitness of textbook crypto for real world applications is necessary for these readers. Moreover, these readers should have a good understanding of the security principles behind the fit-for-application schemes and protocols and so they can apply the schemes and the principles correctly. The self-contained mathematical foundations material in Part II makes the book a suitable self-teaching text for these readers.

- Information security systems administration staff in an enterprise and software/hardware systems developers whose products have security consequences. For these readers, Part I is a simple and essential course for cultural and "trade" training; Parts III and IV form a suitable cut-down set of knowledge in cryptography and information security. These three parts contain many basic crypto schemes and protocols accompanied with plenty of attacking tricks and prevention measures which should be known to and can be grasped by this population of readers without demanding them to be burdened by theoretical foundations.

- New Ph.D. candidates beginning their research in cryptography or computer security. These readers will appreciate a single-point reference book which covers formal treatment of strong security notions and elaborates these notions adequately. Such a book can help them to quickly enter into the vast area of study. For them, Parts II, IV, V and VI constitute a suitable level of literature survey material which can lead them to find further literatures, and can help them to shape and specialize their own research topics.

- A cut-down subset of the book (e.g., Part I, II, III and VI) also form a suitable course in applied cryptography for undergraduate students in computer science, information science and applied mathematics courses.

## Acknowledgements

I am deeply grateful to Feng Bao, Colin Boyd, Richard DeMillo, Steven Galbraith, Dieter Gollmann, Keith Harrison, Marcus Leech, Helger Lipmaa, Hoi-Kwong Lo, Javier Lopez, John Malone-Lee, Cary Meltzer, Christian Paquin, Kenny Paterson, David Pointcheval, Vincent Rijmen, Nigel Smart, David Soldera, Paul van Oorschot, Serge Vaudenay and Stefek Zaba. These people gave generously of their time to review chapters or the whole book and provide invaluable comments, criticisms and suggestions which make the book better.

The book also benefits from the following people answering my questions: Mihir Bellare, Jan Camenisch, Neil Dunbar, Yair Frankel, Shai Halevi, Antoine Joux, Marc Joye, Chalie Kaufman, Adrian Kent, Hugo Krawczyk, Catherine Meadows, Bill Munro, Phong Nguyen, Radia Perlman, Marco Ricca, Ronald Rivest, Steve Schneider, Victor Shoup, Igor Shparlinski and Moti Yung.

I would also like to thank Jill Harry at Prentice-Hall PTR and Susan Wright at HP Professional Books for introducing me to book writing and for the encouragement and professional support they provided during the lengthy period of manuscript writing. Thanks also to Jennifer Blackwell, Robin Carroll, Brenda Mulligan, Justin Somma and Mary Sudul at Prentice-Hall PTR and to Walter Bruce and Pat Pekary at HP Professional Books.

I am also grateful to my colleagues at Hewlett-Packard Laboratories Bristol, including David Ball, Richard Cardwell, Liqun Chen, Ian Cole, Gareth Jones, Stephen Pearson and Martin Sadler for technical and literature services and management support.

Please send suggestions and corrections to the author (`wenbo.mao@hp.com`). Many thanks! Corrections will be listed on the website for the book:

`www-uk.hpl.hp.com/people/wm/mctp.html`


Bristol, England

May 2003

# CONTENTS

# LIST OF FIGURES

# LIST OF ALGORITHMS, PROTOCOLS AND ATTACKS

# Part I

# INTRODUCTION

The first part of this book consists of two introductory chapters. They introduce us to some of the most basic concepts in cryptography and information security, to the environment in which we communicate and handle sensitive information, to several well known figures who act in that environment and the standard modus operandi of some of them who play role of bad guys, to the culture of the communities for research and development of cryptographic and information security systems, and to the fact of extreme error proneness of these systems.

As an elementary-level introduction, this part is intended for newcomers to the areas.

# Chapter 1

# BEGINNING WITH A SIMPLE COMMUNICATION GAME

We begin this book with a simple example of applying cryptography to solve a simple problem. This example of cryptographic application serves three purposes from which we will unfold the topics of this book:

- To provide an initial demonstration on the effectiveness and practicality of using cryptography for solving subtle problems in applications

- To suggest an initial hint on the foundation of cryptography

- To begin our process of establishing a required mindset for conducting the development of cryptographic systems for information security

To begin with, we shall pose a trivially simple problem and then solve it with an equally simple solution. The solution is a two-party game which is very familiar to all of us. However, we will realize that our simple game soon becomes troublesome when our game-playing parties are physically remote from each other. The physical separation of the game-playing parties eliminates the basis for the game to be played fairly. The trouble then is, the game-playing parties cannot trust the other side to play the game fairly.

The need for a fair playing of the game for remote players will "inspire" us to strengthen our simple game by protecting it with a shield of armor. Our strengthening method follows the long established idea for protecting communications over open networks: hiding information using cryptography.

After having applied cryptography and reached a quality solution to our first security problem, we shall conduct a series of discussions on the quality criteria for cryptographic systems (§1.2). The discussions will serve as a background and cultural introduction to the areas in which we research and develop technologies for protecting sensitive information.

## 1.1   A Communication Game

Here is a simple problem. Two friends, Alice and Bob[a], want to spend an evening out together, but they cannot decide whether to go to the cinema or the opera. Nevertheless, they reach an agreement to let a coin decide: playing a coin tossing game which is very familiar to all of us.

Alice holds a coin and says to Bob, "You pick a side then I will toss the coin." Bob does so and then Alice tosses the coin in the air. Then they both look to see which side of the coin landed on top. If Bob's choice is on top, Bob may decide where they go; if the other side of the coin lands on top, Alice makes the decision.

In the study of communication procedures, a multi-party-played game like this one can be given a "scientific sounding" name: protocol. A protocol is a well-defined procedure running among a plural number of participating entities. We should note the importance of the plurality of the game participants; if a procedure is executed entirely by one entity only then it is a procedure and cannot be called a protocol.

### 1.1.1   Our First Application of Cryptography

Now imagine that the two friends are trying to run this protocol over the telephone. Alice offers Bob, "You pick a side. Then I will toss the coin and tell you whether or not you have won." Of course Bob will not agree, because he cannot verify the outcome of the coin toss.

However we can add a little bit of cryptography to this protocol and turn it into a version workable over the phone. The result will become a cryptographic protocol, our first cryptographic protocol in this book! For the time being, let us just consider our "cryptography" as a mathematical function $f(x)$ which maps over the integers and has the following magic properties:

**Property 1.1:** Magic Function $f$

    I) *For every integer $x$, it is easy to compute $f(x)$ from $x$, while given any value $f(x)$ it is impossible to find any information about a pre-image $x$, e.g., whether $x$ is an odd or even number.*

---

[a]They are the most well-known figures in the area of cryptography, cryptographic protocols and information security; they will appear in most of the cryptographic protocols in this book.

---

**Protocol 1.1:** Coin Flipping Over Telephone

PREMISE
Alice and Bob have agreed:

   i) a "magic function" $f$ with properties specified in Property 1.1

   ii) an even number $x$ in $f(x)$ represents HEADS and the other case represents TAILS

($*$ Caution: due to (ii), this protocol has a weakness, see Ex 1.2 $*$)

   1. Alice picks a large random integer $x$ and computes $f(x)$;

      she reads $f(x)$ to Bob over the phone;

   2. Bob tells Alice his guess of $x$ as even or odd;

   3. Alice reads $x$ to Bob;

   4. Bob verifies $f(x)$ and sees the correctness/incorrectness of his guess.

---

*II) It impossible to find a pair of integers $(x, y)$ satisfying $x \neq y$ and $f(x) = f(y)$.*

In Property 1.1, the adjectives "easy" and "impossible" have meanings which need further explanations. Also because these words are related to a degree of difficulty, we should be clear about their quantifications. However, since for now we view the function $f$ as a magic one, it is safe for us to use these words in the way they are used in the common language. In Chapter 4 we will provide mathematical formulations for various uses of "easy" and "impossible" in this book. One important task for this book is to establish various quantitative meanings for "easy," "difficult" or even "impossible." In fact, as we will eventually see in the final technical chapter of this book (Chapter 19) that in our final realization of the coin-flipping protocol, the two uses of "impossible" for the "magic function" in Property 1.1 will have very different quantitative measures.

Suppose that the two friends have agreed on the magic function $f$. Suppose also that they have agreed that, e.g., an even number represents HEADS and an odd number represents TAILS. Now they are ready to run our first cryptographic protocol, Prot 1.1, over the phone.

It is not difficult to argue that Protocol "Coin Flipping Over Telephone" works quite well over the telephone. The following is a rudimentary "security analysis." (Warning: the reason for us to quote "security analysis" is because our analysis provided here is far from adequate.)

#### 1.1.1.1 A Rudimentary "Security Analysis"

First, from "Property II" of $f$, Alice is unable to find two different numbers $x$ and $y$, one is odd and the other even (this can be expressed as $x \neq y \pmod{2}$) such that $f(x) = f(y)$. Thus, once having read the value $f(x)$ to Bob over the phone (Step 1), Alice has committed to her choice of $x$ and cannot change her mind. That's when Alice has completed her coin flipping.

Secondly, due to "Property I" of $f$, given the value $f(x)$, Bob cannot determine whether the pre-image used by Alice is odd or even and so has to place his guess (in Step 2) as a real guess (i.e., an uneducated guess). At this point, Alice can convince Bob whether he has guessed right or wrong by revealing her pre-image $x$ (Step 3). Indeed, Bob should be convinced if his own evaluation of $f(x)$ (in Step 4) matches the value told by Alice in Step 1 and if he believes that the properties of the agreed function hold. Also, the coin-flipping is fair if $x$ is taken from an adequately large space so Bob could not have a guessing advantage, that is, some strategy that gives him a greater than 50-50 chance of winning.

We should notice that in our "security analysis" for Prot 1.1 we have made a number of simplifications and omissions. As a result, the current version of the protocol is far from a concrete realization. Some of these simplifications and omissions will be discussed in this chapter. However, necessary techniques for a proper and concrete realization of this protocol and methodologies for analyzing its security will be the main topics for the remainder of the whole book. We shall defer the proper and concrete realization of Prot 1.1 (more precisely, the "magic function" $f$) to the final technical chapter of this book (Chapter 19). There, we will be technically ready to provide a formal security analysis on the concrete realization.

### 1.1.2 An Initial Hint on Foundations of Cryptography

Although our first protocol is very simple, it indeed qualifies as a cryptographic protocol because the "magic function" the protocol uses is a fundamental ingredient for modern cryptography: **one-way function**. The two magic properties listed in Property 1.1 pose two **computationally intractable** problems, one for Alice, and the other for Bob.

From our rudimentary security analysis for Prot 1.1 we can claim that the existence of one-way function implies a possibility for secure selection of recreation venue. The following is a reasonable generalization of this claim:

*The existence of a one-way function implies the existence of a secure cryptographic system.*

It is now well understood that the converse of this claim is also true:

> *The existence of a secure cryptographic system implies the existence of a one-way function.*

It is widely believed that one-way function does exist. Therefore we are optimistic on securing our information. Our optimism is often confirmed by our everyday experience: many processes in our world, mathematical or otherwise, have a one-way property. Consider the following phenomenon in physics (though not an extremely precise analogy for mathematics): it is an easy process for a glass to fall on the floor and break into pieces while dispersing a certain amount of energy (e.g., heat, sound or even some dim light) into the surrounding environment. The reverse process, recollecting the dispersed energy and using it to reintegrate the broken pieces back into a whole glass, must be a very hard problem if not impossible. (If possible, the fully recollected energy could actually bounce the reintegrated glass back to the height where it started to fall!)

In Chapter 4 we shall see a class of mathematical functions which provide the needed one-way properties for modern cryptography.

## 1.1.3   Basis of Information Security: More than Computational Intractability

We have just claimed that information security requires certain mathematical properties. Moreover, we have further made an optimistic assertion in the converse direction: mathematical properties imply (i.e., guarantee) information security.

However, in reality, the latter statement is not unconditionally true! Security in real world applications depends on many real world issues. Let us explain this by continuing using our first protocol example.

We should point out that many important issues have not been considered in our rudimentary security analysis for Prot 1.1. In fact, Prot 1.1 itself is a much simplified specification. It has omitted some details which are important to the security services that the protocol is designed to offer. The omission has prevented us from asking several questions.

For instance, we may ask: has Alice really been forced to stick to her choice of $x$? Likewise, has Bob really been forced to stick to his even-odd guess of $x$? By "forced," we mean whether voice over telephone is sufficient for guaranteeing the strong mathematical property to take effect. We may also ask whether Alice has a good random number generator for her to acquire the random number $x$. This quality can be crucially important in a more serious application which requires making a fair decision.

All these details have been omitted from this simplified protocol specification and therefore they become hidden assumptions (more on this later). In fact, if this protocol is used for making a more serious decision, it should include some *explicit* instructions. For example, both participants may consider recording the other party's voice when the value $f(x)$ and the even/odd guess are pronounced over the phone, and replay the record in case of dispute.

Often cryptographic systems and protocols, in particular, those introduced by a textbook on cryptography, are specified with simplifications similar to the case in Protocol "Coin Flipping Over Telephone." Simplifications can help to achieve presentation clarity, especially when some agreement may be thought of as obvious. But sometimes a hidden agreement or assumption may be subtle and can be exploited to result in a surprising consequence. This is somewhat ironic to the "presentation clarity" which is originally intended by omitting some details. A violation of an assumption of a security system may allow an attack to be exploited and the consequence can be the nullification of an intended service. It is particularly difficult to notice a violation of a hidden assumption. In §1.2.5 we shall provide a discussion on the importance of explicit design and specification of cryptographic systems.

A main theme of this book is to explain that security for real world applications has many application related subtleties which must be considered seriously.

### 1.1.4   Modern Role of Cryptography: Ensuring Fair Play of Games

Cryptography was once a preserve of governments. Military and diplomatic organizations used it to keep messages secret. Nowadays, however, cryptography has a modernized role in addition to keeping secrecy of information: ensuring fair play of "games" by a much enlarged population of "game players." That is part of the reasons why we have chosen to begin this book on cryptography with a communication game.

Deciding on a recreation venue may not be seen as a serious business, and so doing it via flipping a coin over the phone can be considered as just playing a small communication game for fun. However, there are many communications "games" which must be taken much more seriously. With more and more business and e-commerce activities being and to be conducted electronically over open communications networks, many cases of our communications involve various kinds of "game playing." (In the Preface of this book we have listed various business and services examples which can be conducted or offered electronically over open networks; all of them involve some interactive actions of the participants by following a set of rules, which can be viewed as "playing communication games".) These "games" can be very important!

In general, the "players" of such "games" are physically distant from each other and they communicate over open networks which are notorious for lack of security. The physical distance combined with the lack of security may help and/or encourage some of the "game players" (some of whom can even be uninvited) to try to defeat the rule of game in some clever way. The intention for defeating the rule of game is to try to gain some unentitled advantage, such as causing disclosure of confidential information, modification of data without detection, forgery of false evidence, repudiation of an obligation, damage of accountability or trust, reduction of availability or nullification of services, and so on. The importance of our modern communications in business, in the conduct of commerce and in providing services (and many more others, such as securing missions of companies, personal information, military actions and state affairs) mean that no unentitled advantage should be gained to a player who does not conform the rule of game.

In our development of the simple "Coin-Flipping-Over-Telephone" cryptographic protocol, we have witnessed the process whereby an easy-to-sabotage communication game evolves to a cryptographic protocol and thereby offers desired security services. Our example demonstrates the effectiveness of cryptography in maintaining the order of "game playing." Indeed, the use of cryptography is an effective and the *only practical* way to ensure secure communications over open computers and communications networks. Cryptographic protocols are just communication procedures armored with the use of cryptography and thereby have protective functions designed to keep communications in good order. The endless need for securing communications for electronic commerce, business and services coupled with another need for anticipating the ceaseless temptation of "breaking the rules of the game" have resulted in the existence of many cryptographic systems and protocols, which form the subject matter of this book.

## 1.2    Criteria for Desirable Cryptographic Systems and Protocols

We should start by asking a fundamental question:

What is a good cryptographic system/protocol?

Undoubtedly this question is not easy to answer! One reason is that there are many answers to it depending on various meanings the word *good* may have. It is a main task for this book to provide comprehensive answers to this fundamental question. However, here in this first chapter we should provide a few initial answers.

### 1.2.1    Stringency of Protection Tuned to Application Needs

Let us begin with considering our first cryptographic protocol we designed in §1.1.1.

We can say that Protocol "Coin Flipping Over Telephone" is good in the sense that it is conceptually very simple. Some readers who may already be familiar with many practical one-way hash functions, such as SHA-1 (see §10.3.1), might further consider that the function $f(x)$ is also easy to implement even in a pocket calculator. For example, an output from SHA-1 is a bit string of length of 160 bits, or 20 bytes (1 byte = 8 bits); using the hexadecimal encoding scheme (see

Example 5.17) such an output can be encoded into 40 hexadecimal characters[b] and so it is just not too tedious for Alice (Bob) to read (and jot down) over the phone. Such an implementation should also be considered sufficiently secure for Alice and Bob to decide their recreation venue: if Alice wants to cheat, she faces a non-trivial difficulty in order to find $x \neq y \pmod 2$ with $f(x) = f(y)$; likewise, Bob will also have to face a non-trivial difficulty, that is, given $f(x)$, to determine whether $x$ is even or odd.

However, our judgement on the quality of Protocol "Coin Flipping Over Telephone" realized using SHA-1 is based on a level of non-seriousness that the game players expect on the consequence of the game. In many more serious applications (e.g., one which we shall discuss in §1.2.4), a fair coin-flipping primitive for cryptographic use will in general require much stronger one-way and commitment-binding properties than a practical one-way hash function, such as SHA-1, can offer. We should notice that a function with the properties specified in Property 1.1, if we take the word "impossible" literally, is a *completely secure* one-way function. Such a function is not easily implementable. Worse, even its very existence remains an open question (even though we are optimistic about the existence, see our optimistic view in §1.1.2, we shall further discuss the condition for the existence of a one-way function in Chapter 4). Therefore, for more serious applications of fair coin-flipping, practical hash functions won't be considered good; much more stringent cryptographic techniques are necessary. On the other hand, for deciding a recreation venue, use of heavyweight cryptography is clearly unnecessary or overkill.

We should point out that there are applications where a too-strong protection will even prevent an intended security service from functioning properly. For example, Rivest and Shamir propose a micropayment scheme, called MicroMint [244], which works by making use of a known deficiency in an encryption algorithm to their advantage. That payment system exploits a reasonable assumption that only a resourceful service provider (e.g., a large bank or financial institute) is able to prepare a large number of "collisions" under a practical one-way function, and do so economically. This is to say that the service provider can compute $k$ distinct numbers $(x_1, x_2, \ldots, x_k)$ satisfying

$$f(x_1) = f(x_2) = \cdots = f(x_k).$$

The numbers $x_1$, $x_2$, ..., $x_k$, are called collision under the one-way function $f$. A pair of collisions can be checked efficiently since the one-way function can be evaluated efficiently, they can be considered to have been issued by the resourceful service provider and hence can represent a certified value. The Data Encryption Standard (DES, see §7.6) is suggested as a suitable algorithm for implementing such a one-way function ([244]) and so to achieve a relatively small output space (64 binary bits). Thus, unlike in the normal cryptographic use of one-way functions

---

[b]Hexadecimal characters are those in the set $\{0, 1, 2, \ldots, 9, A, B, \ldots, F\}$ representing the 16 cases of 4-bit numbers.

where a collision almost certainly constitutes a successful attack on the system (for example, in the case of Protocol "Coin Flipping Over Telephone"), in MicroMint, collisions are used in order to enable a fancy micropayment service! Clearly, a strong one-way function with a significantly larger output space (i.e., $\gg 64$ bits, such as SHA-1 with 160 bits) will nullify this service even for a resourceful service provider (in §3.6 we will study the computational complexity for finding collisions under a hash function).

Although it is understandable that using heavyweight cryptographic technologies in the design of security systems (for example, wrapping with layers of encryption, arbitrarily using digital signatures, calling for online services from a trusted third party or even from a large number of them) may provide a better feeling that a stronger security may have been achieved (it may also ease the design job), often this feeling only provides a false sense of assurance. Reaching the point of overkill with unnecessary armor is undesirable because in so doing it is more likely to require stronger security assumptions and to result in a more complex system. A complex system can also mean an increased difficulty for security analysis (hence more likelihood to be error-prone) and secure implementation, a poorer performance, and a higher overhead cost for running and maintenance.

It is more interesting and a more challenging job to design cryptographic or security systems which use only necessary techniques while achieving adequate security protection. This is an important element for cryptographic and security systems to qualify as *good*.

## 1.2.2   Confidence in Security Based on Established "Pedigree"

How can we be confident that a cryptographic algorithm or a protocol is secure? Is it valid to say that an algorithm is secure because nobody has broken it? The answer is, unfortunately, *no*. In general, what we can say about an unbroken algorithm is merely that we do not know how to break it yet. Because in cryptography, the meaning of a broken algorithm sometimes has quantitative measures; if such a measure is missing from an unbroken algorithm, then we cannot even assert whether or not an unbroken algorithm is more secure than a known broken one.

Nevertheless, there are a few exceptions. In most cases, the task of breaking a cryptographic algorithm or a scheme boils down to solving some mathematical problems, such as to find a solution to an equation or to invert a function. These mathematical problems are considered "hard" or "intractable." A formal definition for "hard" or "intractable" will be given in Chapter 4. Here we can informally, yet safely, say that a mathematical problem is intractable if it cannot be solved by any known methods within a reasonable length of time.

There are a number of well-known intractable problems that have been frequently used as standard ingredients in modern cryptography, in particular, in public-key or asymmetric cryptography (see §8.3—§8.14). For example, in public-key cryptography, intractable problems include the integer factorization problem, the discrete logarithm problem, the Diffie-Hellman problem, and a few associated problems (we will define and discuss these problems in Chapter 8). These problems can be referred to as established "pedigree" ones because they have sustained a long history of study by generations of mathematicians and as a result, they are now trusted as really hard with a high degree of confidence.

Today, a standard technique for establishing a high degree of confidence in security of a cryptographic algorithm is to conduct a formal proof which demonstrates that an attack on the algorithm can lead to a solution to one of the accepted "pedigree" hard problems. Such a proof is an efficient mathematical transformation, or a sequence of such transformations, leading from an attack on an algorithm to a solution to a hard problem. Such an efficient transformation is called a reduction which "reduces" an attack to a solution to a hard problem. Since we are highly confident that the resultant solution to the hard problem is unlikely to exist (especially under the time cost measured by the attack and the reduction transformation), we will be able to derive a measurable confidence that the alleged attack should not exist. This way of security proof is therefore named "reduction to contradiction:" an easy solution to a hard problem.

Formally provable security, in particular under various powerful attacking model called *adaptive attacks*, forms an important criterion for cryptographic algorithms and protocols to be regarded as *good*. We shall use *fit-for-application security* to name security qualities which are established through formal and reduction-to-contradiction approach under powerful attacking models.

As an important topic of this book, we shall study fit-for-application security for many cryptographic algorithms and protocols.

## 1.2.3  Practical Efficiency

When we say that a mathematical problem is efficient or is efficiently solvable, we basically assert that the problem is solvable in time which can be measured by a polynomial in the size of the problem. A formal definition for efficiency, which will let us provide precise measures of this assertion, will be provided in Chapter 4.

Without looking into quantitative details of this assertion for the time being, we can roughly say that this assertion divides all the problems into two classes: tractable and intractable. This division plays a fundamental role in the foundations for modern cryptography: a complexity-theoretically based one. Clearly, a cryptographic algorithm must be designed such that it is tractable on the one hand and so is usable by a legitimate user, but is intractable on the other hand and so constitutes a difficult problem for a non-user or an attacker to solve.

We should however note that this assertion for solubility covers a vast span of quantitative measures. If a problem's computing time for a legitimate user is measured by a huge polynomial, then the "efficiency" is in general impractical, i.e., can have no value for a practical use. Thus, an important criterion for a cryptographic algorithm being *good* is that it should be *practically efficient* for a legitimate user. In specific, the polynomial that measures the resource cost for the user should be small (i.e., have a small degree, the degree of a polynomial will be introduced in Chapter 4).

In Chapter 14 we will discuss several pioneering works on provably strong public-key cryptosystems. These works propose public-key encryption algorithms under a common motivation that many basic versions of public-key encryption algorithms are insecure (we name those insecure schemes "textbook crypto" because most text-books in cryptography introduce them up to their basic and primitive versions; they will be introduced in Part III of this book). However, most pioneering works on provably strong public-key cryptosystems resort to a bit-by-bit encryption method, [127, 212, 243], some even take extraordinary steps of adding proofs of knowledge on the correct encryption of each individual bit [212] plus using public-key authentication framework [243]. While these early pioneering works are important in providing insights to achieve strong security, the systems they propose are in general too inefficient for applications. After Chapter 14, we will further study a series of subsequent works following the pioneering ones on probably strongly secure public-key cryptosystems and digital signature schemes. The cryptographic schemes proposed by these latter works propose have not only strong security, but also practical efficiency. They are indeed very good cryptographic schemes.

A cryptographic protocol is not only an algorithm, it is also a communication procedure which involves transmitting of messages over computer networks between different protocol participants under a set of agreed rules. So a protocol has a further dimension for efficiency measure: the number of communication interactions which are often called communication rounds. Usually a step of communication is regarded to be more costly than a step of local computation (typically an execution of a set of computer instructions, e.g. a multiplication of two numbers on a computing device). Therefore it is desirable that a cryptographic protocol should have few communication rounds. The standard efficiency criterion for declaring an algorithm as being efficient is if its running time is bounded by a small polynomial in the size of the problem. If we apply this efficiency criterion to a protocol, then an efficient protocol should have its number of communication rounds bounded by a polynomial of an *extremely* small degree: a constant (degree 0) or at most a linear (degree 1) function. A protocol with communication rounds exceeding a linear function should not be regarded as practically efficient, that is, no *good* for any practical use.

In §18.2.3 we will discuss some zero-knowledge proof protocols which have communication rounds measured by non-linear polynomials. We should note that those protocols were not proposed for real applications; instead, they have importance in the theory of cryptography and computational complexity. In Chapter 18 we will witness much research effort for designing practically efficient zero-knowledge protocols.

## 1.2.4    Use of Practical and Available Primitives and Services

A level of security which is good for one application needn't be good enough for another. Again, let us use our coin-flipping protocol as an example. In §1.2.1 we have agreed that, if implemented with the use of a practical one-way hash function, Protocol "Coin Flipping Over Telephone" is good enough for Alice and Bob to decide their recreation venue over the phone. However, in many cryptographic applications of a fair coin-flipping primitive, security services against cheating and/or for fairness are at much more stringent levels; in some applications the stringency must be in an absolute sense.

For example, in Chapter 18 we will discuss a zero-knowledge proof protocol which needs random bit string input and such random input must be mutually trusted by both proving/verification parties, or else serious damages will occur to one or both parties. In such zero-knowledge proof protocols, if the two communication parties do not have access to, or do not trust, a third-party-based service for supplying random numbers (such a service is usually nicknamed "random numbers from the sky" to imply its impracticality) then they have to generate their mutually trusted random numbers, bit-by-bit via a fair coin-flipping protocol. Notice that here the need for the randomness to be generated in a bit-by-bit (i.e., via fair coin-flipping) manner is in order to satisfy certain requirements, such as the correctness and zero-knowledge-ness of the protocol. In such a situation, a level of practically good (e.g., in the sense of using a practical hash function in Protocol "Coin Flipping Over Telephone") is most likely to be inadequate.

A challenging task in applied research on cryptography and cryptographic protocols is to build high quality security services from *practical* and *available* cryptographic primitives. Once more, let us use a coin-flipping protocol to make this point clear. The protocol is a remote coin-flipping protocol proposed by Blum [44]. Blum's protocol employs a *practically secure* and *easily implementable* "one-way" function but achieves a high-quality security in a *very strong* fashion which can be expressed as:

- First, it achieves a quantitative measure on the difficulty against the coin flipping party (e.g., Alice) for cheating, i.e., for preparing a pair of collision $x \neq y$ satisfying $f(x) = f(y)$. Here, the difficulty is quantified by that for factoring a large composite integer, i.e., that for solving a "pedigree" hard problem.

- Second, there is *absolutely no way* for the guessing party to have a guessing strategy biased away from the 50-50 chance. This is in terms of a complete security.

Thus, Blum's coin-flipping protocol is *particularly good* in the sense of having achieved a strong security while using only practical cryptographic primitives. As a strengthening and concrete realization for our first cryptographic protocol, we will describe Blum's coin-flipping protocol as the final cryptographic protocol of this book.

Several years after the discovery of public-key cryptography [98, 99, 248], it became gradually apparent that several basic and best-known public-key encryption algorithms (we will refer to them as "textbook crypto") generally have two kinds of weakness: (i) they leak partial information about the message encrypted; (ii) they are extremely vulnerable to active attacks (see Chapter 14). These weaknesses mean that "textbook crypto" are not fit for applications. Early approaches to a general fix for the weaknesses in "textbook crypto" invariantly apply bit-by-bit style of encryption and even apply zero-knowledge proof technique at bit-by-bit level as a means to prevent active attacks, plus authentication framework. These results, while valuable in the development of provably secure public-key encryption algorithms, are not suitable for most encryption applications since the need for zero-knowledge proof or for authentication framework is not practical for the case of encryption algorithms.

Since the successful initial work of using a randomized padding scheme in the strengthening of a public key encryption algorithm [25], a general approach emerges which strengthens popular textbook public-key encryption algorithms into ones with provable security by using popular primitives such as hash functions and pseudo-random number generators. These strengthened encryption schemes are practical since they use practical primitives such as hash functions, and consequently their efficiency is similar to the underlying "textbook crypto" counterparts. Due to this important quality element, some of these algorithms enhanced from using practical and popular primitives become public-key encryption and digital signature standards. We shall study several such schemes in Chapters 15 and 16.

Designing cryptographic schemes, protocols and security systems using available and popular techniques and primitives is also desirable in the sense that such results are more likely to be secure as they attract a wider interest for public scrutiny.

## 1.2.5   Explicitness

In the late 1960's, software systems grew very large and complex. Computer programmers began to experience a crisis, the so-called "software crisis." Large and complex software systems were getting more and more error prone, and the cost of debugging a program became far in excess of the cost of the program design and development. Soon computer scientists discovered a few perpetrators who helped to set-up the crisis which resulted from bad programming practice. Bad programming practice includes:

- Arbitrary use of the GOTO statement (jumping up and down seems very convenient)

- Abundant use of global variables (causing uncontrolled change of their values, e.g., in an unexpected execution of a subroutine)

- The use of variables without declaration of their types (implicit types can be used in Fortran, so, for example, a real value may be truncated to an integer one without being noticed by the programmer)

- Unstructured and unorganized large chunk of codes for many tasks (can be thousands of lines a piece)

- Few commentary lines (since they don't execute!)

These were a few "convenient" things for a programmer to do, but had proved to be capable of causing great difficulties in program debugging, maintenance and further development. Software codes designed with these "convenient" features can be just too obscure to be comprehensible and maintained. Back then it was not uncommon that a programmer would not be able to to understand a piece of code s/he had written merely a couple of months or even weeks ago.

Once the disastrous consequences resulting from the bad programming practice were being gradually understood, *Program Design Methodology* became a subject of study in which *being explicit* became an important principle for programming. Being explicit includes limiting the use of GOTO and global variables (better not to use them at all), explicit (via mandatory) type declaration for any variables, which permits a compiler to check type flaws systematically and automatically, modularizing programming (dividing a large program into many smaller parts, each for one task), and using abundant (as clear as possible) commentary material which are texts inside a program and documentation outside.

A security system (cryptographic algorithm or protocol) includes program parts implemented in software and/or hardware, and in the case of protocol, the program parts run on a number of separate hosts (or a number of programs concurrently and interactively running on these hosts). The explicitness principle for software engineering applies to a security system's design by default (this is true in particular for protocols). However, because a security system is assumed to run in a hostile environment in which even a legitimate user may be malicious, a designer of such systems must also be explicit about many additional things. Here we list three important aspects to serve as general guidelines for security system designers and implementors. (In the rest of the book we will see many attacks on algorithms and protocols due to being implicit in design or specification of these systems.)

1. **Be explicit about all assumptions needed.**

   A security system operates by interacting with an environment and therefore it has a set of requirements which must be satisfied by that environment. These requirements are called assumptions (or premises) for a system to run. A violation of an assumption of a protocol may allow the possibility of exploiting an attack on the system and the consequence can be the nullification of some intended services. It is particularly difficult to notice a violation of an assumption which has not been clearly specified (a hidden assumption). Therefore all assumptions of a security system should be made explicit.

For example, it is quite common that a protocol has an implicit assumption or expectation that a computer host upon which the protocol runs can supply good random numbers, but in reality few desktop machines or hand-held devices are capable of satisfying this assumption. A so-called low-entropy attack is applicable to protocols using a poor random source. A widely publicized attack on an early implementation of the Secure Sockets Layer (SSL) Protocol (an authentication protocol for World Wide Web browser and server, see §12.5) is a well-known example of the low-entropy attack [125].

Explicit identification and specification of assumptions can also help the analysis of complex systems. DeMillo et al. (Chapter 4 of [92]), DeMillo and Merritt [93] suggest a two-step approach to cryptographic protocol design and analysis, which are listed below (after a modification by Moore [206, 207]):

i) Identify **all** assumptions made in the protocol.

ii) For each assumption in step (i), determine the effect on the security of the protocol if that assumption were violated.

2. **Be explicit about exact security services to be offered.**

A cryptographic algorithm/protocol provides certain security services. Examples of some important security services include: confidentiality (a message cannot be comprehended by a non-recipient), authentication (a message can be recognized to confirm its integrity or its origin), non-repudiation (impossibility for one to deny a connection to a message), proof of knowledge (demonstration of evidence without disclosing it), and commitment (e.g., a service offered to our first cryptographic protocol "Coin Flipping Over Telephone" in which Alice is forced to stick to a string without being able to change).

When designing a cryptographic protocol, the designer should be very clear regarding exactly what services the protocol intends to serve and should explicitly specify them as well. The explicit identification and specification will not only help the designer to choose correct cryptographic primitives or algorithms, but also help an implementor to correctly implement the protocol. Often, an identification of services to the refinement level of the general services given in these examples is not adequate, and further refinement of them is necessary. Here are a few possible ways to further refine some of them:

Confidentiality      $\Rightarrow$ privacy, anonymity, invisibility, indistinguishability

Authentication      $\Rightarrow$ data-origin, data-integrity, peer-entity

Non-repudiation     $\Rightarrow$ message-issuance, message-receipt

Proof of knowledge $\Rightarrow$ knowledge possession, knowledge structure

A misidentification of services in a protocol design can cause misuse of crypto-graphic primitives, and the consequence can be a security flaw in the protocol. In Chapter 2 and Chapter 11 we will see disastrous examples of security flaws in authentication protocols due to misidentification of security services be-tween confidentiality and authentication.

There can be many more kinds of security services with more ad hoc names (e.g., message freshness, non-malleability, forward secrecy, perfect zero-know-ledge, fairness, binding, deniability, receipt freeness, and so on). These may be considered as derivatives or further refinement from the general services that we have listed earlier (a derivative can be in terms of negation, e.g., de-niability is a negative derivative from non-repudiation). Nevertheless, explicit identification of them is often necessary in order to avoid design flaws.

3. **Be explicit about special cases in mathematics.**

As we have discussed in §1.2.2, some hard problems in computational com-plexity theory can provide a high confidence in the security of a cryptographic algorithm or protocol. However, often a hard problem has some special cases which are not hard at all. For example, we know that the problem of fac-torization of a large composite integer is in general very hard. However the factorization of a *large* composite integer $N = PQ$ where $Q$ is the next prime number of a *large* prime number $P$ is not a hard problem at all! One can do so efficiently by computing $\lfloor \sqrt{N} \rfloor$ ($\lfloor \cdot \rfloor$ is called the floor function and denotes the integer part of $\cdot$ ) and followed by a few trial divisions around that number to pinpoint $P$ and $Q$.

Usual algebraic structures upon which cryptographic algorithms work (such as groups, rings and fields, to be studied in Chapter 5) contain special cases which produce exceptionally easy problems. Elements of small multiplica-tive orders (also defined in Chapter 5) in a multiplicative group or a finite field provide such an example; an extreme case of this is when the base for the Diffie-Hellman key exchange protocol (see §8.3) is the unity element in these algebraic structures. Weak cases of elliptic curves, e.g., "supersingu-lar curves" and "anomalous curves," form another example. The discrete logarithm problem on "supersingular curves" can be reduced to the discrete logarithm problem on a finite field, known as the Menezes-Okamoto-Vanstone attack [199] (see §13.3.4.1). An "anomalous curve" is one with the number of points on it being equal to the size of the underlying field, which allows a polynomial time solution to the discrete logarithm problem on the curve, known as the attack of Satoh-Araki [254], Semaev [260] and Smart [280].

An easy special case, if not understood by an algorithm/protocol designer and/or not clearly specified in an algorithm/protocol specification, may easily go into an implementation and can thus be exploited by an attacker. So an algorithm/protocol designer must be aware of the special cases in mathematics, and should explicitly specify the procedures for the implementor to eliminate such cases.

It is not difficult to list many more items for explicitness (for example, a key-management protocol should stipulate explicitly the key-management rules, such as separation of keys for different usages, and the procedures for proper key disposal, etc.). Due to the specific nature of these items we cannot list all of them here. However, explicitness as a general principle for cryptographic algorithm/protocol design and specification will be frequently raised in the rest of the book. In general, the more explicitly an algorithm/protocol is designed and specified, the easier it is for the algorithm/protocol to be analyzed; therefore the more likely it is for the algorithm/protocol to be correctly implemented, and the less likely it is for the algorithm/protocol to suffer an unexpected attack.

## 1.2.6   Openness

Cryptography was once a preserve of governments. Military and diplomatic organizations used it to keep messages secret. In those days, most cryptographic research was conducted behind closed doors; algorithms and protocols were secrets. Indeed, governments did, and they still do, have a valid point in keeping their cryptographic research activities secret. Let us imagine that a government agency publishes a cipher. We should only consider the case that the cipher published is provably secure; otherwise the publication can be too dangerous and may actually end up causing embarrassment to the government. Then other governments may use the provably secure cipher and consequently undermine the effectiveness of the code-breakers of the government which published the cipher.

Nowadays, however, cryptographic mechanisms have been incorporated in a wide range of civilian systems (we have provided a non-exhaustive list of applications in the very beginning of this chapter). Cryptographic research for civilian use should take an open approach. Cryptographic algorithms do use secrets, but these secrets should be confined to the cryptographic keys or keying material (such as passwords or PINs); the algorithms themselves should be made public. Let's explore the reasons for this stipulation.

In any area of study, quality research depends on the open exchange of ideas via conference presentations and publications in scholarly journals. However, in the areas of cryptographic algorithms, protocols and security systems, open research is more than just a common means to acquire and advance knowledge. An important function of open research is public expert examination. Cryptographic algorithms, protocols and security systems have been notoriously error prone. Once a cryptographic research result is made public it can be examined by a large number of experts. Then the opportunity for finding errors (in design or maybe in security analysis) which may have been overlooked by the designers will be greatly increased. In contrast, if an algorithm is designed and developed in secret, then in order to keep the secret, only few, if any, experts can have access to and examine the details. As a result the chance for finding errors is decreased. A worse scenario can be that a designer may know an error and may exploit it secretly.

It is now an established principle that cryptographic algorithms, protocols, and security systems for civilian use must be made public, and must go through a lengthy public examination process. Peer review of a security system should be conducted by a hostile expert.

## 1.3   Chapter Summary

In this chapter we began with an easy example of applied cryptography. The three purposes served by the example are:

i) Showing the effectiveness of cryptography in problem solving

ii) Aiming for a fundamental understanding of cryptography

iii) Emphasizing the importance of non-textbook aspects of security

They form the main topics to be developed in the rest of this book.

We then conducted a series of discussions which served the purpose for an initial background and cultural introduction to the areas of study. Our discussions in these directions are by no means of complete. Several other authors have also conducted extensive study on principles, guidelines and culture for the areas of cryptography and information security. The following books form good further reading material: Schneier [256], Gollmann [131] and Anderson [14]. Schneier's monthly distributed "Crypto-Gram Newsletters" are also good reading material. To subscribe for receiving the newsletters, send an email to `schneier@counterpane.com`.

## Exercises

1.1 What is the difference between a protocol and an algorithm?

1.2 In Prot 1.1 Alice can decide HEADS or TAILS. This may be an unfair advantage for some applications. Modify the protocol so that Alice can no longer have this advantage.

Hint: let a correct guess decide the side.

1.3 Let function $f$ map from the space of 200-bit integers to that of 100-bit ones with the following mapping rule:

$$f(x) \overset{\text{def}}{=} \text{(the most significant 100 bits of } x) \oplus$$
$$\text{(the least significant 100 bits of } x)$$

here "$\oplus$" denotes bit-by-bit XOR operation, i.e.,

$$a \oplus b = \begin{cases} 0 & \text{if } a = b \\ 1 & \text{otherwise} \end{cases}$$

   i) Is $f$ efficient?

   ii) Does $f$ have the "Magic Property I"?

   iii) Does $f$ have the "Magic Property II"?

   iv) Can this function be used in Prot 1.1?

1.4 Is an unbroken cryptographic algorithm more secure than a known broken one? If not, why?

1.5 Complex systems are error-prone. Give an additional reason for a complex security system to be even more error-prone.

# Chapter 2

# WRESTLING BETWEEN SAFEGUARD AND ATTACK

## 2.1  Introduction

One reason for the existence of many cryptographic protocols is the consequence of a fact: it is very difficult to make cryptographic protocols correct. Endless endeavors have been made to design correct protocols. Many new protocols were proposed as a result of fixing existing ones in which security flaws were discovered. A security flaw in a cryptographic protocol can always be described by an attack scenario in which some security services that the protocol purports to provide can be sabotaged by an attacker or by a number of them via their collusion. In the area of cryptographic protocols it is as if there is a permanent wrestling between protocol designers and attackers: A protocol is proposed, an attack is discovered, a fix follows, then another attack, and another fix ...

In this chapter we shall demonstrate a series of examples of a wrestling battle between attack and fix. We shall start from an artificial protocol which is made flawed deliberately. From that protocol we will go through a "fix, attack, fix again and attack again" process. Eventually we will reach two protocols which have been proposed for solving information security problems in the real world (all of the flawed and "fixed" then broken protocols prior to these two final results are artificial protocols). The two real protocol results from our "attack, fix, attack, fix, ..." process are not only real protocols, but also well-known ones for two reasons. They have played seminal roles both in applications and in underlying an important study on formal analysis of cryptographic protocols.

Unfortunately, these two real protocols from our fixing attempts still contain security flaws which were only discovered *long* after their publication. One flaw in one of them was found three years after the publication, and another flaw in the other protocol was exposed after another fourteen years passed! Having revealed these flaws, we will make a final attempt for fixing, although we will delay the revelation of some further security problems in the result from our final fixation to a later chapter when we become technically better prepared to deal with the problems. Leaving security problems unsolved in this chapter, we intend this chapter to serve an "early-warning" message: cryptographic algorithms, protocols and systems readily contain security flaws.

This chapter also serves a technical introduction to material and ideas that will enable us (in particular, readers who are new to the areas of cryptography, cryptographic protocols and information security) to establish some common and important concepts, definitions and agreements in the areas of study. These include some basic terminologies and the meanings behind them (a term appearing for the first time will be in **bold** form), and the naming convention for the protocol participants whom we will frequently be meeting throughout the book. Also, the attacks on these flawed protocols will let us become familiar with some typical behavior of a special role in our game play: the enemy, against whom we design cryptographic protocols.

### 2.1.1   Chapter Outline

In §2.2 we introduce a simplified notion of encryption which will be used for this chapter only. In §2.3—§2.5 we introduce the standard threat model, environment and goal for cryptographic, in particular authentication, protocols. Finally, in §2.6 we develop a series of authentication protocols.

## 2.2   Encryption

All protocols to be designed in this chapter will use **encryption**. We should provide an early warning on this "one-thing-for-all-purpose" style of using encryption: in many cases such uses are incorrect and some other cryptographic primitives should be used instead. In this book we will gradually develop the sense of precisely using cryptographic primitives for obtaining precise security services. However, to ease our introduction, let us rely on encryption solely in this chapter.

Encryption (sometimes called **encipherment**) is a process to transform a piece of information into an incomprehensible form. The input to the transformation is called **plaintext (or cleartext)** and the output from it is called **ciphertext (or cryptogram)**. The reverse process of transforming ciphertext into plaintext is called **decryption (or decipherment)**. Notice that plaintext and ciphertext are a pair of respective notions: the former refers to messages input to, and the latter,

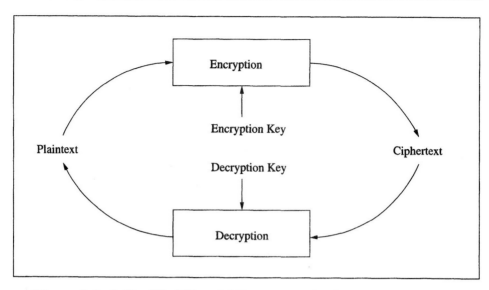

**Figure 2.1.** A Simplified Pictorial Description of a Cryptographic System

output from, an encryption algorithm. Plaintext needn't be in a comprehensible form; for example, in the case of double encryption, a ciphertext can be in the position of a plaintext for re-encryption; we will also see many times in this chapter that encryption of random number is very common in cryptographic protocols. Usually, cleartext means messages in a small subset of all possible messages which have certain recognizable distributions. In §3.7 we will study the distribution of a message.

The encryption and decryption algorithms are collectively called **cryptographic algorithms** (**cryptographic systems** or **cryptosystems**). Both encryption and decryption processes are controlled by a cryptographic **key**, or keys. In a **symmetric** (or **shared-key**) cryptosystem, encryption and decryption use the same (or essentially the same) key; in an **asymmetric** (or **public-key**) cryptosystem, encryption and decryption use two different keys: an **encryption key** and a (**matching**) **decryption key**, and the encryption key can be made public (and hence is also called **public key**) without causing the matching decryption key being discovered (and thus a decryption key in a public-key cryptosystem is also called a **private key**). Fig 2.1 illustrates a simplified pictorial description of a cryptographic system. A more complete view of a cryptosystem will be given in Chapter 7 (Fig 7.1).

We should point out that, within the scope of this chapter, the terms "plaintext," "ciphertext," "encryption," "decryption," "encryption key" and "decryption key" are pairs of relative notions. For a message $M$ (whether it is plaintext or ciphertext), a crypto algorithm $A$ (whether it represents encryption or decryption) and a cryptographic key $K$ (whether an encryption key or a decryption key), we may denote by

$$M' = A(K, M),$$

a **cryptographic transformation** which is represented by the functionality of either the upper box or the lower box in Fig 2.1. Thus, we can use $A'$ and $K'$ to denote

$$M = A'(K', M'),$$

namely,

$$M = A'(K', A(K, M))$$

completes the circle in Fig 2.1. In the case of symmetric cryptosystem, we may view $K' = K$, and in the case of asymmetric cryptosystem, $K'$ represents the matching public or private component of $K$. In this chapter ciphertext in a protocol message will be conventionally specified as

$$\{M\}_K.$$

Later when we have learned probability distributions of messages (to be introduced in §3.7–§3.8), we will know that plaintext (more precisely, cleartext or comprehensible) messages are in a small subset of the entire message space, while ciphertext messages are much more widely distributed in that space. This is the essential difference between plaintext and ciphertext.

We should notice that, in this chapter, our notation for ciphertext always means a result of using a "perfect" cryptographic algorithm in the following two senses:

**Property 2.1:** Perfect Encryption with Notation $\{M\}_K$

i) *Without the key $K$ (in the case of a symmetric cryptosystem), or the matching private key of $K$ (in the case of an asymmetric cryptosystem), the ciphertext $\{M\}_K$ does not provide any cryptanalytic means for finding the plaintext message $M$.*

ii) *The ciphertext $\{M\}_K$ and maybe together with some known information about the plaintext message $M$ do not provide any cryptanalytic means for finding the key $K$ (in the case of a symmetric cryptosystem), or the matching private key of $K$ (in the case of an asymmetric cryptosystem).*

Perfect encryption with these two properties (there will be an additional property which we shall discuss in §2.6.3) is an idealization from the encryption algorithms that exist in the real world. The idealization is a convenient treatment which allows a segregation of responsibilities of the protocol design and analysis from those of the underlying cryptographic algorithm design and analysis. The segregation eases the job of protocol design and analysis. We shall see in a moment that perfect encryption does not prevent a protocol from containing a security flaw. In fact, for every attack on each protocol to be demonstrated in this chapter, none of them depends on any deficiency in the underlying cryptosystems.

We will introduce the formal notion of encryption and number of encryption algorithms in several later chapters (Chapters 7, 8, 13 and 15). Nevertheless the abstract-level description on the functionality of encryption/decryption given here shall suffice for our use in this chapter. It is harmless now for us to think of an encryption algorithm as a keyed padlock and a piece of ciphertext as a box of texts with the box being padlocked.

The reader is also referred to [268] for a useful glossary in information security.

## 2.3 Vulnerable Environment (the Dolev-Yao Threat Model)

A large network of computers, devices and resources (for example, the Internet) is typically open, which means that a **principal** (or **entity**, **agent**, **user**), which can be a computer, a device, a resource, a service provider, a person or an organization of these things, can join such a network and start sending and receiving messages to and from other principals across it, without a need of being authorized by a "super" principal. In such an open environment we must anticipate that there are **bad guys** (or **attacker**, **adversary**, **enemy**, **intruder**, **eavesdropper**, **impostor**, etc.) out there who will do all sorts of bad things, not just passively eavesdropping, but also actively altering (maybe using some unknown calculations or methods), forging, duplicating, rerouting, deleting or injecting messages. The injected messages can be malicious and cause a destructive effect to the principals on the receiving end. In the literature of cryptography such a bad guy is called an **active attacker**. In this book we shall name an attacker **Malice** (someone who does harm or mischief, and often does so under the masquerade of a different identity). Malice can be an individual, a coalition of a group of attackers, and, as a special case, a legitimate principal in a protocol (an **insider**).

In general, it is assumed that Malice is very clever in manipulating communications over the open network. His manipulation techniques are unpredictable because they are unspecified. Also because Malice can represent a coalition of bad guys, he may simultaneously control a number of network nodes which are geographically far apart. The real reason why Malice can do these things will be discussed in §12.2.

In anticipation of such a powerful adversary over such a vulnerable environment, Dolev and Yao propose a **threat model** which has been widely accepted as the standard threat model for cryptographic protocols [102]. In that model, Malice has the following characteristics:

- He can obtain any message passing through the network.

- He is a legitimate user of the network, and thus in particular can initiate a conversation with any other user.

- He will have the opportunity to become a receiver to any principal.

- He can send messages to any principal by impersonating any other principal.

Thus, in the **Dolev-Yao threat model**, any message sent to the network is considered to be sent to Malice for his disposal (according to whatever he is able to compute). Consequently, any message received from the network is treated to have been received from Malice after his disposal. In other words, Malice is considered to have the complete control of the entire network. In fact, it is harmless to just think of the open network as Malice.

However, unless explicitly stated, we do not consider Malice to be *all powerful*. This means that there are certain things that Malice cannot do, even in the case that he represents a coalition of bad guys and thereby may use a large number of computers across the open network in parallel. We list below a few things Malice cannot do without quantifying the meaning of "cannot do;" precise quantification will be made in Chapter 4:

- Malice cannot guess a random number which is chosen from a sufficiently large space.

- Without the correct secret (or private) key, Malice cannot retrieve plaintext from given ciphertext, and cannot create valid ciphertext from given plaintext, with respect to the perfect encryption algorithm.

- Malice cannot find the private component, i.e., the private key, matching a given public key.

- While Malice may have control of a large public part of our computing and communication environment, in general, he is not in control of many private areas of the computing environment, such as accessing the memory of a principal's offline computing device.

The Dolev-Yao threat model will apply to all our protocols.

## 2.4  Authentication Servers

Suppose that two principals **Alice** and **Bob** (whom we have already met in our first cryptographic protocol "Coin Flipping Over Telephone", Prot 1.1) wish to communicate with each other in a secure manner. Suppose also that Alice and Bob have never met before, and therefore they do not already share a secret key between them and do not already know for sure the other party's public key. Then how can they communicate securely over completely insecure networks?

It is straightforward to see that at least Alice and Bob can make an arrangement to meet each other physically and thereby establish a shared secret key between them, or exchange sure knowledge on the other party's public key. However, in a system with $N$ users who wish to hold private conversations, how many trips do these users need to make in order to securely establish these keys? The answer is $N(N-1)/2$. Unfortunately, this means a prohibitive cost for a large system. So this straightforward way for secure key establishment is not practical for use in modern communication systems.

It is nevertheless feasible for each principal who chooses to communicate securely to obtain an **authentication** (and a **directory**) service. Needham and Schroeder suggest that such a service can be provided by an **authentication server** [215]. Such a server is like a name registration authority; it maintains a database indexed by names of the principals it serves, and can deliver identifying information computed from a requested principal's cryptographic key that is already shared between the server and the principal.

An authentication server is a special principal who has to be trusted by its users (**client principals**) to always behave honestly. Namely, upon a client principal's request it will respond exactly according to the protocol's specification, and will not engage in any other activity which will deliberately compromise the security of its clients (so, for instance, it will never disclose any secret key it shares with its clients to any third party). Such a principal is called a **trusted third party** or **TTP** for short. In this book we shall use **Trent** to name a trusted third party.

We suppose that both Alice and Bob use authentication services offered by their respective authentication servers. In an extended network it is inexpedient to have a single central authentication server. Needham and Schroeder proposed to use multiple authentication servers who know each other. Thus, principals served by an authentication server have names of the form "AuthenticationAuthority.SimpleName." The idea of using multiple authentication servers has also been proposed by Diffie and Hellman [98].

However, in order to describe our protocols in this chapter with simplicity and clarity we suppose that Alice and Bob use the same authentication server Trent. In Chapter 12 we will introduce the network authentication basis for Windows 2000 operating system, the Kerberos authentication protocol [91], where a general architecture of multiple authentication servers serving in different network realms will be considered.

Being served by the same Trent, we assume that Alice (Bob) shares a cryptographic key with Trent; let the key be denoted by $K_{AT}$ ($K_{BT}$). Later we shall see that such a key is called **key-encryption key** because its use is mainly for encryption of other cryptographic keys. Also due to the high cost in the establishment of such a key, it should be used for a prolonged period of time, and hence is also called a **long-term key**.

## 2.5   Security Properties for Authenticated Key Establishment

All protocols to be described in this chapter are of a kind: they achieve **authenticated key-establishment**. The precise meaning of this **security service** can be elaborated by the following three properties.

Let $K$ denote a shared secret key to be established between Alice and Bob, the protocols to be designed in this chapter should achieve a security service with the following three properties:

At the end of the protocol run:

1. Only Alice and Bob (or perhaps a principal who is trusted by them) should know $K$.

2. Alice and Bob should know that the other principal knows $K$.

3. Alice and Bob should know that $K$ is newly generated.

The first property follows the most basic meaning of authentication: identifying the principal who is the intended object of communication. Alice (respectively, Bob) should be assured that the other end of the communication, if "padlocked" by the key $K$, can only be Bob (respectively, Alice). If the key establishment service is achieved with the help of Trent, then Trent is trusted that he will not impersonate these two principals.

The second property extends authentication service to an additional dimension, that is, **entity authentication**, or the **liveness** of an identified principal who is the intended object of the communication. Alice (respectively, Bob) should be assured that Bob (respectively, Alice) is alive and responsive to the communications in the current protocol run. We shall see later that this property is necessary in order to thwart an attacking scenario based on replaying of old messages.

The need for the third property follows a long established **key management** principle in cryptography. That principle stipulates that a secret cryptographic key should have a short lifetime if it is a shared key and is used for bulk data encryption. Such a key usage is rather different from that of a "key-encryption key" or a long-term key which we have described at the end of §2.4. There are two reasons behind this key management principle. First, if a key for data encryption is a shared one, then even if one of the sharing party, say, Alice, is very careful in her key management and disposal, compromise of the shared key by the other sharing party, say, Bob, due to Bob's carelessness which is totally out of Alice's control, will still result in Alice's security being compromised. Secondly, most data in confidential communications usually contain (possibly a large volume of) known or predictable information or structure. For example, a piece of computer program contains a large quantity of known texts such as "begin," "end," "class," "int," "if," "then," "else," "++," etc. Such data are said to contain a large quantity of **redundancy** (definition see §3.8). Encryption of such data makes the key a target for **cryptanalysis** which aims for finding the key or the plaintext. Prolonged such use of a key for encryption of such data may ease the difficulty of cryptanalysis. We should also consider that Malice has unlimited time to spend on finding an old data-encryption key and then reusing it as though it were new. The well established and widely accepted principle for key management thus stipulates that a shared data-encryption key should be used for *one* communication session only. Hence, such a key is also referred to as a **session key** and a **short-term key**. The third property of authenticated key establishment service assures Alice and Bob that the session key $K$ established is one that has been newly generated.

## 2.6  Protocols for Authenticated Key Establishment Using Encryption

Now we are ready to design protocols for authenticated key establishment. The first protocol to be designed merely intends to realize straightforwardly the following simple idea: Alice and Bob, though they do not know each other, both know Trent and share respective long-term keys with Trent; so it is possible for Trent to securely pass messages between them.

### 2.6.1  Protocols Serving Message Confidentiality

Since the environment for our protocols to run is a vulnerable one, our protocols will use encryption to safeguard against any threat. At this initial stage of our step-by-step discussions to follow, we shall restrict our attention to a threat which aims for undermining message confidentiality.

#### 2.6.1.1  Protocol "From Alice to Bob"

Let Alice initiate a run of such a protocol. She starts by generating a session key at random, encrypts it under the key she already shares with Trent, and sends to Trent the resultant ciphertext together with the identities of herself and Bob. Upon receipt of Alice's request for session key delivery, Trent shall first find from his database the shared long-term keys of the two principals mentioned in Alice's request. He shall then decrypt the ciphertext using Alice's key, re-encrypt the result using Bob's key, and then send to Bob the resultant ciphertext. Finally, upon receipt and decryption of the delivered session key material, Bob shall acknowledge the receipt by sending an encrypted message to Alice using the newly received session key. Prot 2.1 illustrates a protocol description which realizes delivery of a session key from Alice to Bob. In this protocol, Alice is an **initiator**, and Bob, a **responder**.

In this chapter we shall introduce most of our protocols (and attacks on them)

**Protocol 2.1:** From Alice To Bob

PREMISE  Alice and Trent share key $K_{AT}$; Bob and Trent share key $K_{BT}$.

GOAL   Alice and Bob want to establish a new and shared secret key $K$.

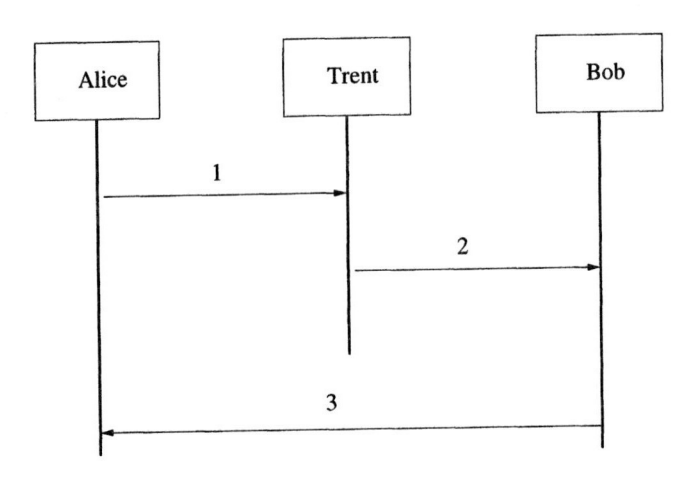

1. Alice generates $K$ at random, creates $\{K\}_{K_{AT}}$, and sends to Trent:
   *Alice, Bob,* $\{K\}_{K_{AT}}$;

2. Trent finds keys $K_{AT}$, $K_{BT}$, decrypts $\{K\}_{K_{AT}}$ to reveal $K$, creates $\{K\}_{K_{BT}}$ and sends to Bob: *Alice, Bob,* $\{K\}_{K_{BT}}$;

3. Bob decrypts $\{K\}_{K_{BT}}$ to reveal $K$, forms and sends to Alice:
   $\{Hello\ Alice,\ I'm\ Bob!\}_{K}$.

in two parts, a pictorial part which illustrates message flows among principals, and a specification part which provides the details of the actions performed by principals regarding the messages sent or received. Although the specification part alone should be sufficient for us to describe a protocol with needed precision (the specification part alone will be the protocol description method in the rest of the book beyond this chapter), by adding pictorial presentation of message flows we intend to allow those readers who are new to the area of cryptographic protocols an easy start. This is a purpose that this chapter should serve.

Before investigating whether Protocol "From Alice To Bob" contains any security flaw we should comment on a design feature of it. The protocol lets Alice generate a session key to be shared with Bob. Will Bob be happy about this? If it turns out that the session key generated by Alice is not sufficiently random (a cryptographic key should be random to make it difficult to be determined by guessing), then Bob's security can be compromised since the key is a shared one. Maybe Alice does not care whether the session key is strong, or maybe she just wants the key to be easily memorable. So long as Bob does not trust Alice (may not even know her prior to a protocol run), he should not feel comfortable accepting a session key generated by her and sharing with her. We shall modify this protocol by removing this design feature and discuss security issues of the modified protocol.

### 2.6.1.2   Protocol "Session Key from Trent"

Since Trent is trusted by both client principals, he should be trusted to be able to properly generate the session key. Prot 2.1 is thus modified to Prot 2.2. It starts with Alice sending to Trent the identities of herself and Bob, the two principals who intend to share a session key for secure communications between them. Upon receipt of Alice's request, Trent shall find from his database the respective keys of the two principals, shall generate a new session key to be shared between the two principals and shall encrypt the session key under each of the principals' keys. Trent should then send the encrypted session key material back to Alice. Alice shall process her own part and shall relay to Bob the part intended for him. Finally, Bob shall process his share of the protocol which ends by sending out an acknowledgement for the receipt of the session key. We shall name the modified Protocol "Session Key From Trent."

With the session key $K$ being encrypted under the perfect encryption scheme, a passive eavesdropper, upon seeing the communications in a run of Protocol "Session Key From Trent" and without the encryption keys $K_{AT}$ and $K_{BT}$, will not gain anything about the session key $K$ since it may only be read by the legitimate recipients via decryption using the respective keys they have.

## 2.6.2   Attack, Fix, Attack, Fix ...

We now illustrate a standard scene of this book, that is, attack, fix, attack, fix ...

### 2.6.2.1   An Attack

However, Protocol "Session Key From Trent" is flawed. The problem with the protocol is that the information about *who* should get the session key is not protected. An attack is shown in Attack 2.1. In the attack, Malice intercepts some messages

---

**Protocol 2.2:** Session Key From Trent

PREMISE    Alice and Trent share key $K_{AT}$; Bob and Trent share key $K_{BT}$.

GOAL       Alice and Bob want to establish a new and shared secret key $K$.

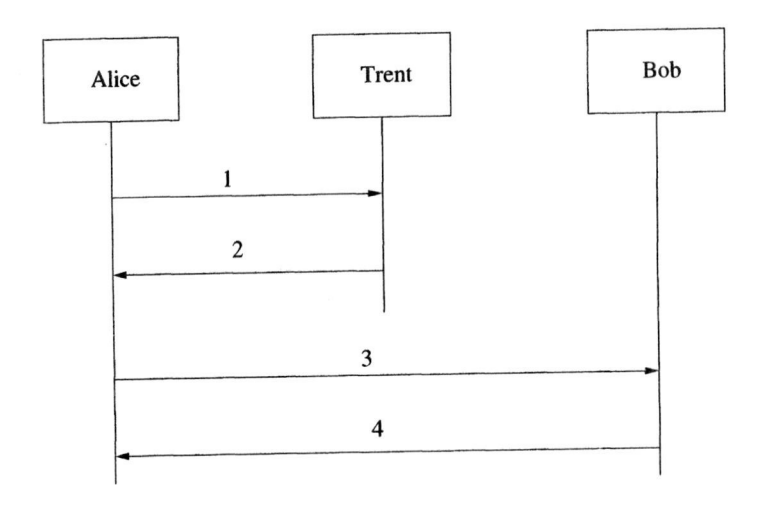

1. Alice sends to Trent: *Alice, Bob*;

2. Trent finds keys $K_{AT}$, $K_{BT}$, generates $K$ at random and sends to Alice: $\{K\}_{K_{AT}}$, $\{K\}_{K_{BT}}$;

3. Alice decrypts $\{K\}_{K_{AT}}$, and sends to Bob: *Trent, Alice*, $\{K\}_{K_{BT}}$;

4. Bob decrypts $\{K\}_{K_{BT}}$ to reveal $K$, forms and sends to Alice: $\{Hello\ Alice,\ I'm\ Bob!\}_K$.

---

transmitted over the network, modifies them and sends them to some principals by impersonating some other principals. In the attack shown in Attack 2.1 we write

     Alice sends to Malice("Trent"): ...

to denote Malice's action of intercepting Alice's message intended for Trent, and we

**Attack 2.1:** An Attack on Protocol "Session Key From Trent"

PREMISE   In addition to that in Protocol "Session Key From Trent,"
Malice and Trent share key $K_{MT}$.

RESULT OF ATTACK
Alice thinks she is sharing a key with Bob
while actually sharing it with Malice.

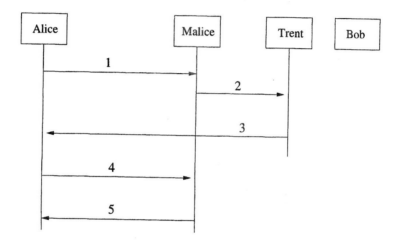

1 Alice sends to Malice("Trent"): *Alice, Bob*;

2 Malice("Alice") sends to Trent: *Alice, Malice*;

3 Trent finds keys $K_{AT}$, $K_{MT}$, generates $K_{AM}$ at random and sends to
Alice: $\{K_{AM}\}_{K_{AT}}$, $\{K_{AM}\}_{K_{MT}}$;

4 Alice decrypts $\{K_{AM}\}_{K_{AT}}$, and sends to Malice("Bob"):   *Trent,
Alice*, $\{K_{AM}\}_{K_{MT}}$;

5 Malice("Bob") sends to Alice: $\{Hello\ Alice,\ I'm\ Bob!\}_{K_{AM}}$.

use

    Malice("Alice") sends to Trent: ...

to denote Malice's action of sending message to Trent by impersonating Alice. We should note that according to the Dolev-Yao threat model for our protocol environment that we have agreed to in §2.3, Malice is assumed to have the entire control of the vulnerable network. So Malice is capable of performing the above malicious actions. We can imagine that the symbol ("principal_name") is a mask worn by Malice when he is manipulating protocol messages passing along the network. In §12.2 we shall see technically how Malice could manipulate messages transmitted over the network this way.

    Malice begins with intercepting the initial message from Alice to Trent. That message is meant for instructing Trent to generate a session key to share with Alice and Bob. Malice alters it by replacing Bob's identity with his own and then sends the altered message to Trent. Trent will think that Alice wants to talk to Malice. So he generates a new session key $K_{AM}$ to share between Alice and Malice, and encrypts it with the respective keys that he shares with these two principals. Since Alice cannot distinguish between encrypted messages meant for other principals she will not detect the alteration. Malice then intercepts the message from Alice intended for Bob so that Bob will not know that he is requested to run the protocol. The result of the attack is that Alice will believe that the protocol has been successfully completed with Bob whereas in fact Malice knows $K_{AM}$ and so can masquerade as Bob as well as learn all the information that Alice intends to send to Bob. Notice that this attack will only succeed if Malice is a legitimate user known to Trent. This, again, is a realistic assumption – an insider attacker is often more of a threat than outsiders.

    We have seen that the above attack works as a result of Malice's alteration of Bob's identity. We should notice the fact that the alteration is possible because Bob's identity is sent in cleartext. This suggests to us to repair the protocol by hiding Bob's identity.

### 2.6.2.2   A Fix

Having seen the attack in which Malice alters Bob's identity, it seems straightforward to repair Protocol "Session Key From Trent." For example, we can modify the protocol into one with Bob's identity in the first message line being treated as a secret and encrypted under the key shared between Alice and Trent. Namely, the first message line in Protocol "Session Key From Trent" should be correctly modified into

    1. Alice sends to Trent: *Alice*, $\{Bob\}_{K_{AT}}$;

Notice that it is necessary for Alice's identity to remain in cleartext so Trent will be able to know which key he should use to decrypt the ciphertext part.

### 2.6.2.3 Another Attack

However, the above way of "repair" does not provide a sound fix for Protocol "Session Key From Trent." For example, it is easy to see that Malice can do the following:

1. Malice("Alice") sends to Trent: $Alice, \{Malice\}_{K_{AT}}$;

while the rest of the attack runs exactly the same as that in Attack 2.1. If initially Malice did not know to whom Alice was intending to run the protocol, he would know that piece of information when he intercepts Alice's message to Bob since that message has to contain Bob's address in order for the network to correctly deliver the message. So Malice can in the end still successfully masquerade as Bob. Notice that in this attack we assume that Malice has the ciphertext $\{Malice\}_{K_{AT}}$; this is possible as it can be the case that Malice has recorded it from a previous protocol run (a correct run) between Alice and Malice.

### 2.6.2.4 Yet Another Attack

In fact, another way to attack Protocol "Session Key From Trent" (or its "fix" shown above) does not rely on change of any principal's identity. Instead, Malice can alter the message from Trent to Alice (message line 2 in Protocol "Session Key From Trent") into the following:

Malice("Trent") sends to Alice: $\{K'\}_{K_{AT}}, \ldots$;

Here $K'$ is a session key transported in a previous protocol run (a correct run) between Alice and Malice such that Malice has recorded the ciphertext part $\{K'\}_{K_{AT}}$. The rest of the attack run is similar to that in the attack in Attack 2.1: Malice should intercept the subsequent message from Alice to Bob, and finally acknowledges Alice by masquerading as Bob:

Malice("Bob") sends to Alice: $\{Hello\ Alice,\ I'm\ Bob!\}_{K'}$.

The fact that the "fixed" versions of Protocol "Session Key From Trent" can be attacked with or without altering Bob's identity clearly shows that to have Bob's identity in the first line of Protocol "Session Key From Trent" protected in terms of confidentiality cannot be a correct security service. The attacks demonstrated so far have shown possibilities for Malice to alter some protocol messages without detection. This suggests that the protocol needs a security service which can guard against tampering of messages.

This brings us to the following security service.

## 2.6.3 Protocol with Message Authentication

We have seen in the attacks shown so far that Malice has always been able to alter some protocol messages without detection. Indeed, none of the protocols designed so far has provided any cryptographic protection against message alteration. Thus, one way to fix these protocols is to provide such protection. The protection should enable legitimate principals who have the right cryptographic keys to detect any unauthorized alteration of any protected protocol messages. Such protection or security service is called **message authentication** (in some texts this notion is also called **data integrity**, but we shall differentiate these two notions in Chapter 11).

### 2.6.3.1   Protocol "Message Authentication"

We observe that Malice's alteration of the protocol messages has caused the following two effects. Either a session key is shared between wrong principals, or a wrong session key gets established. Therefore we propose that the message authentication protection should provide a cryptographic binding between the session key to be established and its intended users. This leads to a new protocol: Prot 2.3, where the identities of Alice and Bob are included in the encrypted message parts sent by Trent. We should name the new protocol "Message Authentication."

We should pay a particular attention to the specification part of Protocol "Message Authentication" where it instructs

3. Alice (decrypts $\{Bob,\ K\}_{K_{AT}}$), **checks Bob's identity**, ...

4. Bob (decrypts $\{Alice,\ K\}_{K_{BT}}$), **checks Alice's identity**, ...

Here in Protocol "Message Authentication," steps for checking the intended principals' identities make a crucial distinction between this protocol and its predecessors (i.e., Protocol "Session Key From Trent" and its "fixes"). These checking steps are possible only after correct decryption of the respective ciphertext blocks using the correct cryptographic keys. Thus, the cryptographic operation "decryption-and-checking" performed by the recipient attempts to achieve a message authentication service which enables the recipient to verify the cryptographic bindings between the session key to be established and its intended users. A correct decryption result should imply that the ciphertext message blocks in question have not been altered in transition. That is how Protocol "Message Authentication" should thwart the attacks shown so far.

We should point out that to achieve message authentication, the operation of "decryption-and-checking" (performed by a recipient) is not a correct "mode of operation". In Chapter 17 we shall see that the correct mode of operation should be "re-encryption-and-checking" (again performed by a recipient). The reason that we use an incorrect or imprecise mode of operation in this chapter is merely because "encryption-by-sender" and "decryption-by-recipient" are the only available cryptographic operations for us to use at this stage.

Since we will use an incorrect mode of operation to realize the message authentication service, it is necessary for us to explicitly state an additional property requirement that our encryption algorithm must satisfy. The property is given be-

---

**Protocol 2.3:** Message Authentication

PREMISE    Alice and Trent share key $K_{AT}$; Bob and Trent share key $K_{BT}$.

GOAL       Alice and Bob want to establish a new and shared secret key $K$.

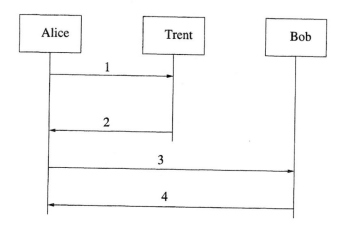

1. Alice sends to Trent: *Alice, Bob*;

2. Trent finds keys $K_{AT}$, $K_{BT}$, generates $K$ at random and sends to Alice: $\{Bob,\ K\}_{K_{AT}}$, $\{Alice,\ K\}_{K_{BT}}$;

3. Alice decrypts $\{Bob,\ K\}_{K_{AT}}$, checks Bob's identity, and sends to Bob: *Trent*, $\{Alice,\ K\}_{K_{BT}}$;

4. Bob decrypts $\{Alice,\ K\}_{K_{BT}}$, checks Alice's identity, and sends to Alice: $\{Hello\ Alice,\ I'm\ Bob!\}_K$.

---

low (its enumeration (iii) follows the enumeration of the other two properties for "The Perfect Encryption with Notation $\{M\}_K$" that we have listed in §2.2).

**Property 2.2:** Perfect Encryption with Notation $\{M\}_K$ (for message authentication service)

*iii) Without the key $K$, even with the knowledge of the plaintext $M$, it should be impossible for someone to alter $\{M\}_K$ without being detected by the recipient during the time of decryption.*

In order to show the importance of this property, below we demonstrate an attack on Protocol "Message Authentication" supposing that our perfect encryption algorithm does not possess the above message authentication property (namely, we assume that the encryption algorithm only possesses the perfect confidentiality properties listed in §2.2). For ease of exposition, we modify the presentation of the ciphertext blocks

$$\{Bob,\ K\}_{K_{AT}}, \quad \{Alice,\ K\}_{K_{BT}},$$

in the protocol into the following presentation

$$\{Bob\}_{K_{AT}}, \quad \{K\}_{K_{AT}}, \quad \{Alice\}_{K_{BT}}, \quad \{K\}_{K_{BT}}.$$

With this presentation of ciphertext blocks, we imply that the cryptographic binding between principals' identities and the session key has been destroyed while the encryption retains the perfect confidentiality service for any plaintext message being encrypted. Protocol "Message Authentication" using this "perfect" encryption scheme should have its message lines 2, 3 and 4 look like the following:

2. Trent ..., sends to Alice: $\{Bob\}_{K_{AT}}, \{K\}_{K_{AT}}, \{Alice\}_{K_{BT}}, \{K\}_{K_{BT}}$;

3. Alice decrypts $\{Bob\}_{K_{AT}}$ and $\{K\}_{K_{AT}}$, checks Bob's identity, ...

4. Bob decrypts $\{Alice\}_{K_{BT}}$ and $\{K\}_{K_{BT}}$, checks Alice's identity, ...

Obviously, the confidentiality protection provided on the principals identities does not make a point; by simply observing the protocol messages flowing over the network (from senders and to recipients) Malice should be able to determine exactly the plaintext content inside the ciphertext blocks $\{Bob\}_{K_{AT}}$ and $\{Alice\}_{K_{BT}}$. Thus, the modified protocol is essentially the same as Protocol "Session Key From Trent," and thus can be attacked by essentially the same attacks demonstrated in §2.6.2. The reader can apply these attacks as an exercise.

### 2.6.3.2 Attack on Protocol "Message Authentication"

Even considering that the encryption algorithm used possesses the message authentication property, Protocol "Message Authentication" can still be attacked. The problem stems from the difference in quality between the long-term key-encrypting keys shared initially between Trent and its clients, and the session keys generated for each protocol run.

First, we note that the relationship between Trent and each of his clients is a long-term based one. This means that a shared key between him and his client is a long-term key. In general, to establish a key between an authentication server and a client is more difficult and more costly than to establish a session key between two client principals (it should require thorough security checking routines, even maybe based on a face-to-face contact). Fortunately, such a key is mainly used in authentication protocols, with infrequent use for encrypting few messages with little redundancy, and hence such use of a key provides little information available for cryptanalysis. Therefore, secret keys shared between an authentication server and its clients can be used for a long period of time. Often they are called long-term keys.

On the other hand, we should recall a key management principle we have discussed in §2.5, which stipulates that a session key should be used for one session only. Consequently, no run of a session-key establishment protocol should establish a session key which is identical to one which was established in a previous run of the protocol. However, this is not the case for Protocol "Message Authentication." An attack run of the protocol will breach the session key management principle. In this attack, all Malice needs to do is first to intercept Alice's request (see Prot 2.3):

1. Alice sends to Malice("Trent"): ...

and then inject a message line 2 as follows:

2. Malice("Trent") sends to Alice: $\{Bob,\ K'\}_{K_{AT}}$, $\{Alice,\ K'\}_{K_{BT}}$

Here, the two ciphertext blocks containing $K'$ are a **replay** of old messages which Malice has recorded from a previous run of the protocol (a normal run between Alice and Bob), and therefore this attack will cause Alice and Bob to reuse the old session key $K'$ which they should not use. Notice that, since $K'$ is old, it may be possible for Malice to have discovered its value (maybe because it has been discarded by a careless principal, or maybe due to other vulnerabilities of a session key that we have discussed in §2.5). Then he can either eavesdrop the confidential session communications between Alice and Bob, or impersonate Bob to talk to Alice.

An attack in the above fashion is called a **message replay attack**.

## 2.6.4   Protocol With Challenge-Response

There are several mechanisms that may be employed to allow users to check that a message in a protocol is not a replay of an old message. These mechanisms will be considered in detail in Chapter 11. However for now we will improve our protocol using a well known method called **challenge-response** (also called **handshake**). Using this method Alice will generate a new random number $N_A$ at the start of the protocol and send this to Trent with the request for a new session key. If this same value ($N_A$) is returned with a session key such that the two pieces are bound together cryptographically and the cryptographic binding provides a message authentication service (i.e., Alice can verify the message integrity regarding the ciphertext containing $N_A$), then Alice can deduce that the cryptographic binding has been created by Trent after having received her random number $N_A$. Moreover, recall our stipulation on the trustworthiness of Trent (see §2.4); Alice knows that Trent will always follow the protocol honestly. So Trent has indeed created a new session key *after* receiving Alice's random challenge. Consequently, the session key should be new (or **fresh, current**), namely, is not a replay of an old key. The random number $N_A$ created by Alice for enabling the challenge-response mechanism is called a **nonce** which stands for a **number** used **once** [62].

### 2.6.4.1    Protocol "Challenge Response" (Needham-Schroeder)

Prot 2.4 specifies a new protocol which utilizes the challenge-response mechanism for Alice to check the freshness of the session key. We shall temporarily name it "Challenge Response" (we will soon change its name).

In Protocol "Challenge Response," Bob also creates a nonce ($N_B$), but this nonce is not sent to Trent since in this protocol Bob does not directly contact Trent. Instead, Bob's nonce is sent to Alice and then is replied from her after her slight modification (subtracting 1). So if Alice is satisfied that the session key $K$ is fresh and uses it in her response to Bob's freshly created nonce, then Bob should deduce the freshness of the session key. Thus, the mutual confidence in the session key is established.

Protocol "Challenge Response," which we have reached by a series of steps, is probably the most celebrated in the subject of authentication and key establishment protocols. It is exactly the protocol of Needham and Schroeder which they published in 1978 [215]. Below we rename the protocol the Needham-Schroeder Symmetric-key Authentication Protocol. This protocol has also been the basis for a whole class of related protocols.

### 2.6.4.2    Attack on the Needham-Schroeder Symmetric-key Authentication Protocol

Unfortunately the Needham-Schroeder Protocol is vulnerable to an attack discovered by Denning and Sacco in 1981 [95]. In the attack of Denning and Sacco, Malice intercepts the messages sent by and to Alice in the message lines 3, 4 and 5, and replaces them with his own version. The attack is given in Attack 2.2.

In the attack, Malice becomes active in message line 3 and intercepts Alice's message sent to Bob. He then completely blockades Alice's communication channel and replays old session key material $\{K', \ Alice\}_{K_{BT}}$ which he recorded from a previous run of the protocol between Alice and Bob. By our assumption on the vulnerability on an old session key, Malice may know the value $K'$ and therefore he can launch this attack to talk to Bob by masquerading as Alice.

We should point out that the vulnerability of an old session key is only one aspect of the danger of this attack. Another danger of this attack is Malice's successful

**Protocol 2.4:** Challenge Response

PREMISE   Alice and Trent share key $K_{AT}$; Bob and Trent share key $K_{BT}$.

GOAL       Alice and Bob want to establish a new and shared secret key $K$.

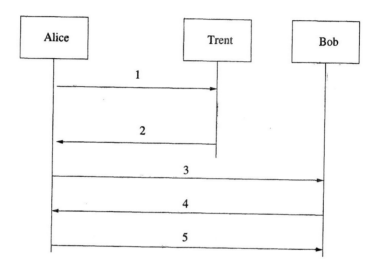

1. Alice creates $N_A$ at random and sends to Trent: *Alice, Bob, $N_A$*;

2. Trent generates $K$ at random and sends to Alice: $\{N_A,\ K,\ Bob,\ \{K,\ Alice\}_{K_{BT}}\}_{K_{AT}}$;

3. Alice decrypts, checks her nonce $N_A$, checks Bob's ID and sends to Bob: *Trent*, $\{K,\ Alice\}_{K_{BT}}$;

4. Bob decrypts, checks Alice's ID, creates random $N_B$ and sends to Alice: $\{I'm\ Bob!\ N_B\}_K$;

5. Alice sends to Bob: $\{I'm\ Alice!\ N_B - 1\}_K$.

**Attack 2.2:** An Attack on the Needham-Schroeder Symmetric-key
Authentication Protocol

RESULT OF ATTACK
Bob thinks he is sharing a new session key with Alice
while actually the key is an old one and may be known to Malice.

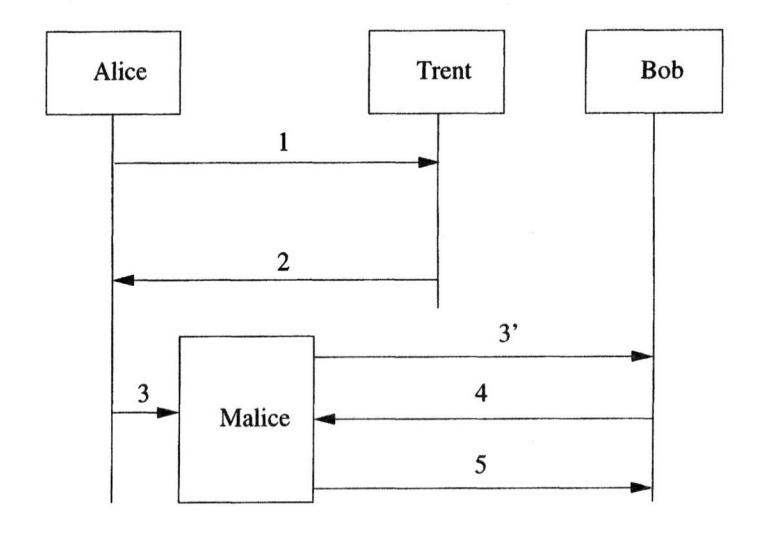

1   and 2. (same as in a normal run)

3.  Alice sends to Malice("Bob"): ...

3'. Malice("Alice") sends to Bob: $\{K', Alice\}_{K_{BT}}$;

4.  Bob decrypts, checks Alice's ID and sends to Malice("Alice"):
    $\{I'm\ Bob!\ N_B\}_{K'}$;

5.  Malice("Alice") sends to Bob: $\{I'm\ Alice!\ N_B - 1\}_{K'}$.

defeat of an important goal of authentication. We shall specify that goal in §11.2.2 and see how the goal is easily defeated by Malice in §11.7.1.

## 2.6.5   Protocol With Entity Authentication

The challenge-response mechanism used in the Needham-Schroeder Protocol (the interaction part between Alice and Trent) provides a security service called **entity authentication**. Like message authentication, the service of entity authentication is also obtained via verifying a cryptographic operation (by a verification principal). The difference between the two services is that in the latter case, an evidence of liveness of a principal (proving principal) is shown. The liveness evidence is shown if the proving principal has performed a cryptographic operation *after* an event which is known as *recent* to the verification principal. In the case of the Needham-Schroeder Protocol, when Alice receives the message line 2, her decryption operation revealing her nonce $N_A$ shows her that Trent has only operated the encryption *after* the event of her sending out the nonce $N_A$ (since the key used is shared between she and Trent). So Alice knows that Trent is alive after that event. This accomplishes an entity authentication from Trent to Alice.

However, in Bob's position in the Needham-Schroeder Protocol, he has no evidence of entity authentication regarding Trent's liveness.

As usual, once a problem has been spotted, it becomes relatively easy to suggest ways of fixing it: Trent should have himself authenticated in entity authentication to *both* of the client principals. This can be done by, for instance, Bob sending a nonce to Trent too, which will be included by Trent in the session key message returned from Trent. This way of fixing will add more message flows to the protocol (an additional handshake between Bob and Trent). Denning and Sacco suggest using **timestamps** to avoid adding message flows [95].

### 2.6.5.1   Timestamps

Let $T$ denote a timestamp. The following fix was suggested by Denning and Sacco:

1. Alice sends to Trent: *Alice, Bob*;
2. Trent sends to Alice: $\{Bob, K, T, \{Alice, K, T\}_{K_{BT}}\}_{K_{AT}}$;
3. Alice sends to Bob: $\{Alice, K, T\}_{K_{BT}}$;

4. ...  ⎫
5. ...  ⎬ Same as in the Needham-Schroeder Protocol.
        ⎭

When Alice and Bob receive their protocol messages from Trent, they can verify that their messages are not replays by checking that

$$| \, Clock - T \, | < \Delta t_1 + \Delta t_2$$

where $Clock$ gives the recipient's local time, $\Delta t_1$ is an interval representing the normal discrepancy between Trent's clock and the local clock, and $\Delta t_2$ is an interval representing the expected network delay time. If each client principal sets its clock manually by reference to a standard source, a value of about one or two minutes for $\Delta t_1$ would suffice. As long as $\Delta t_1 + \Delta t_2$ is less than the interval since the last use of the protocol, this method will protect against the replay attack in Attack 2.2. Since timestamp $T$ is encrypted under the secret keys $K_{AT}$ and $K_{BT}$, impersonation of Trent is impossible given the perfectness of the encryption scheme.

Needham and Schroeder have considered the use of timestamps, but they reject it on the grounds that it requires a good-quality time value to be universally available [214].

## 2.6.6    A Protocol Using Public-key Cryptosystems

The final protocol to be introduced in this chapter is called the Needham-Schroeder Public-key Authentication Protocol [215]. We introduce this protocol here with two reasons, both of which fall within the agenda of this chapter. First, the protocol lets us obtain an initial familiarity with the use of public-key cryptosystems. Secondly, we shall show a subtle attack on this protocol. Even though the protocol looks simple, the attack was found seventeen years after the publication of the protocol.

### 2.6.6.1   Public-key Cryptosystems

We use key labels such as $K_A$ for Alice's public key and $K_A^{-1}$ for the matching private key (Alice's private key). It is supposed that Alice is the only person who is in possession of her private key. The ciphertext block

$$\{M\}_{K_A}$$

denotes the perfect encryption of the plaintext $M$ using Alice's public key $K_A$. It is supposed that to decrypt the above ciphertext one must use the matching private key $K_A^{-1}$. Since it is supposed that Alice is the only person to possess the private key, only she is able to perform decryption to retrieve the plaintext $M$. Analogously, the ciphertext block

$$\{M\}_{K_A^{-1}}$$

denotes the perfect encryption of the plaintext $M$ using Alice's private key $K_A^{-1}$, and decryption is only possible with the use of Alice's public key $K_A$. With the knowledge of $K_A$ being Alice's public key, an action of decryption using $K_A$ provides one with further knowledge that the ciphertext $\{M\}_{K_A^{-1}}$ is created by Alice since the creation requires the use of a key that only she has in possession. For this reason, the ciphertext $\{M\}_{K_A^{-1}}$ is also called Alice's (**digital**) **signature** of message $M$, and an action of decryption using $K_A$ is called verification of Alice's signature of message $M$.

**Protocol 2.5:** Needham-Schroeder Public-key Authentication Protocol

PREMISE    Alice's public key is $K_A$,
Bob's public key is $K_B$,
Trent's public key is $K_T$.

GOAL      Alice and Bob establish a new and shared secret.

1. Alice sends to Trent: *Alice, Bob*;

2. Trent sends to Alice: $\{K_B,\ Bob\}_{K_T^{-1}}$;

3. Alice verifies Trent's signature on "$K_B$, *Bob*," creates her nonce $N_A$ at random, and sends to Bob: $\{N_A,\ Alice\}_{K_B}$;

4. Bob decrypts, checks Alice's ID and sends to Trent: *Bob, Alice*;

5. Trent sends to Bob: $\{K_A,\ Alice\}_{K_T^{-1}}$;

6. Bob verifies Trent's signature on "$K_A$, *Alice*," creates his nonce $N_B$ at random, and sends to Alice: $\{N_A,\ N_B\}_{K_A}$;

7. Alice decrypts, and sends to Bob: $\{N_B\}_{K_B}$.

### 2.6.6.2  Needham-Schroeder Public-key Authentication Protocol

Suppose that Trent has in his possession the public keys of all the client principals he serves. Also, every client principal has an authenticated copy of Trent's public key. Prot 2.5 specifies the Needham-Schroeder Public-key Authentication Protocol.

Here Alice is an initiator who seeks to establish a session with responder Bob, with the help of Trent. In step 1, Alice sends a message to Trent, requesting Bob's public key. Trent responds in step 2 by returning the key $K_B$, along with Bob's identity (to prevent the sort of attacks in §2.6.2), encrypted using Trent's private key $K_T^{-1}$. This forms Trent's digital signature on the protocol message which assures Alice that the message in step 2 is originated from Trent (Alice should verify the signature using Trent's public key). Alice then seeks to establish a connection with Bob by selecting a nonce $N_A$ at random, and sending it along with her identity to Bob (step 3), encrypted using Bob's public key. When Bob receives this message, he decrypts the message to obtain the nonce $N_A$. He requests (step 4) and receives (step 5) the authentic copy of Alice's public key. He then returns the nonce $N_A$, along with his own new nonce $N_B$, to Alice, encrypted with Alice's public key (step 6). When Alice receives this message she should be assured that she is talking to Bob, since only Bob should be able to decrypt message 3 to obtain $N_A$ and this must have been done *after* her action of sending the nonce out (a recent action). Alice then returns the nonce $N_B$ to Bob, encrypted with Bob's public key. When Bob receives this message he should, too, be assured that he is talking to Alice, since only Alice should be able to decrypt message 6 to obtain $N_B$ (also a recent action). Thus, a successful run of this protocol does achieve the establishment of the shared nonces $N_A$ and $N_B$ and they are shared secrets exclusively between Alice and Bob. Further notice that since both principals contribute to these shared secrets recently, they have the freshness property. Also, each principal should trust the randomness of the secrets as long as her/his part of the contribution is sufficiently random.

Needham and Schroeder suggest that $N_A$ and $N_B$, which are from a large space, can be used to initialize a shared secret key ("as the base for seriation of encryption blocks") [215] for subsequent secure communications between Alice and Bob.

Denning and Sacco have pointed out that this protocol provides no guarantee that the public keys obtained by the client principals are current, rather than replays of old, possibly compromised keys [95]. This problem can be overcome in various ways, for example by including timestamps in the key deliveries[a]. Below we assume that the clients' public keys that are obtained from Trent are current and good.

### 2.6.6.3  Attack on the Needham-Schroeder Public-key Authentication Protocol

Lowe discovers an attack on the Needham-Schroeder Public-key Authentication Protocol [182].

Lowe observes that this protocol can be considered as the interleaving of two logically disjoint protocols; steps 1, 2, 4 and 5 are concerned with obtaining public keys, whereas steps 3, 6 and 7 are concerned with the authentication of Alice and Bob. Therefore, we can assume that each principal initially has the authentic copies of each other's public key, and restrict our attention to just the following steps (we only list message flows; the reader may refer to Prot 2.5 for details):

3. Alice sends to Bob: $\{N_A, Alice\}_{K_B}$;

---

[a]Denning and Sacco propose such a fix [95]. However, their fix is flawed for a different reason. We will see their fix and study the reason of the flaw in §11.7.7.

6. Bob sends to Alice: $\{N_A, N_B\}_{K_A}$;

7. Alice sends to Bob: $\{N_B\}_{K_B}$.

We shall consider how Malice can interact with this protocol. We assume that Malice is a legitimate principal in the system, and so other principals may try to set up standard sessions with Malice. Indeed, the attack below starts with Alice trying to establish a session with Malice. Attack 2.3 describes the attack.

The attack involves two simultaneous runs of the protocol; in the first run (steps 1-3, 1-6 and 1-7), Alice establishes a valid session with Malice; in the second run (steps 2-3, 2-6 and 2-7), Malice impersonates Alice to establish a bogus session with Bob. In step 1-3, Alice starts to establish a normal session with Malice, sending him a nonce $N_A$. In step 2-3, Malice impersonates Alice to try to establish a bogus session with Bob, sending to Bob the nonce $N_A$ from Alice. Bob responds in step 2-6 by selecting a new nonce $N_B$, and trying to return it, along with $N_A$, to Alice. Malice intercepts this message, but cannot decrypt it because it is encrypted with Alice's public key. Malice therefore seeks to use Alice to do the decryption for him, by forwarding the message to Alice in step 1-6; note that this message is of the form expected by Alice in the first run of the protocol. Alice decrypts the message to obtain $N_B$, and returns this to Malice in step 1-7 (encrypted with Malice's public key). Malice can then decrypt this message to obtain $N_B$, and returns this to Bob in step 2.7, thus completing the second run of the protocol. Hence Bob believes that Alice has correctly established a session with him and they share exclusively the secret nonces $N_A$ and $N_B$.

A crucial step for Malice to succeed in the attack is Alice's decryption of Bob's nonce $N_B$ for Malice unwittingly. We say that a principal is used as an **oracle** or providing an **oracle service** when the principal performs a cryptographic operation inadvertently for an attacker. We will see many cases of oracle services in this book and will gradually develop a general methodology that cryptographic algorithms and protocols should be designed such that they are secure even if their users provide oracle services to attackers.

We can imagine the following consequences of this attack. Malice may include the shared nonces within a subsequent message suggesting a session key, and Bob will believe that this message originated from Alice. Similarly, if Bob is a bank, then Malice could impersonate Alice to send a message such as:

Malice("Alice") sends to Bob:

$\{N_A, N_B, \text{ Transfer } £1,000,000 \text{ from my account to Malice's"}\}_{K_B}$.

### 2.6.6.4   A Fix

It is fairly easy to change the protocol so as to prevent the attack. If we include the responder's identity in message 6 of the protocol

6. Bob sends to Alice: $\{Bob, N_A, N_B\}_{K_A}$;

**Attack 2.3:** Lowe's Attack on the Needham-Schroeder Public-key Authentication Protocol

PREMISE    Alice's public key is $K_A$, Bob's public key is $K_B$,
                  Malice's public key is $K_M$.

RESULT OF ATTACK
         Bob thinks he is sharing secrets $N_A, N_B$ with Alice
         while actually sharing them with Malice.

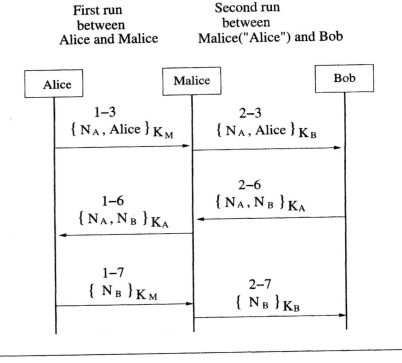

then step 2-6 of the attack would become

2-6. Bob sends to Malice("Alice"): $\{Bob, N_A, N_B\}_{K_A}$.

Now because Alice is expecting a message with Malice's identity, Malice cannot successfully replay this message in step 1-6 with an intention to use Alice as a decryption oracle.

This fix represents an instance of a principle for cryptographic protocols design suggested by Abadi and Needham [1]:

> If the identity of a principal is essential to the meaning of a message, it is prudent to mention the principal's name explicitly in the message.

However, we should refrain from claiming that this way of "fixing" should result in a secure protocol. In §17.2.1 we will reveal several additional problems in this protocol due to an undesirable design feature which can be referred to as "message authentication via decryption-and-checking" (we have labeled it a wrong mode of operation, see §2.6.3.1). That design feature appears generally in authentication protocols using secret-key or public-key cryptographic techniques and has appeared in all protocols in this chapter (the design feature has been retained in our "fix" of the Needham-Schroeder Public-key Authentication Protocol, and hence our "fix" is still not a correct one). Methodical fixes for the Needham-Schroeder Authentication Protocols (both symmetric-key and public-key) will be given in §17.2.3.

The error-prone nature of authentication protocols has inspired the consideration of systematic approaches to the development of correct protocols. That topic will be introduced in Chapter 17.

## 2.7 Chapter Summary

Some design protection mechanisms, others want to crack them. This is a fact of life and there is nothing special about it. However, in this chapter we have witnessed a rather sad part of this fact of life in authentication protocols: they, as protection mechanisms, are very easily compromised.

Actually, all complex systems easily contain design errors. However, unlike in the case of systems which provide security services, users and the environment of other complex system are generally non-hostile or even friendly. For example, a careful user of a buggy software may learn to avoid certain usages in order to avoid a system crash. However, for an information security system, its environment and some of its users are always hostile: the whole reason for their existence is to attack the system. Exploiting design errors is of course an irresistible source of tricks for them.

We have used authentication protocols as a means to manifest the error-prone nature of security systems. Although it seems that protocols are more notoriously error-prone due to their communication nature, the real reason for us to use authentication protocols is that they require relatively simpler cryptographic techniques and therefore are more suitable for serving our introductory purpose at this early stage of the book. We should remember that it is the hostility of the environment for all security systems that should always alert us to be careful when we develop security systems.

We will return to studying authentication protocols in several later chapters. The further study will include a study on the principles and structures of authentication protocols and a taxonomy of attacks on authentication protocols (Chapter 11), case studies of several protocols for real world applications (Chapter 12), and formalism approaches to the development of correct authentication protocols (Chapter 17).

## Exercises

2.1 What sort of things can an active attacker do?

2.2 Under the Dolev-Yao Threat Model, Malice is very powerful because he is in control of the entire open communications network. Can he decrypt or create a ciphertext message without using the correct key? Can he find the key encryption key from a ciphertext message? Can he predict a nonce value?

2.3 What is the role of Trent in authenticated key establishment protocols?

2.4 What is a long-term key, a key-encryption key, a short-term key and a session key?

2.5 Why with the perfect encryption and the perfect message authentication services, can authentication protocols still be broken?

2.6 What is a nonce? What is a timestamp? What are their roles in authentication or authenticated key establishment protocols?

2.7 Why must some messages transmitted in authentication or authenticated key establishment protocols be fresh?

2.8 How can a principal decide the freshness of a protocol message?

2.9 For the perfect encryption notation $\{M\}_K$, differentiate the following three properties: (i) message confidentiality, (ii) key secrecy, and (iii) message authentication.

2.10 Provide another attack on Protocol "Session Key From Trent" (Prot 2.2), which allows Malice to masquerade not only as Bob toward Alice as in Attack 2.1, but at the same time also as Alice toward Bob, and hence Malice can relay "confidential" communications between Alice and Bob.

Hint: run another instance of Attack 2.1 between Malice("Alice") and Bob.

2.11 What is the difference between message authentication and entity authentication?

2.12 Provide another attack on the Needham-Schroeder Authentication Protocol in which Alice (and Trent) stays offline completely.

2.13 Does digital signature play an important role in the Needham-Schroeder Public-key Authentication Protocol?

Hint: consider that that protocol can be simplified to the version which only contains message lines 2, 6 and 7.

# Part II

# MATHEMATICAL FOUNDATIONS

This part is a collection of mathematical material which provides the basic notations, methods, basis of algebraic operations, building blocks of algorithmic procedures and references for modeling, specifying, analyzing, transforming and solving various problems to appear in the rest of this book.

This part has four chapters: probability and information theory (Chapter 3), computational complexity (Chapter 4), algebraic foundations (Chapter 5) and number theory (Chapter 6). This part serves as a self-contained mathematical reference guide. In the rest of the book whenever we meet non-trivial mathematical problems we will be able to refer to precise places in these four chapters to obtain supporting facts and/or foundations. Therefore our way of including the mathematical material in this book will help the reader to conduct an active and interactive way of learning the mathematical foundations for modern cryptography.

We will pay in-depth attention to, and provide sufficiently detailed elaborations for, the algorithms and theorems which are important to the theoretical foundations and practical applications of modern cryptography. We will provide a proof for a theorem if we believe that the proof will help the reader to develop skills which are relevant to the study of the cryptographic topics in this book. Sometimes, our development of mathematical topics has to make use of facts from other branches of mathematics (e.g., linear algebra) which do not have a direct relevance to the cryptographic skills to be developed here; in such cases we will simply use the needed facts without proof.

# STANDARD NOTATION

The following standard notation is used throughout the rest of the book. Some notation will be defined locally near its first use, other notation will be used without further definition.

| | |
|---|---|
| $\emptyset$ | empty set |
| $S \cup T$ | union of sets $S$ and $T$ |
| $S \cap T$ | intersection of sets $S$ and $T$ |
| $S \setminus T$ | difference of sets $S$ and $T$ |
| $S \subseteq T$ | $S$ is a subset of $T$ |
| $\#S$ | number of elements in set $S$ (e.g., $\#\emptyset = 0$) |
| $x \in S$, $x \notin S$ | element $x$ in (not in) set $S$ |
| $x \in_U S$ | sampling element $x$ uniformly random in set $S$ |
| $x \in (a, b)$, $x \in [a, b]$, | $x$ in open interval $(a, b)$ ($x$ in closed interval $[a, b]$) |
| $\mathbb{N}, \mathbb{Z}, \mathbb{Q}, \mathbb{R}, \mathbb{C}$ | sets of natural numbers, integers, rationals, reals and complex numbers |
| $\mathbb{Z}_n$ | integers modulo $n$ |
| $\mathbb{Z}_n^*$ | multiplicative group of integers modulo $n$ |
| $\mathbb{F}_q$ | finite field of $q$ elements |

| | |
|---|---|
| $\mathrm{desc}(A)$ | description of algebraic structure $A$ |
| $x \leftarrow D$ | value assignment according to the distribution $D$ |
| $x \leftarrow_U S$ | value assignment according to the uniform distribution in $S$ |
| $a \ (\mathrm{mod}\ b)$ | modulo operation: remainder of $a$ divided by $b$ |
| $x \mid y,\ x \nmid y$ | integer $y$ is divisible (not divisible) by integer $x$ |
| $\stackrel{\mathrm{def}}{=}$ | defined to be |
| $\forall$ | for all |
| $\exists$ | there exists |
| $\gcd(x, y)$ | greatest common divisor of $x$ and $y$ |
| $\mathrm{lcm}(x, y)$ | least common multiple of $x$ and $y$ |
| $\log_b x$ | logarithm to base $b$ of $x$; natural log if $b$ is omitted |
| $\lfloor x \rfloor$ | the maximum integer less than or equal to $x$ |
| $\lceil x \rceil$ | the least integer greater than or equal to $x$ |
| $\lvert x \rvert$ | length of integer $x$ $(= 1 + \lfloor \log_2 x \rfloor$ for $x \geq 1)$, also absolute value of $x$ |
| $\phi(n)$ | Euler's function of $n$ |
| $\lambda(n)$ | Carmichael's function of $n$ |
| $\mathrm{ord}(x)$ | order of a group element |
| $\mathrm{ord}_n(x)$ | order of $x \ (\mathrm{mod}\ n)$ |
| $\langle g \rangle$ | cyclic group generated by $g$ |
| $\left( \dfrac{x}{y} \right)$ | Legendre-Jacobi symbol of integer $x$ modulo integer $y$ |
| $\mathrm{J}_n(1)$ | $\left\{\, x \mid x \in \mathbb{Z}_n^*,\ \left( \dfrac{x}{n} \right) = 1 \,\right\}$ |

$\mathrm{QR}_n$        the set of quadratic residues modulo integer $n$;

$\mathrm{QNR}_n$        the set of quadratic non-residues modulo integer $n$;

$\deg(P)$        degree of a polynomial $P$

$\displaystyle\sum_{i=1}^{n} v_i, \sum_{i\in S} v_i$        sum of values $v_i$ for $i = 1, 2, \ldots, n$, or for $i \in S$

$\displaystyle\prod_{i=1}^{n} v_i, \prod_{i\in S} v_i$        product of values $v_i$ for $i = 1, 2, \ldots, n$, or for $i \in S$

$\overline{E}$        complement of event $E$

$E \cup F$        sum of events $E$, $F$, i.e., either $E$ or $F$ occurs

$E \cap F$        product of events $E$, $F$, i.e., both $E$ and $F$ occur

$E \subseteq F$        event $F$ contains event $E$,
i.e., occurrence of $E$ implies occurrence of $F$

$E \setminus F$        difference of events $E$, $F$ $(= E \cap \overline{F})$

$\displaystyle\bigcup_{i=1}^{n} E_i, \bigcup_{i\in S} E_i$        sum of events $E_i$ for $i = 1, 2, \ldots, n$, or for $i \in S$

$\displaystyle\bigcap_{i=1}^{n} E_i, \bigcap_{i\in S} E_i$        product of events $E_i$ for $i = 1, 2, \ldots, n$, or for $i \in S$

$\mathrm{Prob}\,[E]$        probability of event $E$ occurring

$\mathrm{Prob}\,[E \mid F]$        conditional probability of event $E$ occurring
given that event $F$ has occurred

$n!$        factorial of $n$ $(= n(n-1)(n-2)\cdots 1$ with $0! = 1)$

$\dbinom{n}{k}$        ways of picking $k$ out of $n$ $\left(= \dfrac{n!}{k!(n-k)!}\right)$

$b(k; n, p)$        binomial distribution of $k$ successes in $n$ Bernoulli trials
with the success probability being $p$

| | |
|---|---|
| $O(f(n))$ | function $g(n)$ such that $|g(n)| \leq c|f(n)|$ for some constant $c > 0$ and all sufficiently large $n$ |
| $O_B()$ | $O()$ in the bitwise computation mode |
| $\neg x$ | logical operation NOT ($x$ is a Boolean variable), also bit operation: bit-wise negation ($x$ is a bit string) |
| $x \wedge y$ | logical operation AND ($x$, $y$ are Boolean variables), also bit operation: bit-wise and ($x$, $y$ are bit strings) |
| $x \vee y$ | logical operation OR ($x$, $y$ are Boolean variables), also bit operation: bit-wise or ($x$, $y$ are bit strings) |
| $x \oplus y$ | logical operation XOR ($x$, $y$ are Boolean variables), also bit operation: bit-wise xor ($x$, $y$ are bit strings) |
| $(* \ldots *)$ | non-executable comment parts in algorithms or protocols |
| $\square$ | end of proof, remark or example |

# Chapter 3

# PROBABILITY AND INFORMATION THEORY

## 3.1 Introduction

Probability and information theory are essential tools for the development of modern cryptographic techniques.

Probability is a basic tool for the analysis of security. We often need to estimate *how probable* it is that an insecure event may occur under certain conditions. For example, considering Protocol "Coin Flipping Over Telephone" in Chapter 1, we need to estimate the probability for Alice to succeed in finding a collision for a given one-way function $f$ (which should desirably be bounded by a very small quantity), and that for Bob to succeed in finding the parity of $x$ when given $f(x)$ (which should desirably be very close to $\frac{1}{2}$).

Information theory is closely related to probability. An important aspect of security for an encryption algorithm can be referred to as "uncertainty of ciphers:" an encryption algorithm should desirably output ciphertext which has a random distribution in the entire space of its ciphertext message space. Shannon quantifies the uncertainty of information by a notion which he names entropy. Historically, the desire for achieving a high entropy in ciphers comes from the need for thwarting a cryptanalysis technique which makes use of the fact that natural languages contain redundancy, which is related to frequent appearance of some known patterns in natural languages.

Recently, the need for modern cryptographic systems, in particular public-key cryptosystems, to have probabilistic behavior has reached a rather stringent degree: semantic security. This can be described as the following property: if Alice encrypts either 0 or 1 with equal probability under a semantically secure encryption algorithm, sends the resultant ciphertext $c$ to Bob and asks him to answer which is the case, then Bob, without the correct decryption key, should not have an algorithmic strategy to enable him to discern between the two cases with any "advantage" better than a random guessing. We notice that many "textbook" versions of encryption algorithms do not have this desirable property.

### 3.1.1  Chapter Outline

The basic notions of probability which are sufficient for our use in this book will be introduced in §3.2—§3.6. Information theory will be introduced in §3.7—§3.8.

## 3.2  Basic Concept of Probability

Let $\mathbb{S}$ be an arbitrary, but fixed, set of points called **probability space** (or **sample space**). Any element $x \in \mathbb{S}$ is called a **sample point** (also called **outcome**, **simple event** or **indecomposable event**; we shall just use **point** for short). An **event** (also called compound event or decomposable event) is a subset of $\mathbb{S}$ and is usually denoted by a capital letter (e.g., $E$). An **experiment** or observation is an action of yielding (taking) a point from $\mathbb{S}$. An occurrence of an event $E$ is when an experiment yields $x \in E$ for some point $x \in \mathbb{S}$.

**Example 3.1:** Consider an experiment of drawing one playing card from a fair deck (here "fair" means drawing a card at random). Here are some examples of probability spaces, points, events and occurrences of events.

1. $\mathbb{S}_1$: The space consists of 52 points, 1 for each card in the deck. Let event $E_1$ be "aces" (i.e., $E_1 = \{A\spadesuit, A\heartsuit, A\diamondsuit, A\clubsuit\}$). It occurs if the card drawn is an ace of any suit.

2. $\mathbb{S}_2 = \{\text{red, black}\}$. Let event $E_2 = \{\text{red}\}$. It occurs if the card drawn is of red color.

3. $\mathbb{S}_3$: This space consists of 13 points, namely, 2, 3, 4, ..., 10, J, Q, K, A. Let event $E_3$ be "numbers." It occurs if the card drawn is 2, or 3, or ..., or 10. $\square$

**Definition 3.1: Classical Definition of Probability** *Suppose that an experiment can yield one of $n = \#\mathbb{S}$ equally probable points and that every experiment must yield a point. Let $m$ be the number of points which form event $E$. Then value $\dfrac{m}{n}$ is called the probability of the event $E$ occurring and is denoted by*

$$\mathrm{Prob}\,[E] = \frac{m}{n}.$$

**Example 3.2:** In Example 3.1:

1. $\mathrm{Prob}\,[E_1] = \dfrac{4}{52} = \dfrac{1}{13}.$

2. $\mathrm{Prob}\,[E_2] = \dfrac{1}{2}$.

3. $\mathrm{Prob}\,[E_3] = \dfrac{9}{13}$.                                             $\square$

**Definition 3.2: Statistical Definition of Probability**  *Suppose that n experiments are carried out under the same condition, in which event E has occurred $\mu$ times. If value $\dfrac{\mu}{n}$ becomes and remains stable for all sufficiently large n, then the event E is said to have probability which is denoted by*

$$\mathrm{Prob}\,[E] \approx \frac{\mu}{n}.$$

In §3.5.3 we will see that Definition 3.2 can be derived as a theorem (a corollary of the law of large numbers) from a few other intuitive notions. We however provide it in the form of a definition because we consider that itself is sufficiently intuitive.

## 3.3   Properties

1. A probability space itself is an event called **sure event**. For example, $\mathbb{S} = \{\mathrm{HEADS}, \mathrm{TAILS}\}$. We have

$$\mathrm{Prob}\,[\mathbb{S}] = 1.$$

2. Denoting by $\mathbb{O}$ the event that contains no point (i.e., the event that never occurs). For example, black $\lozenge \in \mathbb{O}$. It is called an **impossible event**. We have

$$\mathrm{Prob}\,[\mathbb{O}] = 0.$$

3. Any event $E$ satisfies

$$0 \leq \mathrm{Prob}\,[E] \leq 1.$$

4. If $E \subseteq F$, we say that event $E$ implies event $F$, and

$$\mathrm{Prob}\,[E] \leq \mathrm{Prob}\,[F].$$

5. Denote by $\overline{E} = \mathbb{S} \setminus E$ the **complementary event** of $E$. Then

$$\mathrm{Prob}\,[E] + \mathrm{Prob}\,[\overline{E}] = 1.$$

## 3.4   Basic Calculation

Denote by $E \cup F$ the sum of events $E$, $F$ to represent an occurrence of at least one of the two events, and by $E \cap F$ the product of events $E$, $F$ to represent the occurrence of both of the two events.

## 3.4.1   Addition Rules

1. $\text{Prob}\,[E \cup F] = \text{Prob}\,[E] + \text{Prob}\,[F] - \text{Prob}\,[E \cap F]$.

2. If $E \cap F = \mathbb{O}$, we say that the two events are mutually exclusive or disjoint, and
$$\text{Prob}\,[E \cup F] = \text{Prob}\,[E] + \text{Prob}\,[F]\,.$$

3. If $\bigcup_{i=1}^{n} E_i = \mathbb{S}$ with $E_i \cap E_j = \mathbb{O}\ (i \neq j)$ then

$$\sum_{i=1}^{n} \text{Prob}\,[E_i] = 1.$$

**Example 3.3:** Show

$$\text{Prob}\,[E \cup F] = \text{Prob}\,[E] + \text{Prob}\,\left[F \cap \overline{E}\right].\qquad (3.4.1)$$

Because $E \cup F = E \cup (F \cap \overline{E})$ where $E$ and $F \cap \overline{E}$ are mutually exclusive, (3.4.1) holds as a result of Addition Rule 2.                                                               □

**Definition 3.3: Conditional Probability**  *Let $E, F$ be two events with $E$ having non-zero probability. The probability of occurring $F$ given that $E$ has occurred is called the conditional probability of $F$ given $E$ and is denoted by*

$$\text{Prob}\,[F \mid E] = \frac{\text{Prob}\,[E \cap F]}{\text{Prob}\,[E]}.$$

**Example 3.4:** Consider families with two children. Let $g$ and $b$ stand for girl and boy, respectively, and the first letter for the older child. We have four possibilities $gg, gb, bg, bb$ and these are the four points in $\mathbb{S}$. We associate probability $\frac{1}{4}$ with each point. Let event $E$ be that a family has a girl. Let event $F$ be that both children in the family are girls. What is the probability of $F$ given $E$ (i.e., $\text{Prob}\,[F \mid E]$)?

The event $E \cap F$ means $gg$, and so $\text{Prob}\,[E \cap F] = \frac{1}{4}$. Since the event $E$ means $gg$, or $gb$, or $bg$, and hence $\text{Prob}\,[E] = \frac{3}{4}$. Therefore by Definition 3.3, $\text{Prob}\,[F \mid E] = \frac{1}{3}$. Indeed, in one-third of the families with the characteristic $E$ we can expect that $F$ will occur.                                                               □

**Definition 3.4: Independent Events**  *Events $E,\ F$ are said to be independent if and only if*

$$\text{Prob}\,[F \mid E] = \text{Prob}\,[F]\,.$$

## 3.4.2 Multiplication Rules

1. $\text{Prob}[E \cap F] = \text{Prob}[F \mid E] \cdot \text{Prob}[E] = \text{Prob}[E \mid F] \cdot \text{Prob}[F]$.

2. If events $E$, $F$ are independent, then

$$\text{Prob}[E \cap F] = \text{Prob}[E] \cdot \text{Prob}[F].$$

**Example 3.5:** Consider Example 3.1. We expect that the events $E_1$ and $E_2$ are independent. Their probabilities are $\frac{1}{13}$ and $\frac{1}{2}$, respectively (Example 3.2). Since these two events are independent, applying "Multiplication Rule 2," the probability of their simultaneous realization (a red ace is drawn) is $\frac{1}{26}$. $\qquad\square$

## 3.4.3 The Law of Total Probability

The **law of total probability** is a useful theorem.

**Theorem 3.1:** *If* $\bigcup_{i=1}^{n} E_i = \mathbb{S}$ *and* $E_i \cap E_j = \mathbb{O}$ *(*$i \neq j$*), then for* any *event* $A$

$$\text{Prob}[A] = \sum_{i=1}^{n} \text{Prob}[A \mid E_i] \cdot \text{Prob}[E_i].$$

**Proof** Since

$$A = A \cap \mathbb{S} = \bigcup_{i=1}^{n} (A \cap E_i)$$

where $A \cap E_i$ and $A \cap E_j$ ($i \neq j$) are mutually exclusive, the probabilities of the right-hand-side sum of events can be added up using Addition Rule 2, in which each term follows from an application of "Multiplication Rule 1." $\qquad\square$

The law of total probability is very useful. We will frequently use it when we evaluate (or estimate a bound of) the probability of an event $A$ which is conditional given some other mutually exclusive events (e.g. and typically, $E$ and $\overline{E}$). The usefulness of this formula is because often an evaluation of conditional probabilities $\text{Prob}[A \mid E_i]$ is easier than a direct calculation of $\text{Prob}[A]$.

**Example 3.6:** (This example uses some elementary facts of number theory. The reader who finds this example difficult may return to review it after having studied Chapter 6.)

*Let* $p = 2q + 1$ *such that both* $p$ *and* $q$ *are prime numbers. Consider choosing two numbers* $g$ *and* $h$ *at random from the set* $\mathcal{S} = \{1, 2, ..., p-1\}$ *(with replacement). Let event* $A$ *be "*$h$ *is generated by* $g$*," that is,* $h \equiv g^x \pmod{p}$ *for some* $x < p$

*(equivalently, this means "$\log_g h \pmod{p-1}$ exists"). What is the probability of $A$ for random $g$ and $h$?*

It is not very straightforward to evaluate $\text{Prob}[A]$ directly. However, the evaluation can be made easy by first evaluating a few conditional probabilities followed by applying the theorem of total probability.

Denote by $\text{ord}_p(g)$ the (multiplicative) order of $g \pmod p$, which is the least natural number $i$ such that $g^i \equiv 1 \pmod p$. The value $\text{Prob}[A]$ depends on the following four mutually exclusive events.

i) $E_1 : \text{ord}_p(g) = p - 1 = 2q$ and we know $\text{Prob}[E_1] = \frac{\phi(2q)}{p-1} = \frac{q-1}{p-1}$ (here $\phi$ is Euler's phi function; in $S$ there are exactly $\phi(2q) = q - 1$ elements of order $2q$). In this case, any $h < p$ must be generated by $g$ ($g$ is a generator of the set $S$), and so we have $\text{Prob}[A \mid E_1] = 1$.

ii) $E_2 : \text{ord}_p(g) = q$ and similar to case (i) we know $\text{Prob}[E_2] = \frac{q-1}{p-1}$. In this case, $h$ can be generated by $g$ if and only if $\text{ord}_p(h) \mid q$. Since in the set $S$ there are exactly $q$ elements of orders dividing $q$, we have $\text{Prob}[A \mid E_2] = \frac{q}{p-1} = \frac{1}{2}$.

iii) $E_3 : \text{ord}_p(g) = 2$. Because there is only one element, $p - 1$, of order 2, so $\text{Prob}[E_3] = \frac{1}{p-1}$. Only 1 and $p - 1$ can be generated by $p - 1$, so we have $\text{Prob}[A \mid E_3] = \frac{2}{p-1}$.

iv) $E_4 : \text{ord}_p(g) = 1$. Only element 1 is of order 1, and so $\text{Prob}[E_4] = \frac{1}{p-1}$. Also only 1 can be generated by 1, and we have $\text{Prob}[A \mid E_4] = \frac{1}{p-1}$.

The above four events not only are mutually exclusive, but also form all possible cases for the orders of $g$. Therefore we can apply the theorem of total probability to obtain $\text{Prob}[A]$:

$$\text{Prob}[A] = \frac{q-1}{p-1} + \frac{q-1}{2(p-1)} + \frac{2}{(p-1)^2} + \frac{1}{(p-1)^2}. \qquad \square$$

## 3.5  Random Variables and their Probability Distributions

In cryptography, we mainly consider functions defined on discrete spaces (such as an interval of integers used as a cryptographic key-space, or a finite algebraic structure such as finite group or field). Let discrete space $S$ have a finite or countable number of isolated points $x_1, x_2, ..., x_n, ..., x_{\#S}$. We consider the general case that $S$ may contain a countable number of points, and in that case, $\#S = \infty$. This will allow us to conduct computational complexity analysis of our algorithms and protocols in an asymptotic manner (see §4.6).

## Definition 3.5: Discrete Random Variables and their Distribution Function

1) *A (discrete) random variable is a numerical result of an experiment. It is a function defined on a (discrete) sample space.*

2) *Let $\mathbb{S}$ be a (discrete) probability space and $\xi$ be a random variable. A (discrete) distribution function of $\xi$ is a function of type $\mathbb{S} \mapsto \mathbb{R}$ provided by a list of probability values*

$$\mathrm{Prob}\,[\xi = x_i] = p_i \quad (i = 1, 2, ..., \#\mathbb{S})$$

*such that the following conditions are satisfied:*

*i)* $p_i \geq 0$;

*ii)* $\displaystyle\sum_{i=1}^{\#\mathbb{S}} p_i = 1.$

Now let us look at two discrete probability distributions which are frequently used in cryptography. From now on we shall always drop the word "discrete" from "discrete probability space," "discrete probability distribution," etc. All situations in our considerations will always be discrete.

## 3.5.1 Uniform Distribution

The most frequently used random variables in cryptography follows **uniform distribution**:

$$\mathrm{Prob}\,[\xi = x_i] = \frac{1}{\#\mathbb{S}} \quad (i = 1, 2, ..., \#\mathbb{S})$$

**Example 3.7:** Let $S$ be the set of non-negative numbers up to $k$ bits (binary digits). Sample a point in $S$ at random by following the uniform distribution. Show that the probability that the sampled point is a $k$-bit number is $\frac{1}{2}$.

$S = \{0, 1, 2, ..., 2^k - 1\}$ can be partitioned into two disjoint subsets $S_1 = \{0, 1, 2, ..., 2^{k-1} - 1\}$ and $S_2 = \{2^{k-1}, 2^{k-1} + 1, ..., 2^k - 1\}$ where $S_2$ contains all $k$-bit numbers, $\#S_1 = \#S_2 = \frac{\#S}{2}$. Applying "Addition 2," we have

$$\text{Prob}\,[\text{sampled point} \in S_2] \;=\; \text{Prob}\left[\bigcup_{i=2^{k-1}}^{2^k-1} \text{sampled point} = i\right]$$

$$=\; \sum_{i=2^{k-1}}^{2^k-1} \text{Prob}\,[\text{sampled point} = i]$$

$$=\; \sum_{i=2^{k-1}}^{2^k-1} \frac{1}{\#S}$$

$$=\; \frac{\#S_2}{\#S}$$

$$=\; \frac{1}{2}. \qquad\qquad\qquad \square$$

In this example, the instruction "sample (a point) $p$ in (a set) $S$ at random by following the uniform distribution" is quite long while it is also a frequent instruction in cryptography. For this reason, we shall shorten this long instruction into "picking $p$ in $S$ at uniformly random," or into an even shorter notation: $p \in_U S$.

## 3.5.2 Binomial Distribution

Suppose an experiment has two results, titled "success" and "failure" (e.g., tossing a coin results in HEADS or TAILS). Repeated independent such experiments are called **Bernoulli trials** if there are only two possible points for each experiment and their probabilities remain the same throughout the experiments. Suppose that in any one trial

$$\text{Prob}\,[\,\text{"success"}\,] = p, \quad \text{Prob}\,[\,\text{"failure"}\,] = 1 - p$$

then

$$\text{Prob}\,[k \text{ "successes" in } n \text{ trials}] = \binom{n}{k} p^k (1-p)^{n-k}, \qquad (3.5.1)$$

where $\binom{n}{k}$ is the number of ways for "picking $k$ out of $n$."

Here is why (3.5.1) holds. First, event "$n$ trials result in $k$ "successes" and $n-k$ "failures" can happen in the number of ways for "picking $k$ out of $n$," that is, the event has $\binom{n}{k}$ points. Secondly, each point consists of $k$ "successes" and $n-k$ "failures," we have the probability $p^k(1-p)^{n-k}$ for this point.

If random variable $\xi_n$ takes values $0, 1, \ldots, n$, and for value $p$ with $0 < p < 1$

$$\text{Prob}\,[\xi_n = k] = \binom{n}{k} p^k (1-p)^{n-k} \quad (k = 0, 1, \ldots, n)$$

then we say that $\xi_n$ follows **binomial distribution**. Comparing with (3.5.1), we know that Bernoulli trial follows the binomial distribution. We denote by $b(k; n, p)$ a **binomial term** where $k = 0, 1, \ldots, n$ and $0 < p < 1$.

**Example 3.8:**

i) Let a fair coin be tossed 10 times. What is the probability for all possible numbers of "HEADS appearance" (i.e., appears 0, or 1, or, $\ldots$, or 10 times)?

ii) The probability for "HEADS appears 5 times?"

iii) What is that for "HEADS appears less than or equal to 5 times?"

For (i), since this event always occurs, it should have probability 1. Indeed, applying "Addition Rule 2," we have

$$\text{Prob}\left[\bigcup_{i=0}^{10} \text{HEADS appears } i \text{ times}\right] = \sum_{i=0}^{10} \text{Prob}\,[\text{HEADS appears } i \text{ times}]$$

$$= \sum_{i=0}^{10} \binom{10}{i} \left(\frac{1}{2}\right)^i \left(\frac{1}{2}\right)^{10-i}$$

$$= (1+1)^{10} \left(\frac{1}{2}\right)^{10}$$

$$= 1.$$

For (ii), we have

$$\text{Prob}\,[5 \text{ HEADS in 10 tosses}] == \binom{10}{5} \left(\frac{1}{2}\right)^{10} = \frac{252}{1024} \approx 0.246.$$

For (iii), we must sum the probabilities for all cases of 5 or less "HEADS appearances:"

$$\text{Prob}\left[\bigcup_{i=0}^{5} \text{HEADS appears } i \text{ times in 10 tosses}\right] = \left(\frac{1}{2}\right)^{10} \sum_{i=0}^{5} \binom{10}{i} \approx 0.623. \square$$

Fig 3.1 plots the binomial distribution for $p = 0.5$ and $n = 10$, i.e., that used in Example 3.8.

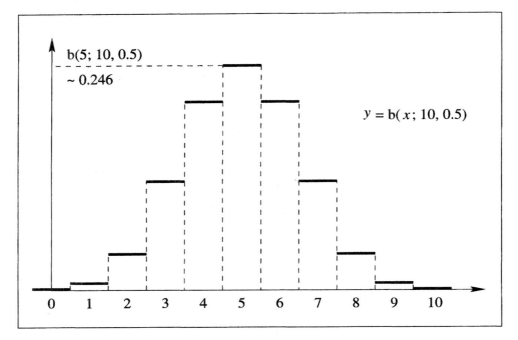

**Figure 3.1.** Binomial Distribution

The reader should pay particular attention to the difference between Example 3.8.(ii) and Example 3.8.(iii). The former is the area of the central rectangular in Fig 3.1 while the latter is the sum of the left six of them.

In applications of binomial distributions (e.g., in §4.4.1, §4.4.5.1 and §18.5.1), the probability of having exactly $r$ "successes" (as in Example 3.8.(ii), a single term) is less interesting than the probability of $r$ or less (or more) "successes" (as in Example 3.8.(iii), the sum of many terms). Moreover, the sum of some terms will be much more significant than that of some others. Let us now investigate "the significant sum" and "the negligible sum" in binomial distributions.

### 3.5.2.1   The Central Term and the Tails

Stacking consecutive binomial terms, we have

$$\frac{b(k; n, p)}{b(k-1; n, p)} = \frac{(n-k+1)p}{k(1-p)} = 1 + \frac{(n+1)p - k}{k(1-p)}. \tag{3.5.2}$$

The second term in the right-hand side is positive when $k < (n+1)p$ and then becomes negative after $k > (n+1)p$. So, the ratio in (3.5.2) is greater than 1 when $k < (n+1)p$ and is less than 1 after $k > (n+1)p$. Consequently, $b(k; n, p)$ increases as $k$ does before $k$ reaches $(n+1)p$ and then decreases after $k > (n+1)p$. Therefore, the binomial term $b(k; n, p)$ reaches the maximum value at the point $k = \lfloor (n+1)p \rfloor$. The binomial term

$$b(\lfloor (n+1)p \rfloor ; n, p) \tag{3.5.3}$$

is called the **central term**. Since the central term reaches the maximum value, the point $\lfloor (n+1)p \rfloor$ is one with "the most probable number of successes." Notice that when $(n+1)p$ is an integer, the ratio in (3.5.2) is 1, and therefore in this case we have two central terms $b((n+1)p - 1; n, p)$ and $b((n+1)p; n, p)$.

Let $r > (n+1)p$, i.e., $r$ is a point somewhere right to the point of "the most probable number of successes." We know that terms $b(k; n, p)$ decrease for all $k \geq r$. We can estimate the speed of the decreasing by replacing $k$ with $r$ in the right-hand side of (3.5.2) and obtain

$$b(k; n, p) < b(k - 1; n, p)s \quad \text{where } s = \frac{(n + 1 - r)p}{r(1 - p)} < 1. \tag{3.5.4}$$

In particular, we have

$$b(k; n, p) < b(r; n, p)s.$$

Notice that (3.5.4) holds for all $k = r + 1, r + 2, \ldots, n$. Therefore we have

$$b(r + i; n, p) < b(r; n, p)s^i \quad \text{for } i = 1, 2, \ldots \tag{3.5.5}$$

Now for $r > np$, let us see an upper bound of the probability of having $r$ or more "successes," which is

$$\text{Prob}\,[\xi_n \geq r] = \sum_{k=r}^{n} b(k; n, p) = \sum_{i=0}^{n-r} b(r + i; n, p). \tag{3.5.6}$$

By (3.5.5), we have

$$\text{Prob}\,[\xi_n \geq r] < b(r; n, p) \sum_{i=0}^{n-r} s^i < b(r; n, p) \sum_{i=0}^{\infty} s^i = b(r; n, p) \frac{1}{1 - s}.$$

Replacing $s$ back to $\frac{(n+1-r)p}{r(1-p)}$, we have

$$\text{Prob}\,[\xi_n \geq r] < b(r; n, p) \frac{r(1 - p)}{r - (n + 1)p}.$$

Now we notice that there are only $r - (n + 1)p$ binomial terms between the central term and $b(r; n, p)$, each is greater than $b(r; n, p)$ and their sum is still less than 1. Therefore it turns out that $b(r; n, p) < (r - (n + 1)p)^{-1}$. We therefore finally reach

$$\text{Prob}\,[\xi_n \geq r] \leq \frac{r(1 - p)}{(r - (n + 1)p)^2} \quad \text{for } r > (n + 1)p . \tag{3.5.7}$$

The bound in (3.5.7) is called a **right tail** of the binomial distribution function. We can see that if $r$ is *slightly* away from the central point $(n+1)p$, then the denominator in the fraction of (3.5.7) is not zero and hence the whole "right tail" is bounded by a quantity which is at the magnitude of $(np)^{-1}$. Hence, a right tail is a small quantity and diminishes to 0 when $n$ gets large.

We can analogously derive the bound for a **left tail**:

$$\text{Prob}\,[\xi_n \le r] \le \frac{(n+1-r)p}{((n+1)p-r)^2} \quad \text{for } r < (n+1)p\,. \tag{3.5.8}$$

The derivation is left for the reader as an exercise (Ex 3.7).

At first sight of (3.5.7) and (3.5.8) it seems that the two tails are bounded by quantities which are at the magnitude of $\frac{1}{n}$. We should however notice that the estimates derived in (3.5.7) and (3.5.8) are only two upper bounds. The real speed that a tail diminishes to 0 is much faster than $\frac{1}{n}$ does. The following numerical example reveals this fact (also see the soundness and completeness properties of Prot 18.4 in §18.5.1.1).

**Example 3.9:** Let $p = 0.5$. For various cases of $n$, let us compute left tails of binomial distribution functions bounded to the point $r = n(p - 0.01)$.

i) For $n = 1,000$, the corresponding left tail is:

$$\text{Prob}\,[\xi < 490] \approx 0.25333.$$

ii) For $n = 10,000$, the corresponding left tail becomes:

$$\text{Prob}\,[\xi < 4,900] \approx 0.02221.$$

iii) If $n$ is increased to $100,000$, then the corresponding tail is trivialized to:

$$\text{Prob}\,[\xi < 49,000] \approx 1.24241 \cdot 10^{-10}$$

Comparing these results, it is evident that a tail diminishes to 0 much faster than $\frac{1}{n}$ does.

Since $p = 0.5$, the distribution density function is symmetric (see Fig 3.1). For a symmetric distribution, a right tail equals a left one if they have the equal number of terms. Thus, for case (iii), the sum of the two tails of 98,000 terms (i.e., 98% of the total terms) is practically 0, while the sum of the terms of the most probable number of successes (i.e., 2% of the total terms around the center, there are 2,001 such terms) is practically 1. □

### 3.5.3  The Law of Large Numbers

Recall Definition 3.2: it states that if in $n$ identical trials $E$ occurs stably $\mu$ times and if $n$ is sufficiently large, then $\frac{\mu}{n}$ is the probability of $E$.

Consider that in Bernoulli trials with probability $p$ for "success," the random variable $\xi_n$ is the number of "successes" in $n$ trials. Then $\frac{\xi_n}{n}$ is the average number of "successes" in $n$ trials. By Definition 3.2, $\frac{\xi_n}{n}$ should be close to $p$.

Now we consider, for example, the probability that $\frac{\xi_n}{n}$ exceeds $p + \alpha$ for any $\alpha > 0$ (i.e., $\alpha$ is arbitrarily small but fixed). Clearly, this probability is

$$\text{Prob}\left[\xi_n > n(p+\alpha)\right] = \sum_{i=n(p+\alpha)+1}^{n} b(i; n, p).$$

By (3.5.7), we have

$$\text{Prob}\left[\xi_n > n(p+\alpha)\right] < \frac{1}{n\alpha}. \qquad (3.5.9)$$

Thus,

$$\text{Prob}\left[\xi_n > n(p+\alpha)\right] \to 0 \quad (n \to \infty). \qquad (3.5.10)$$

Analogously we can also see

$$\text{Prob}\left[\xi_n < n(p-\alpha)\right] \to 0 \quad (n \to \infty).$$

Therefore we have (the **law of large numbers**):

$$\lim_{n \to \infty} \text{Prob}\left[\left|\frac{\xi_n}{n} - p\right| < \alpha\right] = 1.$$

This form of the law of large numbers is also called **Bernoulli's theorem**. It is now clear that Definition 3.2 can be derived as a corollary of the law of large numbers. However, we have provided it in the form of a definition because we consider that itself is sufficiently intuitive.

## 3.6  Birthday Paradox

For any function $f : X \mapsto Y$ where $Y$ is a set of $n$ elements, let us solve the following problem:

> For a probability bound $\epsilon$ (i.e., $0 < \epsilon < 1$), find a value $k$ such that for $k$ pairwise distinct values $x_1, x_2, \ldots, x_k \in_U X$, the $k$ evaluations $f(x_1), f(x_2), \ldots, f(x_k)$ satisfy
>
> $$\text{Prob}\left[f(x_i) = f(x_j)\right] \geq \epsilon \quad \text{for some } i \neq j.$$

That is, in $k$ evaluations of the function, a collision has occurred with the probability no less than $\epsilon$.

This problem asks for a value $k$ to satisfy the given probability bound from below for *any* function. We only need to consider functions which have a so-called random property: such a function maps uniform input values in $X$ to uniform output values in $Y$. Clearly, only a function with such a random property can enlarge the value $k$ for the given probability bound, which can then be able to satisfy other functions for the same probability bound. Consequently, it is necessary that $\#X > \#Y$; otherwise it is possible that for some functions there will be no collision occurring at all.

Thus, we can assume that the function evaluation in our problem has $n$ distinct and equally possible points. We can model such a function evaluation as drawing a ball from a bag of $n$ differently colored balls, recording the color and then replacing the ball. Then the problem is to find the value $k$ such that at least one matching color is met with probability $\epsilon$.

There is no color restriction on the first ball. Let $y_i$ be the color for the $i$th instance of ball drawing. The second ball should not have the same color as the first one, and so the probability for $y_2 \neq y_1$ is $1 - 1/n$; the probability for $y_3 \neq y_1$ and $y_3 \neq y_2$ is $1 - 2/n$, and so on. Upon drawing the $k$th ball, the probability for no collision so far is

$$\left(1 - \frac{1}{n}\right)\left(1 - \frac{2}{n}\right)\cdots\left(1 - \frac{k-1}{n}\right).$$

For sufficiently large $n$ and relatively small $x$, we know

$$\left(1 + \frac{x}{n}\right)^n \approx e^x$$

or

$$1 + \frac{x}{n} \approx e^{x/n}.$$

So

$$\left(1 - \frac{1}{n}\right)\left(1 - \frac{2}{n}\right)\cdots\left(1 - \frac{k-1}{n}\right) = \prod_{i=1}^{k-1}\left(1 + \frac{-i}{n}\right) \approx \prod_{i=1}^{k-1} e^{-i/n} = e^{-\frac{k(k-1)}{2n}}.$$

The equation in the most right-hand side is due to Gauss summation on the exponent value.

This is the probability for drawing $k$ balls without collision. Therefore the probability for at least one collision should be

$$1 - e^{-\frac{k(k-1)}{2n}}.$$

Equalizing this value to $\epsilon$, we have

$$e^{-\frac{k(k-1)}{2n}} \approx 1 - \epsilon$$

or

$$k^2 - k \approx 2n \log \frac{1}{1-\epsilon},$$

that is,

$$k \approx \sqrt{2n \log \frac{1}{1-\epsilon}}. \qquad (3.6.1)$$

Thus, for a random function mapping onto $Y$, we only need to perform this amount of evaluations in order to meet a collision with the given probability $\epsilon$. From (3.6.1) we can see that even if $\epsilon$ is a significant value (i.e., very close to 1), the value $\log \frac{1}{1-\epsilon}$ will remain trivially small, and hence in general $k$ is proportional to $\sqrt{n}$.

If we consider $\epsilon = 1/2$, then

$$k \approx 1.1774\sqrt{n}. \qquad (3.6.2)$$

The square-root relationship between $k$ and $n$ shown in (3.6.1) and in (3.6.2) suggests that for a random function with the cardinality of the output space being $n$, we need only to make roughly $\sqrt{n}$ evaluations of the function and find a collision with a non-negligible probability.

This fact has a profound impact on the design of cryptosystems and cryptographic protocols. For example, for a piece of data (e.g., a cryptographic key or a message) hidden as a pre-image of a cryptographic function (which is typically a random function), if the square root of this data is not a sufficiently large quantity, then the data may be discovered by random evaluation of the function. Such an attack is often called **square-root attack** or **birthday attack**. The latter name is due to the following seemingly "paradoxical phenomenon:" taking $n = 365$ in (3.6.2), we find $k \approx 22.49$; that is, in order for two people in a room of random people to have the same birthday with more than 50% chance, we only need 23 people in the room. This seems to be a little bit of counter-intuition at first glance.

### 3.6.1    Application of Birthday Paradox: Pollard's Kangaroo Algorithm for Index Computation

Let $p$ be a prime number. Under certain conditions (which will become apparent in Chapter 5) the **modulo exponentiation** function $f(x) = g^x \pmod{p}$ is essentially a random function. That is, for $x = 1, 2, \ldots, p-1$, the value $f(x)$ jumps wildly in the range interval $[1, p-1]$. This function has wide applications in cryptography because it has a one-way property: computing $y = f(x)$ is very easy (using Alg 4.3) while inverting the function, i.e., extracting $x = f^{-1}(y)$, is extremely difficult for almost all $y \in [1, p-1]$.

Sometimes for $y = f(x)$ we know $x \in [a, b]$ for some $a$ and $b$. Clearly, evaluations of $f(a), f(a+1), \ldots$, can reveal $x$ before exhausting $b - a$ steps. If $b - a$ is too large, then this exhaustive search method cannot be practical. However, if $\sqrt{b-a}$ is a tractable value (for example, $b - a \approx 2^{100}$ and so $\sqrt{b-a} \approx 2^{50}$, a gaspingly handleable quantity), then birthday paradox can play a role in inverting $f(x)$ in $\sqrt{b-a}$ steps. Pollard discovers such a method [240]; he names the algorithm $\lambda$-**method** and **kangaroo method** for index computation. The meanings of these names will become clear in a moment.

Pollard describes his algorithm using two kangaroos. One is a tame kangaroo $T$ and the other is a wild one $W$. The task of extracting the unknown index value $x$ from $y = g^x \pmod{p}$ is modeled by catching $W$ using $T$. This is done by letting the two kangaroos jump around in the following ways. Let $S$ be an integer set of $J$ elements ($J = \lfloor \log_2(b - a) \rfloor$, hence small):

$$S = \{s(0), s(1), s(2), \ldots, s(J - 1)\} = \{2^0, 2^1, 2^2, \ldots, 2^{J-1}\}.$$

Each jump made by a kangaroo uses a distance which is randomly picked from $S$. Each kangaroo carries a mileageometer to accumulate the distance it has travelled.

$T$ starts its journey from the known point $t_0 = g^b \pmod{p}$. The known point is $b$ which can be considered as the home-base since $T$ is tame. Its path is

$$t(i + 1) = t(i) \cdot g^{s(t(i) \,(\mathrm{mod}\, J))} \pmod{p} \quad \text{for } i = 0, 1, 2, \ldots \qquad (3.6.3)$$

Let $T$ jump $n$ steps then it stops. We will decide how large $n$ should be in a moment. After $n$-th jump, the mileageometer carried by $T$ records the distance so far as

$$d(n) = \sum_{i=0}^{n} s(t(i) \,(\mathrm{mod}\, J)).$$

Using the distance recorded on $T$'s mileageometer, we can re-express (3.6.3) into

$$t(n) = g^{b+d(n-1)} \pmod{p}.$$

$W$ starts its journey from an unknown point hidden in $w_0 = g^x \pmod{p}$. The unknown point is $x$ and that is why this kangaroo is a wild one. Its path is

$$w(j + 1) = w(j) \cdot g^{s(w(j) \,(\mathrm{mod}\, J))} \pmod{p} \quad \text{for } j = 0, 1, 2, \ldots \qquad (3.6.4)$$

The mileageometer carried by $W$ also records the distance so far:

$$D(j) = \sum_{k=0}^{j} s(w_k \,(\mathrm{mod}\, J)).$$

Similar to the expression for $T$'s footprints, using the distance recorded on $W$'s mileageometer we can also re-express (3.6.4) into

$$w(i) = g^{x+D(i-1)} \pmod{p}.$$

It is clear that footprints of the two kangaroos, $t(i)$ and $w(j)$, are two random functions. The former ranges over a set of $i$ points and the latter, $j$ points. Due to birthday paradox, within roughly

$$n \approx \sqrt{b - a}$$

jumps made by $T$ and by $W$, respectively, a collision $t(\xi) = w(\eta)$ should occur for some $\xi \le n$ and $\eta \le n$. This is when $T$ and $W$ landed on the same point. One may imagine this as $W$ landing on a trap set by $T$. Now $W$ is caught. The probability of occurring a collision tends to 1 quickly if the number of random jumps the two kangaroo make exceed $\sqrt{b - a}$.

When the collision $t(\xi) = w(\eta)$ occurs, observing (3.6.3) and (3.6.4), we will have $t(\xi + 1) = w(\eta + 1)$, $t(\xi + 2) = w(\eta + 2)$, ..., etc., that is, eventually $w(m) = t(n)$ will show up for some integers $m \approx n$. One may imaging that the collision equation $t(\xi) = w(\eta)$ represents the point where the two legs of the Greek letter $\lambda$ meet, and after that meeting point, the two kangaroos jumps on the same path which will eventually lead to the detection of $w(m) = t(n)$ (recall that $T$ jumps a fixed $n$ steps). This is explains $\lambda$ as the other name for the algorithm.

When the collision is detected, we have

$$g^x = g^{b + d(n-1) - D(m-1)} \pmod{p}.$$

Namely, we have extracted

$$x = b + d(n - 1) - D(m - 1).$$

Since we have kept the two mileageometers $d(m - 1)$ and $D(n - 1)$, we can compute $x$ using the "miles" accumulated in them. It is possible that the two kangaroos over run a long distance after they have landed on the same point, and so the extracted index value can be $x + o$ for some $o$ satisfying $g^o \pmod{p} = 1$. If this is the case, it's harmless to just consider $x + o$ as the targeted index value.

This is a **probabilistic algorithm**, which means that it may fail without finding a collision (i.e., fail to output the targeted index value). Nevertheless, due to the significant collision probability we have seen in §3.6, the probability of failure can be controlled to adequately small. Repeating the algorithm by offsetting $W$'s starting point with a known offset value $\delta$, the algorithm will terminated within several repetitions.

The value $\sqrt{b - a}$ being feasibly small is the condition for the $\lambda$-algorithm to be practical. Therefore, setting $n = \sqrt{b - a}$ (the number of jumps made by $T$), the algorithm runs in time proportional to computing $\sqrt{b - a}$ modulo exponentiations. The space requirement is trivial: there are only $J = \lfloor \log(b - a) \rfloor$ elements to be stored. The time constraint $\sqrt{b - a}$ means that the algorithm cannot be practical for extracting a large index value. Pollard considers this limitation as that kangaroos cannot jump across continents.

## 3.7    Information Theory

Shannon's definition for **entropy** [264, 265] of a message source is a measure of the amount of information the source has. The measure is in the form of a function of the probability distribution over the set of all possible messages the source may output.

Let $L = \{a_1, a_2, \ldots, a_n\}$ be a language of $n$ different symbols. Suppose a source $S$ may output these symbols with independent probabilities

$$\text{Prob}[a_1], \text{Prob}[a_2], \ldots, \text{Prob}[a_n],$$

respectively, and these probabilities satisfy

$$\sum_{i=1}^{n} \text{Prob}[a_i] = 1. \tag{3.7.1}$$

The entropy of the source $S$ is

$$H(S) = \sum_{i=1}^{n} \text{Prob}[a_i] \log_2 \left( \frac{1}{\text{Prob}[a_i]} \right). \tag{3.7.2}$$

The entropy function $H(S)$ defined in (3.7.2) captures a quantity which we can name "*number of bits per source output.*"

Let us explain the entropy function by assigning ourselves a simple job: considering that the source $S$ is memoryless, we must record the output from $S$. A straightforward way to do the job is to record whatever $S$ outputs. However, from (3.7.1) we know that each output from $S$ will be one of the $n$ symbols $a_1, a_2, \ldots, a_n$ which are already known to us. It can be quite uninteresting and inefficient to record known things. Thus, the question for us is, how can we *efficiently* record something *interesting* in the output from $S$?

Let $S$ output these symbols in a $k$ consecutive sequence, i.e., $S$ outputs a word of $k$ symbols

$$a_{i_1} a_{i_2} \cdots a_{i_k} \quad \text{for} \ \ 1 \leq i_k \leq n.$$

Let $L_k$ denote the minimum expected number of bits we have to use in order to record a $k$-symbol word output from $S$. We have the following theorem for measuring the quantity $L_k$.

**Theorem 3.2: Shannon** [264, 265]

$$\lim_{k \to \infty} \frac{L_k}{k} = H(S).$$

**Proof** The following "sandwich" style relation holds for all integers $k > 0$:

$$kH(S) \leq L_k \leq kH(S) + 1.$$

The statement is in its limit form.

☐

In other words, the minimum average number of bits needed for recording per output from $S$ is $H(S)$.

## 3.7.1   Properties of Entropy

The function $H(S)$ has the minimum value 0 if $S$ outputs some symbol, say $a_1$, with probability 1, since then

$$H(S) = \text{Prob}\,[a_1]\log_2(\frac{1}{\text{Prob}\,[a_1]}) = \log_2 1 = 0.$$

This case captures the fact that when we are sure that $S$ will only and definitely output $a_1$, then why should we waste any bit to record it?

The function $H(S)$ reaches the maximum value of $\log_2 n$ if $S$ outputs each of these $n$ symbols with equal probability $1/n$, i.e., $S$ is a random source of the uniform distribution. This is because under this situation

$$H(S) = \frac{1}{n}\sum_{i=1}^{n}\log_2 n = \log_2 n.$$

This case captures the following fact: since $S$ can output any one of these $n$ symbols with equal probability, we have to prepare $\log_2 n$ bits in order to mark any possible one of the $n$ numbers.

To this end we can think of $H(S)$ as the amount of *uncertainty*, or *information*, contained in each output from $S$.

**Example 3.10:** Consider Prot 1.1 ("Coin Flipping Over Telephone"). Whether running over telephones or on connected computers, that protocol is for Alice and Bob to agree on a random bit. In the protocol, Alice picks a large random integer $x \in_U \mathbb{N}$, then sends $f(x)$ to Bob under the one-way function $f$, and finally reveals $x$ to Bob after his random guess. Viewed by Bob, $x$ as a whole number should not be regarded as a piece of new information since he knows already that $x$ is one element in $\mathbb{N}$ before even receiving $f(x)$. Bob only uses an interesting part of Alice's output: the parity of $x$ is used to compute a random bit agreed with Alice. Thus, we have

$$\begin{aligned}H(\text{Alice}) &= \text{Prob}\,[x \text{ is odd}]\log_2(\frac{1}{\text{Prob}\,[x \text{ is odd}]}) + \\ &\quad \text{Prob}\,[x \text{ is even}]\log_2(\frac{1}{\text{Prob}\,[x \text{ is even}]}) \\ &= \frac{1}{2}\log_2 2 + \frac{1}{2}\log_2 2 = 1.\end{aligned}$$

That is, Alice is a source of 1 bit per output, even though her output is a large integer.

☐

If Alice and Bob repeat running Prot 1.1 $n$ times, they can agree on a string of $n$ bits: a correct guess by Bob outputs 1, while an incorrect guess outputs 0. In this usage of the protocol, both Alice and Bob are 1-bit-per-protocol-run random sources. The agreed bit string is mutually trust by both parties as random because each party has her/his own random input and knows that the other party cannot control the output.

## 3.8  Redundancy in Natural Languages

Consider a source $S(L)$ outputs words in a natural language $L$. Suppose that, on average, each word in $L$ has $k$ characters. Since by Shannon's Theorem (Theorem 3.2), $H(S(L))$ is the minimum average number of bits per output from $S(L)$ (remember that per output from $S(L)$ is a word of $k$ characters), the value

$$r(L) = \frac{H(S(L))}{k}$$

should be the minimum average number of bits per character in language $L$. The value $r(L)$ is called the **rate of language** $L$. Let $L$ be English. Shannon calculated that $r(\text{English})$ is in the range of 1.0 to 1.5 bits/letter [267].

Let $\Sigma = \{a, b, \ldots, z\}$. Then we know $r(\Sigma) = \log_2 26 \approx 4.7$ bits/letter. $r(\Sigma)$ is called **absolute rate of language** with alphabet set $\Sigma$. Comparing $r(\text{English})$ with $r(\Sigma)$, we see that the actual rate of English is considerably less than its absolute rate.

The **redundancy of language** $L$ with alphabet set $\Sigma$ is

$$r(\Sigma) - r(L) \text{ (bits per character)}.$$

Thus for a conservative consideration of $r(\text{English}) = 1.5$, the redundancy of English is $4.7 - 1.5 = 3.2$ bits per letter. In terms of percentage, the redundancy ratio is $3.2/4.7 \approx 68\%$. In other words, about 68% of the letters in an English word are redundant. This means a possibility to compress an English article down to 32% of its original volume without loss of information.

Redundancy in a natural language arises from some known and frequently appearing patterns in the language. For example, in English, letter $q$ is almost always followed by $u$; "the," "ing" and "ed" are a few other known examples of patterns. Redundancy in natural languages provides an important means for **cryptanalysis** which aims for recovering plaintext messages or a cryptographic key from a ciphertext.

**Example 3.11:** We have mentioned in Chapter 1 that in this book we will study many kinds of attacks on cryptographic algorithms and protocols. In a later chapter (Chapter 14) we will introduce and discuss four kinds of attacks on encryption algorithms which have rather long names. They are:

- Passive plaintext indistinguishable attack

- Active plaintext indistinguishable attack in the chosen-plaintext mode

- Active plaintext indistinguishable attack in the non-adaptive chosen-ciphertext mode

- Active plaintext indistinguishable attack in the adaptive chosen-ciphertext mode

Full meanings of these attacks will be explained in that chapter. Here we only need to point out the following two facts about these attacks:

1. The use of long names is very appropriate because behind each of these long-named attacks there is a non-trivial amount of information to convey.

2. In Chapter 14 we will only deal with these four attacks.

Since in Chapter 14 we will only deal with these four attacks, the actual entropy of these names can be as low as 2 bits per name. However, because numbers 0, 1, 2, and 3 and a few other single characters (e.g., letter "a", index "$i$", "$j$", security parameter "$k$", etc.) will appear in Chapter 14, in order to uniquely identify these attacks, we actually have to use more than two bits of information to name these attacks.

Notice that we will not use strings a0, a1, a2, a3 in any part of Chapter 14; we can actually shorten the four long attacking names to these four strings, respectively, without causing any ambiguity. Consequently, within Chapter 14, the entropy for naming these four attacks can reasonably be as low as $4.7 + 2 = 6.7$ (bits per name). Here 4.7 bits are for representing the letter "a", and 2 bits are for representing the numbers 0, 1, 2, 3.

On the other hand, by simple counting the reader can find that the average length of the four long names is 62.75 (letters). Therefore, the average number of bits per letter in these long names is $6.7/62.75 < 0.107$. From this result, we can further calculate the redundancy of these long names as (within the scope of Chapter 14):

$$\frac{6.7 - 0.107}{6.7} > 98\%. \qquad \Box$$

So these long attacking names are very, very redundant!

However, the area of study for cryptographic systems with provable strong security is an environment much larger than Chapter 14. Therefore the extremely shortened names a0, a1, a2, a3 used in Example 3.11 are in fact too short for naming these attacks (using so short names may cause ambiguity in understanding and uncomfortableness). As a matter of fact, the latter three attacking names listed in

Example 3.11 are shortened into IND-CPA, IND-CCA and IND-CCA2, respectively. We will adopt these names in Chapter 14 too.

Finally we point out that the reason why only the latter three long names are shortened is because in the area of study the latter three attacks are discussed more frequently. For "passive (plaintext indistinguishable) attack," we are comfortable enough to use the long name since the attack is a less frequently discussed topic due to its ease of prevention.

## 3.9  Chapter Summary

In this chapter we have conducted a very rudimentary study of probability and information theory. However, the material is sufficient for the use in this book.

In probability, it is very important to understand and be familiar with the basic notions, the properties and the rules for the basic calculations. We should emphasize that a good understanding of the very basics, which is not a difficult task at all, will help the most. We have witnessed that useful theorems and tools, e.g., the law of total probability, the law of large numbers and birthday paradox, can be derived solely from a few basic and intuitive properties and rules.

In the rest of this book we will frequently meet applications of conditional probability, the law of total probability, binomial distributions, and birthday paradox (we have already seen Pollard's $\lambda$-algorithm as a good application of birthday paradox). In these applications we will become more and more familiar with these useful tools.

We have also conducted a basic study of information theory. We now understand that entropy of a message source is a measure on the amount of information contained in messages from the source, or on the degree of randomness (unpredictability) of these messages.

## Exercises

3.1 Throw two dice one after the other. Find the probability of the following events:

    i) sum is 7, 1, and less than or equal to 12;

    ii) second die < first die;

    iii) at least one die is 6;

    iv) given that the first die is 6, the second die is 6.

3.2 In the preceding problem, find the probability that the first die is 3 given that the sum is greater or equal to 8.

3.3 Given that 4.5% of the population and 0.6% of females are color blind, what is the percentage of color blindness in males who consists of 49.9% of the population?

Hint: apply the law of total probability.

3.4 Suppose $\theta$ is uniformly distributed in $[-\pi/2, \pi/2]$. Find the probability that $\sin\theta \le 1/2$, and that $|\sin\theta| \le 1/2$.

3.5 A quarter numbers in a set of numbers are square numbers. Randomly picking 5 numbers from the set, find the probability for majority of them being square numbers.

Hint: analogous to Example 3.8.(iii), sum up the majority cases of number of squares $\ge 3$.

3.6 What are (left, right) tails of a binomial distribution function?

3.7 Derive (3.5.8), an upper bound for a "left tail" of the binomial distribution function.

3.8 Why can Definition 3.2 be viewed as a theorem which can be derived from the law of large numbers?

3.9 Let $n = pq$ with $p$ and $q$ being distinct large primes of roughly equal size. We know that for any $a < n$ and $\gcd(a, n) = 1$, it holds $a^{p+q} = a^{n+1} \pmod{n}$. Prove that $n$ can be factored in $n^{1/4}$ steps of searching.

Hint: search index $p+q$ from $a^{p+q} \pmod{n}$ by applying Pollard's $\lambda$-algorithm, with noticing $p + q \approx n^{1/2}$; then factor $n$ using $p + q$ and $pq$.

3.10 In Protocol "Coin Flipping Over Telephone," Alice picks a large and uniformly random integer. What is the entropy of Alice's source measured at Alice's end, and what is that measured by Bob?

3.11 In Example 3.11 we have measured the redundancy for four very long attacking names to be introduced Chapter 14 with respect to four extremely shortened names: a0, a1, a2, a3. Now, in the scope of that chapter measure the redundancy for the following four reasonably shortened attacking names:

- Passive IND-Attack,
- IND-CPA,
- IND-CCA,
- IND-CCA2.

# Chapter 4

# COMPUTATIONAL COMPLEXITY

## 4.1  Introduction

If a random variable follows the uniform distribution and is independent from *any* given information, then there is *no way* to relate a uniformly random variable to any other information by any means of "computation." This is exactly the security basis behind the *only unconditionally* (or *information-theoretically*) secure encryption scheme: one-time pad, that is, mixing a uniformly random string (called key string) with a message string in a bit by bit fashion (see §7.3.3). The need for independence between the key string and the message string requires the two strings to have the same length. Unfortunately, this poses an almost unpassable limitation for a practical use of the one-time-pad encryption scheme.

Nevertheless (and somewhat ironical), we are still in a "fortunate" position. At the time of writing, the computational devices and methods which are widely available to us (hence to code breakers) are based on a notion of computation which is not very powerful. To date we have not been very successful in relating, via computation, between two pieces of information if one of them merely "looks random" while in fact they are completely dependent one another (for example, plaintext, ciphertext messages in many cryptosystems). As a result, modern cryptography has its security based on a so-called *complexity-theoretic* model. Security of such cryptosystems is *conditional* on various assumptions that certain problems are *intractable*. Here, "intractable" means that the widely available computational methods cannot effectively handle these problems.

We should point out that our "fortunate" position may only be temporary. A new and much more powerful model of computation, *quantum information processing* (QIP), has emerged. Under this new model of computation, exponentially many computation steps can be parallelized by manipulating so-called "super-position" of quantum states. The consequence: many useful hard problems underlying the security bases for complexity-theoretic based cryptography will collapse, that is, will become useless. For example, using a quantum computer, factorization and multiplication of integers will take similar time if the integers processed have similar sizes, and hence, e.g., the famous public-key cryptosystems of Rivest, Shamir and Adleman (RSA) [248] (see §8.5) will be thrown out of stage. However, at the time of writing, the QIP technique is still quite distant from practical applications. The current record for factoring a composite number: 15 (see e.g., [302]), which is the least size, odd and non-square composite integer.

Therefore, let us not worry too much about the QIP for the time being. The rest of this chapter provides an introduction to our "less-powerful" conventional computational model and to the complexity-theoretic based approach to modern cryptography.

### 4.1.1   Chapter Outline

§4.2 introduces the Turing computation model. §4.3 introduces the class of deterministic polynomial-time, several useful deterministic polynomial-time algorithms and expressions for complexity measurement. §4.4 and §4.5 introduce two subclasses of non-deterministic polynomial-time (NP) problems. The first subclass (§4.4) is probabilistic polynomial-time which is further broken down to four subclasses of efficiently solvable problems (§4.4.2–§4.4.5). The second subclass (§4.5) is the problems which are efficiently solvable only with an internal knowledge and play an important role in the complexity-theoretic-based modern cryptography. §4.6 introduces the notion of complexities which are not bound by any polynomial. §4.7 instantiates the non-polynomial bounded problems to a decisional case: polynomial-time indistinguishability. Finally, §4.8 discusses the relationship between the theory of computational complexity and modern cryptography.

## 4.2   Turing Machines

In order to make precise the notion of an effective procedure (i.e., an algorithm), Turing proposed an imaginary computing device, called a **Turing machine**, to provide a primitive yet sufficiently general model of computation. The computational complexity material to be introduced here follows the computation model of Turing machines. Below we introduce a variant version of Turing machines which are sufficient for our purpose of computational complexity study. A general description of Turing machines can be studied in, e.g., §1.6 of [9].

In our variant, a Turing machine (see picture in Fig 4.1) consists of a *finite-state control unit*, some number $k \, (\geq 1)$ of *tapes* and the same number of *tapeheads*. The finite-state control unit controls the operations of the tapeheads which read or write some information from or to the tapes; each tapehead does so by accessing one tape, called *its* tape, and by moving along its tape either to left or to right. Each

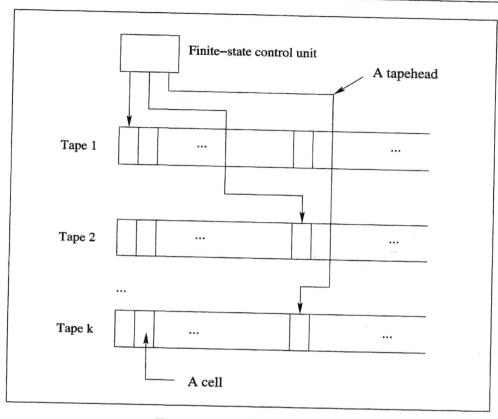

**Figure 4.1.** A Turing Machine

of these tapes is partitioned into an infinite number of *cells*. The machine solves a problem by having a tapehead scanning a string of a finite number of symbols which are placed sequentially in the leftmost cells of one tape; each symbol occupies one cell and the remaining cells to the right on that tape are *blank*. This string is called an *input* of a problem. The scanning starts from the leftmost cell of the tape that contains the input while the machine is in a designated *initial state*. At any time only one tapehead of the machine is accessing its tape. A step of access made by a tapehead on its tape is called a *(legal) move*. If the machine starts from the initial state, makes legal moves one after another, completes scanning the input string, eventually causes the satisfaction of a *terminating condition* and thereby terminates, then the machine is said to *recognize* the input. Otherwise, the machine will at some point have no legal move to make; then it will halt without recognizing the input. An input which is recognized by a Turing machine is called an *instance* in a recognizable *language*.

For a given problem, a Turing machine can be fully specified by a function of its finite-state control unit. Such a function can be given in the form of a table which lists the machine's *next-step move* for each state. We shall provide a problem example and a specification of a Turing machine in a moment (see Example 4.1 below).

Upon termination, the number of moves that a Turing machine $M$ has taken to recognize an input is said to be the running time or the *time complexity* of $M$ and is denoted by $T_M$. Clearly, $T_M$ can be expressed as a function $T_M(n) : \mathbb{N} \mapsto \mathbb{N}$ where $n$ is the *length* or *size* of the input instance, i.e., the number of symbols that consists of the input string when $M$ is in the initial state. Obviously, $T_M(n) \geq n$. In addition to the time requirement, $M$ has also a space requirement $S_M$ which is the number of tape cells that the tapeheads of $M$ have visited in writing access. The quantity $S_M$ can also be expressed as a function $S_M(n) : \mathbb{N} \mapsto \mathbb{N}$ and is said to be the *space complexity* of $M$.

We will see a concrete Turing machine in the next section.

## 4.3 Deterministic Polynomial Time

We begin with considering the class of languages that are recognizable by deterministic Turing machines in **polynomial time**. A function $p(n)$ is a polynomial in $n$ over the integers if it is of the form

$$p(n) = c_k n^k + c_{k-1} n^{k-1} + \cdots + c_1 n + c_0 \qquad (4.3.1)$$

where $k$ and $c_i$ $(i = 0, 1, 2, ..., k)$ are constant integers with $c_k \neq 0$. When $k > 0$, the former is called the **degree**, denoted by $\deg(p(n))$, and the latter, the **coefficients**, of the polynomial $p(n)$.

**Definition 4.1: Class** $\mathcal{P}$   *We write $\mathcal{P}$ to denote the class of languages with the following characteristics. A language $L$ is in $\mathcal{P}$ if there exists a Turing machine $M$ and a polynomial $p(n)$ such that $M$ recognizes any instance $I \in L$ in time $T_M(n)$ with $T_M(n) \leq p(n)$ for all non-negative integers $n$, where $n$ is an integer parameter representing the size of the instance $I$. We say that $L$ is recognizable in polynomial time.*

Roughly speaking, languages which are recognizable in polynomial time are considered as *always* "easy." In other words, polynomial-time Turing machines are considered as *always* "efficient" (we will define the notion of "easy" or "efficient" in §4.4.6). Here let us explain the meaning for *always*. Turing machines which recognize languages in $\mathcal{P}$ are all **deterministic**. A deterministic Turing machine outputs an effect which is entirely determined by the input to, and the initial state of, the machine. In other words, running a deterministic Turing machine twice with the same input and the same initial state, the two output effects will be identical.

We should notice that in Definition 4.1, the universal-style restrictions "any instance $I \in L$" and "for all non-negative integers $n$" are very important. In the study of computational complexity, a problem is considered solved only if *any* instance of the problem can be solved by the same Turing machine (i.e., the same method). Only so, the method is sufficiently general and thereby can indeed be considered as a method. Let us look at the following example for an illustration.

**Example 4.1: Language DIV3**   Let DIV3 be the set of non-negative integers divisible by 3. Show DIV3 $\in \mathcal{P}$.

We do so by constructing a single-tape Turing machine to recognize DIV3 in polynomial time.

We first notice that if we write the input as integers in the base-3 (i.e., ternary) representation, that is, an input is a string of symbols in $\{0, 1, 2\}$, then the recognition problem becomes trivially easy: an input $x$ is in DIV3 if and only if the last digit of $x$ is 0. Consequently, the machine to be constructed should simply make consecutive moves to right until reaching a blank symbol, and then it stops with a YES answer if and only if the final non-blank symbol is 0. Clearly, this machine can recognize any instance in number of moves which is the size of the instance. Hence DIV3 $\in \mathcal{P}$.

However, we want to show that the fact DIV3 $\in \mathcal{P}$ should be independent from the base representation of the input. It suffices for us to show the case when the input is written in the base-2 (i.e., binary) representation. Let this machine be named Div3. The finite-state control of Div3 follows a "next move" function specified in Fig 4.2.

We now argue that the machine Div3 defined by the function in Fig 4.2 is sufficiently general for recognizing all instances in DIV3.

First, we notice that for recognizing whether or not a binary string $x \in$ DIV3, it is sufficient for Div3 to have three states, corresponding to the cases when it (its tapehead) completes scanning strings $3k$, $3k+1$ and $3k+2$ (for $k \geq 0$), respectively. The least input instance 0 stipulates that Div3 must be in an initial state (without loss of generality, let the initial state be $q_0$) upon its completion of scanning input string 0. Without loss of generality, we can assign Div3 to state $q_1$ upon its completion of scanning input string 1, and to state $q_2$ upon its completion of scanning input string 2 $(= (10)_2)$[a].

For any non-negative integer $a$ in the binary representation, postfixing $a$ with symbol 0 (respectively, symbol 1) yields value $2a$ (respectively, value $2a+1$). Thus, after completion of scanning $a = 3k$ (when Div3 is in state $q_0$), Div3 must remain in $q_0$ upon further scanning symbol 0, since at that point it completes scanning $2a = 6k = 3k'$, and must evolve to $q_1$ upon further scanning symbol 1, since at that

---

[a]We use $(a_1 a_2 ... a_n)_b$, with $a_i < b$ and $i = 1, 2, ..., n$, to denote a number written in the base-$b$ representation; the cases of $b = 10$ and $b = 2$ are often omitted if no confusion arises.

| Current state | Symbol on tape | Next move | New state |
|---|---|---|---|
| $q_0$ (initial state) | 0 <br> 1 <br> blank | right <br> right <br> "Ding" & Stop | $q_0$ <br> $q_1$ |
| $q_1$ | 0 <br> 1 | right <br> right | $q_2$ <br> $q_0$ |
| $q_2$ | 0 <br> 1 | right <br> right | $q_1$ <br> $q_2$ |

**Figure 4.2.** The operation of machine Div3

point it completes scanning $2a + 1 = 6k + 1 = 3k' + 1$. Similarly, after completion of scanning $a = 3k + 1$ (when Div3 is in state $q_1$), Div3 must evolve to $q_2$ upon completion of scanning $2a = 6k+2 = 3k'+2$, and must evolve to $q_0$ upon completion of scanning $2a + 1 = 6k + 3 = 3k'$. The remaining two cases for $a = 3k + 2$ are: $2a = 6k + 4 = 3k' + 1$ (Div3 evolves from $q_2$ to $q_1$), and $2a + 1 = 6k + 5 = 3k' + 2$ (Div3 stays in $q_2$).

So, the three states $q_0$, $q_1$ and $q_2$ correspond to Div3's completion of scanning strings $3k$, $3k + 1$ and $3k + 2$, respectively, for any $k \geq 0$. Now upon the head meeting the special symbol "blank," only in state $q_0$ Div3 is configured to ring the bell and stop (meaning to terminate with YES answer) and hence to recognize the input $3k$; in the other two states, Div3 will have no legal move to make and therefore halt with no recognition.

Finally, it is easy to see $T_{\text{Div3}}(n) = n$. Thus, Div3 does recognize language DIV3 in polynomial time. □

**Example 4.2:**

i) The bit string $10101 (= (21)_{10})$ is recognizable; Div3 recognizes the string in $T_{\text{Div3}}(|10101|) = |10101| = 5$ moves;

ii) The bit string $11100001 (= (225)_{10})$ is another recognizable instance; Div3 recognizes it in $T_{\text{Div3}}(|11100001|) = |11100001| = 8$ moves;

iii) The bit string $10 (= (2)_{10})$ is not recognizable; Div3 decides that it is unrecognizable in two moves. $\qquad\Box$

## 4.3.1   Polynomial-Time Computational Problems

By definition, $\mathcal{P}$ is the class of polynomial-time language recognition problems. A language recognition problem is a **decisional problem**. For every possible input, a decisional problem requires YES or NO as output. However, class $\mathcal{P}$ is sufficiently general to enclose polynomial-time **computational problems**. For every possible input, a computational problem requires an output to be more general than a YES/NO answer. Since a Turing machine can write symbols to a tape, it can of course output information more general than a YES/NO answer.

For instance, we can design another Turing machine which will not only recognize any instance $x \in \text{DIV3}$, but will also output $\frac{x}{3}$ upon recognition of $x$. Let this new machine be named Div3-Comp. A very simple way to realize Div3-Comp is to have its input written in the base-3 representation. Then the input is an instance in DIV3 if and only if its final digit is 0, and the output from the machine, upon recognition of the input, should be the content on the input-tape after having erased the last 0 unless 0 is the only symbol on the tape. If one insists that Div3-Comp must only input and output binary numbers, then Div3-Comp can be realized as follows. It first translates an input $x$ from the base-2 representation into the base-3 representation, and upon obtaining $\frac{x}{3}$ in the base-3 representation it translates the number back to the base-2 representation as the final output. It is evident that these translations can be done digit-by-digit *mechanically* in $c \cdot |x|$ moves where $c$ is a constant. To this end we know

$$T_{\text{Div3-Comp}}(|x|) \le C \cdot |x|$$

where $C$ is a constant. From this example we see evidently that the class $\mathcal{P}$ must include the problem which can be solved by Div3-Comp.

A general argument for $\mathcal{P}$ to enclose polynomial-time computational problems can be given as follows. A computing device in the so-called von Neumann architecture (that is, the modern computer architecture we are familiar with, [229]) has a counter, a memory, and a central processor unit (CPU) which can perform one of the following basic instructions, called micro-instructions, at a time:

| | |
|---|---|
| Load: | Loading the content in a memory location to a register (in CPU) |
| Store: | Storing the content of a register to a memory location |
| Add: | Adding contents of two registers |
| Comp: | Complementing the content of a register (for subtraction via "Add") |
| Jump: | Setting the counter to a new value |
| JumpZ: | "Jump" upon zero content of a register (for conditional branching) |
| Stop: | Terminating. |

It is well known (see e.g., §1.4 of [9]) that the above small set of micro-instructions is sufficient for constructing algorithms for solving arbitrary arithmetic problems on a von Neumann computer (however notice that by "arbitrary arithmetic problems" we do not mean to consider instances of arbitrary sizes; we will further discuss this in a moment). It can be shown (e.g., Theorem 1.3 in [9]) that each micro-instruction in the above set can be simulated by a Turing machine in polynomial time. Consequently, a problem that can be solved in polynomial time on a von Neumann computer (which implies that the number of micro-instructions used in the algorithm must be a polynomial in the size of the input to the algorithm) can also be solved by a Turing machine in polynomial time. This is because for any polynomials $p(n)$ and $q(n)$, any ways of arithmetic combining $p(n)$, $q(n)$, $p(q(n))$ and $q(p(n))$ will result in a polynomial in $n$. Notice that we have deliberately excluded multiplication and division from our (simplified) set of micro-instructions. A multiplication between numbers of size $n$ can be done via $n$ additions and hence has its total cost should be measured by $n \times$ cost(Add). Division has the same cost as multiplication since it is repeated subtraction which is addition of a complementary number.

We should mention an unimportant difference between the computation model based on Turing machines and that based on von Neumann computers. By Definition 4.1, we regard a problem solvable on a Turing machine only if *any* instance is solvable on the *same* machine ("one machine to solve them all!"). The cost for solving a problem on a Turing machine is measured by the size of the problem in a *uniform* manner across the whole spectrum of the size of the problem. There is no need to have a pre-determined bound for the size of a problem. Machine Div3 in Example 4.1 shows this evidently. Due to this property in cost measurement we say that the Turing-machine-based computation model uses the **uniform cost measure** to measure complexities. In contrast, registers and logical circuits which are the basic building blocks of a von Neumann computer have fixed sizes. As a result, problems solvable on a von Neumann computer must also have a pre-determined size: for the same problem, the bigger an instance is, the bigger a machine is needed for solving it. In general, machines of different sizes do not agree on a uniform measurement on the cost for solving the same problem. We therefore say that a circuit-based computation model (upon which a von Neumann computer is based) has a **non-uniform cost measure**. However, so far, the difference between the uniform and non-uniform cost measures has not created any new complexity class, or caused any known classes to collapse. That is why we say that this difference is not important.

In the rest of this chapter we shall often neglect the difference between a decisional problem and a computational problem, and the difference among a Turing machine, a modern computer, a procedure, or an algorithm. Decisional or computational problems will be generally called problems, while machines, computers, procedures or algorithms will be generally referred to as methods or algorithms. Occasionally, we will return to describing a language recognition problem, and only then we will return to using Turing machines as our basic instrument of computation.

## 4.3.2    Algorithms and Computational Complexity Expressions

Let us now study three very useful polynomial-time algorithms. Through the study of these algorithms, we shall (i) get familiar with a programming language which we shall use to write algorithms and protocols in this book, (ii) agree on some notation and convention for expressing computational complexity for algorithms and protocols, and (iii) establish the time complexities for a number of arithmetic operations which will be most frequently used in cryptography.

Above we have explained that Turing machines provide us with a general model of computation and with a precise notion for measuring the computational complexity for procedures. However, we do not generally wish to describe algorithms in terms of such a primitive machine, not even in terms of the micro-instructions of a modern computer (i.e., the set of instructions we described in § 4.3.1). In order to describe algorithms and mathematical statements effectively and clearly, we shall use a high-level programming language called "Pseudo Programming Language" which is very close to a number of popular high-level programming languages such as Pascal or C and can be understood without any difficulty due to its plainly self-explanatory feature.

### 4.3.2.1    Greatest Common Divisor

The first algorithm we shall study is the famous algorithm of Euclid for computing greatest common divisor (Alg 4.1). Denoted by $\gcd(a, b)$ the greatest common divisor of integers $a$ and $b$, $\gcd(a, b)$ is defined to be the largest integer that divides both $a$ and $b$.

---

**Algorithm 4.1:** Euclid Algorithm for Greatest Common Divisor

INPUT      Integers $a > b \geq 0$;
OUTPUT    $\gcd(a, b)$.

 1. if $b = 0$ return( $a$ );

 2. return( $\gcd(b, a \bmod b)$ ).

---

In Alg 4.1, "$a \bmod b$" denotes the remainder of $a$ divided by $b$. (In §4.3.2.5 we will formally define the modular operation and provide some useful facts on modular arithmetic.) The condition $a > b \geq 0$ is merely for the purpose of ease of exposition. In the implementation, this condition can be satisfied by replacing $a$, $b$ with their absolute values, and by invoking $\gcd(|b|, |a|)$ in case $|a| < |b|$.

Now let us examine how Alg 4.1 works. For positive integers $a \geq b$, we can always write

$$a = bq + r \tag{4.3.2}$$

for some integer $q \neq 0$ (the quotient of $a$ divided by $b$) and $0 \leq r < b$ (the remainder of $a$ divided by $b$). Since by definition, $\gcd(a, b)$ divides both $a$ and $b$, equation (4.3.2) shows that it must also divide $r$ too. Consequently, $\gcd(a, b)$ equals $\gcd(b, r)$. Since the remainder $r$ (of $a$ divided by $b$) is denoted by $a \bmod b$, we have derived

$$\gcd(a, b) = \gcd(b, \ a \bmod b).$$

This is the fact we have used in Alg 4.1, namely, $\gcd(a, b)$ is defined by $\gcd(b, a \bmod b)$ recursively. The series of recursive calls of gcd compute the following series of equations, each is in the form of (4.3.2) and is formed by a division between the two input values:

$$
\begin{aligned}
a &= bq_1 + r_1 \\
b &= r_1 q_2 + r_2 \\
r_1 &= r_2 q_3 + r_3 \\
&\phantom{=}\ . \\
&\phantom{=}\ . \\
&\phantom{=}\ . \\
r_{k-3} &= r_{k-2} q_{k-1} + r_{k-1} \\
r_{k-2} &= r_{k-1} q_k + r_k
\end{aligned}
\tag{4.3.3}
$$

where $r_k = 0$ (which causes the terminating condition in step 1 being met) and $q_1$, $q_2$, ..., $q_k$, $r_1$, $r_2$, ..., $r_{k-1}$ are non-zero integers. With $r_k = 0$, the last equation in (4.3.3) means $r_{k-1}$ divides $r_{k-2}$, and in the last-but-one equation, it must also divide $r_{k-3}$, ..., eventually, as shown in the first equation in (4.3.3), $r_{k-1}$ must divide both $a$ and $b$. None of other remainders in other equations has this property (that's why they are called remainders, not a divisor; only $r_{k-1}$ is a divisor in the last equation in (4.3.3)). Therefore, $r_{k-1}$ is indeed the greatest common divisor of $a$ and $b$, i.e., $r_{k-1} = \gcd(a, b)$.

For example, $\gcd(108, 42)$ will invoke the following sequence of recursive calls:

$$\gcd(108, 42) = \gcd(42, 24) = \gcd(24, 18) = \gcd(18, 6) = \gcd(6, 0) = 6.$$

### 4.3.2.2   Extended Euclid Algorithm

Alg 4.1 has thrown away all the intermediate quotients. If we accumulate them during the computation of $\gcd(a, b)$, we can obtain something more than just $\gcd(a, b)$.

Let us see what we can obtain.

The first equation in (4.3.3) can be written as

$$a + b(-q_1) = r_1.$$

Multiplying both sides of this equation with $q_2$, we can obtain

$$aq_2 + b(-q_1 q_2) = r_1 q_2.$$

Using this equation and the second equation in (4.3.3), we can derive

$$a(-q_2) + b(1 + q_1 q_2) = r_2. \tag{4.3.4}$$

The same way of calculation can be carried out. In general, for $i = 1, 2, \ldots, k$, we can derive

$$a\lambda_i + b\mu_i = r_i \tag{4.3.5}$$

where $\lambda_i, \mu_i$ are some integers which are, as indicated in (4.3.4), certain form of accumulations of the intermediate quotients. We have seen in §4.3.2.1 that following this way of calculation we will eventually reach $r_k = 0$, and then we have

$$a\lambda_{k-1} + b\mu_{k-1} = r_{k-1} = \gcd(a, b). \tag{4.3.6}$$

An algorithm that inputs $a$, $b$ and outputs the integers $\lambda_{i-1}$, $\mu_{k-1}$ satisfying (4.3.6) is called **extended Euclid algorithm**. Extended Euclid algorithm will have an extensive use in the rest of the book for computing division modulo integers. Let us now specify this algorithm, that is, find a general method for accumulating the intermediate quotients.

Observe the equations in (4.3.3) and denote $r_{-1} = a$, $r_0 = b$, $\lambda_{-1} = 1$, $\mu_{-1} = 0$, $\lambda_0 = 0$, $\mu_0 = 1$. Then for $i = 1, 2, \ldots, k - 1$, the $i$th equation in (4.3.3) relates $r_{i-1}$, $r_i$ and $r_{i+1}$ by

$$r_{i+1} = r_{i-1} - r_i q_{i+1}. \tag{4.3.7}$$

Replacing $r_{i-1}$ and $r_i$ in the right-hand side of (4.3.7) using equation (4.3.5), we derive

$$r_{i+1} = a(\lambda_{i-1} - q_{i+1}\lambda_i) + b(\mu_{i-1} - q_{i+1}\mu_i). \tag{4.3.8}$$

Comparing between (4.3.8) and (4.3.5), we obtain (for $i = 0, 1, \ldots, k - 1$)

$$\begin{array}{rcl} \lambda_{i+1} & = & \lambda_{i-1} - q_{i+1}\lambda_i \\ \mu_{i+1} & = & \mu_{i-1} - q_{i+1}\mu_i \end{array} \tag{4.3.9}$$

These two equations provide us with a general method for accumulating the intermediate quotients while computing greatest common divisor (see Alg 4.2).

---

**Algorithm 4.2:** Extended Euclid Algorithm

INPUT       $a, b$: integers with $a > b \geq 0$;
OUTPUT      integers $\lambda$, $\mu$ satisfying $a\lambda + b\mu = \gcd(a, b)$.

1. $i \leftarrow 0$; $r_{-1} \leftarrow a$; $r_0 \leftarrow b$;
   $\lambda_{-1} \leftarrow 1$; $\mu_{-1} \leftarrow 0$; $\lambda_0 \leftarrow 0$; $\mu_0 \leftarrow 1$;          $(* \text{ initialize } *)$

2. while ( $r_i = a\lambda_i + b\mu_i \neq 0$ ) do    $(* \text{ it always holds } a\lambda_i + b\mu_i = r_i *)$

   (a) $q \leftarrow r_{i-1} \div r_i$;              $(* \div \text{ denotes division in integers } *)$
   (b) $\lambda_{i+1} \leftarrow \lambda_{i-1} - q\lambda_i$; $\mu_{i+1} \leftarrow \mu_{i-1} - q\mu_i$;  $(* \text{ sum up quotients } *)$
   (c) $i \leftarrow i + 1$;

3. return( $(\lambda_{i-1}, \mu_{i-1})$ ).

---

**Remark 4.1:** *In order to expose the working principle of Alg 4.1 and Alg 4.2 in an easily understandable way, we have chosen to sacrifice efficiency. In the next two sections (§4.3.2.3—§4.3.2.4) we will analyze their time complexities and contrast our result with the best known time complexity result for computing greatest common divisor.*                                                                       □

### 4.3.2.3  Time Complexity of Euclid Algorithms

Let us now measure the time complexities for the two Euclid algorithms. It is clear that the number of recursive calls in Alg 4.1 is equal to the number of loops in Alg 4.2 which is in turn equal to $k$ in (4.3.3).

Consider the case $a > b$ and observe (4.3.7) for $i = 0, 1, \ldots, k - 1$. We have either of the following two cases:

$$|r_i| < |r_{i-1}|, \tag{4.3.10}$$

or

$$|r_{i+1}| < |r_{i-1}|. \tag{4.3.11}$$

Further noticing $r_{i+1} < r_i$, so case (4.3.10) also implies case (4.3.11), that is, case (4.3.11) holds invariantly. This means that the maximum value for $k$ is bounded by $2 \cdot |a|$. If we consider the modulo operation as a basic operation which takes one unit of time, then the time complexity of gcd realized in Alg 4.1 is bounded by $2 \cdot |a|$. This is a linear function in the size of $a$.

**Theorem 4.1:** *Greatest common divisor* $\gcd(a, b)$ *can be computed by performing no more than* $2\max(|a|, |b|)$ *modulo operations. Therefore, Alg 4.1 and Alg 4.2 terminate within* $2\max(|a|, |b|)$ *loops.*                                              □

G. Lamé (1795–1870) was the first person who proved the first sentence in the statements of Theorem 4.1. It is considered to be the first theorem ever proved about the theory of computational complexity (page 35 of [178]).

The series of equations in (4.3.3) which are formed by a series of divisions suggest an inherent *sequentiality* characteristic in the computation of greatest common divisor. Since Euclid discovered his algorithm (i.e., Alg 4.1), no significant improvement has been found to cut short this seemingly necessary sequential process.

### 4.3.2.4  Two Expressions for Computational Complexity

When we measure the computational complexity for an algorithm, it is often difficult or unnecessary to pinpoint exactly the constant coefficient in an expression that bounds the complexity measure. **Order notation** allows us to ease the task of complexity measurement.

**Definition 4.2: Order Notation** *We write* $O(f(n))$ *to denote a function* $g(n)$ *such that there exists a constant* $c > 0$ *and a natural number* $N$ *with* $|g(n)| \leq c|f(n)|$ *for all* $n \geq N$.

Using the notation $O()$ we can express the time complexities of Alg 4.1 and Alg 4.2 as $O(\log a)$. Notice that in this expression we have replaced $|a|$ with $\log a$ without explicitly giving the base of the logarithm (though we conventionally agree that the omitted base is natural base $e$). The reader may confirm that any base $b > 1$ will provide a correct measurement expression under the order notation (Ex 4.10).

So far we have considered that computing one modulo operation costs one unit of time, that is, it has the time complexity $O(1)$. As a matter of fact, modulo operation "$a \pmod b$" in the general case involves division $a \div b$, which is actually done in Alg 4.2 in order to keep the quotient. Therefore the time complexity of modulo operation, the same as that of division, should depend on the sizes of the two operands. In practical terms (for the meaning of "practical," see the end of §4.4.6), using $O(1)$ to represent the time for a division is too coarse for a sensible resource management.

A simple modification of the order notation is to measure an arithmetic in terms of **bitwise computation**. In bitwise computation, all variables have the values 0 or 1, and the operations used are logical rather than arithmetic: they are $\wedge$ (for AND), $\vee$ (for OR), $\oplus$ (for XOR, i.e., "exclusive or"), and $\neg$ (for NOT).

**Definition 4.3: Bitwise Order Notation** *We write* $O_B()$ *to denote* $O()$ *under the bitwise computation model.*

Under the bitwise model, addition and subtraction between two integers $i$ and $j$ take $\max(|i|, |j|)$ bitwise operations, i.e., $O_B(\max(|i|, |j|))$ time. Intuitively, multiplication and division between $i$ and $j$ take $|i| \cdot |j|$ bitwise operations, i.e., $O_B(\log i \cdot \log j)$ time. We should point out that for multiplication (and division) a lower time complexity of $O_B(\log(i + j) \log\log(i + j))$ can be obtained if the fast Fourier Transformation (FFT) method is used. However, this lower complexity is an asymptotic one which is associated with a much larger constant coefficient (related to the cost of FFT) and may actually cause a higher complexity for operands having relatively small sizes (e.g., sizes for modern cryptographic use). Therefore in this book we shall not consider the FFT implemented multiplication and division. Consequently we shall only use the intuitive complexity measurement for multiplication and division.

Let us now express the time complexities of Alg 4.1 and Alg 4.2 using the more precise bitwise order notation $O_B()$. In Theorem 4.1 we have obtained that for $a > b$, $\gcd(a, b)$ can be computed in $O(\log a)$ time. Given that both input values are bounded by $a$, and that modulo operation or division cost $O_B((\log a)^2)$, the time complexities of Alg 4.1 and Alg 4.2 are both $O_B((\log a)^3)$.

Now we should recall Remark 4.1: we have chosen to present these algorithms with easily understandable working principles by sacrificing the efficiency. As a matter of fact, our sacrifice on efficiency is rather large!

Careful realizations of these two algorithms should make use of the following two facts:

i) Modulo operation or division for creating $a = bq + r$ cost $O_B((\log a)(\log q))$.

ii) Quotients $q_1, q_2, \ldots, q_k$ in (4.3.3) satisfy

$$\sum_{i=1}^{k} \log q_i = \log \prod_{i=1}^{k} q_i \leq \log a. \tag{4.3.12}$$

Hence the total time for computing greatest common divisor, via a careful realization, can be bounded by

$$\sum_{i=1}^{k} O_B((\log a)(\log q_i)) \leq O_B((\log a)^2).$$

Careful realizations of the counterparts for Alg 4.1 and Alg 4.2 can be found in Chapter 1 of [80].

In the rest of this book, we shall use the best known result $O_B((\log a)^2)$ for expressing the time complexity for computing greatest common divisor, either using Euclid algorithm or the extended Euclid algorithm.

### 4.3.2.5    Modular Arithmetic

An important polynomial-time deterministic algorithm we shall study is one for computing modular exponentiation. Modular exponentiation is widely used in public-key cryptography. Let us first take a short course on modular arithmetic (readers who are familiar with modular arithmetic can skip this section).

**Definition 4.4: Modular Operation** *Given integers $x$ and $n > 1$, the operation "$x \pmod n$" is the remainder of $x$ divided by $n$, that is, a non-negative integer $r \in [0, n-1]$ satisfying*

$$x = kn + r$$

*for some integer $k$.*

**Theorem 4.2: Properties of Modular Operation** *Let $x$, $y$, $n \neq 0$ be integers with $\gcd(y, n) = 1$. The modular operation has the following properties.*

*1. $(x + y) \pmod n = [(x \pmod n) + (y \pmod n)] \pmod n$;*

*2. $(-x) \pmod n = (n - x) \pmod n = n - (x \pmod n)$;*

*3. $(x \cdot y) \pmod n = [(x \pmod n) \cdot (y \pmod n)] \pmod n$;*

*4. Denote by $y^{-1} \pmod n$ the **multiplicative inverse** of $y$ modulo $n$. It is a unique integer in $[1, n-1]$ satisfying*

   *$(y \cdot y^{-1}) \pmod n = 1$.*

**Proof** We shall only show 1 and 4 while leaving 2 and 3 as an exercise (Ex 4.4).

We can write $x = kn + r$, $y = \ell n + s$ for $0 \leq r, s \leq n - 1$.

For 1, we have

$$
\begin{aligned}
(x + y) \pmod n &= [(kn + r) + (\ell n + s)] \pmod n \\
&= [(k + \ell)n + (r + s)] \pmod n \\
&= (r + s) \pmod n \\
&= [(x \pmod n) + (y \pmod n)] \pmod n
\end{aligned}
$$

For 4, because $\gcd(y, n) = 1$, applying extended Euclid algorithm (Alg 4.2) on input $y$, $n$, we obtain integers $\lambda$ and $\mu$ satisfying

$$y\lambda + n\mu = 1. \tag{4.3.13}$$

Without loss of generality, we have $\lambda < n$ because otherwise we can replace $\lambda$ with $\lambda \pmod n$ and replace $\mu$ with $yk + \mu$ for some $k$ while keeping equation (4.3.13).

By Definition 4.4, $y\lambda \pmod{n} = 1$. Therefore we have found $y^{-1} = \lambda < n$ as the multiplicative inverse of $y$ modulo $n$. Below we show the uniqueness of $y^{-1}$ in $[1, n-1]$. Suppose there exists another multiplicative inverse of $y$ mod $n$; denote it by $\lambda' \in [1, n-1]$, $\lambda' \neq \lambda$. We have

$$y(\lambda - \lambda') \bmod n = 0,$$

i.e.,

$$y(\lambda - \lambda') = an, \qquad (4.3.14)$$

for some integer $a$. We know $y = \ell n + 1$ for some integer $\ell$. Therefore equation (4.3.14) is

$$(\ell n + 1)(\lambda - \lambda') = an,$$

or

$$\lambda - \lambda' = bn,$$

for some integer $b$. This contradicts our assumption $\lambda, \lambda' \in [1, n-1]$, $\lambda \neq \lambda'$.  $\square$

Same as in the case of division in rationals $\mathbb{Q}$, division by a number modulo $n$ is defined to be multiplication with the inverse of the divisor, of course, this requires the existence of the inverse, just as in the case in $\mathbb{Q}$. Thus, for any $y$ with $\gcd(y, n) = 1$, we write $x/y \bmod n$ for $xy^{-1} \bmod n$.

Since computing $y^{-1}$ involves applying extended Euclid algorithm, it needs time $O_B((\log n)^2)$. Therefore the time complexity for division modulo $n$ is $O_B((\log n)^2)$.

Theorem 4.2 shows that modular arithmetic is very similar to the integer arithmetic. It is easy to see that addition and multiplication obey the following laws of commutativity and associativity (where "$\circ$" denotes either addition or multiplication):

$$a \circ b \bmod n = b \circ a \bmod n \qquad \text{(Commutativity)}$$

$$a \circ (b \circ c) \bmod n = (a \circ b) \circ c \bmod n \qquad \text{(Associativity)}$$

Finally we should point out that, in the definition for the modular operation $x \bmod n$ (see Definition 4.4), the value of $k$ (the quotient of $x$ divided by $n$) is not an important element. Therefore in equation

$$x \bmod n = y \bmod n \qquad (4.3.15)$$

we should not care whether $x$ and $y$ may differ by a multiple of $n$. In the sequel, the above equation will always be written as either

$$x \equiv y \pmod{n},$$

or

$$x \pmod{n} \equiv y.$$

We shall call this way of denoting equation (4.3.15) a **congruence** modulo $n$, or we say: $x$ is congruent to $y$ modulo $n$.

### 4.3.2.6   Modular Exponentiation

For $x, y < n$, **modular exponentiation** $x^y \pmod{n}$ follows the usual definition of exponentiation in integers as repeated multiplications of $x$ to itself $y$ times, but in terms of modulo $n$:

$$x^y \stackrel{\text{def}}{=} \underbrace{xx \cdots x}_{y} \pmod{n}.$$

Let $y \div 2$ denote $y$ divided by 2 with truncation to integers, that is,

$$y \div 2 = \begin{cases} y/2 & \text{if } y \text{ is even} \\ (y-1)/2 & \text{if } y \text{ is odd} \end{cases}$$

Then applying the "Associativity Law" of modular multiplication, we have

$$x^y = \begin{cases} (x^2)^{y \div 2} & \text{if } y \text{ is even} \\ (x^2)^{y \div 2}x & \text{if } y \text{ is odd} \end{cases}$$

The above computation provides the well-known algorithm for realizing modular exponentiation called "repeated square-and-multiply." The algorithm repeats the following process: dividing the exponent into 2, performing a squaring, and performing an extra multiplication if the exponent is odd. Alg 4.3 specifies a recursive version of the method.

---

**Algorithm 4.3:** Modular Exponentiation

INPUT      $x, y, n$: integers with $x > 0$, $y \geq 0$, $n > 1$;
OUTPUT   $x^y \pmod{n}$.

mod_exp$(x, y, n)$

1. if $y = 0$ return( 1 );

2. if $y \pmod 2 = 0$ return( mod_exp$(x^2 \pmod{n}, y \div 2, n)$ );

3. return( $x \cdot$ mod_exp$(x^2 \pmod{n}, y \div 2, n) \pmod{n}$ ).

---

We should notice a property in Alg 4.3 that is resulted from the recursive definition: the execution of a "return" statement implies that the subsequent step(s) following the "return" statement will never be executed. This is because the statement return( "value" ) causes the program to go back, with "value," to the point where the current call of mod_exp was made. So in Alg 4.3, if step 2 is executed, then step 3 will not be executed.

For example, starting from mod_exp(2, 21, 23), Alg 4.3 will invoke the following five recursive calls:

mod_exp(2, 21, 23)

$= 2 \cdot$ mod_exp($4(\equiv 2^2 \pmod{23})$, 10, 23) $\hspace{3cm}$ (in step 3)

$= 2 \cdot$ mod_exp($16(\equiv 4^2 \pmod{23})$, 5, 23) $\hspace{3cm}$ (in step 2)

$= 2 \cdot 16 \cdot$ mod_exp($3(\equiv 16^2 \pmod{23})$, 2, 23) $\hspace{2.2cm}$ (in step 3)

$= 2 \cdot 16 \cdot$ mod_exp($9(\equiv 3^2 \pmod{23})$, 1, 23) $\hspace{2.4cm}$ (in step 2)

$= 2 \cdot 16 \cdot 9 \cdot$ mod_exp($12(\equiv 9^2 \pmod{23})$, 0, 23) $\hspace{1.6cm}$ (in step 3)

$= 2 \cdot 16 \cdot 9 \cdot 1$ $\hspace{6.4cm}$ (in step 1)

Notice that the above six lines contain five recursive calls of mod_exp. The final line "mod_exp(12, 0, 23)" merely represents "return value 1" and is not a recursive call. The final value returned to mod_exp(2, 21, 23) is 12 which is constructed from several multiplications made in step 3:

$$12 \equiv 2 \cdot 16 \cdot 9 \equiv 2^1 \cdot (2^2)^2 \cdot (((2^2)^2)^2)^2 \pmod{23}.$$

Let us now examine the time complexity of mod_exp realized in Alg 4.3. Since for $y > 0$, the operation "dividing into 2" can be performed exactly $\lfloor \log_2 y \rfloor + 1$ times to reach 0 as the quotient, a run of mod_exp($x$, $y$, $n$) will invoke exactly $\lfloor \log_2 y \rfloor + 1$ recursive calls of the function itself to reach the terminating condition in step 1 (zero exponent). Each recursive call consists of a squaring or a squaring plus a multiplication which costs $O_B((\log x)^2)$. Thus, considering $x, y$ as numbers less than $n$, the time complexity for mod_exp realized in Alg 4.3 is bounded by $O_B((\log n)^3)$.

Similar to a seemingly unavoidable sequentiality in the computation of gcd, there is also an inherent sequentiality in the computation of mod_exp. This is seen as a simple fact in the repeated squaring: $x^4$ can only be computed after $x^2$ has been computed, and so on. Over the years, no significant progress has been made to improve the complexity from $O_B((\log n)^3)$ (without considering using FFT, review our discussion in 4.3.2.4).

Fig 4.3 summarizes our examination on the time complexities for the basic modular arithmetic operations. We should notice that in the case of addition and subtraction, the modulo operation should not be considered to involve division; this is because for $0 \le a, b < n$, we have $-n < a \pm b < 2n$, and therefore

$$a \pm b \pmod{n} = \begin{cases} a \pm b & \text{if } 0 \le a \pm b < n \\ a \pm b - n & \text{if } a \pm b \ge n \\ n + (a \pm b) & \text{if } a \pm b < 0 \end{cases}.$$

| Operation<br>for $a, b \in_U [1, n)$ | Complexity |
|---|---|
| $a \pm b \pmod{n}$ | $O_B(\log n)$ |
| $a \cdot b \pmod{n}$ | $O_B((\log n)^2)$ |
| $b^{-1} \pmod{n}$ | $O_B((\log n)^2)$ |
| $a/b \pmod{n}$ | $O_B((\log n)^2)$ |
| $a^b \pmod{n}$ | $O_B((\log n)^3)$ |

**Figure 4.3.** Bitwise Time Complexities of the Basic Modular Arithmetic Operations

## 4.4   Probabilistic Polynomial Time

It is generally accepted that if a language is not in $\mathcal{P}$ then there is no Turing machine that recognizes it *and* is *always* efficient[b]. However, there is a class of languages with the following property: their membership in $\mathcal{P}$ has not been proven, but they can *always* be recognized *efficiently* by a kind of Turing machine which may *sometimes* make mistakes.

The reason why such a machine may sometimes make a mistake is that in some step of its operation the machine will make a **random move**. While some random moves lead to a correct result, others lead to an incorrect one. Such a Turing machine is called a **non-deterministic Turing machine**. A subclass of decisional problems we are now introducing share the following bounded error property:

> The probability for a non-deterministic Turing machine to make a mistake when answering a decisional problem is bounded by a constant (the probability space is the machine's random tape).

We conventionally call a non-deterministic Turing machine with a bounded error a **probabilistic Turing machine**. For this reason, the name "non-deterministic Turing machine" is actually reserved for a different class of decisional problems which we will introduce in §4.5.

---

[b]The precise meaning for an "efficient machine" will be defined in §4.4.6; here we can roughly say that an efficient machine is a fast one.

A probabilistic Turing machine also has a plural number of tapes. One of these tapes is called a **random tape** which contains some uniformly distributed random symbols. During the scanning of an input instance $I$, the machine will also interact with the random tape, pick up a random symbol and then proceed like a deterministic Turing machine. The random string is called the **random input** to a probabilistic Turing machine. With the involvement of the random input, the recognition of an input instance $I$ by a probabilistic Turing machine is no longer a deterministic function of $I$, but is associated with a random variable, that is, a function of the machine's random input. This random variable assigns certain **error probability** to the event of recognizing $I$.

The class of languages that are recognizable by probabilistic Turing machines is called **probabilistic polynomial-time (PPT)** languages, which we denote by $\mathcal{PP}$.

**Definition 4.5: Class $\mathcal{PP}$** *We write $\mathcal{PP}$ to denote the class of languages with the following characteristics. A language $L$ is in $\mathcal{PP}$ if there exists a probabilistic Turing machine PM and a polynomial $p(n)$, such that PM recognizes any instance $I \in L$ with certain error probability which is a random variable of PM's random move, in time $T_{PM}(n)$ with $T_{PM}(n) \leq p(n)$ for all nonnegative integers $n$, where $n$ is an integer parameter representing the size of the instance $I$.*

In Definition 4.5 we have left one element to have a particularly vague meaning, which is: "*PM* recognizes $I \in L$, with certain error probability." The "certain **error probability**" should be formulated into the following two expressions of conditional probability bounds:

$$\text{Prob}\,[PM \text{ recognizes } I \in L \mid I \in L] \geq \epsilon, \qquad (4.4.1)$$

and

$$\text{Prob}\,[PM \text{ recognizes } I \in L \mid I \notin L] \leq \delta, \qquad (4.4.2)$$

where $\epsilon$ and $\delta$ are constants satisfying

$$\epsilon \in (\frac{1}{2}, 1], \qquad \delta \in [0, \frac{1}{2}). \qquad (4.4.3)$$

The probability space is the random tape of *PM*.

The expression (4.4.1) is the probability bound for a correct recognition of an instance. It is called the **completeness probability (bound)**. Here "completeness" means eventually recognition of an instance in the language. The need for bounding this probability from below is in order to limit the possibility for a mistaken rejection of an instance. A more meaningful manifestation for (4.4.1) is the following equivalent re-expression:

$$\text{Prob}\,[PM \text{ decides } I \notin L \mid I \in L] < 1 - \epsilon. \qquad (4.4.4)$$

In this expression the value $1 - \epsilon$ is the probability bound for a false rejection. We say that the completeness of *PM* is a bounded probability for false rejection.

The expression (4.4.2) is the probability bound for a mistaken recognition of a non-instance. It is called the **soundness probability (bound),** Here "soundness" means no recognition of a non-instance. The need for bounding the probability from above is obvious. We say that the soundness of *PM* is a bounded probability for false recognition.

## 4.4.1   Error Probability Characterizations

We have expressed error probability bounds for a *PM* with two constants $\epsilon$, $\delta$ in two intervals (4.4.3) with no any precision. Now let us explain that the imprecision will not cause any problem.

### 4.4.1.1   Polynomial-time Characterizations

For a probabilistic Turing machine *PM* with error probabilities bounded by any fixed value $\epsilon \in (\frac{1}{2}, 1]$ (for completeness) and and any fixed value $\delta \in [0, \frac{1}{2})$ (for soundness), if we repeatedly run *PM* $n$ times on an input $I$, the repetition, denoted by $PM'(I, n)$, is also a probabilistic Turing machine. We can use "majority election" as the criterion for $PM'(I, n)$ to decide whether to recognize or reject $I$. That is, if $\lfloor \frac{n}{2} \rfloor + 1$ or more runs of $PM(I)$ output recognition (rejection), then $PM'(I, n)$ recognizes (rejects). It is clear that the completeness and soundness probabilities of $PM'(I, n)$ are functions of $n$. We now show that $PM'(I, n)$ remains being polynomial time in the size of $I$.

Since the random moves of the $n$ runs of $PM(I)$ are independent, each run of $PM(I)$ can be viewed as a Bernoulli Trial of $\epsilon$ (or $\delta$ for soundness) probability for "success" and $1 - \epsilon$ (or $1 - \delta$ for soundness) probability for "failure." Applying binomial distribution (see §3.5.2), the majority election criterion made by $PM'(I, n)$ provides the error probability bound for $PM'(I, n)$ as the sum of all probabilities for $n$ Bernoulli Trials with $\lfloor \frac{n}{2} \rfloor + 1$ or more "successes." For completeness, the sum is

$$\epsilon(n) = \text{Prob}\left[\xi_n \geq \left\lfloor \frac{n}{2} \right\rfloor + 1\right] = \sum_{i=\lfloor \frac{n}{2} \rfloor + 1}^{n} b(i; n, \epsilon). \tag{4.4.5}$$

For soundness, we have

$$\delta(n) = \text{Prob}\left[\eta_n \geq \left\lfloor \frac{n}{2} \right\rfloor + 1\right] = \sum_{j=\lfloor \frac{n}{2} \rfloor + 1}^{n} b(j; n, \delta). \tag{4.4.6}$$

These two expressions are accumulative sums of the respective binomial distributions. Because $\epsilon > \frac{1}{2}$ and $\delta < \frac{1}{2}$, the central term (defined in §3.5.2.1) of the first distribution is at the point $(n+1)\epsilon > \lfloor \frac{n}{2} \rfloor + 1$ (where the binomial term reaches the maximum value) and that for latter is at the point $(n+1)\delta < \lfloor \frac{n}{2} \rfloor + 1$.

In §3.5.2.1 we have investigated the behavior of these sums. The sum in (4.4.6) is a "right tail" of the binomial distribution function since $\lfloor \frac{n}{2} \rfloor + 1 > (n+1)\delta$. Applying (3.5.7) using $r = \lfloor \frac{n+1}{2} \rfloor$ and $p = \delta$, we obtain

$$\delta(n) < \frac{2(1-\delta)}{(1-2\delta)^2} \cdot \frac{1}{n+1}.$$

With $\delta$ being constant, we have

$$\delta(n) \to 0 \quad (n \to \infty).$$

The reader may analogously derive the following result

$$\epsilon(n) > 1 - \frac{c}{n}$$

for some constant $c$. The derivation is left as an exercise (Ex 4.7, a hint is given there).

Since the "tails" diminish to zero faster than $\frac{1}{n}$ does[c], we can let $n = |I|$, and hence the machine $PM'(I, n)$ runs in time $|I| \cdot poly(|I|)$ where $poly(|I|)$ is the running time of the machine $PM$ on the input $I$. Therefore, $PM'$ remains being polynomial time.

### 4.4.1.2   Why Bounded Away from $\frac{1}{2}$?

If $\epsilon = \delta = \frac{1}{2}$, then both distributions (4.4.5) and (4.4.6) have central terms at the point $\lfloor \frac{n}{2} \rfloor$. It is easy to check that for odd $n$

$$\epsilon(n) = \delta(n) = \frac{1}{2},$$

and for even $n$

$$\epsilon(n) \approx \delta(n) \approx \frac{1}{2}.$$

That is, $\epsilon(n)$ can never be enlarged and $\delta(n)$ can never be reduced; they will remain at the $\frac{1}{2}$ level regardless of how many times $PM(I)$ is repeated. So machine $PM'(I, n)$, as $n$ independent runs of $PM(I)$, can reach no decision because for both completeness and soundness cases, half of the $n$ runs of $PM(I)$ reach acceptances and the other half of the $n$ runs reach rejections. With $n$ unbounded and $PM(I)$ remaining in the indecision state, machine $PM'(I, n)$ will never terminate and hence cannot be a polynomial-time algorithm.

---

[c]Our estimates derived in (3.5.7) and (3.5.8) are only two upper bounds. The real speed that a tail diminishes to 0 is much faster than that of $\frac{1}{n}$. See Example 3.9 for numerical cases. This will further be confirmed by the soundness and completeness properties of Prot 18.4 in §18.5.1.1.

Therefore, for $\mathcal{PP}$ being the class of languages with membership recognizable in probabilistic polynomial time, we must require both error probabilities expressed in (4.4.1) and (4.4.2) be bounded away from $\frac{1}{2}$.

However, we should notice that the requirement for error probabilities being "bounded-away-from-$\frac{1}{2}$" is only necessary for the most *general case* of language recognition problems in the class $\mathcal{PP}$ which must include the subclass of the "two-sided error" problems (see §4.4.5). If a problem has one-sided error (i.e., either $\epsilon = 1$ or $\delta = 0$, see §4.4.3 and §4.4.4), then bounded away from $\frac{1}{2}$ is unnecessary. This is because, in the case of one-sided error algorithms, we do not have to use the majority election criterion. A "minority election criterion" can be used instead. For example, a "unanimous election criterion" can be used with which $PM'(I, n)$ recognizes (rejects) $I$ only if all $n$ runs of $PM(I)$ reaches the same decision. In such a election criterion, $\epsilon(n) \to 1$ or $\delta(n) \to 0$ in a exponential speed for any quantities $\epsilon, \delta \in (0, 1)$.

In applications, it is possible that some useful problems have $\epsilon \leq \frac{1}{2}$ or $\delta \geq \frac{1}{2}$ (but, as we have reasoned, must not holding of both). For such problems, changing election criterion (e.g., to a minority election one) can provide us with room to enlarge or reduce the error probability. In §18.5.1, we will see a protocol example which has the recognition probability $\epsilon = \frac{1}{2}$, but we can still enlarge the completeness probability by repeating the protocol using a minority election criterion.

## Several Subclasses in $\mathcal{PP}$

The class $\mathcal{PP}$ has several subclasses which are defined by different ways to characterize the error-probability bound expressions in (4.4.1) and in (4.4.2), using different values of $\epsilon$ and $\delta$, respectively. Let us now introduce these subclasses. We will exemplify each subclass with an algorithm. Similar to the case where a deterministic Turing machine simulates a polynomial-time algorithm, a probabilistic Turing machine simulates a **randomized (polynomial-time) algorithm**. Therefore, the algorithm examples shown in our introduction will not be limited to those for language recognition.

## 4.4.2 Subclass "Always Fast and Always Correct"

A subclass of $\mathcal{PP}$ is named $\mathcal{ZPP}$ (which stands for **Zero-sided-error Probabilistic Polynomial time**) if the error probability bounds in (4.4.1) and (4.4.2) have the following characterization: for any $L \in \mathcal{ZPP}$ there exists a randomized algorithm $A$ such that for any instance $I$

$$\text{Prob}\,[A \text{ recognizes } I \mid I \in L] = 1$$

and

$$\text{Prob}\,[A \text{ recognizes } I \mid I \notin L] = 0.$$

This error-probability characterization means that a random operation in a randomized algorithm makes no error at all. So, at a first glance, $\mathcal{ZPP}$ should have no difference from $\mathcal{P}$. However, there are a class of problems which can be solved by deterministic algorithms as well as by randomized algorithms, *both in polynomial time*; while the randomized algorithms can yield no error whatsoever, they are much quicker than their deterministic counterparts. We will provide an example for contrasting the time complexity in a moment.

### 4.4.2.1    An Example of "Zero-sided-error" Algorithms

Some randomized algorithms are so natural that we have been using them instead of their deterministic counterparts for a long history. For example, to weigh an object using a steelyard[d], the user should move around the counterbalance on the scaled arm in a randomized way which will allow one to find the weight much quicker than to do the job in a deterministic way. One such algorithm we all are familiar with is a randomized process for looking up someone's phone number from a phone book. This algorithm is specified in Alg 4.4.

---

**Algorithm 4.4:** Searching Through Phone Book (a $\mathcal{ZPP}$ Algorithm)

INPUT        *Name*: a person's name;
             *Book*: a phone book;
OUTPUT    The person's phone number.

1. Repeat the following until *Book* has one page

   {

   (a) Open *Book* at a random page;

   (b) If *Name* occurs before the page, *Book* ← Earlier_pages(*Book*);

   (c) Else *Book* ← Later_pages(*Book*);

   }

2. Return( Phone number beside *Name* );

---

Clearly, the random operation in Alg 4.4 will not introduce any error to the output result. Therefore this is indeed a "zero-sided-error" randomized algorithm. For a phone book of $N$ pages, Alg 4.4 will only need to execute $O(\log N)$ steps

---

[d]The weighing instrument is called "Gancheng" in Chinese and has been used for more than two thousand years.

and find the page containing the name and the number. We should notice that a deterministic algorithm for "searching through phone book" will execute average $O(N)$ steps.

The reason why Alg 4.4 works so fast is that names in a phone book have been sorted alphabetically. We should notice that sorting is itself a $\mathcal{ZPP}$ problem: "quick-sort" (see, e.g., pages 92–97 of [9]) is a randomized sorting algorithm, can sort $N$ elements in $O(N \log N)$ steps, and its random operations will not introduce any error to the outcome result. In contrast, "bubble-sort" is a deterministic sorting algorithm; it sorts $N$ elements in $O(N^2)$ steps (see e.g., pages 77 of [9]).

We can say that $\mathcal{ZPP}$ is a subclass of languages which can be recognized by randomized algorithms in an "always fast and always correct" fashion.

### 4.4.3 Subclass "Always Fast and Probably Correct"

A subclass of $\mathcal{PP}$ which we name $\mathcal{PP}$(Monte Carlo) ("Monte Carlo" is typically used as a generic term for "randomized") if the error probability bounds in (4.4.1) and (4.4.2) have the following characterization: for any $L \in \mathcal{PP}$(Monte Carlo) there exists a randomized algorithm $A$ such that for any instance $I$

$$\text{Prob}\,[A \text{ recognizes } I \mid I \in L] = 1,$$

and

$$\text{Prob}\,[A \text{ recognizes } I \mid I \notin L] \le \delta,$$

here $\delta$ is any constant in the interval $(0, \frac{1}{2})$. However, as we have pointed out in §4.4.1.2, since for one-sided-error algorithms we do not have to use the majority election criterion in the process of reducing a soundness error probability bound, $\delta$ can actually be any constant in $(0, 1)$.

Notice that now $\delta \ne 0$; otherwise the subclass degenerates to the special case $\mathcal{ZPP}$. Randomized algorithms with this error-probability characterization have **one-sided error** in the soundness side. In other words, such an algorithm may make a mistake in terms of a false recognition of a non-instance. However, if an input is indeed an instance then it will always be recognized. This subclass of algorithms are called **Monte Carlo algorithms**.

From our study in §4.4.1 we know that the error probability of a Monte Carlo algorithm can be reduced to arbitrarily closing to 0 by independent iterating the algorithm and the iterated algorithm remains in polynomial time. We therefore say that a Monte Carlo algorithm is always fast and is probably correct.

We now show that PRIMES (the set of all prime numbers) is in the subclass $\mathcal{PP}$(Monte Carlo).

### 4.4.3.1  An Example of Monte Carlo Algorithms

Since Fermat, it has been known that if $p$ is a prime number and $x$ is relatively prime to $p$, then $x^{p-1} \equiv 1 \pmod{p}$. This forms a basis for the following Monte Carlo method for primality test ([284]), that is, picking $x \in_U (1, p-1]$ with $\gcd(x, p) = 1$ and checking

$$x^{(p-1)/2} \stackrel{?}{\equiv} \pm 1 \pmod{p}. \tag{4.4.7}$$

The test is repeated $k = \log_2 p$ times with the $-1$ case occurring at least once. Alg 4.5 specifies this test algorithm.

---

**Algorithm 4.5:** Probabilistic Primality Test (a Monte Carlo Algorithm)

INPUT       $p$: a positive integer;
OUTPUT    YES if $p$ is prime, NO otherwise.

Prime_Test($p$)

1. repeat $\log_2 p$ times:

    (a)  $x \in_U (1, p-1]$;
    (b)  if $\gcd(x, p) > 1$ or $x^{(p-1)/2} \not\equiv \pm 1 \pmod{p}$ return( NO );

    end_of_repeat;

2. if ( test in 1.(b) never shows $-1$ ) return( NO );

3. return( YES ).

---

First of all, we know from **Fermat's Little Theorem** (Theorem 6.10 in §6.4) that if $p$ is prime then for all $x < p$:

$$x^{p-1} \equiv 1 \pmod{p}. \tag{4.4.8}$$

So if $p$ is prime then Prime_Test($p$) will always return YES, that is, we always have (including the case of $p$ being the even prime)

$$\text{Prob}\left[x^{(p-1)/2} \equiv \pm 1 \pmod{p} \mid p \text{ is prime}\right] = 1.$$

On the other hand, if $p$ is a composite number then congruence (4.4.7) will not hold in general. In fact (a fact in Group Theory, see Example 5.2.3 and Theorem 5.1 (in §5.2.1) if the inequality against congruence (4.4.7) shows for one $x < p$ with

$\gcd(x, p) = 1$ then the inequality must show for at least half the numbers of this kind. Thus we conclude that for $x \in_U (1, p - 1]$ with $\gcd(x, p) = 1$:

$$\text{Prob}\left[ x^{(p-1)/2} \equiv \pm 1 \pmod{p} \mid p \text{ is composite} \right] \leq 1/2. \qquad (4.4.9)$$

Therefore, if the test passes $k$ times for $x$ chosen at uniformly random (remember that the $-1$ case is seen to hold at least once), then the probability that $p$ is not prime is less than $2^{-k}$. Here we have used the "unanimous election criterion": $p$ will be rejected if there is a single failure in $\log_2 p$ tests. Notice that this election criterion is different from the majority election one which we have studied in §4.4.1 (for the general case of two-sided error problems) where failures will be tolerated as long as the number of failures does not exceed half the number of tests. In this "unanimous election" the soundness probability tends to 0 much faster than the majority election case.

We have set $k = \log_2 p$, and so any input instance $p$:

$$\text{Prob}\left[ \text{Prime\_Test}(p) = \text{YES} \mid p \text{ is not prime} \right] \leq 2^{-\log_2 p}.$$

In §4.3 we have seen that computing modulo exponentiation and computing the greatest common divisor with $\log_2 p$ -bit long input value have their time complexities bounded by $O_B((\log_2 p)^3)$. Therefore the time complexity of Prime\_Test($p$) is bounded by $O_B((\log p)^4)$.

To this end we know that PRIMES – the language of all prime numbers – is in $\mathcal{PP}$(Monte Carlo).

Nevertheless without invalidating this statement, in August 2002, three Indian computer scientists, Agrawal, Kayal and Saena, find a *deterministic* polynomial-time primality test algorithm [8]; consequently, PRIMES is in fact in $\mathcal{P}$.

## 4.4.4  Subclass "Probably Fast and Always Correct"

A subclass of $\mathcal{PP}$ which we name $\mathcal{PP}$(Las Vegas) if the error probability bounds in (4.4.1) and (4.4.2) have the following characterization: for any $L \in \mathcal{PP}$(Las Vegas) there exists a randomized algorithm $A$ such that for any instance $I$

$$\text{Prob}\left[ A \text{ recognizes } I \mid I \in L \right] \geq \epsilon,$$

and

$$\text{Prob}\left[ A \text{ recognizes } I \mid I \notin L \right] = 0,$$

here $\epsilon$ is any constant in the interval $(\frac{1}{2}, 1)$. Again, as in the case of one-sided-error in the soundness side (§4.4.3), because there is no need to use the majority election criterion in the process of enlarging the completeness probability bound, $\epsilon$ can actually be any constant in $(0, 1)$.

Also again we should notice $\epsilon \neq 1$; otherwise the subclass degenerates to the special case $\mathcal{ZPP}$. Randomized algorithms with this error-probability characterization have one-sided error in the completeness side. In other words, such an algorithm may make a mistake in terms of a false non-recognition of an instance. However, if an instance is recognized then no mistake is possible: the instance must be a genuine one. This subclass of algorithms are called **Las Vegas algorithms**. The term Las Vegas, first introduced in [16], refers to randomized algorithms which either give the correct answer or no answer at all.

From our analysis in §4.4.1.1, we know that the probability for a Las Vegas algorithm to give YES answer to an instance can be enlarged to arbitrarily closing to 1 by independent iterating the algorithm and the iterated algorithm remains in polynomial time. If we say that Monte Carlo algorithms are always fast and probably correct, then Las Vegas algorithms are always correct and probably fast.

Observing the error probability characterizations of $\mathcal{ZPP}$, $\mathcal{PP}$(Monte Carlo) and $\mathcal{PP}$(Las Vegas), the following equation is obvious

$$\mathcal{ZPP} = \mathcal{PP}(\text{Monte Carlo}) \cap \mathcal{PP}(\text{Las Vegas}).$$

### 4.4.4.1   An Example of Las Vegas Algorithms

Let $p$ be an odd positive integer and let $p - 1 = q_1 q_2 \cdots q_k$ as the complete prime factorization of $p - 1$ (some of the prime factors may repeat). In Chapter 5 we will establish a fact (Theorem 5.12 in §5.4.4): $p$ is prime if and only if there exists a positive integer $g \in [2, p - 1]$ such that

$$
\begin{aligned}
g^{p-1} &\equiv 1 \pmod{p} \\
g^{(p-1)/q_i} &\not\equiv 1 \pmod{p} \quad \text{for } i = 1, 2, \ldots, k.
\end{aligned}
\tag{4.4.10}
$$

This fact provides us with an algorithm for proving primality. Inputting an odd number $p$ and the complete prime factorization of $p - 1$, the algorithm tries to find a number $g$ satisfying (4.4.10). If such a number is found, the algorithm outputs YES and terminates successfully, and $p$ must be prime. Otherwise, the algorithm will be in an undecided state; this means, it does not know if $p$ is prime or not. The algorithm is specified in Alg 4.6.

First we notice $k \leq \log_2(p - 1)$, therefore Alg 4.6 terminates in time polynomial in the size of $p$.

From the fact to be established in Theorem 5.12 (in §5.4.4), we will see that if Alg 4.6 outputs YES, then the input integer $p$ must be prime; no error is possible. Also, if the algorithm outputs NO, the answer is also correct since otherwise Fermat's Little Theorem (4.4.8) will be violated. These two cases reflect the algorithm's "always correct" nature. The error-free property of the algorithm entitles it to be named "Proof of Primality."

**Algorithm 4.6:** Proof of Primality (a Las Vegas Algorithm)

INPUT      $p$: an odd positive number;

            $q_1, q_2, \ldots, q_k$: all prime factors of $p - 1$;

OUTPUT     YES if $p$ is prime, NO otherwise;

            NO_DECISION with certain probability of error.

1. pick $g \in_U [2, p-1]$;

2. for ( $i = 1$, $i{+}{+}$, $k$ ) do
   if $g^{(p-1)/q_i} \equiv 1 \pmod{p}$ output NO_DECISION and terminate;

3. if $g^{p-1} \not\equiv 1 \pmod{p}$ output NO and terminate;

4. output YES and terminate.

However, when Alg 4.6 outputs NO_DECISION, it does not know whether or not the input integer $p$ is prime. It is possible that $p$ is not prime, but it is also possible that an error has occurred. In the latter case $p$ is indeed prime, but the testing number $g$ which the algorithm picks at random is a wrong one. After we have studied Theorem 5.12 in §5.4.4, we will know that the wrong number $g$ is not a "primitive root."

To this end we know that Alg 4.6 is a one-sided-error algorithm in the completeness side, i.e., a Las Vegas algorithm. We may revise the algorithm into one which does not terminate at a NO_DECISION answer, but carries on the testing step by picking another random tester $g$. The modified algorithm is still a Las Vegas algorithm, and becomes "probably fast" since it's possible that it always picks a non-primitive root as a tester. Fortunately, for any odd prime $p$, the multiplicative group modulo $p$ (to be defined in Chapter 5) contains plenty of primitive roots and so such an element can be picked up with a non-trivial probability by random sampling the group modulo $p$ (in Chapter 5 we will establish the proportion of primitive roots in a multiplicative group modulo a prime).

Las Vegas algorithms and Monte Carlo algorithms collectively are referred to as **"randomized algorithms with one-sided error."** Algorithms in this union (recall that the union includes $\mathcal{ZPP}$) are really efficient ones; even they are non-deterministic algorithms, their time-complexity behaviors are similar to those of the algorithms in $\mathcal{P}$.

#### 4.4.4.2   Another Example of Las Vegas Algorithms: Quantum Factorization

A quantum computer can factor an integer in time polynomial in the size of the integer (i.e., FACTORIZATION $\in \mathcal{QP}$). Shor devises such an algorithm ([269], also see, e.g., pages 108–115 of [302]). We now explain that Shor's quantum factorization procedure is also a Las Vegas algorithm.

To factor an integer $N$, a random integer $a$ is picked; a quantum algorithm, which uses Simon's idea of finding period in quantum state by sampling from the Fourier transform [278], can find the period of the function $f(x) = a^x \pmod{N}$, i.e., the least positive integer $r$ satisfying $f(r) = 1$. In Chapter 6 we shall see that for a composite $N$, a non-trivial proportion of integers $a$ satisfying $\gcd(a, N) = 1$ has an even period (called the multiplicative order of the element $a$), i.e., $r$ is even.

Once an even period $r$ is found, if $a^{r/2} \neq \pm 1 \pmod{N}$, then $a^{r/2} \pmod{N}$ is a non-trivial square-root of 1 modulo $N$. In §6.6.2 (Theorem 6.17) we shall show that $\gcd(a^{r/2} \pm 1, N)$ must be a non-trivial factor of $N$, i.e., the algorithm has successfully factored $N$.

If $r$ is odd or if $a^{r/2} = \pm 1 \pmod{N}$, then $\gcd(a^{r/2} \pm 1, N)$ is a trivial factor of $N$, i.e., 1 or $N$; so the algorithm fails with no answer. However, for randomly chosen integer $a < N$, the probability for encountering $a^{r/2} \neq \pm 1 \pmod{N}$ is bounded from below by a constant $\epsilon > 1/2$, and therefore the procedure can be repeated using another random element $a$. By our analysis in §4.4.1.1, Shor's algorithm remains in polynomial time.

### 4.4.5   Subclass "Probably Fast and Probably Correct"

A subclass of $\mathcal{PP}$ is named $\mathcal{BPP}$ (which stands for "**B**ounded error probability **P**robabilistic **P**olynomial time") if the error probability bounds in (4.4.1) and (4.4.2) both hold for the following cases:

$$\epsilon \in [\frac{1}{2} + \alpha, 1) \ \text{ and } \ \delta \in (0, \frac{1}{2} - \beta], \qquad (4.4.11)$$

here $\alpha > 0$ and $\beta > 0$. We should pay attention to two things in this error probability characterization:

1. $\epsilon \neq 1$ and $\delta \neq 0$. Otherwise, the subclass $\mathcal{BPP}$ degenerates to one of the three simpler cases: $\mathcal{ZPP}$, or $\mathcal{PP}$(Monte Carlo), or $\mathcal{PP}$(Las Vegas). Now with $\epsilon \neq 1$ and $\delta \neq 0$, algorithms in $\mathcal{BPP}$ have **two-sided errors**, both false no-recognition (a completeness error) and false recognition (a soundness error) are possible.

2. $\alpha > 0$ and/or $\beta > 0$. This means that algorithms in $\mathcal{BPP}$ have their error probabilities *clearly* bounded away from $\frac{1}{2}$. In §4.4.1 we have reasoned that if $\epsilon \neq \frac{1}{2}$ ($\delta \neq \frac{1}{2}$) then repeating the algorithm with the majority election criterion

can lead to the enlargement of the completeness (reduction of the soundness) error probability. If $\epsilon = \frac{1}{2}$ or $\delta = \frac{1}{2}$, then the majority election technique won't work, since the former (the latter) case means that there is no majority fraction of the random moves to lead to a recognition (rejection). However, a "minority election criterion" may still be used (we will see such an example in §18.5.1). Finally, if $\epsilon = \frac{1}{2}$ and $\delta = \frac{1}{2}$, then no election criterion can work and the problem is not in $\mathcal{PP}$ (i.e., cannot be recognized by a non-deterministic Turing machine regardless of how long a machine runs).

Since besides Monte Carlo and Las Vegas, Atlantic City is another famous gambling place to lure people to increase their winning probabilities by increasing the number of games they play, randomized algorithms with two-sided-errors are also called **Atlantic City algorithms**. Now let us look at an example of Atlantic City algorithms.

### 4.4.5.1 An Example of Atlantic City Algorithms

There is a famous protocol in **quantum cryptography** named the **quantum key distribution protocol** (the QKD protocol, see e.g. [32]). The QKD protocol allows a bit string to be agreed between two communication entities without having the two parties to meet face to face, and yet that the two parties can be sure with a high confidence that the agreed bit string is exclusively shared between them. The QKD protocol is a two-sided-error randomized algorithm. Let us describe this algorithm and examine its two-sided-error property.

Let us first provide a brief description on the physical principle for the QKD protocol. The distribution of a secret bit string in the QKD protocol is achieved by a sender (let Alice be the sender) transmitting a string of four-way-polarized photons. Each of these photons is in a state (called a photon state or a state) denoted by one of the four following symbols:

$$- , \ | \ , \ \diagup , \ \diagdown \ .$$

The first two photon states are emitted by a polarizer which is set with a rectilinear orientation; the latter two states are emitted by a polarizer which is set with a diagonal orientation. Let us denote by $+$ and $\times$ these two differently oriented polarizers, respectively. We can encode information into these four photon states. The following is a bit-to-photon-state encoding scheme:

$$+(0) = - , \ +(1) = \ | \ , \ \times(0) = \diagup , \ \times(1) = \diagdown \ . \qquad (4.4.12)$$

This encoding scheme is the public knowledge. If Alice wants to transmit the conventional bit 0 (respectively, 1), she may choose to use $+$ and consequently send out over a quantum channel $-$ (respectively, $|$ ), or choose to use $\times$ and consequently send out $\diagup$ (respectively, $\diagdown$ ). For each conventional bit to be transmitted in the QKD protocol Alice will set differently oriented polarizers $+$ or $\times$ uniformly random.

To receive a photon state, a receiver (who may be Bob, the intended receiver, or Eve, an eavesdropper) must use a device called a photon observer which is also set with rectilinear or diagonal orientations. We shall also denote by $+$ and $\times$ these two differently oriented observers, respectively. Let $\overset{+}{\Longrightarrow}$ and $\overset{\times}{\Longrightarrow}$ denote the two differently oriented observers receiving and interpreting photon states transmitted from left to right. The observation of the photon states obeys the following rules:

**Correct observations** (states are maintained with probability 1)

$$- \overset{+}{\Longrightarrow} -, \quad | \overset{+}{\Longrightarrow} |, \quad / \overset{\times}{\Longrightarrow} /, \quad \backslash \overset{\times}{\Longrightarrow} \backslash.$$

**Incorrect observations** (states are destroyed)

$$/ \overset{+}{\Longrightarrow} \begin{array}{l} - \\ | \end{array} \quad \begin{array}{l} \text{probability } \frac{1}{2} \\ \text{probability } \frac{1}{2} \end{array}, \quad \backslash \overset{+}{\Longrightarrow} \begin{array}{l} - \\ | \end{array} \quad \begin{array}{l} \text{probability } \frac{1}{2} \\ \text{probability } \frac{1}{2} \end{array},$$

$$- \overset{\times}{\Longrightarrow} \begin{array}{l} / \\ \backslash \end{array} \quad \begin{array}{l} \text{probability } \frac{1}{2} \\ \text{probability } \frac{1}{2} \end{array}, \quad | \overset{\times}{\Longrightarrow} \begin{array}{l} / \\ \backslash \end{array} \quad \begin{array}{l} \text{probability } \frac{1}{2} \\ \text{probability } \frac{1}{2} \end{array}.$$

These observation rules say the following things. Rectilinearly oriented states can be correctly observed by rectilinearly set observers correctly; likewise, diagonally oriented states can be correctly observed by diagonally set observers correctly. However, if a rectilinearly (diagonally) oriented state is observed by a diagonally (rectilinearly) oriented observer, then a $\pm 45°$ "rectification" of the orientation will occur, with 0.5 probability in either directions. These are wrong observations and are an inevitable result of "Heisenberg Uncertainty Principle" which underlies the working principle for the QKD Protocol.

So if the orientation setting of the receiver's observer agrees with (i.e., is the same as) the setting of Alice's polarizer then a photon state will be correctly received. The public bit-to-photon encoding scheme in (4.4.12) is a 1-1 mapping between the conventional bits and the phone states. So in such a case, the conventional bit sent by Alice can be correctly decoded. On the other hand, if the orientation settings of the photon devices in the two ends disagree, a wrong observation must occur and it also necessarily destroys the photon state transmitted, although the receiver can have no idea which photon state has actually been sent and destroyed.

We are now ready to specify the QKD Protocol. The protocol is specified in Prot 4.1.

Let us explain how this protocol works and measure the probabilities for the two-sided errors to occur.

**Protocol 4.1:** Quantum Key Distribution (an Atlantic City Algorithm)

**High-level Description of the Protocol**

**Quantum channel** Alice sends to Bob $m$ photon states, each of them is randomly oriented in $\left\{ -, \mid, \diagup, \diagdown \right\}$.

**Conventional channel, open discussions** They choose $k = \frac{m}{10}$ "sifted bits" which are transmitted as the result of Alice's settings of her polarizers agree with Bob's settings of his observers. They further compare random $\ell (< k)$ "testing bits" in the $k$ sifted bits to detect eavesdropping, and in absence of an eavesdropper, they agree on the remaining $k - \ell$ secrete bits.

1. Alice generates $m$ random conventional bits $a_1, a_2, \ldots, a_m \in_U \{0, 1\}$; she sets $m$ randomly oriented polarizers $p_1, p_2, \ldots, p_m \in_U \{+, \times\}$; she sends to Bob $m$ photon states $p_1(a_1), p_2(a_2), \ldots, p_m(a_m)$ according to the bit-to-photon-state encoding scheme in (4.4.12);

2. Bob sets $m$ randomly oriented photon observers $o_1, o_2, \ldots, o_m \in_U \{+, \times\}$ and uses them to receive the $m$ photon states; using the bit-to-photon-state encoding scheme in (4.4.12) Bob decodes and obtains conventional bits $b_1, b_2, \ldots, b_m$; he tells Alice: "All received!";

3. They openly compare their settings $(p_1, o_1), (p_2, o_2), \ldots, (p_m, o_m)$; if there are more than $k = \frac{m}{10}$ pairs of the settings agree as follows: (∗ without loss of generality we have relabeled the subscripts ∗)
$$p_i = o_i \text{ for } 1 \le i \le k,$$
then they proceed to execute the following steps; otherwise the run fails (∗ the failure is an error in the completeness side ∗);

4. (∗ now the set $\{(a_i, b_i)\}_{i=1}^k$ contains $k$ pairs of sifted bits distributed via the agreed settings of polarizers and observers ∗) Alice and Bob openly compare random $\ell$ pairs in $\{(a_i, b_i)\}_{i=1}^k$; the compared bits are called testing bits; if any pair of the testing bits do not match, they announce "Eavesdropper detected!" and abort the run;

5. They output the remaining $k - \ell$ bits as the distributed secret key; the run terminates successfully (∗ but an error in the soundness side may have occurred ∗).

Steps 1 and 2 are quite straightforward: Alice sends to Bob $m$ random photon states using $m$ random settings $p_1, p_2, \ldots, p_m \in_U \{+, \times\}$ (Step 1) and Bob has to observe them in a random process using $m$ random settings $o_1, o_2, \ldots, o_m \in_U$

$\{+, \times\}$ (Step 2). The $m$ conventional bits Alice encoded and transmitted are $a_1, a_2, \ldots, a_m$ and those Bob received and decoded are $b_1, b_2, \ldots, b_m$.

In Step 3, Alice and Bob discuss over a conventional communication channel to see whether or not in their random $m$ pairs $\{(p_i, o_i)\}_{i=1}^{m}$ of the devices settings there are $k = \frac{m}{10}$ pairs of settings being the same. If there are $k$ agreed settings they will proceed further. Otherwise, the run has failed and this is an error in the completeness side. We shall provide a probability measure for the completeness-side error in a moment.

Suppose that a completeness-side error has not occurred and the two parties are now in Step 4. They now have a set of $k$ sifted bits which are distributed by the $k$ agreed devices settings. Without loss of generality we can relabel the subscripts of these bits; so Alice's sifted bits are $a_1, a_2, \ldots, a_k$ and those of Bob are $b_1, b_2, \ldots, b_k$. They now conduct an open discussion again over the conventional channel: comparing a random $\ell$ pairs of the sifted bits. Any mismatch will be considered as being caused by an eavesdropper Eve. If they do not find the existence of Eve in Step 4, the protocol reaches the happy end in Step 5. Alice and Bob now share $k - \ell$ bits which they consider as not having been eavesdropped. However, it is possible that the reason of non-detection is the occurrence of a soundness-side error. Let us now investigate the probability for this error.

### Probability of the Soundness-side Error

Suppose Eve has listened the quantum channel. The only way for Eve to observe the photon states sent from Alice is to use the same technique that Bob uses. So Eve has to set $m$ random orientations for her observers and she also has to send $m$ states to Bob. Due to "Heisenberg Uncertainty Principle" her wrong observations will destroy Alice's states. Since Eve can have no idea on the correctness of her observations, she will have no idea on what should be passed to Bob. One strategy for Eve is to send to Bob a completely new set of $m$ states which she invents randomly (just as Alice does), hoping that whatever she sends and whatever Alice sends will be observed by Bob without difference; another strategy is to just pass over to Bob whatever she has observed, hoping that she has not destroyed Alice's states. Actually, there will be no difference between these two strategies in terms of effecting the soundness-side error probability which we now derive.

Let us consider the second strategy (the first strategy will lead to the same soundness-side error probability result, see Ex 4.9). For state $p_i(a_i)$, if Eve has set her observer $e_i$ correctly, i.e., $e_i = p_i$, then she will receive the state $p_i(a_i)$ and hence the bit $a_i$ correctly, and consequently Bob will receive the state and the bit correctly too. So in this case there is no way for Alice and Bob to detect Eve's existence. Since the probability for Eve to have correctly set her $i$-th observer is $1/2$, we have $1/2$ as part of the probability value for non-detection (in the $i$-th position).

If Eve has set her $i$-th observer incorrectly then the $i$-th state she observes is incorrect and hence she will send an incorrect state to Bob. Nevertheless, Bob's observer will "rectify" that wrong state by $\pm 45°$, 50:50 chance either way. Thus, Bob may receive that state correctly or incorrectly with probability for either case being $1/2$. A correct receipt will again leave Eve undetected. Notice that this sub-case of non-detection is after Eve's wrong setting of her device which also has the probability $1/2$. Since Eve's and Bob's devices settings are independent, the probability of this sub-case of non-detection is $\frac{1}{2} \times \frac{1}{2} = \frac{1}{4}$.

Summing the probability values obtained in the above two paragraphs, we have derived $\frac{1}{2} + \frac{1}{4} = \frac{3}{4}$ as the probability for non-detection of Eve in her listening of the $i$-th state. Since Eve must listen to all the sifted states in order for her to obtain the distributed key, and Alice and Bob compare random $\ell$ testing bits and any single mismatch will signal a detection (this is a "unanimous election criterion", not even a single failure is tolerated, see §4.4.1.2), the probability for non-detection of Eve in all positions is $(\frac{3}{4})^\ell$. This is the probability for the soundness-side error. This quantity diminishes to 0 very fast.

## Probability of the Completeness-side Error

Finally let us look at the probability for a completeness-side error to occur. Consider Alice's $m$ settings of her devices being a random binary vector $V = (v_1, v_2, \ldots, v_m)$ and those of Bob's, $W = (w_1, w_2, \ldots, w_m)$. A completeness-side error occurs when

$$V \oplus W = (v_1 \oplus w_1, v_2 \oplus w_2, \ldots, v_m \oplus w_m)$$

has less than $\frac{m}{10}$ zeros. Since the settings of Alice and those of Bob are independent and uniform, $V \oplus W$ should also be a uniformly random binary vector of $m$ binary bits. The probability of number of zeros appearing in this vector follows the binomial distribution of $m$ trials with $i$ successes where the probability for success is 0.5. Clearly, the "most probable number of zeros" in vector $V \oplus W$ is $\frac{m}{2}$. That is, the "central term" (see §3.5.2.1) of this binomial distribution is at point $\lfloor \frac{m+1}{2} \rfloor$. So point $\frac{m}{10}$ is far away (far left) from point $\lfloor \frac{m+1}{2} \rfloor$ where the central term is. Thus, the probability of a completeness-side error

$$\text{Prob}\left[\text{zeros\_in}(V \oplus W) < \frac{m}{10}\right]$$

is a "left tail" of this binomial distribution function. By the probability bound for a left tail which we have established in (3.5.8), we derive the following bound for the probability of occurring a completeness-side error:

$$\text{Prob}\left[\text{zeros\_in}(V \oplus W) < \frac{m}{10}\right] < \frac{(m + 1 - \frac{m}{10})0.5}{((m+1)0.5 - \frac{m}{10})^2} < \frac{3}{m} \quad \text{(for } m \geq 2\text{)}.$$

Therefore, the probability for Alice and Bob to run the protocol beyond Step 3 is greater than $1 - \frac{3}{m}$.

**Summary of the Two-sided-error Probabilities**

We summarize the probabilities of two-sided errors for Prot 4.1 as follows. For completeness side we have:

$$\text{Prob}\left[\text{Number of sifted bits} \geq \frac{m}{10} \mid \text{In } m \text{ photon states distributed}\right] > 1 - \frac{3}{m},$$

and for soundness side we have:

$$\text{Prob}\left[\text{Non-detection of Eve} \mid \text{Alice and Bob test } \ell \text{ testing bits}\right] \leq \left(\frac{3}{4}\right)^{\ell}.$$

We should notice that the "left tail" bound $\frac{3}{m}$, obtained from (3.5.8), for the completeness-side error probability is a loose upper bound. The left tail diminishes to zero much faster than $\frac{3}{m}$ does (see the numerical example in Example 3.9).

These error probability results show that the QKD protocol can be practically used for key distribution. Commercial QKD systems are expected to be in practical use in year 2004 or so [270].

In the real application, the conventional communication channel over which Alice and Bob conduct open discussions should have the authentication property. That is necessary in order for them to be sure that they share the secret key with the right communication partner. Authentication will be the topic of Part IV.

## 4.4.6   Efficient Algorithms

To this end of our introduction to the polynomial-time class and to the probabilistic polynomial-time (PPT) subclasses, we have established the following class inclusion relation:

$$\mathcal{P} \subseteq \mathcal{ZPP} \subseteq \begin{array}{c} \mathcal{PP}(\text{Monte Carlo}) \\ \mathcal{PP}(\text{Las Vegas}) \end{array} \subseteq \mathcal{BPP} \subseteq \mathcal{PP}.$$

Algorithms which can solve problems in any of these classes are called efficient algorithms.

**Definition 4.6: Efficient Algorithms**  *An algorithm is said to be efficient if it is deterministic or randomized with execution time expressed by a polynomial in the size of the input.*

This definition characterizes a notion of **tractability**: whether deterministic or randomized, a polynomial-time problem is solvable, i.e., such a problem requires resources which are manageable even if the size of the problem can be very large. Problems outside the tractable class are **intractable**.

However, since polynomials can have vastly different degrees, within $\mathcal{P}$ or $\mathcal{PP}$, problems have vastly different time complexities. Therefore an efficient algorithm for solving a tractable problem need not be efficient in a practical sense. We will see a few protocol examples in a later chapter, which have their time complexities bounded by polynomials in their input sizes. Thus, these protocols are efficient by Definition 4.6), however, they have little value for practical use because the polynomials that bound their time complexities are simply too large (i.e., their degrees are too large). This is in contrast to the situations in applications where some algorithms with non-polynomial (to be defined in §4.6) time complexities are still useful for solving small instances of intractable problems effectively (e.g., Pollard's Kangaroo Method for Index Computation §3.6.1).

We shall use the term **practically efficient** to refer to polynomial-time algorithms where the polynomials have very small degrees. For example, Turing machine Div3, algorithms gcd, mod_exp and Prime_Test, and the QKD protocol are all practically efficient. Now let us see another example of a practically efficient algorithm which is widely used in modern cryptography.

### 4.4.6.1  Efficient Algorithms: An Example

The idea of probabilistic primality test can be translated straightforwardly to an algorithm for generating a random **probabilistic prime** number of a given size. We say that $n$ is a probabilistic prime number if Prime_Test($n$) returns the YES answer. Alg 4.7 specifies how to generate such a number of a given size.

---

**Algorithm 4.7:** Random $k$-bit Probabilistic Prime Generation

INPUT        $k$: a positive integer;
             (* the input is written to have the size of the input *)
OUTPUT       a $k$-bit random prime.

Prime_Gen($k$)

   1. $p \in_U (2^{k-1}, 2^k - 1]$ with $p$ odd;

   2. if  Prime_Test($p$) = NO  return( Prime_Gen($k$) );

   3. return( $p$ ).

---

First, let us suppose that Prime_Gen($k$) terminates. This means that the algorithm eventually finds a number $p$ which satisfies Prime_Test($p$) = YES (in step 2). From our estimate on the error probability bound for Prime_Test, the probability for the output $p$ not being prime is bounded from above by $2^{-k}$ where $k = \log_2 p$.

An obvious question arises: Will Prime_Gen($k$) terminate at all?

The well-known prime number theorem (see e.g., page 28 of [172]) states that the number of primes less than $X$ is bounded below by $\frac{X}{\log X}$. So the number of primes of exactly $k$ binary bits is about

$$\frac{2^k}{k} - \frac{2^{k-1}}{k-1} \approx \frac{2^k}{2k}.$$

Thus, we can *expect* that Prime_Gen($k$) may recursively call itself $2k$ times in step 2 until a probabilistic prime is found, and then it terminates.

With the time complexity for Prime_Test($p$) being bounded by $O_B((\log p)^4)$ $= O_B(k^4)$, after $2k$ calls of Prime_Test, the time complexity of Prime_Gen($k$) is bounded by $O_B(k^5)$.

Another question arises: while $O_B(k^5)$ is indeed a polynomial in $k$, can this quantity be a polynomial in the *size* of the input to Algorithm Prime_Gen($k$), i.e., a polynomial of the size of $k$?

When we write a number $n$ in the base-$b$ representation for any $b > 1$, the size of the number $n$ is $\log_b n$ and is always less than $n$. In order to make Prime_Gen($k$) a polynomial-time algorithm in the size of its input, we have explicitly required in the specification of Prime_Gen($k$) that its input should be written to have the size of the input. Using the **unary**, or base-1, representation, $k$ can indeed be written to have the size $k$.

**Definition 4.7: Unary Representation of a Number**    *The unary representation of a positive natural number $n$ is*

$$1^n = \underbrace{11 \cdots 1}_{n}.$$

From now on we shall use Prime_Gen($1^k$) to denote an invocation instance of the algorithm Prime_Gen. In the rest of this book, the unary representation of a number always provides an explicit emphasis that the size of that number is the number itself.

# 4.5    Non-deterministic Polynomial Time

Consider the following decisional problem:

**Problem** SQUARE-FREENESS

INPUT          $N$: a positive and odd composite integer;

QUESTION    Is $N$ square free?
                      Answer YES if there exists no prime $p$ such that $p^2 | N$.

Problem SQUARE-FREENESS is very difficult. To date there exists no known algorithm (whether deterministic or probabilistic) which can answer it in time polynomial in the size of the input. Of course, there exists algorithms to answer this question. For example, the following is one: on input $N$, perform trial division exhaustively using the square of all odd primes up to $\lfloor \sqrt{N} \rfloor$, and answer YES when all divisions fail. However, for $N$ being a general instance input, this method runs in time $O(\lfloor \sqrt{N} \rfloor) = O(e^{\frac{\log N}{2}})$, i.e., in time exponential in (half) size of $N$.

Nevertheless, Problem SQUARE-FREENESS should not be regarded as too difficult. If we know some "internal information" of the problem, called a **witness** (or a **certificate** or an **auxiliary input**), then an answer can be *verified* in time polynomial in the size of the input. For example, for input $N$, the integer $\phi(N)$, which is named **Euler's phi function** of $N$ and is the number of all positive numbers less than $N$ and co-prime to $N$ (see Definition 5.11 in §5.2.3), can be used as a witness for an efficient verification algorithm to verify an answer to whether $N$ is square free. Alg 4.8 is an efficient verification algorithm.

---

**Algorithm 4.8:** Square-Free$(N, \phi(N))$

1. $d \leftarrow \gcd(N, \phi(N))$;

2. if $d = 1$ or $d^2 \nmid N$ answer YES else answer NO.

---

The reader who is already familiar with the meaning of $\phi(N)$ may confirm the correctness of Alg 4.8 (Ex 4.13). This verification algorithm is due to a basic number theoretic fact which will become apparent to us in Chapter 6 (§6.3). From our study of the time complexity of the great common divisor algorithm (§4.3.2.3), it is clear that this algorithm runs in time polynomial in the size of $N$.

Now let us describe a computation device: it models a method to solve the class of problems which share the same property with Problem SQUARE-FREENESS. The computation of the device can be described by a tree in Fig 4.4.

The device is called a **non-deterministic Turing machine**. This is a variant Turing machine (review our description of Turing machines in §4.2). At each step the machine will have a finite number of choices as to its next-step move. An input string is said to be recognized if there exists at least one sequence of legal moves which starts from the machine's initial state when the machine scans the first input symbol, and leads to a state after the machine has completed scanning the input string where a terminating condition is satisfied. We shall name such a sequence of moves a *recognition sequence*.

We can imagine that a non-deterministic Turing machine finds a solution to a

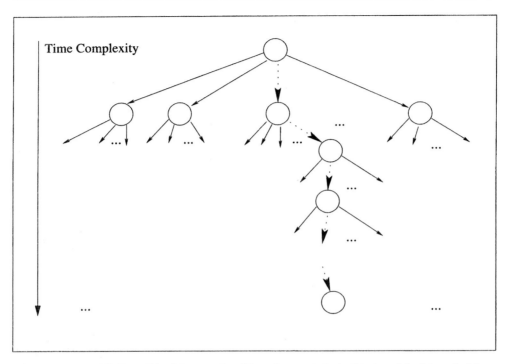

**Figure 4.4.** All Possible Moves of a Non-deterministic Turing Machine (with a recognition sequence)

recognizable input instance by a series of guesses; a sequence of moves that consist of correct guesses forms a recognition sequence. Thus, all possible moves that the machine can make form a tree (called **computational tree** of a non-deterministic Turing machine, see picture in Fig 4.4). The size (the number of nodes) of the tree is obviously an exponential function in the size of the input. However, since the number of moves in a recognition sequence for a recognizable input instance is the depth $d$ of the tree, we have $d = O(\log(\text{number of nodes in the tree}))$ and therefore the number of moves in a recognition sequence must be bounded by a polynomial in the size of the input instance. Thus, the time complexity for recognizing a recognizable input, via a series of correct guesses, is a polynomial in the size of the input.

**Definition 4.8: Class** $\mathcal{NP}$ *We write* $\mathcal{NP}$ *to denote the class of languages recognizable by non-deterministic Turing machines in polynomial time.*

It is straightforward to see

$$\mathcal{P} \subseteq \mathcal{NP}$$

namely, every language (decisional problem) in $\mathcal{P}$ is trivially recognizable by a non-deterministic Turing machine. It is also trivial to see

$$\mathcal{ZPP}, \mathcal{PP}(\text{Monte Carlo}), \mathcal{PP}(\text{Las Vegas}) \subseteq \mathcal{NP}.$$

In fact, $\mathcal{ZPP}$, $\mathcal{PP}(\text{Monte Carlo})$ and $\mathcal{PP}(\text{Las Vegas})$ are all genuine NP problems since they are indeed *non-deterministic polynomial-time* problems[e]. The only reason for these subclasses of NP problems to be efficiently solvable is because these NP problems have abundant witnesses which can be easily found via random guessing. It is only a customary convention that we usually confine $\mathcal{NP}$ to be the class of non-deterministic polynomial-time (decisional) problems which have **sparse witnesses**. Here is the meaning of "sparse witnesses:" in a computational tree of an NP problem, the fraction

$$\frac{\text{number of recognition sequences}}{\text{number of all sequences}}$$

is a negligible quantity (Definition 4.13).

In §18.2.3 we shall further establish the following result

$$\mathcal{NP} \subseteq \mathcal{PP}. \tag{4.5.1}$$

If an NP problem has sparse witnesses, then with the involvement of random guessing steps, a non-deterministic Turing machine does not really offer any useful (i.e., efficient) algorithmic method for recognizing it. This is different from the cases of non-deterministic Turing machines being efficient devices for NP problems with abundant witnesses. For NP problems with sparse witnesses, non-deterministic Turing machines merely model a class of decisional problems which share the following property:

> Given a witness, an answer to a decisional problem can be verified in polynomial time.

A witness for an NP problem is modelled by a recognition sequence in the computational tree for a non-deterministic Turing machine (see the dashed branches in the computational tree in Fig 4.4).

Now we ask: without using a witness, what is the exact time complexity for any given problem in $\mathcal{NP}$? The answer is *not known*. All known algorithms for solving *any* problem in $\mathcal{NP}$ *without using a witness* show polynomially-unbounded time complexities. Yet to date no one has been able to prove if this is necessary, i.e., to prove $\mathcal{P} \neq \mathcal{NP}$. Also, no one has so far been able to demonstrate the opposite case, i.e., to prove $\mathcal{P} = \mathcal{NP}$. The question

$$\mathcal{P} = \mathcal{NP} \ ?$$

---

[e]Recall the reason given in the beginning of §4.4 for renaming a subclass of non-deterministic polynomial-time Turing machines into "probabilistic Turing machines."

is a well-known open question in theoretic computer science.

**Definition 4.9: Lower and Upper Complexity Bounds** *A quantity B is said to be the lower (complexity) bound for a problem P if any algorithm A solving P has a complexity cost $C(A) \geq B$.*

*A quantity U is said to be an upper bound for a problem P if there exists an algorithm A solving P and A has a complexity cost $C(A) \leq U$.*

It is usually possible (and easy) to identify the lower bound for any problem in $\mathcal{P}$, namely, to pinpoint precisely the polynomial bound that declares the *necessary* number of steps needed for solving the problem. Machine Div3 (Example 4.1) provides such an example: it recognizes an $n$-bit string in precisely $n$ steps, i.e., using the least possible number of steps permitted by the way of writing the input instance.

However, for problems in $\mathcal{NP}$, it is always difficult to identify the lower complexity bound or even finding a new (i.e., lowered) upper bound. Known complexity bounds for NP problems are all upper bounds. For example, we have "demonstrated" that $\lfloor \sqrt{N} \rfloor$ is an upper bound for answering Problem SQUARE-FREENESS with input $N$ (via trial division). An upper bound essentially says: "only this number of steps are needed for solving this problem" without adding an important untold part: "but fewer steps may be possible." In fact, for Problem SQUARE-FREENESS, the Number Field Sieve method for factoring $N$ has complexity given by (4.6.1) which has much fewer steps than $\lfloor \sqrt{N} \rfloor$ but is still an upper bound.

One should not be confused by "the lower bound" and "a lower bound." The latter often appears in the literature (e.g., used by Cook in his famous article [81] that discovered "Satisfiability Problem" being "NP-complete") to mean a newly identified complexity cost which is lower than all known ones (hence a lower bound). Even the identification of *a* (not the) lower bound usually requires a proof for the lowest cost. Identification of *the* lower bound for an NP problem qualifies a major breakthrough in the theory of computational complexity.

The difficulty for identifying the lower non-polynomial bound for NP problems has a serious consequence in modern cryptography which has a complexity-theoretic basis for its security. We shall discuss this in §4.8.

## 4.5.1   Non-deterministic Polynomial-time Complete

Even though we do not know whether or not $\mathcal{P} = \mathcal{NP}$, we do know that certain problems in $\mathcal{NP}$ are as difficult as any in $\mathcal{NP}$, in the sense that if we had an efficient algorithm to solve one of these problems, then we could find an efficient algorithm to solve any problem in $\mathcal{NP}$. These problems are called **non-deterministic polynomial-time complete** (**NP-complete** or NPC for short).

**Definition 4.10: Polynomial Reducible**  *We say that a language $L$ is polyno-mially reducible to another language $L_0$ if there exists a deterministic polynomial-time-bounded Turing machine $M$ which will convert each instance $I \in L$ into an instance $I_0 \in L_0$, such that $I \in L$ if and only if $I_0 \in L$.*

**Definition 4.11: NP-Complete**  *A language $L_0 \in \mathcal{NP}$ is non-deterministic poly-nomial time complete (NP-complete) if any $L \in \mathcal{NP}$ can be polynomially reducible to $L_0$.*

A well-known NP-complete problem is so-called SATISFIABILITY problem (identified by Cook [81]), which is the first problem found as NP-complete (page 344 of [229]). Let $E(x_1, x_2, ..., x_n)$ denote a Boolean expression constructed from $n$ Boolean variables $x_1, x_2, ..., x_n$ using Boolean operators, such as $\wedge$, $\vee$ and $\neg$.

**Problem**  SATISFIABILITY

INPUT $\qquad X = (x_1, \neg x_1, x_2, \neg x_2, ..., x_n, \neg x_n);$
$\qquad\qquad E(x_1, x_2, ..., x_n).$

A truth assignment for $E(x_1, x_2, ..., x_n)$ is a sublist $X'$ of $X$ such that for $1 \leq i \leq n$, $X'$ contains either $x_i$ or $\neg x_i$ but not both, and that $E(X') = \mathsf{True}$.

QUESTION   Is $E(x_1, x_2, ..., x_n)$ is satisfiable?
$\qquad\qquad$ That is, does a truth assignment for it exist?
$\qquad\qquad$ Answer YES if $E(x_1, x_2, ..., x_n)$ is satisfiable.

If a satisfiable truth assignment is given, then obviously the YES answer can be verified in time bounded by a polynomial in $n$. Therefore by Definition 4.8 we know SATISFIABILITY $\in \mathcal{NP}$. Notice that there are $2^n$ possible truth assignments, and so far we know of no deterministic polynomial-time algorithm to determine whether there exists a satisfiable one.

A proof for SATISFIABILITY being NP-complete (due to Cook [81]) can be seen in Chapter 10 of [9] (the proof is constructive, which transforms an arbitrary non-deterministic polynomial-time Turing machine to one that solves SATISFIA-BILITY).

A large list of NP-complete problems has been provided in [120].

For an NP-complete problem, any newly identified lowered upper bound can be polynomially "reduced" (transformed) to a new result for a whole class of NP prob-lems. Therefore it is desirable, as suggested by [99], that cryptographic algorithms are designed to have security based on an NP-complete problem. A successful at-tack to such a cryptosystem should hopefully lead to solution to the whole class of difficult problems, which should be unlikely. However, such a reasonable desire has so far not led to fruitful results, either in terms of realizing a secure and practical cryptosystem, or in terms of solving the whole class NP problems using an attack to such a cryptosystem. We shall discuss this seemingly strange phenomenon in §4.8.2.

## 4.6  Non-Polynomial Bounds

There are plenty of functions larger than any polynomial.

**Definition 4.12: Non-Polynomially-Bounded Quantity**  *A function $f(n)$ : $\mathbb{N} \mapsto \mathbb{R}$ is said to be* unbounded by any polynomial in $n$ *if for any polynomial $p(n)$ there exists a natural number $n_0$ such that for all $n > n_0$, $f(n) > p(n)$.*

A function $f(n)$ is said to be **polynomially bounded** if it is not a non-polynomially-bounded quantity.

**Example 4.3:** Show that for any $a > 1$, $0 < \epsilon < 1$, functions

$$f_1(n) = a^{n^\epsilon (\log n)^{1-\epsilon}}, \quad f_2(n) = n^{(\log \log \log n)^\epsilon}$$

are not bounded by any polynomial in $n$.

Let $p(n)$ be any polynomial. Denoting by $d$ its degree and by $c$ its largest coefficient then $p(n) \le cn^d$. First, let $n_0 = \max(c, \lfloor (\frac{d+1}{\log a})^{\frac{2}{\epsilon}} \rfloor)$, then $f_1(n) > p(n)$ for all $n > n_0$. Secondly, let $n_0 = \max(c, \lfloor \exp(\exp(\exp((d+1)^{\frac{1}{\epsilon}}))) \rfloor)$, then $f_2(n) > p(n)$ for all $n > n_0$.  $\square$

In contrast to polynomial-time problems (deterministic or randomized), a problem with time complexity which is non-polynomially bounded is considered to be computationally intractable or infeasible. This is because the resource requirement for solving such a problem grows too fast when the size of the problem instances grows, so fast that it quickly becomes impractically large. For instance, let $N$ be a composite integer of size $n$ (i.e., $n = \log N$); then function $f_1(\log N)$ in Example 4.3 with $a \approx \exp(1.9229994 \cdots + o(1))$ (where $o(1) \approx \frac{1}{\log N}$) and $\epsilon = \frac{1}{3}$ provides a time-complexity expression for factoring $N$ by the Number Field Sieve method (see, e.g., [71]):

$$\exp((1.9229994 \cdots + o(1)) (\log N)^{\frac{1}{3}} (\log \log N)^{\frac{2}{3}}). \tag{4.6.1}$$

Expression (4.6.1) is a **sub-exponential expression** in $N$. If $\frac{1}{3}$ is replaced with 1, then the expression becomes an exponential one. A subexponential function grows much slower than an exponential one, but much faster than a polynomial. For $N$ being a 1024-bit number, expression (4.6.1) provides a quantity larger than $2^{86}$. This quantity is currently not manageable even with the use of a vast number of computers running in parallel. The sub-exponential time complexity formula also applies to the best algorithm for solving a "discrete logarithm problem" in a finite field of magnitude $N$ (see Definition 8.2 in §8.4).

We should, however, notice the **asymptotic** fashion in the comparison of functions used in Definition 4.12 ($f(n)$ in Definition 4.12 is also said to be asymptotically larger than any polynomial, or larger than any polynomial in $n$ for sufficiently large $n$). Even if $f(n)$ is unbounded by any polynomial in $n$, often it is the case that for a quite large number $n_0$, $f(n)$ is less than some polynomial $p(n)$ for $n \leq n_0$. For instance, function $f_2(n)$ in Example 4.3 with $\epsilon = 0.5$ remains being a smaller quantity than the quadratic function $n^2$ for all $n \leq 2^{742762245454927736743541}$, even though $f_2(n)$ is asymptotically larger than $n^d$ for any $d \geq 1$. That is why in practice, some algorithms with non-polynomially-bounded time complexities can still be effective for solving problems of small input size. Pollard's $\lambda$-method for extracting small discrete logarithm, which we have introduced in §3.6.1, is just such an algorithm.

While using the order notation (see Definition 4.2 in §4.3.2.4) we deliberately neglect any constant coefficient in complexity expressions. However, we should notice the significance of a constant coefficient which appears in the exponent position of a non-polynomial-bounded quantity (e.g., $1.9229994\cdots + o(1)$ in the expression (4.6.1)). For example, if a new factoring algorithm advances from the current NFS method by reducing the constant exponent $1.9229994$ in the expression in (4.6.1) to 1, then the time complexity for factoring a 1024-bit composite integer using that algorithm will be reduced from about $2^{86}$ to about $2^{45}$. The latter is no longer regarded a too huge quantity for today's computing technology. In specific for the NFS method, one current research effort for speeding up the method is to reduce the exponent constant, e.g., via time-memory trade-off (and it is actually possible to achieve such a reduction to some extent, though a reduction in time cost may be penalized by an increment in memory cost).

We have defined the notion of non-polynomial bound for large quantities. We can also define a notion for small quantities.

**Definition 4.13: Negligible Quantity** *A function $\epsilon(n) : \mathbb{N} \mapsto \mathbb{R}$ is said to be a negligible quantity (or $\epsilon(n)$ is negligible) in $n$ if its reciprocal, i.e., $\frac{1}{\epsilon(n)}$, is a non-polynomially-bounded quantity in $n$.*

For example, for any polynomial $p$, $\frac{p(n)}{2^n}$ is a negligible quantity. For this reason, we sometimes also say that a subset of $p(n)$ points in the set $\{1, 2, 3, \ldots, 2^n\}$ has a negligible-fraction number of points (with respect to the latter set), or that any $p(n)$ points in $\{1, 2, 3, \ldots, 2^n\}$ are sparse in the set.

If $\epsilon$ is a negligible quantity, then $1 - \epsilon$ is said to be an **overwhelming quantity**. Thus, for example we also say that any **non-sparse** (i.e., **dense**) subset of $\{1, 2, \ldots, 2^n\}$ has an overwhelming-fraction number of points (with respect to the latter set).

A negligible function diminishes to 0 faster than the reciprocal of any polynomial does. If we regard a non-polynomially-bounded quantity as an unmanageable one (for example, in resource allocation), then it should be harmless for us to neglect any quantity at the level of the reciprocal of a non-polynomially-bounded quantity.

More examples:

$$\text{Prob}\left[\text{``Prime\_Gen}(1^k) \text{ is not prime''}\right]$$

is negligible in $k$ and

$$1 - \text{Prob}\left[\text{``Prime\_Gen}(1^k) \text{ is not prime''}\right] = \text{Prob}\left[\text{``Prime\_Gen}(1^k) \text{ is prime''}\right]$$

is overwhelming in $k$.

Review Example 3.6; for $p$ being a $k$ bit prime number ($q = \frac{p-1}{2}$ being also a prime), we can neglect quantities at the level of $\frac{1}{p-1}$ or smaller and thereby obtain $\text{Prob}[A] \approx \frac{3}{4}$.

Finally, if a quantity is not negligible, then we often say it is a non-negligible quantity, or a **significant quantity**. For example, we have seen through a series of examples that for a decisional problem in $\mathcal{PP}$ whose membership is efficiently decidable, there is a significant probability, via random sampling the space of the computational tree (Fig 4.4), for finding a witness for confirming the membership.

## 4.7   Polynomial-time Indistinguishability

We have just considered that neglecting a negligible quantity is harmless. However, sometimes when we neglect a quantity, we feel *hopeless* because we are forced to abandon an attempt *not* to neglect it. Let us now describe such a situation through an example.

Consider two experiments over the space of large odd composite integers of a fixed length. Let one of them be called $E_{2\_\text{Prime}}$, and the other, $E_{3\_\text{Prime}}$. These two experiments yield large and random integers of the same size: every integer yielded from $E_{2\_\text{Prime}}$ is the product of two large distinct prime factors; every integer yielded from $E_{3\_\text{Prime}}$ is the produce of three or more distinct prime factors. Now let someone supply you an integer $N$ by following one of these two experiments. Can you tell with confidence from which of these two experiments $N$ is yielded? (Recall that $E_{2\_\text{Prime}}$ and $E_{3\_\text{Prime}}$ yield integers of the same length.)

By Definition 3.5 (in §3.5), such an experiment result is a random variable of the internal random moves of these experiments. We know that random variables yielded from $E_{2\_\text{Prime}}$ and those yielded from $E_{3\_\text{Prime}}$ have drastically different probability distributions: $E_{2\_\text{Prime}}$ yields a two-prime product with probability 1 while $E_{3\_\text{Prime}}$ never does so. However, it is in fact a very hard problem to distinguish random variables from these two experiments.

Let us now define precisely what we mean by **indistinguishable ensembles** (also called **indistinguishable experiments**).

**Definition 4.14: Distinguisher for ensembles** *Let $E = \{e_1, e_2, \ldots\}$, $E' = \{e_1', e_2', \ldots\}$ be two sets of ensembles in which $e_i$, $e_j'$ are random variables in a finite sample space $\mathbb{S}$. Denote $k = \log_2 \#\mathbb{S}$. Let $a = (a_1, a_2, \ldots, a_\ell)$ be random variables such that all of them are yielded from either $E$ or $E'$, where $\ell$ is bounded by a polynomial in $k$.*

*A distinguisher $\mathcal{D}$ for $(E, E')$ is a probabilistic algorithm which halts in time polynomial in $k$ with output in $\{0, 1\}$ and satisfies (i) $\mathcal{D}(a, E) = 1$ iff $a$ is from $E$; (ii) $\mathcal{D}(a, E') = 1$ iff $a$ is from $E'$.*

*We say that $\mathcal{D}$ distinguishes $(E, E')$ with advantage* Adv $> 0$ *if*

$$\mathrm{Adv}(\mathcal{D}) = |\,\mathrm{Prob}\,[\mathcal{D}(a, E) = 1] - \mathrm{Prob}\,[\mathcal{D}(a, E') = 1]\,|.$$

It is important to notice the use of probability distributions in the formulation of an advantage for a distinguisher $\mathcal{D}$: a distinguisher is probabilistic algorithm; also it is a polynomial-time algorithm: its input has a polynomially bounded size.

Many random variables can be easily distinguished. Here is an example.

**Example 4.4:** Let $E = \{k\text{-bit Primes}\}$ and $E' = \{k\text{-bit Composites}\}$. Define $\mathcal{D}(a, E) = 1$ iff Prime_Test$(a) \to$ YES, and $\mathcal{D}(a, E') = 1$ iff Prime_Test$(a) \to$ NO (Prime_Test is specified in Alg 4.5). Then $\mathcal{D}$ is a distinguisher for $E$ and $E'$. When $a \in E$, we have Prob$[\mathcal{D}(a, E) = 1] = 1$ and Prob$[\mathcal{D}(a, E') = 1] = 0$; when $a \in E'$, we have Prob$[\mathcal{D}(a, E) = 1] = 2^{-k}$ and Prob$[\mathcal{D}(a, E') = 1] = 1 - 2^{-k}$. Hence, Adv$(\mathcal{D}) \geq 1 - 2^{-(k-1)}$. $\qquad\square$

**Definition 4.15: Polynomial-time Indistinguishability** *Let ensembles $E$, $E'$ and security parameter $k$ be those defined in Definition 4.14. $E$, $E'$ are said to be polynomially indistinguishable if there exists no distinguisher for $(E, E')$ with advantage* Adv $> 0$ *non-negligible in $k$ for all sufficiently large $k$.*

The following assumption is widely accepted as plausible in computational complexity theory.

**Assumption 4.1: General Indistinguishability Assumption** *There exist polynomially indistinguishable ensembles.*

Ensembles $E_{2\_\mathrm{Prime}}$ and $E_{3\_\mathrm{Prime}}$ are assumed to be polynomially indistinguishable. In other words, if someone supplies us with a set of polynomially many integers which are either all from $E_{2\_\mathrm{Prime}}$, or all from $E_{3\_\mathrm{Prime}}$, and if we use the best known algorithm as our distinguisher, we will soon feel hopeless and have to abandon our distinguishing attempt.

Notice that since we can factor $N$ and then be able to answer the question correctly, our advantage Adv must be no less than the reciprocal of the function in (4.6.1). However, that value is too small not to be neglected. We say that we are hopeless in distinguishing these two ensembles because the best distinguisher we can have will have a negligible advantage in the size of the integer yielded from the ensembles. Such an advantage is a slow-growing function of our computational resources. Here "slow-growing" means that even if we add our computational resources in a tremendous manner, the advantage will only grow in a marginal manner so that we will soon become hopeless.

Polynomial indistinguishability is an important security criterion for many cryptographic algorithms and protocols. There are many practical ways to construct polynomially indistinguishable ensembles for being useful in modern cryptography. For example, a **pseudo-random number generator** is an important ingredient in cryptography; such a generator generates pseudo-random numbers which have a distribution totally determined (i.e., in a deterministic fashion) by a seed. Yet, a good pseudo-random number generator yields pseudo-random numbers which are polynomially indistinguishable from truly random numbers, that is, the distribution of the random variables output from such a generator is indistinguishable from the uniform distribution of strings which are of the same length as those of the pseudo-random variables. In fact, the following assumption is an instantiation of Assumption 4.1:

**Assumption 4.2: (Indistinguishability between Pseudo-randomness and True Randomness)** *There exist pseudo-random functions which are polynomially indistinguishable from truly random functions.*

In Chapter 8 we shall see a pseudo-random function (a pseudo-random number generator) which is polynomially indistinguishable from a uniformly random distribution. In Chapter 14 we shall further study a well-known **public-key cryptosystem** named the **Goldwasser-Micali cryptosystem**; that cryptosystem has its security based on polynomially indistinguishable ensembles which are related to $E_{2\_\text{Prime}}$ and $E_{3\_\text{Prime}}$ (we shall discuss the relationship in §6.5.1). For a further example, a **Diffie-Hellman tuple** (Definition 13.1 in §13.3.4.3) of four elements in some **abelian group** and a random quadruple in the same group form indistinguishable ensembles which provide security basis for the **ElGamal cryptosystem** and many **zero-knowledge proof protocols**. We will frequently use the notion of polynomial indistinguishability in several later chapters.

# 4.8  Theory of Computational Complexity and Modern Cryptography

In the end of our short course in computational complexity, we shall provide a discussion on the relationship between the computational complexity and modern cryptography.

## 4.8.1 A Necessary Condition

On the one hand, we are able to say that the complexity-theoretic-based modern cryptography uses $\mathcal{P} \neq \mathcal{NP}$ as a necessary condition. Let us call it the $\mathcal{P} \neq \mathcal{NP}$ conjecture[f].

An encryption algorithm should, on the one hand, provide a user who is in possession of correct encryption/decryption keys with efficient algorithms for encryption and/or decryption, and on the other hand, pose an intractable problem for one (an attacker or a cryptanalyst) who tries to extract plaintext from ciphertext, or to construct a valid ciphertext without using correct keys. Thus, a cryptographic key plays the role of a witness, or an auxiliary input (a more suitable name) to an NP-problem-based cryptosystem.

One might want to argue against our assertion on the necessary condition for complexity-theoretic-based cryptography by thinking that there might exist a cryptosystem which would be based on an asymmetric problem in $\mathcal{P}$: encryption would be an $O(n)$-algorithm and the best cracking algorithm would be of order $O(n^{100})$. Indeed, even for the tiny case of $n = 10$, $O(n^{100})$ is a $2^{332}$-level quantity which is *way, way, way beyond* the grasp of the world-wide combination of the most advanced computation technologies. Therefore, if such a polynomial-time cryptosystem exists, we should be in a good shape even if it turns out $\mathcal{P} = \mathcal{NP}$. However, the trouble is, while $\mathcal{P}$ does enclose $O(n^k)$ problems for *any* integer $k$, it does not contain any problem with an *asymmetric* complexity behavior. For any given problem in $\mathcal{P}$, if an instance of size $n$ is solvable in time $n^k$, then time $n^{k+\alpha}$ for any $\alpha > 0$ is unnecessary due to the *deterministic* behavior of the algorithm.

The conjecture also forms a necessary condition for the existence of **one-way function**. In the beginning of this book (§1.1.1) we have assumed that a one-way function $f(x)$ should have a "magic property" (Property 1.1): for all integer $x$, it is easy to compute $f(x)$ from $x$ while given most values $f(x)$ it is extremely difficult to find $x$, except for a negligible fraction of the instances in the problem. Now we know that the class $\mathcal{NP}$ provides us with candidates for realizing a one-way function with such a "magic property." For example, problem Satisfiability defines a one-way function from an $n$-tuple Boolean space to {True, False}.

In turn, the existence of one-way functions forms a necessary condition for the existence of **digital signatures**. A digital signature should have such properties: easy to verify and difficult forge.

Moreover, the notion of polynomial-time indistinguishability which we have studied in §4.7 is also based on the $\mathcal{P} \neq \mathcal{NP}$ conjecture. This is the decisional case of hard problems in $\mathcal{NP}$. In Chapters 14, 15 and 17 we shall see the impor-

---

[f]A recent survey shows that most theoretic computer scientists believe $\mathcal{P} \neq \mathcal{NP}$.

tant role of polynomial-time indistinguishability plays in modern cryptography: the correctness of cryptographic algorithms and protocols.

In particular, we should mention the fundamentally important role that the $\mathcal{P} \neq \mathcal{NP}$ conjecture plays in a fascinating subject of public-key cryptography: **zero-knowledge proof protocols** [128] and interactive proof system.

A zero-knowledge protocol is an interactive procedure running between two principals called a **prover** and a **verifier** with the latter having a polynomially-bounded computational power. The protocol allows the former to prove to the latter that the former knows a YES answer to an NP-problem (e.g., a YES answer to Problem SQUARE-FREENESS, or to question: "Is $N$ from $E_{2\_\text{Prime}}$?"), because the former has in possession of an auxiliary input, without letting the latter learn how to conduct such a proof (i.e., without disclosing the auxiliary input to the latter). Hence the verifier gets "zero-knowledge" about the prover's auxiliary input. Such a proof can be modelled by a non-deterministic Turing machine with an added random tape. The prover can make use of auxiliary input and so the machine can always be instructed (by the prover) to move along a recognition sequence (i.e., to demonstrate the YES answer) regarding the input problem. Consequently, the time complexity for a proof is a polynomial in the size of the input instance. The verifier should challenge the prover to instruct the machine to move either along a recognition sequence, or along a different sequence, and the challenge should be uniformly random. Thus, from the verifier's observation, the proof system behaves precisely in the fashion of a randomized Turing machine (review §4.4). As a matter of fact, it is the property that the error probability of such a randomized Turing machine can be reduced to a negligible quantity by repeated independent executions (as analyzed in §4.4.1.1) that forms the basis for convincing the verifier that the prover does know the YES answer to the input problem.

The $\mathcal{P} \neq \mathcal{NP}$ conjecture plays the following two roles in zero-knowledge protocols: (i) an auxiliary input of an NP problem permits the prover to conduct an efficient proof, and (ii) the difficulty of the problem means that the verifier alone cannot verify the prover's claim. In Chapter 18 we will study zero-knowledge proof protocols.

## 4.8.2 Not a Sufficient Condition

On the other hand, the $\mathcal{P} \neq \mathcal{NP}$ conjecture does not provide a sufficient condition for a secure cryptosystem even if such a cryptosystem is based on an NP-complete problem. The well-known broken NP-complete knapsack problem provides a counterexample [202].

After our course in computational complexity, we are now able to provide two brief but clear explanations on why cryptosystems based on NP (or even NP-complete) problems are often broken.

First, as we have pointed out in an early stage of our course (e.g., review Definition 4.1), the complexity-theoretic approach to computational complexity restricts a language $L$ (a problem) in a complexity class with a universal-style quantifier: "any instance $I \in L$." This restriction results in the **worst-case complexity analysis**: a problem is regarded difficult even if there only exists negligibly few difficult instances. In contrast, a cryptanalysis can be considered successful as long as it can break a non-trivial fraction of the instances. That is exactly why breaking of an NP-complete-based cryptosystem does not lead to a solution to the underlying NP-complete problem. It is clear that the worst-case complexity criterion is hopeless and useless for measuring security for the practical cryptosystems.

The second explanation lies in the *inherent* difficulty of identifying new lower upper bounds for NP problems (notice, phrase "new lower upper bounds" makes sense for NP problems, review our discussion on lower and upper bounds in §4.5). Security basis for an NP-problem-based cryptosystem, even if the basis has been proven to be the intractability of an underlying NP-problem, is at best an open problem since we only know an upper bound complexity for the problem. More often, the underlying intractability for such an NP-based cryptosystem is not even clearly identified.

A further dimension of insufficiency for basing security of modern cryptographic systems on the complexity intractability is the main topic of this book: non-textbook aspects of security for applied cryptography (review §1.1.3). Cryptographic systems for real world applications can be compromised in many practical ways which may have little to do with mathematical intractability properties underlying the security of an algorithm. We will provide abundant explanations and evidence to manifest this dimension in the rest of this book.

A positive attitude toward the design and analysis of secure cryptosystems, which is getting wide acceptance recently, is to formally prove that a cryptosystem is secure (**provable security**) using polynomial reduction techniques (see Definition 4.10): to "reduce" via an efficient transformation *any* efficient attack on the cryptosystem to a solution to an instance of a known NP problem. Usually the NP problem is in a small set of widely accepted "pedigree class." Such a reduction is usually called a **reduction to contradiction** because it is widely believed that the widely accepted "pedigree problem" does not have an efficient solution. Such a proof provides a high confidence of the security of the cryptosystem in question. We shall study this methodology in Chapters 14 and 15.

## 4.9 Chapter Summary

Computational complexity is one of the foundations (indeed, the most important foundation) for modern cryptography. Due to this importance, this chapter provides a self-contained and systematic introduction to this foundation.

We started with the notion of Turing computability as the class of computable problems. Some problems in the class are tractable (efficiently solvable in polynomial time) which are either deterministic (in $\mathcal{P}$) or non-deterministic (several subclasses in $\mathcal{PP}$ which are called probabilistic polynomial time). Others are intractable (the class $\mathcal{NP}$ which is still a subclass in $\mathcal{PP}$, this will become clear in §18.2.3). Problems in $\mathcal{NP}$ do not appear to be solvable by efficient algorithms, deterministic or otherwise, while with their membership in the class being efficiently verifiable given a witness.

In our course, we also introduced various important notions in computational complexity and in its application in modern cryptography. These include efficient algorithms (several important algorithms are constructed with precise time complexity analysis), order notation, polynomial reducibility, negligible quantity, lower, upper and non-polynomial bounds, and indistinguishability. These notions will be frequently used in the rest part of the book.

Finally, we conduct a discussion on the fundamental roles of $\mathcal{NP}$ problems and the complexity-theoretic basis playing in modern cryptography.

# Exercises

4.1 Construct a Turing machine to recognize even integers. Then construct a machine to recognize integers which are divisible by 6.

Hint: the second machine can use an operation table which conjuncts that of the first and that of Div3 in Fig 4.2.

4.2 In the measurement of computational complexity of an algorithm, why is the bit-complexity, i.e., based on counting the number of bit operations, more preferable than a measure based on counting, e.g., the number of integer multiplications?

Hint: consider a problem can have instances of variant sizes.

4.3 Our cost measure for $\gcd(x, y)$ (for $x > y$) given by Theorem 4.1 is $\log x$ modulo operations. With a modulo operation having the cost same as a division $O_B((\log x)^2)$, our measure for $\gcd(x, y)$ turns out to be $O_B((\log x)^3)$. However, in standard textbooks the cost for $\gcd(x, y)$ is $O_B((\log x)^2)$. What we have missed in our measurement?

Hint: observe inequality (4.3.12).

4.4 Prove statements 2 and 3 in Theorem 4.2.

4.5 Show that $\mathcal{PP}$(Monte Carlo) and $\mathcal{PP}$(Las Vegas) are complement to each other (this is denoted by $\mathcal{PP}$(Monte Carlo) = $\mathbf{co}\mathcal{PP}$(Las Vegas)). That is, a Monte Carlo algorithm for recognizing $I \in L$ is a Las Vegas algorithm for recognizing $I \in \bar{L}$, and vise versa. Using the same method to show $\mathcal{BPP} = \mathbf{co}\mathcal{BPP}$.

4.6 In the computational complexity literature, we often see that the class $\mathcal{BPP}$ is defined by $\epsilon = \frac{2}{3}$ (4.4.1) and $\beta = \frac{1}{3}$ for (4.4.2). We have used any constants $\epsilon \in [\frac{1}{2} + \alpha, 1)$, $\delta \in (0, \frac{1}{2} - \beta]$ for $\alpha > 0$, $\beta > 0$. Do these two different ways of formulation make any difference?

4.7 Show that for $\epsilon(k)$ in (4.4.5), $\epsilon(k) \to 1$ when $k \to \infty$.
Hint: consider $1 - \epsilon(k) \to 0$.

4.8 Explain why in the error probability characterization for $\mathcal{BPP}$, error probabilities must be *clearly* bounded away from $\frac{1}{2}$, i.e., $\alpha$ and $\beta$ in (4.4.11) must be some non-zero constant.

Hint: consider a "biased" coin: one side is more likely than the other by a negligible quantity. Are you able to find the more likely side by flipping the coin and using the majority election criterion?

4.9 In our measure of the soundness error probability for the QKD protocol (Prot 4.1), we have mentioned two strategies for Eve: sending to Bob completely new $m$ photon states or forwarding to him whatever she observes. We have only measured the soundness error probability by considering Eve taking the latter strategy. Use the the former strategy to derive the same result for the soundness error probability for the QKD protocol.

4.10 For a positive natural number $n$ we use $|n| = \log_2 n$ as the measure of the size of $n$ (which is the number of bits in $n$'s binary representation). However in most cases the size of $n$ can be written as $\log n$ without giving an explicit base (the omitting case is the natural base $e$). Show that for any base $b > 1$, $\log_b n$ provides a correct size measure for $n$, i.e., the statement "a polynomial in the size of $n$" remains invariant for any base $b > 1$.

4.11 Exceptional to the cases in the preceding problem, we sometimes write a positive number in the unary representation, i.e., write $1^n$ for $n$. Why is this necessary?

4.12 What is an efficient algorithm? What is a practically efficient algorithm?

4.13 If you are already familiar with the properties of the Euler's phi function $\phi(N)$ (to be introduced in §6.3), then confirm the correctness of Alg 4.8.

4.14 Provide two examples of indistinguishable ensembles.

4.15 Why does a cryptosystem with security based on an NP-Complete problem need not be secure?

4.16 Differentiate and relate the following problems:

   i) Turing computable.

   ii) Intractable.

iii) Tractable.

iv) Deterministic polynomial time.

 v) Practically efficient.

# Chapter 5

# ALGEBRAIC FOUNDATIONS

## 5.1 Introduction

Cryptographic algorithms and protocols process messages as numbers or elements in a finite space. Encoding (encryption) and the necessary decoding (decryption) operations must transform messages to messages so that the transformation obeys a *closure* property inside a finite space of the messages. However, the usual arithmetic over numbers such as addition, subtraction, multiplication and division which are familiar to us do not have a closure property within a finite space (integers or numbers in an interval). Therefore, cryptographic algorithms which operate in a finite space of messages are in general not constructed only using the familiar arithmetic over numbers. Instead, they in general operate in spaces with certain algebraic structures to maintain the closure property.

In this chapter we introduce three algebraic structures which not only are central concepts of abstract algebra, but also provide the basic elements and operations for modern cryptography and cryptographic protocols. These three structures are: group, ring and field.

### 5.1.1 Chapter Outline

We study groups in §5.2, rings and fields in §5.3 and the structure of finite fields in §5.4. Finally in §5.5, we provide a realization of a finite group using points on an elliptic curve.

## 5.2 Groups

Roughly speaking, a group is a set of objects with an operation defined between any two objects in the set. The need for an operation over a set of objects is very natural. For example, upon every sunset, an ancient shepherd would have counted his herd of sheep. Maybe the shepherd did not even know numbers; but this would not prevent him from performing his operation properly. He could keep with him a sack of pebbles and match each sheep against each pebble. Then, as long as he always ended up his matching operation when no more pebble were left to match, he knew that his herd of sheep were fine. In this way, the shepherd had actually generated a group using the "add 1" operation. Sheep or pebbles or some other objects, the important point here is to perform an operation over a set of objects and obtain a result which remains in the set.

**Definition 5.1: Group** *A group $(G, \circ)$ is a set $G$ together with an operation $\circ$ satisfying the following conditions:*

1. *$\forall a, b \in G : a \circ b \in G$*                                                  (Closure Axiom)

2. *$\forall a, b, c \in G : a \circ (b \circ c) = (a \circ b) \circ c$*            (Associativity Axiom)

3. *$\exists$ unique element $e \in G : \forall a \in G : a \circ e = e \circ a = a$*    (Identity Axiom)

   *The element $e$ is called the* **identity** *element.*

4. *$\forall a \in G : \exists a^{-1} \in G: a \circ a^{-1} = a^{-1} \circ a = e$*            (Inverse Axiom)

In the denotation of a group $(G, \circ)$, we often omit the operation $\circ$ and use $G$ to denote a group.

**Definition 5.2: Finite and Infinite Groups** *A group $G$ is said to be finite if the number of elements in the set $G$ is finite, otherwise, the group is infinite.*

**Definition 5.3: Abelian Group** *A group $G$ is abelian if for all $a, b \in G$, $a \circ b = b \circ a$.*

In other words, an abelian group is a **commutative group**. In this book we shall have no occasion to deal with non-abelian group. So all groups to appear in the rest of this book are abelian, and we shall often omit the prefix "abelian."

## Example 5.1: Groups

1. The set of integers $\mathbb{Z}$ is a group under addition $+$, i.e., $(\mathbb{Z}, +)$ is a group, with $e = 0$ and $a^{-1} = -a$. This is an **additive** group and is an infinite group (and is abelian). Likewise, the set of rational numbers $\mathbb{Q}$, the set of real numbers $\mathbb{R}$, and the set of complex numbers $\mathbb{C}$ are additive and infinite groups with the same definitions for identity and inverse.

2. Non-zero elements of $\mathbb{Q}$, $\mathbb{R}$ and $\mathbb{C}$ under multiplication $\cdot$ are groups with $e = 1$ and $a^{-1}$ being the multiplicative inverse (defined in the usual way). We denote

by $\mathbb{Q}^*$, $\mathbb{R}^*$, $\mathbb{C}^*$ these groups, respectively. Thus, the full denotations for these groups are: $(\mathbb{Q}^*, \cdot)$, $(\mathbb{R}^*, \cdot)$ and $(\mathbb{C}^*, \cdot)$. They are called **multiplicative** groups. They are infinite.

3. For any $n \geq 1$, the set of integers modulo $n$ forms a finite additive group of $n$ elements; here addition is in terms of modulo $n$, the identity element is 0, and for all element $a$ in the group, $a^{-1} = n - a$ (property 2 of Theorem 4.2, in §4.3.2.5). We denote by $\mathbb{Z}_n$ this group. Thus, the full denotation of this group is $(\mathbb{Z}_n, + \pmod{n})$. (Notice that $\mathbb{Z}_n$ is a short-hand notation for a formal and standard notation $\mathbb{Z}/n\mathbb{Z}$. We shall see the reason in Example 5.5.)

4. The numbers for hours over a clock form $\mathbb{Z}_{12}$ under addition modulo 12. Let us name $(\mathbb{Z}_{12}, + \pmod{12})$ *"clock group."*

5. The subset of $\mathbb{Z}_n$ containing elements relatively prime to $n$ (i.e., $\gcd(a, n) = 1$) forms a finite multiplicative group; here multiplication is in terms of modulo $n$, $e = 1$, and for any element $a$ in the group, $a^{-1}$ can be computed using extended Euclid algorithm (Alg 4.2). We denote by $\mathbb{Z}_n^*$ this group. For example, $(\mathbb{Z}_{15}^*, \cdot \pmod{15}) = (\{1, 2, 4, 7, 8, 11, 13, 14\}, \cdot \pmod{15})$.

6. For set $B = \{F, T\}$, let $\circ = \oplus$ be (logical XOR): $F \oplus F = F$, $F \oplus T = T \oplus F = T$, $T \oplus T = F$. Then $B$ under $\oplus$ is a finite group with $e = F$ and $T^{-1} = T$.

7. The roots of $x^3 - 1 = 0$ is a finite group under multiplication with $e = 1$ (obviously 1 is a root). Denote by $\text{Roots}(x^3 - 1)$ this group. Let us find the other group elements in $\text{Roots}(x^3 - 1)$ and their inverses. As a degree-3 polynomial, $x^3 - 1$ has three roots only. Let $\alpha$, $\beta$ be the other two roots. From $x^3 - 1 = (x - 1)(x^2 + x + 1)$, $\alpha$ and $\beta$ must be the two roots of $x^2 + x + 1 = 0$. By the relation between the roots and the coefficient of a quadratic equation, we have $\alpha\beta = 1$. Thus, $\alpha^{-1} = \beta$ and $\beta^{-1} = \alpha$. The reader may check that Closure Axiom is satisfied (i.e., $\alpha^2$ and $\beta^2$ are roots of $x^3 - 1 = 0$).  □

## Definition 5.4: Shorthand Representation of Repeated Group Operations

*Let $G$ be a group with operation $\circ$. For any element $a \in G$, and for any non-negative integer $i \in \mathbb{N}$, we denote by $a^i \in G$ the following element*

$$\underbrace{a \circ a \circ \cdots \circ a}_{i}.$$

We should pay attention to two points in the following remark.

**Remark 5.1:**

*i) We write $a^i \in G$ only for a shorthand presentation of $\underbrace{a \circ a \circ \cdots \circ a}_{i}$. Notice that the "operation" between the integer $i$ and the element $a$ is not a group operation.*

*ii) Some groups are conventionally written additively, e.g., $(\mathbb{Z}_n, + \pmod{n})$. For these groups, the reader may view $a^i$ as $i \cdot a$. However, in this shorthand view, one must notice that "$\cdot$" here is not a group operation and the integer $i$ is usually not a group element (considering the case $(\mathbb{Z}_n, + \pmod{n})$ with $i > n$).*                                                                                □

**Definition 5.5: Subgroup** *A subgroup of a group $G$ is a non-empty subset $H$ of $G$ which is itself a group under the same operation as that of $G$. We write $H \subseteq G$ to denote that $H$ is a subgroup of $G$, and $H \subset G$ to denote that $H$ is a proper subgroup of $G$ (i.e., $H \neq G$).*

**Example 5.2:**

1. Under addition, $\mathbb{Z} \subseteq \mathbb{Q} \subseteq \mathbb{R} \subseteq \mathbb{C}$;

2. Under addition, the set of even integers plus 0 is a subgroup of the groups in (1); so is the set of odd numbers plus 0.

3. The "clock group" $(\mathbb{Z}_{12}, + \pmod{12})$ has the following subgroups: $(\{0\}, +)$, $(\{0, 6\}, +)$, $(\{0, 4, 8\}, +)$, $(\{0, 3, 6, 9\}, +)$, $(\{0, 2, 4, 6, 8, 10\}, +)$, $(\mathbb{Z}_{12}, +)$.

4. Under multiplication, $\mathbb{Q}^* \subseteq \mathbb{R}^* \subseteq \mathbb{C}^*$.

5. Let $n$ be an odd positive integer and let $\mathrm{Fermat}(n)$ denote the subset of $\mathbb{Z}_n^*$ such that any $a \in \mathrm{Fermat}(n)$ satisfies $a^{\frac{n-1}{2}} \equiv \pm 1 \pmod{n}$. Then

$$\mathrm{Fermat}(n) \subseteq \mathbb{Z}_n^*.$$

   Moreover, if $n$ is a prime number, then by Fermat's Little Theorem (Theorem 6.10 in §6.4), $\mathrm{Fermat}(n) = \mathbb{Z}_n^*$; otherwise, $\mathrm{Fermat}(n)$ is a proper subgroup of $\mathbb{Z}_n^*$.

6. $\{F\}$ is a proper subgroup of the group $B$ in Example 5.1(6). However, $\{T\}$ is not a subgroup of $B$ since it does not contain an identity (i.e., breach of Identity Axiom).

7. (Review Example 4.1) Polynomial-time language DIV3 is a subgroup of $\mathbb{Z}$;

8. Set $\{e\}$ is a subgroup of any group.                                   □

**Definition 5.6: Order of a Group** *The number of elements in a finite group $G$ is called the order of $G$ and is denoted by $\#G$.*

**Example 5.3:**

1. $\#Z_n = n$;

2. In Example 5.1(6), $\#B = 2$;

3. In Example 5.1(7), $\#\mathrm{Roots}(x^3 - 1) = 3$.                         □

## 5.2.1   Lagrange's Theorem

Let us now introduce a beautiful and important theorem in group theory.

**Definition 5.7: Coset** *Let $G$ be a (abelian) group and $H \subseteq G$. For $a \in G$, set $a \circ H \overset{\text{def}}{=} \{a \circ h \mid h \in H\}$ is called a (left) coset of $H$.*

**Theorem 5.1: Lagrange's Theorem** *If $H$ is a subgroup of $G$ then $\#H \mid \#G$, that is, $\#H$ divides $\#G$.*

**Proof** For $H = G$, $\#H \mid \#G$ holds trivially. Let us consider $H \neq G$.

For any $a \in G \setminus H$, by Closure Axiom, coset $a \circ H$ is a subset of $G$. We can show the following two facts:

  i) For any $a \neq a'$, if $a \notin a' \circ H$ then $(a \circ H) \cap (a' \circ H) = \emptyset$.

  ii) $\#(a \circ H) = \#H$.

For (i), suppose $\exists b \in (a \circ H) \cap (a' \circ H)$. So $\exists c, c' \in H$: $a \circ c = b = a' \circ c'$. Applying Inverse Axiom, Identity Axiom, Closure Axiom and Associative Axiom on elements in $H$, we have

$$a = a \circ e = a \circ (c \circ c^{-1}) = b \circ c^{-1} = (a' \circ c') \circ c^{-1} = a' \circ (c' \circ c^{-1}) \in a' \circ H.$$

This contradicts our assumption: $a \notin a' \circ H$. As a special case, for $a \notin H = e \circ H$, we have $H \cap (a \circ H) = \emptyset$.

For (ii), $\#(a \circ H) \leq \#H$ holds trivially by coset's definition. Suppose that the inequality is rigorous. This is only possible because for some $b \neq c$, $b, c \in H$, $a \circ b = a \circ c$. Applying Inverse Axiom in $G$, we reach $b = c$, contradicting to $b \neq c$.

Thus, $G$ is partitioned by $H$ and the family of its mutually disjoint cosets, each has the size $\#H$. Hence $\#H \mid \#G$. (In general, partitioning a set means splitting it into disjoint subsets.) $\qquad\square$

**Example 5.4:**

  1. Check Example 5.2(3): $\#H \mid \#\mathbb{Z}_{12}$ holds for every $H$ as a subgroup of the "clock group" $\mathbb{Z}_{12}$.

  2. Instantiate Example 5.2(5) using $n = 21$; we have $\mathrm{Fermat}(21) = \{1, 8, 13, 20\}$ satisfying $\#\mathrm{Fermat}(21) = 4 \mid 12 = \#\mathbb{Z}_{21}^*$. $\qquad\square$

Lagrange's Theorem is not only very beautiful in group theory, but also very important in applications. Review our probabilistic primality test algorithm Prime_Test in §4.4.3.1. That algorithm tests whether an odd integer $n$ is prime by testing congruence

$$x^{(n-1)/2} \equiv \pm 1 \pmod{n}$$

using random $x \in_U \mathbb{Z}_n^*$. In Example 5.2(5) we have seen that $\text{Fermat}(n)$ is the subgroup of $\mathbb{Z}_n^*$ defined by this congruence, and is a proper subgroup of $\mathbb{Z}_n^*$ if and only if $n$ is not prime. Thus, by Lagrange's Theorem, $\#\text{Fermat}(n) \mid \#\mathbb{Z}_n^*$. Hence, if $n$ is not prime, $\#\text{Fermat}(n)$ can be at most half the quantity $\#\mathbb{Z}_n^*$. This provides us with the error probability bound $\frac{1}{2}$ for each step of test, i.e., the working principle of Prime_Test (the probability space being $\mathbb{Z}_n^*$).

In §5.2.2 we will discuss another important application of Lagrange's Theorem in public-key cryptography.

**Definition 5.8: Quotient Group** *Let $G$ be a (abelian) group and $H \subseteq G$. The quotient group of $G$ modulo $H$, denoted by $G/H$, is the set of all cosets $a \circ H$ with $a$ ranging over $G$, with the group operation $\star$ defined by $(a \circ H) \star (b \circ H) = (a \circ b) \circ H$, and with the identity element being $e \circ H$.*

**Example 5.5:** Let $n > 0$ be an integer. Set $n\mathbb{Z} = \{0, \pm n, \pm 2n, \ldots,\}$ is clearly a subgroup of $\mathbb{Z}$ under the integer addition. Quotient group

$$\mathbb{Z}/n\mathbb{Z} = \{x + n\mathbb{Z} \mid x \in \mathbb{Z}\}$$

can only have $n$ elements. This is because $n + n\mathbb{Z} = 0 + n\mathbb{Z}$, $n + 1 + n\mathbb{Z} = 1 + n\mathbb{Z}$, and so on, and consequently

$$\mathbb{Z}/(n\mathbb{Z}) = \{0 + n\mathbb{Z},\ 1 + n\mathbb{Z},\ 2 + n\mathbb{Z},\ \ldots,\ n - 1 + n\mathbb{Z}\}.$$

Consider that $n\mathbb{Z}$ only contains zero modulo $n$, we can equate

$$\mathbb{Z}/n\mathbb{Z} = \mathbb{Z}_n. \qquad \square$$

In fact, $\mathbb{Z}/n\mathbb{Z}$ is the formal and standard notation for $\mathbb{Z}_n$. However, for presentation convenience, in this book we will always use the short-hand notation $\mathbb{Z}_n$ in place of $\mathbb{Z}/n\mathbb{Z}$.

**Corollary 5.1:** *Let $G$ be a finite (abelian) group and $H \subseteq G$. Then*

$$\#(G/H) = \frac{\#G}{\#H}. \qquad \square$$

**Example 5.6:** Let $m, n$ be positive integers satisfying $m \mid n$. Following Example 5.5, we have

1. $m\mathbb{Z}_n = \{0, m, 2m, \ldots, \lfloor \frac{n-1}{m} \rfloor \cdot m\}$ is a subgroup of $(\mathbb{Z}_n, +)$ with $n/m$ elements;

2. $\mathbb{Z}_n/m\mathbb{Z}_n = \mathbb{Z}_m$; and

3. $\#(\mathbb{Z}_n/m\mathbb{Z}_n) = \#\mathbb{Z}_m = m = \dfrac{n}{n/m} = \dfrac{\#\mathbb{Z}_n}{\#(m\mathbb{Z}_n)}.$

For instance, consider the "clock group" $\mathbb{Z}_{12}$ (i.e., $n = 12$) and its subgroup $3\mathbb{Z}_{12} = \{0, 3, 6, 9\}$ (i.e., $m = 3$). The reader may follow Example 5.5 and confirm $\mathbb{Z}_{12}/3\mathbb{Z}_{12} = \mathbb{Z}_3$. Hence $\#(\mathbb{Z}_{12}/3\mathbb{Z}_{12}) = \#\mathbb{Z}_3 = 3 = 12/4 = \frac{\#\mathbb{Z}_{12}}{\#(3\mathbb{Z}_{12})}$. The reader may also check all other cases of $m|12$. □

## 5.2.2 Order of Group Element

If we say that in a group, the identity element is special in a unique way, then other elements also have some special properties. One of such properties can be thought of as the "distance" from the identity element.

**Definition 5.9: Order of Group Element** *Let $G$ be a group and $a \in G$. The order of the element $a$ is the least positive integer $i \in \mathbb{N}$ satisfying $a^i = e$, and is denoted by $\mathrm{ord}(a)$. If such an integer $i$ does not exist, then $a$ is called an element of infinite order.*

We should remind the reader the shorthand meaning of $a^i$ where $i$ is an integer and $a$ is a group element. The shorthand meaning of the notation has been defined in Definition 5.4 and further explained in Remark 5.1.

**Example 5.7:**

1. In the "clock group" $\mathbb{Z}_{12}$, $\mathrm{ord}(1) = 12$, since 12 is the least positive number satisfying $12 \cdot 1 \equiv 0 \pmod{12}$; the reader may verify the following: $\mathrm{ord}(2) = 6$, $\mathrm{ord}(3) = 4$, $\mathrm{ord}(4) = 3$, $\mathrm{ord}(5) = 12$. Try to find the orders for the rest of the elements.

2. In $B$ in Example 5.1(6), $\mathrm{ord}(F) = 1$ and $\mathrm{ord}(T) = 2$.

3. In $\mathrm{Roots}(x^3 - 1)$ in Example 5.1(7), $\mathrm{ord}(\alpha) = \mathrm{ord}(\beta) = 3$, and $\mathrm{ord}(1) = 1$.

4. In $\mathbb{Z}$, $\mathrm{ord}(1) = \infty$. □

**Corollary 5.2: Lagrange** *Let $G$ be a finite group and $a \in G$ be any element. Then $\mathrm{ord}(a) \mid \#G$.*

**Proof** For any $a \in G$, if $a = e$ then $\mathrm{ord}(a) = 1$ and so $\mathrm{ord}(a) \mid \#G$ is a trivial case. Let $a \neq e$. Since $G$ is finite, we have $1 < \mathrm{ord}(a) < \infty$. Elements

$$a, a^2, \ldots, a^{\mathrm{ord}(a)} = e \tag{5.2.1}$$

are necessarily distinct. Suppose they were not, then $a^r = a^s$ for some non-negative integers $r$ and $s$ satisfying $1 \leq r < s \leq \mathrm{ord}(a)$. Applying "Inverse Axiom" of $(a^r)^{-1}$ to both sides, we will have, $a^{s-r} = e$ where $0 < s - r < \mathrm{ord}(a)$. This contradicts the definition of $\mathrm{ord}(a)$ being the least positive integer satisfying $a^{\mathrm{ord}(a)} = e$.

It is easy to check that the ord($a$) elements in (5.2.1) form a subgroup of $G$. By Lagrange's Theorem, ord($a$)|#$G$.                                                                    □

Corollary 5.2, which we have shown as a direct application of Lagrange's Theorem, provides a relationship between the order of a group and the orders of elements in the group. This relationship has an important application in public-key cryptography: the famous cryptosystems of Rivest, Shamir and Adleman (RSA) [248] work in a group of a secret order which is known exclusively to the key owner. A ciphertext can be considered as a random element in the group. With the knowledge of the group order the key owner can use the relationship between the order of the element and the order of the group to transform the ciphertext back to plaintext (i.e., to decrypt). We will study the RSA cryptosystems in §8.5.

## 5.2.3   Cyclic Groups

Example 5.1(4) indicates that we can conveniently view $\mathbb{Z}_n$ as $n$ points dividing a circle. This circle is (or these $n$ points are) formed by $n$ repeated operations $a^1, a^2, \ldots, a^n$ for some element $a \in \mathbb{Z}_n$. This is a *cyclic view* of $\mathbb{Z}_n$. For addition modulo $n$ as the group operation, $a = 1$ provides a cyclic view of $\mathbb{Z}_n$. The reader may check that for the case of $n = 12$ as in Example 5.1(4), $5, 7, 11$ are the other three elements which can also provide cyclic views for $\mathbb{Z}_{12}$.

Informally speaking, if a group has a cyclic view, then we say that the group is a **cyclic group**. Cyclic groups are groups with nice properties. They have wide applications in cryptography.

**Definition 5.10: Cyclic Group, Group Generator**  *A group $G$ is said to be cyclic if there exists an element $a \in G$ such that for any $b \in G$, there exists an integer $i \geq 0$ such that $b = a^i$. Element $a$ is called a generator of $G$. $G$ is also called the group generated by $a$.*

*When a group is generated by $a$, we can write $G = \langle a \rangle$.*

A generator of a cyclic group is also called a **primitive root** of the group's identity element. The meaning of this name will become clear in §5.4.3 (Theorem 5.11).

**Example 5.8:**

1. For $n \geq 1$, the additive $\mathbb{Z}_n$ is cyclic because, obviously, 1 is a generator.

2. $B$ in Example 5.1(6) is cyclic and is generated by $T$.

3. Roots($x^3 - 1$) in Example 5.1(7) is cyclic and is generated by $\alpha$ or $\beta$.

4. Let $p$ be a prime number. Then the multiplicative group $\mathbb{Z}_p^*$ is cyclic. This is because $\mathbb{Z}_p^*$ contains element of order $p - 1 = \#\mathbb{Z}_p^*$ and hence such an element generates the whole group. In Alg 4.6 we have seen informally an evidence for

$\mathbb{Z}_p^*$ containing a generator. We will provide a formal proof of $\mathbb{Z}_p^*$ being cyclic in Theorem 5.12.

5. In group $\mathbb{Z}_7^*$, 3 is a generator. This element provides a cyclic view for $\mathbb{Z}_7^*$ as follows (remember the group operation being multiplication modulo 7):

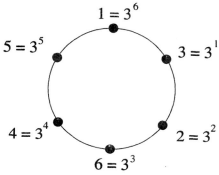

□

**Definition 5.11: Euler's Function**  *For $n \in \mathbb{N}$ with $n \geq 1$, Euler's function $\phi(n)$ is the number of integers $k$ with $0 \leq k < n$ and $\gcd(k, n) = 1$.*

A number of useful results can be derived for cyclic groups.

## Theorem 5.2:

1. *Every subgroup of a cyclic group is cyclic.*

2. *For every positive divisor $d$ of $\# \langle a \rangle$, $\langle a \rangle$ contains precisely one subgroup of order $d$.*

3. *If $\# \langle a \rangle = m$, then $\# \langle a^k \rangle = \mathrm{ord}(a^k) = m/\gcd(k, m)$.*

4. *For every positive divisor $d$ of $\# \langle a \rangle$, $\langle a \rangle$ contains $\phi(d)$ elements of order $d$.*

5. *Let $\# \langle a \rangle = m$. Then $\langle a \rangle$ contains $\phi(m)$ generators. They are elements $a^r$ such that $\gcd(r, m) = 1$.*

## Proof

1. Let $H \subseteq \langle a \rangle$. If $H = \langle e \rangle$ or $H = \langle a \rangle$ then $H$ is obviously cyclic. So we only consider other cases of $H$. Let $d > 1$ be the least integer such that $a^d \in H$, and let $a^s \in H$ for some $s > d$. Dividing $s$ by $d$: $s = dq + r$ for some $0 \leq r < d$. Since $a^{dq} \in H$ we have $a^r = a^{s-dq} \in H$. The minimality of $d$ and $H \neq \langle a \rangle$ imply $r = 0$. So $s$ is a multiple of $d$. So $H$ only contains the powers of $a^d$, and hence is cyclic.

2. Let $d > 1$ and $d|m = \#\langle a \rangle$. Then $\langle a^{\frac{m}{d}} \rangle$ is an order-$d$ subgroup of $\langle a \rangle$ since $d$ is the least integer satisfying $(a^{\frac{m}{d}})^d = e$. Let us assume that there exists another order-$d$ subgroup of $\langle a \rangle$ which is different from $\langle a^{\frac{m}{d}} \rangle$. By 1, such a subgroup must be cyclic and hence be $\langle a^k \rangle$ for some $k > 1$. From $a^{kd} = e$ with minimality of $m$ we have $m|kd$, or equivalently, $\frac{m}{d}|k$. So $a^k \in \langle a^{\frac{m}{d}} \rangle$, i.e., $\langle a^k \rangle \subseteq \langle a^{\frac{m}{d}} \rangle$. The same order of these two groups means $\langle a^k \rangle = \langle a^{\frac{m}{d}} \rangle$. This contradicts our assumption $\langle a^k \rangle \neq \langle a^{\frac{m}{d}} \rangle$.

3. Let $d = \gcd(k, m)$. Then by 2 there exists a unique order-$d$ subgroup of $\langle a \rangle$. Let this subgroup be $\langle a^{\ell} \rangle$ for some least $\ell > 1$, i.e., $\ell$ is the least integer satisfying $a^{d\ell} = e$. By the minimality of $m$, we have $m|d\ell$, or equivalently, $\frac{m}{d}|\ell$. The least case for $\ell$ is when $d = \gcd(\ell, m)$, i.e., $\ell = k$.

4. Let $d|m = \#\langle a \rangle$ and let $a^k$ be any element in $\langle a \rangle$ for $0 \leq k < m$. By 3, element $a^k$ is of order $\frac{m}{d}$ if and only if $\frac{m}{d} = \gcd(k, m)$. Write $k = c\frac{m}{d}$ with $0 \leq c < d$. Then $\gcd(k, m) = \frac{m}{d}$ is equivalent to $\gcd(c, d) = 1$. By Definition 5.11, there are $\phi(d)$ such $c$.

5. For $m = \#\langle a \rangle$, by 4, $\langle a \rangle$ contains $\phi(m)$ elements of order $m$, and they are of order $m$ and hence are generators of $\langle a \rangle$. Further by 3, these generators are $a^r$ with $\gcd(r, m) = 1$. □

**Corollary 5.3:** *A prime-order group is cyclic, and any non-identity element in the group is a generator.*

**Proof** Let $G$ be a group of prime order $p$. Let $a \in G$ be any non-identity element. From Corollary 5.2, $\text{ord}(a)|\#G = p$. Since $a \neq e$, $\text{ord}(a) \neq 1$. Then it has to be the case $\text{ord}(a) = p$. Therefore $\langle a \rangle = G$, i.e., $a$ is a generator of $G$. □

**Example 5.9:** Consider the "clock group" $\mathbb{Z}_{12}$ which is cyclic:

- for $1|12$, it contains an order-1 subgroup $\{0\}$; because $\phi(1) = 1$, the only element of order 1 is 0;

- for $2|12$, it contains an order-2 subgroup $\{0, 6\}$; because $\phi(2) = 1$, the only element of order 2 is 6;

- for $3|12$, it contains an order-3 subgroup $\{0, 4, 8\}$; 4 and 8 are the $2 = \phi(3)$ elements of order 3;

- for $4|12$, it contains an order-4 subgroup $\{0, 3, 6, 9\}$; 3 and 9 are the $2 = \phi(4)$ elements of order 4;

- for $6|12$, it contains an order-6 subgroup $\{0, 2, 4, 6, 8, 10\}$; 2 and 10 are the $2 = \phi(6)$ elements of order 6;

- for $12|12$, it contains an order-12 subgroup $\mathbb{Z}_{12}$; in it, 1, 5, 7 and 11 are the $4 = \phi(12)$ elements of order 12.

The reader may analyze the multiplicative group $\mathbb{Z}_7^*$ analogously. $\qquad\square$

## 5.2.4 The Multiplicative Group $\mathbb{Z}_n^*$

Let $n = pq$ for $p$ and $q$ being distinct odd prime numbers. The multiplicative group $\mathbb{Z}_n^*$ is very important in modern cryptography. Let us now have a look at its structure. We stipulate that all $n$ in this subsection is such a composite.

Since elements in $\mathbb{Z}_n^*$ are positive integers less than $n$ and co-prime to $n$. By Definition 5.11, this group contains $\phi(n) = (p-1)(q-1)$ elements (see Lemma 6.1 to confirm $\phi(n) = (p-1)(q-1)$).

**Theorem 5.3:** Any element in $\mathbb{Z}_n^*$ has an order dividing $\text{lcm}(p-1, q-1)$.

**Proof** Let $a \in \mathbb{Z}_n^*$. By Fermat's Little Theorem (Theorem 6.10 in §6.4) we know

$$a^{(p-1)} \equiv 1 \pmod{p}.$$

Denoting $\lambda = \text{lcm}(p-1, q-1)$, trivially we have

$$a^\lambda \equiv 1 \pmod{p}.$$

Symmetrically we can also derive

$$a^\lambda \equiv 1 \pmod{q}.$$

These two congruences actually say that $a^\lambda - 1$ is a multiple of $p$ and also a multiple of $q$. Since $p$ and $q$ are distinct prime numbers, $a^\lambda - 1$ must be a multiple of $n = pq$. This means

$$a^\lambda \equiv 1 \pmod{n}.$$

Therefore, $\lambda$ is a multiple of the order of $a$ modulo $n$. $\qquad\square$

Notice that both $p-1$ and $q-1$ are even, therefore $\lambda = \text{lcm}(p-1, q-1) < (p-1)(q-1) = \phi(n)$. Theorem 5.3 says that there is no element in $\mathbb{Z}_n^*$ is of order $\phi(n)$. That is, $\mathbb{Z}_n^*$ contains no generator. So by Definition 5.10, $\mathbb{Z}_n^*$ is non-cyclic. Value $\lambda(n)$ is called **Carmichael number** of $n$.

**Example 5.10:** For $n = 5 \times 7 = 35$, let $a \in \mathbb{Z}_{35}^*$ be such an element: (i) $a \pmod 5 \in \mathbb{Z}_5^*$ has the maximum order 4 and hence it provides a cyclic view for the cyclic group $\mathbb{Z}_5^*$ (the left circle below, of period 4); (ii) $a \pmod 7 \in \mathbb{Z}_7^*$ has the maximum order 6 and hence it provides a cyclic view for the cyclic group $\mathbb{Z}_7^*$ (the right circle below, of period 6).

Then the order of $a \in \mathbb{Z}_{35}^*$ can be viewed as the period decided by two engaged toothed wheels. One has four teeth and the other has six teeth. We initially chalk-mark a large dot (see the picture below) at the engaged point of the two wheels. Now let the engaged gear revolve, and the large chalk mark becomes two separate marks on the two wheels. These two separate marks will meet again after the mark on the four-toothed wheel has travelled 3 revolutions, and that on the six-toothed wheel, 2 revolutions. Therefore, the order (period) of $a \in \mathbb{Z}_{35}^*$ is exactly the distance between the separation and the reunion of the large chalk mark, and is $3 \times 4 = 2 \times 6 = 12 = \mathrm{lcm}((5-1), (7-1))$.

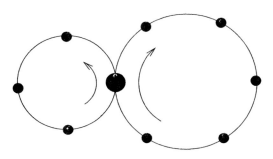

Let $\mathrm{ord}_x(a)$ denote the order of an element modulo a positive number $n$. In general, any element $a \in \mathbb{Z}_n^*$ has the order $\mathrm{ord}_n(a)$ defined by $\mathrm{ord}_p(a)$ and $\mathrm{ord}_q(a)$ in the following relation:

$$\mathrm{ord}_n(a) = \mathrm{lcm}(\mathrm{ord}_p(a), \mathrm{ord}_q(a)). \qquad (5.2.2)$$

Since $\mathbb{Z}_p^*$ and $\mathbb{Z}_q^*$ are both cyclic, they have elements of maximum orders $p-1$ and $q-1$, respectively. Consequently, $\mathbb{Z}_n^*$ contains elements of the maximum order $\mathrm{lcm}(p-1, q-1)$. On the other hand, some maximum-order element $a \in \mathbb{Z}_n^*$ can satisfy the cases of $\mathrm{ord}_p(a) < p-1$ and/or $\mathrm{ord}_q(a) < q-1$. For example, because $\mathrm{lcm}(4,3) = \mathrm{lcm}(4,6)$ and because $\mathbb{Z}_7^*$ contains an element of order 3, group $\mathbb{Z}_{35}^*$ contains an element of the maximum period 12 which is represented by two engaged toothed wheels of four teeth and three teeth.

In the next chapter we will provide a 1-1 onto mapping between the elements in $\mathbb{Z}_n^*$ and the pairs of elements in $\mathbb{Z}_p^* \times \mathbb{Z}_q^*$. The mapping is computable and hence it provides a method to construct elements in $\mathbb{Z}_n^*$ out of those in the cyclic groups $\mathbb{Z}_p^*$ and $\mathbb{Z}_q^*$. The latter job is usually easier because it can make use of the nice properties of the later two groups (cyclic groups). For example, because computing square roots in $\mathbb{Z}_p^*$ and $\mathbb{Z}_q^*$ is easy, we can use the mapping to construct square roots in $\mathbb{Z}_n^*$ using the square roots computed in $\mathbb{Z}_p^*$ and $\mathbb{Z}_q^*$.

# 5.3  Rings and Fields

One day our ancient shepherd settled down and became a farmer.  He needed to figure out with his neighbors the areas of their lands.  The shepherds-turned-farmers began to realize that it was no longer possible for them to use one basic operation for everything: they needed not only sum, but also product.  The need for *two* operations over a set of objects started then.

**Definition 5.12: Ring** *A ring R is a set together with two operations: (addition) + and (multiplication) ·, and has the following properties:*

1. *Under addition +, R is an abelian group; denote by* **0** *the additive identity (called the* **zero-element***);*

2. *Under multiplication ·, R satisfies* Closure Axiom, Associativity Axiom *and* Identity Axiom*; denote by* **1** *the multiplicative identity (called the* **unity-element***);* $1 \neq 0$*;*

3. $\forall a, b \in R : a \cdot b = b \cdot a$          (Commutative Axiom)

4. $\forall a, b, c \in R : a \cdot (b + c) = a \cdot b + a \cdot c$     (Distribution Axiom)

In this definition, the bold form **0** and **1** are used to highlight that these two elements are abstract elements and are not necessarily their integer counterparts (see, e.g., Example 5.11(3) in a moment).

Similar to our confinement of ourselves to the commutative groups, in Definition 5.12 we have stipulated multiplication to satisfy the Commutative Axiom.  So Definition 5.12 defines a **commutative ring** and that is the ring to be considered in this book.  We should also stress that + and · are abstract operations: that is, they are not necessarily the ordinary addition and multiplication between integers.  Whenever possible, we shall shorten $a \cdot b$ into $ab$; explicit presentation of the operation "·" will only be needed where the operation is written without operands.

## Example 5.11:  Rings

1. $\mathbb{Z}$, $\mathbb{Q}$, $\mathbb{R}$ and $\mathbb{C}$ are all rings under usual addition and multiplication with **0** = 0 and **1** = 1.

2. For any $n > 0$, $Z_n$ is a ring under addition and multiplication modulo $n$ with **0** = 0 and **1** = 1.

3. Let $B$ be the additive group defined in Example 5.1(6) with the zero-element $F$.  Let the multiplication operation be $\wedge$ (logical And): $F \wedge F = F$, $F \wedge T = T \wedge F = F$, $T \wedge T = T$.  Then $B$ is a ring with the unity-element $T$.   □

At first glance, Definition 5.12 has only defined multiplication for non-zero elements. In fact, multiplication between the zero-element and other elements has been defined by Distribution Axiom. For example, $\mathbf{0}a = (b + (-b))a = ba + (-b)a = ba - ba = \mathbf{0}$. Moreover, a ring can have **zero-divisors**, that is, elements $a, b$ satisfying $ab = \mathbf{0}$ with $a \neq \mathbf{0}$ and $b \neq \mathbf{0}$. For example, for $n = k\ell$ being a nontrivial factorization of $n$, both $k$ and $\ell$ are non-zero elements in the ring $\mathbb{Z}_n$, and the product $k\ell = n = 0 \pmod{n}$ is the zero-element.

**Definition 5.13: Field**  *If the non-zero elements of a ring forms a group under multiplication, then the ring is called a field.*

The Closure Axiom for the multiplicative group (i.e., the non-zero elements) of a field implies that a field $F$ cannot contain a zero-divisor, that is, for any $a, b \in F$, $ab = \mathbf{0}$ implies either $a = \mathbf{0}$ or $b = \mathbf{0}$.

**Example 5.12: Fields**

1. $\mathbb{Q}$, $\mathbb{R}$ and $\mathbb{C}$ are all fields under usual addition and multiplication with $\mathbf{0} = 0$ and $\mathbf{1} = 1$.

2. The two-element ring $B$ in Example 5.11(3) is a field.

3. For $p$ being a prime number, $\mathbb{Z}_p$ is a field under addition and multiplication modulo $p$ with $\mathbf{0} = 0$ and $\mathbf{1} = 1$.                                            □

We shall see more examples of fields in a moment.

Note that $\mathbb{Z}$ under integer addition and multiplication is not a field because any non-zero element does not have a multiplicative inverse in $\mathbb{Z}$ (a violation of the Inverse Axiom). Also, for $n$ being a composite, $\mathbb{Z}_n$ is not a field too since we have seen that $\mathbb{Z}_n$ contains zero-divisors (a violation of the Closure Axiom).

Sometimes there will be no need for us to care about the difference among a group, a ring or a field. In such a situation we shall use an **algebraic structure** to refer to either of these structures.

The notions of finite group, subgroup, quotient group and the order of group can be extended straightforwardly to rings and fields.

**Definition 5.14:** *An algebraic structure is said to be finite if it contains a finite number of elements. The number of elements is called the order of the structure.*

*A substructure of an algebraic structure $A$ is a non-empty subset $S$ of $A$ which is itself an algebraic structure under the operation(s) of $A$. If $S \neq A$ then $S$ is called a proper substructure of $A$.*

*Let $A$ be an algebraic structure and $B \subseteq A$ be a substructure of $A$. The quotient structure of $A$ modulo $B$, denoted by $A/B$, is the set of all cosets $a \circ B$ with a* *ranging over A, with the operation $\star$ defined by $(a \circ B) \star (b \circ B) = (a \circ b) \circ B$, and with the identity elements being $\mathbf{0} \circ B$ and $\mathbf{1} \circ B$.*

From Definition 5.14, a ring (respectively, a field) not only can have a subring (respectively, a subfield), but also can have a subgroup (respectively, a subring and a subgroup). We shall see such examples in §5.4.

## 5.4   The Structure of Finite Fields

Finite fields find wide applications in cryptography and cryptographic protocols. The pioneer work of Diffie and Hellman in public-key cryptography, the Diffie-Hellman key exchange protocol [99] (§8.3), is originally proposed to work in finite fields of a particular form. Since the work of Diffie and Hellman, numerous finite-fields-based cryptosystems and protocols have been proposed: the ElGamal cryptosystems [103], the Schnorr identification protocol and signature scheme [259], the zero-knowledge undeniable signatures of Chaum, and the zero-knowledge proof protocols of Chaum and Pedersen [74], are well-known examples. Some new cryptosystems, such as the Advanced Encryption Standard [221] (§7.7) and the XTR cryptosystems [177], work in finite fields of a more general form. Finite fields also underlie elliptic curves which in turn form the basis of a class of cryptosystems (e.g., [168]).

Let us now conduct a self-contained course in the structure of finite fields.

### 5.4.1   Finite Fields of Prime Numbers of Elements

Finite fields with the simplest structure are those of orders (i.e., the number of elements) as prime numbers. Yet, such fields have been the most widely used ones in cryptography.

**Definition 5.15: Prime Field**   *A field that contains no proper subfield is called a prime field.*

For example, $\mathbb{Q}$ is a prime field whereas $\mathbb{R}$ is not, since $\mathbb{Q}$ is a proper subfield of $\mathbb{R}$. But $\mathbb{Q}$ is an infinite field. In finite fields, we shall soon see that a prime field must contain a prime number of elements, that is, must have a prime order.

**Definition 5.16: Homomorphism and Isomorphism**   *Let A, B be two algebraic structures. A mapping $f : A \mapsto B$ is called a homomorphism of A into B if f preserves operations of A. That is, if $\circ$ is an operation of A and $\star$, an operation of B, then $\forall x, y \in A$, we have $f(x \circ y) = f(x) \star f(y)$. If f is a one-to-one homomorphism of A onto B, then f is called an isomorphism and we say that A and B are isomorphic.*

If $f : A \mapsto B$ is a homomorphism and $e$ is an identity element in $A$ (either additive or multiplicative), then

$$f(e) \star f(e) = f(e \circ e) = f(e),$$

so that $f(e)$ is the identity element in $B$. Also, for any $a \in A$

$$f(a) \star f(a^{-1}) = f(a \circ a^{-1}) = f(e),$$

so that $f(a^{-1}) = f(a)^{-1}$ for all $a \in A$. Moreover, if the mapping is one-one onto (i.e., $A$ and $B$ are isomorphic), then $A$ and $B$ have the same number of elements. Two isomorphic algebraic structures will be viewed to have the same structure.

## Example 5.13: Isomorphic Algebraic Structures

i) Denote by $\mathbb{F}_2$ the set $\{0,1\}$ with operations $+$ and $\cdot$ being integer addition modulo 2 and integer multiplication, respectively. Then $\mathbb{F}_2$ must be a field because it is isomorphic to field $B$ in Example 5.12(2). It is routine to check that mapping $f(0) = F$, $f(1) = T$ is an isomorphism.

ii) For any prime number $p$, additive group $\mathbb{Z}_{p-1}$ is isomorphic to multiplicative group $\mathbb{Z}_p^*$. It is routine to check that function $f(x) = g^x \pmod{p}$ is an isomorphism between these two sets. $\qquad\square$

Clearly, all fields of two elements are isomorphic to each other and hence to $\mathbb{F}_2$. A field of two elements is the simplest field: it contains the two necessary elements, namely, the zero-element and the unity-element, and nothing else. Since under isomorphisms, there is no need to differentiate these fields, we can treat $\mathbb{F}_2$ as the unique field of order 2.

**Example 5.14: Finite Field of Prime Order**   Let $p$ be any prime number. Then $\mathbb{Z}_p$, the integers modulo $p$, is a finite field of order $p$ (i.e., of $p$ elements) with addition and multiplication modulo $p$ as the field operations. Indeed, we have already shown, in Example 5.11(2) that $\mathbb{Z}_p$ is an additive ring, and in Example 5.1(5) that the non-zero elements of $\mathbb{Z}_p$, denoted by $\mathbb{Z}_p^*$, forms a multiplicative group. $\quad\square$

**Definition 5.17: Field $\mathbb{F}_p$** *Let $p$ be a prime number. We denote by $\mathbb{F}_p$ the finite field $\mathbb{Z}_p$.*

Let $F$ be any finite field of a prime-order $p$. Since we can construct a one-one mapping from $F$ onto $\mathbb{F}_p$ (i.e., the mapping is an isomorphism), any finite field of order $p$ is isomorphic to $\mathbb{F}_p$. As there is no need for us to differentiate fields which are isomorphic to each other, we can harmlessly call $\mathbb{F}_p$ *the* finite field of order $p$.

Let $A$ be a finite algebraic structure with additive operation "+," and let $a$ be any non-zero element in $A$. Observe the following sequence:

$$a, \ 2a = a + a, \ 3a = a + a + a, \ \ldots \tag{5.4.1}$$

Since $A$ is finite, the element $a$ has a finite order and therefore in this sequence there must exist a pair $(ia, ja)$ with $i < j$ being integers and $ja - ia = (j-i)a = \mathbf{0}$.

We should remind the reader to notice Definition 5.4 and Remark 5.1 for the shorthand meaning of writing multiplication $ia$ where $i$ is an integer and $a$ is an algebraic element.

**Definition 5.18: Characteristic of an Algebraic Structure**  *The characteristic of an algebraic structure $A$, denoted by $char(A)$, is the least positive integer $n$ such that $na = \mathbf{0}$ for every $a \in A$. If no such positive integer $n$ exists, then $A$ is said to have the characteristic $0$.*

**Theorem 5.4:**  *Every finite field has a prime characteristic.*

**Proof**  Let $F$ be a finite field and $a \in F$ be any non-zero element. With $(j-i)a = \mathbf{0}$ and $j > i$ derived from the sequence in (5.4.1) we know $F$ must have a positive characteristic. Let it be $n$. Since $F$ has at least two elements (i.e., the zero-element and the unity-element), $n \geq 2$. If $n > 2$ were not prime, we could write $n = k\ell$ with $k, \ell \in \mathbb{Z}$, $1 < k, \ell < n$. Then

$$\mathbf{0} = n\mathbf{1} = (k\ell)\mathbf{1} = (k\ell)\mathbf{1}\mathbf{1} = (k\mathbf{1})(\ell\mathbf{1}).$$

This implies either $k\mathbf{1} = \mathbf{0}$ or $\ell\mathbf{1} = \mathbf{0}$ since non-zero elements of $F$ form a multiplicative group (which does not contain $\mathbf{0}$). It follows either $ka\mathbf{1} = (k\mathbf{1})a = \mathbf{0}$ for all $a \in F$ or $\ell a\mathbf{1} = (\ell\mathbf{1})a = \mathbf{0}$ for all $a \in F$, in contradiction to the definition of the characteristic $n$. $\square$

## 5.4.2   Finite Fields Modulo Irreducible Polynomials

The order of a finite prime field is equal to the characteristic of the field. However, this is not the general case for finite fields. A more general form of finite fields can be constructed using polynomials.

### 5.4.2.1   Polynomials Over an Algebraic Structure

In Chapter 4 we have already used polynomials over integers. Now let us be familiar with polynomials over an abstract algebraic structure.

**Definition 5.19: Polynomials Over an Algebraic Structure**  *Let $A$ be an algebraic structure with addition and multiplication. A polynomial over $A$ is an* *expression of the form*

$$f(x) = \sum_{i=0}^{n} a_i x^i$$

*where $n$ is a non-negative integer, the coefficients $a_i$, $0 \leq i \leq n$ are elements in $A$, and $x$ is a symbol not belonging to $A$. The coefficient $a_n$ is called the leading coefficient and is not the zero-element in $A$ for $n \neq 0$. The integer $n$ is called the degree of $f(x)$ and is denoted by $n = \deg(f(x)) = \deg(f)$. If the leading coefficient is $a_0$, then $f$ is called a constant polynomial. If the leading coefficient is $a_0 = \mathbf{0}$, then $f$ is called the zero-polynomial and is denoted by $f = 0$. We denote by $A[x]$ the set of all polynomials over algebraic structure $A$.*

For $f, g \in A[x]$ with

$$f(x) = \sum_{i=0}^{n} a_i x^i \quad \text{and} \quad g(x) = \sum_{i=0}^{m} b_i x^i,$$

we have

$$f(x) + g(x) = \sum_{i=0}^{\max(n,m)} c_i x^i \quad \text{where} \quad c_i = \begin{cases} a_i + b_i & i = 0, 1, \ldots, \min(n, m) \\ a_i & i = m+1, \ldots, n \\ b_i & i = n+1, \ldots, m \end{cases} \quad (5.4.2)$$

and

$$f(x)g(x) = \sum_{k=0}^{n+m} c_k x^k \quad \text{where} \quad c_k = \sum_{\substack{i+j=k \\ 0 \leq i \leq n \\ 0 \leq j \leq m}} a_i b_j. \quad (5.4.3)$$

It is easy to see that if $A$ is a ring, then $A[x]$ is a ring with $A$ being a subring of $A[x]$. Addition and multiplication between polynomials over a ring will result in the following relationship on the polynomial degrees:

$$\deg(f + g) \leq max(\deg(f), \deg(g)),$$

$$\deg(fg) \leq \deg(f) + \deg(g).$$

Now if $A$ is a field, then because a field has no zero-divisors, we will have $c_{n+m} = a_n b_m \neq \mathbf{0}$ for $a_n \neq \mathbf{0}$ and $b_m \neq \mathbf{0}$. So if $A$ is a field, then

$$\deg(fg) = \deg(f) + \deg(g).$$

Let $f, g \in A[x]$ such that $g \neq 0$. Analogous to the case of division between integers (see §4.3.2.1), we can always write

$$f = gq + r \quad \text{for } q, r \in A[x] \text{ with } \deg(r) < \deg(g). \quad (5.4.4)$$

**Example 5.15:** Consider $f(x) = x^5 + x^4 + x^3 + x^2 + x + 1 \in \mathbb{F}_2[x]$, $g(x) = x^3 + x + 1 \in \mathbb{F}_2[x]$. We can compute $q, r \in \mathbb{F}_2[x]$ by long division

$$
\begin{array}{r}
x^2 \ + \ x \qquad\qquad\qquad\qquad\qquad \\
x^3 + x + 1 \ \overline{\big)\ x^5 \ + \ x^4 \ + \ x^3 \ + \ x^2 \ + \ x \ + \ 1} \\
x^5 \qquad\quad + \ x^3 \ + \ x^2 \qquad\qquad \\
\hline
x^4 \qquad\qquad\qquad\quad + \ x \ + \ 1 \\
x^4 \qquad\quad + \ x^2 \ + \ x \qquad\quad \\
\hline
x^2 \qquad\qquad\quad + \ 1
\end{array}
$$

Therefore $q = x^2 + x$ and $r = x^2 + 1$.    $\square$

**Definition 5.20: Irreducible Polynomial** *Let $A$ be an algebraic structure. A polynomial $f \in A[x]$ is said to be irreducible over $A$ (or irreducible in $A[x]$, or prime in $A[x]$) if $f$ has a positive degree and $f = gh$ with $g, h \in A[x]$ implies that either $g$ or $h$ is a constant polynomial. A polynomial is said to be reducible over $A$ if it is not irreducible over $A$.*

Notice that the reducibility of a polynomial depends on the algebraic structure over which the polynomial is defined. A polynomial can be reducible over one structure, but is irreducible over another.

**Example 5.16:** For quadratic polynomial $f(x) = x^2 - 2x + 2$: (i) Discuss its reducibility over the usual infinite algebraic structures; (ii) Investigate its reducibility over finite fields $\mathbb{F}_p$ for any odd prime number $p$; (iii) Factor $f(x)$ over $\mathbb{F}_p$ for $p < 10$.

Using the rooting formula in elementary algebra, we can compute the two roots of $f(x) = 0$ as

$$ \alpha = 1 + \sqrt{-1}, \quad \beta = 1 - \sqrt{-1}. $$

i) Since $\sqrt{-1}$ is not in $\mathbb{R}$, $f(x)$ is irreducible over $\mathbb{R}$ (and hence is irreducible over $\mathbb{Z}$ or $\mathbb{Q}$). But because $\sqrt{-1} = i \in \mathbb{C}$, therefore $f(x)$ is reducible over $\mathbb{C}$:

$$ f(x) = (x - 1 - i)(x - 1 + i). $$

ii) Clearly, $f(x)$ is reducible over $\mathbb{F}_p$ for any odd prime $p$ if and only if $\sqrt{-1}$ is an element in $\mathbb{F}_p$, or equivalently, $-1$ is a square number modulo $p$.

A number $x$ is a square modulo $p$ if and only if there exists $y \pmod{p}$ satisfying $y^2 \equiv x \pmod{p}$. By Fermat's Little Theorem (Theorem 6.10 in §6.4), we know that all $x \pmod{p}$ satisfies $x^{p-1} \equiv 1 \pmod{p}$. For $p$ being an odd prime, Fermat's Little Theorem is equivalent to

$$ x^{\frac{p-1}{2}} \equiv \pm 1 \pmod{p}, \tag{5.4.5} $$

for all $x$ with $0 < x < p$ (where $-1$ denotes $p - 1$). If $x$ is a square modulo $p$, then (5.4.5) becomes

$$ x^{\frac{p-1}{2}} \equiv (y^2)^{\frac{p-1}{2}} \equiv y^{p-1} \equiv 1 \pmod{p}. $$

Therefore, we know that (5.4.5) provides a criterion for testing whether $x$ is a square modulo an odd prime $p$: $x$ is a square (respectively, non-square) modulo $p$ if the test yields 1 (respectively, $-1$).

To this end we know that for any odd prime $p$, $f(x)$ is reducible over $\mathbb{F}_p$ if and only if $(-1)^{\frac{p-1}{2}} \equiv 1 \pmod{p}$, and is irreducible if and only if $(-1)^{\frac{p-1}{2}} \equiv -1 \pmod{p}$. In other words, $f(x)$ is reducible (or irreducible) over $\mathbb{F}_p$ if $p \equiv 1 \pmod{4}$ (or $p \equiv 3 \pmod{4}$).

iii) For $p = 2$, $f(x) = x^2 - 2x + 2 = x^2 - 0x + 0 = x^2$ and is reducible over $\mathbb{F}_2$.

The only odd prime less than 10 and congruent to 1 modulo 4 is 5. Since $-1 \equiv 4 \equiv 2^2 \pmod{5}$, i.e., $\sqrt{-1} \equiv 2 \pmod{5}$, we can completely factor $f(x)$ over $\mathbb{F}_5$:

$$f(x) = (x - 1 - \sqrt{-1})(x - 1 + \sqrt{-1}) = (x - 1 - 2)(x - 1 + 2) = (x + 2)(x + 1).$$

The other square root of $-1$ in $\mathbb{F}_5$ is 3. The reader may check that the root 3 will provide the same factorization of $f(x)$ over $\mathbb{F}_5$ as does the root 2.　　　　□

### 5.4.2.2　Field Construction Using Irreducible Polynomial

Let us construct finite field using an irreducible polynomial.

**Definition 5.21: Set $A[x]$ Modulo a Polynomial** *Let $A$ be an algebraic structure and let $f, g, q, r \in A[x]$ with $g \neq 0$ satisfy the division expression (5.4.4), we say $r$ is the remainder of $f$ divided by $g$ and denote $r \equiv f \pmod{g}$.*

*The set of the remainders of all polynomials in $A[x]$ modulo $g$ is called the polynomials in $A[x]$ modulo $g$, and is denoted by $A[x]_g$.*

Analogous to the integers modulo a positive integer, $A[x]_f$ is the set of all polynomials of degrees less than $\deg(f)$.

**Theorem 5.5:** *Let $F$ be a field and $f$ be a non-zero polynomial in $F[x]$. Then $F[x]_f$ is a ring, and is a field if and only if $f$ is irreducible over $F$.*

**Proof** First, $F[x]_f$ is obviously a ring under addition and multiplication modulo $f$ defined by (5.4.2), (5.4.3) and (5.4.4) with the zero-element and the unity-element the same as those of $F$.

Secondly, let $F[x]_f$ be a field. Suppose $f = gh$ for $g, h$ being non-constant polynomials in $F[x]$. Then because $0 < \deg(g) < \deg(f)$ and $0 < \deg(h) < \deg(f)$, $g$ and $h$ are non-zero polynomials in $F[x]_f$ whereas $f$ is the zero polynomial in $F[x]_f$. This violates the Closure Axiom for the multiplicative group of $F[x]_f$. So $F[x]_f$ cannot be a field. This contradicts the assumption that $F[x]_f$ is a field.

Finally, let $f$ be irreducible over $F$. Since $F[x]_f$ is a ring, it suffices for us to show that any non-zero element in $F[x]_f$ has a multiplicative inverse in $F[x]_f$. Let $r$ be a non-zero polynomial in $F[x]_f$ with $\gcd(f, r) = c$. Because $\deg(r) < \deg(f)$ and $f$ is irreducible, $c$ must be a constant polynomial. Writing $r = cs$, we have $c \in F$ and $s \in F[x]_f$ with $\gcd(f, s) = 1$. Analogous to the integer case, we can use the extended Euclid algorithm for polynomials to compute $s^{-1} \pmod{f} \in F[x]_f$. Also since $c \in F$, there exists $c^{-1} \in F$. Thus we obtain $r^{-1} = c^{-1}s^{-1} \in F[x]_f$.    $\square$

For finite field $F[x]_f$, let us call the irreducible polynomial $f$ **definition polynomial** of the field $F[x]_f$.

**Theorem 5.6:** *Let $F$ be a field of $p$ elements, and $f$ be a degree-n irreducible polynomial over $F$. Then the number of elements in the field $F[x]_f$ is $p^n$.*

**Proof** From Definition 5.21 we know $F[x]_f$ is the set of all polynomials in $F[x]$ of degrees less than $\deg(f) = n$ with the coefficients ranging through $F$ of $p$ elements. There are exactly $p^n$ such polynomials in $F[x]_f$.    $\square$

**Corollary 5.4:** *For every prime $p$ and for every positive integer $n$ there exists a finite field of $p^n$ elements.*    $\square$

As indicated by Corollary 5.4, for $F$ being a prime field $\mathbb{F}_p$, the structure of the field $\mathbb{F}_p[x]_f$ is very clear: it is merely the set of all polynomials of degree less than $n$ with coefficients in $\mathbb{F}_p$. Under isomorphism, we can even say that $\mathbb{F}_p[x]_f$ is *the* finite field of order $p^n$.

**Example 5.17: Integer Representation of Finite Field Element**    Polynomial $f(x) = x^8 + x^4 + x^3 + x + 1$ is irreducible over $\mathbb{F}_2$. The set of all polynomials modulo $f(x)$ over $\mathbb{F}_2$ forms a field of $2^8$ elements; they are all polynomials over $\mathbb{F}_2$ of degree less than 8. So any element in field $\mathbb{F}_2[x]_f$ is

$$b_7x^7 + b_6x^6 + b_5x^5 + b_4x^4 + b_3x^3 + b_2x^2 + b_1x + b_0$$

where $b_7, b_6, b_5, b_4, b_3, b_2, b_1, b_0 \in \mathbb{F}_2$. Thus, any element in this field can be represented as an integer of 8 binary bits $b_7b_6b_5b_4b_3b_2b_1b_0$, or a byte. In the hexadecimal encoding, we can use a letter to encode an integer value represented by 4 bits:

'0' $= 0000(= 0), \ldots,$ '9' $= 1001(= 9),$ 'A' $= 1010(= 10), \ldots,$ 'F' $= 1111(= 15).$

Since a byte has eight bits, the hexadecimal encoding of a byte can use two quoted characters 'XY' such that '0' $\leq$ 'X' $\leq$ 'F' and '0' $\leq$ 'Y' $\leq$ 'F'. That is, any element in field $\mathbb{F}_2[x]_f$ can be viewed as a byte in the interval ['00', 'FF'].

Conversely, any byte in the interval ['00', 'FF'] can be viewed as an element in field $\mathbb{F}_2[x]_f$. For example, the byte 01010111 (or the hexadecimal value '57') corresponds to the element (polynomial)

$$x^6 + x^4 + x^2 + x + 1.$$    $\square$

From Corollary 5.4 and Example 5.17, we can view field $\mathbb{F}_2[x]_f$ as the field of all non-negative integers up to $\deg(f)$ binary bits. Clearly, this field has $2^{\deg(f)}$ elements. Therefore, for any natural number $n > 0$, the set $\{0, 1\}^n$ forms a field of $2^n$ elements. Let us use "$n$-bit binary field" to name this field. Operations in this field follows the operations between polynomials of degrees less than $n$ over $\mathbb{F}_2$. Addition is very simple as shown in Example 5.18.

**Example 5.18:** Let $f$ be a degree-8 irreducible polynomial over $\mathbb{F}_2$. In the 8-bit binary field, addition follows polynomial addition by adding coefficients modulo 2 (so $1 + 1 = 0$). For example (in hexadecimal) '57' + '83' = 'D4':

$$(x^6 + x^4 + x^2 + x + 1) + (x^7 + x + 1) = x^7 + x^6 + x^4 + x^2.$$

So, addition in this field is independent from the definition polynomial $f$.     $\square$

Multiplication in field $\mathbb{F}_2[x]_f$ depends on the definition polynomial $f$: it is multiplication between two polynomials modulo $f$. The modulo operation can be done by applying the extended Euclid algorithm for polynomials. Later (in Example 5.19) we shall show another method for achieving field multiplication which is based on a different way for the field representation.

The $n$-bit binary field is a useful field because of its natural interpretation of integers. It has many applications in coding and cryptography. A new encryption standard, the Advanced Encryption Standard (AES), works in the 8-bit binary field. We will introduce the AES in Chapter 7.

Finally we notice that in Theorem 5.6 we have never assumed $p$ as prime. In fact, in Theorem 5.5, $F$ can be any field, and $F[x]_f$ is called an **extended field** from the **underlying subfield** $F$ via **field extension**. Since $F$ can be any field, it can of course be an extended field from another underlying subfield. In many applications of finite fields, we need to know more information about the relation between extended fields and underlying subfields (for example, we will need to know this relation when we study the AES later). Also, a different way for finite fields representation may also ease computation (e.g., the multiplication in Example 5.18 can be eased without using the Euclid algorithm if we use a different field representation). The next section serves the purpose for a better understanding of the structure of finite fields.

## 5.4.3   Finite Fields Constructed Using Polynomial Basis

This section is intended to provide the knowledge for helping a better understanding of some cryptosystems based on a general form of finite fields. We present it by assuming that the reader is familiar with the knowledge of vector space in linear algebra. However, this section may be skipped without causing difficulty for reading most parts of the rest of this book.

In §5.4.2 we have shown that under isomorphism, field $\mathbb{F}_p[x]_f$ is *the* finite field of order $p^{\deg(f)}$. However, often it may not be very convenient for us to use fields modulo an irreducible polynomial. In this final part of our course in algebraic foundations, let us construct finite fields using the roots of an irreducible polynomial over a finite field $F$. Fields constructed this way are more frequently used in applications.

Let $F$ be a finite field and $n$ be any positive integer. Let $f(x)$ be an irreducible polynomial over $F$ of degree $n$. We know that $f(x)$ has exactly $n$ roots in somewhere since $f(x)$ can be factored into $n$ linear polynomials there. We shall see in a moment that "somewhere" or "there" is exactly the space we are constructing.

Denote these $n$ roots of $f(x) = 0$ by

$$\theta_0, \ \theta_1, \ \ldots, \ \theta_{n-1} \tag{5.4.6}$$

Since $f(x)$ is irreducible over $F$, none of these roots can be in $F$.

**Theorem 5.7:** *Let $F$ be any finite field and let $f(x) \in F[x]$ be an irreducible polynomial of degree $n$ over $F$. Then for $\theta$ being any root of $f(x) = 0$, elements*

$$1, \ \theta, \ \theta^2, \ \ldots, \ \theta^{n-1}$$

*are linearly independent over $F$, that is, for $r_i \in F$ with $i = 0, 1, 2, \ldots, n-1$:*

$$r_0 + r_1\theta + r_2\theta^2 + \cdots + r_{n-1}\theta^{n-1} = 0 \ \text{ implies } \ r_0 = r_1 = \cdots = r_{n-1} = 0. \tag{5.4.7}$$

**Proof**  Let $\theta$ be any root of $f(x) = 0$. We know $\theta \neq 1$ since $f(x)$ is irreducible over field $F$ which contains 1. Suppose that the elements $1, \theta, \theta^2, \ldots, \theta^{n-1}$ were not linearly independent over $F$. That is, the linear combination (5.4.7) is possible for some $r_i \in F$ which are not all zero ($i = 0, 1, 2, \ldots, n-1$). This is equivalent to $\theta$ being a root of

$$r(x) = r_0 + r_1 x + r_2 x^2 + \cdots + r_{n-1} x^{n-1} = 0.$$

With $r_i \in F$ ($i = 0, 1, \ldots, n-1$), by Definition 5.21, $r(x)$ is an element in the field $F[x]_f$ and therefore $r(x) = 0$ means $r(x) \equiv 0 \pmod{f(x)}$. Let $a_n$ be the leading coefficient of $f(x)$. Then $a_n \in F$, $a_n \neq 0$ and $a_n^{-1} f(x) | r(x)$. But this is impossible since $a_n^{-1} f(x)$ is of degree $n$ while $r(x)$ is of degree less than $n$, unless $r(x)$ is the zero polynomial. This contradicts the supposed condition that $r_i \in F$ are not all zero ($i = 0, 1, \ldots, n-1$). $\square$

**Definition 5.22: Polynomial Basis**  *Let $F$ be a finite field and $f(x)$ be a degree-$n$ irreducible polynomial over $F$. Then for any root $\theta$ of $f(x) = 0$, elements $1, \theta, \theta^2, \ldots, \theta^{n-1}$ are called a (polynomial) basis (of a finite vector space) over $F$.*

We know from a fact in linear algebra that a basis of $n$ elements spans an $n$-dimension vector space. The spanning uses the scalars in $F$, that is, the space so spanned has the following structure

$$\left\{ \sum_{i=0}^{n-1} r_i \theta^i \mid r_0, r_1, \ldots, r_{n-1} \in F \right\}. \tag{5.4.8}$$

**Theorem 5.8:** *Let $F$ be a finite field and $f(x)$ be a degree-$n$ irreducible polynomial over $F$. Then for any root $\theta$ of $f(x) = 0$, the vector space in (5.4.8) is a finite field of $(\#F)^n$ elements.*

**Proof** First, we show that the space in (5.4.8) is a ring. The only non-trivial part is to show that Closure Axiom holds for multiplication. To do so, we note that from

$$f(\theta) = a_n \theta^n + a_{n-1} \theta^{n-1} + \cdots + a_0 = 0 \tag{5.4.9}$$

with $a_n \in F$ and $a_n \neq 0$, we have

$$\theta^n = a_n^{-1}(-a_{n-1}\theta^{n-1} - \cdots - a_0)$$

and so $\theta^n$ is a linear combination of the basis $1, \theta, \theta^2, \ldots, \theta^{n-1}$. Multiplying $\theta$ to (5.4.9), we can further derive that for any positive integer $m \geq n$, $\theta^m$ can be expressed as a linear combination of the same basis. Therefore, for any $u, v$ in the space in (5.4.8), $uv$, as a linear combination of $1, \theta, \ldots, \theta^m$ for $m \leq 2(n-1)$, must be a linear combination of the basis $1, \theta, \ldots, \theta^{n-1}$, and hence is in the space in (5.4.8). So we have shown Closure Axiom.

Secondly, to show that the space in (5.4.8) is a field, we only need to show that the space does not contain zero-divisors. To do so, we can use the linear independence relation in (5.4.7) and check that for $uv = 0$, either the scalars of $u$, or those of $v$, must all be zero, and hence either $u = 0$ or $v = 0$.

Finally, notice that since the spanning process uses $\#F$ elements of $F$ as scalars and the basis of $n$ elements, the space spanned has exactly $(\#F)^n$ elements.  □

**Definition 5.23: Finite Field $\mathbb{F}_{q^n}$** *Let $q$ be the number of elements in a finite field $F$. The finite field spanned by a basis of $n$ elements over $F$ is denoted by $\mathbb{F}_{q^n}$.*

**Theorem 5.9:** *Let $F$ be a finite field of $q$ elements and let $\mathbb{F}_{q^n}$ be a finite field spanned over $F$. Then*

*i) the characteristic of $\mathbb{F}_{q^n}$ is that of $F$;*

*ii) $F$ is a subfield of $\mathbb{F}_{q^n}$;*

*iii) any element $a \in \mathbb{F}_{q^n}$ satisfying $a^q = a$ if and only if $a \in F$.*

**Proof** Let $1, \theta, \theta^2, \ldots, \theta^{n-1}$ be a basis of $\mathbb{F}_{q^n}$ over $F$.

i) Let $\mathrm{char}(F)$ denote the characteristic of $F$. Then adding any element in $\mathbb{F}_{q^n}$ to itself $\mathrm{char}(F)$ times we obtain

$$\sum_{i=0}^{n-1} \mathrm{char}(F) r_i \theta^i = \sum_{i=0}^{n-1} 0 \theta^i = 0.$$

Thus $\mathrm{char}(\mathbb{F}_{q^n}) = \mathrm{char}(F)$.

ii) Since the basis contain 1, using scalars in $F$, any element in $F$ is a linear combination of 1 and hence is a linear combination of the basis.

iii) ($\Leftarrow$) Consider the subfield $F = \{0\} \cup F^*$ where $F^*$ is a multiplicative group of the non-zero elements. So for any $a \in F$, either $a = 0$ or $a \in F^*$. The former case satisfies $a^q = a$ trivially. For the latter case, by Lagrange's Theorem (Corollary 5.2), $\mathrm{ord}(a) | \# F^* = q - 1$ and therefore $a^{q-1} = 1$. So $a^q = a$ is also satisfied.

($\Rightarrow$) Any $a \in \mathbb{F}_{q^n}$ satisfying $a^q = a$ must be a root of polynomial $x^q - x = 0$. This polynomial has degree $q$ and therefore has at most $q$ roots in $\mathbb{F}_{q^n}$ including 0. By (ii), $F$ is a subfield of $\mathbb{F}_{q^n}$, which already contains all the roots of $x^q - x = 0$. No other elements of $\mathbb{F}_{q^n}$ can be a root of $x^q - x$.  $\square$

In our course of spanning the field $\mathbb{F}_{q^n}$ over a field $F$ of $q$ elements, we have never assumed or required that $q$ be a prime number, that is, we have not assumed or required that $F$ be a prime field. The following theorem provides the relationship between $F$ and field $\mathbb{F}_{q^n}$ spanned over $F$ and stipulates the nature of $q$.

**Theorem 5.10: Subfield Criterion** *Let $p$ be a prime number. Then $F$ is a subfield of $\mathbb{F}_{p^n}$ if and only if $F$ has $p^m$ elements for $m$ being a positive divisor of $n$.*

**Proof** ($\Rightarrow$) Let $F$ be a subfield of $\mathbb{F}_{p^n}$. $F = \mathbb{F}_p$ or $F = \mathbb{F}_{p^n}$ are the two trivial cases. Let $F$ be a proper subfield of $\mathbb{F}_{p^n}$ other than $\mathbb{F}_p$. By Theorem 5.9(i), $\mathbb{F}_{p^n}$ has characteristic $p$. Consequently $F$ must also have characteristic $p$. So $F$ contains $\mathbb{F}_p$ as a subfield and is spanned over $\mathbb{F}_p$ by a basis of $m$ elements for some $m$ with $1 \leq m \leq n$. We only need to show $m | n$. The two multiplicative groups $\mathbb{F}_{p^n}^*$ and $F^*$ have $p^n - 1$ and $p^m - 1$ elements, respectively. Since the latter is a subgroup of the former, by Lagrange's Theorem (Theorem 5.1), $p^m - 1 | p^n - 1$. This is only possible if $m | n$.

($\Leftarrow$) Let $m$ be a positive proper divisor of $n$ and let $F$ be a field of $p^m$ elements. Since $n/m$ is a positive integer, using a degree-$(n/m)$ irreducible polynomial over $F$ we can span a field of $(p^m)^{n/m} = p^n$ elements. Denote by $\mathbb{F}_{p^n}$ the spanned field, by Theorem 5.9(ii), $F$ is a subfield of $\mathbb{F}_{p^n}$.  $\square$

Let $f(x)$ be any degree-$n$ irreducible polynomial over $\mathbb{F}_p$. Reviewing Theorem 5.6, we now know $\mathbb{F}_{p^n}$ is isomorphic to $\mathbb{F}_p[x]_f$. Even though two isomorphic fields should be viewed without essential difference, one can be much easier to work with than the other. Indeed, the ease of proving the Subfield Criterion Theorem for $\mathbb{F}_{p^n}$ provides such a clear evidence. The following example provides another evidence.

**Example 5.19: Field $\mathbb{F}_{2^8}$** We have seen that $\mathbb{F}_2[x]_{x^8+x^4+x^3+x+1}$ (in Example 5.18) is the set of all polynomials modulo the irreducible polynomial $x^8 + x^4 + x^3 + x + 1$ over $\mathbb{F}_2$ and has $2^8$ elements. Now we know that $\mathbb{F}_{2^8}$ is also a field of $2^8$ elements and can be represented by the following space

$$\{b_7\theta^7 + b_6\theta^6 + b_5\theta^5 + b_4\theta^4 + b_3\theta^3 + b_2\theta^2 + b_1\theta + b_0\}$$

where $\theta$ is a root of (e.g.) the equation $x^8 + x^4 + x^3 + x + 1 = 0$, and the scalars $b_7, b_6, b_5, b_4, b_3, b_2, b_1, b_0 \in \mathbb{F}_2$. Clearly, these two fields are isomorphic; in particular, we can also use a byte to represent an element in the latter representation of $\mathbb{F}_{2^8}$.

In Example 5.18 we mentioned that multiplication in $\mathbb{F}_2[x]_{x^8+x^4+x^3+x+1}$ is a bit complicated and needs modulo polynomial which requires the Euclid algorithm for polynomial division. Multiplication in $\mathbb{F}_{2^8}$ spanned from polynomial basis can be easier: straightforward multiplying two elements and representing any resultant terms with $\theta^i$ for $i > 7$ using a linear combination of the basis $1, \theta, \ldots, \theta^7$.

For example, let us compute '57' $\cdot$ '83', or

$$(\theta^6 + \theta^4 + \theta^2 + \theta + 1) \cdot (\theta^7 + \theta + 1) = \theta^{13} + \theta^{11} + \theta^9 + \theta^8 + \theta^6 + \theta^5 + \theta^4 + \theta^3 + 1.$$

Since

$$\theta^8 + \theta^4 + \theta^3 + \theta + 1 = 0,$$

we have the following linear combinations (notice $-1 = 1$ in $\mathbb{F}_2$):

$$\theta^8 = \theta^4 + \theta^3 + \theta + 1,$$
$$\theta^9 = \theta^5 + \theta^4 + \theta^2 + \theta,$$
$$\theta^{11} = \theta^7 + \theta^6 + \theta^4 + \theta^3,$$
$$\theta^{13} = \theta^9 + \theta^8 + \theta^6 + \theta^5.$$

Thus,

$$\theta^{13} + \theta^{11} + \theta^9 + \theta^8 + \theta^6 + \theta^5 + \theta^4 + \theta^3 + 1 = \theta^7 + \theta^6 + 1.$$

That is, we have '57' $\cdot$ '83' = 'C1'. $\qquad\square$

We now provide a remark as a summary on our study of finite fields.

**Remark 5.2:** *We have studied two methods for constructing finite fields: field modulo an irreducible polynomial (§5.4.2) and field spanned from a polynomial basis (§5.4.3). In our study of finite fields we have used $\mathbb{F}_q$ to denote a field of the latter construction. However, under isomorphism, two fields of the same number of elements can be viewed without difference. Therefore from now on, we will denote by $\mathbb{F}_q$ any finite field of $q$ elements where $q$ is a prime power.* $\qquad\square$

## 5.4.4   Primitive Roots

We asserted in §4.5 that the complete factorization of $n - 1$ provides a piece of "internal information" (i.e., auxiliary input for verifying a problem in $\mathcal{NP}$) for answering whether $n$ is prime with an efficient deterministic algorithm. Now with the knowledge of finite fields, that assertion can be easily proved.

**Theorem 5.11:** *The multiplicative group* $(\mathbb{F}_{p^n})^*$ *of field* $\mathbb{F}_{p^n}$ *is cyclic.*

**Proof** By Theorem 5.9(iii), the entire roots of polynomial $x^{p^n-1} - 1 = 0$ forms $(\mathbb{F}_{p^n})^*$. However, the entire roots of this polynomial are the $p^n - 1$ distinct (non-trivial) roots of 1, spread over the unity circle. So there exists a $(p^n - 1)$-th root of 1, which generates the group $(\mathbb{F}_{p^n})^*$. Hence $(\mathbb{F}_{p^n})^*$ is cyclic. □

**Definition 5.24: Primitive Root** *A multiplicative generator of the group* $(\mathbb{F}_{p^n})^*$ *is called a primitive root of field* $\mathbb{F}_{p^n}$.

**Theorem 5.12:** *Let* $n$ *be a positive integer with* $n - 1 = r_1 r_2 \cdots r_k$ *as the complete prime factorization of* $n-1$ *(some of the prime factors may repeat). Then* $n$ *is prime if and only if there exists a positive integer* $a < n$ *such that* $a^{n-1} \equiv 1 \pmod{n}$ *and* $a^{(n-1)/r_i} \not\equiv 1 \pmod{n}$ *for* $i = 1, 2, \ldots, k$.

**Proof** ($\Rightarrow$) If $n$ is prime, then by Theorem 5.11, the group $(\mathbb{F}_n)^*$ is cyclic and has a generator which is an $(n-1)$-th root of 1. Denoting by $a$ this root, then $a$ satisfies the conditions in the theorem statement.

($\Leftarrow$) Let integer $a < n$ satisfy the conditions in the theorem statement. Then $a, a^2, \ldots, a^{n-1}$ are solutions of $x^{n-1} - 1 \equiv 0 \pmod{n}$. For any $1 \leq i < j \leq n - 1$, it is necessary $a^i \not\equiv a^j \pmod{n}$. Suppose otherwise $a^{j-i} \equiv 1 \pmod{n}$ for some $i, j$ with $0 < j - i < n - 1$; then by Definition 5.9 $\mathrm{ord}(a)|j - i|n - 1$, contradicting to the conditions in the theorem statement. Now we know that $\langle a \rangle$ is a multiplicative group of $n - 1$ elements (multiplication modulo $n$). This group can contain at most $\phi(n)$ elements. So $\phi(n) = n - 1$. Hence $n$ is prime by definition of Euler's function (Definition 5.11). □

Theorem 5.12 suggests an efficient algorithm for finding a primitive root modulo a prime $p$, i.e., a generator of the group $\mathbb{Z}_p^*$. The algorithm is specified in Alg 5.1.

By Theorem 5.2(4), we know that in the group $\mathbb{Z}_p^*$ there are exactly $\phi(p - 1)$ elements of order $p - 1$, and these elements are generators of the group. Therefore Alg 5.1 is expected to terminate in

$$\frac{p-1}{\phi(p-1)} < 6 \log \log p - 1$$

(see e.g., page 65 of [200]) steps of recursive calls. Since the number of prime factors of $p - 1$ is bounded by $\log p$, the time complexity of the algorithm is bounded by $O_B((\log p)^4 \log \log p)$.

**Algorithm 5.1:** Random Primitive Root Modulo Prime

INPUT       $p$: a prime; $q_1, q_2, \ldots, q_k$: all prime factors of $p - 1$;
OUTPUT     $g$: a random primitive root modulo $p$.

PrimitiveRoot$(p, q_1, q_2, \ldots, q_k)$

  1. pick $g \in_U [2, p - 1)$;

  2. for ( $i = 1$, $i{+}{+}$, $k$ ) do
      if ( $g^{(p-1)/q_i} \equiv 1 \pmod{p}$ ) return( PrimitiveRoot$(p, q_1, q_2, \ldots, q_k)$ );

  3. return( $g$ ).

## 5.5  Group Constructed Using Points on an Elliptic Curve

A class of groups which are very important to modern cryptography is those constructed by points on **elliptic curves**. Miller [205] and Koblitz [168] originally suggest to use elliptic curve groups for realizing public-key cryptography.

Elliptic curves for cryptography are defined over finite algebraic structures such as finite fields. For ease of exposition, let us confine ourselves to the easy case of prime fields $\mathbb{F}_p$ of characteristic $p > 3$. Such a curve is the set of geometric solutions $P = (x, y)$ to an equation of the following form

$$E : y^2 = x^3 + ax + b \pmod{p}. \tag{5.5.1}$$

where $a$ and $b$ are constants in $\mathbb{F}_p$ $(p > 3)$ satisfying $4a^3 + 27b^2 \not\equiv 0 \pmod{p}$.[a] To have the points on $E$ to form a group, an extra point denoted by $\mathcal{O}$ is included. This extra point is called the **point at infinity** and can be formulated as

$$\mathcal{O} = (x, \infty).$$

So for the group format, we write

$$E = \{ P = (x, y) \mid x, y \in \mathbb{F}_p \text{ solved from } (5.5.1) \} \cup \{\mathcal{O}\}. \tag{5.5.2}$$

This set of points form a group under a group operation which is conventionally written additively using the notation  "$+$" . We will define the operation in a moment.

---

[a]Reason to be given after Definition 5.25.

Denote by $f(x)$ the cubic polynomial in the right-hand side of (5.5.1). If $f(x)$ is reducible over $\mathbb{F}_p$ then for $\xi \in \mathbb{F}_p$ being a zero of $f(x)$ (i.e. $f(\xi) \equiv 0 \pmod{p}$), point $(\xi, 0) \in E$. We will see in a moment that these points have order 2 under the group operation "+" . Since $f(x)$ is a cubic polynomial, there are at most three such points (either 1 or 3 depending on the reducibility of $f(x)$ over $\mathbb{F}_p$; answer why by doing Ex 5.13).

All other points apart form $\mathcal{O}$ are made from $\eta \in \mathbb{F}_p$ such that $f(\eta) \not\equiv 0 \pmod{p}$ is a quadratic residue element in $\mathbb{F}_p$ (i.e., a square number modulo $p$, see §6.5). In such cases, for each such $\eta$, there are two distinct solutions for $y$ (every quadratic residue element in $\mathbb{F}_p$ has two square roots modulo $p$, see Corollary 6.2). Since $f(\eta)$ is a constant, the two square roots will be $\sqrt{f(\eta)}$ and $-\sqrt{f(\eta)}$. Thus, we can denote by $(\eta, \sqrt{f(\eta)})$ and $(\eta, -\sqrt{f(\eta)})$ such two points of solutions.

To this end we know that the points on the curve $E(\mathbb{F}_p)$ are $\mathcal{O}$, $(\xi, 0)$, $(\eta, \sqrt{f(\eta)})$ and $(\eta, -\sqrt{f(\eta)})$ for all $\xi$, $\eta$ in $\mathbb{F}_q$ satisfying $f(\xi) \equiv 0 \pmod{p}$ and $f(\eta)$ being a quadratic residue in $\mathbb{F}_q$.

## 5.5.1  The Group Operation

The set $E$ defined in (5.5.2) forms an abelian group under the operation "+" defined as follows.

**Definition 5.25: Elliptic Curve Group Operation ("tangent and chord method")**    *Let $P, Q \in E$, $\ell$ be the line containing $P$ and $Q$ (tangent line to $E$ if $P = Q$), and $R$, the third point of intersection of $\ell$ with $E$. Let $\ell'$ be the line connecting $R$ and $\mathcal{O}$. Then $P$ "+" $Q$ is the point such that $\ell'$ intersects $E$ at $R$, $\mathcal{O}$ and $P$ "+" $Q$.*

For the moment let us suppose that under Definition 5.25, $(E, "+")$ does form a group. We should first explain why we have required the coefficients of the cubic polynomial in (5.5.1) to satisfy $4a^3 + 27b^2 \not\equiv 0 \pmod{p}$. Notice that

$$\Delta = -4a^3 - 27b^2$$

is the discriminant of the cubic polynomial $f(x) = x^3 + ax + b$. If $\Delta \equiv 0 \pmod{p}$ then $f(x) \equiv 0 \pmod{p}$ has at least a double zero $X$ (root which makes $f(X) \equiv 0 \pmod{p}$) and clearly $(X, 0)$ is on $E$. For $E(x, y) = y^2 - x^3 - ax - b = 0$, this point satisfies

$$\frac{\partial E}{\partial y} = 2y \Big|_{y=0} = \frac{\partial E}{\partial x} \Big|_{x=X} = 0.$$

That is, $(X, 0)$ is a singular point at which there is no definition for a real tangent value. With the tangent-and-chord operation failing at the singular point $(X, 0)$, $E$ containing this point cannot be a group.

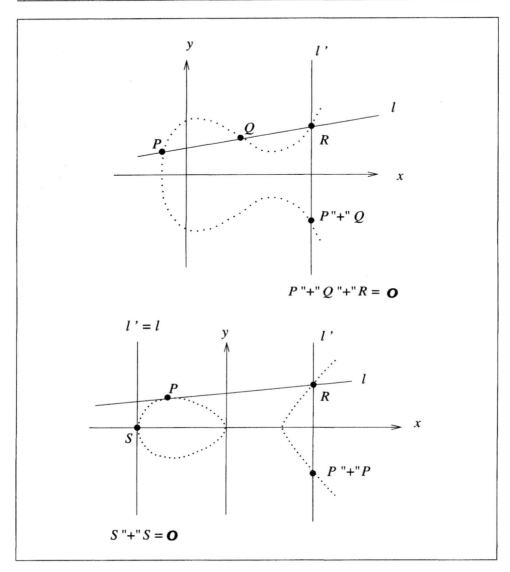

**Figure 5.1.** Elliptic Curve Group Operation

Fig 5.1 illustrates the tangent-and-chord operation. The top curve is the case of $\Delta < 0$ (the cubic polynomial has only one real root) and the lower, $\Delta > 0$.

Now let us show that $(E, \text{ "+" })$ does form a group under the tangent-and-chord operation.

First, for any $P = (X, Y) \in E$, let us apply Definition 5.25 to a special case of $Q$ being $\mathcal{O}$ (since we have included $\mathcal{O}$ in $E$). Line $\ell$ intersecting $P$ and $\mathcal{O}$ is

$$\ell : x = X.$$

Since $P \in E$ means $f(X) = X^3 + aX + b \pmod{p}$ being a quadratic residue in $\mathbb{F}_p$, therefore $-Y$ is the other solution to $y^2 = f(X)$ (i.e., the other square root of $f(X)$ modulo $p$). That is, $\ell$ also intersects point $R = (X, -Y) \in E$. Clearly, because $\ell' = \ell$, it intersects the same three points on $E$ as $\ell$ does. By Definition 5.25, we obtain

$$P = P \text{ "+" } \mathcal{O}$$

for any $P \in E$. Moreover, for all $(x, y) \in E$, we have also derived

$$(x, y) \text{ "+" } (x, -y) = \mathcal{O}.$$

By denoting $(x, -y) = \text{ "} - \text{"}(x, y)$, we see that point $\mathcal{O}$ behaves exactly as the identity element under the operation "+" . Therefore we have obtained Identity Axiom and Inverse Axiom for $(E, \text{ "+" })$.

A special case of this special case is $y_1 = -y_2 = 0$. This is the case of $P = \text{ "} - \text{"} P$ (point $S$ on the lower curve in Fig 5.1). At this doubly special point we have $P \text{ "+" } P = \mathcal{O}$. That is, $P$ is an order-2 element. We have mentioned this special element earlier: it is a solution of $y^2 = f(x) \equiv 0 \pmod{p}$. Such special points only exist when $f(x)$ has zeros in $\mathbb{F}_p$, i.e., when $f(x)$ is reducible over $\mathbb{F}_p$.

Now let us consider the general case of $\ell$ being a non-vertical line. The formula for $\ell$ is

$$\ell : y - y_1 = \lambda(x - x_1) \tag{5.5.3}$$

where

$$\lambda = \begin{cases} \dfrac{y_1 - y_2}{x_1 - x_2} & \text{if } x_1 \neq x_2 \\[2mm] \dfrac{3x_1^2 + a}{2y_1} & \text{if } x_1 = x_2 \text{ and } y_1 = y_2 \neq 0 \end{cases} \tag{5.5.4}$$

is the slope of the line $\ell$. Since $\ell$ will meet $R = (x_3, y_3)$ on the curve, we can use formulae (5.5.1) and (5.5.3) to find the point $R$. The $x$ part of the point $R$ is a solution of

$$\ell \cap E : [\lambda(x - x_1) + y_1]^2 - (x^3 + ax + b) = 0$$

Notice that $\ell \cap E$ is a cubic polynomial which has solutions $x_1$, $x_2$, $x_3$, we can also write it as

$$\ell \cap E : c(x - x_1)(x - x_2)(x - x_3) = 0$$

where $c$ is some constant. Comparing the coefficients in these two ways of writing $\ell \cap E$ (the coefficients of $x^3$ and $x^2$) we obtain $c = -1$ and

$$x_3 = \lambda^2 - x_1 - x_2.$$

Finally, by Definition 5.25, and the fact that $P$ "+" $Q$ = " $-$ "$R$, we obtain the coordinates of the point $P$ "+" $Q$ as

$$x_3 = \lambda^2 - x_1 - x_2$$
$$y_3 = \lambda(x_1 - x_3) - y_1 \tag{5.5.5}$$

where $\lambda$ is defined in (5.5.4). We notice that because line $\ell$ intersects $P, Q$ and $R$, $R$ must be on the curve, and consequently, $P$ "+" $Q$ = " $-$ "$R$ must also be on the curve. Thus, we have obtained Closure Axiom for $(E,$ "+" $)$.

Associativity Axiom can be verified step by step applying the formulae (5.5.5). Because of the tedious nature, we shall not conduct the demonstration here and leave it as exercise for the reader.

To this end, we know that $(E,$ "+" $)$ is indeed a group. Moreover, it is clearly an abelian group.

**Example 5.20:** *The equation $E : y^2 = x^3 + 6x + 4$ over $\mathbb{F}_7$ defines an elliptic curve group since $4 \times 6^3 + 27 \times 4^2 \equiv 1 \neq 0 \pmod 7$. The following points are on $E(\mathbb{F}_7)$:*

$$E(\mathbb{F}_7) = \{\mathcal{O}, (0,2), (0,5), (1,2), (1,5), (3,0), (4,1), (4,6), (6,2), (6,5)\}.$$

*Some applications of the addition law are $(3,0)$ "+" $(3,0) = \mathcal{O}$, $(3,0)$ "+" $(4,1) = (1,2)$ and $(1,2)$ "+" $(1,2) = (0,2)$. The reader may check, e.g., $(1,2)$, is a generator of the group. Therefore $E(\mathbb{F}_7)$ is cyclic.* □

We have introduced elliptic curve groups for the simplest case of $E$ defined over a prime field $\mathbb{F}_p$ with $p > 3$. In general, $E$ can be defined over $\mathbb{F}_q$ where $q$ is a prime power. The cases for $p = 2$ and 3 are a little more complex and need to use curve equations other than (5.5.1). This is because with (5.5.1), we will have

$$\frac{\partial E}{\partial y} = 2y \equiv 0 \pmod 2$$

for characteristic 2, and

$$\frac{\partial E}{\partial x} = 3x^2 + a \equiv a \pmod 3$$

for characteristic 3. These cases cause degeneration for the tangent-and-chord group operation because the "tangent line" at any point will have a wrong slope value (i.e., $\lambda$ given by the second case of (5.5.4) is wrong). However, if different equations other than (5.5.1) are used, the degeneration can be avoided while the working principle for these two cases of field characteristic will remain the same as the simple case we have studied. We recommend [274] to more interested readers for further study.

## 5.5.2   Point Multiplication

From now on, we shall drop the quotation mark from the operation "$+$" and "$-$".

For $m$ being an integer and $P \in E$, we denote

$$[m]P = \begin{cases} \underbrace{P + P + \cdots + P}_{m} & \text{for } m > 0 \\ \mathcal{O} & \text{for } m = 0 \\ [-m] - P & \text{for } m < 0 \end{cases}$$

The computation of $[m]P$ (or a multiple number of the group operation in any additive group) is analogous to exponentiation in a multiplicative group and is given in Alg 5.2.

---

**Algorithm 5.2:** Point Multiplication for Elliptic Curve Element

INPUT       point $P \in E$; integer $m > 0$;
OUTPUT    $[m]P$.

EC_Multiply($P, m$)

1. if $m = 0$ return( $\mathcal{O}$ );

2. if $m \pmod 2 = 0$ return( EC_Multiply($P + P, m \div 2$) );
   (* $\div$ denotes division in integers, i.e., $m \div 2 = \lfloor m/2 \rfloor$ *)

3. return( $P + $ EC_Multiply($P + P, m \div 2,$ ) ).

---

For example, executing EC_Multiply($P, 14$), Alg 5.2 will invoke the following four recursive calls:

EC_Multiply($P, 14$)
$= \text{EC\_exp}(P + P, 7)$                                                   (in step 2)
$= [2]P + \text{EC\_Multiply}([2]P + [2]P, 3)$                    (in step 3)
$= [2]P + [4]P + \text{EC\_Multiply}([4]P + [4]P, 1)$         (in step 3)
$= [2]P + [4]P + [8]P + \text{EC\_Multiply}([8]P + [8]P, 0)$   (in step 3)
$= [2]P + [4]P + [8]P + \mathcal{O}$                                      (in step 1)

The result is $[14]P$.

Considering that $m \approx p$ and that the computations in (5.5.4) and (5.5.5) involve squaring and multiplying numbers of $p$'s magnitude, the time complexity of Alg 5.2 is $O_B((\log p)^3)$. We should notice that Alg 5.2 does not make use of any properties of the underlying field, and hence it is not an efficient realization, rather, it is only for the purpose of providing a succinct exposition for how to compute a point multiplication. Several point multiplication methods with implementation considerations for an improved efficiency, such as precomputations and making use of special field properties, can be found in, e.g., [36].

### 5.5.3   Elliptic Curve Discrete Logarithm Problem

To reverse the effect of a multiplication, that is, given a pair of points $(P, [m]P)$, find the integer $m$, is a problem with a very different nature from that of point multiplication. The problem is called **elliptic-curve discrete logarithm problem**,, or **ECDLP** for short. It is widely believed that the ECDLP is difficult to solve (computationally infeasible) when the point $P$ has a large prime order.

In general, the order of an arbitrary point in a group is proportionally related to the order of the group. Coarsely estimated, a curve defined over a field $\mathbb{F}_q$ ($q$ is a prime power) should have roughly $q$ points since roughly $q/2$ cases of $x^3 + ax + b \in \mathbb{F}_q$ yield quadratic residues in $\mathbb{F}_q$ (if $x^3 + ax + b$ is a permutation over $\mathbb{F}_q$ then precisely $(q-1)/2$ of such values are quadratic residues in the even order group $\mathbb{F}_q^*$) and each quadratic residue case solves two $y$ values in $\mathbb{F}_q$. Hasse's theorem (an important theorem in elliptic curves over finite fields) states a more precise estimate:

$$\#E(\mathbb{F}_q) = q + 1 - t \text{ with } -2\sqrt{q} \le t \le 2\sqrt{q}. \tag{5.5.6}$$

Here $t$ is called the "trace of Frobenious" at $q$. For a curve defined over $\mathbb{F}_q$ (general case), it is very easy to devise a large prime $r$ of size slightly less than $q$ such that $E(\mathbb{F}_q)$ contains a subgroup of order $r$. Thus, the best known algorithm for solving the ECDLP has a time complexity expression $O(\sqrt{r}) \approx O(\sqrt{q})$ (because $|r| \approx |q|$). This is more-or-less a result of a bruteforce search method helped with the birthday paradox (see §3.6). Such a result applies to discrete logarithm problems in any abelian group of orders roughly $q$. Indeed, Pollard's $\lambda$-method (see §3.6.1) can easily be modified to the case for the ECDLP. Therefore, we can say that a solution with complexity $O(\sqrt{q})$ for the ECDLP is *not* a solution at all due to its irrelevance to the group structure in question.

In the case of the discrete logarithm problem in a finite field (to be formally defined in Definition 8.2), there exist algorithmic methods called index calculus for solving the problem. The time complexity of an index calculus method for discrete logarithm in a finite field $\mathbb{F}_q$ has a subexponential expression sub_exp($q$) given in (8.4.2).

The complexity expression $O(\sqrt{q})$ is exponential in the size of $q$. For the same input, $O(\sqrt{q})$ as a function of large quantity grows much faster than the subexponential function sub_exp$(q)$ does. This means that the underlying field for the ECDLP can have a size much smaller than that of a finite field on which an ordinary discrete logarithm problem is based, while both requiring similar lengths of time for solving the respective discrete logarithm problems. For the ECDLP, the common sense is to set $q \approx 2^{160}$. This allows a $2^{80}$-level difficulty of countering bruteforce search methods. To obtain a similar difficulty of the discrete logarithm problem in a finite field, the subexponential expression (8.4.2) will require $q$ to have a magnitude at the level of $2^{1000}$. We should further notice that the progress of the hardware computing technology mean that $q$ should grow accordingly. With the drastically different asymptotic behaviors of $\sqrt{q}$ and sub_exp$(q)$, $q$ for the elliptic curve case can grow much slower than that for the finite field case.

The computational infeasibility maintained by the ECDLP over a relatively small field means that elliptic curve groups have a good application in the realization of more efficient public-key cryptographic systems. Since public-key cryptography is also called asymmetric cryptography, meaning encryption with a public key is easy and decryption without the correct private key is hard. Thus we may say that public-key cryptography based on elliptic curve group is more asymmetric than that based on finite fields.

However, we should provide an early warning that there are weak cases in elliptic curves. For weak cases an underlying field of magnitude $2^{160}$ will be too small. We will see such a weak case, and surprisingly, its positive applications in Chapter 13.

## 5.6 Chapter Summary

After our study of abstract algebraic structure in this chapter we now know that algebraic structures such as group, ring, and field have finite versions of arithmetic operations. For example, we have seen that for any natural number $n$, all non-negative integers up to $n$ binary bits can form a finite field of $2^n$ elements, i.e., the structure is closed in addition and multiplication (hence also closed in subtraction, division, and all other algebraic operations such as exponentiation, rooting, etc., since they are all derived from the most basic addition and multiplication operations). Algebraic structures with the closure property in finite spaces provide the basic building blocks for constructing cryptographic algorithms and protocols.

Our course is not only self-contained for reference purpose for most readers, but also accompanied by plenty of digestion and explanation material so that an in-depth understanding of these subjects can be achieved by more mathematically inclined readers. A more comprehensive study of abstract algebraic topics can be found in [179] and for elliptic curves can be found in e.g., [274].

# Exercises

5.1 In Example 5.2(5) we have shown that Fermat($n$) is a subgroup of $\mathbb{Z}_n^*$. Show that for $n$ being an odd composite integer, #Fermat($n$) $<$ #$\mathbb{Z}_n^*/2$. Argue that this inequality is the basis for the working principle of the probabilistic primality test Alg 4.5.

5.2 Show that DIV3 $= \{0\} \cup 3\,\mathbb{N}$ (set DIV3 is defined in §4.3, Example 4.1).

5.3 In group $\mathbb{Z}_{11}^*$: (i) how many generators in it? (ii) Find all the generators of it. (iii) Find all subgroups of it.

5.4 Let $n$ be an odd composite and is not a power of a prime. Does the group $\mathbb{Z}_n^*$ have a generator?

5.5 Use "chalk-marking-on-toothed-wheels" method given in Example 5.10 to confirm that the largest order elements in group $\mathbb{Z}_{35}^*$ is 12, and the order of any elements must divide 12.

5.6 Let $n = pq$ with $p$, $q$ being odd distinct primes. Prove the generalization case for the preceding problem, that is: (i) the largest order of elements in $\mathbb{Z}_n^*$ is $\lambda(n) = \mathrm{lcm}(p - 1, q - 1)$; (ii) the order of every element in $\mathbb{Z}_n^*$ divides $\lambda(n)$.

5.7 Why must the characteristic of a finite ring or field be prime?

5.8 Using long division for polynomials as a subroutine, construct the extended Euclid algorithm for polynomials.

5.9 Let $n$ be any natural number. Construct a finite field of $n$-bit integers $\{0, 1\}^n$. Hint: map between $\mathbb{F}_2[x]_f$ and $\{0, 1\}^n$ using the mapping method given in Example 5.17, here $f$ is a degree-$n$ polynomial over $\mathbb{F}_2$.

5.10 How many isomorphic subfields does $\mathbb{F}_{2^{36}}$ have? Is $\mathbb{F}_{2^8}$ one of them?

5.11 Why is a group generator also called a primitive root?

5.12 For an odd integer $p$, knowing the complete factorization of $p-1$, construct an efficient algorithm to answer the question "Is $p$ prime?" with the correctness probability 1 (not using Prime_Test($p$) since it cannot achieve the correctness probability 1, also not using trial division since it is not efficient).

5.13 For an elliptic curve $E : y^2 = x^3 + ax + b$ over $\mathbb{F}_p$ with $p > 3$, show that $E(\mathbb{F}_p)$ has no order-2 point if $f(x) = x^3 + ax + b$ is irreducible over $\mathbb{F}_p$ and has 1 or 3 such points otherwise.

5.14 Confirm Associativity Axiom for group $(E, \text{ "+" })$ defined in §5.5.1.

5.15 Confirm that the point $(1, 2)$ in Example 5.20 is a group generator.

# Chapter 6

# NUMBER THEORY

## 6.1 Introduction

Problems such as factorization or primality of large integers, root extraction, solution to simultaneous equations modulo different moduli, etc., are among the frequently used ingredients in modern cryptography. They are also fascinating topics in the theory of numbers. In this chapter we study some basic facts and algorithms in number theory, which have important relevance to modern cryptography.

### 6.1.1 Chapter Outline

§6.2 introduces the basic notions and operations of congruences and residue classes. §6.3 introduces Euler's phi function. §6.4 shows a unified view of the theorems of Fermat, Euler and Lagrange. §6.5 introduces the notion of quadratic residues. §6.6 introduces algorithms for computing square roots modulo an integer. Finally, §6.7 introduces the Blum integers.

## 6.2 Congruences and Residue Classes

In §4.3.2.5 we have defined congruence system modulo a positive integer $n > 1$ and studied a few properties of such systems. Here we shall study a few more facts of the congruence systems.

**Theorem 6.1:** *For integer $n > 1$, the relation of congruence* (mod $n$) *is reflexive, symmetric and transitive. That is, for every $a, b, c \in \mathbb{Z}$,*

  *i)* $a \equiv a \pmod{n}$;

  *ii) If $a \equiv b \pmod{n}$, then $b \equiv a \pmod{n}$;*

  *iii) If $a \equiv b \pmod{n}$ and $b \equiv c \pmod{n}$, then $a \equiv c \pmod{n}$.* $\square$

A relation having the three properties in Theorem 6.1 is called an **equivalence relation**. It is well known that an equivalence relation over a set partitions the set into **equivalence classes**. Let us denote by "$\equiv_n$" the equivalence relation of congruence modulo $n$. This relation is defined over the set $\mathbb{Z}$, and therefore it partitions $\mathbb{Z}$ into exactly $n$ equivalence classes, each class contains integers which are congruent to an integer modulo $n$. Let us denote these $n$ classes by

$$\overline{0}, \ \overline{1}, \ \ldots, \ \overline{n-1},$$

where

$$\overline{a} = \{\, x \in \mathbb{Z} \mid x \ (\text{mod } n) \equiv a \,\}. \tag{6.2.1}$$

We call each of them a **residue class** modulo $n$. Clearly, we can view

$$\mathbb{Z}_n = \{\, \overline{0}, \ \overline{1}, \ \ldots, \ \overline{n-1} \,\}. \tag{6.2.2}$$

On the other hand, if we consider $\mathbb{Z}$ as a (trivial) subset of $\mathbb{Z}$, then coset $n\mathbb{Z}$ (Definition 5.7 in §5.2.1) is the set all integers which are multiples of $n$, i.e.,

$$n\mathbb{Z} = \{0, \ \pm n, \ \pm 2n, \ \ldots \}. \tag{6.2.3}$$

Now consider quotient group (Definition 5.8 in §5.2.1) with addition as the group operation:

$$\mathbb{Z}/n\mathbb{Z} = \{\, x + n\mathbb{Z} \mid x \in \mathbb{Z} \,\}. \tag{6.2.4}$$

If we unfold (6.2.4) using $n\mathbb{Z}$ in (6.2.3), we have

$$
\begin{aligned}
\mathbb{Z}/n\mathbb{Z} \ &= \ \{\ x + n\mathbb{Z} \mid x \in \mathbb{Z} \ \} \\
&= \ \{\ 0 + \{\, 0, \ \pm n, \ \pm 2n, \ \ldots \}, \\
&\qquad 1 + \{\, 0, \ \pm n, \ \pm 2n, \ \ldots \}, \\
&\qquad 2 + \{\, 0, \ \pm n, \ \pm 2n, \ \ldots \}, \\
&\qquad \ldots, \\
&\qquad (n-1) + \{\, 0, \ \pm n, \ \pm 2n, \ \ldots \} \ \} \\
&= \ \{\ \{\, 0, \ \pm n, \ \pm 2n, \ \ldots \}, \\
&\qquad \{\, 1, \ \pm n + 1, \ \pm 2n + 1, \ \ldots \}, \\
&\qquad \{\, 2, \ \pm n + 2, \ \pm 2n + 2, \ \ldots \}, \\
&\qquad \ldots, \\
&\qquad \{\, (n-1), \ \pm n + (n-1), \ \pm 2n + (n-1), \ \ldots \} \ \}.
\end{aligned}
\tag{6.2.5}
$$

There are only $n$ distinct elements in the structure (6.2.5). No more case is possible. For example

$$n + \{0, \ \pm n, \ \pm 2n, \ \ldots \} = \{0, \ \pm n, \ \pm 2n, \ \ldots \},$$

and

$$(n+1) + \{0, \ \pm n, \ \pm 2n, \ \ldots \} = \{1, \ \pm n + 1, \ \pm 2n + 1, \ \ldots \},$$

and so on. Comparing (6.2.2) and (6.2.5) with noticing the definition of $\bar{a}$ in (6.2.1), we now know exactly that for $n > 1$:

$$\mathbb{Z}_n = \mathbb{Z}/n\mathbb{Z}.$$

$\mathbb{Z}/n\mathbb{Z}$ is the standard notation (in fact, the definition) for the residue classes modulo $n$, although for presentation convenience, in this book we will always use the short notation $\mathbb{Z}_n$ in place of $\mathbb{Z}/n\mathbb{Z}$.

**Theorem 6.2:** *For any $a, b \in \mathbb{Z}$, define addition and multiplication between the residue classes $\bar{a}$ and $\bar{b}$ by*

$$\bar{a} + \bar{b} = \overline{a+b}, \qquad \bar{a} \cdot \bar{b} = \overline{ab}.$$

*Then for any $n > 1$, the mapping $f : \mathbb{Z} \mapsto \mathbb{Z}_n$ defined by " (mod $n$)" is a homomorphism from $\mathbb{Z}$ onto $\mathbb{Z}_n$.* $\square$

## 6.2.1   Congruent Properties for Arithmetic in $\mathbb{Z}_n$

The homomorphism from $\mathbb{Z}$ onto $\mathbb{Z}_n$ means that arithmetic in $\mathbb{Z}_n$ (arithmetic modulo $n$) inheres the properties of arithmetic in $\mathbb{Z}$, as shown in the following theorem.

**Theorem 6.3:** *For integer $n > 1$, if $a \equiv b \pmod{n}$ and $c \equiv d \pmod{n}$, then $a \pm c \equiv b \pm d \pmod{n}$ and $ac \equiv bd \pmod{n}$.*

Although the statements in this theorem hold trivially as an immediate result of the homomorphic relationship between $\mathbb{Z}$ and $\mathbb{Z}_n$, we provide a proof which is based purely on using the properties of arithmetic in $\mathbb{Z}_n$.

**Proof** If $n|a - b$ and $n|c - d$ then $n|(a \pm c) - (b \pm d)$.

Also $n|(a - b)(c - d) = (ac - bd) - b(c - d) - d(a - b)$. So $n|(ac - bd)$. $\square$

The properties of the arithmetic in $\mathbb{Z}_n$ shown in Theorem 6.3 are called **congruent properties**, meaning performing the same calculation on both sides of an equation derives a new equation. However, Theorem 6.3 has left out division. Division in $\mathbb{Z}$ has the congruent property as follows:

$$\forall d \neq 0 : ad = bd \text{ implies } a = b. \tag{6.2.6}$$

The counterpart congruent property for division in $\mathbb{Z}_n$ will take a formula which is slightly different from (6.2.6). Before we find out what this formula is, let us provide an explanation on (6.2.6) in $\mathbb{Z}$. We may imagine that $\mathbb{Z}$ is the case of $\mathbb{Z}_n$ for $n = \infty$, and that $\infty$ is divisible by any integer and the resultant quotient is still $\infty$. Thus, we may further imagine that the first equation in (6.2.6) holds in terms of modulo $\infty$ while the second equation holds in terms of modulo $\infty/d$. Since $\infty/d = \infty$, the two equations in (6.2.6) take the same formula. This congruent property for division in $\mathbb{Z}$ is inhered into $\mathbb{Z}_n$ in the following formula.

**Theorem 6.4:** *For integer* $n > 1$ *and* $d \neq 0$, *if* $ad \equiv bd$ (mod $n$) *then* $a \equiv b$ (mod $\frac{n}{\gcd(d,n)}$).

**Proof** Denote $k = \gcd(d, n)$. Then $n|(ad - bd)$ implies $(n/k)|(d/k)(a - b)$. Since $\gcd(d/k, n/k) = 1$, we know $(n/k)|(k/k)(a - b)$ implies $(n/k)|(a - b)$.    □

To this end we know that the arithmetic in $\mathbb{Z}_n$ fully preserves the congruent properties of the arithmetic in $\mathbb{Z}$. Consequently, we have

**Corollary 6.1:** *If* $f(x)$ *is a polynomial over* $\mathbb{Z}$, *and* $a \equiv b$ (mod $n$) *for* $n > 1$, *then* $f(a) \equiv f(b)$ (mod $n$).    □

## 6.2.2   Solving Linear Congruence in $\mathbb{Z}_n$

In Theorem 4.2 (in §4.3.2.5) we have defined the multiplicative inverse modulo $n$ and shown that for an integer $a$ to have the multiplicative inverse modulo $n$, i.e., a unique number $x < n$ satisfying $ax \equiv 1$ (mod $n$), it is necessary and sufficient for $a$ to satisfy $\gcd(a, n) = 1$. The following theorem provides the condition for general case of solving linear congruence equation.

**Theorem 6.5:** *For integer* $n > 1$, *a necessary and sufficient condition that the congruence*

$$ax \equiv b \text{ (mod } n), \tag{6.2.7}$$

*be solvable is that* $\gcd(a, n)|b$.

**Proof** By Definition 4.4 (in §4.3.2.5), the congruence (6.2.7) is the linear equation

$$ax + kn = b, \tag{6.2.8}$$

for some integer $k$.

($\Rightarrow$) Let (6.2.8) hold. Since $\gcd(a, n)$ divides the left-hand side, it must divide the right-hand side.

($\Leftarrow$) For $a$ and $n$, using Extended Euclid Algorithm (Alg 4.2) we can compute

$$a\lambda + \mu n = \gcd(a, n).$$

Since $b/\gcd(a, n)$ is an integer, multiplying this integer to both sides, we obtain (6.2.8) or (6.2.7), where $x = \frac{\lambda b}{\gcd(a,n)}$ (mod $n$) is one solution.    □

It is easy to check that given solution $x$ for (6.2.7),

$$x + \frac{ni}{\gcd(a,n)} \text{ (mod } n) \quad \text{for } i = 0, 1, 2, \ldots, \gcd(a, n) - 1$$

are $\gcd(a, n)$ different solutions less than $n$. Clearly, $\gcd(a, n) = 1$ is the condition for the congruence (6.2.8) to have a unique solution less than $n$.

**Example 6.1:** Congruence

$$2x \equiv 5 \ (\text{mod } 10)$$

is unsolvable since $\gcd(2, 10) = 2 \nmid 5$. In fact, the left-hand side, $2x$, must be an even number, while the right-hand side, $10k + 5$, can only be an odd number, and so trying to solve this congruence is an attempt to equalize an even number to an odd number, which is of course impossible.

On the other hand, congruence

$$6x \equiv 18 \ (\text{mod } 36)$$

is solvable because $\gcd(6, 36)|18$. The six solutions are 3, 9, 15, 21, 27, and 33.   □

**Theorem 6.6:** *For integer $n > 1$, if $\gcd(a, n) = 1$, then $ai + b \not\equiv aj + b \ (\text{mod } n)$ for all $b, i, j$ such that $0 \leq i < j < n$.*

**Proof** Suppose on the contrary $ai + b \equiv aj + b \ (\text{mod } n)$. Then by Theorem 6.4 we have $i \equiv j \ (\text{mod } n)$, a contradiction to $0 \leq i < j < n$.   □

This property implies that for $a, n$ satisfying $\gcd(a, n) = 1$, $ai + b \ (\text{mod } n)$ $(i = 0, 1, \ldots, n-1)$ is a **complete residue system** modulo $n$, that is, the expression $ai + b \ (\text{mod } n)$ ranges through $\mathbb{Z}_n$ for $i$ ranging through $\mathbb{Z}_n$.

## 6.2.3   The Chinese Remainder Theorem

We have studied the condition for solving a single linear congruence in the form of (6.2.7). Often we will meet the problem of solving a system of simultaneous linear congruences with different moduli:

$$
\begin{aligned}
a_1 x &\equiv b_1 \ (\text{mod } n_1) \\
a_2 x &\equiv b_2 \ (\text{mod } n_2) \\
&\ \ \vdots \\
a_r x &\equiv b_r \ (\text{mod } n_r)
\end{aligned}
\tag{6.2.9}
$$

where $a_i, b_i \in \mathbb{Z}$ with $a_i \neq 0$ for $i = 1, 2, \ldots, r$.

For this system of congruences to be solvable it is clearly necessary for each congruence to be solvable. So for $i = 1, 2, \ldots, r$ and denoting

$$d_i = \gcd(a_i, n_i),$$

by Theorem 6.5, it is necessary $d_i | b_i$. With this being the case, the congruent properties for multiplication (Theorem 6.3) and for division (Theorem 6.4) allow us to transform the system (6.2.9) into the following linear congruence system which is equivalent to but simpler than the system (6.2.9):

$$x \equiv c_1 \pmod{m_1}$$
$$x \equiv c_2 \pmod{m_2}$$

. (6.2.10)

.

.

$$x \equiv c_r \pmod{m_r}$$

where for $i = 1, 2, \ldots, r$:

$$m_i = n_i / d_i$$

and

$$c_i = (b_i/d_i)(a_i/d_i)^{-1} \pmod{m_i}.$$

Notice that $(a_i/d_i)^{-1} \pmod{m_i}$ exists since $\gcd(a_i/d_i, \ m_i) = 1$ (review Theorem 4.2 in §4.3.2.5).

In linear algebra, the system (6.2.10) can be represented by the following vector-space version:

$$A\vec{X} = \vec{C} \tag{6.2.11}$$

where

$$A = \begin{pmatrix} \bar{1}_{m_1} & & & & \\ & \bar{1}_{m_2} & & & \\ & & \cdot & & \\ & & & \cdot & \\ & & & & \bar{1}_{m_r} \end{pmatrix}, \tag{6.2.12}$$

$$\vec{X} = \begin{pmatrix} x \\ x \\ \cdot \\ \cdot \\ \cdot \\ x \end{pmatrix}, \tag{6.2.13}$$

$$\vec{C} = \begin{pmatrix} c_1 \\ c_2 \\ \cdot \\ \cdot \\ \cdot \\ c_r \end{pmatrix}. \tag{6.2.14}$$

Notice that because the $i$-th equation (for $i = 1, 2, \ldots, r$) in the congruence system (6.2.10) holds modulo $m_i$, in the diagonal part of the the matrix $A$, $\bar{1}_{m_i}$ denotes the residue class 1 modulo $m_i$, that is,

$$\bar{1}_{m_i} = k_i m_i + 1 \tag{6.2.15}$$

for some integer $k_i$ $(i = 1, 2, \ldots, r)$. The blank part of the matrix $A$ represents 0 modulo respective modulus (i.e., zeros in the $i$ row are means zeros modulo $m_i$).

Thus, given any $r$-dimension vector $\vec{C}$, the problem of solving the system (6.2.10), or its vector-space version (6.2.11), boils down to that of identifying the diagonal matrix $A$, or in other words, finding the residue class 1 modulo $m_i$ as required in (6.2.15) for $i = 1, 2, \ldots, r$. We know from a fact in linear algebra that if the matrix $A$ exists, then because none of the elements in its diagonal line is zero, the matrix has the full rank $r$ and consequently, there *exists* a *unique* solution.

When the moduli in (6.2.10) are pairwise relatively prime to each other, it is not difficult to find a system of residue classes 1. This is according to the useful **Chinese Remainder Theorem (CRT)**.

**Theorem 6.7: Chinese Remainder Theorem** *For the linear congruence system (6.2.10), if* $\gcd(m_i, m_j) = 1$ *for* $1 \le i < j \le r$, *then there exists* $\bar{1}_{m_i}$ *satisfying*

$$\bar{1}_{m_i} \equiv 0 \;(\mathrm{mod}\; m_j). \tag{6.2.16}$$

*Consequently, there exists* $x \in \mathbb{Z}_M$ *as the unique solution to the system (6.2.10) where* $M = m_1 m_2 \cdots m_r$.

**Proof** We prove first the existence and then the uniqueness of the solution.

**Existence** For each $i = 1, 2, \ldots, r$, $\gcd(m_i, M/m_i) = 1$. By Theorem 4.2 (§4.3.2.5), there exists $y_i \in \mathbb{Z}_{m_i}$ satisfying

$$(M/m_i)y_i \equiv 1 \;(\mathrm{mod}\; m_i). \tag{6.2.17}$$

Moreover, for $j \ne i$, because $m_j | (M/m_i)$, we have

$$(M/m_i)y_i \equiv 0 \;(\mathrm{mod}\; m_j). \tag{6.2.18}$$

So $(M/m_i)y_i$ is exactly the number that we are looking for to play the role of $\bar{1}_{m_i}$. Let

$$x \leftarrow \sum_{i=1}^{r} \bar{1}_{m_i} c_i \;(\mathrm{mod}\; M). \tag{6.2.19}$$

Then $x$ is a solution to the system (6.2.10) and is a residue class modulo $M$.

**Uniqueness** View the linear system defined by (6.2.11), (6.2.12), (6.2.13) and (6.2.14) such that the elements of the matrix $A$ and those of the vector $\vec{C}$ are all in $\mathbb{Z}$ (i.e., they are all integers). Notice that in $\mathbb{Z}$

$$\det(A) = \bar{1}_{m_1} \bar{1}_{m_2} \cdots \bar{1}_{m_r} \ne 0. \tag{6.2.20}$$

This means that the $r$ columns (vectors) of the matrix $A$ form a basis for the $r$-dimension vector space $\underbrace{\mathbb{Z} \times \mathbb{Z} \times \cdots \times \mathbb{Z}}_{r}$ (this basis is similar to a so-called "natural basis" in linear algebra where the only non-zero element in any basis-vector is 1). Therefore, for any vector $\vec{C} \in \underbrace{\mathbb{Z} \times \mathbb{Z} \times \cdots \times \mathbb{Z}}_{r}$, the system (6.2.11) has a unique solution $\vec{X} \in \underbrace{\mathbb{Z} \times \mathbb{Z} \times \cdots \times \mathbb{Z}}_{r}$. We have seen in the existence part of the proof that the unique elements of $\vec{X}$ are given by (6.2.19).                                          □

The proof of Theorem 6.7 is constructive, that is, we have constructed an algorithm for finding the solution to the system (6.2.10). This algorithm is now specified in Alg 6.1.

---

**Algorithm 6.1:** Chinese Remainder

INPUT        integer tuple $(m_1, m_2, \ldots, m_r)$, pairwise relatively prime;
             integer tuple $(c_1 \pmod{m_1}, c_2 \pmod{m_2}, \ldots, c_r \pmod{m_r})$.
OUTPUT    integer $x < M = m_1 m_2 \cdots m_r$ satisfying the system (6.2.10).

1. $M \leftarrow m_1 m_2 \cdots m_r$;

2. for ( $i$ from 1 to $r$ ) do

    (a) $y_i \leftarrow (M/m_i)^{-1} \pmod{m_i}$; (* by Extended Euclid Algorithm *)

    (b) $\bar{1}_{m_i} \leftarrow y_i M/m_i$;

3. return( $\displaystyle\sum_{i=1}^{r} \bar{1}_{m_i} c_i \pmod{M}$ ).

---

In Alg 6.1, the only time-consuming part is in step 2(a) where a multiplicative inversion of a large number is computed. This can be done by applying the Extended Euclid Algorithm (Alg 4.2). Considering $m_i < M$ for $i = 1, 2, \ldots, r$, the time complexity of Alg 6.1 is $O_B(r(\log M)^2)$.

It is also easy to see the following results from Theorem 6.7:

i) every $x \in \mathbb{Z}_M$ yields a vector $\vec{C} \in \mathbb{Z}_{m_1} \times \mathbb{Z}_{m_2} \times \cdots \times \mathbb{Z}_{m_r}$; from (6.2.19) we can see that the elements in $\vec{C}$ are computed by (for $i = 1, 2, \ldots, r$)

$$c_i \leftarrow x \pmod{m_i};$$

ii) in particular, 0 and 1 in $\mathbb{Z}_M$ yield $\vec{0}$ and $\vec{1}$ in $\mathbb{Z}_{m_1} \times \mathbb{Z}_{m_2} \times \cdots \times \mathbb{Z}_{m_r}$, respectively;

iii) for $x, x'$ yielding $\begin{pmatrix} c_1 \\ c_2 \\ \cdot \\ \cdot \\ \cdot \\ c_r \end{pmatrix}$, $\begin{pmatrix} c'_1 \\ c'_2 \\ \cdot \\ \cdot \\ \cdot \\ c'_r \end{pmatrix}$, respectively, $x \cdot x'$ yields

$$\begin{pmatrix} c_1 \cdot c'_1 \ (\text{mod } m_1) \\ c_2 \cdot c'_2 \ (\text{mod } m_2) \\ \cdot \\ \cdot \\ \cdot \\ c_r \cdot c'_r \ (\text{mod } m_r) \end{pmatrix}.$$

Thus, we have also proven the following theorem (following Definition 5.16):

**Theorem 6.8:** *If* $\gcd(m_i, m_j) = 1$ *for* $1 \leq i < j \leq r$, *then for* $M = m_1 m_2 \cdots m_r$, $\mathbb{Z}_M$ *is isomorphic to* $\mathbb{Z}_{m_1} \times \mathbb{Z}_{m_2} \times \cdots \times \mathbb{Z}_{m_r}$, *and the isomorphism*

$$f : \mathbb{Z}_M \mapsto \mathbb{Z}_{m_1} \times \mathbb{Z}_{m_2} \times \cdots \times \mathbb{Z}_{m_r}$$

*is*

$$f(x) = ( x \ (\text{mod } m_1), \ x \ (\text{mod } m_2), \ \ldots, \ x \ (\text{mod } m_r) ). \qquad \square$$

Theorem 6.8 is very useful in the study of cryptographic systems or protocols which use groups modulo composite integers. In many places in the rest of this book we will need to make use of the isomorphism between $\mathbb{Z}_n^*$ and $\mathbb{Z}_p^* \times \mathbb{Z}_q^*$ where $n = pq$ with $p$, $q$ prime numbers. For example, we will make use of a property that the non-cyclic group $\mathbb{Z}_n^*$ is generated by two generators of the cyclic groups $\mathbb{Z}_p^*$ and $\mathbb{Z}_q^*$, respectively.

Let us now look at an application of the Chinese Remainder Theorem: a calculation is made easy by applying the isomorphic relationship.

**Example 6.2:** At this stage we do not yet know how to compute square root modulo an integer (we will study the techniques in §6.6). However in some cases a square number in some space (such as in $\mathbb{Z}$) is evident and so square rooting in that space is easy without need of using modulo arithmetic. Let us apply Theorem 6.8 to compute one of the square roots of 29 in $\mathbb{Z}_{35}$.

Limited to our knowledge for the moment, it is not evident to us that 29 is a square number in $\mathbb{Z}_{35}$ and so for the time being we do not know how to root it directly. However, if we apply Theorem 6.8 and map 29 to the isomorphic space $\mathbb{Z}_5 \times \mathbb{Z}_7$, we have

$$29 \ (\text{mod } 5) \mapsto 4, \quad 29 \ (\text{mod } 7) \mapsto 1,$$

that is, the image is $(4, 1)$. Both 4 and 1 are evident square numbers with 2 being a square root of 4 and 1 being a square root of 1. By isomorphism, we know one of the square roots of 29 in $\mathbb{Z}_{35}$ corresponds to $(2, 1)$ in $\mathbb{Z}_5 \times \mathbb{Z}_7$. Applying the Chinese Remainder Algorithm (Alg 6.1), we obtain

$$\bar{1}_5 = 21, \quad \bar{1}_7 = 15,$$

and

$$\sqrt{29} \equiv 21 \cdot 2 + 15 \cdot 1 \equiv 22 \ (\text{mod } 35).$$

Indeed, $22^2 = 484 \equiv 29 \ (\text{mod } 35)$.    □

As a matter of fact, 29 has four distinct square roots in $\mathbb{Z}_{35}^*$. For an exercise, the reader may find the other three square roots of 29 (Ex 6.4).

## 6.3   Euler's Phi Function

In §5.2.3 we have defined Euler's phi function in Definition 5.11. Now let us study some useful properties of it.

**Lemma 6.1:** *Let $\phi(n)$ be Euler's phi function defined in Definition 5.11. Then*

i) $\phi(1) = 1$.

ii) *If $p$ is prime then $\phi(p) = p - 1$.*

iii) *Euler's phi function is multiplicative. That is, if $\gcd(m, n) = 1$, then $\phi(mn) = \phi(m)\phi(n)$.*

iv) *If $n = p_1^{e_1} p_2^{e_2} \cdots p_k^{e_k}$ is the prime factorization of $n$, then*

$$\phi(n) = n \left( 1 - \frac{1}{p_1} \right) \left( 1 - \frac{1}{p_2} \right) \cdots \left( 1 - \frac{1}{p_k} \right).$$

**Proof** (i) and (ii) are trivial from Definition 5.11.

iii) Since $\phi(1) = 1$, the equation $\phi(mn) = \phi(m)\phi(n)$ holds when either $m = 1$ or $n = 1$. So suppose $m > 1$ and $n > 1$. For $\gcd(m, n) = 1$, consider the array

$$
\begin{array}{ccccc}
0 & 1 & 2 & \cdots & m-1 \\
m & m+1 & m+2 & \cdots & m+(m-1) \\
\cdot & \cdot & \cdot & \cdots & \cdot \\
\cdot & \cdot & \cdot & \cdots & \cdot \\
\cdot & \cdot & \cdot & \cdots & \cdot \\
(n-1)m & (n-1)m+1 & (n-1)m+2 & \cdots & (n-1)m+(m-1)
\end{array}
\qquad (6.3.1)
$$

On the one hand, (6.3.1) consists of $mn$ consecutive integers, so it is all the numbers modulo $mn$ and therefore contains $\phi(mn)$ elements prime to $mn$.

On the other hand, observe (6.3.1). The first row is all the numbers modulo $m$, and all the elements in any column are congruent modulo $m$. So there are $\phi(m)$ columns consisting entirely of integers prime to $m$. Let

$$b, m + b, 2m + b, \ldots, (n - 1)m + b$$

be any such column of $n$ elements. With $\gcd(m, n) = 1$, by Theorem 6.6, such a column is a complete residue system modulo $n$. So in each such column there are $\phi(n)$ elements prime to $n$. To this end we know that in (6.3.1) there are $\phi(m)\phi(n)$ elements prime to both $m$ and $n$. Further notice that any element prime to both $m$ and to $n$ if and only if it is prime to $mn$.

Combining the results of the above two paragraphs, we have derived $\phi(mn) = \phi(m)\phi(n)$.

iv) For any prime $p$, in $1, 2, \ldots, p^e$, the elements which are not prime to $p^e$ are the multiples of $p$, i.e., $p, 2p, \ldots, p^{e-1}p$. Clearly, there are exactly $p^{e-1}$ such numbers. So

$$\phi(p^e) = p^e - p^{e-1} = p^e \left( 1 - \frac{1}{p} \right).$$

This holds for each prime power $p^e | n$ with $p^{e+1} \nmid n$. Noticing that different such prime powers of $n$ are relatively prime to each other, the targeted result follows from (iii).  $\square$

In §4.5 we considered a problem named SQUARE-FREENESS: answering whether a given odd composite integer $n$ is square free. There we used $\phi(n)$ to serve an auxiliary input to show that SQUARE-FREENESS is in $\mathcal{NP}$. Now from Property (iv) of Lemma 6.1 we know that for any prime $p > 1$, if $p^2 | n$ then $p | \phi(n)$. This is why we used $\gcd(n, \phi(n)) = 1$ as a witness for $n$ being square free. The reader may consider the case $\gcd(n, \phi(n)) > 1$ (be careful of the case, e.g., $n = pq$ with $p | \phi(q)$, see Ex 6.5).

Euler's phi function has the following elegant property.

**Theorem 6.9:** *For integer $n > 0$, $\sum_{d|n} \phi(d) = n$.*

**Proof**   Let $S_d = \{ x \mid 1 \leq x \leq n, \gcd(x, n) = d \}$. It is clear that set $S = \{1, 2, \ldots, n\}$ is partitioned into disjoint subsets $S_d$ for each $d|n$. Hence

$$\bigcup_{d|n} S_d = S.$$

Notice that for each $d|n$, $\#S_d = \phi(n/d)$, therefore

$$\sum_{d|n} \phi(n/d) = n.$$

However, for any $d|n$, we have $(n/d)|n$, therefore

$$\sum_{d|n} \phi(n/d) = \sum_{(n/d)|n} \phi(n/d) = \sum_{d|n} \phi(d). \qquad \square$$

**Example 6.3:** For $n = 12$, the possible values of $d|12$ are 1, 2, 3, 4, 6, and 12. We have $\phi(1) + \phi(2) + \phi(3) + \phi(4) + \phi(6) + \phi(12) = 1 + 1 + 2 + 2 + 2 + 4 = 12$. $\qquad \square$

## 6.4   The Theorems of Fermat, Euler and Lagrange

We have introduced Fermat's Little Theorem in Chapter 4 (congruence (4.4.8)) and have since used it for a few times but without having proved it. Now we prove Fermat's Little Theorem by showing that it is a special case of another famous theorem in number theory: Euler's Theorem.

**Theorem 6.10: Fermat's Little Theorem** *If $p$ is prime and $p \nmid a$, then $a^{p-1} \equiv 1 \pmod{p}$.*

Since $\phi(p) = p - 1$ for $p$ being prime, Fermat's Little Theorem is a special case of the following theorem.

**Theorem 6.11: Euler's Theorem** *If $\gcd(a, n) = 1$ then $a^{\phi(n)} \equiv 1 \pmod{n}$.*

**Proof** For $\gcd(a, n) = 1$, we know $a \pmod{n} \in \mathbb{Z}_n^*$. Also $\#\mathbb{Z}_n^* = \phi(n)$. By Corollary 5.2, we have $\mathrm{ord}_n(a) \mid \#\mathbb{Z}_n^*$ which implies $a^{\phi(n)} \equiv 1 \pmod{n}$. $\qquad \square$

Since Corollary 5.2 used in the proof of Theorem 6.11 is a direct application of Lagrange's Theorem (Theorem 5.1), we therefore say that Fermat's Little Theorem and Euler's Theorem are special cases of the beautiful Theorem of Lagrange.

In Chapter 4 we have seen the important role of Fermat's Little Theorem in probabilistic primality test, which is useful for the generation of key material for many public-key cryptographic systems and protocols. Euler's Theorem will have an important application for the RSA cryptosystem which will be introduced in §8.5.

## 6.5   Quadratic Residues

Quadratic residues play important roles in number theory. For example, integer factorization algorithms invariantly involve using quadratic residues. They also have frequent uses in encryption and interesting cryptographic protocols.

**Definition 6.1: Quadratic Residue** *Let integer $n > 1$. For $a \in \mathbb{Z}_n^*$, $a$ is called a quadratic residue modulo $n$ if $x^2 \equiv a \pmod{n}$ for some $x \in \mathbb{Z}_n$; otherwise, $a$ is* *called a quadratic non-residue modulo n. The set of quadratic residues modulo n is denoted by* $QR_n$, *and the set of quadratic non-residues modulo n is denoted by* $QNR_n$.

**Example 6.4:** Let us compute $QR_{11}$, the set of all quadratic residues modulo 11.
$QR_{11} = \{\, 1^2,\ 2^2,\ 3^2,\ 4^2,\ 5^2,\ 6^2,\ 7^2,\ 8^2,\ 9^2,\ 10^2 \,\}\ (\mathrm{mod}\ 11) = \{\, 1,\ 3,\ 4,\ 5,\ 9 \,\}$. □

In this example, we have computed $QR_{11}$ by exhaustively squaring elements in $\mathbb{Z}_{11}^*$. However, this is not necessary. In fact, the reader may check

$$QR_{11} = \{\, 1^2,\ 2^2,\ 3^2,\ 4^2,\ 5^2 \}\ (\mathrm{mod}\ 11),$$

i.e., exhaustively squaring elements up to half the magnitude of the modulus suffices. The following theorem claims so for any prime modulus.

**Theorem 6.12:** *Let p be a prime number. Then*

   *i)* $QR_p = \{\, x^2\ (\mathrm{mod}\ p) \mid 0 < x \le (p-1)/2 \,\}$;

  *ii) There are precisely* $(p-1)/2$ *quadratic residues and* $(p-1)/2$ *quadratic non-residues modulo p, that is,* $\mathbb{Z}_p^*$ *is partitioned into two equal-size subsets* $QR_p$ *and* $QNR_p$.

**Proof**   (i) Clearly, set $S = \{\, x^2\ (\mathrm{mod}\ p) \mid 0 < x \le (p-1)/2 \,\} \subseteq QR_p$. To show $QR_p = S$ we only need to prove $QR_p \subseteq S$.

Let any $a \in QR_p$. Then $x^2 \equiv a\ (\mathrm{mod}\ p)$ for some $x < p$. If $x \le (p-1)/2$ then $a \in S$. Suppose $x > (p-1)/2$. Then $y = p - x \le (p-1)/2$ and $y^2 \equiv (p-x)^2 \equiv p^2 - 2px + x^2 \equiv x^2 \equiv a\ (\mathrm{mod}\ p)$. So $QR_p \subseteq S$.

ii) To show $\#QR_p = (p-1)/2$ it suffices to show that for $0 < x < y \le (p-1)/2$, $x^2 \not\equiv y^2\ (\mathrm{mod}\ p)$. Suppose on the contrary, $x^2 - y^2 \equiv (x+y)(x-y) \equiv 0\ (\mathrm{mod}\ p)$. Then $p \mid x + y$ or $p \mid x - y$. Only the latter case is possible since $x + y < p$. Hence $x = y$, a contradiction.

Then $\#QNR_p = (p-1)/2$ since $QNR_p = \mathbb{Z}_p^* \setminus QR_p$ and $\#\mathbb{Z}_p^* = p - 1$.   □

In the proof of Theorem 6.12(i) we have actually shown the following:

**Corollary 6.2:** *Let p be a prime number. Then for any* $a \in QR_p$, *there are exactly two square roots of a modulo p. Denoting by x one to them, then the other is* $-x$ *($= p - x$).*   □

## 6.5.1   Quadratic Residuosity

Often we need to decide if a number is a quadratic residue element modulo a given modulus. This is the so-called **quadratic residuosity problem**.

**Theorem 6.13: Euler's Criterion**    *Let $p$ be a prime number.    Then for any*
$x \in \mathbb{Z}_p^*$, $x \in \mathrm{QR}_p$ *if and only if*

$$x^{(p-1)/2} \equiv 1 \pmod{p}. \tag{6.5.1}$$

**Proof**  ($\Rightarrow$) For $x \in \mathrm{QR}_p$, there exists $y \in \mathbb{Z}_p^*$ such that $y^2 \equiv x \pmod{p}$. So $x^{(p-1)/2} \equiv y^{p-1} \equiv 1 \pmod{p}$ follows from Fermat's Theorem (Theorem 6.10).

($\Leftarrow$) Let $x^{(p-1)/2} \equiv 1 \pmod{p}$. Then $x$ is a root of polynomial $y^{(p-1)/2} - 1 \equiv 0 \pmod{p}$. Notice that $\mathbb{Z}_p$ is a field, by Theorem 5.9(iii) (in §5.4.3) every element in the field is a root of the polynomial $y^p - y \equiv 0 \pmod{p}$. In other words, every non-zero element of the field, i.e., every element in the group $\mathbb{Z}_p^*$, is a root of

$$y^{p-1} - 1 \equiv (y^{(p-1)/2} - 1)(y^{(p-1)/2} + 1) \equiv 0 \pmod{p}.$$

These roots are all distinct since this degree-$(p-1)$ polynomial can have at most $p-1$ roots. Consequently, the $(p-1)/2$ roots of polynomial $y^{(p-1)/2} - 1 \equiv 0 \pmod{p}$ must all be distinct. We have shown in Theorem 6.12 that $\mathrm{QR}_p$ contains exactly $(p-1)/2$ elements, and they all satisfy $y^{(p-1)/2} - 1 \equiv 0 \pmod{p}$. Any other element in $\mathbb{Z}_p^*$ must satisfy $y^{(p-1)/2} + 1 \equiv 0 \pmod{p}$. Therefore $x \in \mathrm{QR}_p$.    □

In the proof of Theorem 6.13 we have shown that if the criterion is not met for $x \in \mathbb{Z}_p$, then

$$x^{(p-1)/2} \equiv -1 \pmod{p}. \tag{6.5.2}$$

Euler's Criterion provides a criterion to test whether or not an element in $\mathbb{Z}_p^*$ is a quadratic residue: if congruence (6.5.1) is satisfied, then $x \in \mathrm{QR}_p$; otherwise (6.5.2) is satisfied and $x \in \mathrm{QNR}_p$.

Let $n$ be a composite natural number with its prime factorization as

$$n = p_1^{e_1} p_2^{e_2} \cdots p_k^{e_k}. \tag{6.5.3}$$

Then by Theorem 6.8, $\mathbb{Z}_n$ is isomorphic to $\mathbb{Z}_{p_1^{e_1}} \times \mathbb{Z}_{p_2^{e_2}} \times \cdots \times \mathbb{Z}_{p_k^{e_k}}$. Since isomorphism preserves arithmetic, we have:

**Theorem 6.14:** *Let $n$ be a composite integer with complete factorization in (6.5.3). Then $x \in \mathrm{QR}_n$ if and only if $x \pmod{p_i^{e_i}} \in \mathrm{QR}_{p_i^{e_i}}$ and hence if and only if $x \pmod{p_i} \in \mathrm{QR}_{p_i}$ for prime $p_i$ with $i = 1, 2, \ldots, k$.*    □

Therefore, if the factorization of $n$ is known, given $x \in \mathbb{Z}_n^*$, the quadratic residuosity of $x$ modulo $n$ can be decided by deciding the residuosity of $x \pmod{p}$ for each prime $p | n$. The latter task can be done by testing Euler's criterion.

However, if the factorization of $n$ is unknown, deciding quadratic residuosity modulo $n$ is a non-trivial task.

### Definition 6.2: Quadratic Residuosity (QR) Problem

INPUT    $n$: *a composite number;*
$x \in \mathbb{Z}_n^*$.

OUTPUT    YES *if $x \in \mathrm{QR}_n$*.

The QRP is a well-known hard problem in number theory and is one of the main four algorithmic problems discussed by Gauss in his "Disquisitiones Arithmeticae" [121]. An efficient solution for it would imply an efficient solution to some other open problems in number theory. In Chapter 14 we will study a well-known public-key cryptosystem named the **Goldwasser-Micali cryptosystem**; that cryptosystem has its security based on the difficult for deciding the QRP.

Combining Theorem 6.12 and Theorem 6.14 we can obtain:

**Theorem 6.15:** *Let $n$ be a composite integer with $k > 1$ distinct prime factors. Then exactly $\frac{1}{2^k}$ fraction of elements in $\mathbb{Z}_n^*$ are quadratic residues modulo $n$.* $\qquad\square$

Thus, for a composite number $n$, an efficient algorithm for deciding quadratic residuosity modulo $n$ will provide an efficient statistic test on the proportion of quadratic residues in $\mathbb{Z}_n^*$, and hence by Theorem 6.15, provide an efficient algorithm for answering the question whether $n$ has two or three distinct prime factors. This is because, by Theorem 6.15, in the former case ($n$ has two distinct prime factors), exactly a quarter of elements in $\mathbb{Z}_n^*$ are quadratic residues, and in the latter case, exactly one-eighth of them are. Consequently, ensembles $E_{2-\mathrm{Prime}}$ and $E_{3-\mathrm{Prime}}$ (see §4.7) can be distinguished.

To date, for a composite $n$ of unknown factorization, no algorithm is known to be able to decide quadratic residuosity modulo $n$ in time polynomial in the size of $n$.

## 6.5.2    Legendre-Jacobi Symbols

Testing quadratic residuosity modulo a prime using Euler's criterion (6.5.1) involves evaluating modulo exponentiation which is quite computation intensive. However, quadratic residuosity can be tested by a much faster algorithm. Such an algorithm is based on the notion of Legendre-Jacobi symbol.

### Definition 6.3: Legendre-Jacobi Symbol    *For each prime number $p$ and for any $x \in \mathbb{Z}_p^*$, let*

$$\left(\frac{x}{p}\right) \overset{\text{def}}{=} \begin{cases} 1 & \text{if } x \in \mathrm{QR}_p \\ -1 & \text{if } x \in \mathrm{QNR}_p. \end{cases}$$

$\left(\dfrac{x}{p}\right)$ *is called Legendre symbol of $x$ modulo $p$.*

*Let $n = p_1 p_2 \cdots p_k$ be the prime factorization of $n$ (some of these prime factors may repeat). Then*

$$\left(\frac{x}{n}\right) \overset{\text{def}}{=} \left(\frac{x}{p_1}\right)\left(\frac{x}{p_2}\right)\cdots\left(\frac{x}{p_k}\right)$$

*is called Jacobi symbol of $x$ modulo $n$.*

In the rest of this book $\left(\frac{a}{b}\right)$ will always be referred to as Jacobi symbol whether or not $b$ is prime.

For $p$ being prime, comparing (6.5.1), (6.5.2) with Definition 6.3, we know

$$\left(\frac{x}{p}\right) = x^{(p-1)/2} \pmod{p}. \tag{6.5.4}$$

Moreover, Jacobi symbol has the following properties.

**Theorem 6.16:** *Jacobi symbol has the following properties:*

*i)* $\left(\dfrac{1}{n}\right) = 1$;

*ii)* $\left(\dfrac{xy}{n}\right) = \left(\dfrac{x}{n}\right)\left(\dfrac{y}{n}\right)$;

*iii)* $\left(\dfrac{x}{mn}\right) = \left(\dfrac{x}{m}\right)\left(\dfrac{x}{n}\right)$;

*iv) if $x \equiv y \pmod{n}$ then* $\left(\dfrac{x}{n}\right) = \left(\dfrac{y}{n}\right)$;

*(below $m, n$ are odd numbers)*

*v)* $\left(\dfrac{-1}{n}\right) = (-1)^{(n-1)/2}$;

*vi)* $\left(\dfrac{2}{n}\right) = (-1)^{(n^2-1)/8}$;

*vii) if $\gcd(m, n) = 1$ and $m, n > 2$ then* $\left(\dfrac{m}{n}\right)\left(\dfrac{n}{m}\right) = (-1)^{(m-1)(n-1)/4}$.

In Theorem 6.16, (i–iv) are immediate from the definition of Jacobi symbol. A proof for (v–vii) uses no special technique either. However, due to the lengthiness and lack of immediate relevance to the topic of this book, we shall not include a proof but refer the reader to the standard textbooks for number theory (e.g., [172, 178]).

Theorem 6.16(vii) is known as the Gauss' Law of Quadratic Reciprocity. Thanks to this law, it is not hard to see that the evaluation of $\left(\dfrac{x}{n}\right)$ for $\gcd(x, n) = 1$ has a fashion and hence the same computational complexity of computing the greatest common divisor.

**Remark 6.1:** *When we evaluate Jacobi symbol by applying Theorem 6.16, the evaluation of the right-hand sides of (v–vii) must not be done via exponentiations. Since* $\mathrm{ord}(-1) = 2$ *(in multiplication), all we need is the parity of these exponents. In Alg 6.2 we realize the evaluation by testing whether 2 divides these exponents.*   □

Alg 6.2 provides a recursive specification of the properties of Jacobi symbol listed in Theorem 6.16.

---

**Algorithm 6.2:** Legendre/Jacobi Symbol

INPUT       odd integer $n > 2$, integer $x \in \mathbb{Z}_n^*$.
OUTPUT    $\left(\dfrac{x}{n}\right)$.

Jacobi($x$, $n$)

1. if ( $x == 1$ ) return ( 1 );

2. if ( $2 \,|\, x$ )

   (a) if ( $2 \,|\, (n^2 - 1)/8$ ) return ( Jacobi($x/2$, $n$) );
   (b) return( $-$Jacobi($x/2$, $n$) );

   ($*$ now $x$ is odd $*$)

3. if ( $2 \,|\, (x-1)(n-1)/4$ ) return( Jacobi($n \bmod x$, $x$) );

4. return( $-$Jacobi($n \bmod x$, $x$) ).

---

In Alg 6.2, each recursive call of the function Jacobi(,) will cause either the first input value being divided by 2, or the second input value being reduced modulo the first. Therefore there can be at most $\log_2 n$ calls and the first input value is reduced to 1, reaching the terminating condition. So rigorously expressed, because each modulo operation costs $O_B((\log n)^2)$ time, Alg 6.2 computes $\left(\dfrac{x}{n}\right)$ can be computed in $O_B((\log n)^3)$ time.

However we should notice that, in order to present the algorithm with ease of understanding, we have again chosen to sacrifice efficiency!

Instead of bounding each modulo operation with $O_B((\log n)^2)$, via a careful realization, *total* modulo operations in steps 3, 4 can be bounded by $O_B((\log n)^2)$. This situation is exactly the same as that for computing greatest common divisor with a carefully designed algorithm: to exploit the fact expressed in (4.3.12). Consequently, for $x \in \mathbb{Z}_n^*$, $\left(\dfrac{x}{n}\right)$ can be computed in $O_B((\log n)^2)$ time. A careful realization of the counterpart for Alg 6.2 can be found in Chapter 1 of [80].

Compared with the complexity of evaluating Euler's criterion (5.4.5), which is $O_B((\log p)^3)$ due to modulo exponentiation, testing quadratic residuosity modulo prime $p$ using Alg 6.2 is $\log p$ times faster.

**Example 6.5:** Let us show that $384 \in \mathrm{QNR}_{443}$.

Going through Alg 6.2 step by step, we have

$$
\begin{aligned}
\mathrm{Jacobi}(384, 443) &= -\mathrm{Jacobi}(192, 443) \\
&= \mathrm{Jacobi}(96, 443) \\
&= -\mathrm{Jacobi}(48, 443) \\
&= \mathrm{Jacobi}(24, 443) \\
&= -\mathrm{Jacobi}(12, 443) \\
&= \mathrm{Jacobi}(6, 443) \\
&= -\mathrm{Jacobi}(3, 443) \\
&= \mathrm{Jacobi}(2, 3) \\
&= -\mathrm{Jacobi}(1, 3) \\
&= -1.
\end{aligned}
$$

Therefore $384 \in \mathrm{QNR}_{443}$.

$\square$

Finally, we should notice that evaluation of Jacobi symbol $\left(\dfrac{x}{n}\right)$ using Alg 6.2 does not need to know the factorization of $n$. This is a very important property which has a wide application in public-key cryptography, e.g., in Goldwasser-Micali cryptosystem (§14.3.3) and in Blum's coin-flipping protocol (Chapter 19).

## 6.6  Square Roots Modulo Integer

In Example 6.2 we have had an experience of "computing a square root modulo an integer." However the "algorithm" used there should not qualify as an algorithm because we were lucky to have managed to map, using the isomorphism in Theorem 6.8, a seemingly difficult task to two trivially easy ones: computing square roots of 1 and 4, which happen to be square numbers in $\mathbb{Z}$ and the "rooting algorithm" is known even to primary school pupils. In general, the isomorphism in Theorem 6.8 will not be so kind to us: for overwhelming cases the image should not be a square number in $\mathbb{Z}$.

Now we introduce algorithmic methods for computing square roots of a quadratic residue element modulo a positive integer. We start by considering prime modulus. By Corollary 6.2, the two roots of a quadratic residue complements to one another modulo the prime modulus; so it suffices for us to consider computing one square root of a quadratic residue element.

For most of the odd prime numbers, the task is very easy. These cases include primes $p$ such that $p \equiv 3, 5, 7 \pmod 8$.

## 6.6.1 Computing Square Roots Modulo Prime

**Case** $p \equiv 3, 7 \pmod 8$

In this case, $p + 1$ is divisible by 4. For $a \in \mathrm{QR}_p$, let

$$x \stackrel{\text{def}}{=} a^{(p+1)/4} \pmod p.$$

Then because $a^{(p-1)/2} \equiv 1 \pmod p$, we have

$$x^2 \equiv a^{(p+1)/2} \equiv a^{(p-1)/2} \, a \equiv a \pmod p$$

So indeed, $x$ is a square root of $a$ modulo $p$.

**Case** $p \equiv 5 \pmod 8$

In this case, $p + 3$ is divisible by 8; also because $(p-1)/2$ is even, $-1$ meets Euler's criterion as a quadratic residue. For $a \in \mathrm{QR}_p$, let

$$x \stackrel{\text{def}}{=} a^{(p+3)/8} \pmod p. \tag{6.6.1}$$

From $a^{(p-1)/2} \equiv 1 \pmod p$ we know $a^{(p-1)/4} \equiv \pm 1 \pmod p$; this is because in field $\mathbb{Z}_p^*$, 1 has only two square roots: 1 and $-1$. Consequently

$$x^2 \equiv a^{(p+3)/4} \equiv a^{(p-1)/4} \, a \equiv \pm a \pmod p.$$

That is, we have found that $x$ computed in (6.6.1) is a square root of either $a$ or $-a$. If the sign is $+$ we are done. If the sign is $-$, then we have

$$-x^2 \equiv (\sqrt{-1}\, x)^2 \equiv a \pmod p.$$

Therefore

$$x \stackrel{\text{def}}{=} \sqrt{-1}\, a^{(p+3)/8} \pmod p \tag{6.6.2}$$

will be the solution. So the task boils down to computing $\sqrt{-1} \pmod p$. Let $b$ be any quadratic non-residue mod $p$. Then by Euler's criterion

$$(b^{(p-1)/4})^2 \equiv b^{(p-1)/2} \equiv -1 \pmod p,$$

so $b^{(p-1)/4} \pmod p$ can be used in place of $\sqrt{-1}$. By the way, since

$$p^2 - 1 = (p+1)(p-1) = (8k+6)(8k+4) = 8(4k'+3)(2k''+1),$$

and the right-hand side is 8 times an odd number; so by Theorem 6.16(vi) $2 \in \mathrm{QNR}_p$. That is, for this case of $p$ we can use $2^{(p-1)/4}$ in place of $\sqrt{-1}$. Then, one may check that (6.6.2) becomes

$$2^{(p-1)/4} a^{(p+3)/8} \equiv (4a)^{(p+3)/8}/2 \pmod{p}. \qquad (6.6.3)$$

We can save one modulo exponentiation by using the right-hand-side of (6.6.3).

---

**Algorithm 6.3:** Square Root Modulo $p \equiv 3, 5, 7 \pmod{8}$

INPUT        prime $p$ satisfying $p \equiv 3, 5, 7 \pmod{8}$; integer $a \in \mathrm{QR}_p$.
OUTPUT     a square root of $a$ modulo $p$.

1. if ( $p \equiv 3, 7 \pmod{8}$ ) return( $a^{(p+1)/4} \pmod{p}$ );

(* below $p \equiv 5 \pmod{8}$ *)

2. if ( $a^{(p-1)/4} \equiv 1 \pmod{p}$ ) return( $a^{(p+3)/8} \pmod{p}$ );

3. return( $(4a)^{(p+3)/8}/2$ ).

---

The time complexity of Alg 6.3 is $O_B((\log p)^3)$.

## Computing Square Roots Modulo Prime in General Case

The method described here is due to Shanks (see §1.5.1 of [80]).

For general case of prime $p$, we can write

$$p - 1 = 2^e q$$

with $q$ odd and $e \geq 1$. By Theorem 5.2 (in §5.2.3), cyclic group $\mathbb{Z}_p^*$ has a unique cyclic subgroup $G$ of order $2^e$. Clearly, quadratic residues in $G$ have orders as powers of 2 since they divide $2^{e-1}$. For $a \in \mathrm{QR}_p$, since

$$a^{(p-1)/2} \equiv (a^q)^{2^{e-1}} \equiv 1 \pmod{p},$$

so $a^q \pmod{p}$ is in $G$ and is of course a quadratic residue. So there exists an even integer $k$ with $0 \leq k < 2^e$ such that

$$a^q g^k \equiv 1 \pmod{p}, \qquad (6.6.4)$$

where $g$ is a generator of $G$. Suppose that we have found the generator $g$ and the even integer $k$. Then setting

$$x \overset{\text{def}}{=} a^{(q+1)/2} g^{k/2},$$

it is easy to check that $x^2 \equiv a \pmod{p}$.

Thus, the task boils down to two sub-tasks: (i) finding a generator $g$ of group $G$, and (ii) finding the least non-negative even integer $k$, such that (6.6.4) is satisfied.

Sub-task (i) is rather easy. For any $f \in \mathrm{QNR}_p$, because $q$ is odd, $f^q \in \mathrm{QNR}_p$ and $\mathrm{ord}_p(f^q) = 2^e$; hence $f^q$ is a generator of $G$. Finding $f$ is rather easy: picking a random element $f \in \mathbb{Z}_p^*$ and testing $\left(\dfrac{f}{p}\right) = -1$ (using Alg 6.2). Since half the elements in $\mathbb{Z}_p^*$ are quadratic non-residues, the probability of finding a correct $f$ in one go is one-half.

Sub-task (ii) is not too difficult either. The search of $k$ from (6.6.4) is fast by utilizing the fact that non-unity quadratic-residue elements in $G$ have orders as powers of 2. Thus, letting initially

$$b \overset{\text{def}}{=} a^q \equiv a^q g^{2^e} \pmod{p}, \qquad (6.6.5)$$

then $b \in G$. We can search the least integer $m$ for $0 \le m < e$ such that

$$b^{2^m} \equiv 1 \pmod{p} \qquad (6.6.6)$$

and then modify $b$ into

$$b \leftarrow bg^{2^{e-m}} \equiv a^q g^{2^{e-m}} \pmod{p}. \qquad (6.6.7)$$

Notice that $b$, after the modification in (6.6.7), has its order been reduced from that in (6.6.5) while remaining a quadratic residue in $G$ and so the reduced order should remain being a power of 2. Therefore, the reduction must be in terms of a power of 2, and consequently, repeating (6.6.6) and (6.6.7), $m$ in (6.6.6) will strictly decrease. Upon $m = 0$, (6.6.6) shows $b = 1$, and thereby (6.6.7) becomes (6.6.4) and so $k$ can be found by accumulating $2^m$ in each loop of repetition. The search will terminate in at most $e$ loops.

It is now straightforward to put our descriptions into Alg 6.4.

Since $e < \log_2 p$, the time complexity of Alg 6.4 is $O_B((\log p)^4)$.

**Remark 6.2:** *For the purpose of better exposition, we have presented Alg 6.4 by following our explanation on the working principle of Shanks' algorithm; in particular, we have followed precisely the explanation on Sub-task (ii) for searching the even exponent $k$. In so doing, our presentation of Shanks' algorithm sacrifices a little bit of efficiency: explicitly finding $k$, while is unnecessary since $g^{k/2}$ can be obtained as a byproduct in step 3, costs an additional modulo exponentiation in step 4. For the optimized version of Shanks' algorithm, see Algorithm 1.5.1 in [80].* $\square$

Finally we should point out that Alg 6.4 contains Alg 6.3 as three special cases.

**Algorithm 6.4:** Square Root Modulo Prime

INPUT        prime $p$; integer $a \in \mathrm{QR}_p$.
OUTPUT    a square root of $a$ modulo $p$.

1. (∗ initialize ∗)
   set $p - 1 = 2^e q$ with $q$ odd; $b \leftarrow a^q \pmod{p}$; $r \leftarrow e$; $k \leftarrow 0$;

2. (∗ sub-task (i), using Alg 6.2 ∗)
   find $f \in \mathrm{QNR}_p$; $g \leftarrow f^q \pmod{p}$;

3. (∗ sub-task (ii), searching even exponent $k$ ∗)
   while ( $b \neq 1$ ) do

   3.1 find the least non-negative integer $m$ such that $b^{2^m} \equiv 1 \pmod{p}$;

   3.2 $b \leftarrow bg^{2^{r-m}} \pmod{p}$; $k \leftarrow k + 2^{r-m}$; $r \leftarrow m$;

4. return( $a^{(q+1)/2} g^{k/2} \pmod{p}$ ).

## 6.6.2  Computing Square Roots Modulo Composite

Thanks to Theorem 6.8, we know that, for $n = pq$ with $p$, $q$ primes, $\mathbb{Z}_n^*$ is isomorphic to $\mathbb{Z}_p^* \times \mathbb{Z}_q^*$. Since isomorphism preserves the arithmetic, relation

$$x^2 \equiv y \pmod{n}$$

holds if and only if it holds modulo both $p$ and $q$. Therefore, if the factorization of $n$ is given, square rooting modulo $n$ can computed using Alg 6.5.

Clearly, the time complexity of Alg 6.5 is $O_B((\log n)^4)$.

By Corollary 6.2, $y \pmod{p}$ has two distinct square roots, which we denote by $x_p$ and $p - x_p$, respectively. So does $y \pmod{q}$, which we denote by $x_q$ and $q - x_q$, respectively. By the isomorphic relationship between $\mathbb{Z}_n^*$ and $\mathbb{Z}_p^* \times \mathbb{Z}_q^*$ (Theorem 6.8), we know that $y \in \mathrm{QR}_n$ has exactly four square roots in $\mathbb{Z}_n^*$. By Alg 6.5, these four roots are

$$\left.\begin{array}{llll} x_1 \equiv & \bar{1}_p \, x_p & + & \bar{1}_q \, x_q \\ x_2 \equiv & \bar{1}_p \, x_p & + & \bar{1}_q \, (q - x_q) \\ x_3 \equiv & \bar{1}_p \, (p - x_p) & + & \bar{1}_q \, x_q \\ x_4 \equiv & \bar{1}_p \, (p - x_p) & + & \bar{1}_q \, (q - x_q) \end{array}\right\} \pmod{n} \qquad (6.6.8)$$

Thus, if we apply (6.6.8) in Step 2 of Alg 6.5, we can compute all four square roots of the element input to the algorithm.

---

**Algorithm 6.5:** Square Root Modulo Composite

INPUT       primes $p, q$ with $n = pq$; integer $y \in \mathrm{QR}_n$.
OUTPUT     a square root of $y$ modulo $n$.

1. $x_p \leftarrow \sqrt{y \ (\mathrm{mod} \ p)}$;

   $x_q \leftarrow \sqrt{y \ (\mathrm{mod} \ q)}$;                         (∗ applying Alg 6.3 or Alg 6.4 ∗)

2. return( $\overline{1}_p x_p + \overline{1}_q x_q \ (\mathrm{mod} \ n)$).              (∗ applying Alg 6.1 ∗)

---

For an exercise, we ask: if $n = pqr$ with $p, q, r$ distinct prime numbers, how many square roots for each $y \in \mathrm{QR}_n$?

We now know that if the factorization of $n$ is known, then computing square roots of any given element in $\mathrm{QR}_n$ can be done efficiently. Now, what can we say about square rooting modulo $n$ without knowing the factorization of $n$? The third part of the following theorem answers this question.

**Theorem 6.17:** *Let $n = pq$ with $p$, $q$ being distinct odd primes and let $y \in \mathrm{QR}_n$. Then the four square roots of $y$ constructed in (6.6.8) have the following properties:*

*i) they are distinct from one another;*

*ii) $x_1 + x_4 = x_2 + x_3 = n$;*

*iii) $\gcd(x_1 + x_2, n) = \gcd(x_3 + x_4, n) = q$,   $\gcd(x_1 + x_3, n) = \gcd(x_2 + x_4, n) = p$.*

**Proof**

i) Noticing the meaning of $\overline{1}_p$ and $\overline{1}_q$ defined by (6.2.15) and (6.2.16), we have, e.g., $x_1 \ (\mathrm{mod} \ q) = x_q$ and $x_2 \ (\mathrm{mod} \ q) = q - x_q$. Remember, $x_q$ and $q - x_q$ are two distinct square roots of $y \ (\mathrm{mod} \ q)$. So $x_1 \not\equiv x_2 \ (\mathrm{mod} \ q)$ implies $x_1 \not\equiv x_2 \ (\mathrm{mod} \ n)$, i.e., $x_1$ and $x_2$ are distinct. Other cases can be shown analogously.

ii) From (6.6.8) we have

$$x_1 + x_4 = x_2 + x_3 = \overline{1}_p \, p + \overline{1}_q \, q.$$

The right-hand side value is congruent to 0 modulo $p$ and modulo $q$. From these roots' membership in $\mathbb{Z}_n^*$, we have $0 < x_1 + x_4 = x_2 + x_3 < 2n$. Clearly, $n$ is the only value in the interval $(0, 2n)$ and is congruent to 0 modulo $p$ and $q$. So $x_1 = n - x_4$ and $x_2 = n - x_3$.

iii) We only study the case $x_1 + x_2$; other cases are analogous. Observing (6.6.8) we have

$$x_1 + x_2 = 2 \cdot \overline{1}_p \, x_p + \overline{1}_q \, q.$$

Therefore $x_1 + x_2 \pmod{p} \equiv 2x_p \neq 0$ and $x_1 + x_2 \equiv 0 \pmod{q}$. Namely, $x_1 + x_2$ is a non-zero multiple of $q$, but not a multiple of $p$. This implies $\gcd(x_1 + x_2, n) = q$. $\qquad\qquad\square$

Suppose there exists an efficient algorithm $A$, which, on input $(y, n)$ for $y \in \mathrm{QR}_n$, outputs $x$ such that $x^2 \equiv y \pmod{n}$. Then we can run $A(x^2, n)$ to obtain a square root of $x^2$ which we denote by $x'$. By Theorem 6.17(iii), the probability for $1 < \gcd(x + x', n) < n$ is exactly one half (the probability space being the four square roots of $y$). That is, the algorithm $A$ is an efficient algorithm for factoring $n$.

Combining Alg 6.5 and Theorem 6.17(iii), we have

**Corollary 6.3:** *Let $n = pq$ with $p$ and $q$ being distinct odd primes. Then factoring $n$ is computationally equivalent to computing square root modulo $n$.* $\qquad\square$

Also from Theorem 6.17(ii) and the fact that $n$ is odd, we have

**Corollary 6.4:** *Let $n = pq$ with $p$ and $q$ being distinct odd primes. Then for any $y \in \mathrm{QR}_n$, two square roots of $y$ are less than $n/2$, and the other two roots are larger than $n/2$.* $\qquad\square$

## 6.7 Blum Integers

Blum integers have wide applications in public-key cryptography.

**Definition 6.4: Blum Integer** *A composite integer $n$ is called a Blum integer if $n = pq$ where $p$ and $q$ are distinct prime numbers satisfying $p \equiv q \equiv 3 \pmod{4}$.*

A Blum integer has many interesting properties. The following are some of them which are very useful in public-key cryptography and cryptographic protocols.

**Theorem 6.18:** *Let $n$ be a Blum integer. Then the following properties hold for $n$:*

*i)* $\left( \dfrac{-1}{p} \right) = \left( \dfrac{-1}{q} \right) = -1$ *(hence* $\left( \dfrac{-1}{n} \right) = 1$*);*

*ii)* *For $y \in \mathbb{Z}_n^*$, if $\left( \dfrac{y}{n} \right) = 1$ then either $y \in \mathrm{QR}_n$ or $-y = n - y \in \mathrm{QR}_n$;*

*iii) Any $y \in \mathrm{QR}_n$ has four square roots $u$, $-u$, $v$, $-v$ and they satisfy (w.l.o.g.)*

*a)* $\left(\dfrac{u}{p}\right) = 1$, $\left(\dfrac{u}{q}\right) = 1$, *i.e.*, $u \in \mathrm{QR}_n$;

*b)* $\left(\dfrac{-u}{p}\right) = -1$, $\left(\dfrac{-u}{q}\right) = -1$;

*c)* $\left(\dfrac{v}{p}\right) = -1$, $\left(\dfrac{v}{q}\right) = 1$;

*d)* $\left(\dfrac{-v}{p}\right) = 1$, $\left(\dfrac{-v}{q}\right) = -1$;

*iv) Function $f(x) = x^2 \pmod{n}$ is a permutation over $\mathrm{QR}_n$;*

*v) For any $y \in \mathrm{QR}_n$, exactly one square root of $y$ with Jacobi symbol 1 is less than $n/2$;*

*vi) $\mathbb{Z}_n^*$ is partitioned into four equivalence classes: one multiplicative group $\mathrm{QR}_n$, and three cosets $(-1)\mathrm{QR}_n$, $\xi\mathrm{QR}_n$, $(-\xi)\mathrm{QR}_n$; here $\xi$ is a square root of 1 with Jacobi symbol $-1$.*

## Proof

i) Notice that $p \equiv 3 \pmod 4$ implies $\frac{p-1}{2} = 2k+1$. Then by Euler's Criterion (6.5.1), we have

$$\left(\frac{-1}{p}\right) = (-1)^{\frac{p-1}{2}} = (-1)^{2k+1} = -1.$$

Analogously, $\left(\dfrac{-1}{q}\right) = -1$.

ii) $\left(\dfrac{y}{n}\right) = 1$ implies either $\left(\dfrac{y}{p}\right) = \left(\dfrac{y}{q}\right) = 1$, or $\left(\dfrac{y}{p}\right) = \left(\dfrac{y}{q}\right) = -1$. For the first case, $y \in \mathrm{QR}_n$ due to the definition of Legendre symbol (Definition 6.3) and Theorem 6.14. For the second case, (i) implies $\left(\dfrac{-y}{p}\right) = \left(\dfrac{-y}{q}\right) = 1$. Hence $-y \in \mathrm{QR}_n$.

iii) First of all, by Theorem 6.17(ii), we can indeed denote the four distinct square roots of $x$ by $u$, $-u\,(=n-u)$, $v$ and $-v$.

Next, from $u^2 \equiv v^2 \pmod{n}$, we have $(u+v)(u-v) \equiv 0 \pmod{p}$, that is, $u \equiv \pm v \pmod{p}$. Similarly, $u \equiv \pm v \pmod{q}$. However, by Theorem 6.17(i), $u \not\equiv \pm v \pmod{n}$, so only the following two cases are possible:

$$u \equiv v \pmod{p} \text{ and } u \equiv -v \pmod{q},$$

or
$$u \equiv -v \pmod{p} \text{ and } u \equiv v \pmod{q}.$$

These two cases plus (i) imply $\left(\dfrac{u}{n}\right) = -\left(\dfrac{v}{n}\right)$.

Thus, if $\left(\dfrac{u}{n}\right) = 1$ then $\left(\dfrac{v}{n}\right) = -1$ and if $\left(\dfrac{u}{n}\right) = -1$ then $\left(\dfrac{v}{n}\right) = 1$. Without loss of generality, the four distinct Legendre-symbol characterizations in (a)-(d) follow the multiplicative property of Legendre-Jacobi symbol and (i).

iv) For any $y \in \mathrm{QR}_n$, by (iii) there exists a unique $x \in \mathrm{QR}_n$ satisfying $f(x) = y$. Thus, $f(x)$ is a 1-1 and onto mapping, i.e., a permutation, over $\mathrm{QR}_n$.

v) By (iii), the square root with Jacobi symbol 1 is either $u$ or $n - u$. Only one of them can be less than $n/2$ since $n$ is odd. (So, exactly one square root with Jacobi symbol $-1$ is less than $n/2$; the other two roots are larger than $n/2$ and have the opposite Jacobi symbols.)

vi) It is trivial to check that $\mathrm{QR}_n$ forms a group under multiplication modulo $n$ with 1 as the identity. Now by (iii), the four distinct square roots of 1 have the four distinct Legendre-symbol characterizations in (a), (b), (c), and (d), respectively. Therefore the four sets $\mathrm{QR}_n$, $(-1)\mathrm{QR}_n$, $\xi\mathrm{QR}_n$, $(-\xi)\mathrm{QR}_n$ are pair-wise disjoint. These four sets make up $\mathbb{Z}_n^*$ because by Theorem 6.15, $\#\mathrm{QR}_n = \frac{\#\mathbb{Z}_n^*}{4}$.      □

## 6.8   Chapter Summary

In this chapter we have conducted a study in the following topics of elementary number theory:

- Linear congruences

- Chinese Remainder Theorem (with algorithm)

- Lagrange's, Euler's and Fermat's theorems

- Quadratic residues and Legendre-Jacobi symbols (with algorithm)

- Square roots modulo integers and the relation to factorization (with algorithm for root extraction)

- Blum integers and their properties

In addition to introducing the basic knowledge and facts, we have also studied several important algorithms (Chinese Remainder, Jacobi symbol, square-rooting), with their working principles explained and their time complexity behaviors analyzed. In so doing, we considered that these algorithms not only have theoretic importance, but also have practical importance: these algorithms are frequently used in cryptography and cryptographic protocols.

In the rest of this book we will frequently apply the knowledge, facts, skills and algorithms which we have learned in this chapter.

## Exercises

6.1 Let $m, n$ be positive integers satisfying $m|n$. Show that operation " (mod $m$)" partitions $\mathbb{Z}_n$ into $n/m$ equivalence classes, each has $m$ elements.

6.2 Under the same condition of the preceding problem, show $\mathbb{Z}_n/m\mathbb{Z}_n = \mathbb{Z}_m$.

6.3 Use the Chinese Remainder Algorithm (Alg 6.1) to construct an element in $\mathbb{Z}_{35}$ which maps to $(2,3) \in \mathbb{Z}_5 \times \mathbb{Z}_7$ under the isomorphism in Theorem 6.8. Prove that this element has the maximum order.

6.4 Use the method in Example 6.2 to find the other three square roots of 29 in $\mathbb{Z}_{35}^*$. Find analogously the four square roots of 1 in $\mathbb{Z}_{35}^*$.

Hint: 29 (mod 5) = 4 which has square roots 2 and 3 ($= -2$ (mod 5)), and 29 (mod 7) = 1 which has square roots 1 and 6 ($= -1$ (mod 7)); the four square roots of 29 modulo 35 are isomorphic to $(2, 1)$, $(2, 6)$, $(3, 1)$ and $(3, 6)$ in $\mathbb{Z}_5 \times \mathbb{Z}_7$.

6.5 Construct an odd composite number $n$ such that $n$ is square free, i.e., there exists no prime $p$ such that $p^2|N$, however $\gcd(n, \phi(n)) > 1$.

6.6 Let $m|n$. Prove that for any $x \in \mathbb{Z}_n^*$, $\mathrm{ord}_m(x)|\mathrm{ord}_n(x)$.

6.7 Let $n = pq$ with $p, q$ being distinct primes. Since $p - 1|\phi(n)$, there exists elements in $\mathbb{Z}_n^*$ of order dividing $p - 1$. (Similarly, there are elements of order dividing $q - 1$.) Prove that for any $g \in \mathbb{Z}_n^*$, if $\mathrm{ord}_n(g)|p - 1$ and $\mathrm{ord}_n(g) \nmid q - 1$, then $\gcd(g - 1, n) = q$. (Similarly, any $h \in \mathbb{Z}_n^*$ of $\mathrm{ord}_n(h)|q - 1$ and $\mathrm{ord}_n(h) \nmid p - 1$, $\gcd(h - 1, n) = p$.)

6.8 Let $n = pq$ with $p, q$ being distinct primes. Show that for any $g \in \mathbb{Z}_n^*$, it holds $g^{p+q} \equiv g^{n+1} \pmod{n}$. For $|p| \approx |q|$, show that an upper bound for factoring $n$ is $n^{1/4}$.

Hint: find $p + q$ from $g^{n+1} \pmod{n}$ using Pollard's $\lambda$-algorithm; then factor $n$ using $p + q$ and $pq$.

6.9 Let $p$ be a prime. Show that a generator of the group $\mathbb{Z}_p^*$ must be a quadratic non-residue. Analogously, let $n$ be an odd composite; show that elements in $\mathbb{Z}_n^*$ of the maximum order must be quadratic non-residues.

6.10 Testing quadratic residuosity modulo $p$ using Euler's criterion is $\log p$ times slower than doing so via evaluation of Legendre symbol. Why?

6.11 Factor 35 using the square roots computed in Ex 6.4.

6.12 Show that $QR_n$ is a subgroup of $J_n(1)$ and the latter is a subgroup of $\mathbb{Z}_n^*$.

6.13 Let $n = pq$ with $p$ and $q$ being distinct primes. Under what condition $-1 \in$ $QR_n$? Under what condition $\left(\dfrac{-1}{n}\right) = -1$?

6.14 Let $n$ be a Blum integer. Construct the inversion of the function $f(x) = x^2 \pmod{n}$ over $QR_n$.

Hint: apply the Chinese Remainder Theorem (Alg 6.1) to Case 1 of Alg 6.3.

6.15 Let $n = pq$ be a Blum integer satisfying $\gcd(p-1, q-1) = 2$. Show that group $J_n(1)$ is cyclic.

Hint: apply Chinese Remainder Theorem to construct an element using a generator of $\mathbb{Z}_p^*$ and one of $\mathbb{Z}_q^*$. Prove that this element is in $J_n(1)$ and is o order $\#J_n(1)$.

# Part III

# BASIC CRYPTOGRAPHIC TECHNIQUES

This part contains four chapters which introduce the most basic cryptographic techniques for confidentiality and data integrity. Chapter 7 introduces symmetric encryption techniques, Chapter 8 introduces asymmetric encryption techniques, Chapter 9 considers an important security quality possessed by the basic and popular asymmetric cryptographic functions when they are used in an ideal world (where data are random), and finally, Chapter 10 introduces basic techniques for data integrity.

The basic cryptographic algorithms and schemes to be introduced in this part can be considered as "textbook crypto" since they can be found in many textbooks on cryptography. In this part we shall expose various weaknesses of these "textbook crypto" algorithms and schemes by demonstrating abundant attacks, even though we will not, in fact cannot for the moment, fix these weaknesses for the time being. However, this book will not stop at "textbook crypto" level of introduction to cryptography. Fit-for-application, i.e., non-textbook, versions of encryption algorithms and data-integrity mechanisms will be introduced in later chapters, and most of them are results of enhancement to their "textbook crypto" counterparts.

For readers who do not plan to proceed an in-depth study of fit-for-application crypto and their strong security notions, this "textbook crypto" part will still provide them with explicit early warning signals on general insecurity of "textbook crypto."

# Chapter 7

# ENCRYPTION — SYMMETRIC TECHNIQUES

## 7.1 Introduction

Secrecy is at the heart of cryptography. **Encryption** is a practical means to achieve information secrecy. Modern encryption techniques are mathematical transformations (algorithms) which treat messages as numbers or algebraic elements in a space and transform them between a region of "meaningful messages" and a region of "unintelligible messages". A messages in the meaningful region and input to an encryption algorithm is called **cleartext** and the unintelligible output from the encryption algorithm is called **ciphertext**. If we disregard the intelligibility of a message, then a message input to an encryption algorithm is conventionally called **plaintext** which may or may not be intelligible. For example, a plaintext message can be a random nonce or a ciphertext message; we have seen such cases in some protocols studied Chapter 2. Therefore, plaintext and ciphertext are a pair of respective notions: the former refers to messages input to, and the latter, output from, an encryption algorithm.

In order to restore information, an encryption transformation must be reversible and the reversing transformation is called **decryption**. Conventionally, encryption and decryption algorithms are parameterized by cryptographic keys. An encryption algorithm and a decryption algorithm plus the description on the format of messages and keys form a cryptographic system or a **cryptosystem**.

Semantically, Shannon characterizes a desired property for a cryptosystem as follows: the ciphertext message space is the space of all possible messages while the cleartext (notice: not plaintext according to our convention given the first paragraph above) message space is a sparse region inside the message space, in which messages have a certain fairly simple statistical structure, i.e., they are meaningful; a (good) encryption algorithm is a mixing-transformation which distributes the meaningful messages from the sparse and meaningful region fairly uniformly over the entire message space (pages 711-712 of [266]). Shannon characterizes this mixing property as follows:

$$\lim_{n\to\infty} \bigcup_n F^n R = \Omega. \tag{7.1.1}$$

Here, $F$ denotes a mapping (an encryption algorithm) of a space $\Omega$ (message space) into itself, $R$ denotes an initial and small region (the cleartext region) in $\Omega$. Shannon's semantic characterization for encryption expresses that a good encryption algorithm should have such a mix-transformation behavior: it can map a small initial region of a space into the entire space.

Although nowadays, in particular after the invention of public-key cryptography, it needn't be the case an encryption algorithm is a mapping from a space into the space itself, (this is still true for most cryptosystems, secret-key or public-key), Shannon's semantic characterization for encryption as a mixing-transformation remains very meaningful. The contemporary definition for **semantic security** of an encryption algorithm, which will be given in §14.3, essentially means that a ciphertext has a distribution in the message space which is indistinguishable from the uniform distribution in the same space.

### 7.1.1 Chapter Outline

In this chapter we will introduce the notion of cryptosystems, several well-known symmetric cryptosystems and the standard modes of operations. We begin by providing a formal syntactic definition for cryptosystems to be used in the rest of this book (§7.2). We then introduce several important classical ciphers (§7.3—§7.4). We will make explicit the importance of the classical cipher techniques by showing their widespread roles in modern ciphers and in cryptographic protocols (§7.5). After classical ciphers, two important modern block ciphers will be described: the Data Encryption Standard (DES, §7.6) and the Advanced Encryption Standard (AES, §7.7), and their design strategies will be explained. We will also provide a brief discussion on the AES's positive impact on applied cryptography (§7.7.5). The part on symmetric techniques will also include various standard modes of operations for using block ciphers which achieve probabilistic encryption (7.8). We end our introduction to symmetric encryption techniques by posing the classical problem of key channel establishment (§7.9).

## 7.2 Definition

Syntactically, a cryptosystem can be defined as follows.

**Definition 7.1: Cryptographic System** *A cryptographic system consists of the following:*

- *a plaintext message space $\mathcal{M}$: a set of strings over some alphabet*

- *a ciphertext message space $\mathcal{C}$: a set of possible ciphertext messages*

- *an encryption key space $\mathcal{K}$: a set of possible encryption keys, and a decryption key space $\mathcal{K}'$: a set of possible decryption keys*

- *an efficient key generation algorithm $\mathcal{G} : \mathbb{N} \mapsto \mathcal{K} \times \mathcal{K}'$*

- *an efficient encryption algorithm $\mathcal{E} : \mathcal{M} \times \mathcal{K} \mapsto \mathcal{C}$*

- *an efficient decryption algorithm $\mathcal{D} : \mathcal{C} \times \mathcal{K}' \mapsto \mathcal{M}$.*

*For integer $1^\ell$, $\mathcal{G}(1^\ell)$ outputs a key pair $(ke, kd) \in \mathcal{K} \times \mathcal{K}'$ of length $\ell$. For $ke \in \mathcal{K}$ and $m \in \mathcal{M}$, we denote by*

$$c = \mathcal{E}_{ke}(m)$$

*the encryption transformation and read it as "c is an encryption of m under key ke," and we denote by*

$$m = \mathcal{D}_{kd}(c)$$

*the decryption transformation and read it as "m is the decryption of c under key kd." It is necessary that for all $m \in \mathcal{M}$ and all $ke \in \mathcal{K}$, there exists $kd \in \mathcal{K}'$:*

$$\mathcal{D}_{kd}(\mathcal{E}_{ke}(m)) = m. \tag{7.2.1}$$

In the rest of the book we will use this set of syntactic notation to denote abstract cryptosystems, except in the some places where different notations have been conventionally used in the literature. Fig 7.1 provides an illustration of cryptosystems.

Definition 7.1 applies to cryptosystems which use secret keys as well as public keys (public-key cryptosystems will be introduced in the next chapter). In a **secret-key cryptosystems** encryption and decryption use the same key. The principal who encrypts a message must share the encryption key with the principal who will be receiving and decrypting the encrypted message. The fact $kd = ke$ provides secret-key cryptosystem another name: **symmetric cryptosystems**. In a **public-key cryptosystem**, encryption and decryption use different keys; for every key $ke \in \mathcal{K}$, there exists $kd \in \mathcal{K}'$, the two keys are different and match each other; the encryption key $ke$ needn't be kept secret, and the principal who is the owner of $ke$ can decrypt a ciphertext encrypted under $ke$ using the matching private key $kd$. The fact $kd \neq ke$ provides public-key cryptosystems another name: **asymmetric cryptosystems**.

By requiring encryption algorithms efficient, we consider that such algorithms include probabilistic polynomial-time ones. Hence, although the abstract notation $\mathcal{E}$ looks a deterministic, it can have a internal random move, and so an output ciphertext can be a random variable of this internal random move. Also notice that

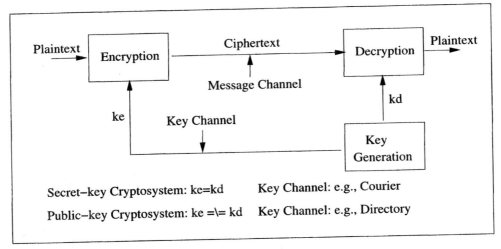

**Figure 7.1.** Cryptographic Systems

the integer input to the key generation algorithm $\mathcal{G}$ provides the size of the output encryption/decryption keys. Since the key generation algorithm is efficient with running time polynomial in the size of its input, the input integer value should use the unary representation (reason explained in §4.4.6.1).

In 1883, Kerchoffs wrote a list of requirements for the design cryptosystems (see page 14 of [200]). One of the items in Kerchoffs' list has evolved into a widely accepted convention known as **Kerchoffs' principle**:

> Knowledge of the algorithm and key size as well as the availability of known plaintext, are standard assumptions in modern cryptanalysis. Since an adversary may obtain this information eventually, it is preferable not to rely on its secrecy when assessing cryptographic strength.

Combining Shannon's semantic characterization for cryptosystem and Kerchoffs' principle, we can provide a summary for a good cryptosystem as follows:

- Algorithms $\mathcal{E}$ and $\mathcal{D}$ contain no component or design part which is secret;

- $\mathcal{E}$ distributes meaningful messages fairly uniformly over the entire ciphertext message space; it may even be possible that the random distribution is due to some internal random operation of $\mathcal{E}$;

- With the correct cryptographic key, $\mathcal{E}$ and $\mathcal{D}$ are *practically* efficient;

- Without the correct key, the task for recovering from a ciphertext the correspondent plaintext is a problem of a difficulty determined solely by the size of the key parameter, which usually takes a size $s$ such that solving the problem requires computational resource of a quantitative measure beyond $p(s)$ for $p$ being any polynomial.

We should notice that this list of desirable properties for a cryptosystem have become inadequate for cryptosystems for modern day applications. More stringent requirements will be developed through our study of cryptosystems.

# 7.3  Substitution Ciphers

In a **substitution cipher**, the encryption algorithm $\mathcal{E}_k(m)$ is a substitution function which replaces each $m \in \mathcal{M}$ with a corresponding $c \in \mathcal{C}$. The substitution function is parameterized by a secret key $k$. The decryption algorithm $\mathcal{D}_k(c)$ is merely the reverse substitution. In general, the substitution can be given by a mapping $\pi : \mathcal{M} \mapsto \mathcal{C}$, and the reverse substitution is just the corresponding inverse mapping $\pi^{-1} : \mathcal{C} \mapsto \mathcal{M}$.

## 7.3.1  Simple Substitution Ciphers

**Example 7.1: A Simple Substitution Cipher**  Let $\mathcal{M} = \mathcal{C} = \mathbb{Z}_{26}$ and interpret $A = 0, B = 1, \ldots, Z = 25$. Define encryption algorithm $\mathcal{E}_k(m)$ as the following permutation over $\mathbb{Z}_{26}$

$$\begin{pmatrix} 0 & 1 & 2 & 3 & 4 & 5 & 6 & 7 & 8 & 9 & 10 & 11 & 12 \\ 21 & 12 & 25 & 17 & 24 & 23 & 19 & 15 & 22 & 13 & 18 & 3 & 9 \end{pmatrix}$$

$$\begin{pmatrix} 13 & 14 & 15 & 16 & 17 & 18 & 19 & 20 & 21 & 22 & 23 & 24 & 25 \\ 5 & 10 & 2 & 8 & 16 & 11 & 14 & 7 & 1 & 4 & 20 & 0 & 6 \end{pmatrix}.$$

Then the corresponding decryption algorithm $\mathcal{D}_K(C)$ is given by

$$\begin{pmatrix} 0 & 1 & 2 & 3 & 4 & 5 & 6 & 7 & 8 & 9 & 10 & 11 & 12 \\ 24 & 21 & 15 & 11 & 22 & 13 & 25 & 20 & 16 & 12 & 14 & 18 & 1 \end{pmatrix}$$

$$\begin{pmatrix} 13 & 14 & 15 & 16 & 17 & 18 & 19 & 20 & 21 & 22 & 23 & 24 & 25 \\ 9 & 19 & 7 & 17 & 3 & 10 & 6 & 23 & 0 & 8 & 5 & 4 & 2 \end{pmatrix}.$$

Plaintext messages

`proceed meeting as agreed`

will be encrypted into the following ciphertext messages (spaces are not transformed)

`cqkzyyr jyyowft vl vtqyyr`

□

In this simple substitution cipher example, the message spaces $\mathcal{M}$ and $\mathcal{C}$ coincide with the alphabet $\mathbb{Z}_{26}$. In other words, a plaintext or ciphertext message is a single character in the alphabet. For this reason, the plaintext message string proceedmeetingasagreed is not a single message, but comprises 22 messages; likewise, the ciphertext message string cqkzyyrjyyowftvlvtqyyr comprises 22 messages. The key space of this cipher has the size $26! > 4 \times 10^{26}$, which is huge in comparison with the size of the message space. However, this cipher is in fact very weak: each plaintext character is encrypted to a unique ciphertext character. This weakness renders this cipher extremely vulnerable to a **cryptanalysis** technique called **frequency analysis** which exploits the fact that natural languages contain a high volume of redundancy (see §3.8). We will further discuss the security of simple substitution cipher in §7.5.

Several special cases of simple substitution ciphers appear in history. The simplest and the most well-known case is called **shift ciphers**. In shift ciphers, $\mathcal{K} = \mathcal{M} = \mathcal{C}$; let $N = \#\mathcal{M}$, the encryption and decryption mappings are defined by

$$\begin{cases} \mathcal{E}_k(m) \leftarrow m + k \pmod{N} \\ \\ \mathcal{D}_k(c) \leftarrow c - k \pmod{N} \end{cases} \tag{7.3.1}$$

with $m, c, k \in \mathbb{Z}_N$. For the case of $\mathcal{M}$ being the capital letters of the Latin alphabet, i.e., $\mathcal{M} = \mathbb{Z}_{26}$, the shift cipher is also known as **Caesar cipher**, because Julius Caesar used it with the case of $k = 3$ (§2.2 of [94]).

By Theorem 6.6 (in §6.2.2) we know that if $\gcd(k, N) = 1$, then for every $m < N$:

$$km \pmod{N}$$

ranges over the entire message space $\mathbb{Z}_N$. Therefore for such $k$ and for $m, c < N$

$$\begin{cases} \mathcal{E}_k(m) \leftarrow km \pmod{N} \\ \\ \mathcal{D}_k(c) \leftarrow k^{-1}c \pmod{N} \end{cases} \tag{7.3.2}$$

provide a simple substitution cipher. Similarly,

$$k_1 m + k_2 \pmod{N}$$

can also define a simple substitution cipher called **affine cipher**:

$$\begin{cases} \mathcal{E}_k(m) \leftarrow k_1 m + k_2 \pmod{N} \\ \\ \mathcal{D}_k(c) \leftarrow k_1^{-1}(c - k_2) \pmod{N} \end{cases} . \tag{7.3.3}$$

It is not difficult to see that using various arithmetic operations between keys in $\mathcal{K}$ and messages in $\mathcal{M}$, various cases of simple substitution ciphers can be designed.

These ciphers are called **monoalphabetic ciphers**: for a given encryption key, each element in the plaintext message space will be substituted into a unique element in the ciphertext message space. Therefore, monoalphabetic ciphers are extremely vulnerable to frequency analysis attacks.

However, due to their simplicity, simple substitution ciphers have been widely used in modern secret-key encryption algorithms. We will see the kernel role that simple substitution ciphers play in the Data Encryption Standard (DES) (§7.6) and in the Advanced Encryption Standard (AES) (§7.7). It has been agreed that a combination of several simple cipher algorithms can result in a strong cipher algorithm. That is why simple ciphers are still in wide use. Simple substitution ciphers are also widely used in cryptographic protocols; we will illustrate a protocol's application of a simple substitution cipher in §7.5 and see many further such examples in the rest of the book.

## 7.3.2 Polyalphabetic Ciphers

A substitution cipher is called a **polyalphabetic cipher** if a plaintext message element in $\mathcal{P}$ may be substituted into many, possibly any, ciphertext message element in $\mathcal{C}$.

We shall use the **Vigenère cipher** to exemplify a polyalphabetic cipher since the Vigenère cipher is the best known among polyalphabetic ciphers.

The Vigenère cipher is a string-based substitution cipher: a key is a string comprising a plural number of characters. Let $m$ be the key length. Then a plaintext string is divided into sections of $m$ characters, that is, each section is a string of $m$ characters with possibly an exception that the final section of string may have fewer characters. The encryption algorithm operates that of the shift cipher between the key string and a plaintext string, one plaintext string at a time with the key string being repeated. The decryption follows the same manner, using the decryption operation of the shift cipher.

**Example 7.2: Vigenère Cipher** Let the key string be gold. Using the encoding rule $A = 0, B = 1, \ldots, Z = 25$, the numerical representation of this key string is $(6, 14, 11, 3)$. The Vigenère encryption of the plaintext string

proceed meeting as agreed

has the following operation which is character-wise addition modulo 26:

| 15 | 17 | 14 | 2 | 4 | 4 | 3 | 12 | 4 | 4 | 19 |
|----|----|----|----|----|----|----|----|----|----|----|
| 6 | 14 | 11 | 3 | 6 | 14 | 11 | 3 | 6 | 14 | 11 |
| 21 | 5 | 25 | 5 | 10 | 18 | 14 | 15 | 10 | 18 | 4 |

| 8 | 13 | 6 | 0 | 18 | 0 | 6 | 17 | 4 | 4 | 3 |
|----|----|----|----|----|----|----|----|----|----|----|
| 3 | 6 | 14 | 11 | 3 | 6 | 14 | 11 | 3 | 6 | 14 |
| 11 | 19 | 20 | 11 | 21 | 6 | 20 | 2 | 7 | 10 | 17 |

Thus, the ciphertext string is

`vfzfkso pkseltu lv guchkr`                    □

Other well-known polyalphabetic ciphers include the **book cipher** (also called the **Beale cipher**) where the key string is an agreed text in a book, and the **Hill cipher**. See, e.g., §2.2 of [94] or §1.1 of [286], for detailed description of these substitution ciphers.

### 7.3.3   The Vernam Cipher and the One-Time Pad

The **Vernam cipher** is one of the simplest cryptosystems. If we assume that the message is a string of $n$ binary bits

$$m = b_1 b_2 \ldots b_n \in \{0,1\}^n$$

then the key is also a string of $n$ binary bits

$$k = k_1 k_2 \ldots k_n \in_U \{0,1\}^n,$$

(notice here the symbol "$\in_U$:" $k$ is chosen at uniformly random). Encryption takes place one bit at a time and the ciphertext string $c = c_1 c_2 \ldots c_n$ is found by the bit operation XOR (exclusive or) each message bit with the corresponding key bit

$$c_i = b_i \oplus k_i$$

for $1 \leq i \leq n$, where the operation $\oplus$ is defined by

| $\oplus$ | 0 | 1 |
|---|---|---|
| 0 | 0 | 1 |
| 1 | 1 | 0 |

Decryption is the same as encryption, since $\oplus$ is addition modulo 2, and thereby subtraction is identical to addition.

Considering $\mathcal{M} = \mathcal{C} = \mathcal{K} = \{0,1\}^*$, the Vernam cipher is a special case of substitution ciphers. If the key string is used for one time only, then the Vernam cipher satisfies two strong security conditions for substitution ciphers which we will be summarizing in §7.5. There we shall argue that confidentiality offered by the one-time-key Vernam cipher is in the information-theoretically secure sense, or is, unconditional. A simple way to see this security quality is the following: a ciphertext message string $c$ provides (an eavesdropper) no information whatsoever about the plaintext message string $m$ since any $m$ could have yield $c$ if the key $k$ is equal to $c \oplus m$ (bit by bit).

The one-time-key Vernam cipher is also called the **one-time pad cipher**. In principle, as long as the usage of encryption key satisfies the two conditions for secure substitution ciphers which we will list in §7.5, then any substitution cipher is a one-time pad cipher. Conventionally however, only the cipher using the bit-wise XOR operation is called the one-time pad cipher.

In comparison with other substitution ciphers (e.g., the shift cipher using addition modulo 26), the bit-wise XOR operation (which is addition modulo 2) can be easily realized by an electronic circuit. Because of this reason, the bit-wise XOR operation is a widely used ingredient in the design of modern secret-key encryption algorithms. It will be used in two important modern ciphers the DES (§7.6) and the AES (§7.7).

The one-time pad style of encryption is also widely used in cryptographic protocols. We will see such a protocol in §7.5.1.

## 7.4   Transposition Ciphers

A **transposition cipher** (also called **permutation cipher**) transforms a message by rearranging the positions of the elements of the message without changing the identities of the elements. Transposition ciphers are an important family of classical ciphers, in additional substitution ciphers, which are widely used in the constructions of modern block ciphers.

Consider that the elements of a plaintext message are letters in $\mathbb{Z}_{26}$; let $b$ be a fixed positive integer representing the size of a message block; let $\mathcal{P} = \mathcal{C} = (\mathbb{Z}_{26})^b$; finally, let $\mathcal{K}$ be all permutations, i.e., rearrangements, of $(1, 2, \ldots, b)$.

Then a permutation $\pi = (\pi(1), \pi(2), \ldots, \pi(b))$ is a key since $\pi \in \mathcal{K}$. For a plaintext block $(x_1, x_2, \ldots, x_b) \in \mathcal{P}$, the encryption algorithm of this transposition cipher is

$$e_\pi(x_1, x_2, \ldots, x_b) = (x_{\pi(1)}, x_{\pi(2)}, \ldots, x_{\pi(b)}).$$

Let $\pi^{-1}$ denote the inverse of $\pi$, i.e., $\pi^{-1}(\pi(i)) = i$ for $i = 1, 2, \ldots, b$. Then the corresponding decryption algorithm of this transposition cipher is

$$d_\pi = (y_1, y_2, \ldots, y_b) = (y_{\pi^{-1}(1)}, y_{\pi^{-1}(2)}, \ldots, y_{\pi^{-1}(b)}).$$

For a message of length larger than the block size $b$, the message is divided into multiple blocks and the same procedures are repeated block by block.

Since for message block size $b$ there are $b!$ different number of keys, a plaintext message block can be transposition-enciphered to $b!$ possible ciphertexts. However, since the identities of the letters do not change, transposition cipher is also extremely vulnerable to the frequency analysis techniques.

**Example 7.3: Transposition Cipher**   Let $b = 4$ and

$$\pi = (\pi(1), \pi(2), \pi(3), \pi(4)) = (2, 4, 1, 3).$$

Then the plaintext message

proceed meeting as agreed

is first divided into 6 blocks of four letters each:

proc eedm eeti ngas agre ed

which can then be transposition-enciphered to the following ciphertext

rcpoemedeietgsnagearde

Notice that the final short block of plaintext ed is actually padded as ed⊔⊔ and then enciphered into d⊔e⊔, followed by deleting the padded spaces from the ciphertext block.

The decryption key is

$$\pi^{-1} = (\pi(1)^{-1}, \pi(2)^{-1}, \pi(3)^{-1}, \pi(4)^{-1}) = (2^{-1}, 4^{-1}, 1^{-1}, 3^{-1}).$$

The fact that the final shortened ciphertext block de containing only two letters means that in the corresponding plaintext block there is no letter to match the positions for $3^{-1}$ and $4^{-1}$. Therefore spaces should be re-inserted into the shortened ciphertext block *at these positions* to restore the block into the padded form d⊔e⊔, before the decryption procedure can be applied properly.                           □

Notice that in the case of the final plaintext block is a short one (as in the case of Example 7.3), leaving the padded letters, such as ⊔, in the ciphertext message, should be avoided because the padded letters expose information about the key used.

## 7.5 Classical Ciphers: Usefulness and Security

First of all we should point out that the two basic working principles of the classical ciphers: substitution and transposition, are still the most important kernel techniques in the construction of modern symmetric encryption algorithms. We will clearly see combinations of substitution and transposition ciphers in two important modern symmetric encryption algorithms: DES and AES, which we shall introduce in §7.6 and §7.7.

Consider character-based substitution ciphers. Because the plaintext message space coincides with the alphabet, each message is a character in the alphabet and encryption is to substitute character-by-character each plaintext character with a ciphertext character and the substitution is according to a secret key. If a key is fixed for encrypting a long string of characters, then the same character in the plaintext messages will be encrypted to a fixed character in the ciphertext messages.

It is well known that letters in a natural language have stable frequencies (review §3.8). The knowledge of the frequency distribution of letters in a natural language provides clue for cryptanalysis, a technique aiming at finding information about the plaintext or the encryption key from given ciphertext messages. This phenomenon is shown in Example 7.1, where the ciphertext message show a high frequent appearance of the letter y, and suggest that a fixed letter must appear in the corresponding plaintext message with the same frequency (in fact the letter is e which appears in English with a high frequency). Simple substitution ciphers are not secure for hiding natural-language-based information. For details of the cryptanalysis technique based on studying the frequencies of letters, see any standard texts in cryptography, e.g., §2.2 of [94], or §7.3.5 of [200].)

Polyalphabetic ciphers and transposition ciphers are stronger than simple substitution ciphers. However, if the key is short and the message is long, then various cryptanalysis techniques can be applied to break such ciphers.

However, classical ciphers, even simple substitution ciphers can be secure in a *very strong sense* if the use of cryptographic keys follows certain conditions. In fact, with the proper key usages, simple substitution ciphers are widely used in cryptographic systems and protocols.

## 7.5.1 Usefulness of Classical Ciphers

Let us now look at an example of the shift cipher (i.e., the simplest substitution cipher) being securely used in a cryptographic protocol. After showing the example, we will summarize two important conditions for secure use of classical ciphers.

Suppose we have a function $f(x)$ over $\mathbb{Z}_n$ with the following two properties:

**One-way:** given any $x \in \mathbb{Z}_n$, evaluation of $f(x)$ can be done efficiently (review §4.4.6 for the meaning of efficient computation) while for almost all $y \in \mathbb{Z}_n$ and for any efficient algorithms $A$, $\text{Prob}[x \leftarrow A(y) \wedge f(x) = y]$ is a negligible quantity in size of $y$ (review 4.6 for the meaning of negligible quantity);

**Homomorphic:** for all $x_1, x_2 \in \mathbb{Z}_n$, $f(x_1 + x_2) = f(x_1) \cdot f(x_2)$.

There are many functions which apparently satisfy these two properties; we shall see many such functions later in this book.

Using this function, we can construct a so-called "zero-knowledge proof" protocol, which allows a **prover** (let it be Alice) to show a **verifier** (let it be Bob) that she knows the pre-image of $f(z)$ (which is $z < n$) without disclosing to the latter the pre-image. This can be achieved by a simple protocol which uses the shift cipher. The protocol is specified in Prot 7.1.

Prot 7.1 is a very useful one. In applications, the value $X = f(z)$ can be Alice's cryptographic credential for proving her identity or entitlement to a service. Only

---

**Protocol 7.1:** A Zero-knowledge Protocol Using Shift Cipher

COMMON INPUT    i) $f()$: a one-way and homomorphic function over $\mathbb{Z}_n$;
                ii) $X = f(z)$ for some $z \in \mathbb{Z}_n$.

Alice's INPUT       $z < n$. (* prover's private input *)

OUTPUT to Bob       Alice knows $z \in \mathbb{Z}_n$ such that $X = f(z)$.

Repeat the following steps $m$ times:

1. Alice picks $k \in_U \mathbb{Z}_n$, computes Commit $\leftarrow f(k)$ and sends it to Bob;

2. Bob picks Challenge $\in_U \{0, 1\}$ and sends it to Alice;

3. Alice computes Response $\leftarrow \begin{cases} k & \text{if Challenge} = 0 \\ k + z \pmod{n} & \text{if Challenge} = 1 \end{cases}$

   She sends Response to Bob;

   (* when Challenge $= 1$, Response is a ciphertext output from shift cipher encryption of $z$ under the one-time key $k$, see (7.3.1) *)

4. Bob checks $f(\text{Response}) \overset{?}{=} \begin{cases} \text{Commit} & \text{if Challenge} = 0 \\ \text{Commit} \cdot X & \text{if Challenge} = 1 \end{cases}$

   he rejects and aborts the run if any checking step shows an error;

Bob accepts.

---

Alice can use the credential because only she knows how to use it as a result of the fact that only she knows the pre-image $z$. This protocol shows how Alice should use her credential without the verifier Bob know *any* information about the pre-image $z$.

In Chapter 18 we will make an extensive use of this protocol and its several variations when we study the subject of zero-knowledge proof protocols. For this moment, all we should concern is the quality of confidentiality service that this protocol provides for hiding Alice's private information $z$.

## 7.5.2    Security of Classical Ciphers

Let us now see the quality of confidentiality service that the shift-cipher encryption offers in Prot 7.1. We claim that the quality is *perfect*. That is, after running this protocol Bob gets absolutely *no* new information about $z \in \mathbb{Z}_n$ beyond what he may have already obtained from the common input $f(z)$ (the common input only provides *apriori* information).

We should notice that the shift cipher encryption

$$\mathsf{Response} = z + k \ (\mathrm{mod} \ n)$$

forms a permutation over $\mathbb{Z}_n$. With $k \in_U \mathbb{Z}_n = \mathcal{K} = \mathcal{M}$, the permutation renders $\mathsf{Response} \in_U \mathbb{Z}_n$ since a permutation maps the uniform distribution to the uniform distribution. This means that for a given ciphertext $\mathsf{Response}$, *any* key in $\mathbb{Z}_n$ could have been used with the same probability in the creation of $\mathsf{Response}$ (the probability space being the key space and the message space). This is equivalent to say that *any* $x \in \mathbb{Z}_n$ is equally likely to have been encrypted inside $\mathsf{Response}$. So the plaintext $z$ is independent from the ciphertext $\mathsf{Response}$, or the ciphertext leaks no information whatsoever about the plaintext.

If a cipher achieves independence between the distributions of its plaintext and ciphertext, then we say that the cipher is secure in an **information-theoretically secure** sense. In contrast to a security in the complexity-theoretic sense which we have established in Chapter 4, the security in the information-theoretic sense is *unconditional* and is immune to any method of cryptanalysis. In Prot 7.1, this sense of security means that runs of the protocol will not provide Bob with any knowledge regarding Alice's private input $z$, except the conviction that Alice has the correct private input.

The notion of information-theoretic-based cryptographic security is developed by Shannon [266]. According to Shannon's theory, we can summarize two conditions for secure use of classical ciphers:

**Conditions for Secure Use of Classical Ciphers**

i) $\#\mathcal{K} \geq \#\mathcal{M}$;

ii) $k \in_U \mathcal{K}$ and is used once in each encryption only.

So if a classical cipher (whether it is a simple substitution cipher in character-based or string-based, a polyalphabetic cipher, or the Vernam cipher) encrypts a message string of length $\ell$, then in order for the encryption to be secure, the length of a key string should be at least $\ell$, and the key string should be used once only. While this requirement may not be very practical for applications which involve encryption of bulk volumes of messages, it is certainly practical for encrypting small data, such as a nonce (see §2.6.4) or a session key (see §2.5). Prot 7.1 is just such an example.

In the rest of this book we will meet numerous cryptographic systems and protocols which apply various forms of substitution ciphers such as shift ciphers (as in Prot 7.1), multiplication ciphers (defined in (7.3.2)), affine ciphers (defined in (7.3.3)), and substitution ciphers under the general form of permutations (as in Example 7.1). Most of such applications follow the two conditions for secure use of classical ciphers.

## 7.6    The Data Encryption Standard (DES)

Without doubt the first and the most significant modern symmetric encryption algorithm is that contained in the Data Encryption Standard (DES) [213]. The DES was published by the United States' National Bureau of Standards in January 1977 as an algorithm to be used for unclassified data (information not concerned with national security). The algorithm has been in wide international use, a primary example being its employment by banks for funds transfer security. Originally approved for a five-year period, the standard stood the test of time and was subsequently approved for three further five-year periods.

### 7.6.1    A Description of the DES

The DES is a **block cipher** in which messages are divided into data blocks of a fixed length and each block is treated as one message either in $\mathcal{M}$ or in $\mathcal{C}$. In the DES, we have $\mathcal{M} = \mathcal{C} = \{0, 1\}^{64}$ and $\mathcal{K} = \{0, 1\}^{56}$; namely, the DES encryption and decryption algorithms take as input a 64-bit plaintext or ciphertext message and a 56-bit key, and output a 64-bit ciphertext or plaintext message.

The operation of the DES can be described in the following three steps:

1. Apply a fixed "initial permutation" IP to the input block. We can write this initial permutation as

$$(L_0, R_0) \leftarrow \text{IP(Input Block)}. \tag{7.6.1}$$

Here $L_0$ and $R_0$ are called "(left, right)-half blocks," each is a 32-bit block. Notice that $IP$ is a fixed function (i.e., is not parameterized by the input key) and is publicly known; therefore this initial permutation has no apparent cryptographic significance.

2. Iterate the following 16 **rounds** of operations (for $i = 1, 2, \ldots, 16$)

$$L_i \leftarrow R_{i-1} \tag{7.6.2}$$
$$R_i \leftarrow L_{i-1} \oplus f(R_{i-1}, k_i). \tag{7.6.3}$$

Here $k_i$ is called "round key" which is a 48-bit substring of the 56-bit input key; $f$ is called "S-box Function" ("S" for substitution, we will provide a brief description on this function in §7.6.2) and is a substitution cipher (§7.3). This operation features swapping two half blocks, that is, the left half block input to a round is the right half block output from the previous round. The swapping operation is a simple transposition cipher (§7.4) which aims to achieve a big degree of "message diffusion," essentially the mixing property modeled by Shannon in (7.1.1). From our discussion we can see that this step of DES is a combination of a substitution cipher and a transposition cipher.

3. The result from round 16, $(L_{16}, R_{16})$, is input to the inverse of IP to cancel the effect of the initial permutation. The output from this step is the output of the DES algorithm. We can write this final step as

$$\text{Output Block} \leftarrow \text{IP}^{-1}(R_{16}, L_{16}). \tag{7.6.4}$$

Please pay a particular attention to the input to $\text{IP}^{-1}$: the two half blocks output from round 16 take an additional swap before being input to $\text{IP}^{-1}$.

These three steps are shared by the encryption and the decryption algorithms, with the only difference in that, if the round keys used by one algorithm are $k_1, k_2, \ldots, k_{16}$, then those used by the other algorithm should be $k_{16}, k_{15}, \ldots, k_1$. This way of arranging round keys is called "key schedule," and can be denoted by

$$(k_1', k_2', \ldots, k_{16}') = (k_{16}, k_{15}, \ldots, k_1). \tag{7.6.5}$$

**Example 7.4:** Let a plaintext message $m$ be encrypted to a ciphertext message $c$ under an encryption key $k$. Let us go through the DES algorithm to confirm the proper working of the decryption function, i.e., decryption of $c$ under $k$ will output $m$.

The decryption algorithm starts by inputing the ciphertext $c$ as "Input Block." By (7.6.1) we have

$$(L_0', R_0') \leftarrow \text{IP}(c).$$

But since $c$ is actually "Output Block" from the final step of the encryption algorithm, by (7.6.4) we have

$$(L_0', R_0') = (R_{16}, L_{16}). \tag{7.6.6}$$

In round 1, from (7.6.2), (7.6.3) and (7.6.6), we have

$$L_1' \leftarrow R_0' = L_{16},$$
$$R_1' \leftarrow L_0' \oplus f(R_0', k_1') = R_{16} \oplus f(L_{16}, k_1').$$

In the right-hand sides of these two assignments, $L_{16}$ should be replaced with $R_{15}$ due to (7.6.2), $R_{16}$ should be replaced with $L_{15} \oplus f(R_{15}, k_{16})$ due to (7.6.3), and $k_1' = k_{16}$ due to the key schedule (7.6.5). Thus, the above two assignments are in fact the following two:

$$L_1' \leftarrow R_{15},$$
$$R_1' \leftarrow [L_{15} \oplus f(R_{15}, k_{16})] \oplus f(R_{15}, k_{16}) = L_{15}.$$

So, after round 1 of decryption, we obtain

$$(L_1', R_1') = (R_{15}, L_{15}).$$

Therefore, at the beginning of round 2, the two half blocks are $(R_{15}, L_{15})$.

It is routine to check that, in the subsequent 15 rounds, we will obtain

$$(L_2', R_2') = (R_{14}, L_{14}), \quad \ldots \ldots, \quad (L_{16}', R_{16}') = (R_0, L_0).$$

The two final half blocks from round 16, $(L_{16}', R_{16}')$ are swapped to $(R_{16}', L_{16}') = (L_0, R_0)$ and are input to $\text{IP}^{-1}$ (notice (7.6.4) for the additional swapping) to cancel the effect of the IP in (7.6.1). Indeed, the output from the decryption function is the original plaintext block $m$. $\qquad \square$

We have shown that the DES encryption and decryption algorithms do keep equation (7.2.1) to hold for all $m \in \mathcal{M}$ and all $k \in \mathcal{K}$. It is clear that these algorithms work with no regard of the internal details of the "S-box Function" and the key schedule function.

The DES iterations which use (7.6.2) and (7.6.3) to process two half blocks in a swapping fashion is called the **Feistel cipher**. Fig 7.2 illustrates the swapping structure of one round Feistel cipher. Feistel proposed this cipher originally [108]. As we have mentioned earlier, the swapping feature aims to achieve a big degree of data diffusion. Feistel cipher also has an important application in public-key cryptography: a structure named **Optimal Asymmetric Encryption Padding (OAEP)** is essentially a two-round Feistel cipher. We will study OAEP in §15.2.

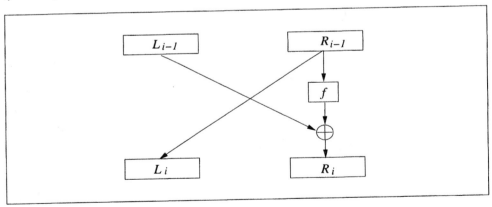

**Figure 7.2.** Feistel Cipher (One Round)

## 7.6.2   The Kernel Functionality of the DES: Random and Non-linear Distribution of Message

The kernel part of the DES is inside the "S-box Function" $f$. This is where the DES realizes a random and non-linear distribution of plaintext messages over the ciphertext message space.

In the $i$-th round, $f(R_{i-1}, k_i)$ does the following two sub-operations:

i) add the round key $k_i$, via bit-wise XOR, to the half block $R_{i-1}$; this provides the randomness needed in message distribution;

ii) substitute the result of (i) under a fixed permutation which consists of eight "substitution boxes" (S-boxes), each S-box is a non-linear permutation function; this provides the non-linearity needed in message distribution.

The non-linearity of the S-boxes is very important to the security of the DES. We notice that the general case of the substitution cipher (e.g., Example 7.1 with random key) is non-linear while the shift cipher and the affine cipher are linear sub-cases. These linear sub-cases not only drastically reduce the size of the key space from that of the general case, but also render the resultant ciphertext vulnerable to a **differential cryptanalysis** (DC) technique [34]. DC attacks a cipher by exploiting the linear difference between two plaintext messages and that between two ciphertext messages. Let us look at such an attack using the affine cipher (7.3.3) for example. Suppose Malice (the attacker) somehow knows the difference $m - m'$ but he does not know $m$ nor $m'$. Given the corresponding ciphertexts $c = k_1 m + k_2 \pmod{N}$, $c' = k_1 m' + k_2 \pmod{N}$, Malice can calculate

$$k_1 = (c - c')/(m - m') \pmod{N}.$$

With $k_1$, it becomes much easier for Malice to further find $k_2$, e.g., $k_2$ can be found if Malice has a known plaintext-ciphertext pair. Subsequent to its discovery in 1990, DC has been shown as very powerful against many known block ciphers. However, it is not very successful against the DES. It turned out that the designer of the DES had anticipated DC 15 years earlier [82] through the non-linear design of the S-boxes.

An interesting feature of the DES (in fact, the Feistel cipher) is that the S-boxes in function $f(R_{i-1}, k_i)$ need not be invertible. This is shown in Example 7.4 as encryption and decryption working for arbitrary $f(R_{i-1}, k_i)$. This feature saves space for the hardware realization of the DES.

We shall omit the description of the internal details of the S-boxes, of the key-schedule function and of the initial-permutation function. These details are out of the scope of the book. The interested reader is referred to §2.6.2 of [94] for these details.

## 7.6.3 The Security of the DES

Debates on the security of the DES started soon after the DES was proposed as the encryption standard. Detailed discussions and historical accounts can be found in various cryptographic texts, e.g., §2 of [281], §3.3 of [286], and §7.4.3 of [200]. Later, it became more and more clear that these debates reached a single main critique:

the DES has a relatively short key length. This is regarded as the only most serious weakness of the DES. Attacks related to this weakness involve exhaustively testing keys, using a known pair of plaintext and ciphertext messages, until the correct key is found. This is the so-called **brute-force** or **exhaustive key search attack**.

However, we should not regard a brute-force key search attack as a real attack. This is because the cipher designers not only have anticipated it, but also have hoped this to be the only means for an adversary. Therefore, given the computation technology of the 1970s, the DES is a very successful cipher.

One solution to overcome the short-key limitation is to run the DES algorithm a multiple number of times using different keys. One such proposal is called encryption-decryption-encryption-**triple DES** scheme [292]. Encryption under this scheme can be denoted by

$$c \leftarrow \mathcal{E}_{k_1}(\mathcal{D}_{k_2}(\mathcal{E}_{k_1}(m))),$$

and decryption by

$$m \leftarrow \mathcal{D}_{k_1}(\mathcal{E}_{k_2}(\mathcal{D}_{k_1}(c))).$$

In addition to achieving an effect of enlarging the key space, this scheme also achieves an easy compatibility with the single-key DES, if $k_1 = k_2$ is used. The triple DES can also use three different keys, but then is not compatible with the single-key DES.

The short-key weakness of the DES became evident in the 1990s. In 1993, Wiener argued that a special-purpose VLSI DES key search machine can be built at the cost of US$1,000,000. Given a pair of plaintext-ciphertext messages, this machine can be expected to find the key in 3.5 hours [301]. On July 15, 1998, a coalition of Cryptography Research, Advanced Wireless Technologies and Electronic Frontier Foundation announced a record-breaking DES key search attack: they built a key search machine, called the DES Cracker (also know as Deep Crack), with a cost under US$250,000, and successfully found the key of the RSA's DES Challenge after searching for 56 hours [111]. This result demonstrates that a 56-bit key is too short for a secure secret-key cipher for the late 1990s computation technology.

## 7.7　The Advanced Encryption Standard (AES)

On January 2, 1997, the United States' National Institute of Standards and Technology (NIST) announced the initiation of a new symmetric-key block cipher algorithm as the new encryption standard to replace the DES. The new algorithm would be named the Advanced Encryption Standard (AES). Unlike the closed design process for the DES, an open call for the AES algorithms was formally made on September 12, 1997. The call stipulated that the AES would specify an unclassified, publicly disclosed symmetric-key encryption algorithm(s); the algorithm(s) must support (at a minimum) block sizes of 128-bits, key sizes of 128-, 192-, and 256-bits, and should have a strength at the level of the triple DES, but should be more efficient then the triple DES. In addition, the algorithm(s), if selected, must be available royalty-free, worldwide.

On August 20, 1998, NIST announced a group of fifteen AES candidate algorithms. These algorithms had been submitted by members of the cryptographic community from around the world. Public comments on the fifteen candidates were solicited as the initial review of these algorithms (the period for the initial public comments was also called the Round 1). The Round 1 closed on April 15, 1999. Using the analyses and comments received, NIST selected five algorithms from the fifteen. The five AES finalist candidate algorithms were MARS [63], RC6 [249], Rijndael [87], Serpent [15], and Twofish [257]. These finalist algorithms received further analysis during a second, more in-depth review period (the Round 2). In the Round 2, comments and analysis were sought on any aspect of the candidate algorithms, including, but not limited to, the following topics: cryptanalysis, intellectual property, cross-cutting analyses of all of the AES finalists, overall recommendations and implementation issues. After the close of the Round 2 public analysis period on May 15, 2000, NIST studied all available information in order to make a selection for the AES. On October 2, 2000, NIST announced that it has selected Rijndael to propose for the AES.

Rijndael is designed by two Belgium cryptographers: Daemen and Rijmen.

## 7.7.1  An Overview of the Rijndael Cipher

Rijndael is a block cipher with a variable block size and variable key size. The key size and the block size can be independently specified to 128, 192 or 256 bits. For simplicity we will only describe the minimum case of the 128-bit key size and the same block size. Our confined description will not cause any loss of generality to the working principle of the Rijndael cipher.

In this case, a 128-bit message (plaintext, ciphertext) block is segmented into 16 bytes (a byte is a unit of 8 binary bits, so $128 = 16 \times 8$):

$$\text{InputBlock} = m_0, m_1, \ldots, m_{15}.$$

So is a key block:

$$\text{InputKey} = k_0, k_1, \ldots, k_{15}.$$

The data structure for their internal representation is a $4 \times 4$ matrix:

$$\text{InputBlock} = \begin{pmatrix} m_0 & m_4 & m_8 & m_{12} \\ m_1 & m_5 & m_9 & m_{13} \\ m_2 & m_6 & m_{10} & m_{14} \\ m_3 & m_7 & m_{11} & m_{15} \end{pmatrix},$$

$$\mathrm{InputKey} = \begin{pmatrix} k_0 & k_4 & k_8 & k_{12} \\ k_1 & k_5 & k_9 & k_{13} \\ k_2 & k_6 & k_{10} & k_{14} \\ k_3 & k_7 & k_{11} & k_{15} \end{pmatrix}.$$

Like the DES (and most modern symmetric-key block ciphers), the Rijndael algorithm comprises a plural number of iterations of a basic unit of transformation: "round." In the minimum case of 128-bit message-block and key-block size, the number of rounds is 10. For larger message sizes and key sizes, the number of rounds should be increased accordingly and is given in Figure 5 of [221].

A round transformation in Rijndael is denoted by

$$\mathsf{Round}(State, RoundKey).$$

Here $State$ is a round-message matrix and is treated as both input and output; $RoundKey$ is a round-key matrix and is derived from the input key via key schedule. The execution of a round will cause the elements of $State$ to change value (i.e., to change its state). For encryption (respectively, decryption), $State$ input to the first round is Input Block which is the plaintext (respectively, ciphertext) message matrix, and $State$ output from the final round is the ciphertext (respectively, plaintext) message matrix.

The round (other than the final round) transformation is composed of four different transformations which are internal functions to be described in a moment:

Round($State, RoundKey$) {

    SubBytes($State$);

    ShiftRows($State$);

    MixColumns($State$);

    AddRoundKey($State, RoundKey$);

    }

The final round, denoted by

$$\mathsf{FinalRound}(State, RoundKey),$$

is slightly different: it is equal to Round($State, RoundKey$) with the MixColumns function removed. This is analogous to the situation of the final round in the DES where an additional swap between the output half data blocks is applied.

The round transformations are invertible for the purpose of decryption. The respective reverse round transformations should be denoted by

$$\mathsf{Round}^{-1}(State, RoundKey), \text{ and}$$

FinalRound$^{-1}$(*State*, *RoundKey*),

respectively. We shall see below that the four internal functions are all invertible.

## 7.7.2   The Internal Functions of the Rijndael Cipher

Let us now describe the four internal functions of the Rijndael cipher. We shall only describe the functions for the encryption direction. Because each of the four internal functions is invertible, decryption in Rijndael merely applies their respective inversions in the reverse direction.

The internal functions of the Rijndael cipher work in a finite field. The field is realized as all polynomials modulo the irreducible polynomial

$$f(x) = x^8 + x^4 + x^3 + x + 1$$

over $\mathbb{F}_2$. That is, specifically, the field used by the Rijndael cipher is $\mathbb{F}_2[x]_f$ for $f$ in the above formula. Any element in this field is a polynomial over $\mathbb{F}_2$ of degree less than 8 and the operations are done modulo $f(x)$. Let us name this field the "Rijndael field." Due to isomorphism, we will often use $\mathbb{F}_{2^8}$ to denote this field which has $2^8 = 256$ elements.

We have actually studied the Rijndael field in Chapter 5, Examples 5.17, 5.18 and 5.19, where we demonstrated the following operations:

- A 1-1 mapping between an integer byte and a field element (Example 5.17)

- Addition between two field elements (Example 5.18)

- Multiplication between two field elements (Example 5.19)

Our study there can now help us to describe the Rijndael internal functions.

First of all, as we have already described, a block of message (a state) and a block of key in the Rijndael cipher are segmented into bytes. From the simple 1-1 mapping scheme described in Example 5.17, these bytes will be viewed as field elements and will be processed by several Rijndael internal functions which we now describe.

### 7.7.2.1   Internal Function SubBytes(*State*)

This function provides a non-linear substitution on each byte (i.e., $x$) of *State*. Any non-zero byte $x \in (\mathbb{F}_{2^8})^*$ is substituted by the following transformation:

$$y = Ax^{-1} + b. \tag{7.7.1}$$

where

$$
A = \begin{pmatrix}
1 & 0 & 0 & 0 & 1 & 1 & 1 & 1 \\
1 & 1 & 0 & 0 & 0 & 1 & 1 & 1 \\
1 & 1 & 1 & 0 & 0 & 0 & 1 & 1 \\
1 & 1 & 1 & 1 & 0 & 0 & 0 & 1 \\
1 & 1 & 1 & 1 & 1 & 0 & 0 & 0 \\
0 & 1 & 1 & 1 & 1 & 1 & 0 & 0 \\
0 & 0 & 1 & 1 & 1 & 1 & 1 & 0 \\
0 & 0 & 0 & 1 & 1 & 1 & 1 & 1
\end{pmatrix}
\quad \text{and} \quad
b = \begin{pmatrix}
1 \\ 1 \\ 0 \\ 0 \\ 0 \\ 1 \\ 1 \\ 0
\end{pmatrix}.
$$

If $x$ is the zero byte, then $y = b$ is the **SubBytes** transformation result.

We should notice that the non-linearity of the transformation in (7.7.1) comes from the inversion $x^{-1}$ only. Should the transformation be applied on $x$ directly, the affine equation in (7.7.1) would then be *absolutely linear*!

Since the $8 \times 8$ constant matrix $A$ is an invertible one (i.e., its rows are linearly independent in $\mathbb{F}_{2^8}$), the transformation in (7.7.1) is invertible. Hence, function SubBytes($State$) is invertible.

### 7.7.2.2   Internal Function ShiftRows($State$)

This function operates on each row of $State$. For the case of 128-bit block size, it is the following transformation:

$$
\begin{pmatrix}
s_{0,0} & s_{0,1} & s_{0,2} & s_{0,3} \\
s_{1,0} & s_{1,1} & s_{1,2} & s_{1,3} \\
s_{2,0} & s_{2,1} & s_{2,2} & s_{2,3} \\
s_{3,0} & s_{3,1} & s_{3,2} & s_{3,3}
\end{pmatrix}
\rightarrow
\begin{pmatrix}
s_{0,0} & s_{0,1} & s_{0,2} & s_{0,3} \\
s_{1,1} & s_{1,2} & s_{1,3} & s_{1,0} \\
s_{2,2} & s_{2,3} & s_{2,0} & s_{2,1} \\
s_{3,3} & s_{3,0} & s_{3,1} & s_{3,2}
\end{pmatrix}.
\qquad (7.7.2)
$$

This operation is actually a transposition cipher (§7.4). It only rearranges the positions of the elements without changing their identities: for elements in the $i$th row ($i = 0, 1, 2, 3$), the position rearrangement is "cyclic shifting to right" by $4 - i$ positions.

Since the transposition cipher only rearranges positions of the row elements, the transformation is of course mechanically invertible.

### 7.7.2.3   Internal Function MixColumns($State$)

This function operates on each column of $State$. So for $State$ of four columns of the right-hand-side matrix in (7.7.2), MixColumns($State$) repeats four iterations. The following description is for one column only. The output of an iteration is still a column.

First, let

$$
\begin{pmatrix}
s_0 \\
s_1 \\
s_2 \\
s_3
\end{pmatrix}
$$

be a column in the right-hand-side matrix in (7.7.2). Notice that we have omitted the column number for clarity in exposition.

This column is interpreted into a degree-3 polynomial:

$$s(x) = s_3 x^3 + s_2 x^2 + s_1 x + s_0.$$

Notice that because the coefficients of $s(x)$ are bytes, i.e., are elements in $\mathbb{F}_{2^8}$, this polynomial is *over* $\mathbb{F}_{2^8}$, and hence is *not* an element in the Rijndael field.

The operation on the column $s(x)$ is defined by multiplying this polynomial with a fixed degree-3 polynomial $c(x)$, modulo $x^4 + 1$:

$$c(x) \cdot s(x) \ (\mathrm{mod}\ x^4 + 1), \tag{7.7.3}$$

where the fixed polynomial $c(x)$ is

$$c(x) = c_3 x^3 + c_2 x^2 + c_1 x + c_0 = \text{`03'} x^3 + \text{`01'} x^2 + \text{`01'} x + \text{`02'}.$$

The coefficients of $c(x)$ are also elements in $\mathbb{F}_{2^8}$ (denoted by the hexadecimal representations of the respective bytes, or field elements).

We should notice that the multiplication in (7.7.3) is *not* an operation in the Rijndael field: $c(x)$ and $s(x)$ are not even Rijndael field elements. Also because $x^4 + 1$ is reducible over $\mathbb{F}_2$ $(x^4 + 1 = (x + 1)^4)$, the multiplication in (7.7.3) is not even an operation in any field (review Theorem 5.5 in §5.4.2.2). The only reason for this multiplication being performed modulo a degree-4 polynomial is in order for the operation to output a degree-3 polynomial, that is, to achieve a transformation from a column (a degree-3 polynomial) to a column (a degree-3 polynomial). This transformation can be viewed as a polyalphabetic substitution (multiplication) cipher using a known key.

The reader may apply the long division method in Example 5.15 (in page 157) to confirm the following equation computed over $\mathbb{F}_2$ (noticing that subtraction in this ring is identical to addition):

$$x^i \ (\mathrm{mod}\ x^4 + 1) = x^{i\ (\mathrm{mod}\ 4)}.$$

Therefore, in the product (7.7.3), the coefficient for the $x^i$ term (for $i = 0, 1, 2, 3$) must be the sum of $c_j s_k$ satisfying $j + k = i$ (mod 4) (where $j, k = 0, 1, 2, 3$). For example, the coefficient for the $x^2$ term in the product is

$$c_2 s_0 + c_1 s_1 + c_0 s_2 + c_3 s_3.$$

The multiplication and addition are in $\mathbb{F}_{2^8}$. For this reason, it is now easy to check that the polynomial multiplication in (7.7.3) can be achieved by taking the following linear algebraic one:

$$
\begin{pmatrix} d_0 \\ d_1 \\ d_2 \\ d_3 \end{pmatrix} = \begin{pmatrix} c_0 & c_3 & c_2 & c_1 \\ c_1 & c_0 & c_3 & c_2 \\ c_2 & c_1 & c_0 & c_3 \\ c_3 & c_2 & c_1 & c_0 \end{pmatrix} \begin{pmatrix} s_0 \\ s_1 \\ s_2 \\ s_3 \end{pmatrix}
$$
$$
= \begin{pmatrix} `02' & `03' & `01' & `01' \\ `01' & `02' & `03' & `01' \\ `01' & `01' & `02' & `03' \\ `03' & `01' & `01' & `02' \end{pmatrix} \begin{pmatrix} s_0 \\ s_1 \\ s_2 \\ s_3 \end{pmatrix}. \tag{7.7.4}
$$

We further notice that because $c(x)$ is relatively prime to $x^4 + 1$ over $\mathbb{F}_2$, the inversion $c(x)^{-1} \pmod{x^4 + 1}$ exists in $\mathbb{F}_2[x]$. This is equivalent to saying that the matrix and hence the transformation in (7.7.4) are invertible.

### 7.7.2.4   Internal Function AddRoundKey($State, RoundKey$)

This function merely adds, byte by byte and bit by bit, the elements of $RoundKey$ to those of $State$. Here "add" is addition in $\mathbb{F}_2$ (i.e., bit-wise XOR) and is trivially invertible; the inversion is "add" itself.

The $RoundKey$ bits have been "scheduled," i.e., the key bits for different rounds are different, and are derived from the key using a fixed (non-secret) "key schedule" scheme. For details for "key schedule" see Figure 12 of [221].

To this end we have completed the description of the Rijndael internal functions and hence the encryption operation.

### 7.7.2.5   Decryption Operation

As we have seen that each of the four internal functions are invertible, the decryption is merely to invert the encryption in the reverse direction, i.e., applying

AddRoundKey($State, RoundKey$)$^{-1}$;

MixColumns($State$)$^{-1}$;

ShiftRows($State$)$^{-1}$;

SubBytes($State$)$^{-1}$.

We should notice that, unlike in the case of a Feistel cipher where encryption and decryption use the same circuit (hardware) or code (software), the Rijndael cipher must implement different circuits and codes for encryption and decryption, respectively.

### 7.7.3 Summary of the Roles of the Rijndael Internal Functions

At the end of our description of the Rijndael cipher let us provide a summary on the roles of the four internal functions.

- SubBytes is intended to achieve a non-linear substitution cipher. As we have discussed in §7.6.2, non-linearity is an important property for a block cipher to prevent differential cryptanalysis.

- ShiftRows and MixColumns are intended to achieve a mixture of the bytes positioned in different places of a plaintext message block. Typically, plaintext messages have a low-entropy distribution in the message space due to the high redundancy contained in natural languages and business data (that is, typical plaintexts concentrate in a small subspace of the whole message space). A mixture of the bytes in different positions of a message block causes a wider distribution of messages in the whole message space. This is essentially the mixing property modeled by Shannon in 7.1.1.

- AddRoundKey provides the necessary secret randomness to the message distribution.

These functions repeat a plural number of times (minimum 10 for the case of 128-bit key and data size), and the result is the Rijndael cipher.

### 7.7.4 Fast and Secure Implementation

We have seen that the Rijndael internal functions are very simple and operate in trivially small algebraic spaces. As a result, implementations of these internal functions can be done with extremely good efficiency. From our descriptions of the Rijndael internal functions, we see that only SubBytes and MixColumns have non-trivial algebraic operations and hence are worthy of fast implementation considerations.

First, in SubBytes, the calculation of $x^{-1}$ can be efficiently done using a "table lookup" method: a small table of $2^8 = 256$ pairs of bytes can be built once and used forever (i.e., the table can be "hardwired" into hardware or software implementations). In this table of pairs, the zero byte is paired with the zero byte; the rest of the 255 entries in the table are the 255 cases of the pair $(x, x^{-1})$. The "table lookup" method not only is efficient, but also prevents a **timing analysis attack** which is based on observing the operation time difference for different data which may suggest whether an operation is performed on bit 0 or bit 1 (see §12.5.4).

Because the matrix $A$ and the vector $b$ in (7.7.1) are constants, the "table lookup" method can actually include the whole transformation (7.7.1) altogether, that is, the table of 256 entries are the pairs $(x, y)$ with $x, y \in \mathbb{F}_{2^8}$ with $(0, b)$ being a special case of $(x, y)$.

Clearly, inversion is merely to use the inversion table. Therefore, SubBytes can be implemented by two small tables, each of the size 256 bytes.

Next, in MixColumns, multiplication between elements in $\mathbb{F}_{2^8}$, i.e., that between coefficients of $c(x)$ and $s(x)$, or more precisely, that between an element of the fixed matrix and that in a column vector in (7.7.4), can also be realized via a "table lookup" method: $z = x \cdot y$ (field multiplication) where $x \in \{\text{'01'}, \text{'02'}, \text{'03'}\}$ and $y \in \mathbb{F}_{2^8}$. Further notice that the byte '01' is simply the multiplicative identity in the field, i.e., $\text{'01'} \cdot y = y$. Thus, implementation (either in software or hardware) of this multiplication table only needs $2 \times 256 = 512$ entries. This small table is not much larger than one which every primary school pupil has to recite. This realization not only is fast, but also decreases the risk of the timing analysis attack.

The linear algebraic operation in (7.7.4) and its inversion also have a fast "hardwired" implementation method. The reader with a more investigative appetite is referred to [88].

## 7.7.5  Positive Impact of the AES on Applied Cryptography

The introduction of the AES will in turn introduce a few positive changes in applied cryptography.

First, multiple encryption, such as triple-DES, will become unnecessary with the AES: the enlarged and variable key and data-block sizes of 128, 192 and 256 can accommodate a wide spectrum of security strengths for various application needs. Since multiple encryption uses a plural number of keys, the avoidance of using multiple encryption will mean a reduction on the number of cryptographic keys that an application has to manage, and hence will simplify the design of security protocols and systems.

Secondly, wide use of the AES will lead to the emergence of new hash functions of compatible security strengths. In several ways, block cipher encryption algorithms are closely related to hash functions (see §10.3.1). It has been a standard practice that block cipher encryption algorithms are often used to play the role of one-way hash functions. The logging-in authentication protocol of the UNIX[a] operating system [208] is a well-known example; we shall see in §11.5.1 a typical "one-way transformation" usage of the DES function in the realization of the UNIX password scheme. Another example of using block cipher encryption algorithms to realize (keyed) one-way hash functions can be seen in §10.3.3. In practice, hash functions are also commonly used as pseudo-random number functions for generating keys for block cipher algorithms. With the AES's variable and enlarged key and data-block sizes, hash functions of compatible sizes will be needed. However, due to the square-root attack (the birthday attack, see §3.6 and §10.3.1), a hash function should have a size which doubles the size of a block cipher's key or data-block size. Thus, matching the AES's sizes of 128, 192 and 256, new hash functions of output

---

[a]UNIX is a trademark of Bell Laboratories.

sizes of 256, 384 and 512 are needed. The ISO/IEC are currently in the process of standardizing hash functions SHA-256, SHA-384 and SHA-512 [153].

Finally, as in the case that the DES's standard position had attracted much cryptanalysis attention trying to break the algorithm, and that these efforts have contributed to the advance of knowledge in block cipher cryptanalysis, the AES as the new block cipher standard will also give rise to a new resurgence of high research interest in block cipher cryptanalysis which will certainly further advance the knowledge in the area.

# 7.8   Confidentiality Modes of Operation

A block cipher processes (encrypts or decrypts) messages as data blocks. Usually, the size of a bulk message (i.e., a message string) is larger than the size of the message block of a block cipher, the long message is divided into a series of sequentially listed message blocks, and the cipher processes these blocks one at a time.

A number of different modes of operation have been devised on top of an underlying block cipher algorithm. These modes of operation (except a trivial case of them) provide several desirable properties to the ciphertext blocks, such as adding nondeterminism (randomness) to a block cipher algorithm, padding plaintext messages to an arbitrary length (so that the length of a ciphertext needn't be related to that of the corresponding plaintext), control of error propagation, generation of key stream for a stream cipher, etc.

However, we should not consider that the use of these modes of operations can turn a "textbook crypto" block cipher into a fit-for-application one. This point will be made clear in the study (in particular, in §7.8.2.1 where we will see an active attack which is applicable to several protocols in wide use in the real world).

We describe here five usual modes of operation. They are **electronic code-book (ECB)** mode, **cipher block chaining (CBC)** mode, **output feedback (OFB)** mode, **cipher feedback (CFB)** mode, and **counter (CTR)** mode. Our description follow the most recent NIST recommendation [220].

In our description, we will use the following notation:

- $\mathcal{E}()$: the encryption algorithm of the underlying block cipher;

- $\mathcal{D}()$: the decryption algorithm of the underlying block cipher;

- $n$: the binary size of the message block of the underlying block cipher algorithm (in all block ciphers we consider, the plaintext and ciphertext message spaces coincide, and so $n$ is the block size of both input and output of the block cipher algorithm);

- $P_1, P_2, \ldots, P_m$: $m$ successive segments of plaintext messages input to a mode of operation;

- the $m$-th segment may have a smaller size than the other segments and in that case a padding is applied to make the $m$-th segment the same size as the other segments;

- the size of a message segment is equal to $n$ (the block size) in some modes of operation, and is any positive number less than or equal to $n$ in other modes of operation;

- $C_1, C_2, \ldots, C_m$: $m$ successive segments of ciphertext messages output from a mode of operation;

- $\mathrm{LSB}_u(B)$, $\mathrm{MSB}_v(B)$: the least $u$, and the most $v$, significant bits of the block $B$, respectively; for example

$$\mathrm{LSB}_2(1010011) = 11, \quad \mathrm{MSB}_5(1010011) = 10100;$$

- $A \parallel B$: concatenation of the data blocks $A$ and $B$; for example,

$$\mathrm{LSB}_2(1010011) \parallel \mathrm{MSB}_5(1010011) = 11 \parallel 10100 = 1110100.$$

## 7.8.1  The Electronic Codebook Mode (ECB)

The most straightforward way of encrypting (or decrypting) a series of sequentially listed message segments is just to encrypt (or decrypt) them one another separately. In this case, a message segment is just a message block. Analogous to the assignment of code words in a codebook, this natural and simple method gets an official name: electronic codebook mode of operation (ECB). The ECB mode is defined as follows:

**ECB Encryption**  $C_i \leftarrow \mathcal{E}(P_i)$, $i = 1, 2, \ldots, m$;

**ECB Decryption**  $P_i \leftarrow \mathcal{E}(C_i)$, $i = 1, 2, \ldots, m$.

The ECB mode is deterministic, that is, if $P_1, P_2, \ldots, P_m$ are encrypted twice under the same key, the output ciphertext blocks will be the same. In applications, data usually have partial information which can be guessed. For example, a salary figure has a guessable range. A ciphertext from a deterministic encryption scheme can allow an attacker to guess the plaintext by trial-and-error if the plaintext message is guessable. For example, if a ciphertext from the ECB mode is known to encrypt a salary figure, then a small number of trials will allow an attacker to recover the figure. In general, we do not wish to use a deterministic cipher, and hence the ECB mode should not be used in most applications.

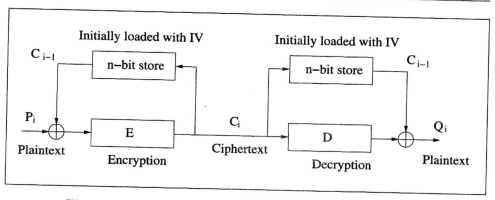

**Figure 7.3.** The Cipher Block Chaining Mode of Operation

## 7.8.2    The Cipher Block Chaining Mode (CBC)

The cipher block chaining (CBC) mode of operation is a common block-cipher algorithm for encryption of general data. Working with the CBC mode, the output is a sequence of $n$-bit cipher blocks which are chained together so that each cipher block is dependent, not just on the plaintext block from which it immediately came, but on all the previous data blocks. The CBC mode has the following operations:

**CBC Encryption**  INPUT: $IV, P_1, \ldots, P_m$;   OUTPUT: $IV, C_1, \ldots, C_m$;

$$C_0 \leftarrow IV;$$
$$C_i \leftarrow \mathcal{E}(P_i \oplus C_{i-1}), \quad i = 1, 2, \ldots, m;$$

**CBC Decryption**  INPUT: $IV, C_1, \ldots, C_m$;   OUTPUT: $P_1, \ldots, P_m$;

$$C_0 \leftarrow IV;$$
$$P_i \leftarrow \mathcal{D}(C_i) \oplus C_{i-1}, \quad i = 1, 2, \ldots, m$$

The computation of the first ciphertext block $C_1$ needs a special input block $C_0$ which is conventionally called the "initial vector" (IV). An IV is a random $n$-bit block. In each session of encryption a new and random IV should be used. Since an IV is treated as a ciphertext block, it need not be secret, but it must be unpredictable. From the encryption procedure we know that the first ciphertext block $C_1$ is randomized by the IV; and in the same way and in turn, a subsequent output ciphertext block is randomized by the immediate preceding ciphertext block. Hence, the CBC mode outputs randomized ciphertext blocks. The ciphertext messages sent to the receiver should include the IV. Thus, for $m$ blocks of plaintext, the CBC mode outputs $m + 1$ ciphertext blocks.

Let $Q_1, Q_2, \ldots, Q_m$ be the data blocks output from decryption of the ciphertext blocks $C_0, C_1, C_2, \ldots, C_m$. Then since

$$Q_i = \mathcal{D}(C_i) \oplus C_{i-1} = (P_i \oplus C_{i-1}) \oplus C_{i-1} = P_i,$$

indeed, the decryption works properly. Fig 7.3 provides an illustration of the CBC mode.

### 7.8.2.1  A Common Misconception

It seems that, because in CBC the data blocks are chained together, the mode may provide a protection against unauthorized data modification such as deletion and insertion (such a protection is **data integrity** which we will study in Chapter 10). Some block cipher algorithms therefore specify algorithmic methods using the CBC mode as a means for serving data integrity. For example, the RC5-CBC-PAD mode [17] specifies the following **CBC plaintext padding scheme** for processing plaintext message blocks before applying encryption in the CBC mode:

1. The plaintext message string is divided into a sequence of bytes (a byte is 8 bits); every eight message bytes form a (plaintext) message block (so the block size is 64).

2. The final plaintext message block of eight bytes must be a "padded block". It starts with the final $a$ plaintext message bytes where $0 \leq a \leq 7$, followed by $8 - a$ "padding bytes." Each of the "padding bytes" has the fixed hexadecimal value $8 - a$. For example, if the final message block has seven plaintext message bytes, then these message bytes are trailed by one "padding byte" which is '01'; therefore the padded block is

   message byte$_1$ ‖ message byte$_2$ ‖ … ‖ message byte$_7$ ‖ '01'

   whereas if the final message block has only one plaintext message byte, then the padded block is

   message byte ‖ '07' ‖ '07' ‖ '07' ‖ '07' ‖ '07' ‖ '07' ‖ '07'

   If the number of message bytes is divisible by 8, then the message bytes are trailed by the following padded block of all "padding bytes":

   '08' ‖ '08' ‖ '08' ‖ '08' ‖ '08' ‖ '08' ‖ '08' ‖ '08'

Other CBC encryption schemes use similar padding schemes. For example, in "IP Encapsulating Security Payload (ESP)" used for IPSec [164] (to be introduced in Chapter 12), $X$ "padding bytes" (for $1 \leq X \leq 255$) are

$$\text{'01' ‖ '02' ‖ } \cdots \text{ ‖ 'xy'}$$

Here '0' $\leq$ 'x' $\leq$ 'F' and '0' $\leq$ 'y' $\leq$ 'F', symbol 'xy' is the hexadecimal presentation for the integer $X$. In the decryption time, the revealed "padding bytes" will be deleted from the retrieved plaintext message (of course, after checking of the "data integrity" consistency).

Several authentication protocols in two early draft documents from the International Organization for Standards (ISO) [146, 147] also suggested to "data-integrity protection" serviced by the CBC encryption mode (general guideline for these protocols to use CBC is documented in [148, 144]).

However, it is in fact utterly wrong to believe that CBC can provide data-integrity protection *in any sense.*

For a CBC "padding byte" scheme, if the use of the scheme intends to provide data-integrity protection, Vaudenay demonstrates an attack [296] which betrays the absence of the protection. In Vaudenay's attack, Malice (the attacker) sends to a principal (a key holder, who is named a **decryption oracle**[b] and provides **oracle service**) two adaptively manipulated ciphertext blocks

$$r, C_i$$

where $r$ is a random data block and $C_i = \mathcal{E}(P \oplus C_{i-1})$ is a ciphertext block for which Malice is interested in knowing the information about the corresponding plaintext message $P$ (e.g., $P$ is a password). From "CBC Decryption" we know that the corresponding decryption will be

$$P \oplus C_{i-1} \oplus r.$$

The "data-integrity" checking method will instruct how the decryption oracle should behave. From the behavior of the decryption oracle Malice may have a good chance to figure out certain information about the plaintext message $P$. For example, if the "data-integrity protection mechanism" instructs the decryption oracle to answer YES upon seeing a "valid padding," then most likely the "valid padding" is the case of the final "padding byte" being '01'. The probability of this event is close to $2^{-8}$ since the probability space is a byte which has eight bits. This is under the condition that, because of the randomness of $r$, other cases of "correct padding" will have much lower probability (due to a much larger probability space of two or more bytes) for the decryption oracle to answer YES and can be neglected. Then Malice discovers

$$\mathrm{LSB}_8(P) = \mathrm{LSB}_8(r) \oplus \text{'01'},$$

i.e., Malice has successfully retrieved the final byte of $P$, a significant amount of information about $P$!

---

[b]The term "oracle" appears frequently in the literature of cryptography, usually for naming any unknown algorithm or method which is alleged to be able to solve a difficult problem. An oracle service means a user providing (often inadvertently) an attacker with cryptographic operations using a key which is not available to the attacker.

If the decryption procedure detects that a padding error has occurred (with probability close to $1 - 2^{-8}$ as reasoned above), the oracle may give an explicit NO answer, or may give no answer at all (the procedure terminates as if the oracle explodes, and hence Vaudenay names this oracle a **bomb oracle**). However, "no answer" is in fact an answer, which is NO in this case. In the case of the answer being NO (explicit or implicit), Malice fails to extract the last byte. But he can change $r$ and retry. This is an **active attack** which mainly targets a principal which provides an oracle service. We will formally define an active attack in §8.6. More scenarios on principals playing the role of an oracle service provider will be seen in many places in the rest of this book.

Vaudenay applies his attacking technique on several cryptographic protocols which are in widespread use in many real-world applications, such as IPSec, SSH and SSL (these protocols will be introduced in Chapter 12). In these real-world applications, a YES/NO answer is easily available to Malice even if answers are not given in an explicit way (e.g., answers are encrypted).

In the basic form of this attack the decryption oracle only answers the last byte with a rather small probability $\approx 2^{-8}$ if the oracle "does not explode". Nevertheless, under fairly standard settings in many applications there are ways to maintain an oracle to be a non-explosive one, and so it can answer further questions to allow Malice to extract further plaintext bytes. Suppose that after giving a YES answer with respect to the final plaintext byte, the oracle is still in one piece. Then Malice can modify $r$ into $r'$ such that

$$\mathrm{LSB}_8(r') \leftarrow \mathrm{LSB}_8(r) \oplus \text{`01'} \oplus \text{`02'}.$$

Then sending $r', C$ to the oracle, Malice can aim to extract the last but one byte of the plaintext with the same probability $2^{-8}$. If the oracle can be maintained to be non-explosive, the attack can carry on, and allow Malice to extract the whole plaintext block in $8 \times 2^8 = 2048$ oracle calls.

In §12.5.4 we will see Vaudenay's attack applied to a CBC-plaintext-padding implementation of an e-mail application which uses the SSL/TLS Protocol. In that attack, the decryption oracle is an e-mail server which never explodes and hence allows Malice to extract the whole block of plaintext message which is a user's password for accessing e-mails. The attack utilizes **side channel** information which is available via **timing analysis**. The attack is therefore called a **side channel attack**.

The ISO protocols which use CBC for data-integrity protection are also fatally flawed [186, 187]. We shall demonstrate the flaw in §17.2.1.2 by analyzing an authentication protocol in which the use of encryption follows the standard CBC implementation; the protocol is designed to expect that the use of CBC should provide data-integrity protection on the ciphers, however, the protocol is flawed precisely due to the missing of this service.

To randomize output ciphertext appears to be the only security service that the CBC mode offers. Data integrity of ciphertexts output from CBC will have to be served by additional cryptographic techniques which we shall study in Chapter 10.

### 7.8.2.2 A Warning

Knudsen observes a confidentiality limitation in CBC [167] which can be described as follows. When two ciphertext blocks $C_i$, $C'_j$ are equal, then from CBC Encryption we have

$$C_{i-1} \oplus C'_{j-1} = P_i \oplus P'_j.$$

Since plaintext usually contains redundancy, this equation helps to recover the plaintexts from the ciphertexts which are available to an eavesdropper. To make an attack using this equation infeasible, we must always use random IVs for each encryption session and so the probability for two ciphertexts to be equal is negligibly small (a random IV provides a very large probability space).

## 7.8.3 The Cipher Feedback Mode (CFB)

The cipher feedback (CFB) mode of operation features feeding the successive cipher segments which are output from the mode back as input to the underlying block cipher algorithm. A message (plaintext or ciphertext) segment has a size $s$ such that $1 \le s \le n$. The CFB mode requires an IV as the initial random $n$-bit input block. The IV need not be secret since in the system it is in the position of a ciphertext. The CFB mode has the following operations:

**CFB Encryption** INPUT: $IV, P_1, \ldots, P_m$; OUTPUT: $IV, C_1, \ldots, C_m$;

$$
\begin{aligned}
&I_1 \leftarrow IV; \\
&I_i \leftarrow \mathrm{LSB}_{n-s}(I_{i-1}) \parallel C_{i-1} && i = 2, \ldots, m; \\
&O_i \leftarrow \mathcal{E}(I_i) && i = 1, 2, \ldots, m; \\
&C_i \leftarrow P_i \oplus \mathrm{MSB}_s(O_i) && i = 1, 2, \ldots, m.
\end{aligned}
$$

**CFB Decryption** INPUT: $IV, C_1, \ldots, C_m$; OUTPUT: $P_1, \ldots, P_m$;

$$
\begin{aligned}
&I_1 \leftarrow IV; \\
&I_i \leftarrow \mathrm{LSB}_{n-s}(I_{i-1}) \parallel C_{i-1} && i = 2, \ldots, m; \\
&O_i \leftarrow \mathcal{E}(I_i) && i = 1, 2, \ldots, m; \\
&P_i \leftarrow C_i \oplus \mathrm{MSB}_s(O_i) && i = 1, 2, \ldots, m.
\end{aligned}
$$

Observe that, in the CFB mode, the encryption function of the underlying block cipher is used in both ends of the encryption and the decryption. As a result, the underlying cipher function $E$ can be any (keyed) one-way transformation, such as a one-way hash function. The CFB mode can be considered as a key stream generator

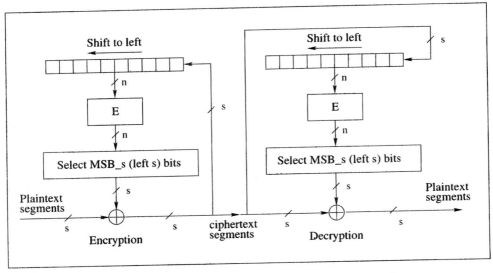

**Figure 7.4.** The Cipher Feedback Mode of Operation

for a stream cipher with the encryption being the Vernam cipher between the key stream and the message segments. Similar to the CBC mode, a ciphertext segment is a function of all preceding plaintext segment and the IV. Fig 7.4 provides an illustration of the CFB mode.

## 7.8.4   The Output Feedback Mode (OFB)

The output feedback (OFB) mode of operation features feeding the successive output blocks from the underlying block cipher back to it. These feedback blocks form a string of bits which is used as the key stream of the Vernam cipher, that is, the key stream is XOR-ed with the plaintext blocks. The OFB mode requires an IV as the initial random $n$-bit input block. The IV need not be secret since in the system it is in the position of a ciphertext. The OFB mode has the following operations:

**OFB Encryption**  INPUT: $IV, P_1, \ldots, P_m$;  OUTPUT: $IV, C_1, \ldots, C_m$;

$$I_1 \leftarrow IV;$$
$$I_i \leftarrow O_{i-1} \qquad i = 2, \ldots, m;$$
$$O_i \leftarrow \mathcal{E}(I_i) \qquad i = 1, 2, \ldots, m;$$
$$C_i \leftarrow P_i \oplus O_i \qquad i = 1, 2, \ldots, m.$$

**OFB Decryption**  INPUT: $IV, C_1, \ldots, C_m$;   OUTPUT: $P_1, \ldots, P_m$;

$$I_1 \leftarrow IV;$$
$$I_i \leftarrow O_{i-1} \qquad i = 2, \ldots, m;$$
$$O_i \leftarrow \mathcal{E}(I_i) \qquad i = 1, 2, \ldots, m;$$
$$P_i \leftarrow C_i \oplus O_i \qquad i = 1, 2, \ldots, m.$$

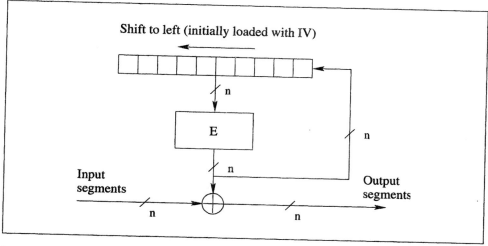

**Figure 7.5.** The Output Feedback Mode of Operation (for both encryption and decryption)

In the OFB mode, the encryption and the decryption are identical: XORing the input message blocks with the key stream which is generated by the feedback circuit. The feedback circuit actually forms a finite state machine with the state solely determined by the encryption key for the underlying block cipher algorithm and the IV. Thus, if a transmission error occurred to a cipher block, then only the plaintext block in the corresponding position can be garbled. Therefore, the OFB mode is suitable for encryption messages for which retransmission is not possible, like radio signals. Similar to the CFB mode, the underlying block cipher algorithm can be replaced with a keyed one-way hash function. Fig 7.5 provides an illustration of the CFB mode.

## 7.8.5   The Counter Mode (CTR)

The counter (CTR) mode features feeding the underlying block cipher algorithm with a counter value which counts up from an initial value. With the counter counting up, the underlying block cipher algorithm outputs successive blocks to form a string of bits. This string of bits is used as the key stream of the Vernam cipher, that is, the key stream is XOR-ed with the plaintext blocks. The CTR mode has the following operations (where $Ctr_1$ is an initial non-secret value of the counter):

**CTR Encryption**  INPUT: $Ctr_1, P_1, \ldots, P_m$;  OUTPUT: $Ctr_1, C_1, \ldots, C_m$;

$$C_i \leftarrow P_i \oplus \mathcal{E}(Ctr_i) \quad i = 1, 2, \ldots, m.$$

**CTR Decryption**  INPUT: $Ctr_1, C_1, \ldots, C_m$;  OUTPUT: $P_1, \ldots, P_m$;

$$P_i \leftarrow C_i \oplus \mathcal{E}(Ctr_i) \quad i = 1, 2, \ldots, m.$$

Without feedback, the CTR mode encryption and decryption can be performed in parallel. This is the advantage that the CTR mode has over the CFB and OFB modes. Due to its simplicity, we omit the illustration for the CTR mode.

## 7.9   Key Channel Establishment for Symmetric Cryptosystems

Before two principals can start confidential communications by using symmetric cryptosystems, they must first establish correct cryptographic keys shared between them. Here, "correct" not only means that a key established is bit-by-bit correct, i.e., not corrupted, but also means that both parties must be assured that the key is exclusively shared with the intended communication partner.

A communication channel over which a key is correctly established is called a **key channel** (see Fig 7.1). A key channel is a separate channel from a message channel. The difference between them is that a key channel is a protected one, while a communication channel is an unprotected one. In symmetric cryptosystems, since the encryption key is equal to the decryption key, the key channel must preserve both the confidentiality and the authenticity of the key.

A key channel for a symmetric cryptosystem can be established by three means: conventional techniques, public-key techniques, and the Quantum Key Distribution (QKD) technique.

**Conventional Techniques**  In the system setting-up time, a physically secure means, e.g., a courier delivery service, can be employed to make two users exclusively share an initial key. Usually, one of these two users is a trusted third party (TTP) who will be providing authentication service (see §2.4 for the meaning of this trust). Once an initial key is shared between an end-user principal and a TTP, which a long-term key channel, any two end-users can run an authentication protocol to maintain establish a secure key channel between them. The use of TTP reduces the burden of key management for end-users: an end-user does not have to manage many keys as she/he would have to should long-term key channels be between any two pair of end-user principals. In Chapter 2 we have seen a few examples of authentication and key establishment protocols which serve for setting up session keys between any two end-user principals using long-term key channels between end-user principals and an authentication server. We will see more such protocols in Chapters 11, 12 and 17 when we study authentication protocols, systems and formal methodologies for their security analysis.

A serious drawback of the conventional key channel establishment technique is the necessary relying on an on-line authentication service. This disadvantage limits the scalability of the technique for any open systems applications. In reality, this technique so far only finds good applications in an enterprise environment; we shall conduct a detailed study of that application in §12.4.

**Public-key Techniques**  An important advantage of public-key cryptography is the ease of establishing a key channel between any two remote end-user principals without having them to meet each other or using an on-line authentication service. This overcomes precisely the drawback of the conventional techniques. Therefore, public-key based techniques can easily scale up for a large open systems. There are a number of public-key techniques for key channel establishment. We shall introduce public-key cryptography in the next chapter, and study public-key based techniques for authentication framework in Chapter 13.

However, with public-key cryptography, there is still a need for establishing a secure key channel from a user toward the system. Here, "secure" means authentication: a given public key can be identified as really owned by a claimed principal. Nevertheless, key channel establishment using public-key techniques does not involve handling of any secret. Indeed, the setting up of a key channel regarding a public key is purely an authentication problem. In Fig 7.1 we have illustrated that a public key channel can be based on a directory service. We will study some practical authentication techniques for establishing a public-key authentication channel in Chapter 12 (§12.3) and the general techniques for setting up public-key authentication framework in Chapter 13.

**The Quantum Key Distribution Technique**  In §4.4.5.1 we have seen a technique for achieving Quantum Key Distribution (QKD, Prot 4.1). The QKD Protocol allows two principals to agree on a secret key although they may have never physically met. Similar to the case of public-key techniques, there is still a need to initially establish an authentication channel from a user toward the system. This authentication channel can be based on some one-way functions such that an end-user has in possession of a secret pre-image of a one-way function allowing its communication partner to verify without the former disclosing the secret to the latter. Using the authentication channel, participants of the QKD Protocol can be sure that the protocol is run with the intended communication partner. Commercial QKD systems are expected to be in practical use in year 2004 or so [270].

We must emphasize the future importance of the QKD technique for key channel establishment. Most practical complexity-theoretic based public-key techniques (based on difficulties for finding the period of a periodical function) would fall upon the availability of practical quantum computing technologies. The QKD technique, nevertheless, is quantum-technology immune (and there seems to exist non-periodical one-way functions which are quantum-technology immune and can serve the authentication purpose). Therefore, even when quantum computing technologies become practically available, the QKD technique will stand for serving key channel establishment without a need for the key sharing parties to meet physically or rely on *on-line* authentication service from a trusted third party.

Finally, we should notice that the public-key based techniques and the QKD technique manifest that a confidentiality communication channel can be established though pure public discussions. This is a well-known principle (see e.g., [190, 191]).

## 7.10   Chapter Summary

In this chapter we have studied the principle of symmetric encryption algorithms and introduced several symmetric encryption schemes.

We started with introducing classical ciphers and considering their conditional security under Shannon's information theory. We point out that the working principle of the classical ciphers: substitution, is still the most important kernel technique in the construction of modern symmetric encryption algorithms.

Two modern block encryption algorithms, the DES and the AES, are introduced. The DES is introduced for the reasons of its historical position and the still-alive usefulness of its Feistel cipher design structure. The AES, as the newly established encryption standard, is described with detailed explanations on its working principle. We also consider methods for fast and secure realization of the AES, and discuss the positive impact the AES may have on applied cryptography.

We then introduced various standard modes of operation for using block ciphers. A common mode of operation, CBC, is studied with a common misconception exposed. The misconception is that CBC provides data-integrity service, which we have demonstrated being false. More clear evidence of this misconception will be given in Chapter 17 when we study authentication protocols which apply CBC encryption.

Finally we listed three techniques for the establishment of secure key channels between communication partners who wish to communicate confidential information. Among the three, the QKD technique, although in its initial and primitive shape, is vitally important for the future owing to its immunization from the quantum computation technology.

## Exercises

7.1 Why should not an encryption algorithm contain secret design parts?

7.2 Uneven frequencies of certain letters in English is an example of plaintext being in a small region of the entire message space. Give two other examples which also contribute to the fact that English plaintext messages have a small region distribution.

7.3 Let $S_P$, $S_C$ denote a plaintext message source and the corresponding ciphertext message source, respectively. Use the entropy formulation given in §3.7 to explain that ciphertext messages output from the simple substitution or transposition ciphers do not change the distribution of the corresponding plaintext messages, that is, the ciphertexts remain in a small region of the entire message space.

Hint: $H(S_P) = H(S_C)$.

7.4 Is the Vernam cipher a substitution cipher? Is it monoalphabetic or polyalphabetic?

7.5 What is the difference between the Vernam cipher and one-time pad?

7.6 Why is the one-time pad encryption unconditionally secure against eavesdropping?

7.7 The shift cipher in Prot 7.1 is a perfectly secure encryption scheme since a one-time key is used and the key has the same size as that of the message. If the shift cipher is computed as addition without modulo reduction, can it still be a perfectly secure encryption scheme?

7.8 Why are simple substitution ciphers and transposition ciphers, even though extremely vulnerable to the frequency analysis attack, still in wide use in modern day encryption algorithms and cryptographic protocols?

7.9 A modern cipher is usually constructed as a combination of several classical cipher techniques. Identify parts in the DES and the AES where (i) substitution cipher techniques are used, (ii) transposition cipher techniques are used, and (iii) the Vernam cipher is used.

7.10 (i) Why is the AES regarded very efficient? (ii) How should multiplication in the finite field $\mathbb{F}_{2^8}$ be realized in the implementation of the AES?

7.11 In the cipher block chaining (CBC) mode of operation for block cipher, if the decryption of a received ciphertext "has the right padding," will you consider that the transmitted plaintext has a valid data integrity?

# Chapter 8

# ENCRYPTION
# — ASYMMETRIC
# TECHNIQUES

## 8.1  Introduction

Early ciphers (such as the Caesar cipher) depended on keeping the entire encryption process secret. Modern ciphers such as the DES and the AES follow Kerchoffs' principle (see §7.1): the algorithmic details of these ciphers are made public for open scrutiny. In so doing, the designers of these ciphers wish to demonstrate that the security of their cryptosystems reside solely in the choice of the secret encryption keys.

There is further room to practice Kerchoffs' principle of reducing the secret component in an encryption algorithm. Consider Shannon's semantic property of encryption [266]: a mixing-transformation which distributes meaningful messages from the plaintext region $\mathcal{M}$ fairly uniformly over the entire message space $\mathcal{C}$ (review equation (7.1.1) in page 206). We now know that such a random distribution can be achieved without using any secret. Diffie and Hellman first realized this in 1975 [98] (the publication date of this paper was 1976, but the paper was first distributed in December 1975 as a preprint, see [97]). They named their discovery **public-key cryptography**. At that time it was a totally new understanding of cryptography.

In a public-key cryptosystem, encryption uses no secret key; secret key is only needed in decryption time. In [98], Diffie and Hellman sketched several mathematical transformations, which they termed **one-way trapdoor** functions, as possible candidates for realizing public-key cryptography. Informally speaking, a one-way trapdoor function has the following property:

**Property 8.1: One-way Trapdoor Function** *A one-way trapdoor function, which we denote by $f_t(x) : \mathcal{D} \mapsto \mathcal{R}$, is a one-way function, i.e., it is easy to evaluate for* *all $x \in \mathcal{D}$ and difficult to invert for almost all values in $\mathcal{R}$. However, if the trapdoor information t is used, then for all values $y \in \mathcal{R}$ it is easy to compute $x \in \mathcal{D}$ satisfying $y = f_t(x)$.*

The notion of one-way trapdoor function forms the enabler for public-key cryptography. Opposing to the notion of secret-key or symmetric cryptosystems, a public-key cryptosystem based on a one-way trapdoor function is also referred to as **asymmetric cryptosystems** due to the asymmetric property of one-way trapdoor functions. Although the several one-way trapdoor functions considered in the first paper of Diffie and Hellman on public-key cryptography (i.e., [98]) were not very plausible due to their poor asymmetry, Diffie and Hellman soon proposed a successful function: modulo exponentiation, and used it to demonstrate the famous cryptographic protocol: the **Diffie-Hellman key exchange protocol** [99] (see §8.3). To this day, this first successful realization of public-key crypto-algorithm is still in wide use and under endless further development.

In 1974, Merkle discovered a mechanism to realize cryptographic key agreeme via an apparent asymmetric computation, which is now known as *Merkle's puzzle* [201]. The asymmetric computation in Merkle's puzzle means that the computational complexity for legitimate participants of a key agreement protocol and that for an eavesdropper are drastically different: the former is feasible and the latter is not. Merkle's puzzle was the first effective realization of a one-way trapdoor function. Although Merkle's puzzle may not be considered suitable for modern cryptographic applications (as the asymmetry is between $n$ and $n^2$), the insight it revealed was monumental to the discovery of public-key cryptography.

It is now known that Cocks, a British cryptographer, invented the first public-key cryptosystem in 1973 (see e.g., [279]). Cocks' encryption algorithm, named "non-secret key encryption," is based on the difficulty of integer factorization and is essentially the same as the RSA cryptosystem (see §8.5). Unfortunately, Cocks' algorithm was classified. In December 1997, the British government's Communications Services Electronics Security Group (CESG), released Cocks' algorithm.

Although it happened that the discovery of public-key cryptography by the open research community took place after the notion was known in a closed circle, we must point out that it was the open research community that identified the two most important applications of public-key cryptography: (i) digital signatures (see §10.4), and (ii) secret key establishment over public communications channels (see §8.3). These two applications have enabled today's proliferation of secure electronic commerce over the Internet.

## 8.1.1    Chapter Outline

We begin the technical part of this chapter with an introduction to a "textbook crypto" security notion and providing an early warning that all public key cryptographic algorithms to be introduced in this chapter are actually insecure for standard application scenarios in the real world (§8.2). We then introduce several well-known public-key cryptographic primitives. These are: the Diffie-Hellman key exchange protocol (§8.3), the textbook versions of the RSA (§8.5), Rabin (§8.10) and ElGamal (§8.12) cryptosystems. These basic public-key cryptographic primitives are introduced together with formal and complexity-theoretic based statements on the respective underlying intractability assumptions. These are: the Diffie-Hellman problem and the discrete logarithm problem (§8.4), the RSA problem (§8.7) and the integer factorization problem (8.8). We will also begin in this chapter to develop formal notions for describing various attacking models against public-key cryptosystems (§8.6). Insecurity of the textbook versions of the cryptographic algorithms will be demonstrated in §8.9 (RSA), §8.11 (Rabin) and §8.13 (ElGamal). We will consider the need for a stronger security notion for public-key encryption (§8.14). Having introduced both symmetric and asymmetric cryptosystems, we will introduce their combination: hybrid encryption schemes (§8.15).

## 8.2   Insecurity of "Textbook Encryption Algorithms"

We should notice that the encryption algorithms to be introduced in this chapter should be labeled textbook crypto. They are so labeled because these algorithms can be found in most textbooks on cryptography. However, these basic encryption algorithms are actually not suitable for use in real-world applications. Within the scope of public-key cryptosystems, a textbook encryption algorithm in general has a confidentiality property stated in Property 8.2.

**Property 8.2: Insecurity Property of Textbook Encryption Algorithms**
*Within the scope of this chapter, security (confidentiality) for a cryptosystem is considered in the following two senses:*

i) **All-or-nothing secrecy**   *For a given ciphertext output from a given encryption algorithm, the attacker's task is to retrieve the whole plaintext block which in general has a size stipulated by a security parameter of the cryptosystem; or for a given pair of plaintext and ciphertext under a given encryption algorithm, the attacker's task is to uncover the whole block of the underlying secret key. The attacker either succeeds with obtaining the whole block of the targeted secret, or fails with nothing. We should pay particular attention to the meaning of "nothing:" it means that the attacker does not have any knowledge about the targeted secret before or after its attacking attempt.*

ii) **Passive attacker**   *The attacker does not manipulate or modify ciphertexts using data she/he has in possession, and does not ask a key owner for providing encryption or decryption services.*

This notion of security (confidentiality) is extremely weak, in fact, is uselessly weak and therefore should be better named "a notion of insecurity."

Let us first explain why Property 8.2.(i) is an insecurity property. In applications, plaintext data are likely to have some non-secret "partial information" which can be known to an attacker. For example, some data are always in a small range: a usual salary figure should be less than one million which is, though a large salary, a small number in cryptographic sense. For another example, a usual password is a bit string up to eight characters. Often, the known partial information will permit an attacker to succeed and obtain the whole plaintext message, rather than "fail with nothing."

Now let us explain further why Property 8.2.(ii) is also an insecurity property. We should never expect an attacker to be so nice and remain in passive. The typical behavior of an attacker is that it will try all means available to it. This particularly includes the attacker engaging in interactions with a targeted user, sending a ciphertext to the latter for being decrypted with the plaintext returned to the former. This way of interaction is known as a user (a public key owner) to provide an **oracle decryption service** for an attacker. We will see in this chapter and a few later chapters that it is hard to avoid providing oracle services.

The nice algebraic properties that are generally held by textbook cryptographic algorithms can often enable an attacker who is served with oracle services to break a textbook cryptographic algorithm. We will see a few such examples in this chapter and will further see the general applicability of such attacking techniques in a few later chapters.

While in this chapter we will sometimes provide warnings that a user should not be used as an oracle service provider, we should notice that ordinary users of a public-key algorithm are too naive to be educated not to provide an oracle service to an attacker. Also, avoiding being used as an oracle is a very hard problem (we will see this point in §12.5.4). The correct strategy is to design fit-for-application cryptosystems to be securely used by naive users.

By stating Property 8.2, we make it explicit that within the scope of this chapter, we will not consider a stronger notion of security for public-key encryption algorithms, and consequently, for the textbook encryption algorithms to be introduced here, we will not hope that they are secure in any strong sense. On the contrary, we will demonstrate, but not try to fix, a number of confidentiality flaws with the textbook encryption algorithms in both insecurity properties, i.e., partial information leakage and/or results of active attacks.

Definitions for a number of more stringent security notions against stronger (i.e., more real) attacking scenarios will be introduced in Chapter 14. Fit-for-application counterparts to the textbook encryption algorithms will be followed up in Chapter 15.

# 8.3   The Diffie-Hellman Key Exchange Protocol

With a symmetric cryptosystem it is necessary to transfer a secret key to both communicating parties before secure communication can begin. Prior to the birth of public-key cryptography, the establishment of a shared secret key between communication parties had always been a difficult problem because the task needed a secure confidential channel, and often such a channel meant physical delivery of keys by a special courier. An important advantage that public key cryptography provides over symmetric cryptography is the achievement of exchanging a secret key between remote communication parties with no need of a secure confidential channel. The first practical scheme to achieve this was proposed by Diffie and Hellman, known as the Diffie-Hellman exponential key exchange protocol [99].

To begin with, users Alice and Bob are assumed to have agreed on a finite field $\mathbb{F}_q$ and an element $g \in \mathbb{F}_q$ which generates a group of a large order. For simplicity, we consider the case of field $\mathbb{F}_p$ where $p$ is a large prime, i.e., $\mathbb{F}_p$ is a prime number. The two parties may test the primality of $p$ using Alg 4.5 where they have constructed $p$ such that they know the complete factorization of $p - 1$; and then they may find a generator $g$ (e.g., of $\mathbb{F}_p^*$) using Alg 5.1. By Theorem 5.11, each number in $[1, p)$ can be expressed as $g^x \pmod{p}$ for some $x$. Now $p$ and $g$ are the common input to the participants in a basic version of a so-called **Diffie-Hellman Key Exchange** protocol which is specified in Prot 8.1.

---

**Protocol 8.1:** The Diffie-Hellman Key Exchange Protocol

COMMON INPUT   $(p, g)$: $p$ is a large prime, $g$ is a generator element in $\mathbb{F}_p^*$.

OUTPUT   An element in $\mathbb{F}_p^*$ shared between Alice and Bob.

1. Alice picks $a \in_U [1, p - 1]$; computes $g_a \leftarrow g^a \pmod{p}$; sends $g_a$ to Bob;

2. Bob picks $b \in_U [1, p - 1]$; computes $g_b \leftarrow g^b \pmod{p}$; sends $g_b$ to Alice;

3. Alice computes $k \leftarrow g_b^a \pmod{p}$;

4. Bob computes $k \leftarrow g_a^b \pmod{p}$.

---

It is easy to see from Prot 8.1 that for Alice

$$k = g^{ba} \pmod{p},$$

and for Bob

$$k = g^{ab} \pmod{p}.$$

We note that since $ab \equiv ba \pmod{p-1}$, the two parties have computed the same value. This is how the Diffie-Hellman key exchange protocol achieves a shared key between two communication parties.

A system-wide users may share the common public parameters $p$ and $g$.

**Example 8.1:** Let $p = 43$. Applying Alg 5.1 we find that 3 is a primitive root modulo 43. Let Alice and Bob share the public material elements $(p, g) = (43, 3)$.

For Alice and Bob to agree a secret key, Alice picks her random secret exponent 8, and sends to Bob $3^8 \equiv 25 \pmod{43}$. Bob picks his random secret 37, and sends to Alice $3^{37} \equiv 20 \pmod{43}$. The secret key agreed between them is

$$9 \equiv 20^8 \equiv 25^{37} \pmod{43}. \qquad \square$$

We should add a few cautionary details to the implementation and the use of the Diffie-Hellman key exchange protocol.

- The common input $p$ should be such a prime (or a prime power) that $p - 1$ has a sufficiently large prime factor $p'$; here "sufficiently large" means $p' > 2^{160}$. The need for $p$ to have this property will be discussed in §8.4.

- The common input $g$ needn't be a generator of $\mathbb{F}_p^*$ itself; but it is necessary to be a generator of a large-order subgroup of $\mathbb{F}_p^*$, e.g., a subgroup of order $p'$. In this case, Alice and Bob should check $g \neq 1$ and $g^{p'} \equiv 1 \pmod{p}$. For this purpose, $p'$ should be part of the common input to the protocol.

- Alice (respectively, Bob) should check $g_b \neq 1$ (respectively, $g_a \neq 1$). Then for their respective exponents chosen from $(1, p')$, these checking steps will guarantee that the shared key $g^{ab}$ will be one in the order-$p'$ subgroup of $\mathbb{F}_p$, that is, in a sufficiently large subgroup.

- Alice (respectively, Bob) should erase her exponent $a$ (respectively, his exponent $b$) upon termination of the protocol. In so doing, they will have a **forward secrecy** property on the exchanged key $g^{ab}$ if they also properly dispose the exchanged key after their session communication ends. We will further discuss the "forward secrecy" property in §8.15 and §11.6.1.

## 8.3.1 The Man-in-the-Middle Attack

It should be noted that the Diffie-Hellman key exchange protocol does not support the authenticity of the key agreed. An active adversary in the middle of the communications between Alice and Bob can manipulate the protocol messages to succeed an attack called **man-in-the-middle attack**. Attack 8.1 illustrates such an attack.

**Attack 8.1:** Man-in-the-Middle Attack on the Diffie-Hellman Key Exchange Protocol

COMMON INPUT: Same as Prot 8.1.

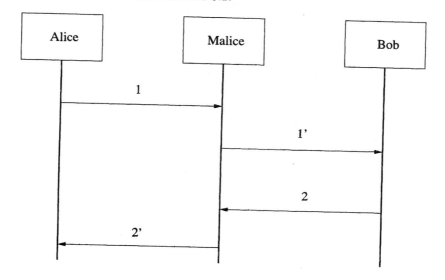

1   Alice picks $a \in_U [1, p-1)$, computes $g_a \leftarrow g^a \pmod{p}$;
    she sends $g_a$ to Malice("Bob");

1'  Malice("Alice") computes $g_m \leftarrow g^m \pmod{p}$ for some $m \in [1, p-1)$;
    he sends $g_m$ to Bob;

2   Bob picks $b \in_U [1, p-1)$, computes $g_b \leftarrow g^b \pmod{p}$;
    he sends to $g_b$ Malice("Alice");

2'  Malice("Bob") sends to Alice: $g_m$;

3   Alice computes $k_1 \leftarrow g_m^a \pmod{p}$;
    ($*$ this key is shared between Alice and Malice
    since Malice can compute $k_1 \leftarrow g_a^m \pmod{p}$. $*$)

4   Bob computes $k_2 \leftarrow g_m^b \pmod{p}$.
    ($*$ this key is shared between Bob and Malice
    since Malice can compute $k_2 \leftarrow g_m^b \pmod{p}$. $*$)

In an attack to a run of the protocol, Malice (the bad guy) intercepts and blocks Alice's first message to Bob, $g_a$, and he masquerades as Alice and sends to Bob

Malice("Alice") sends to Bob: $g_m(\stackrel{\text{def}}{=} g^m)$ (mod $p$);

(The reader may recall our convention agreed in §2.6.2 for denoting Malice's action of masquerading as other principals.) Bob will follow the protocol instructions by replying $g_b$ to Malice("Alice"). This means that the value transmitted is again intercepted and blocked by Malice. Now Malice and Bob have agreed a key $g^{bm}$ (mod $p$) which Bob thinks to share with Alice.

Analogously, Malice can masquerade as Bob and agree another key with Alice (e.g., $g^{am}$ (mod $p$)). After this, Malice can use these two keys to read and relay "confidential" communications between Alice and Bob, or to impersonate one of them to the other.

The man-in-the-middle attack on the Diffie-Hellman key exchange protocol is possible because the protocol does not provide an authentication service on the source of the protocol messages. In order to agree on a key which is exclusively shared between Alice and Bob, these principals must make sure that the messages they receive in a protocol run are indeed from the intended principals. In Chapter 11 we will study authentication techniques; there (§11.6) we will introduce methods for securely applying the Diffie-Hellman key exchange protocol.

# 8.4  The Diffie-Hellman Problem and the Discrete Logarithm Problem

The secrecy of the agreed shared key from the Diffie-Hellman key exchange protocol is exactly the problem of computing $g^{ab}$ (mod $p$) given $g_a$ and $g_b$. This problem is called **computational Diffie-Hellman problem** (CDH problem).

**Definition 8.1: Computational Diffie-Hellman Problem (CDH Problem)**
*(in finite field)*

INPUT       desc($\mathbb{F}_q$): *the description of finite field* $\mathbb{F}_q$;
            $g \in \mathbb{F}_q^*$: *a generator element of* $\mathbb{F}_q^*$;
            $g^a, g^b \in \mathbb{F}_q^*$ *for some integers* $0 < a, b < q$.

OUTPUT   $g^{ab}$.

We have formulated the problem in a general form working in a finite field $\mathbb{F}_q$. The Diffie-Hellman key exchange protocol in §8.3 uses a special case. For formalism purpose, in definition of a general problem, an assumption, etc., we will try to be as general as possible, while in explanations outside formal definitions we will often use special cases which help to expose ideas with clarity.

If the CDH problem is easy, then $g^{ab}$ (mod $p$) can be computed from the values $p$, $g$, $g_a$, $g_b$, which are transmitted as part of the protocol messages. According to our assumptions on the ability of our adversary (see §2.3), these values are available to an adversary.

The CDH problem lies, in turn, on the difficulty of the **discrete logarithm problem (DL problem)**.

**Definition 8.2: Discrete Logarithm Problem (DL Problem)** *(in finite field)*

INPUT       $\mathrm{desc}(\mathbb{F}_q)$: *the description of finite field* $\mathbb{F}_q$;
             $g \in \mathbb{F}_q^*$: *a generator element of* $\mathbb{F}_q^*$;
             $h \in_U \mathbb{F}_q^*$.

OUTPUT      *the unique integer* $a < q$ *such that* $h = g^a$.

*We denote the integer* $a$ *by* $\log_g h$.

The DL problem looks similar to taking ordinary logarithms in the reals. But unlike logarithms in the reals where we only need approximated "solutions," the DL problem is defined in a discrete domain where a solution must be *exact*.

We have discussed in Chapter 4 that the security theory of modern public-key cryptography is established on a complexity-theoretic foundation. Upon this foundation, the security of a public-key cryptosystem is *conditional* on some assumptions that certain problems are intractable. The CDH problem and the DL problem are two assumed intractable problems. Intuitively we can immediately see that the difficulties of these problems depend on the size of the problems (here, it is the size of the field $\mathbb{F}_q$), as well as on the choice of the parameters (here, it is the choice of the public parameter $g$ and the private data $a$, $b$). Clearly, these problems need not be difficult for small instances. In a moment we will further see that these problems need not be difficult for poorly chosen instances. Thus, a precise description of the difficulty must formulate properly both the problem size and the choice of the instances. With the complexity-theoretic foundations that we have established in Chapter 4, we can now describe precisely the assumptions on the intractabilities of these two problems. The reader may review Chapter 4 to refresh several notions to be used in the following formulations (such as "$1^k$," "probabilistic polynomial time," and "negligible quantity in $k$").

**Assumption 8.1: Computational Diffie-Hellman Assumption (CDH Assumption)** *A CDH problem solver is a PPT algorithm* $\mathcal{A}$ *with an advantage* $\epsilon > 0$ *defined by*

$$\epsilon = \mathrm{Prob}\left[g^{ab} \leftarrow \mathcal{A}(\mathrm{desc}(\mathbb{F}_q), g, g^a, g^b)\right]$$

*where the input to* $\mathcal{A}$ *is defined in Definition 8.1.*

Let $\mathcal{IG}$ be an instance generator that on input $1^k$, runs in time polynomial in $k$, and outputs (i) $\mathrm{desc}(\mathbb{F}_q)$ with $|q| = k$, (ii) a generator element $g \in \mathbb{F}_q^*$.

We say that $\mathcal{IG}$ satisfies the computational Diffie-Hellman (CDH) assumption if there exists no CDH problem solver for $\mathcal{IG}(1^k)$ with advantage $\epsilon > 0$ non-negligible in $k$ for all sufficiently large $k$.

**Assumption 8.2: Discrete Logarithm Assumption (DL Assumption)**   *A DL problem solver is a PPT algorithm $\mathcal{A}$ with an advantage $\epsilon > 0$ defined by*

$$\epsilon = \mathrm{Prob}\left[ \log_g h \leftarrow \mathcal{A}(\mathrm{desc}(\mathbb{F}_q), g, h) \right]$$

*where the input to $\mathcal{A}$ is defined in Definition 8.2.*

Let $\mathcal{IG}$ be an instance generator that on input $1^k$, runs in time polynomial in $k$, and outputs (i) $\mathrm{desc}(\mathbb{F}_q)$ with $|q| = k$, (ii) a generator element $g \in \mathbb{F}_q^*$, (iii) $h \in \mathbb{F}_q^*$.

We say that $\mathcal{IG}$ satisfies the discrete logarithm (DL) assumption if there exists no DL problem solver for $\mathcal{IG}(1^k)$ with advantage $\epsilon > 0$ non-negligible in $k$ for all sufficiently large $k$.

In a nutshell, these two assumptions state that in finite fields for all sufficiently large instances, there exists no efficient algorithm to solve the CDH problem or the DL problem for almost all instances. A negligible fraction of exceptions are due to the existence of weak instances.

However, much more decent elaborations are needed for these two assumptions. Let us first make a few important remarks, in which we will keep the "formal tone".

**Remark 8.1:**

1. *In Assumptions 8.1 and 8.2, the respective probability space should consider (i) the instance space, i.e., arbitrary finite fields and arbitrary elements are sampled (the importance of this will be discussed in §8.4.1), and (ii) the space of the random operations in an efficient algorithm. The need for considering (ii) is because by "polynomial-time" or "efficient" algorithm we include randomized algorithms (see Definition 4.6 in §4.4.6).*

2. *The number $k$ in the both formulations is called a **security parameter**. $\mathcal{IG}(1^k)$ is a random instance of the field and the element(s). From our study of the probabilistic prime generation in §4.4.6.1 and the field construction in §5.4 we know that $\mathcal{IG}(1^k)$ indeed terminates in polynomial time in $k$. It is now widely accepted that $k = 1024$ is the lower bound setting of security parameter for the DLP in finite fields. This lower bound is a result of a subexponential time algorithm (index calculus) for solving the DLP in finite fields. The subexponential complexity expression is in (8.4.2). For $|q| = 1024$, the expression yields a quantity greater than $2^{80}$. This is why the setting of $k = 1024$*

*becomes the widely agreed lower bound. Thus, as stipulated by the phrase "for all sufficiently large k" in both assumptions, we should only consider k greater than this lower bound.*

3. *Holding of the DL assumption means that the function*

$$g^x : \mathbb{Z}_q \mapsto \mathbb{F}_q^* \tag{8.4.1}$$

*is one-way. Therefore, holding of the DL assumption implies the existence of one-way function. It is widely believed that the DL assumption should actually hold (a case under the belief $\mathcal{P} \neq \mathcal{NP}$, see §4.5), or the function in (8.4.1) should be one-way, or in other words, one-way function should exist.*

4. *It is not known to date whether or not the function in (8.4.1) is a trap-door function (see Property 8.1 in §8.1 for the meaning of one-way trapdoor function). That is, no one knows how to embed trapdoor information inside this function to enable an efficient inversion of the function (i.e., an efficient method to compute x from $g^x$ using trapdoor information). However, if the function uses a composite modulus (the function remains one-way), then the function becomes a trapdoor where the prime factorization of the modulus forms the trapdoor information. The reader is referred to [231, 226, 230] for the technical details.* $\square$

We still need more "common-language" explanations for these two assumptions.

These two assumptions essentially say that "there is no polynomial in $k$ algorithms for solving these two problems". However, we must read this statement with great care. A "poly($k$) solver", if it exists, runs in time $k^n$ for some integer $n$. On the other hand, we know there exists a "subexponential solver" for the DLP running in time

$$\text{sub\_exp}(q) = \exp(c\,(\log q)^{\frac{1}{3}}\,(\log\log q)^{\frac{2}{3}}) \tag{8.4.2}$$

where $c$ is a small constant (e.g., $c < 2$). Combining "no poly($k$) solver" and "having an sub\_exp($q$) solver", we are essentially saying that $k^n$ is much much smaller than sub\_exp($k\log 2$) (for $k = |q| = \log_2 q$, we have $\log q = k\log 2$). However, this "much much smaller" relation can only be true when $n$ is fixed and $k$ is sufficiently large. Let us make this point explicit.

Suppose $k$ is not sufficiently large. Taking natural logarithm on poly($k$) = $k^n$ and on sub\_exp($k\log 2$), we become comparing the following two quantities:

$$n\log k \quad \text{and} \quad ck^{\frac{1}{3}}[\log(k\log 2)]^{\frac{2}{3}}.$$

This is comparison is simplified to one between

$$n(\log k)^{\frac{1}{3}} \quad \text{and} \quad ck^{\frac{1}{3}}.$$

Now we see that the known subexponential solver will be quicker than a supposedly "non-existing poly solver" when $n$ is at the level of $ck^{\frac{1}{3}}$. The real meaning of "no poly($k$) solver" is when $k$ is considered as a variable which is not bounded (and hence can be "sufficiently large" as stated in the two assumptions), while $n$ is a fixed constant. In reality, $k$ cannot be unbounded. In particular, for the commonly agreed lower bound setting for security parameter: $k = 1024$, and for $c < 2$, there does exist a "poly($k$) solver" which has a running time bounded by a degree-9 polynomial in $k$ (confirm this by doing Ex 8.4).

From our discussions so far, we reach an *asymptotic* explanation for "no poly($k$) solver": $k$ is unbound and is sufficiently large. In reality $k$ *must be bounded*, and hence a poly($k$) solver *does exist*. Nevertheless, we can set a lower bound for $k$ so that we can be content that the poly solver will run in time which is an unmanageable quantity. In fact, the widely agreed lower bound $k = 1024$ is worked out this way.

This asymptotic meaning of "no poly solver" will apply to all complexity-theoretic based intractability assumptions to appear in the rest of the book.

Finally let us look at the relationship between these two problems.

Notice that the availability of $a = \log_g g_1$ or $b = \log_g g_2$ will permit the calculation of

$$g^{ab} = g_1^b = g_2^a.$$

That is, an efficient algorithm which solves the DLP will lead to an efficient algorithm to solve the CDH problem. Therefore if the DL assumption does not hold, then we cannot have the CDH assumption. We say that the CDH problem is weaker than the DL problem, or equivalently, the CDH assumption is a stronger assumption than the DL assumption. The converse of this statement is an open question:

*Can the DL assumption be true if the CDH assumption is false?*

Maurer and Wolf give a strong heuristic argument on the relation between these two problems; they suggest that it is very likely that these two problems are equivalent [192].

## 8.4.1  Importance of Arbitrary Instances for Intractability Assumptions

We should emphasize the importance of arbitrary instances required in the DL assumption. Let us consider $\mathbb{F}_p^*$ with $p$ being a $k$-bit prime and the problem of extracting $a$ from $h \equiv g^a \pmod{p}$.

We know that $a$ is an element in $\mathbb{Z}_{p-1}$. If $p - 1 = q_1 q_2 \cdots q_\ell$ with each factor $q_i$ being small (meaning, $q_i \leq$ polynomial($k$) for $i = 1, 2, \ldots, \ell$), then the discrete-logarithm-extraction problem can be turned into extracting $a_i \equiv a \pmod{q_i}$ from $h^{(p-1)/q_i} \pmod{p}$ but now $a_i$ are small and can be extracted in time polynomial in $k$. After $a_1, a_2, \cdots, a_\ell$ are extracted, $a$ can be constructed by applying the Chinese

Remainder Theorem (Theorem 6.7). This is the idea behind the polynomial-time algorithm of Pohlig and Hellman [233] for solving the DL problem modulo $p$ if $p - 1$ has no large prime factor. Clearly, if every prime factor of $p - 1$ is bounded by a polynomial in $k$, then the Pohlig-Hellman algorithm has a running time in polynomial in $k$.

A prime number $p$ with $p-1$ containing no large prime factor is called a **smooth prime**. But sometimes we also say "$p - 1$ is smooth" with the same meaning. A standard way to avoid the smooth-prime weak case is to construct the prime $p$ such that $p-1$ is divisible by another large prime $p'$. By Theorem 5.2(2), the cyclic group $\mathbb{F}_p^*$ contains the unique subgroup of order $p'$. If $p'$ is made public, the users of the Diffie-Hellman key exchange protocol can make sure that the protocol is working in this large subgroup; all they need to do is to find an element $g \in \mathbb{F}_p^*$ such that

$$g^{(p-1)/p'} \not\equiv 1 \pmod{p}.$$

This element $g$ generates the group of the prime order $p'$. The Diffie-Hellman key exchange protocol should use $(p, p', g)$ so generated as the common input. An accepted value for the size of the prime $p'$ is at least 160 (binary bits), i.e., $p' > 2^{160}$. (Also see our discussion in §10.4.8.1.)

The DLP and the CDH problem are also believed as intractable in a general finite abelian group of a large order, such as a large prime-order subgroup of a finite field, or a group of points on an elliptic curve defined over a finite field (for group construction: §5.5, and for the elliptic-curve discrete logarithm problem, ECDLP: §5.5.3). Thus, the Diffie-Hellman key exchange protocol will also work well in these groups.

There are several exponential-time algorithms which are very effective for extracting the discrete logarithm when the value to be extracted is known to be small. We have described Pollard's $\lambda$-method (§3.6.1). Extracting small discrete logarithms has useful applications in many cryptographic protocols.

Research into the DLP is very active. Odlyzko provided a survey of the area which included an extensive literature on the topic [223].

## 8.5   Encryption in RSA (Textbook Version)

The best known public-key cryptosystem is the RSA, named after its inventors Rivest, Shamir and Adleman [248]. The RSA is the first practical realization of public-key cryptography based on the notion of one-way trapdoor function which Diffie and Hellman envision [98, 99].

The RSA cryptosystem is specified in Alg 8.1. We notice that this is a textbook version for encryption in RSA.

We now show that the system specified in Alg 8.1 is indeed a cryptosystem, i.e.,

---

**Algorithm 8.1:** The RSA Cryptosystem

**Key Setup**
To set up a user's key material, user Alice performs the following steps:

1. choose two random prime numbers $p$ and $q$ such that $|p| \approx |q|$;

   ($*$ this can be done by applying a Monte-Carlo prime number finding algorithm, e.g., Alg 4.7 $*$)

2. compute $N = pq$;

3. compute $\phi(N) = (p-1)(q-1)$;

4. choose a random integer $e < \phi(N)$ such that $\gcd(e, \phi(N)) = 1$, and compute the integer $d$ such that

$$ed \equiv 1 \ (\mathrm{mod}\ \phi(N));$$

   ($*$ since $\gcd(e, \phi(N)) = 1$, this congruence does have a solution for $d$ which can be found by applying the Extended Euclid Algorithm (Alg 4.2). $*$)

5. publicize $(N, e)$ as her public key, safely destroy $p$, $q$ and $\phi(N)$, and keep $d$ as her private key.


**Encryption**
To send a confidential message $m < N$ to Alice, the sender Bob creates the ciphertext $c$ as follows
$$c \leftarrow m^e \ (\mathrm{mod}\ N).$$

($*$ viewed by Bob, the plaintext message space is the set of all positive numbers less $N$, although in fact the space is $\mathbb{Z}_N^*$. $*$)

**Decryption**
To decrypt the ciphertext $c$, Alice computes

$$m \leftarrow c^d \ (\mathrm{mod}\ N).$$

Alice's decryption procedure will actually return the same plaintext message that Bob has encrypted.

From the definition of the modulo operation (see Definition 4.4 in §4.3.2.5), congruence $ed \equiv 1 \pmod{\phi(N)}$ in Alg 8.1 means

$$ed = 1 + k\phi(N)$$

for some integer $k$. Therefore, the number returned from Alice's decryption procedure is

$$c^d \equiv m^{ed} \equiv m^{1+k\phi(N)} \equiv m \cdot m^{k\phi(N)} \pmod{N}. \qquad (8.5.1)$$

We should notice that for $m < N$, it is almost always the case that $m \in \mathbb{Z}_N^*$ (the multiplicative group of integers relatively prime to $N$). In fact, the cases for $m \notin \mathbb{Z}_N^*$ are $m = up$ or $m = vq$ for some $u < q$ or $v < p$. In such cases, Bob can factor $N$ by computing $\gcd(m, N)$. Assuming that the factoring is difficult (we will formulate the factorization problem and an assumption on its difficulty in a moment), we can assume that any message $m < N$ prepared by Bob satisfies $m \in \mathbb{Z}_N^*$.

For $m \in \mathbb{Z}_N^*$, by Lagrange's Theorem (Corollary 5.2), we have

$$\mathrm{ord}_N(m) \,|\, \#\mathbb{Z}_N^* = \phi(N).$$

This is true for all $m \in \mathbb{Z}_N^*$. By the definition of the order of a group element (see Definition 5.9 in §5.2.2), this means that for all $m \in \mathbb{Z}_N^*$

$$m^{\phi(N)} \equiv 1 \pmod{N}.$$

Obviously, this further implies

$$m^{k\phi(N)} \equiv (m^{\phi(N)})^k \equiv 1 \pmod{N}$$

for any integer $k$. Thus, the value in (8.5.1) is, indeed, $m$.

**Example 8.2:** Let Alice set $N = 7 \times 13 = 91$ and $e = 5$. Then $\phi(N) = 6 \times 12 = 72$. Applying Alg 4.2 (by inputting $(a, b) = (72, 5)$), Alice obtains:

$$72 \times (-2) + 5 \times 29 = 1,$$

that is, $5 \times 29 \equiv 1 \pmod{72}$. Therefore Alice has computed 29 to be her private decryption exponent. She publicizes $(N, e) = (91, 5)$ as her public key material for the RSA cryptosystem.

Let Bob encrypt a plaintext $m = 3$. Bob performs encryption by computing

$$c = 3^5 = 243 \equiv 61 \pmod{91}.$$

The resultant ciphertext message is 61.

To decrypt the ciphertext message 61, Alice computes

$$61^{29} \equiv 3 \pmod{91}. \qquad \qquad \square$$

## 8.6  Cryptanalysis Against Public-key Cryptosystems

It makes sense to say "Cryptosystem X is secure against attack Y but is insecure against attack Z," that is, the security of a cryptosystem is defined by an attack. Active attacks have been modeled into three usual modes. These modes of active attacks will be used in the analysis of the cryptosystems to be introduced in rest of this chapter. They are defined as follows.

**Definition 8.3: Active Attacks on Cryptosystems**

**Chosen-plaintext attack (CPA)**  *An attacker chooses plaintext messages and gets encryption assistance to obtain the corresponding ciphertext messages. The task for the attacker is to weaken the targeted cryptosystem using the obtained plaintext-ciphertext pairs.*

**Chosen-ciphertext attack (CCA)**  *An attacker chooses ciphertext messages and gets decryption assistance to obtain the corresponding plaintext messages. The task for the attacker is to weaken the targeted cryptosystem using the obtained plaintext-ciphertext pairs. The attacker is successful if he can retrieve some secret plaintext information from a "target ciphertext" which is given to the attacker after the decryption assistance is stopped. That is, upon the attacker receipt of the target ciphertext, the decryption assistance is no longer available.*

**Adaptive chosen-ciphertext attack (CCA2)**  *This is a CCA where the decryption assistance for the targeted cryptosystem will be available forever, except for the target ciphertext.*

We may imagine these attacks with the following scenarios:

- In a CPA, an attacker has in its possession an encryption box.

- In a CCA, an attacker is entitled to a conditional use of a decryption box: the box will be switched off before the target ciphertext is given to the attacker.

- In a CCA2, an attack has in its possession a decryption box for use as long as he wishes, before or after the target ciphertext is made available to the attacker, provided that he does not feed the target ciphertext to the decryption box. This single restriction on CCA2 is reasonable since otherwise there will be no difficult problem for the attacker to solve.

In all cases, the attacker should not have in its possession the respective cryptographic keys.

CPA and CCA are originally proposed as active cryptanalysis models against secret-key cryptosystems where the objective of an attacker is to weaken the targeted cryptosystem using the plaintext-ciphertext message pairs he obtains from the attacks (see e.g., §1.2 of [286]). They have been adopted for modeling active cryptanalysis on public-key cryptosystems. We should notice the following three points which are specific to public-key cryptosystems.

- The encryption assistance of a public-key cryptosystem is always available to anybody since given a public key anyone has *complete* control of the encryption algorithm. In other words, CPA can always be mounted against a public-key cryptosystem. So, we can call an attack against a public-key cryptosystem CPA if the attack does not make use of any decryption assistance. Consequently and obviously, any public-key cryptosystem must resist CPA or else it is not a useful cryptosystem.

- In general, the mathematics underlying most public-key cryptosystems has some nice properties of an algebraic structure underlying these cryptosystems, such as closure, associativity, and homomorphism, etc., (review Chapter 5 for these algebraic properties). An attacker may explore these nice properties and make up a ciphertext via some clever calculations. If the attacker is assisted by a decryption service, then his clever calculations may enable him to obtain some plaintext information, or even the private key of the targeted cryptosystem, which otherwise should be computationally infeasible for him to obtain. Therefore, public-key cryptosystems are particularly vulnerable to CCA and CCA2. We will see that every public-key cryptosystem to be introduced in this chapter is vulnerable to CCA or CCA2. As a general principle, we have provided in Property 8.2.(ii) an advice that the owner of a public key should always be careful not to allow oneself to provide any decryption assistance to anybody. This advice must be followed for every public-key cryptosystem introduced in this chapter. In Chapter 14 we will introduce stronger public-key cryptosystems. Such cryptosystems do not require users to keep in such an alert state all the time.

- It seems that CCA is too restrictive. In applications a user under attack (i.e., is asked to provide decryption assistance) actually does not know the attack. Therefore the user can never know when (s)he should begin to stop providing decryption assistance. We generally assume that normal users are too naive to know the existence of attackers, and hence decryption assistance should be generally available *all the time*. On the other hand, any public-key cryptosystem must be secure against CPA since an attacker can always help himself to perform encryption "assistance" on chosen plaintext messages. For these reasons, we will mainly consider techniques to counter CCA2.

## 8.7 The RSA Problem

Against CPA, the security of RSA lies on the difficulty of computing the $e$-th root of a ciphertext $c$ modulo a composite integer $n$. This is the so-called the **RSA** problem.

## Definition 8.4: RSA Problem

INPUT        $N = pq$ *with* $p$, $q$ *prime numbers;*
             $e$: *an integer such that* $\gcd(e, (p-1)(q-1)) = 1$*;*
             $c \in \mathbb{Z}_N^*$*.*

OUTPUT       *the unique integer* $m \in \mathbb{Z}_N^*$ *satisfying* $m^e \equiv c \pmod{N}$*.*

No difference from all underlying difficult problems for the security of public-key cryptosystems, it is also assumed that the RSA problem is only difficult under properly chosen parameters.

**Assumption 8.3: RSA Assumption**    *An RSA problem solver is a PPT algorithm* $\mathcal{A}$ *with an advantage* $\epsilon > 0$ *defined by*

$$\epsilon = \mathrm{Prob}\left[m \leftarrow \mathcal{A}(N, e, m^e \pmod{N})\right],$$

*where the input to* $\mathcal{A}$ *is defined in Definition 8.4.*

*Let* $\mathcal{IG}$ *be an RSA instance generator that on input* $1^k$*, runs in time polynomial in* $k$*, and outputs (i) a* $2k$*-bit modulus* $N = pq$ *where* $p$ *and* $q$ *are two distinct uniformly random primes, each is* $k$*-bit long, (ii)* $e \in \mathbb{Z}_{(p-1)(q-1)}^*$*.*

*We say that* $\mathcal{IG}$ *satisfies the RSA assumption if there exists no RSA problem solver for* $\mathcal{IG}(1^k)$ *with advantage* $\epsilon > 0$ *non-negligible in* $k$ *for all sufficiently large* $k$*.*

Similar to our discussion in Remark 8.1(3) (in §8.4), we know that holding of the RSA assumption implies the existence of one-way function. Also related to our discussion in Remark 8.1(4), the one-way function implied by the RSA assumption is a trapdoor function: the prime factorization of the modulus enables an efficient inversion procedure.

We should notice that the probability space in this assumption includes the instance space, the plaintext message space and the space of the random operations of a randomized algorithm for solving the RSA problem.

We further notice that in the description of the RSA assumption, the (alleged) algorithm takes the encryption exponent $e$ as part of its input. This precisely describes the target of the problem: breaking the RSA problem under a given encryption exponent. There is a different version of the RSA problem called **strong RSA problem** ([18, 113, 86]); its target is: for some odd encryption exponent $e > 1$, which may be the choice of the algorithm, solve the RSA problem under this $e$ (i.e., $e$ can be an output of the algorithm, rather than an input). Clearly, solving the strong RSA problem is easier than doing that for the RSA problem which is for a fixed encryption exponent. It is widely believed (assumed) that the strong RSA problem is still an intractable one. Therefore some encryption algorithms or protocols base their security on that intractability (**strong RSA assumption**).

It is clear that for public key $(N, e)$, if $m < N^{1/e}$ then encryption $c = m^e \pmod{N}$ will take no modulo reduction, and hence $m$ can be found efficiently by extracting the $e$-th root in integers. This is one of the reasons why the case $e = 3$ should be avoided. In the case of $e = 3$, if one message $m$ is encrypted in three different moduli: $c_i = m^3 \pmod{N_i}$ for $i = 1, 2, 3$, then because the moduli are pair-wise co-prime, the Chinese Remainder Algorithm (Alg 6.1) can be applied to construct $C = m^3 \pmod{N_1 N_2 N_3}$. Now because $m < (N_1 N_2 N_3)^{1/3}$, the encryption exponentiation is actually the same as it is performed in the integer space. So decryption of $C$ is to extract the 3rd root in integers and can be efficiently done (see hint in Ex. 8.8).

Coppersmith [83] further extends this trivial case to a non-trivial one: for $m' = m + t$ where $m$ is known and $t$ is unknown but $t < N^{1/e}$, given $c = m'^e \pmod{N}$, $t$ can be extracted efficiently. Because in applications, partially known plaintext is not uncommon (we will see a case in Chapter 15), it is now widely agreed that RSA encryption should avoid using very small encryption exponents. A widely accepted encryption exponent is $e = 2^{16} + 1 = 65537$ which is also a prime number. This exponent makes encryption sufficiently efficient while refuting a small exponent attack.

RSA is also CPA insecure if the decryption exponent $d$ is small. Wiener discovers a method based on continued fraction expansion of $e/N$ to find $d$ if $d < N^{1/4}$ [300]. This result has been improved to $d < N^{0.292}$ [51].

# 8.8   The Integer Factorization Problem

The difficulty of the RSA problem depends, in turn, on the difficulty of the **integer factorization problem**.

### Definition 8.5: Integer Factorization Problem (IF Problem)

INPUT     *N: odd composite integer with at least two distinct prime factors.*

OUTPUT    *prime p such that p|N.*

Again, it is assumed that the IF problem is difficult only under properly chosen parameters.

**Assumption 8.4: Integer Factorization Assumption (IF Assumption)** *An integer factorizer is a PPT algorithm $\mathcal{A}$ with an advantage $\epsilon > 0$ defined by*

$$\epsilon = \text{Prob}\left[\mathcal{A}(N) \text{ divides } N \text{ and } 1 < \mathcal{A}(N) < N\right]$$

*where the input to $\mathcal{A}$ is defined in Definition 8.5.*

*Let $\mathcal{IG}$ be an integer instance generator that on input $1^k$, runs in time polynomial in $k$, and outputs a $2k$-bit modulus $N = pq$ where $p$ and $q$ are each a $k$-bit uniformly random odd prime.*

*We say that $\mathcal{IG}$ satisfies the integer factorization (IF) assumption if there exists no integer factorizer for $\mathcal{IG}(1^k)$ with advantage $\epsilon > 0$ non-negligible in $k$ for all sufficiently large $k$.*

Obviously, an algorithm which solves the IF problem will solve the RSA problem since Alice decrypts an RSA ciphertext exactly by first computing $d \equiv e^{-1} \pmod{(p-1)(q-1)}$, i.e., from the knowledge of the factorization of $N$. Similar to the relation between the CDH problem and the DL problem, the converse is also an open question: Can the IF assumption be true if the RSA assumption is false?

Similar to the situation of a smooth prime making a weak case DL problem, a smooth prime factor of $N$ will also make a weak case IF problem. One such a weak case is shown by Pollard using an efficient factorization algorithm known as **Pollard's p − 1-algorithm** [239]. The idea behind Pollard's $p - 1$ algorithm can be described as follows. Let $p$ be a prime factor of $N$ where the largest prime factor of $p - 1$ is bounded by $B = \text{Poly}(k)$ where $k = |N|$ and $\text{Poly}(k)$ is a polynomial in $k$ ($B$ is called "the smoothness bound of $p - 1$"). We can construct

$$A = \prod_{\text{primes } r < B} r^{\lfloor \log N / \log r \rfloor}.$$

By this construction, $p - 1 | A$, and so $a^A \equiv 1 \pmod{p}$ for any $a$ with $\gcd(a, p) = 1$ due to Fermat's Little Theorem (Theorem 6.10). If $a \not\equiv 1 \pmod{q}$ for some other prime factor $q$ of $N$ (this is easily satisfiable), then $a^A - 1 \pmod{N} = \ell p$ for some integer $\ell$ which is not a multiple of $q$. Thus, $\gcd(a^A - 1 \pmod{N}, N)$ must be a proper prime factor of $N$, and it must be $p$ if $N = pq$. It remains to show that the size of $A$ is a polynomial in $k$, and so computing $a^A \pmod{N}$ takes time in a polynomial in $k$.

By the prime number theorem (see e.g., page 28 of [172]), there are no more than $B/\log B$ prime numbers less than $B$. So we have

$$A < B^{\lfloor \log N \rfloor \frac{B}{\log B}} < B^{k \frac{B}{\log B}}$$

that is,

$$|A| < kB \log 2 < k\text{Poly}(k).$$

Clearly, the right-hand side is a polynomial in $k$. Thus, $a^A \pmod N$ can be computed in a number of multiplications modulo $N$ (using Alg 4.3) where the number is a polynomial in $k$. Notice that the explicit construction of $A$ is unnecessary; $a^A \pmod N$ can be computed by computing $a^{r^{\lfloor \log N / \log r \rfloor}} \pmod N$ for all prime $r < B$.

It is very easy to construct an RSA modulus $N = pq$ such that the smoothness bound of $p - 1$ and that of $q - 1$ are non-polynomially (in $|N|$) small, and so the modulus would resist this factoring method. One may start by finding large prime $p'$ such that $p = 2p' + 1$ is also a prime; and large prime $q'$ such that $q = 2q' + 1$ is also prime. A prime of this format is called a **safe prime** and an RSA modulus with two safe prime factors is called a **safe-prime RSA modulus**. There is a debate on the need of using safe-prime RSA modulus for the RSA cryptosystems. The point against the use (see e.g., [275]) is that an RSA modulus should be as random as possible, and that for a randomly chosen prime $p$, the probability that $p - 1$ has a large prime factor is overwhelming. However, many cryptographic protocols based on the IF problem do require using safe-prime RSA moduli in order to achieve the correctness of the effects served by the protocols.

It is also well-known that partial information of a prime factor of $N$ can produce efficient algorithms to factor $N$. For instance, for $N = pq$ with $p$ and $q$ primes of roughly equal size, knowledge of up to half the bits of $p$ will suffice to factor $N$ in polynomial time in the size of $N$, see e.g., [83].

If not using any *apriori* information about the prime factors of the input composite, then the current best factorization algorithm is the number field sieve (NFS) method which has the time complexity expressed in (4.6.1). Thus, similar to the setting of the security parameter for the DLP in finite fields, 1024 is the widely agreed lower bound setting for the size of an RSA modulus in order to achieve a high confidence in security.

Recently, the number field sieve method demonstrated an effectiveness of massive parallelization: in early 2000, a coalition of 9,000 workstations worldwide ran a parallel algorithm and factored a 512-bit RSA modulus (the RSA-512 Challenge) after more than four months of running the parallel algorithm [71].

Research into integer factorization is very active and it is impossible to rule out a decisive advance. Boneh provided a survey on the RSA problem [49]. Discussions on the progress in the area of IF problem with a literature review can be found in Chapter 3 of [200].

## 8.9 Insecurity of the Textbook RSA Encryption

We have labeled the RSA encryption algorithm in Alg 8.1 a textbook version because that version is what the RSA encryption algorithm is in most textbook on cryptography. Now let us look at the security (or insecurity) properties of the textbook RSA encryption algorithm.

For random key instance and random message instance, by Definition 8.4 and Assumption 8.3, the existence of an efficient CPA against the RSA cryptosystem means the RSA assumption must be false. Therefore we have

**Theorem 8.1:** *The RSA cryptosystem is "all-or-nothing" secure against CPA if and only if the RSA assumption holds.* □

Here, the meaning of "all-or-nothing" secure is explained in Property 8.2.(i); while CPA means the attacker remains passive as stipulated in Property 8.2.(ii).

However, confidentiality of this quality is actually not a very useful one for reasons we now explain.

## 8.9.1 Meet-in-the-Middle Attack and Active Attack on the Textbook RSA

First, let us consider "all-or-nothing" security. Notice that "all" here means to find the whole block of plaintext message in the general case: the message has the size of the modulus. This needn't be the case in applications. In real-world applications, a plaintext typically contains some non-secret partial information which is known to an attack. The textbook RSA does not hide some partial information about a plaintext. For example, if a plaintext is known as a number less than 1,000,000 (e.g., a secret bid or a salary figure), then given a ciphertext, an attacker can pinpoint the plaintext in less than 1,000,000 trial-and-error encryptions.

In general, for a plaintext $m(< N)$, with a non-negligible probability, only $\sqrt{m}$ number of trials are needed to pinpoint $m$ if $\sqrt{m}$ size of memory is available. This is due to a clever observation made by Boneh, Joux and Nguyen [53] which exploits the fact that factorization of small plaintext message is not a hard problem and the multiplicative property of the RSA function. The multiplicative property of the RSA function is as follows

$$(m_1 \times m_2)^e \equiv m_1^e \times m_2^e \equiv c_1 \times c_2 \ (\text{mod } N). \tag{8.9.1}$$

That is, factorization of plaintext implies that of the corresponding ciphertext. It is normally a hard problem to factor an RSA ciphertext since the mix-transformation property of the encryption function will almost always cause a ciphertext to have the size of that of the modulus. However, the multiplicative property indicates that if a plaintext is easy to factor, then so is the corresponding ciphertext. The ease of factoring the latter leads to a **meet-in-the-middle attack**. This is explained in Attack 8.2.

Let's measure Malice's cost. The database has a space cost of $2^{\frac{\ell}{2}} \cdot \log N$ bits. For time cost: creating elements in the database costs $O_B(2^{\frac{\ell}{2}} \cdot \log^3 N)$, sorting the

---

**Attack 8.2:** Meet-in-the-Middle Attack on the Textbook Encryption in RSA

CONDITION:

Let $c = m^e \pmod{N}$ such that Malice knows $m < 2^\ell$. With non-negligible probability $m$ is a composite number satisfying

$$m = m_1 \cdot m_2 \quad \text{with} \quad m_1, m_2 < 2^{\frac{\ell}{2}}. \tag{8.9.2}$$

The multiplicative property of the RSA function yields

$$c = m_1^e \cdot m_2^e \pmod{N}. \tag{8.9.3}$$

MALICE PERFORMS THE FOLLOWING:

1. Builds a sorted database

$$\{1^e, 2^e, 3^e, \ldots, (2^{\frac{\ell}{2}})^e\} \pmod{N}.$$

2. Searches through the sorted database trying to find $c/i^e \pmod{N}$ (for $i = 1, 2, \ldots, 2^{\frac{\ell}{2}}$) from the database trying to find

$$c/i^e \equiv j^e \pmod{N}. \tag{8.9.4}$$

($*$ Because of (8.9.2) and (8.9.3), a "meet-in-the-middle", signaled by (8.9.4) will show up before $2^{\frac{\ell}{2}}$ steps of computing $i^e \pmod{N}$. Now that Malice knows plaintexts $i, j$, he uncovers $m = i \cdot j$. $*$)

---

database costs $O_B(\frac{\ell}{2} \cdot 2^{\frac{\ell}{2}})$, and finally, searching through the sorted database to find $j^e \pmod{N}$ costs $O_B(2^{\frac{\ell}{2}} \cdot (\frac{\ell}{2} + \log^3 N))$. This final part comprises time for modulo exponentiation plus that for binary search (using Alg 4.4). So the total time cost measured in bit-complexity is $O_B(2^{\frac{\ell}{2}+1} \cdot (\frac{\ell}{2} + \log^3 N))$. If the space of $2^{\frac{\ell}{2}} \cdot \log N$ bits is affordable, then the time complexity is significantly less than $2^\ell$. This attack achieves a square-root level reduction in time complexity.

For cases of a plaintext message having sizes ranging from 40-64 bits, the probabilities that the plaintext can be factored to two similar size integers range from 18%-50% (see Table 1 of [53]).

**Example 8.3: A Real-life Instantiation of Attack 8.2** Now imagine a scenario of using an 1024-bit RSA to encrypt a DES key of 56 bits in the textbook style.

For a random DES key, the discovery of the key can be done with a non-negligible probability (of factoring the DES key into two integers of 28 bits), using $2^{28} \cdot 1024 = 2^{38}$-bit storage (= 32 gigabytes) and computing $2^{29}$ modulo exponentiations. Both the space and time costs can be realistically handled by a good personal computer, while direct searching for the DES key from the encryption requires computing $2^{56}$ modulo exponentiations which can be quite prohibitive even using a dedicated device. $\qquad\square$

Now we know that we *must not* use the textbook RSA to encrypt a short key or a password which are less than $2^{64}$. What happens if in an application we have to perform RSA encryption of small numbers, even the message is as small as a single bit? We suggest that the reader should use the encryption methods (including an RSA-based scheme) to be introduced in Chapter 15.

The next example further shows the inadequacy of the CPA security of the textbook RSA: against an active attack, the textbook RSA fails more miserably.

**Example 8.4:** Let Malice be in a conditional control of Alice's RSA decryption box. The condition is quite "reasonable:" if the decryption result of a ciphertext submitted by Malice is not meaningful (looks random), then Alice should return the plaintext to Malice. We say that this condition is "reasonable" for the following two reasons:

i) "A random response for a random challenge" is quite a standard mode of operation in many cryptographic protocols, and hence, a user should follow such a "challenge-response" instruction. Indeed, *often* cryptographic protocols have been designed to allow this kind of conditional control of a decryption box by a protocol participant. For example, the Needham-Schroeder public-key authentication protocol (see Prot 2.5) has exactly such a feature: Alice is instructed to decrypt a ciphertext from Bob.

ii) Anyway, we would like to hope that a random-looking decryption result should not provide an attacker with any useful information.

Now suppose Malice wants to know the plaintext of a ciphertext $c \equiv m^e \pmod N$ which he has eavesdropped or intercepted from a previous confidential communication between Alice and someone else (not with him!). He picks a random number $r \in_U \mathbb{Z}_N^*$, computes $c' = r^e c \pmod N$ and sends his chosen ciphertext $c'$ to Alice. The decryption result by Alice will be

$$c'^d \equiv rm \pmod N$$

which can be completely random for Alice since the multiplication of $r$ is a **permutation** over $\mathbb{Z}_N^*$. So Alice returns the decryption result $rm$ back to Malice. Alas, Malice has $r$ and thereby can obtain $m$ with a division modulo $N$. $\qquad\square$

Attack 8.2 and Example 8.4 show that the textbook RSA is too weak to fit for real-world applications. A systematic fix for these weaknesses is necessary. We will conduct a fix work in two steps:

- in Chapter 14 we will strengthen security notions for public-key encryption schemes into fit-for-application ones;

- in Chapter 15 we will study a fit-for-application version of the RSA encryption which is also a standard for encryption in RSA; we will show formal evidence of its security under the strong and fit-for-application security notion.

## 8.10  Encryption in Rabin (Textbook Version)

Rabin developed a public-key cryptosystem based on the difficulty of computing a square root modulo a composite integer [242]. Rabin's work has a theoretic importance; it provided the first provable security for public-key cryptosystems: the security of the Rabin cryptosystem is exactly the intractability of the IF problem. (Recall our discussion for the case of the RSA: it is not known if the RSA problem is equivalent to the IF problem.) The encryption algorithm in the Rabin cryptosystem is also extremely efficient and hence is very suitable in certain applications such as encryption performed by hand-held devices.

The Rabin cryptosystem is specified in Alg 8.2. We notice that this is a textbook version for encryption in Rabin.

We now show that the system specified in Alg 8.2 is indeed a cryptosystem, i.e., Alice's decryption procedure will actually return the same plaintext message that Bob has encrypted.

We know from elementary mathematics that the general solution to this equation can be written as

$$m \equiv \frac{-b + \sqrt{\Delta_c}}{2} \pmod{N}, \qquad (8.10.1)$$

where

$$\Delta_c \overset{\text{def}}{=} b^2 + 4c \pmod{N}. \qquad (8.10.2)$$

Since $c$ is formed using $m \in \mathbb{Z}_N^*$, of course the quadratic equation

$$m^2 + bm - c \equiv 0 \pmod{N}$$

has solutions in $\mathbb{Z}_N^*$, and these solutions include $m$ sent from Bob. This implies that $\Delta_c$ must be a quadratic residue modulo $N$, i.e., an element in $\mathrm{QR}_N$.

The decryption computation involves computing square roots modulo $N$. From our study of the square-rooting problem in §6.6.2 we know that the difficulty of this problem is computationally equivalent to that of factoring $N$ (Corollary 6.3). Therefore, the only person who can compute (8.10.1) is Alice since only she knows

---

**Algorithm 8.2:** The Rabin Cryptosystem

**Key Setup**
To set up a user's key material, user Alice performs the following steps:

1. choose two random prime numbers $p$ and $q$ such that $|p| \approx |q|$
   ($*$ same as generating an RSA modulus in Alg 8.1 $*$)

2. compute $N = pq$;

3. pick a random integer $b \in_U \mathbb{Z}_N^*$;

4. publicize $(N, b)$ as her public key material, and keep $(p, q)$ as her private key.

**Encryption**
To send a confidential message $m \in \mathbb{Z}_N^*$ to Alice, the sender Bob creates ciphertext $c$ as follows:

$$c \leftarrow m(m + b) \pmod{N}.$$

**Decryption**
To decrypt the ciphertext $c$, Alice solves the quadratic equation

$$m^2 + bm - c \equiv 0 \pmod{N}$$

for $m < N$.

---

the factorization of $N$. Alice can compute $\sqrt{\Delta_c}$ using Alg 6.5. In §6.6.2 we also know that for each ciphertext $c$ sent by Bob, there are four distinct values for $\sqrt{\Delta_c}$ and hence there are four different decryption results. We assume that, in applications, a plaintext message should contain *redundant information* to allow Alice to recognize the correct plaintext from the four decryption results. We will provide in §10.4.3 the meaning for "recognizable redundancy" and a common method for a message to be formated to contain recognizable redundancy.

We notice that if $N$ is a so-called **Blum integer**, that is, $N = pq$ with $p \equiv q \equiv 3 \pmod 4$, then it is easier to compute square roots modulo $N$ (by computing square roots modulo $p$ and $q$ using Alg 6.3, Case $p \equiv 3, 7 \pmod 8$ and then constructing the square roots by applying the Chinese Remainder Theorem). Therefore, in practice, the public modulus in the Rabin cryptosystem is set to be a Blum integer.

The Rabin encryption algorithm only involves one multiplication and one addition and hence is much faster than the RSA encryption.

**Example 8.5:** Let Alice set $N = 11 \times 19 = 209$ and $b = 183$. She publicizes $(N, b) = (209, 183)$ as her public key material for the Rabin cryptosystem.

Let Bob encrypt a plaintext message $m = 31$. Bob performs Rabin encryption:

$$c = 31 \times (31 + 183) \equiv 155 \ (\text{mod } 209).$$

The resultant ciphertext is 155.

To decrypt the ciphertext 155, Alice first computes $\Delta_c$ using (8.10.2):

$$\Delta_c = b^2 + 4c = 183^2 + 4 \times 155 \equiv 42 \ (\text{mod } 209).$$

Now applying Alg 6.5, Alice finds that the four square roots of 42 modulo 209 are $135, 173, 36, 74$. Finally, she can apply equation 8.10.1 and obtains the four decryption results: $185, 204, 31, 50$. In real application of the Rabin cryptosystem, the plaintext should contain additional information for the receiver to pinpoint the correct decryption result. $\qquad\qquad\square$

## 8.11 Insecurity of the Textbook Rabin Encryption

We have a more devastating active attack against the textbook Rabin. The following theorem manifests this attack in a "provable" way.

**Theorem 8.2:**

I) *The Rabin cryptosystem is provably "all-or-nothing" secure against CPA if and only if the IF problem is hard.*

II) *The Rabin cryptosystem is completely insecure if it is attacked under CCA.*

**Proof** (I) Because the specified decryption procedure of the Rabin cryptosystem uses the factorization of an RSA modulus, the security of the Rabin encryption therefore implies the intractability of factoring of RSA moduli. Thus for (I), we only need to prove the statement for the other direction: the intractability of the IF problem implies the security of the Rabin cryptosystem.

Suppose that there exists an oracle $\mathcal{O}$ which breaks the Rabin cryptosystem with a non-negligible advantage $\epsilon$, i.e.,

$$\text{Prob}\left[ \mathcal{O}(c, N) = \frac{-b + \sqrt{\Delta_c}}{2} \ (\text{mod } N) \mid c \in_U \mathbb{Z}_N^* \right] \geq \epsilon.$$

We choose a random message $m$, computes $c = m(m + b) \ (\text{mod } N)$ and call $\mathcal{O}(c, N)$ which will return $m' \equiv \frac{-b + \sqrt{\Delta_c}'}{2} \ (\text{mod } N)$ with advantage $\epsilon$. Here $\sqrt{\Delta_c}'$ denotes any one of the four square roots of $\Delta_c$. By Theorem 6.17 (in §6.6.2) we know with probability $1/2$:

$$m' + \frac{b}{2} \equiv \frac{\sqrt{\Delta_c}'}{2} \not\equiv \pm\frac{\sqrt{\Delta_c}}{2} \equiv \pm(m + \frac{b}{2}) \ (\mathrm{mod}\ N).$$

But because

$$(m' + \frac{b}{2})^2 \equiv \frac{\Delta_c}{4} \equiv [\pm(m + \frac{b}{2})]^2 \ (\mathrm{mod}\ N),$$

so as shown in Theorem 6.17,

$$\gcd(m' + \frac{b}{2} \pm (m + \frac{b}{2}),\ N) = p \text{ or } q. \tag{8.11.1}$$

That is, $N$ can be factored with the non-negligible advantage $\epsilon/2$. This contradicts the assumed intractability of factoring of RSA moduli (the IF assumption). We have thus shown (I).

Statement (II) holds trivially true if an attacker can obtain a decryption assistance: the decryption assistance plays exactly the role of the oracle used in the proof of statement (I)! Since the attacker will generate (choose) ciphertext for the decryption oracle to decrypt, such an attack is CCA.      □

Theorem 8.2 tells us two opposite things. First, the Rabin cryptosystem is provably secure, in an "all-or-nothing" sense in Property 8.2.(i), with respect to the difficulty of factorization (N.B. provided the plaintext itself is "all-or-nothing" secret, i.e., does not have known *apriori* information). This is a strong and desirable result because it relates the (textbook) security of the Rabin encryption scheme to a reputably hard problem. If the IF problem is indeed intractable, then the alleged oracle $\mathcal{O}$ in the proof of (I) should not exist. However, we should pay particular attention to the modifier "all-or-nothing" for the CPA security property. Here "all" means to find the whole block of plaintext message in the *general case*: the message has the size of the modulus. Clearly, due to the fact that the Rabin encryption is deterministic, finding some special messages, such as short ones, needn't be as hard as factorization. We will come back to this point when we discuss meet-in-the-middle attack on the Rabin scheme at the end of this section.

Secondly, it is now clear that, in the Rabin cryptosystem, one should *never* allow oneself to be used as a decryption oracle. CCA is devastating against the Rabin cryptosystem: the consequence of such an attack is not merely finding *some* plaintext information (as in the case of CCA2 against the RSA cryptosystem as illustrated in Example 8.4), it is the discovery of the private key of the key owner, and hence the attacker will be able to read *all* confidential messages encrypted under the targeted public key.

**Example 8.6:** In Example 8.5 for the Rabin cryptosystem we have seen that for public key material $(N, b) = (209, 183)$, the four decryption results of the ciphertext 31 are $185, 204, 31, 50$.

If these numbers are made available to a non-owner of the public key, e.g., via a CCA, they can be used to factor the modulus 209. For example, applying (8.11.1):

$$\gcd(204 - 185, 209) = 19,$$

or

$$\gcd((31 + 183/2) + (50 + 183/2), 209) = gcd(264, 209) = 11. \qquad \square$$

Although we have warned that a public key owner of the Rabin encryption scheme should never provide a decryption service, it is unrealistic for a user to keep this high degree of vigilance in real world applications. Therefore, the text-book Rabin encryption scheme is not a fit-for-application one. In Chapter 15 we shall introduce a fit-for-application method for encrypting in Rabin (and in RSA). There we will also provide formal argument on fit-for-application security for those encryption schemes.

We should also notice that since the modulus of the Rabin cryptosystem is the same as that of the RSA cryptosystem, the cautionary measures that we have discussed for the proper choice of the RSA modulus apply to the Rabin modulus.

Finally, meet-in-the-middle attack also applies to the following variation of the textbook Rabin encryption scheme:

**Encryption:**  $c = m^2 \pmod{N}$.

**Decryption:**  Computing square root of $c$ modulo $N$.

Similar to case for the textbook RSA encryption, ease of factoring a small plain-text message and the multiplicative property (explained in §8.9) of this Rabin encryption scheme enables a meet-in-the-middle attack as we have shown in Attack 8.2 for the textbook RSA case.

## 8.12  Encryption in ElGamal (Textbook Version)

ElGamal works out an ingenious public-key cryptosystem [103]. The cryptosystem is a successful application of the Diffie-Hellman one-way trapdoor function which turns the function into a public-key encryption scheme. ElGamal's work inspires great interest in both research and applications which has remained high to this day. We will see two further development of this cryptosystem in Chapter 13 (an identity-based ElGamal encryption scheme), and in Chapter 15 (a variation with a strong provable security).

One reason for the great momentum following up ElGamal's work is its enabling of the use of the widely believed reliable intractability for underlying the security of public-key cryptosystems: the CDH problem, which is widely believed to be as hard as the DL problem and the latter is considered to be a good alternative to the other widely accepted reliable intractability: the IF problem (the basis for the RSA and Rabin).

---

**Algorithm 8.3:** The ElGamal Cryptosystem

**Key Setup**
To set up a user's key material, user Alice performs the following steps:

1. choose a random prime number $p$;

2. compute a random multiplicative generator element $g$ of $\mathbb{F}_p^*$;

3. pick a random number $x \in_U \mathbb{Z}_{p-1}$ as her private key;

4. compute her public key by

$$y \leftarrow g^x \pmod{p};$$

5. publicize $(p, g, y)$ as her public key, and keep $x$ as her private key.

($*$ similar to the case of the Diffie-Hellman key exchange protocol, a system-wide users may share the common public parameters $(p, g)$. $*$)

**Encryption**
To send a confidential message $m < p$ to Alice, the sender Bob picks $k \in_U \mathbb{Z}_{p-1}$ and computes ciphertext pair $(c_1, c_2)$ as follows:

$$\begin{cases} c_1 \leftarrow g^k \pmod{p}, \\ c_2 \leftarrow y^k m \pmod{p}. \end{cases} \qquad (8.12.1)$$

**Decryption**
To decrypt ciphertext $(c_1, c_2)$, Alice computes

$$m \leftarrow c_2 / c_1^x \pmod{p}. \qquad (8.12.2)$$

---

The ElGamal cryptosystem is specified in Alg 8.3. We notice that this is a textbook version for encryption in ElGamal.

We now show that the system specified in Alg 8.3 is indeed a cryptosystem, i.e., Alice's decryption procedure will actually return the same plaintext message that Bob has encrypted.

Since

$$c_1^x \equiv (g^k)^x \equiv (g^x)^k \equiv y^k \equiv c_2/m \pmod{p},$$

the decryption calculation (8.12.2) does indeed restore the plaintext $m$.

The division in the decryption step (8.12.2) needs to use the extended Euclid algorithm (Alg 4.2) which is generally more costly than a multiplication. However Alice may avoid the division by computing

$$m \leftarrow c_2 c_1^{-x} \pmod{p}.$$

One may verify that this decryption method works, but notice that $-x$ here means $p - 1 - x$.

**Example 8.7:** From Example 8.1 we know that 3 is a primitive root modulo 43. Let Alice choose 7 as her private key. She computes her public key as

$$37 \equiv 3^7 \pmod{43}.$$

Alice publicizes her public key material $(p, g, y) = (43, 3, 37)$.

Let Bob encrypt a plaintext message $m = 14$. Bob picks a random exponent 26 and computes

$$c_1 = 15 \equiv 3^{26} \pmod{43}, \quad c_2 = 31 \equiv 37^{26} \times 14 \pmod{43}.$$

The resultant ciphertext message pair is $(15, 31)$.

To decrypt the ciphertext message $(15, 31)$, Alice computes

$$14 = 31/36 \equiv 31/15^7 \pmod{43}.$$

Division requires application of Alg 4.2. But Alice can avoid it by computing:

$$14 = 31 \times 15^{42-7} \equiv 31 \times 6 \pmod{43}. \qquad \square$$

# 8.13   Insecurity of the Textbook ElGamal Encryption

The encryption algorithm (8.12.1) of the ElGamal cryptosystem is probabilistic: it uses a random input $k \in_U \mathbb{Z}_{p-1}$. Suppose that Alice's private key $x$ is relatively prime to $p - 1$; then by Theorem 5.2(3) (in §5.2.3), her public key $y \equiv g^x \pmod{p}$ remains being a generator of $\mathbb{F}_p^*$ (since $g$ is), and thereby $y^k \pmod{p}$ will range over $\mathbb{F}_p^*$ when $k$ ranges over $\mathbb{Z}_{p-1}$. Since multiplication modulo $p$ is a permutation over $\mathbb{F}_p^*$, for any plaintext message $m \in \mathbb{F}_p^*$, $c_2 \equiv y^k m \pmod{p}$ will range over $\mathbb{F}_p^*$ when $k$ ranges over $\mathbb{Z}_{p-1}$ (Theorem 6.6 in §6.2.2). Consequently, we have $c_2 \in_U \mathbb{F}_p^*$ for $k \in_U \mathbb{Z}_{p-1}$. This means that the ElGamal encryption achieves the distribution of the plaintext message *uniformly* over the entire message space. This is the ideal semantic property for an encryption algorithm.

However, we should not be too optimistic! The ciphertext of the ElGamal encryption is not just the single block $c_2$, but the pair $(c_1, c_2)$, and these two blocks *are* statistically *related*. Therefore, like all other public-key cryptosystems, the security of the ElGamal cryptosystem is conditional under an intractability assumption. Moreover, we shall see in a moment (§8.13.1) that in order for the ideal semantic property to hold, the plaintext message must be in the group $\langle g \rangle$. Unfortunately, this is usually not the case in the real-world applications.

First, we present an "all-or-nothing" security result for the ElGamal encryption scheme.

**Theorem 8.3:** *For a plaintext message uniformly distributed in the plaintext message space, the ElGamal cryptosystem is "all-or-nothing" secure against CPA if and only if the CDH problem is hard.*

**Proof** ($\Rightarrow$) We need to show that if the ElGamal cryptosystem is secure, then the CDH assumption holds.

Suppose on the contrary the CDH assumption does not hold. Then given any ciphertext $(c_1, c_2) \equiv (g^k, y^k m) \pmod p$ constructed under the public key $y \equiv g^x \pmod p$, a CDH oracle will compute from $(p, g, g^x, g^k)$ to $g^{xk} \equiv y^k \pmod p$ with a non-negligible advantage. Then $m \leftarrow c_2/y^k \pmod p$ with the same advantage. This contradicts the assumed security of the ElGamal cryptosystem.

($\Leftarrow$) We now need to show that if the CDH assumption holds, then there exists no efficient algorithm that can recover plaintext message encrypted in an ElGamal ciphertext with non-negligible advantage.

Suppose on the contrary there exists an efficient oracle $\mathcal{O}$ against the ElGamal cryptosystem, that is, given any public key $(p, g, y)$ and ciphertext $(c_1, c_2)$, $\mathcal{O}$ outputs

$$m \leftarrow \mathcal{O}(p, g, y, c_1, c_2)$$

with a non-negligible advantage $\delta$ such that $m$ satisfies

$$c_2/m \equiv g^{(\log_g y \log_g c_1)} \pmod p.$$

Then for an arbitrary CDH problem instance $(p, g, g_1, g_2)$, we set $(p, g, g_1)$ as public key and set $(g_2, c_2)$ as ciphertext pair for a random $c_2 \in \mathbb{F}_p^*$. Then with the advantage $\delta$, $\mathcal{O}$ outputs

$$m \leftarrow \mathcal{O}(p, g, g_1, g_2, c_2)$$

with $m$ satisfying

$$c_2/m \equiv g^{(\log_g g_1 \log_g g_2)} \pmod p.$$

This contradicts the holding of the CDH assumption.                    $\square$

Since the CPA security of the ElGamal cryptosystem is equivalent to the CDH problem, our discussions for the CDH problem and DL problem in §8.4), such as the cautionary considerations on the settings of the public-key parameters, all apply to the ElGamal cryptosystem. As in the Diffie-Hellman key exchange protocol, the ElGamal cryptosystem can also work in a large prime-order subgroup of $\mathbb{F}_q$, or in a large group of points on an elliptic curve defined over a finite field.

## 8.13.1    Meet-in-the-Middle Attack and Active Attack on the Textbook ElGamal Encryption

The reason we have labeled the ElGamal cryptosystem specified in Alg 8.3 a textbook scheme is because it is a very weak encryption scheme. Now let us see why.

The ElGamal encryption scheme, in a usual form used in applications, may leak partial information even to a passive attacker. In practice, the ElGamal cryptosystem often uses $g$ of order $r = \mathrm{ord}_p(g) \ll p$ as a means to obtain an improved efficiency. In such a case, if a message $m$ is not in the subgroup $\langle g \rangle$, then a meet-in-the-middle attack similar to that on the textbook RSA (see Attack 8.2) can also be applied to the textbook ElGamal. This is because, for ciphertext $(c_1, c_2) = (g^k, y^k m) \pmod{p}$, Malice can obtain

$$c_2^r \equiv m^r \pmod{p}.$$

That is, Malice has transformed the "probabilistic" encryption scheme of ElGamal into a *deterministic* version! Moreover, it has the multiplicative property just as the textbook RSA does (explained in §8.9). Therefore, for a small message which is easy to be factored, Malice can launch the meet-in-the-middle attack on $m^r \pmod{p}$ exactly the same way as he does on the textbook RSA (this meet-in-the-middle attack on the textbook ElGamal encryption scheme is observed in [53]).

From this attack we now know that when a plaintext message is not in the subgroup generated by $g$, the ElGamal cryptosystem becomes a deterministic scheme. A deterministic encryption scheme of course leaks partial information since it permits a trial-and-error method to find small plaintext messages, such as a secret bid or a salary figure.

Finally we provide an example of ElGamal's vulnerability to active attack.

**Example 8.8:** Let Malice be in a conditional control of Alice's ElGamal decryption box. As in Example 8.4, the condition is a "reasonable" one in that if a decryption of a ciphertext submitted by Malice results in a message which is not meaningful (looks random), then Alice should return the decryption result to Malice.

Let Malice have a ciphertext $(c_1, c_2) \equiv (g^k, y^k m) \pmod{p}$ which he has eavesdropped or intercepted from a previous confidential communication between Alice and someone else (not with Malice!). If Malice wants to know the corresponding plaintext. He picks a random number $r \in_U \mathbb{F}_p^*$, computes $c_2' = rc_2 \pmod{p}$ and sends his chosen ciphertext $(c_1, c_2')$ to Alice. The decryption result by Alice will be

$$rm \pmod{p}$$

which, viewed by Alice, is completely random since the multiplication of $r < p$ is a permutation over $\mathbb{F}_p^*$. So Alice returns the decryption result $rm$ back to Malice. Alas, Malice has $r$ and thereby can obtain $m$ with a division modulo $p$.    □

## 8.14    Need for Stronger Security Notions for Public-key Cryptosystems

We have introduced several basic and textbook public-key cryptosystems. These basic schemes can be viewed as direct applications of various one-way trapdoor functions. (The meaning of one-way trapdoor functions has been given in Property 8.1.).

Now it is time to provide a summary on the insecurity features of these textbook schemes. We should provide a brief discussion here on two aspects of vulnerabilities that a textbook public-key cryptosystem has.

First, as having stated in Property 8.2.(i), within the scope of this chapter we have only considered a very weak notion of security: secrecy in an "all-or-nothing" sense. In most applications of public-key cryptosystems, such a weak notion of secrecy is far from being good enough and is also not very useful. In many applications plaintext messages contain *apriori* information known to an attacker. For example, if a cipher encrypts a vote, then the *apriori* information can be "YES" or "NO," or a handful names of the candidates; thus, regardless of how strong a trapdoor function is, an attacker only needs several trial-and-error to pinpoint the correct plaintext. In some other applications, some partial *apriori* information about the plaintext will provide an attacker an unentitled advantage (we will see such an attack in §14.3.2). In general, a textbook encryption algorithm does not hide such partial information very well. Thus, stronger public-key cryptosystems secure for hiding any *apriori* information about the plaintext are needed.

Secondly, as having stated in Property 8.2.(ii), within the scope of this chapter we have only considered a very weak mode of attack: "passive attacker." However, for each textbook scheme introduced in this chapter we have demonstrated an active attack on it (Examples 8.4, 8.6, 8.8). In such an attack, the attacker can prepare a cleverly calculated ciphertext message and submit it to a key owner for an oracle decryption service in CCA or CCA2 modes. Our attacks show that textbook public-key cryptosystems are in general vulnerable to CCA or CCA2. Although we have provided an advice as a general principle for a user to anticipate an active attacker: a public key owner should always be vigilant not to provide a decryption service, however, considering that it will be impractical to require an innocent user to keep in an alert state all the time, advising a user not to respond to a decryption request cannot be a correct strategy against an active attacker.

Public-key cryptosystems with stronger notions of security with respect to these two aspects have been proposed by various authors. In Chapter 14 we will study the course of establishing various stronger confidentiality notions and how to achieve **formally provable security**. In Chapter 15 we shall introduce fit-for-application public-key cryptosystems which are provably secure under a very strong security notion.

# 8.15 Combination of Asymmetric and Symmetric Cryptography

Public-key cryptography solves the key distribution problem very nicely. However, in general, public-key cryptographic functions operate in very large algebraic structures which mean expensive algebraic operations. Comparatively, symmetric cryptographic functions are in general much more efficient. Considering the AES for example, it works in a field of 256 elements; the basic operations such as multiplication and inversion can be conducted by "table lookup" method (review §7.7.4) which is extremely efficient. In general, public-key cryptosystems are comparatively much more computationally intensive than their symmetric-key counterparts.

In applications, in particular in those which need encryption of bulk data, it is now a standard approach that encryption uses a **hybrid scheme**. In such a scheme, public-key cryptography is used to encrypt a so called **ephemeral key** for keying a symmetric cryptosystem; this establishes the shared ephemeral key between a sender and a receiver; the bulk data payload is then encrypted under the shared ephemeral key using a symmetric cryptosystem. Such a combined scheme achieves the best out of the two kinds of cryptosystems: the ease of key distribution from public-key cryptosystems and the efficiency from the symmetric cryptosystems.

A widely used combination of public-key and symmetric-key cryptosystems in cryptographic protocols is a so-called **digital envelope** technique. This is the combination of the RSA cryptosystem with a symmetric-key cryptosystem such as the DES, the triple-DES or the AES. This common combination (RSA + DES or RSA + triple DES) is the basic mode for the **secure sockets layer (SSL)** protocol ([138], we will introduce the SSL protocol in Chapter 12) which has been used in popular Web browsers such as Netscape and Internet Explorer and Web servers. In the SSL protocol, the initiator of the protocol (let it be Alice, usually in the position of a Web client) will first download the public-key material of the other communication party (let it be Bob, usually in the position of a Web server); then Alice (in fact, her web-browser software) will generate a random session key, encrypts ("envelopes") the session key using Bob's public key and send the "envelope" to Bob. After Bob (in fact, his web-server software) has decrypted the "envelope" and retrieved the session key, the two parties can then use the session key to key a symmetric encryption scheme for their subsequent confidential communications.

In the context of protocols, the simple hybrid encryption scheme is conceptually very simple. But it has two limitations. First, the scheme uses a session key which is created by one party (the message sender or the protocol initiator); the other party (the message receiver or the protocol responder) will have to completely rely on the sender's or the protocol initiator's competence (or honesty) in key generation for security. This may not be desirable in some circumstances, for instance, in the SSL protocol's client-server setting where the client is the sender and is implemented in software which is notoriously weak in generation of randomness.

The second limitation of the simple hybrid encryption scheme is due to its non-evanescent property. In hybrid encryption scheme, an eavesdropper who can coerce the receiver into revealing her/his private key can then recover the full Payload_Message. This weakness is often referred to as lack of "forward secrecy property." The forward secrecy property means it is impossible for an eavesdropper to recover the plaintext message in a future time using the ciphertext messages sent in the past, either by means of cryptanalysis or even by means of *coercion*.

These two limitations can be overcome if the public-key cryptographic part of a hybrid encryption scheme uses the Diffie-Hellman key exchange protocol.

Let us first look at how the first limitation disappears if a hybrid scheme uses the Diffie-Hellman key exchange protocol. In the Diffie-Hellman key exchange protocol run between Alice and Bob, the shared secret $g^{ab}$ contains randomness input from the both parties: Alice's contribution is from $a$ and Bob's, from $b$. Given that $g$ generates a prime-order group and that the protocol messages satisfy $g^a \neq 1$ and $g^b \neq 1$ (see the "cautionary details" that we have provided in §8.3), Alice (respectively, Bob) can be sure that the shared secret session key derived from $g^{ab}$ will be random as long as she (respectively, he) has used a random exponent. This is because the mappings $g^b \mapsto (g^b)^a$ and $g^a \mapsto (g^a)^b$ are permutations in the group in question and thereby a uniform exponent (less than the group order) will cause $g^a$ (respectively, $g^b$) being mapped to a uniform group element $g^{ab}$.

Secondly, let us look at how the second limitation is overcome. We note that a hybrid encryption scheme using the Diffie-Hellman key exchange protocol has the forward secrecy property if Alice and Bob run the key exchange protocol in a cautionary manner which we have recommended in §8.3, and if they also properly process the subsequent session communications. To run the Diffie-Hellman key exchange protocol in a cautionary manner, Alice and Bob should exchange the session key $g^{ab}$ and then erase the exponents $a$ and $b$ upon termination of the protocol. To properly process the subsequent session communications, Alice and Bob should destroy the session key after the session ends and should properly dispose of the plaintext messages they have communicated. If they follow these rather *standard* procedures, then obviously coercion will not enable an eavesdropper to find out the plaintext messages that Alice and Bob have communicated. Cryptanalysis won't do the job for the eavesdropper either since the forward secrecy property (of the Diffie-Hellman key exchange protocol) is simply due to the difficulty of the CDH problem (see §8.4).

Finally we point out that a hybrid encryption scheme can be designed to have a **provable security** under a very strong notion of confidentiality. In Chapter 15 we shall conduct an overview of a series of such schemes.

# 8.16   Key Channel Establishment for Public-key Cryptosystems

The well-known man-in-the-middle attack on the Diffie-Hellman key exchange protocol (see §8.3.1) is general in public-key cryptosystems. In general, to send a confidential message to a recipient by encrypting under her/his public key, the sender must first make sure that that the key to be used really belongs to the intended recipient. Likewise, upon receipt a "digital envelope," the recipient must make sure that the "envelope" is really from the claimed source before engaging in a confidential communications using the symmetric key retrieved from the "envelope."

Thus, no matter how "unconventional" public-key cryptographic techniques are, there is still a need for establishing a secure key channel between communication parties. However, in public-key cryptography we have $ke \neq kd$ (see Fig 7.1) and therefore transporting an encryption key $ke$ to the message sender need not involve handling of any secret. Therefore, the task for establishing a secure key channel is purely an authentication problem, namely, the key channel involves no handling of any secret and should only preserve the authenticity of the encryption key.

Authenticated key channel establishment for public keys will be the topic of Chapter 13. Directory based techniques for public-key channel setting-up will be introduced in §13.2 while some identity based techniques will be introduced in §13.3.

# 8.17   Chapter Summary

In this chapter we have introduced several well-known and widely used public-key encryption schemes: Diffie-Hellman key exchange protocol, the RSA, Rabin and ElGamal encryption algorithms. Along with these basic public-key schemes, we introduce respective hard problems as complexity-theoretic assumptions which are the security underpins for the basic public-key encryption algorithms.

We declared that the quality of security considered in this chapter, all-or-nothing secrecy and passive attacker, is a low one: it is labeled as a textbook security notion and is only suitable for an ideal world in which data are already random and bad guys are nice (in that they do not mount active attacks). All public-key schemes introduced in this chapter are textbook ones. Various attacks on them have been demonstrated to manifest their insecurity qualities.

We then discussed the need for more stringent and fit-for-application security notions for public-key encryption schemes, and the need for schemes which are secure under the stronger notions. However, we decided to defer their introduction to several later chapters (in Part V). The reader who does not plan to study Part V should carefully review the attacks given in this chapter, especially if (s)he plans to use a textbook crypto scheme introduced in this chapter.

## Exercises

8.1 What are the two prominent characteristics of a textbook crypto algorithm?

8.2 A cipher block chaining (CBC) mode of operation for a block cipher (introduced in §7.8.2) has a random input and as a result any partial information of a plaintext can be well hidden. Is CBC still a textbook crypto algorithm? Why?

8.3 Let an attacker in a man-in-the-middle attack on the Diffie-Hellman key exchange only relay messages between Alice and Bob (i.e., the "man in the middle" does not alter the conversations of Alice and Bob, apart from performing decryption and encryption using the keys the attacker shares with Alice and Bob). Is the attack a passive one or an active one?

Hint: the attack takes place before the message relays.

8.4 For the commonly agreed lower bound size setting for finite field $F_q$: $|q| = 1204$ and for $c < 2$ in the subexponential expression sub_exp$(q)$ in (8.4.2), confirm that there is a "poly solver" for the DLP in $\mathbb{F}_q$ where the "poly solver" runs in time bounded by a degree-9 polynomial in the size of $q$.

8.5 Let group $\langle g \rangle$ have a non-secret order ord$(g)$. Is the following problem hard? Given $g^c$, find $g^a$ and $g^b$ such that $ab \equiv c \pmod{\text{ord}(g)}$, that is, to construct a Diffie-Hellman tuple $(g, g^a, g^b, g^c)$ from $(g, g^c)$.

8.6 What is the relationship between the discrete logarithm problem and the computational Diffie-Hellman problem?

8.7 In RSA public-key material $(e, N)$, why must the encryption exponent $e$ be relatively prime to $\phi(N)$?

8.8 Factoring an odd composite integer is in general a difficult problem. Is factoring a prime power a difficult problem too? (A prime power is $N = p^i$ where $p$ is a prime number and $i$ is an integer. Factor $N$.)

Hint: for any $i > 1$, how many index values $i$ need to be tried in computing the $i$-th root of $N$?

8.9 For $N$ being a prime power, one method for "computing the $i$-th root of $N$" in the preceding problem is binary search. Design a binary search algorithm to root $p^i$ ($i$ is known). Prove that this algorithm is efficient.

Hint: consider binary searching primes of $\frac{\log_2}{i}$ bits.

8.10 An RSA encryption function is a permutation in the multiplicative group modulo the RSA modulus. RSA function is therefore also called a one-way trapdoor permutation. Is Rabin (ElGamal) encryption function a one-way trapdoor permutation?

8.11 Let $N \approx 2^{1024}$. Randomly sampling elements in $\mathbb{Z}_N^*$, what is the probability for a sampling result being less than $2^{64}$? Use this result to explain why a 64-bit random password should not be regarded as a random plaintext for the RSA (Rabin, ElGamal) encryption algorithms.

8.12 Under what condition can the encryption function of the ElGamal cryptosystem be viewed as a deterministic algorithm?

8.13 What are CPA, CCA and CCA2? Explain these notions.

8.14 We have used "all-or-nothing" as a modifier in the descriptions of the CPA security properties for the RSA and Rabin cryptosystems (Theorem 8.1 and Theorem 8.2(I), respectively). Why is this necessary?

8.15 Why must any public-key encryption algorithm (even a textbook crypto one) resist CPA?

8.16 What is the main reason for textbook crypto algorithms being generally vulnerable to active attacks?

8.17 What is an oracle (encryption, decryption) service? For a public-key encryption algorithm, does an attacker need an oracle encryption service?

8.18 Since textbook crypto algorithms are generally vulnerable to active attacks, we have advised that one should be careful not to provide any (oracle) decryption service. Is this actually a correct attitude or a practical strategy?

8.19 Since an active attack generally involves modification of (ciphertext) message transmitted over the network, will an active attack still work if a public-key encryption algorithm has a data integrity protection mechanism which detects unauthorized alteration of ciphertext messages?

8.20 What is the virtue of a hybrid cryptosystem?

# Chapter 9

# IN AN IDEAL WORLD: BIT SECURITY OF THE BASIC PUBLIC-KEY CRYPTOGRAPHIC FUNCTIONS

## 9.1 Introduction

We have seen from several examples that the basic public-key cryptographic functions introduced in the preceding chapter in general do not hide partial information *about* plaintext messages very well, especially when a plaintext message is not random. However, these basic cryptographic primitive functions are not bad at all if they are used in an ideal world in which plaintext messages are random. In such a situation, each of these basic functions is actually very strong.

In this chapter we shall study the **bit security** of the basic public-key cryptographic functions. We shall see that each of the basic and popular public-key cryptographic primitive functions introduced in the preceding chapter has a strong bit security in that, provided the plaintext messages are random, to find an individual bit of the plaintext from a ciphertext is just as difficult as finding the whole plaintext block.

The positive results on bit security for the basic and popular public-key cryptographic functions suggest that as long as a plaintext message is random, then the problem of finding any information about the plaintext can be as hard as inverting these basic functions, since the latter is the problem of finding the whole block of the plaintext message.

This observation has been applied by many researchers to constructing strong public-key encryption schemes out of using the basic and popular public-key crypto-graphic primitive functions. The idea is to randomize the plaintext messages using some randomization schemes before applying a primitive function. In Part V, we will study a general methodology for security proof which is called **random oracle model**. Under the random oracle model, public-key encryption schemes (in fact, digital signature schemes too) which are based on the popular public-key crypto-graphic functions introduced in the preceding chapter can be proved secure under a strong notion of security. An important step for these proofs to go through is an assumption that the plaintext (or message) input to these schemes have been randomized.

We should notice that "an ideal world" is one in which plaintext messages are random. Such a world is not "the ideal world." In the latter, in addition to random messages, Malice is also a nice guy who never mounts an active attack. Therefore, the basic and popular public-key cryptographic functions are still very weak in an ideal world. We will see such examples in this chapter.

This chapter may be skipped by a reader who does not plan to find "know-why" about the fit-for-application cryptographic schemes which we will study in Part V.

### 9.1.1   Chapter Outline

§9.2 studies the RSA bit security. §9.3 studies the Rabin bit security and a technique for using the Rabin bit to generate strong pseudo-random numbers. §9.4 studies the ElGamal bit security. Finally, §9.5 studies the bit security of the discrete logarithm function.

## 9.2   The RSA Bit

If an RSA ciphertext encrypts a message which contains no *apriori* guessable infor-mation (for example, when a message is a uniformly random number in $\mathbb{Z}_N^*$), then it is known that the problem of extracting a single bit of the plaintext message from a ciphertext is as hard as extracting the whole block of the plaintext [130, 77, 76]. Without loss of generality, "one bit of the plaintext" can be the least significant bit, i.e., the parity bit, of the plaintext message. What we are trying to say here is the following statement.

**Theorem 9.1:** *Let N be an RSA modulus. The following two problems are equally hard (or equally easy):*

I) *given the RSA encryption of a message, retrieve the message;*

II) *given the RSA encryption of a message, retrieve the least significant bit of the message.*

If one can solve (I) then obviously one can solve (II). The converse seems not so straightforward. One may think that these two problems can hardly be computationally equivalent: (I) is a computational problem, while for uniformly random plaintext message, (II) is a decisional problem and sheer guessing will entitle one to solve half the instances.

Nevertheless, if one can have possession an oracle which can answer (II) *reliably*, then one can indeed solve (I) by calling this oracle $\log_2 N$ times, and we shall show such a method. Since $\log_2 N$ is the size of $N$, such a method "reduces" (I) to (II) in polynomial time in the size of the input, and is therefore called a **polynomial time reduction**. Consequently, (I) can be solved in time polynomial in the size of the input, *on top of the time* for the oracle to solve (II). We view these two problems to have the same time complexity because we do not differentiate complexities which are different up to a polynomial.

Now let us describe a polynomial reduction method from (I) to (II). Let us call the oracle solving (II) "RSA parity oracle" and denote it by $PO_N$, namely,

$$m \ (\mathrm{mod}\ 2) \leftarrow PO_N(m^e \ (\mathrm{mod}\ N)).$$

In our proof of Theorem 9.1, we denote by $x \in (a, b)$ an integer $x$ in the open interval $(a, b)$ where $a$ and/or $b$ may or may not be integer. Since $x$ is an integer, $x \in (a, b)$ implies that $x$ is in the closed interval $[\lceil a \rceil, \lfloor b \rfloor]$.

The crux of the proof is a **binary search** technique which is enabled by the following observation.

**Lemma 9.1:** *Let $N$ be an odd integer and $x \in (0, N)$. Then $2x \ (\mathrm{mod}\ N)$ is even if and only if $x \ (\mathrm{mod}\ N) \in (0, \frac{N}{2})$.*

**Proof** For all $x \in (0, \frac{N}{2})$, multiplication $2x \ (\mathrm{mod}\ N)$ takes no modulo operation and therefore the result is $2x$ and is an even number in $(0, N)$. Conversely, if $2x \ (\mathrm{mod}\ N)$ is even then it can be divided by 2 and the division takes no modulo operation. Consequently $x \in (0, \frac{N}{2})$.  □

Since all $x \in (0, \frac{N}{2})$ occupy exactly half the integers in $(0, N)$, Lemma 9.1 also says that $2x \ (\mathrm{mod}\ N)$ is odd if and only if $x \in (\frac{N}{2}, N)$.

Now let us prove Theorem 9.1.

**Proof** (of Theorem 9.1) We only need to show (II) $\Rightarrow$ (I). The proof is constructive. We construct a binary search algorithm which makes use of a reliable $PO_N$ and finds $m$ from an RSA ciphertext $c = m^e \ (\mathrm{mod}\ N)$. The algorithm will maintain an interval $(a, b)$, called "current interval," ($CI$ for short). In the starting of the algorithm, the initial case for current interval is $(a, b) = (0, N)$. The binary search algorithm will maintain the following two invariant conditions:

- each iteration will cause $CI$ to halve its length;

- the targeted plaintext remains in $CI$.

For clarity in exposition, we shall only consider the first two iterations of the search procedure.

**Iteration 1** We know that the plaintext is in $(a, b) = (0, N)$. We ask $PO_N$ by feeding it $2^e c \pmod{N}$. Noticing $2^e c \equiv (2m)^e \pmod{N}$, from $PO_N(2^e c)$ we can deduce from Lemma 9.1 whether $m \in (0, N - \frac{N}{2})$ or $m \in (0 + \frac{N}{2}, N)$. We therefore obtain a new $CI$ which contains the plaintext and with the length halved. So when entering this iteration, $(a, b) = (0, N)$; when out of this iteration, we have either $(a, b) = (0, \frac{N}{2})$ or $(a, b) = (\frac{N}{2}, N)$.

**Iteration 2** Consider the case $(a, b) = (\frac{N}{2}, N)$ out of Iteration 1. Let us feed $2^{2e} c \equiv (2^2 m)^e \pmod{N}$ to $PO_N$. If $PO_N(2^{2e} c) = 0$, then the plaintext $2^2 m \equiv 4m \pmod{N}$ is even. By Lemma 9.1 we have $2m \pmod{N} \in (0, \frac{N}{2})$. But remember $2m < 2N$; so for $2m \pmod{N} < \frac{N}{2}$ it is only possible for $2m < 2N - \frac{N}{2} = \frac{3N}{2}$, and thereby $m < \frac{3N}{4}$. So we reach $m \in (\frac{N}{2}, \frac{3N}{4})$. Now we update $CI$ by performing $(a, b) \leftarrow (a, b - \frac{N}{2^2})$. Thus, the invariant conditions are maintained.

The reader may check the correctness of the following two general case for updating $CI$

- If $PO_N$ answers 0, the plaintext is in the lower half of $CI = (a, b)$, and therefore $b$ should be reduced by quantity $\frac{|CI|}{2}$;

- Otherwise, the plaintext is in the upper half of $CI = (a, b)$, and therefore $a$ should be increased by quantity $\frac{|CI|}{2}$.

Clearly, after $i = \lfloor \log_2 N \rfloor + 1$ steps of search, we will reach the case $|CI| = b - a < 1$. The search algorithm terminates and outputs $m = b$. To this end we have proven Theorem 9.1.    □

Alg 9.1 summarizes the general description of the binary search algorithm which we have constructed in the proof of Theorem 9.1.

**Example 9.1:** For RSA public key $(N, e) = (15, 3)$, ciphertext $c = 13$, let us ask $PO_N$ 4 questions and pinpoint the secret plaintext $m$. We feed $PO_N$ the following random-looking ciphertext queries:

$$(2^3 \times 13, \; 4^3 \times 13, \; 8^3 \times 13, \; 16^3 \times 13) \equiv (14, 7, 11, 13) \pmod{15}.$$

$PO_N$ answers: $0, 1, 1, 1$. From these answers we deduce:

1st answer $0 \Rightarrow m \in (0, 15 - \frac{15}{2}) = (0, \frac{15}{2})$, i.e., $m \in [1, 7]$;

2nd answer $1 \Rightarrow m \in (0 + \frac{15}{4}, \frac{15}{2}) = (\frac{15}{4}, \frac{15}{2})$, i.e., $m \in [4, 7]$;

3rd answer $1 \Rightarrow m \in (\frac{15}{4} + \frac{15}{8}, \frac{15}{2}) = (\frac{45}{8}, \frac{15}{2})$, i.e., $m \in [6, 7]$;

---

**Algorithm 9.1:** Binary Searching RSA Plaintext Using a Parity Oracle

INPUT       $(N, e)$: RSA public-key material;
            $c = m^e \pmod{N}$: an RSA ciphertext;
            $PO_N$: a parity oracle, on inputting an RSA ciphertext,
            it returns the least significant bit of the corresponding plaintext.
OUTPUT   $m$.

1. Initialize $(a, b) \leftarrow (0, N)$;

   (∗ the length of "current interval" $CI = (a, b)$ will be halved in each iteration while $m \in (a, b)$ is maintained. ∗)

2. For $i = 1, 2, \ldots, \lfloor \log_2 N \rfloor + 1$ do
   {
   (∗ the length of $(a, b)$ is always under $\frac{N}{2^{i-1}}$. ∗)

   2.1 If ( $PO_N(2^{ie}c) = 0$ ) then $b \leftarrow b - \frac{N}{2^i}$;
        (∗ $m$ is in the lower half of $(a, b)$ ∗)
   2.2 Else $a \leftarrow a + \frac{N}{2^i}$;
        (∗ $m$ is in the upper half of $(a, b)$ ∗)

   }

3. Return( $\lfloor b \rfloor$ ).

---

4th answer $1 \Rightarrow m \in (\frac{45}{8} + \frac{15}{16}, \frac{15}{2}) = (\frac{105}{16}, \frac{15}{2})$, i.e., $m \in [7, 7]$.

So we have found $m = 7$. Indeed, 7 is the plaintext: $7^3 = 13 \pmod{15}$.   □

Theorem 9.1 tells us that the RSA least significant bit can be as strong as the whole block of the plaintext.

In Example 8.4 we have seen that it is dangerous for a user, as the owner of an RSA public key, to act as a decryption oracle to return a plaintext as a whole data block to a decryption request. Now from the "RSA least significant bit security" result we further know that the user must also not act as an "parity oracle," or an "$N/2$-oracle" (due to Lemma 9.1) to answer any cipher query on the parity bit of the corresponding plaintext (or to answer whether the plaintext is less than $N/2$).

We should warn the reader that an attacker may embed such queries in an innocent-looking protocol. See the following example.

**Example 9.2:** When Alice and Malice need to agree on a secret session key to be shared exclusively between them, Malice may provide a reasonable suggestion as follows:

> "Alice, how about we send to each other 1,000 ciphertext messages encrypted under our respective public keys? Let the session key be the bit string from XORing the parity bits of each pair of the exchanged plaintext messages. By the way, to assure you that the session key will be random, let me send my 1,000 blocks to you first!"

Alice not only agrees, she is also grateful for the trust Malice has shown her (in making the session key random)! However, the 1,000 ciphertext messages Malice sends to her will be $(2^i)^e c \pmod{N}$ $(i = 1, 2, \ldots, 1000)$ where $c$ is a ciphertext someone else sent to Alice and was eavesdropped by Malice.

After the protocol, Malice pretends to have erred in the computation of the session key:

> "Alice, I'm sorry for having messed up my computation. Would you be so kind and send me the session key? Please encrypt it under my public key."

Poor Alice offers help. Alas, from the session key, Malice can extract the needed parity bits and then applies Alg 9.1 to discover the plaintext encrypted inside $c$! □

Here Malice is an active attacker: he modifies the ciphertext $c$ by binding it using multipliers $(2^i)^e \pmod{N}$. Therefore, although the RSA least significant bit is as strong as the whole block of the plaintext message, the function is still hopelessly weak against an active attack.

## 9.3    The Rabin Bit

Alg 9.1 can be easily modified and applied to the Rabin encryption if the encryption takes the simple form of $c = m^2 \pmod{N}$ (i.e., the case of encryption exponent being $e = 2$, and that is all the "modification").

However, there is some complication. For $N$ having two distinct prime factors, by Theorem 6.17 (in §6.6.2), any given $c \in \text{QR}_N$ has four distinct square roots modulo $N$, i.e., the ciphertext $c$ has four different plaintexts. If an parity-oracle answers the parity of a random square root of $c$ (i.e., random among the four), then this oracle is not a reliable one and hence cannot be used. Nevertheless, if a square root has certain properties which allow an oracle to do the job deterministically (and hence reliably), then the binary-search technique can still be applied to the Rabin encryption.

One example of such a deterministic oracle is one which answers the parity bit of a smaller square root of the positive Jacobi symbol. By Theorem 6.18 (in §6.7), we know that if $N$ is a Blum integer, then any quadratic residue $c$ has two roots $m$, $-m$ of the positive Jacobi symbol. Since $N$ is odd, only one of these two roots is less than $\dfrac{N}{2}$, and so we can call it the "smaller root of $c$ of the positive Jacobi symbol."

Now if we confine $N$ to a more restricted form of Blum integer, such that $\left(\dfrac{2}{N}\right) = 1$ ($N = pq$ with $p \equiv q \pmod 8$ will do), then a parity oracle which answers the parity bit of a smaller square root of the positive Jacobi symbol will work. Notice that with $\left(\dfrac{2}{N}\right) = 1$, an $i$-th query made to this reliable parity oracle will have the plaintext $\dfrac{m}{2^i} \pmod N$ and so will keep the sign of Jacobi symbol for all $i$ plaintext queries. For details of a modified binary search algorithm for the Rabin encryption case, see [130].

## 9.3.1 The Blum-Blum-Shub Pseudo-random Bits Generator

The fact that a binary search algorithm working for the Rabin encryption function suggests that the Rabin least significant bit is strong if the IF assumption holds (Assumption 8.4 in §8.8). The strength of the Rabin least significant bit has an important application: **cryptographically strong pseudo-random bits** (CSPRB) generation [43]. The so-called **Blum-Blum-Shub pseudo-random number generator** uses a seed $x_0 \in \mathrm{QR}_N$ where $N$ is a $k$-bit Blum integer. Then the pseudo-random bits generated from the BBS generator using the seed $x_0$ are composed of the least significant bit of each number in the following sequence

$$x_0, \ x_1 = x_0^2, \ \ldots, \ x_i = x_{i-1}^2, \ \ldots \pmod N \qquad (9.3.1)$$

It can be shown [43, 130] that, without knowing the seed $x_0$, predicting the least significant bits in the sequence in (9.3.1) is computationally equivalent to factoring the Blum integer $N$.

**Remark 9.1:** *It is also known [13, 297] that the problem of extracting the simultaneous* $\log_2 \log_2 N$ *least significant bits from a Rabin ciphertext is equivalent to factoring $N$.* ☐

Blum and Goldwasser applied this result and proposed an efficient cryptosystem which has a strong security called **semantic security**. We will study semantic security in Chapter 14, there we shall also introduce the semantically secure cryptosystem of Blum and Goldwasser based on the strength of the Rabin bit.

## 9.4    The ElGamal Bit

For the ElGamal cryptosystem given in the form of Alg 8.3, since the plaintext message space is $\mathbb{F}_p^*$ where $p$ is a large prime number (hence odd), it is straightforward that the binary search technique can also be applied. To find the plaintext message encrypted under a ciphertext pair $(c_1, c_2)$, the querying ciphertext messages sent to a parity oracle should be

$$(c_1,\ 2^i c_2) \pmod{p},\quad i = 1, 2, \ldots, \lfloor \log_2 p \rfloor + 1.$$

If the parity oracle is a human being (this is very likely, see Example 9.2), then in order to avoid suspicion, the attacker can blind the queries, for instance, as follows:

$$(g^{r_i} c_1,\ 2^i y^{r_i} c_2) \pmod{p} \text{ with } r_i \in_U \mathbb{Z}_{p-1},\ i = 1, 2, \ldots, \lfloor \log_2 p \rfloor + 1,$$

where $(g, y)$ are the public key material of the parity oracle. These $\lfloor \log_2 p \rfloor + 1$ pairs of ciphertext messages are completely independent one another, however, they encrypt the related message series $2^i m \pmod{p}$ for $i = 1, 2, \ldots, \lfloor \log_2 p \rfloor + 1$:

$$(g^{k+r_i}, y^{k+r_i} 2^i m) \pmod{p},\ i = 1, 2, \ldots, \lfloor \log_2 p \rfloor + 1.$$

To this end we can conclude that the bit security of the ElGamal cryptosystem is as hard as the block data security. On the other hand, a public key owner should be careful not to be tricked to play the game as in Example 9.2.

## 9.5    The Discrete Logarithm Bit

In §8.4 we have discussed that in an abelian group in the general case, the discrete logarithm problem is hard: the function $g^x$ is believed to be one-way. Moreover, it is so far not known whether the function is a trapdoor. So extraction of $x$ from $g^x$ with the help of an oracle is a strange idea. However, in order to investigate the relation between the bit security to the block security for the discrete logarithm function, let us assume that there exists an oracle which can answer some bit-level partial information of $x$ upon being fed a pair $(g, g^x)$.

If the element $g$ has an odd order, then the value $\frac{1}{2} \pmod{\operatorname{ord}(g)}$ is available if $\operatorname{ord}(g)$ is not secret (this is the usual case). In this situation, the problem of extracting the discrete logarithm using a parity oracle is in fact, bit-by-bit, the reverse operation of the modulo exponentiation algorithm (see Alg 4.3). Since the modulo exponentiation algorithm is also called "squaring-and-multiplying" method, the reverse algorithm should be called "square-rooting-and-dividing" method. Alg 9.2 specifies such a method.

Now what happens if $g$ has an even order? For example, if $g$ is a generator element of $\mathbb{F}_p^*$ with $p$ being a prime number, then $\operatorname{ord}_p(g) = p - 1$ is even and is not

---

**Algorithm 9.2:** Extracting Discrete Logarithm Using a Parity Oracle

INPUT      $(g, h)$: $g$ is a group element of an odd order, $h = g^x$;
                $PO_{\mathrm{desc}(g)}$: a parity oracle, $PO_{\mathrm{desc}(g)}(g, h) = \log_g h \pmod 2$.

OUTPUT   integer $x$.

1. Set $x \leftarrow 0$; $y \leftarrow \frac{1}{2} \pmod{\mathrm{ord}(g)}$;

2. Repeat the following steps until $h = 1$ (∗ including $h = 1$ ∗)

   {

        2.1 If ( $PO_{\mathrm{desc}(g)}(g, h) == 1$ ) then $h \leftarrow h/g$; $x \leftarrow x + 1$;
            (∗ when $\log_g h$ is odd, do "division and plus 1," as reverse to "multiplication and minus 1" in modulo exponentiation ∗)

        2.2 $h \leftarrow h^y$; $x \leftarrow 2x$;
            (∗ now $\log_g h$ is even, do "square rooting and doubling" as reverse to "squaring and halving" in modulo exponentiation ∗)

   }

3. Return( $x$ ).

---

relatively prime to 2. Therefore $\frac{1}{2} \pmod{p-1}$ does not exist. So square-rooting of $h$ cannot be done in the form of Step 2.2 in Alg 9.2.

However, in this case (i.e., when $g$ is a generator element in $\mathbb{F}_p^*$), we can still compute square roots of $h$ modulo $p$ using Alg 6.4. For any quadratic residue element $h \in \mathrm{QR}_p$, that square-rooting algorithm will return two square roots of $h$, which we should denote by $\pm\sqrt{h}$. Since $g$ is a generator of $\mathbb{F}_p^*$, it holds $g \in \mathrm{QNR}_p$; but $h \in \mathrm{QR}_p$, therefore $\log_g h$ must be an even number. Thus, without loss of generality, we can write the discrete logarithms of the two square roots of $h$ to the base $g$ as follows:

$$\log_g \sqrt{h} = \frac{\log_g h}{2}, \quad \log_g(-\sqrt{h}) = \frac{p-1}{2} + \frac{\log_g h}{2}. \qquad (9.5.1)$$

Notice because addition in (9.5.1) is computed modulo $p - 1$, exactly one of the two values in (9.5.1) is less than $\frac{p-1}{2}$, the other must be greater than or equal to $\frac{p-1}{2}$. Clearly, the square root which has the smaller discrete logarithm to the base $g$ is the correct square root. The trouble is, from $\sqrt{h}$ and $-\sqrt{h}$, we cannot see which one of the two square roots has the smaller discrete logarithm to the base $g$!

---

**Algorithm 9.3:** Extracting Discrete Logarithm Using a "Half-order Oracle"

INPUT       $(g, h, p)$: $g$ is a generator of $\mathbb{F}_p^*$ with $p$ prime; $h = g^x \pmod{p}$;
            $PO_{(p,g)}$: a half-order oracle,
$$PO_{(p,g)}(g, y, -y) = \begin{cases} y & \text{if } \log_g y < \log_g(-y) \\ -y & \text{otherwise} \end{cases}.$$

OUTPUT    integer $x$.

1. Set $x \leftarrow 0$;

2. Repeat the following steps until $h = 1$ (∗ including $h = 1$ ∗)

   {

   2.1 If ( $h \in \text{QNR}_p$ ) then $h \leftarrow h/g$; $x \leftarrow x + 1$;
       (∗ $h \in \text{QNR}_p$ implies that $\log_g h$ is odd; this can be done by
       testing Legendre symbol $\left( \dfrac{h}{p} \right) = -1$. ∗)

   2.2 $h \leftarrow PO_{(p,g)}(g, \sqrt{h}, -\sqrt{h})$; $x \leftarrow 2x$;
       (∗ we can do square-rooting with no difficulty, but we need the
       oracle to tell us which root is the correct one, i.e., has the smaller
       discrete logarithm $\dfrac{\log_g h}{2}$. ∗)

   }

3. Return( $x$ ).

---

Nevertheless, if we have a different "one-bit-information oracle" which, upon being fed $(g, y, -y)$, answers $y$ or $-y$, whichever has the smaller discrete logarithm to the base $g$, then we can use this oracle (call it "half-order oracle") to pick the correct square root for us. Alg 9.3, which is modified from Alg 9.2, does the job using the "half-order oracle."

Since testing Legendre symbol and computing square roots modulo a prime can be efficiently done, from Alg 9.3 we know that being able to decide from $(g, h)$ whether $\log_g h$ is less than $\frac{\text{ord}(g)}{2}$ is equivalent to extracting $\log_g h$ from $(g, h)$.

Alg 9.3 is more general than Alg 9.2 in that, it will also work with $g$ of odd order. Let us therefore go through Alg 9.3 with a small numerical example.

**Example 9.3:** Suppose we have a "half-order oracle." For group $\mathbb{Z}_{23}^*$, generator

$g = 5$ and element $h = 9$, let us extract $x = \log_5 9 \pmod{22}$ by calling the "half-order oracle."

An execution tree of Alg 9.3 on input $(5, 9, 23)$ can be given as follows. Each double arrow stands for the "square-rooting," of which the horizontal ones ($\Rightarrow$) are those chosen by the "half-order oracle." Each single arrows ($\rightarrow$) stands for "dividing-$g$" ($g = 5$). All computations are performed modulo 23.

$$
\begin{array}{ccccccccccc}
9 & \Rightarrow & 20 & \rightarrow & 4 & \Rightarrow & 2 & \Rightarrow & 5 & \rightarrow & 1 & \Rightarrow & 1 \\
\Downarrow & & & & \Downarrow & & \Downarrow & & & & \Downarrow & & \\
3 & & & & 21 & & 18 & & & & 22 & &
\end{array}
$$

At the starting of the algorithm, $x$ is initialized to 0 (step 1). For each double arrow $\Rightarrow$, operation $x \leftarrow 2x$ will be performed (step 2.2), and for each single arrow $\rightarrow$, operation $x \leftarrow x + 1$ will be performed (step 2.1). Upon termination of the algorithm, the final value for $x$ is 10. Indeed, $9 = 5^{10} \pmod{23}$. $\qquad\square$

These results show that the individual bits of discrete logarithm are in general as hard as the whole block. We now also know that if a generator element is a quadratic residue, then all bits including the least significant bit of a discrete logarithm to this base are hard. This leads to a "semantically secure" version of the ElGamal cryptosystem, which we shall introduce in Chapter 14.

## 9.6   Chapter Summary

Our investigations on the hardness of the bit-level security for the basic and popular public-key cryptographic algorithms have invariantly reached very positive results: every single plaintext bit hidden under these functions is as hard as the whole plaintext block. These positive results suggest the following observation: if a plaintext message is random, then the problem of finding any information about the plaintext can be as hard as inverting these basic functions.

This observation has been applied by many researchers to constructing stronger public-key encryption schemes out of the basic and popular public-key cryptographic primitives. The idea is to randomize the plaintext messages using some randomization schemes. In Part V, we will study a general methodology named **random oracle model** to achieve the construction of strong and provably secure public-key encryption schemes (in fact, digital signature schemes too) out of using the basic and popular public-key cryptographic primitives.

Through our investigation on several basic and popular public-key cryptographic functions we have also witnessed an invariant weakness of these functions: they are extremely vulnerable to active attacks. The general methodology for strengthening public-key encryption algorithms to be studied in Part V will also include mechanisms for foiling active attacks.

## Exercises

9.1 Complete the other three cases of "Iteration 2" in the proof of Theorem 9.1, i.e.,

    i) $(a, b) = (\frac{N}{2}, N)$, $PO_N(2^{2e}c) = 1$;

    ii) $(a, b) = (0, \frac{N}{2})$, $PO_N(2^{2e}c) = 0$;

    ii) $(a, b) = (0, \frac{N}{2})$, $PO_N(2^{2e}c) = 1$.

9.2 Under what condition the RSA encryption algorithm can have a strong bit security?

Hint: if a plaintext has some verifiable partial information, can the encryption algorithm have a strong block security?

9.3 Does the strong bit security of the basic public-key encryption algorithms imply that these algorithms are secure?

9.4 What is the security basis for the Blum-Blum-Shub pseudo-random number generator?

9.5 Let $p$ be a prime and $g$ be a generator element in $\mathbb{F}_p^*$. The ease of computing Legendre symbol of $g^x \pmod{p}$ means the ease of computing the parity bit of $x$. Why is the extraction of $x$ from $g^x \pmod{p}$ still a hard problem?

# Chapter 10

# DATA INTEGRITY TECHNIQUES

## 10.1 Introduction

In Chapter 2 we made a realistic and standard assumption on the vulnerability of the open communications network: all communications go through an adversary named Malice who is free to eavesdrop, intercept, relay, modify, forge or inject messages. When Malice injects modified or forged messages, he will try to fool the targeted receivers into believing that the messages are sent from some other principals. To use such a vulnerable communications medium in a secure manner, as is required for secure electronic commerce transactions, cryptographic mechanisms which can provide the security service in terms of message confidentiality (i.e., protection against eavesdropping) are inadequate. We need mechanisms which can enable a message receiver to verify that a message has indeed come from the claimed source and has not been altered in an unauthorized way during the transmission. **Data integrity** is the security service against unauthorized modification of messages.

Data integrity in modern cryptography is closely related to, and evolves from, a classical subject in communications: error-detection code. The latter is a procedure for detecting errors which can be introduced into messages due to fault in communications. It is considered that using information which has been modified in a malicious way is at the same risk as using information which contains defects due to errors introduced in communications or data processing. As a result, the working principle of the techniques providing data integrity and that of techniques providing error-detection codes are essentially the same: a transmitter of a message creates a "checking value" by encoding some redundancy into the message to be transmitted and appends the checking value to the message; a receiver of the message then verifies the correctness of the message received using the appended checking value according to a set of rules which are agreed with the transmitter [277]. In error-detection codes, the redundancy is encoded in such a way that the receiver can use a maximum likelihood detector to decide which message he should infer as having most likely been transmitted from the possibly altered codes that were received. In data integrity protection, the redundancy is encoded in such a way that the appended checking value will be distributed as uniform as possible to the entire message space of the checking values and so to minimize the probability for an attacker to forge a valid checking value. The cryptographic transformation for the latter way of adding redundancy is similar to the mixing-transformation property for encryption that we have described in §7.1), although for the case of encryption the mix-transformation is not based on adding verifiable redundancy.

Like an encryption algorithm, the cryptographic transformations for achieving data integrity should also be parameterized by keys. Thus, in the usual sense, a correct data-integrity verification result will also provide the verifier with the knowledge of the message source, that is, the principal who had created the data integrity protection. However, recently a notion of "data integrity without source identification" has emerged. This new notion is important in the study of public-key cryptosystems secure against adaptive attackers. We will use an example ' introduce this notion. The example will serve a preparation for a later chapt where we study the public-key cryptosystems secure against adaptive attackers.

### 10.1.1  Chapter Outline

We begin the technical part of this chapter with providing a syntactic definition for data integrity protection (10.2). Cryptographic techniques for providing data integrity services will be introduced. The introduction will be divided into symmetric techniques (§10.3), asymmetric ones (§10.4) and the notion of data integrity without source identification §10.5.

## 10.2  Definition

**Definition 10.1: Data Integrity Protection** *Let* Data *be arbitrary information. Let Ke denote an encoding key and Kv denote a verification key which matches the encoding key. Data integrity protection on* Data *comprises the following crypto-graphic transformations:*

*Manipulation detection code creation:*

$$\mathsf{MDC} \leftarrow f(Ke, \mathsf{Data});$$

*Manipulation detection code verification:*

$g(Kv, \mathsf{Data}, \mathsf{MDC})$

$$= \begin{cases} \text{True, with probability 1} & \text{if } \mathsf{MDC} = f(Ke, \mathsf{Data}) \\ \text{False, with an overwhelming probability} & \text{if } \mathsf{MDC} \neq f(Ke, \mathsf{Data}) \end{cases}$$

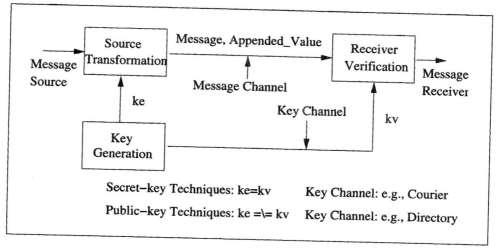

**Figure 10.1.** Data Integrity Systems

*Here f and g are efficient cryptographic transformations; the former is parameter-
ized by an auxiliary input Ke (encoding key) and the latter is parameterized by an
auxiliary input Kv (verification key);* MDC *stands for* **manipulation detection
code.** *The probability space*[a] *includes the space of all possible cases of* Data, MDC
*and keys, and perhaps a random input space if the signing/verification algorithms
are probabilistic ones.*

Fig 10.1 provides an illustration of data integrity systems.

We should notice that although in our introductory discussions (and in Fig 10.1)
we have used a communications scenario to introduce the notion of data integrity
protection, Definition 10.1 needn't be confined to communications; for example, the
pair (**Data, MDC**) can be data stored to or retrieved from an insecure data storage.

Similar to the case of cryptosystems, data integrity protection also have symmetric techniques and asymmetric techniques. However we should notice a difference
between the two systems in the case of public-key techniques. In cryptosystems
realized by asymmetric techniques, public key and private key have fixed usages:
public key is for message encoding (encryption) and private key is for message decoding (decryption). In data-integrity systems realized by asymmetric techniques,
public (private) key can have both encoding and verification usages. These two
different usages will be the respective topics for §10.4 and §10.5.

---

[a]The meaning for the "overwhelming" probability follows the "overwhelming" notion we have
defined in §4.6.

## 10.3   Symmetric Techniques

In symmetric techniques for achieving data integrity, the cryptographic transformations $f$ and $g$ (see Definition 10.1) are a symmetric cryptographic algorithm which means $f = g$ and $Ke = Kv$, that is, the creation and the verification of the consistency between Data and MDC use the identical cryptographic operation.

Due to a close relation between data integrity and message authentication (we will study message authentication in Chapter 11), MDC created by a symmetric cryptographic technique is often called a **message authentication code (MAC** for short). A MAC can be created and verified using a keyed hash function technique, or using a block cipher encryption algorithm.

### 10.3.1   Cryptographic Hash Functions

A common method for realizing a MAC is to use a so-called keyed **hash function** technique. We first introduce cryptographic hash functions.

A hash function is a deterministic function which maps a bit string of an arbitrary length to a hashed value which is a bit string of a fixed length. Let $h$ denote a hash function whose fixed output length is denoted by $|h|$. It is desired that $h$ should have the following properties:

**Property 10.1: Properties of a Hash Function**

- **Mixing-transformation** On any input $x$, the output hashed value $h(x)$ should be computationally indistinguishable from a uniform binary string in the interval $[0, 2^{|h|})$. Here, the computational indistinguishability follows Definition 4.15 (in §4.7). By Assumption 4.2 (also in §4.7), this property is a reasonable one.

- **Collision resistance** It should be computationally infeasible to find two inputs $x, y$ with $x \neq y$ such that $h(x) = h(y)$. For this assumption to be reasonable, it is necessary that the output space of $h$ should be sufficiently large. The least value for $|h|$ is 128 while a typical value is 160.

- **Pre-image resistance** Given a hashed value $h$, it should be computationally infeasible to find an input string $x$ such that $h = h(x)$. This assumption also requires the output space of $h$ be sufficiently large.

- **Practical efficiency** Given input string $x$, the computation of $h(x)$ can be done in time bounded by a small-degree polynomial (ideally linear) in the size of $x$.

The mixing-transformation and collision resistance properties of a hash function can be realized by using operations similar to those used in the design of a block cipher algorithm (see §7.6–§7.7). The pre-image resistance property can be realized using some data compression techniques which render partial loss of some input data and therefore make the function non-invertible.

We shall not describe the design details of any real hash function. More inquisitive readers may find them in the literature (e.g. Chapter 9 of [200]).

### 10.3.1.1 Hash Functions' Applications in Cryptography

Hash functions are widely used in cryptography. We can list here several important uses of hash functions.

- In digital signatures, hash functions are generally used for generating "message digests" or "message fingerprints." This usage is to add certain verifiable redundancy to a message to be signed so that the hashed message contains recognizable information. We will see this general usage of hash functions in digital signatures in this chapter (§10.4). There we will realize that security of a digital signature scheme (unforgeability) crucially depends on some recognizable redundant information contained in the message signed. Formal arguments that this usage of hash functions offers provable security for digital signature schemes will be described in Chapter 16.

- In public-key cryptosystems with fit-for-application security, hash functions are widely used for realizing a ciphertext correctness verification mechanism. Such a mechanism is necessary for an encryption scheme to achieve a provable security against active attackers. We will see an example of this usage in this chapter (§10.5). Formal evidence that this usage of hash functions offers provable security for public-key encryption will be provided in Chapter 15 where we will further see the more fundamental role of hash functions play in making public-key encryption provably secure.

- In a wide range of cryptographic applications where pseudo-randomness is required, hash functions are widely used as practical pseudo-random functions. These applications include: key agreement (e.g., two principals providing their own random seed input to a hash and obtaining a shared key value), authentication protocols (e.g., for two protocol participants to confirm the completion of a protocol run by exchanging some hashed values), electronic commerce protocols (e.g., to achieve micro-payment aggregation via gambling [299, 203]), proof of knowledge protocols (e.g., to achieve a non-interactive mode of proof, see §18.3.2.2). We will see abundant examples of such usages of hash functions in the rest of this book.

### 10.3.1.2  Random Oracle

Let us recap the "mixing-transformation" property of a hash function: on any input, the distribution of the output hashed value is computationally indistinguishable from the uniform distribution in the function's output space. If we change "is computationally indistinguishable from the uniform distribution" into "is uniform," then we turn the hash function into a very powerful and imaginary function named **random oracle**.

We regard random oracle a *very powerful* function because of the combination of the three properties, i.e.: *deterministic, efficient* and *uniform* output. The reason for us to have labeled random oracle an imaginary function is because from all computational models we know of, there exists no computing mechanism or machinery which can be so powerful.

On the one hand, we know how to output uniformly distributed random values efficiently, e.g., tossing a fair coin. However this way of outputting randomness is not a deterministic procedure. On the other hand, we can also relate a set of uniformly independent values deterministically, e.g., by sorting a set of such values so that any two of them have a deterministic relation as the distance between them in the sorted list. However, this relation cannot be computed in time polynomial in the size of these random values (sorting a list of $n$ items needs $n \log n$ steps).

In fact, a random oracle's properties of determinism and uniform output mean that the output of a random oracle has an entropy greater than that of its input (review §3.7 for the definition of entropy). However, according to Shannon's entropy theory (Theorem 3.2, in §3.7), a deterministic function can never "amplify" entropy. Therefore, random oracle does not exist in the real world.

Since the mixing-transformation property of a hash function is only a computational assumption (Assumption 4.2, in §4.7), a hash function in the real world should have this property only up to a computational indistinguishability given by Definition 4.15 (in §4.7), i.e., its output values follow some probability distribution (in the output message space) which may not be discernible by a polynomially bounded distinguisher. Thus, a real-world hash function only emulates the random oracle behavior to a precision where the difference is hopefully a negligible quantity.

Nevertheless, hash function's emulated behavior of a random oracle plays an important role in public-key cryptography. In essence, to hash a message is to add quality redundancy to the message in a deterministically verifiable manner.

### 10.3.1.3  Birthday Attack

Assuming that a hash function $h$ really behaves as a random oracle, the square-root attack (the birthday attack, see §3.6) suggests that

$$2^{|h|/2} = \sqrt{2^{|h|}}$$

random evaluations of the hash function will suffice an attacker to obtain a collision with a non-negligible probability. To mount a birthday attack, the attacker should generate random message-hash pairs

$$(m_1, h(m_1)), \ (m_2, h(m_2)), \ \ldots$$

until he ends up with finding two messages $m$ and $m'$ satisfying

$$m \neq m', \ h(m) = h(m'). \tag{10.3.1}$$

Such a pair of messages is called a collision under the hash function $h$. Of course, in order for a birthday attack to be useful for the attacker, the collision message $m$ and $m'$ should contain some meaningful sub-messages. For example, let a message to be hashed (and digitally signed, see §10.4) be a payment authorization statement in the following form

$$M = \text{Price, Goods\_Description, } R$$

where $R$ is a random number to make the protocol messages randomized (it is always desirable that protocol messages are randomized). Then an interesting birthday attack can be

$$m = \text{Price\_1, Goods\_Description, } r$$

and

$$m' = \text{Price\_2, Goods\_Description, } r'$$

where Price_1 $\neq$ Price_2 and Goods_Description are fixed message parts, and the collision is on the random numbers $r \neq r'$. Collision finding for such messages has the same complexity as collision finding for random messages as in (10.3.1) since we can view

$$h'(x) \stackrel{\text{def}}{=} h(\text{Price\_1, Goods\_Description, } x)$$

and

$$h''(x) \stackrel{\text{def}}{=} h(\text{Price\_2, Goods\_Description, } x)$$

as two random functions.

It is obvious that fewer evaluations will be needed if a hash function is not a truely random function.

Thus, the size of the output space of a cryptographic hash function must have a lower bound. The current widely used hash functions in applied cryptography are SHA-1 [219] and RIPEMD-160 [54]. Both have the output length $|h| = 160$. Their strength against the square-root attack is therefore $2^{80}$. This is compatible to the strength of a block cipher algorithm of the key length up to 80 bits. The previous popular hash function MD5 [245] has the case $|h| = 128$ which was tailored to suit the DES's key length of 56 bits and block length of 64 bits.

With the introduction of the AES-128, AES-192 and AES-256 (the AES of key lengths 128, 192 and 256 bits, respectively, see §7.7), standard bodies (e.g., the ISO/IEC [153]) are currently standardizing hash functions of compatible output lengths $|h| \in \{256, 384, 512\}$.

## 10.3.2   MAC Based on a Keyed Hash Function

Cryptographic hash functions naturally form a cryptographic primitive for data integrity. For use in a shared-key scenario, a hash function takes a key as part of its input. The other part of the input is the message to be authenticated. Thus, to authenticate a message $M$, a transmitter computes

$$\text{MAC} = h(k \parallel M),$$

where $k$ is a secret key shared between the transmitter and a receiver, and "$\parallel$" denotes the bit string concatenation.

From the properties of a hash function listed in §10.3.1, we can assume that in order to create a valid MAC using a hash function with respect to a key $k$ and a message $M$, a principal must actually be in possession of the correct key and the correct message. The receiver who shares the key $k$ with the transmitter should recalculate the MAC from the received message $M$ and check that it agrees with the MAC received. If so the message can be believed to have come from the claimed transmitter.

Because such a MAC is constructed using a hash function, it is also called an HMAC. It is often a prudent practice that an HMAC is computed in the following format

$$\text{HMAC} = h(k \parallel M \parallel k),$$

that is, the key is pre-fixed and post-fixed to the message to be authenticated [290]. This is in order to prevent an adversary from exploiting a "round-function iteration" structure of some hash functions. Without guarding the both ends of the message with a secret key, such a known structure of certain hash functions may allow an adversary to modify the message by pre-fixing or post-fixing some chosen data to the message without need of knowing the secret key $k$.

## 10.3.3   MAC Based on a Block Cipher Encryption Algorithm

A standard method for forming a keyed hash function is to apply the CBC mode of operation using a block cipher algorithm. Conventionally, a keyed hash function so constructed is called a MAC.

Let $\mathcal{E}_k(m)$ denote a block cipher encryption algorithm keyed with the key $k$ on inputing the message $m$. To authenticate a message $M$, the transmitter first divide $M$ as

$$M = m_1 m_2 \ldots m_\ell$$

where each sub-message block $m_i$ $(i = 1, 2, \ldots, \ell)$ has the size of the input of the block cipher algorithm. Padding of a random value to the last sub-message block $m_\ell$ may be necessary if the final block is not of the full block size. Let $C_0 = IV$ be a random initializing vector. Now the transmitter applies the CBC encryption:

$$C_i \leftarrow \mathcal{E}_k(m_i \oplus C_{i-1}), \quad i = 1, 2, \ldots, \ell.$$

Then the pair

$$(IV, C_\ell)$$

will be used as the MAC to be appended with $M$ and sent out.

It is obvious that the computation for creating a CBC-MAC involves non-invertible data compression (in essence, a CBC-MAC is a "short digest" of the whole message), and so a CBC-MAC is a one-way transformation. Moreover, the mixing-transformation property of the underlying block cipher encryption algorithm adds a hash feature to this one-way transformation (i.e., distributes a MAC over the MAC space as uniform as the underlying block cipher should do over its ciphertext message space). Thus, we can assume that in order to create a valid CBC-MAC, a principal actually has to be in possession of the key $k$ which keys the underlying block cipher algorithm. The receiver who shares the key $k$ with the transmitter should recalculate the MAC from the received message and check that it agrees with the version received. If so the message can be believed to have come from the claimed transmitter.

We will sometimes denote by $\text{MAC}(k, M)$ a MAC which provides the integrity service on the message $M$ for principals who share the key $k$. In this denotation we ignore the implementation details such as what underlying one-way transformation has been used for the MAC's realization.

# 10.4 Asymmetric Techniques I: Digital Signatures

In public-key cryptography, a principal can use her/his private key to "encrypt" a message and the resultant "ciphertext" can be "decrypted" back to the original message using the principal's public key. Evidently, the "ciphertext" so created can play the role of a manipulation detection code (MDC) accompanying the "encrypted" message, that is, provide data integrity protection for the message. Here, the public-key "decryption" process forms a step of verification of the MDC.

Moreover, while the verification of such an MDC can be performed by anybody since the public key is available to anybody, it is considered that only the owner of the public key used for the MDC verification could have created the MDC using the corresponding private key. Thus, this usage of public key cryptography can model precisely the property of a signature, a **digital signature**, for proving the authorship of a message. In other words, public-key cryptography, more precisely, a one-way trapdoor function (see Property 8.1, in §8.1) can be used to realize a digital signature scheme[b]. Diffie and Hellman envision the notion of digital signature first [98] (the publication date of this paper is 1976, but the paper was first distributed in December 1975 as a preprint, see [97]).

---

[b]Although the more fundamental basis for digital signatures is one-way function, see [175], one-way *trapdoor* function is the basis for *practical* digital signatures.

The ability to provide a digital signature forms a great advantage of public-key cryptography over secret-key cryptography (the other significant advantage of public-key cryptography is the possibility of achieving key distribution between remote parties, see, e.g., §8.15). Now that only a single entity is able to create a digital signature of a message which can be verified by anybody, it is easy to settle a dispute over who has created the signature. This allows provision of a security service called **non-repudiation** which means no denial of a connection with a message. Non-repudiation is a necessary security requirement in electronic commerce applications.

Syntactically, Definition 10.2 specifies the definition of a digital signature scheme.

**Definition 10.2: Digital Signature Scheme** *A digital signature scheme consists of the following attributes:*

- *a plaintext message space $\mathcal{M}$: a set of strings over some alphabet*

- *a signature space $\mathcal{S}$: a set of possible signatures*

- *a signing key space $\mathcal{K}$: a set of possible keys for signature creation, and a verification key space $\mathcal{K}'$: a set of possible keys for signature verification*

- *an efficient key generation algorithm* Gen $: \mathbb{N} \mapsto \mathcal{K} \times \mathcal{K}'$ *where $\mathcal{K}$, $\mathcal{K}'$ are private, public key spaces, respectively.*

- *an efficient signing algorithm* Sign $: \mathcal{M} \times \mathcal{K} \mapsto \mathcal{S}$

- *an efficient verification algorithm* Verify $: \mathcal{M} \times \mathcal{S} \times \mathcal{K}' \mapsto \{$True, False$\}$.

*For any $sk \in \mathcal{K}$ and any $m \in \mathcal{M}$, we denote by*

$$s \leftarrow \mathsf{Sign}_{sk}(m)$$

*the signing transformation and read it as "s is a signature of m created using key sk."*

*For any secret key $sk \in \mathcal{K}$, let $pk$ denote the public key matching $sk$, and for $m \in \mathcal{M}$, $s \in \mathcal{S}$, it is necessary*

$$\mathsf{Verify}_{pk}(m, s) = \begin{cases} \text{True, with probability 1} & \text{if } s \leftarrow \mathsf{Sign}_{sk}(m) \\ \text{False, with an overwhelming probability} & \text{if } s \nleftarrow \mathsf{Sign}_{sk}(m) \end{cases}$$

*where the probability space includes $\mathcal{S}$, $\mathcal{M}$, $\mathcal{K}$ and $\mathcal{K}'$, and perhaps a random input space if the signing/verification algorithms are probabilistic ones.*

This definition can be viewed as a special case of Definition 10.1: (Sign, Verify), $(sk, pk)$ and $(m, s)$ in the former correspond to $(f, g)$, $(Ke, Kv)$ and (Data, MDC) in the latter, respectively.

Notice that the integer input to the key generation algorithm Gen provides the size of the output signing/verification keys. Since the key generation algorithm is efficient with running time polynomial in the size of its input, the input integer value should be unary encoded (reason see Definition 4.7 in §4.4.6.1). This integer is the security parameter of the signature scheme and defines the size of the signature space.

With the size of the signature space defined by the security parameter, the meaning for the "overwhelming" probability for the case of $\mathsf{Verify}_{pk}(m, s) = \mathsf{False}$ when $s \not\leftarrow \mathsf{Sign}_{sk}(m)$ follows the "overwhelming" notion defined in §4.6. However, this probability must disregard an easy forgery case to be remarked in Remark 10.1. Quantitative measure for "overwhelming" will be given for several "fit-for-application" signature schemes when we study formal proof of security for digital signatures in Chapter 16.

Semantically, Shannon's mixing-transformation characterization for encryption algorithms (see §7.1) also makes a great sense for a digital signature scheme. Algorithm Sign should also be a good mixing-transformation function: output signature values which are fairly uniformly distributed over the entire signature space $\mathcal{S}$. This property prevents an easy way of creating a valid signature without using the corresponding signing key.

## 10.4.1 Textbook Security Notion for Digital Signatures

Analogous to the case of Property 8.2 (in §8.2) being a textbook security notion for the basic public-key encryption algorithms introduced in Chapter 8, we shall also consider a very weak security notion for digital signature schemes to be introduced in this chapter.

**Property 10.2: Textbook Security Notion for Digital Signatures** *Within the scope of this chapter we only consider a restricted notion of security for digital signatures. We say that a digital signature is secure if it is computationally infeasible for an attacker to forge (i.e., to create) a valid message-signature pair "from scratch." That is, the attacker is given a public key and the description of a signature scheme, and is required to output a valid message-signature pair which has never been issued by a targeted signer (i.e., the owner of the given public key). The attacker is non-adaptive, that is, it does not try to ease its forgery task via, e.g., using some other available message-signature pairs or interacting with the targeted signer for the signer to issue valid signatures on the messages of the attacker's choice.*

We should notice that this notion of security for digital signatures is inadequate for applications because it assumes that the attacker is unreasonably weak or that the environment is extremely harsh to the attacker. In reality, message-signature pairs with respect to a given public key and a signature scheme are abundantly available since they are not secret information. Also in general the attacker should be entitled to ask a signer to issue signatures on messages of its choice. Such an attacker is an adaptive one because it can choose messages in an adaptive way. In such an "adaptive chosen-message attack", the attacker is given a **target message**, it can choose messages based on the target message (maybe doing some algebraic transformation on the target message) and send the chosen messages to a targeted signer to get them signed. This is like the signer providing the attacker with a training course for signature forgery. The task for the attacker is to forge a signature on the target message. As we have discussed in §8.6 on the severity of adaptive attacks on cryptosystems, with the same reasons, an adaptive chosen-message attack on signature schemes, although much severer than a non-adaptive one, is a reasonable attacking scenario and hence should be seriously considered.

Recall that when we consider textbook security notion for textbook public-key encryption algorithms in the preceding chapter, we have explicitly warned many times that a public key owner must not provide a "naive decryption service" to an attacker. That level of vigilance may be possible if a key owner is smart enough, even though demanding a user to keep a high degree of vigilance is not a correct solution to adaptive attacks. Now in the signature case, we can no longer demand or warn the user not to provide "naive signing services." Signing service may be unavoidable: to issue signatures of given messages can be a perfectly normal service in many applications.

A strong notion of security for digital signature, which can be called unforgeability against **adaptive chosen-message attack** and is a fit-for-application security notion for digital signatures as the counterpart to CCA2 (Definition 8.3, in §8.6) for cryptosystems, will be introduced in Chapter 16. Formal security arguments for some digital signature schemes under the strong security notion will also be studied there.

We remark on an easy but benign form of signature forgery:

**Remark 10.1: Existential forgery** *The algorithms* $(\mathsf{Sign}_{sk}, \mathsf{Verify}_{pk})$ *form a one-way trapdoor function pair. The one-way part is* $\mathsf{Verify}_{pk}$ *and the trapdoor part is* $\mathsf{Sign}_{ak}$. *In general, the function* $\mathsf{Verify}_{pk}(s, m)$ *is computed in the direction from* $s$ *to* $m$. *Therefore, many digital signature schemes based on a one-way trapdoor function generally provide an efficient method for forging "valid message-signature" pairs using the one-way function* $\mathsf{Verify}_{pk}$ *computing from* $s$ *to* $m$. *However, thanks to the mixing-transformation property which must also be possessed by the one-way function* $\mathsf{Verify}_{pk}$, *a "message" generated from a "signature" using function* $\mathsf{Verify}_{pk}$ *will look random and is almost certainly meaningless. This easy way of forgery is part of a forgery technique called* **existential forgery**. *Digital signature schemes based on one-way trapdoor functions generally permit existential forgery. A usual method to prevent existential forgery is to add recognizable redundancy to the message to be signed which permits a verifier to verify non-random distribution of a message.* □

---

**Algorithm 10.1:** The RSA Signature Scheme

**Key Setup**

The key setup procedure is the same as that for the RSA cryptosystems (Alg 8.1).

(* thus, user Alice's public-key material is $(N, e)$ where $N = pq$ with $p$ and $q$ being two large prime numbers of roughly equal size, and $e$ is an integer such that $\gcd(e, \phi(N)) = 1$. She also finds an integer $d$ such that $ed \equiv 1 \pmod{\phi(N)}$. The integer $d$ is Alice's private key. *)

**Signature Generation**

To create a signature of message $m \in \mathbb{Z}_N^*$, Alice creates

$$s = \mathsf{Sign}_d(m) \leftarrow m^d \pmod{N}.$$

**Signature Verification**

Let Bob be a verifier who knows that the public-key material $(N, e)$ belongs to Alice. Given a message-signature pair $(m, s)$, Bob's verification procedure is

$$\mathsf{Verify}_{(N,e)}(m, s) = \mathsf{True} \ \text{ if } \ m \equiv s^e \pmod{N}.$$

(* N.B., Message $m$ must be a recognizable one, see §10.4.3. *)

---

Let us now introduce several well-known digital signature schemes.

## 10.4.2  Signing in RSA (Textbook Version)

The RSA signature scheme is the first digital signature scheme following the envision of Diffie and Hellman. It is realized by Rivest, Shamir and Adleman [248]. The RSA signature scheme is specified in Alg 10.1. We notice that this is a textbook version for signing in RSA.

It is easy to see that the RSA digital signature procedures are in the same format as those for the RSA encryption and decryption (see §8.5), except that now Alice performs "encryption" first using her private key, and Bob (or anybody) performs "decryption" later using Alice's public key. The holding of the verification congruence for a valid signature follows exactly the argument we have made in §8.5 for the cases of the RSA encryption and decryption.

## 10.4.3    Informal Security Argument for the RSA Signature

If the RSA signature scheme is just as simple as we have described, then it is not difficult at all for anybody to forge Alice's signature. For example, Bob can pick a random number $s \in \mathbb{Z}_N^*$ and compute

$$m \leftarrow s^e \pmod{N}. \tag{10.4.1}$$

Of course, for such a prepared "message"-signature pair, the verification will return True. Also, the multiplicative property of the RSA function (see (8.9.1) in §8.9) provides an easy-to-forge new message-signature pair from existing ones, e.g., a new message-signature pair $(m_1 m_2, s_1 s_2)$ from existing message-signature pairs $(m_1, s_1)$ and $(m_2, s_2)$.

As we have remarked in Remark 10.1, the above methods of forgery are existential forgeries. Since $m$ created in (10.4.1) or by multiplication should look random, the existential forgery is usually prevented by adding *recognizable* redundant information to $m$ so that $m$ becomes non-random or is "meaningful." The simplest method for adding recognizable information into a message is to have a message contain a recognizable part, e.g., $m = M \parallel I$ where $M$ is the message really signed and $I$ is a recognizable string such as the signer's identity.

The most commonly used method for adding recognizable information to a message is to "hash" the message using a cryptographic hash function (§10.3.1). Let $h$ be such a hash function mapping from $\{0, 1\}^*$ to $\mathcal{M}$. Then a message $m \in \mathcal{M}$ is regarded as recognizable or meaningful if there exists a string $M \in \{0, 1\}^*$ such that

$$m = h(M).$$

Under such a notion of message recognizability, forging an RSA signature should no longer be an easy job. Computing $m$ from $s$ as in (10.4.1) does not constitute a useful forgery if the attacker cannot also come up with a message $m$ which is recognizable, e.g., the attacker has in its possession a pre-image of $m$ under the cryptographic hash function used. If we assume that the hash function behaves like a random oracle does (the random oracle behavior is described in §10.3.1.2), then "forging from scratch" an RSA signature for a given message should have the difficulty of solving the RSA problem, i.e., that of extracting the $e$th root modulo $N$ (Definition 8.4, in §8.7).

However, we must notice that we have not provided any formal evidence (i.e., proof) for this result. The textbook RSA signature scheme in Alg 10.1 certainly does not have a provable security. For the simple version using hash function on the message, no one knows how to prove its security under adaptive chosen-message attack. Hence, this simple version should also be labeled a textbook RSA signature.

A better algorithm for signing in RSA using hash functions will be introduced in Chapter 16. That algorithm is a probabilistic one, meaning a signature output from the signing algorithm has a random distribution in the signature space, which is indistinguishable from a uniform distribution. That algorithm is also a fit-for-application version of the RSA signature scheme. Formal argument for security of that RSA signature scheme will be considered under a stronger and fit-for-application security notion which will also be introduced in Chapter 16.

### 10.4.4 Signing in Rabin (Textbook Version)

The Rabin signature scheme [242] is very similar to the RSA signature scheme. The difference between the two schemes is that they use different kinds of verification exponents. In the case of RSA, the verification exponent $e$ is an odd integer since it is required that $\gcd(e, \phi(N)) = 1$ where $\phi(N)$ is an even number, while in the case of the Rabin, $e = 2$.

The Rabin signature scheme is specified in Alg 10.2. We notice that this is a textbook version for signing in Rabin.

The Rabin signature has a couple of advantages over RSA. First, forgery is provably as hard as factoring (formal argument deferred). Secondly, verification is faster, and is suitable to use in applications where signature verification uses small computing devices, such as handheld ones.

Following Remark 10.1, if $m$ is not a recognizable message, then it is trivially easy to forge a valid "message"-signature pair for the Rabin signature scheme. This is an existential forgery. The usual prevention method is to hash a message as in §10.4.3 so that the message becomes recognizable.

### 10.4.5 A Paradoxical Security Basis for Signing in Rabin

Using the same idea in Theorem 8.2 (in §8.11) we can also show that if there exists an algorithm for forging a Rabin signature, then the forging algorithm can be used for factoring the composite modulus used in the signature scheme. This is a desirable property because it relates signature forgery to a reputably hard problem (factorization).

However, this strong security property also means that the Rabin signature scheme is fatally insecure against an adaptive attack in which an attacker can ask the signer to issue the signatures of messages of its choice. For example, the attacker can pick an arbitrary $s \in \mathbb{Z}_N^*$, and submit $m = s^2 \pmod{N}$ to Alice for her to return a Rabin signature of message $m$. Alice's reply, let it be $s'$, is any one of four square roots of $m$. If $s' \not\equiv \pm s \pmod{N}$, then her modulus can be factored by the adaptive attacker.

Therefore, the textbook Rabin signature scheme specified in Alg 10.2 is absolutely unusable in any real world application where an adaptive attack is unavoidable. Signing in Rabin for any real world application must prevent an adaptive attacker from obtaining two different square roots of one message.

---

**Algorithm 10.2:** The Rabin Signature Scheme

**Key Setup**
User Alice sets up her public modulus same as an RSA modulus.
(∗ so her modulus is $N = pq$ with $p$, $q$ being distinct odd primes. $N$ is her public key and $p$, $q$ form her private key. ∗)

**Signature Generation**
To create a signature of message $m \in \mathbb{Z}_N^*$, Alice creates signature

$$s \leftarrow m^{1/2} \pmod{n}.$$

(∗ for this calculation to be possible, it is necessary for $m \in \mathrm{QR}_N$; from §6.6.2 we know that for $N$ being an RSA modulus, $\#\mathrm{QR}_N = \#\mathbb{Z}_N^*/4$, i.e., a quarter of the elements in $\mathbb{Z}_N^*$ are in $\mathrm{QR}_N$; thus, Alice can employ a suitable message formatting mechanism so that she can make sure $m \in \mathrm{QR}_N$; for such $m$, Alice can use Alg 6.5 to compute a square root of $m$. ∗)

**Signature Verification**
Let Bob be a verifier who knows that the public modulus $N$ belongs to Alice. Given a message-signature pair $(m, s)$, Bob's verification procedure is
$$\mathsf{Verify}_N(m, s) = \mathsf{True} \ \text{if} \ m \equiv s^2 \pmod{B}.$$

(∗ N.B., Message $m$ must be a recognizable one, see §10.4.3. ∗)

---

A better and fit-for-application scheme for signing in Rabin using hash functions will be introduced in Chapter 16. That algorithm is a probabilistic one which guarantees that multiple issuances of signatures for the same message will be randomized so that an adaptive attacker cannot obtain two different square roots of one message. That Rabin signature scheme is therefore a fit-for-application one. Formal argument for security of that Rabin signature scheme will be considered under a stronger and fit-for-application security notion which will also be introduced in Chapter 16.

We summarize a paradoxical result regarding security for signing in Rabin.

On the one hand, using the same method in Theorem 8.2 (in §8.11), the textbook sense of unforgeability for the textbook Rabin signature can be shown as equivalent to factorization. This result not only is a very strong one since it is formal evidence (i.e., a proof), but also is a desirable one since it relates forgery to a reputably hard problem: integer factorization.

On the other hand, the textbook version of the Rabin signature scheme is hopelessly weak and absolutely unusable in real world applications where adaptive chosen-message attacks are common. Such attacks totally destroy the scheme. A fit-for-application variation for signing in Rabin is necessary and such a variation will be introduced in Chapter 16. Unfortunately however, as we shall see in that chapter, our proof of security (formal evidence of security) for that scheme will no longer relate unforgeability to integer factorization.

### 10.4.6   The ElGamal Signature

In addition to his elegant public-key cryptosystem in §8.12, ElGamal also works out an ingenious digital signature scheme. Similar to the case of the ElGamal public-key cryptosystem inspiring great follow-up research and application interests which last to this day, the ElGamal signature scheme is also the origin of many further digital signature schemes which belong to the family of ElGamal-like signature schemes (some of them will be introduced in §10.4.8 and their security properties further studied in Chapter 16).

The ElGamal signature scheme is specified in Alg 10.3.

### 10.4.7   Informal Security Argument for the ElGamal Signature

Let us now investigate a few security issues in the ElGamal signature scheme.

#### 10.4.7.1   Warnings

We notice a few warnings in the ElGamal signature schemes.

**Warning 1**

The first warning is the importance of checking $r < p$ in the signature verification. Bleichenbacher [42] discovers the following attack if Bob would accept signatures where $r$ is larger than $p$. Let $(r, s)$ be a signature on message $m$. Malice can forge a new signature on an arbitrary message $m'$ as follows:

1. $u \leftarrow m'm^{-1} \pmod{p-1}$

2. $s' \leftarrow su \pmod{p-1}$

3. compute $r'$ satisfying: $r' \equiv ru \pmod{p-1}$ and $r' \equiv r \pmod{p}$; this can be done by applying the Chinese Remainder Theorem (Alg 6.1)

Then it is routine to go through the following congruence:

$$y_A^{r'} r'^{s'} \equiv y_A^{ru} r^{su} \equiv (y_A^r r^s)^u \equiv g^{mu} \equiv g^{m'} \pmod{p}.$$

**Algorithm 10.3:** The ElGamal Signature Scheme

**Key Setup**

The key setup procedure is the same as that for the ElGamal cryptosystems (see §8.12).

(∗ thus, user Alice's public-key material is a tuple $(g, y, p)$ where $p$ is a large prime number, $g \in \mathbb{F}_p^*$ is a random multiplicative generator element, and $y_A \equiv g^{x_A} \pmod{p}$ for a secret integer $x_A < p - 1$; Alice's private key is $x_A$. ∗)

**Signature Generation**

To create a signature of message $m \in \mathbb{F}_p^*$, Alice picks a random number $\ell \in_U \mathbb{Z}_{p-1}^*$ (i.e., $\ell < p - 1$ and $\gcd(\ell, p - 1) = 1$) and creates a signature pair $(r, s)$ where

$$r \leftarrow g^\ell \pmod{p},$$
$$s \leftarrow \ell^{-1}(m - x_A r) \pmod{p - 1}.$$

(10.4.2)

(∗ $\ell^{-1}$ can be computed using the extended Euclid's algorithm (Alg 4.2). ∗)

**Signature Verification**

Let Bob be a verifier who knows that the public-key material $(g, y_A, p)$ belongs to Alice. Given a message-signature pair $(m, (r, s))$, Bob's verification procedure is

$$\mathsf{Verify}_{(g, y_A, p)}(m, (r, s)) = \mathsf{True} \quad \text{if}$$

$$r < p \quad \text{and} \quad y_A{}^r r^s \equiv g^m \pmod{p}.$$

(∗ N.B., Message $m$ must be a recognizable one, see §10.4.7.2. ∗)

The attack is prevented if Bob checks $r < p$. This is because $r'$ computed from the Chinese Remainder Theorem in step 3 above will be a value of a magnitude $p(p-1)$.

## Warning 2

The second warning is also discovered by Bleichenbacher [42]: Alice should pick the public parameter $g$ randomly in $\mathbb{F}_p^*$. If this parameter is not chosen by Alice (e.g., in the case of the system-wide users share the same public parameters $g, p$), then a publicly known procedure must be in place for users to check the random choice of $g$ (e.g., $g$ is output from a pseudo-random function).

Now let us suppose that public parameters $g, p$ are chosen by Malice. Parameter $p$ can be setup in a standard way which we have recommended in §8.4.1: let $p-1 = bq$ where $q$ can be a sufficiently large prime but $b$ can be smooth (i.e., $b$ only has small prime factors and so computing discrete logarithm in group of order $b$ is easy, see §8.4.1).

Malice generates $g$ as follows

$$g = \beta^t \pmod{p}$$

for some $\beta = cq$ with $c < b$.

For Alice's public key $y_A$, we know that the extraction of the discrete logarithm of $y_A$ to the base $g$ is hard. However, the extraction of the discrete logarithm of $y_A{}^q$ to the base $g^q$ is easy. The discrete logarithm is $z \equiv x_A \pmod{b}$, that is the following congruence holds:

$$y_A{}^q \equiv (g^q)^z \pmod{p}.$$

With $z$, Malice can forge Alice's signature as follows:

$$r \leftarrow \beta = cq$$

$$s \leftarrow t(m - cqz) \pmod{p-1}$$

Then it is routine to go through the following congruence:

$$y_A{}^r r^s \equiv y_A{}^{cq} (\beta^t)^{(m-cqz)} \equiv g^{cqz} g^{m-cqz} \equiv g^m \pmod{p}.$$

Hence, $(r, s)$ is indeed a valid signature on $m$, which is created without using $x_A$ (but using $x_A \pmod{b}$).

We notice that in this signature forgery attack, $r$ is a value divisible by $q$. So in the standard parameter setting for $p$ satisfying $p = bq$ where $q$ is a large prime, this attack of Bleichenbacher can be prevented if in the verification time Bob checks $q \nmid r$ (suppose that the standard setting up of $p$ makes $q$ part of the public parameter). Related to this point, later in §16.3.2.1 when we will conduct a formal prove for unforgeability of the ElGamal signature scheme, we will see that the condition $q \nmid r$ must be in place in order for the formal proof to go through.

## Warning 3

The third warning is the care of the ephemeral key $\ell$. Similar to the case of the ElGamal encryption: the ElGamal signature generation is also a randomized algorithm. The randomization is due to the randomness of the ephemeral key $\ell$.

Alice should never reuse an ephemeral key in different instances of signature issuance. If an ephemeral key $\ell$ is reused to issue two signatures for two messages

$m_1 \not\equiv m_2 \pmod{p-1}$, then from the second equation in (10.4.2), we have

$$\ell(s_1 - s_2) \equiv m_1 - m_2 \pmod{p-1}.$$

Since $\ell^{-1} \pmod{p-1}$ exists, $m_1 \not\equiv m_2 \pmod{p-1}$ implies

$$\ell^{-1} \equiv (s_1 - s_2)/(m_1 - m_2) \pmod{p-1}, \qquad (10.4.3)$$

i.e., $\ell^{-1}$ is disclosed. In turn, Alice's private key $x_A$ can be computed from the second equation in (10.4.2) as

$$x_A \equiv (m_1 - \ell s_1)/r \pmod{p-1}. \qquad (10.4.4)$$

Notice also that the ephemeral key must be picked uniformly randomly from the space $\mathbb{Z}_{p-1}^*$. A particular caution should be taken when a signature is generated by a small computer such as a smartcard or a handheld device: one must make sure that such devices should be equipped with adequately reliable randomness source.

As long as $\ell$ is used once only per signature and is generated uniformly random, the second equation for signature generation (10.4.2) shows that it essentially provides a one-time multiplication cipher to encrypt the signer's private key $x$. Therefore, these two secrets protect one another in the information-theoretical secure sense.

### 10.4.7.2    Prevention of Existential Forgery

Existential forgery given in Remark 10.1 applies to the ElGamal signature too if the message signed does not contain recognizable redundancy. That is, it is not difficult to forge a valid "message"-signature pair under the ElGamal signature scheme where the resultant "message" is not a recognizable one.

For example, let $u$, $v$ be any integers less than $p-1$ such that $\gcd(v, p-1) = 1$; set

$r \leftarrow g^u y_A{}^v \pmod{p}$,

$s \leftarrow -rv^{-1} \pmod{p-1}$,

$m \leftarrow -ruv^{-1} \pmod{p-1}$;

then $(m, (r, s))$ is indeed a valid "message"-signature pair for the ElGamal signature scheme related to Alice's public key $y_A$ since

$$
\begin{aligned}
y^r r^s &\equiv y_A{}^r r^{-rv^{-1}} \\
&\equiv y_A{}^r (g^u y_A{}^v)^{-rv^{-1}} \\
&\equiv y_A{}^r (g^u)^{-rv^{-1}} (y_A{}^v)^{-rv^{-1}} \\
&\equiv y_A{}^r g^{-ruv^{-1}} y_A{}^{-r} \\
&\equiv g^{-ruv^{-1}} \\
&\equiv g^m \pmod{p}.
\end{aligned}
$$

However, in this forgery, "message" $m$ is not recognizable due to the good mixing-transformation property of the modulo exponentiation.

A message formatting mechanism can defeat this forgery. The simplest message formatting mechanism is to have $m$ to contain a recognizable part, e.g., $m = M \parallel I$ where $M$ is the message to be signed and $I$ is a recognizable string such as the signer's identity.

The most commonly used message formatting mechanism is to have $m$ to be a hashed value of the message to be signed. An example of such a hashed message can be

$$m = H(M, r)$$

where $H$ is a cryptographic hash function and $M$ is a bit string representing a message. Now the signature is of the message $M$. The verification step includes verifying $m = H(M, r)$. The one-way property of the hash function effectively stops the existential forgery shown above.

If we assume that the hash function $H$ behaves like a random oracle does (see §10.3.1.2), then formal evidence to relate the unforgeability of ElGamal signature to the discrete logarithm problem (a reputably hard problem) can be obtained. However, at this moment we do not have sufficient tool to demonstrate such formal evidence. The formal demonstration will be deferred to Chapter 16.

For the same reason, we will also defer to Chapter 16 formal proof of security for other signature schemes in the ElGamal signature family.

## 10.4.8 Signature Schemes in the ElGamal Signature Family

After ElGamal's original work, several variations of the ElGamal signature scheme emerged. Two influential ones are the Schnorr signature scheme [258, 259] and the Digital Signature Standard (DSS) [217, 218].

### 10.4.8.1 The Schnorr Signature

The Schnorr signature scheme is a variation of the ElGamal signature scheme but possesses a feature which forms an important contribution to public-key cryptography: a considerably shortened representation of prime field elements without having degenerated the underlying intractable problem (which is the DL problem, see §8.4). This idea is later further developed to finite fields of a more general form in a new cryptosystem: the XTR public-key system [177].

The shortened representation is realized by constructing a field $\mathbb{F}_p$ such that it contains a much smaller subgroup of prime order $q$. We notice that the current standard parameter setting for $p$ in ElGamal-like cryptosystems is $p \approx 2^{1024}$. We should further notice that the size for $p$ is likely to grow to suit the advances in solving the DL problem. However, after Schnorr's work, it has become a standard convention (a rule of thumb) that parameter setting for $q$ is $q \approx 2^{160}$. It is quite possible that this setting is more or less a constant regardless of the growth of the size of $p$. This is because that the subgroup information does not play a role in general methods for solving the DL problem in $\mathbb{F}_p$, even if the target element is known in the given subgroup. The constant-ish $2^{160}$ setting for $q$ is merely imposed by the lower-bound requirement due to the square-root attack (see §3.6).

The Schnorr signature scheme is specified in Alg 10.4

Notice that in the setting-up of public parameters, a generator $g$ can be found quickly. This is because for $q|p-1$,

$$\text{Prob}\left[\gcd(\text{ord}(f), q) = 1 \mid f \in_U \mathbb{Z}_p^*\right] \le 1/q,$$

i.e., the probability of random chosen $f$ satisfying $g \leftarrow f^{\frac{p-1}{q}} \equiv 1 \pmod{p}$ is negligibly small. By Fermat's Little Theorem (Theorem 6.10 in §6.4), we have

$$g^q \equiv 1 \pmod{p}.$$

Therefore $g$ indeed generates a subgroup of $q$ elements.

The signature verification works correctly because if $(m, (s, e))$ is a valid message-signature pair created by Alice, then

$$r' \equiv g^s y^e \equiv g^{xe+\ell} y^e \equiv y^{-e} g^\ell y^e \equiv g^\ell \equiv r \pmod{p}.$$

As we have discussed earlier, working in the order-$q$ subgroup of $\mathbb{F}_p$, a signature in the Schnorr signature scheme is much shorter than that of a signature in the ElGamal signature scheme: $2|q|$ bits are required for transmitting a Schnorr signature, in comparison with $2|p|$ bits for transmitting an ElGamal signature. The shortened signature also means fewer operations in signature generation and verification: $O_B(\log_2 q \log^2 p)$ in Schnorr vs. $O_B(\log^3 p)$ in ElGamal. Further notice that in signature generation, the modulo $p$ part of the computation can be conducted in an off-line manner. With this consideration, real-time signature generation only needs to compute one multiplication modulo $q$, the hardwork is done in offline time. Such a design arrangement is suitable for a small device to perform.

Same as the case of the ElGamal signature, the ephemeral key $\ell$ should never be reused, and should be uniformly random. Under these conditions, the ephemeral key and the signer's private key protect one another in an information-theoretical secure sense.

### 10.4.8.2  The Digital Signature Standard (DSS)

In August 1991, the US standards body, National Institute of Standards and Technology (NIST), announced a new proposed digital signature scheme called the Digital Signature Standard (DSS) [217, 218]. The DSS is essentially the ElGamal

**Algorithm 10.4:** The Schnorr Signature Scheme

**Setup of System Parameters**

1. Setup two prime numbers $p$ and $q$ such that $q|p-1$;

   (* typical sizes for these parameters: $|p| = 1024$ and $|q| = 160$ *)

2. Setup an element $g \in \mathbb{Z}_p^*$ of order $q$;

   (* this can be done by picking $f \in_U \mathbb{Z}_p^*$ and setting

   $g \leftarrow f^{(p-1)/q} \pmod{p}$. If $g = 1$, repeat the procedure until $g \neq 1$ *)

3. Setup a cryptographic hash function $H : \{0,1\}^* \mapsto \mathbb{Z}_q$;

   (* for example, SHA-1 is a good candidate for $H$ *)

The parameters $(p, q, g, H)$ are publicized for use by system-wide users.

**Setup of a Principal's Public/Private Key**
User Alice picks a random number $x \in_U \mathbb{Z}_q$ and computes

$$y \leftarrow g^{-x} \pmod{p}.$$

Alice's public-key material is $(p, q, g, y, H)$; her private key is $x$.

**Signature Generation**
To create a signature of message $m \in \{0,1\}^*$, Alice picks a random number
$\ell \in_U \mathbb{Z}_q$ and computes a signature pair $(e, s)$ where

$$
\begin{aligned}
r &\leftarrow g^\ell \pmod{p}; \\
e &\leftarrow H(m \parallel r); \\
s &\leftarrow \ell + xe \pmod{q}.
\end{aligned}
$$

**Signature Verification**
Let Bob be a verifier who knows that the public-key material $(p, q, g, y, H)$
belongs to Alice. Given a message-signature pair $(m, (e, s))$, Bob's verification procedure is

$$
\begin{aligned}
r' &\leftarrow g^s y^e \pmod{p}, \\
e' &\leftarrow H(m \parallel r'), \\
\mathsf{Verify}_{(p,q,g,y,h)}(m, (s, e)) &= \mathsf{True} \ \text{ if } \ e' = e.
\end{aligned}
$$

---

**Algorithm 10.5:** The Digital Signature Standard

**Setup of System Parameters**
(* the system parameters are identical to those for the Schnorr signature scheme; thus, parameters $(p, q, g, H)$, which have the same meaning as those in Alg 10.4, are publicized for use by the system-wide users. *)

**Setup of a Principal's Public/Private Key**
User Alice picks a random number $x \in_U \mathbb{Z}_q$ as her private key, and computes her public key by

$$y \leftarrow g^x \pmod{p}.$$

Alice's public-key material is $(p, q, g, y, H)$; her private key is $x$.

**Signature Generation**
To create a signature of message $m \in \{0, 1\}^*$, Alice picks a random number $\ell \in_U \mathbb{Z}_q$ and computes a signature pair $(r, s)$ where

$$r \leftarrow (g^\ell \pmod{p}) \pmod{q},$$
$$s \leftarrow \ell^{-1}(H(m) + xr) \pmod{q}.$$

**Signature Verification**
Let Bob be a verifier who knows that the public-key material $(p, q, g, y, h)$ belongs to Alice. Given a message-signature pair $(m, (r, s))$, Bob's verification procedure is

$w \leftarrow s^{-1} \pmod{q}$,
$u_1 \leftarrow H(m)w \pmod{q}$,
$u_2 \leftarrow rw \pmod{q}$,
$\mathsf{Verify}_{(p,q,g,y,h)}(m, (r, s)) = \mathsf{True}$ if $r = (g^{u_1} y^{u_2} \pmod{p}) \pmod{q}$.

---

signature scheme, but like the Schnorr signature scheme, it works in a much smaller prime-order subgroup of a larger finite field in which the DL problem is believed to be hard. Therefore, the DSS has a much reduced signature size than that for the ElGamal signature scheme.

The DSS is specified in Alg 10.5

Signature verification works correctly because if $(m, (r, s))$ is a valid message-signature pair created by Alice, then

$$g^{u_1} y^{u_2} \equiv g^{H(m)s^{-1}} y^{rs^{-1}} \equiv g^{(H(m)+xr)s^{-1}} \equiv g^\ell \pmod{p};$$

comparing the right-hand side with the first equation for signature generation, this congruence should return $r$ if is further operated modulo $q$.

The communication bandwidth and the computational requirements for the DSS are the same as those for the Schnorr signature scheme if the public parameters of these two schemes have the same size.

The DSS has been standardized together with a compatible standardization process for its hash function, namely SHA-1 [219]. The use of the standard hash function provides the needed property for message recognizability and so prevents existential forgery.

Finally, the caution for the ephemeral key is also necessary as in all signature schemes in the ElGamal signature family.

## 10.4.9 Formal Security Proof for Digital Signature Schemes

Analogous to our discussion in §8.14 on the need for stronger security notions for public-key cryptosystems, we should also provide a brief discussion on the issue of provable security for digital signature schemes.

The reader may have noticed that in this chapter we have not provided any formal evidence on showing security for the digital signature schemes introduced. Indeed, as we have remarked in Remark 10.2, in this chapter we will not consider formal proof for signature schemes. There are two reasons behind this.

To explain the first reason, we notice that it is reasonable to expect that forging a signature "from scratch" should be harder than doing the job by making use of some available message-signature pairs which an attacker may have in possession before it starts to forge. The forgery task may be further eased if the attacker can interact with a targeted signer and persuade the latter to provide a signing service, i.e., to issue signatures of messages chosen by the attacker. Signature forgery based on making use of a targeted signer's signing service is called forgery via **adaptive chosen-message attack**.

In reality, message-signature pairs with respect to a given public key are abundantly available. Also, adaptive attacks are hard to prevent in applications of digital signatures: to issue signatures of given messages can be a perfectly legitimate service in many applications. Consequently, a fit-for-application notion of security for digital signatures is necessary. Such a security notions will be defined in Chapter 16. This is the first reason why we have deferred formal security proof for digital signature schemes.

For the second reason, we have also seen that it is generally easy to forge a message-signature pair, even to forge it "from scratch" if the "message" is not recognizable (in general, see Remark 10.1 for ease of existential forgery and in specific, review many concrete cases of existential forgery in our description of various concrete schemes). To prevent such easy ways of forgery, any digital signature scheme must be equipped with a message formatting mechanism which renders a message to be signed into a recognizable one. Most frequently, message formatting mechanisms use cryptographic hash functions. It is thus reasonable to expect that a formal evidence for security of a digital signature scheme should be supplied together with a formally modeled behavior of a cryptographic hash function. In absence of a formally modeled hash function behavior, we have not been able to provide formal argument on security for digital signature schemes introduced so far in this chapter. This is the second reason why we have deferred formal security proof for digital signature schemes.

We have discussed in §10.3.1.2 that cryptographic hash functions try to emulate random functions. For cryptographic schemes which use hash functions, a notion for establishing formal evidence for their security is called **random oracle model (ROM)** for provable security. This notion will be available in Chapter 16. There, we shall see that under the ROM, we will be able to provide formal evidence to relate the difficulty of signature forgery (even via adaptive chosen-message attack) to some well-known computational assumptions in the theory of computational complexity.

# 10.5   Asymmetric Techniques II: Data Integrity Without Source Identification

In a data integrity mechanism realized by a digital signature scheme, the usual setting for key parameters stipulates that $Ke$ is a private key and $Kv$ is the matching public key. Under this setting, a correct integrity verification result of a message provides the message verifier the identity of the message transmitter who is the signer of the message, i.e., the owner of the public key $Kv$.

We should notice however that this "usual setting for key parameters," while being a necessary element for achieving a digital signature scheme, is unnecessary for a data-integrity system. In fact, in Definition 10.1 we have never put any constraint on the two keys for constructing and for verifying MDC.

Thus, for example, we can actually set the two keys, $Ke$ and $Kv$, opposite to that for a digital signature scheme, that is, let $Ke$ be a public key and $Kv$ be a private key. Under such a key setting, anybody is able to use the public key $Ke$ to create a consistent (i.e., cryptographicly integral) pair (Data, MDC) or a "message-signature pair" $(m, s)$, while only the holder of the private key $Kv$ is able to verify the consistency of the pair (Data, MDC) or the validity of the "signature" $(m, s)$. Of course, under such an unusual key setting, the system can no longer be regarded as a digital signature scheme. However, we must notice that, according to Definition 10.1, the system under such an unusual key setting remains a data-integrity system!

Since anybody can have used the public key $Ke$ to create the consistent pair (Data, MDC), we shall name this kind of data-integrity system **data-integrity**

**without source identification.** From our familiarity with the behavior of Malice (the bad guy), there is no danger for us to conveniently rename this data-integrity service "*data integrity from Malice.*"

Let us now look at an example of a public-key encryption scheme which provides this sort of service. This is a scheme with such a property: Malice can send to Alice a confidential message such that the message is "non-malleable" (e.g., by other friends of Malice), that is, it's computationally hard for any other member in the clique of Malice to modify the message without being detected by Alice, the message receiver. This algorithm, with its RSA instantiation being specified in Alg 10.6, is named **Optimal Asymmetric Encryption Padding (OAEP)** and is invented by Bellare and Rogaway [25].

If the ciphertext has not been modified after its departure from the sender, then from the encryption algorithm we know that Alice will retrieve the random number $r$ correctly, and therefore

$$v = s \oplus G(r) = (m \parallel 0^{k_1}) \oplus G(r) \oplus G(r) = m \parallel 0^{k_1}.$$

Therefore, Alice will see $k_1$ zeros trailing the retrieved plaintext message.

On the other hand, any modification of the ciphertext will cause an alteration of the message sealed under the RSA function. This alteration will further cause "uncontrollable" alteration to the plaintext message, including the random input and the redundancy of $k_1$ zeros trailing the plaintext message, which have been input to the OAEP function. Intuitively, the "uncontrollable" alteration is due to a so-called "random oracle" property of the two hash functions used in the scheme (see our discussions of random oracles in §10.3.1.2). The uncontrollable alteration will show itself up by damaging the redundancy (the string of $k_1$ zeros) added into the plaintext with a probability at least $1 - 2^{-k_1}$. Given $2^{-k_1}$ being negligible, $1 - 2^{-k_1}$ is significant. Thus, indeed, the scheme provides a data-integrity protection on the encrypted message.

Notice that the data-integrity protection provided by the RSA-OAEP encryption algorithm is a strange one: although upon seeing the string of $k_1$ zeros Alice is assured that the ciphertext has not been modified, she can have no idea who the sender is. That is why in Alg 10.6 we have deliberately specified Malice as the sender. The notion of "data integrity from Malice" is very useful and important. This notion became apparent as a result of advances in public-key encryption schemes secure with respect to adaptively chosen ciphertext attack (CCA2, see Definition 8.3, in §8.6). In a public-key cryptosystems secure with respect to CCA2, the decryption procedure includes a data-integrity verification step. Such a cryptosystem is considered to be invulnerable even in the following extreme form of abuse by an attacker:

- The attacker and a public-key owner play a challenge-response game. The attacker is in the position of a challenger and is given freedom to send, as many

**Algorithm 10.6:** Optimal Asymmetric Encryption Padding for RSA
(RSA-OAEP) [25]

**Key Parameters**
Let $(N, e, d, G, H, n, k_0, k_1) \leftarrow_U \mathsf{Gen}(1^k)$ satisfy: $(N, e, d)$ is the RSA key
material where $d = e^{-1} \pmod{\phi(N)}$ and $|N| = k = n + k_0 + k_1$ with $2^{-k_0}$
and $2^{-k_1}$ being negligible quantities; $G, H$ are two hash functions satisfying

$$G : \{0,1\}^{k_0} \mapsto \{0,1\}^{k-k_0}, \quad H : \{0,1\}^{k-k_0} \mapsto \{0,1\}^{k_0};$$

$n$ is the length for the plaintext message.
Let $(N, e)$ be Alice's RSA public key and $d$ be her private key.

**Encryption**
To send a message $m \in \{0,1\}^n$ to Alice, Malice performs the following steps:

1. $r \leftarrow_U \{0,1\}^{k_0}$; $s \leftarrow (m \parallel 0^{k_1}) \oplus G(r)$; $t \leftarrow r \oplus H(s)$;

2. if[a] ( $s \parallel t \geq N$ ) go to 1;

3. $c \leftarrow (s \parallel t)^e \pmod{N}$.

The ciphertext is $c$.
(∗ here, "$\parallel$" denotes the bit string concatenation, "$\oplus$," the bit-wise XOR
operation, and "$0^{k_1}$," the string of $k_1$ zeros functioning as redundancy for
data-integrity checking in decryption time. ∗)

**Decryption**
Upon receipt of the ciphertext $c$, Alice performs the following steps:

1. $s \parallel t \leftarrow c^d \pmod{N}$ satisfying $|s| = n + k_1 = k - k_0$, $|t| = k_0$;

2. $u \leftarrow t \oplus H(s)$; $v \leftarrow s \oplus G(u)$;

3. output $\begin{cases} m & \text{if } v = m \parallel 0^{k_1} \\ \text{REJECT} & \text{otherwise} \end{cases}$

    (∗ when REJECT is output, the ciphertext is deemed invalid ∗)

---

[a]We use trial-and-error test in order to guarantee that the padding result as an integer
is always less than $N$. The probability of repeating the test $i$ times is $2^{-i}$. An alternative
way is to make $r$ and $H$, and hence $t$, one-bit shorter than the length of $N$, see a "PSS
Padding" algorithm in §16.4.2.

as he wishes (of course the attacker is polynomially bounded), *"adaptively chosen ciphertext"* messages to the owner of the public key for decryption in an oracle-service manner (review our discussion on "oracle services" in §8.2 and see a concrete example of an oracle encryption service in §8.2).

- The owner of the public key is in the position of a responder. If the data-integrity verification in the decryption procedure passes, the key owner should simply send the decryption result back regardless of the fact that the decryption request may even be from an attacker who may have created the ciphertext in some clever and unpublicized way with the intention to break the target cryptosystem (either to obtain a plaintext message which the attacker is not entitled to see, or to discover the private key of the key owner).

If a ciphertext has the correct data integrity, then it is considered that the sender should have known already the plaintext encrypted in. This is a notion known as **"plaintext awareness."** If the attacker has known already the encrypted plaintext, then an oracle decryption service should provide him no new information, not even in terms of providing him with a cryptanalysis training for how to break the target cryptosystem. On the other hand, if the attacker has tried an adaptive way to modify the ciphertext, then with an overwhelming probability the data integrity checking will fail, and then the decryption will be a null message. So against a cryptosystem with data integrity protection on the ciphertext, an active attacker won't be effective.

In Chapter 14 we will introduce a formal model for capturing the security notion under adaptively chosen ciphertext attack (CCA2). We will also study some public-key cryptosystems which are formally provably secure with respect to such attacks in Chapter 15. The RSA-OAEP is one of them. In §15.2 we shall provide a detailed analysis on the security of the RSA-OAEP encryption scheme. The analysis will be a formal proof that the RSA-OAEP is secure under a very strong attacking scenario: indistinguishability against an adaptively chosen ciphertext attacker. Due to this stronger security quality, the RSA-OAEP is no longer a textbook encryption algorithm; it is a fit-for-application public-key cryptosystem.

As having been shown in the RSA-OAEP algorithm, the usual method to achieve a CCA2-secure cryptosystem is to have the cryptosystem include a data-integrity checking mechanism without having the least concern of **message source identification**.

Message source identification is part of authentication service called data-origin authentication. Authentication is the topic for the next chapter.

## 10.6  Chapter Summary

In this chapter we have introduced the basic cryptographic techniques for providing data-integrity services. These techniques include (i) symmetric techniques based on using MACs constructed from hash functions or from block cipher algorithms, and (ii) asymmetric techniques based on digital signatures. Data-integrity served by these techniques comes together with a sub-service: message source identification.

The security notion for digital signature schemes provided is this chapter is a textbook version and hence is a very weak one. For some digital signature schemes introduced here we have also provided early warning signals on their (textbook) insecurity. The strengthening work for both security notions and for constructing strong signature schemes will be conducted in Chapter 16.

Finally, we also identified a peculiar data-integrity service which does not come together with identification of the message source, and exemplified the service by introducing a public-key cryptosystem which makes use of this service for obtaining a strong security (not reasoned here). In Chapter 15 we will see the important role played by this peculiar data-integrity service in formalizing a general methodology for achieving fit-for-application cryptosystems.

## Exercises

10.1 What is a manipulation detection code (MDC)? How is an MDC generated and used? Is a message authentication code (MAC) an MDC? Is a digital signature (of a message) an MDC?

10.2 What is a random oracle? Does a random oracle exist? How is the random oracle behavior approximated in the real world?

10.3 Let the output space of a hash function have magnitude $2^{160}$. What is the expected time cost for finding a collision under this hash function?

10.4 Why is a hash function practically non-invertible?

10.5 What is the main difference between a symmetric data-integrity technique and an asymmetric one?

10.6 What is existential forgery of a digital signature scheme? What are practical mechanisms to prevent existential forgery?

10.7 Why is the textbook security notion for digital signatures inadequate?

Hint: consider the fatal vulnerability of the Rabin signature against an active attacker.

10.8 What is the security notion "data integrity from Malice?"

10.9 Is a ciphertext output from the RSA-OAEP algorithm (Alg 10.6) a valid MDC?

# Part IV

# AUTHENTICATION

Nowadays, many commerce activities, business transactions and government services have been, and more and more of them will be, conducted and offered over an open and vulnerable communications network such as the Internet. It is vitally essential to establish that the intended communication partners and the messages transmitted are bona fide. The security service needed here is authentication, which can be obtained by applying cryptographic techniques. This part has three chapters on various protocol techniques of authentication. In Chapter 11 we study authentication protocols on their basic working principles, examine typical errors in authentication protocols and investigate causes. In Chapter 12 we examine case studies of several important authentication protocol techniques applied in the real world. In Chapter 13 we introduce the authentication framework for public-key infrastructure.

# Chapter 11

# AUTHENTICATION
# PROTOCOLS
# — PRINCIPLES

## 11.1   Introduction

In Chapter 2 we have exposed ourselves to a number of authentication protocols. Most protocols there are fictional ones (with two exceptions): we have deliberately designed them to be flawed in several ways in order for them to serve as an introduction to a culture of caution and vigilance in the areas of cryptography and information security.

In this chapter we return to the topic of authentication. The purpose of returning to the topic is for us to have a more comprehensive study of the area. Our study in this chapter will be divided into two categories:

### An Introduction to Various Authentication Techniques

In this category we shall study various basic techniques for authentication. These include the very basic mechanisms and protocol constructions for message and entity authentication, password-based authentication techniques and some important authenticated key establishment techniques. We believe that a number of basic authentication mechanisms and protocol constructions in several international standards are the ones which have been selected from the literature and subsequently gone through a careful (and long) process of expert review and improvement revision. Therefore, in our introduction to the basic authentication techniques, we shall pay particular attention to the mechanisms which have been standardized by international standard bodies. In addition, we shall introduce a few other reputable authentication and authenticated key establishment protocols. We believe that authentication mechanisms and protocols introduced in this category have a value for serving as building blocks and guidelines for designing good protocols. We therefore consider that this category provides the model authentication techniques for protocol designers.

**An Exemplified Study of a Wide Range of Protocol Flaws**

This is an inevitable part in the subject of authentication. We shall list various known and typical attacking techniques which can be mounted on authentication protocols. We shall analyze and discuss each attacking technique using some flawed protocols with the applicable attacks demonstrated. Through this study, we shall become familiar with a common phenomenon that authentication protocols are likely to contain security flaws even when they have been designed by experts. The comprehensive list of typical protocol flaws and the related attacking techniques provide essential knowledge for a protocol designer: "Did you know this sort of attack?"

Unlike in the cases of Chapter 2 where we have deliberately designed fictional protocols with artificial flaws, the security flaws in the protocols to be demonstrated in this chapter are not artificial ones; indeed, none of them is! These flaws were all discovered after the flawed protocols were published by reputable authors in information security and/or cryptography. A fact we shall see through the study in this chapter is that, even though conforming to standard documents, following well-thought-out design principles, and even being familiar with many typical protocol flaws, design of authentication protocol remains extremely error-prone, even for experts in the areas.

Due to the notorious error-prone nature of authentication protocols, this chapter plus the next, as follow-up of Chapter 2, are still not an end for the topic of authentication in this book. Systematic approaches (i.e., formal methods) to the development of correct authentication protocols are currently serious research topics. We shall study the topics of formal approaches to correct authentication protocols in Chapter 17.

## 11.1.1   Chapter Outline

In §11.2 we discuss the notion of authentication by introducing several refined notions. In §11.3 we agree on conventions for expressing components in authentication protocol and for the default behavior of protocol participants. The next three sections form the first category of our study in this chapter: in §11.4 we study the very basic and standard constructions for authentication protocols; in §11.5 we study some password based authentication techniques, and in §11.6 we study an important protocol which achieves authentication and authenticated key exchange using cryptographic techniques which are alternatives to those used in the previous two sections. The second category of our study is contained in §11.7 where we list and demonstrate typical attacking techniques applicable to authentication protocols.

Finally, we end this chapter in §11.8 by recommending a brief but important list of literature references in the area.

## 11.2   Authentication and Refined Notions

For a very short description of authentication, we may say that it is a procedure by which an entity establishes a claimed property to another entity. For example, the former is a subject claiming a legitimate entry to, or use of, the latter which is a system or a service, and by authentication, the latter establishes the claimed legitimacy. From this short description we can already see that authentication involves at least two separate entities in communication. Conventionally, a communication procedure run between or among co-operative principals is called a protocol. An authentication procedure is hence an authentication protocol.

The notion of authentication can be broken down to three sub-notions: **data-origin authentication, entity authentication** and **authenticated key establishment**. The first concerns validating a claimed property of a message; the second pays more attention to validating a claimed identity of a message transmitter; and the third further aims to output a secure channel for a subsequent, application-level secure communication session.

### 11.2.1   Data-Origin Authentication

Data-origin authentication (also called **message authentication**) relates closely to data integrity. Early textbooks in cryptography and information security viewed these two notions with no essential difference (e.g., Chapter 5 of [90] and §1.2-§1.3 of [94]). Such a view was based on a consideration that using information which has been modified in a malicious way is at the same risk as using information which has no reputable source.

However, data-origin authentication and data integrity are two *very* different notions. They can be clearly differentiated from a number of aspects.

First, data-origin authentication necessarily involves communications. It is a security service for a message receiver to verify whether a message is from a purported source. Data integrity needn't have a communication feature: the security service can be provided on stored data.

Secondly, data-origin authentication necessarily involves identifying the source of a message, while data integrity needn't do so. In §10.5, we have shown and argued with a convincing example that data integrity as a security service can be provided without message source identification. We have even coined a phrase "data integrity from Malice" to label a data-integrity service with such a property. We should remember that according to our stipulation made in Chapter 2 Malice is a faceless principal whose identity has the least to do with a reputable source of a message. In Chapter 15 we shall realize that "data integrity from Malice" is a general mechanism for achieving a provably secure public-key cryptosystems.

Thirdly and the most significantly, data-origin authentication necessarily involves establishing **freshness** of a message, while, again, data integrity needn't do so: a piece of stale data can have perfect data integrity. To obtain data-origin authentication service, a message receiver should verify whether or not the message has been sent sufficiently *recently* (that is, the time interval between the message issuance and its receipt is sufficiently small). A message which is deemed by the receiver to have been issued sufficiently recently is often referred to as a fresh message. Requiring that a message be fresh follows a common sense that a fresh message implies a good *correspondence* between the communication principals, and this may further imply less likelihood that, e.g., the communication principals, apparatus, systems, or the message itself may have been sabotaged. In §2.6.4 we have seen an attack on the Needham-Schroeder Symmetric-key Authentication Protocol (the attack of Denning and Sacco, Attack 2.2) in which a replayed old message has absolutely valid data integrity but has invalid authenticity. Authentication failure of this kind can be referred to as *valid data integrity without liveness of the message source*.

Notice that whether or not a message is fresh should be determined by applications. Some applications require a rather short time interval for a message being fresh which can be a matter of seconds (as in many challenge-response based real-time secure communication applications). Some applications allow a longer freshness period; for example, in World War II, the German military communications encrypted by the famous Enigma machine stipulated a rule that each day all Enigma machines must be set to a new "day-key" [279]. This rule has become a widely used key-management principle for many security systems today, though "day-key" may have been changed to "hour-key" or even "minute-key." Some other applications permit a much longer time interval for message freshness. For example, a bank check may have passed examinations in terms of its integrity and source identification; then its validity (authenticity) for authorizing the payment should be determined by the age of the check, that is, the time interval between the date of the check's issuance and that of the check's deposit. Most banks permit three months as the valid age for a check.

Finally, we point out that some anonymous credential enabled by some cryptographic schemes (e.g., blind signature) also provide a good differentiation between data-origin authentication and data integrity. A user can be issued an anonymous credential which enables the holder to gain a service by proving membership to a system anonymously. Notice that here, the data integrity evidence can even be demonstrated in a lively correspondent fashion, however, the system is prevented from performing source identification. We will study such cryptographic techniques in a later chapter.

From our discussions so far, we can characterize the notion of data-origin authentication as follows:

i) It consists of transmitting a message from a purported source (the transmitter) to a receiver who will validate the message upon reception.

ii) The message validation conducted by the receiver aims to establish the identity of the message transmitter.

iii) The validation also aims to establish the data integrity of the message subsequent to its departure from the transmitter.

iv) The validation further aims to establish liveness of the message transmitter.

## 11.2.2  Entity Authentication

Entity authentication is a communication process (i.e., protocol) by which a principal establishes a *lively correspondence* with a second principal whose claimed identity should meet what is sought by the first. Often, the word "entity" is omitted, as in this statement: "An important goal of an authentication protocol is to establish lively correspondence of a principal."

Often, a claimed identity in a protocol is a protocol message in its own right. In such a situation, confidence about a claimed identity and about the liveness of the claimant can be established by applying data-origin authentication mechanisms. Indeed, as we shall see in many cases in this chapter, for a claimed identity being in the position of a protocol message, treating it as a subject of data-origin authentication does form a desirable approach to entity authentication.

There are several types of entity authentication scenarios in distributed systems depending on various ways of classifying principals. We list several usual scenarios which are by no means exhaustive.

**Host-host type**  Communication partners are computers called "nodes" or platforms in a distributed system. Host-level activities often require cooperation among them. For example, in remote "reboot"[a] of a platform, upon reboot, the platform must identify a trusted server to supply necessary information, such as a trusted copy of an operating system, trusted clock setting, or the current trusted environment settings. The establishment of the trusted information is usually achieved via running an authentication protocol. A customary case in this host-host type of communication is a **client-server** setting where one host (client) requests certain services from the other (server).

**User-host type**  A user gains access to a computer system by logging in to a host in the system. The simplest examples are to login in to a computer via telnet,

---

[a] "Reboot" is a technical term in computer science for re-initialization of a computer system from some simple preliminary instructions or a set of information which may be hardwired in the system.

or to conduct file transfer via ftp (file transfer protocol); both can be achieved via running a password authentication protocol. In a more serious application where a compromised host will cause a serious loss (e.g., when a user makes an electronic payment via a smart card), **mutual authentication** is necessary.

**Process-host type**  Nowadays distributed computing has been so highly advanced that a great many functionalities and services are possible. A host may grant a foreign process various kinds of access rights. For example, a piece of "mobile code" or a "Java$^{TM}$ applet"[b] can travel to a remote host and run on it as a remote process. In sensitive applications, it is necessary and possible to design authentication mechanisms so that an applet can be deemed a friendly one by a host and be granted an appropriate access right on it.

**Member-club type**  A proof of holding a credential by a member to a club can be viewed as a generalization of the "user-host type." Here a club may need only to be concerned with the validation of the member's credential without necessarily knowing further information such as the true identity of the member. Zero-knowledge identification protocols and undeniable signature schemes can enable this type of entity authentication scenario. We shall study these authentication techniques in Chapter 18.

## 11.2.3  Authenticated Key Establishment

Often, communication partners run an entity authentication protocol as a means to bootstrap further secure communications at a higher or application level. In modern cryptography, cryptographic keys are the basis for secure communication channels. Therefore, entity authentication protocols for bootstrapping higher or application-level secure communications generally feature a sub-task of (authenticated) key establishment, or **key exchange**, or **key agreement**.

As in the case where entity authentication can be based on data-origin authentication regarding the identity of a claimant, in protocols for authenticated key establishment, key establishment material also forms important protocol messages which should be the subject for data-origin authentication.

In the literature, (entity) authentication protocols, authenticated key establishment (key exchange, key agreement) protocols, security protocols, or sometimes even cryptographic protocols, often refer to the same set of communication protocols.

---

[b]A Java$^{TM}$ applet is an executable code to run by a "web browser" on a remote host in order to effect a function on the issuing host's behalf.

## 11.2.4 Attacks on Authentication Protocols

Since the goal of an authentication protocol (data-origin, entity, key establishment) is to establish a claimed property, cryptographic techniques are inevitably used. Also inevitably, the goal of an authentication protocol will be matched with a counter-goal: attack. An attack on an authentication protocol consists of an attacker or a coalition of them (who we name collectively Malice, see §2.3) achieving an unentitled gain. Such a gain can be a serious one such as Malice obtaining a secret message or key, or a less serious one such as Malice successfully deceiving a principal to establish a wrong belief about a claimed property. In general, an authentication protocol is considered flawed if a principal concludes a normal run of the protocol with its intended communication partner while the intended partner would have a different conclusion.

We must emphasize that attacks on authentication protocols are mainly those which do *not* involve breaking the underlying cryptographic algorithms. Usually, authentication protocols are insecure not because the underlying cryptographic algorithm they use are weak, but because of protocol design flaws which permit Malice to break the goal of authentication without necessarily breaking any cryptographic algorithm. We shall see many such attacks in this chapter. For this reason, in the analysis of authentication protocols, we usually assume that the underlying cryptographic algorithms are *"perfect"* without considering their possible weakness. Those weakness are usually considered in other subjects of cryptography.

## 11.3 Convention

In authentication protocols to appear in the rest of this chapter, we stipulate a set of conventions for the semantical meanings of some protocol messages according to their syntactic structures. This convention set is as follows:

- *Alice, Bob, Trent, Malice, ...* : principal names appear as protocol messages; sometimes they may be abbreviated to $A$, $B$, $T$, $M$, ...;

- Alice $\rightarrow$ Bob: $M$; Alice sends to Bob message $M$; a protocol specification is a sequence of several such message communications;

- $\{M\}_K$: a ciphertext which encrypts the message $M$ under the key $K$;

- $K$, $K_{AB}$, $K_{AT}$, $K_A$, ... : cryptographic keys, where $K_{XY}$ denotes a key shared between principals $X$ and $Y$, and $K_X$ denotes a public key of principal $X$;

- $N$, $N_A$, ... : nonces, which stands for "number use for once" [62]; these are random numbers sampled from a sufficiently large space; $N_X$ is generated by principal $X$;

- $T_X$: a timestamp created by principal $X$;

- $\text{sig}_A(M)$: a digital signature on message $M$ created by principal $A$.

**Remark 11.1:** *We should notice that the semantical meanings of protocol messages which are associated to their syntactic structures (types) as above are not necessarily comprehensible by a protocol participant (say Alice). In general, for any message or part of a message in a protocol, if the protocol specification does not require Alice to perform a cryptographic operation on that message or message part, then Alice (in fact, her protocol compiler) will only understand that message part at the syntactic level. At the syntactic level, Alice may misinterpret the semantical meanings of a protocol message. We exemplify various possibilities of misinterpretations in Example 11.1.* □

**Example 11.1:** At the syntactic level, Alice may make wrong interpretations on protocol messages. Here are a few examples:

- She may consider a message chunk as a ciphertext and may try to decrypt it if she thinks she has the right key, or forward it to Bob if she thinks that the chunk is for him. However, the message chunk may in fact be a principal's identity (e.g., *Alice* or *Bob*) or a nonce or a timestamp.

- She may decrypt a ciphertext and sends the result out by "following protocol instruction," where the ciphertext is in fact one which was created earlier by herself, perhaps in a different context.

- She may view a key parameter as a nonce; etc.

It may seem that Alice is very "stupid" in understanding protocol messages. No, we should rather consider that she is too innocent and cannot always anticipate the existence of "clever" Malice who may have already "recompiled" a protocol by misplacing various message parts in order to cause the misinterpretation. □

In general, we have a further set of conventions for the behavior of a protocol participant, whether a legitimate one or an uninvited one:

- An honest principal in a protocol does not understand the semantical meanings of any protocol message before a run of the protocol terminates successfully.

- An honest principal in a protocol cannot recognize $\{M\}_K$ or create it or decompose it unless the principal has in its possession the correct key.

- An honest principal in a protocol cannot recognize a random-looking number such as a nonce, a sequence number or a cryptographic key, unless the random-looking number either has been created by the principal in the current run of the protocol, or is an output to the principal as a result of a run of the protocol.

- An honest principal in a protocol does not record any protocol messages unless the protocol specification instructs so. In general, an authentication protocol is *stateless*, that is, it does not require a principal to maintain any state information after a protocol run terminates successfully, except for information which is deemed to be the output of the protocol to the principal.

- Malice, in addition to his capability specified in §2.3, knows the "stupidities" (to be more fair, the weaknesses) of honest principals which we have exemplified in Example 11.1, and will always try to exploit them.

Authentication protocols are meant to transmit messages in a public communication network, which is assumed to be under Malice's control, and to thwart his attacks in such an environment although Malice is "clever" and honest principals are "stupid."

Now let us see how this is achieved.

## 11.4 Basic Authentication Techniques

There are numerous protocol-based techniques for realizing (data-origin, entity) authentication and authenticated key establishment. However, the basic protocol constructions, in particular those which should be regarded as good ones, and the simple technical ideas behind the good constructions, are not so diverse.

In this section let us study basic authentication techniques through introducing some basic but important protocol constructions. In our study, we shall pay particular attention to constructions which have been documented in a series of international standards. We consider that these constructions should serve as models for the design of authentication protocols. We shall also argue why some constructions are more desirable than others, exemplify a few bad ones and explain why they are bad.

The following basic authentication techniques will be studied in this section:

- Standard mechanisms for establishing message freshness and principal liveness (§11.4.1)

- Mutual authentication vs. unilateral authentication (§11.4.2)

- Authentication involving a trusted third party (§11.4.3)

### 11.4.1 Message Freshness and Principal Liveness

To deem whether a message is fresh is a necessary part of data-origin authentication (please notice the difference between message source identification and data-origin *authentication* which we have discussed in §11.2.1), as well as in the case of entity authentication where a principal is concerned with lively correspondence of an intended communication partner. Therefore, mechanisms which establish message freshness or principal liveness are the most basic components in authentication protocols.

Let us now describe the basic and standard mechanisms to achieve these functions. In our descriptions, we shall let Alice be in the position of a claimant regarding a property (e.g., her liveness, or freshness of a message), and Bob be in the position of a verifier regarding the claimed property. We assume that Alice and Bob share a secret key $K_{AB}$ if a mechanism uses symmetric cryptographic techniques, or that Bob knows Alice's public key via a public-key certification framework[c] if a mechanism uses asymmetric cryptographic techniques.

### 11.4.1.1  Challenge-Response Mechanisms

In a **challenge-response mechanism**, Bob (the verifier) has his input to a composition of a protocol message and the composition involves a cryptographic operation performed by Alice (the claimant) so that Bob can verify the lively correspondence of Alice via the freshness of his own input. The usual form of Bob's input can be a random number (called a nonce) which is generated by Bob and passed to Alice beforehand. Let $N_B$ denote a nonce generated by Bob. This message freshness mechanism has the following interactive format:

$$
\begin{array}{ll}
\text{1.} & \text{Bob} \;\rightarrow\; \text{Alice: } N_B; \\
\text{2.} & \text{Alice} \;\rightarrow\; \text{Bob: } \mathcal{E}_{K_{AB}}(M, N_B); \\
\text{3.} & \text{Bob decrypts the cipher chunk and} 
\begin{cases}
\text{accepts} & \text{if he sees } N_B \\
\text{rejects} & \text{otherwise.}
\end{cases}
\end{array}
\qquad (11.4.1)
$$

Here, the first message transmission is often called Bob's **challenge** to Alice, and the second message transmission is thereby called Alice's **response** to Bob. Bob is in a position of an **initiator** while Alice is in a position of a **responder**.

The specified mechanism uses symmetric cryptographic technique: symmetric encryption. Therefore, upon receipt of Alice's response, Bob has to decrypt the ciphertext chunk using the shared key $K_{AB}$. If the decryption extracts his nonce *correctly* (be careful of the meaning of "correctly," it actually means correct data integrity, as we shall see in a moment) then Bob can conclude that Alice has indeed performed the required cryptographic operation *after* his action of sending the challenge; if the time interval between the challenge and the response is acceptably small (according to an application requirement as we have discussed in §11.2.1), then the message $M$ is deemed to be fresh. The intuition behind this message freshness mechanism is a confidence that Alice's cryptographic operation must have taken place after her receipt of Bob's nonce. This is because Bob's nonce has been

---

[c]Public-key certification frameworks will be introduced in Chapter 13.

sampled at random from a sufficiently large space and so no one can have predicted its value before his sampling.

Now let us explain what we meant by Bob's decryption and extraction of his nonce "correctly" (as we warned in the previous paragraph). The use of symmetric encryption in this mechanism may deceptively imply that the cryptographic service provided here is confidentiality. In fact, the necessary security service for achieving message freshness should be data integrity. The reader might want to argue that the two principals may want to keep the message $M$ confidential, e.g., $M$ may be a cryptographic key to be used for securing a higher-level communication session later (and thus this basic construction includes a sub-task of session key establishment). This does constitute a legitimate reason for using encryption. We could actually further consider that the two parties may also like to keep Bob's nonce secret and so in that case Bob should also encrypt the first message transmission. Therefore, we are not saying that the use of encryption for providing the confidentiality service is wrong here provided such a service is needed. What we should emphasize here is that if the encryption algorithm does not provide a proper data-integrity service (an encryption algorithm usually doesn't), then the specified mechanism is a dangerous one because the necessary service needed here, data integrity, is missing! In §17.2.1 we shall see with convincing evidence the reason behind the following statement:

**Remark 11.2:** *If the encryption algorithm in authentication mechanism (11.4.1) does not offer a proper data-integrity service then Bob cannot establish the freshness of the message M.*
□

The really correct and a standard approach to achieving data-integrity service using symmetric cryptographic techniques is to use a manipulation detection code (MDC, see Definition 10.1 in §10.1). Therefore, in mechanism (11.4.1), the encryption should be accompanied by an MDC which is keyed with a shared key and inputs the ciphertext chunk which needs integrity protection. If the message $M$ does not need confidentiality protection, then the following mechanism is a proper one for achieving message freshness:

1. Bob → Alice: $N_B$;
2. Alice → Bob: $M$, MDC$(K_{AB}, M, N_B)$;
3. Bob reconstructs MDC$(K_{AB}, M, N_B)$ and (11.4.2)
   $\begin{cases} \text{accepts} & \text{if two MDCs are identical} \\ \text{rejects} & \text{otherwise.} \end{cases}$

Notice that in order for Bob to be able to reconstruct the MDC in step 3, the message $M$ now must be sent in cleartext in step 2. Of course, $M$ can be a ciphertext encrypting a confidential message.

In §17.2.1 we shall argue with convincing evidence that, in terms of achieving authentication using symmetric cryptographic techniques, mechanism (11.4.2) is a correct approach while mechanism (11.4.1) is an incorrect one. There we shall also see that, without proper data-integrity, confidentiality of $M$ in (11.4.1) needn't be in place even if the mechanism uses a strong encryption algorithm.

The challenge-response mechanism can also be achieved by applying an asymmetric cryptographic technique, as in the following mechanism:

1. Bob $\rightarrow$ Alice: $N_B$;
2. Alice $\rightarrow$ Bob: $\text{sig}_A(M, N_B)$;
3. Bob verifies the signature using his nonce and                    (11.4.3)
   $\begin{cases} \text{accepts} & \text{if signature verification passes} \\ \text{rejects} & \text{otherwise.} \end{cases}$

Notice that in this mechanism, Alice's free choice of the message $M$ is very important. Alice's free choice of $M$ should be part of the measure to prevent this mechanism from being exploited by Bob to trick Alice to sign inadvertently a message of Bob's preparation. For example, Bob may have prepared his "nonce" as

$$N_B = h(\text{Transfer £1000 to Bob's Acc.No. 123 from Alice's Acc.No. 456.})$$

where $h$ is a hash function.

In some applications, a signer in the position of Alice in mechanism (11.4.3) may not have freedom to choose $M$. In such situations, specialized keys can be defined to confine the usages of keys. For example, the public key for verifying Alice's signature in mechanism (11.4.3) can be specified for the specific use in this mechanism. Specialization of cryptographic keys is a subject in **key management** practice.

### 11.4.1.2   Standardization of the Challenge-response Mechanisms

The ISO (the International Organization for Standardization) and the IEC (the International Electrotechnical Commission) have standardized the three challenge-response mechanisms introduced so far as the basic constructions for **unilateral entity authentication** mechanisms. The standardization for mechanism (11.4.1) is called "ISO Two-Pass Unilateral Authentication Protocol" and is as follows [149]:

1. $B \rightarrow A : R_B \parallel \text{Text1}$;

2. $A \rightarrow B : \text{Token}AB$.

   Here $\text{Token}AB = \text{Text3} \parallel \mathcal{E}_{K_{AB}}(R_B \parallel B \parallel \text{Text2})$.

   Upon receipt of $\text{Token}AB$, Bob should decrypt it; he should accept the run if the decryption reveals his nonce $R_B$ correctly, or reject the run otherwise.

Here and below in the ISO/IEC standards, we shall use precisely the notation of the ISO/IEC for protocol specification. In the ISO/IEC specification, Text1, Text2, etc. are optional fields, $\|$ denotes bit string concatenation, $R_B$ is a nonce generated by Bob.

We should remind the reader of the importance for the encryption algorithm to provide data integrity service which is a necessary condition to allow testing whether or not a decryption result is correct (review Remark 11.2 in §11.4.1.1).

Notice also that while we regard (11.4.1) as a basic message freshness mechanism, its ISO/IEC standard version is an entity authentication mechanism. Therefore the inclusion of the message "$B$," i.e., Bob's identity, in place of $M$ in (11.4.1) becomes vitally important: the inclusion makes it explicit that the ISO/IEC mechanism is for the purpose of establishing Bob's lively correspondence, is an entity authentication protocol in which Bob is the subject of authentication. Abadi and Needham propose a list of prudent engineering principles for cryptographic protocols design [1]; making explicit the identity of the intended authentication subject is an important principle in their list. In §11.7.7 we shall see the danger of omission of the principal's identity in authentication protocols.

The ISO/IEC standardization for mechanism (11.4.2) is called "ISO Two-Pass Unilateral Authentication Protocol Using a Cryptographic Check Function (CCF)," and is as follows [151]:

1. $B \to A : R_B \parallel \text{Text1};$

2. $A \to B : \text{Token}AB.$

   Here[d] $\text{Token}AB = \text{Text2} \parallel f_{K_{AB}}(R_B \parallel B \parallel \text{Text2});$ $f$ is a CCF, and is essentially a cryptographic hash function. The use of the CCF here is keyed.

   Upon receipt of $\text{Token}AB$, $B$ should reconstruct the keyed CCF using the shared key, his nonce, his identity and Text2; he should accept the run if the reconstructed CCF block is identical to the received block, or reject the run otherwise.

The ISO/IEC standardization for mechanism (11.4.3) is called "ISO Public Key Two-Pass Unilateral Authentication Protocol," and is as follows [150]:

1. $B \to A : R_B \parallel \text{Text1};$

2. $A \to B : \text{Cert}A \parallel \text{Token}AB.$

   Here $\text{Token}AB = R_A \parallel R_B \parallel B \parallel \text{Text3} \parallel \text{sig}_A(R_A \parallel R_B \parallel B \parallel \text{Text2});$ $\text{Cert}A$ is Alice's public key certificate (we shall study public-key certification in the next chapter).

   Upon receipt of $\text{Token}AB$, $B$ should verify the signature; he should accept the run if the verification passes, or reject the run otherwise.

---

[d] In [151], Text2 in the cleartext part is mistaken to Text3. Without Text2 in cleartext, $B$ cannot verify the CCF by reconstructing it.

As we have discussed regarding mechanism (11.4.3), in this ISO/IEC protocol, $A$'s free choice of $R_A$ forms part of the measure preventing $A$ from inadvertently signing a message of $B$'s preparation.

### 11.4.1.3  Timestamp Mechanisms

In a **timestamp mechanism**, Alice adds the current time to her message composition which involves a cryptographic operation so that the current time is cryptographically integrated in her message.

Let $T_A$ denote a timestamp created by Alice when she composes her message. This message freshness mechanism has the following non-interactive format:

$$
\begin{array}{ll}
1. & \text{Alice} \;\rightarrow\; \text{Bob: } \mathcal{E}_{K_{AB}}(M, T_A); \\
2. & \text{Bob decrypts the cipher chunk and} \\
& \left\{ \begin{array}{ll} \text{accepts} & \text{if } T_A \text{ is deemed valid} \\ \text{rejects} & \text{otherwise.} \end{array} \right.
\end{array}
\tag{11.4.4}
$$

Analogous to mechanism (11.4.1), the decryption performed by Bob must be tested for data-integrity correctness (review §11.4.1.1 and Remark 11.2 given there). After decryption, Bob can compare the revealed $T_A$ with his own time (we assume that the protocol participants use a global standard time, such as Greenwich Mean Time). If the time difference is sufficiently small as allowed by the application in Bob's mind, then the message $M$ is deemed fresh.

Analogous to our criticism in §11.4.1.1 on encryption without data-integrity as misuse of security service, a more desirable version of the timestamp mechanism using symmetric cryptographic techniques should be as follows:

$$
\begin{array}{ll}
1. & \text{Alice} \;\rightarrow\; \text{Bob: } M, T_A, \mathtt{MDC}(K_{AB}, M, T_A); \\
2. & \text{Bob reconstructs } \mathtt{MDC}(K_{AB}, M, T_A) \text{ and} \\
& \left\{ \begin{array}{ll} \text{accepts} & \text{if two MDCs are identical and } T_A \text{ is deemed valid} \\ \text{rejects} & \text{otherwise.} \end{array} \right.
\end{array}
\tag{11.4.5}
$$

In this version, Bob performs data-integrity validation by checking a one-way transformation style of cryptographic integration between the timestamp and message. Of course, if $M$ also needs confidentiality protection, then it is necessary to use encryption; however, the use of encryption does not rule out the necessity of data-integrity protection.

Obviously, a timestamp mechanism can also be obtained by applying asymmetric cryptographic techniques:

$$
\begin{array}{ll}
1. & \text{Alice} \;\rightarrow\; \text{Bob: } \mathrm{sig}_A(M, T_A); \\
2. & \text{Bob verifies the signature and} \\
& \left\{ \begin{array}{ll} \text{accepts} & \text{if signature verification passes \& } T_A \text{ is deemed valid} \\ \text{rejects} & \text{otherwise.} \end{array} \right.
\end{array}
\tag{11.4.6}
$$

A timestamp mechanism avoids the need for interaction, and is therefore suitable for applications which involves no interaction, e.g., in an electronic mail application. However, the disadvantage of a timestamp mechanism is that synchronized time clocks are required and must be maintained securely. This can be difficult. Difficulties, precautions and objections to timestamps have been well-documented in the literature [29, 35, 117, 100].

In the basic protocol constructions introduced so far, a nonce or a timestamp are special message components. They play the role of identifying the freshness of other messages which are cryptographically integrated with them. We shall use **freshness identifier** to refer to a nonce or a timestamp.

### 11.4.1.4 Standardization of Timestamp Mechanisms

The ISO/IEC have also standardized timestamp mechanisms for authentication protocols.

The ISO/IEC standardization for mechanism (11.4.4) is called "ISO Symmetric Key One-Pass Unilateral Authentication Protocol" [149] and is as follows:

1. $A \to B : \mathrm{Token}AB$.

Here $\mathrm{Token}AB = \mathrm{Text2} \parallel \mathcal{E}_{K_{AB}}( \genfrac{}{}{0pt}{}{T_A}{N_A} \parallel B \parallel \mathrm{Text1})$.

Again, because this simple mechanism uses an encryption-decryption approach, we should recall Remark 11.2 in §11.4.1.1 for the importance for the encryption algorithm to serve data-integrity protection.

Here $\genfrac{}{}{0pt}{}{T_A}{N_A}$ denotes the choice between the use of $T_A$, which is a timestamp, and $N_A$, which is a **sequence number**. In the case of using a sequence number, Alice and Bob maintain a synchronized sequence number (e.g., a counter) so that the sequence number $N_A$ will increase in a manner known to Bob. After a successful receipt and validation of a sequence number, each of the two principals should update its sequence-number keeper to the new state.

There are two disadvantages in a sequence-number mechanism. First, a set of state information must be maintained for each potential communication partner; this can be difficult for applications in an open environment where each principal may communicate with many other principals. Therefore a sequence-number mechanism does not scale well. Secondly, management of a sequence-number keeper can be very troublesome in the presence of communication errors, either genuine ones or deliberate ones (such as a result of a **denial-of-service attack**). Recall our convention made in §11.3 that an authentication protocol should be stateless; a stateful protocol cannot function properly in a hostile environment. We therefore do not recommend a sequence-number mechanism even though such mechanisms have been documented in ISO/IEC standards.

The ISO/IEC standardization for mechanism (11.4.5) is called "ISO One-Pass Unilateral Authentication with Cryptographic Check Functions" [151], and is as follows:

1. $A \rightarrow B : \text{Token}AB$.

Here[e] $\text{Token}AB = \begin{matrix} T_A \\ N_A \end{matrix} \parallel B \parallel \text{Text1} \parallel f_{K_{AB}}(\begin{matrix} T_A \\ N_A \end{matrix} \parallel B \parallel \text{Text1}); f$ is a keyed CCF, e.g., a keyed hash function.

The reader may have already predicted the following named protocol as the public-key counterpart for encryption and cryptographic-check-function versions: "ISO Public Key One-Pass Unilateral Authentication Protocol" [150]:

1. $A \rightarrow B : \text{Cert}A \parallel \text{Token}AB$.

Here $\text{Token}AB = \begin{matrix} T_A \\ N_A \end{matrix} \parallel B \parallel \text{Text2} \parallel \text{sig}_A(\begin{matrix} T_A \\ N_A \end{matrix} \parallel B \parallel \text{Text1})$.

### 11.4.1.5  Non-standard Mechanisms

We have introduced so far several basic constructions for building authentication protocols. It is not difficult at all to imagine numerous other variations which can achieve the same purpose as has been achieved by the introduced basic constructions. For example, a variation for mechanism (11.4.1) using symmetric cryptographic techniques can be

$$
\begin{array}{lll}
1. & \text{Bob} \rightarrow \text{Alice}: & Bob, \mathcal{E}_{K_{AB}}(M, N_B); \\
2. & \text{Alice} \rightarrow \text{Bob}: & N_B; \\
3. & \text{Bob} & \left\{ \begin{array}{ll} \text{accepts} & \text{if the returned nonce is correct} \\ \text{rejects} & \text{otherwise.} \end{array} \right.
\end{array} \quad (11.4.7)
$$

For another example, a variation for mechanism (11.4.3) using asymmetric cryptographic techniques can be:

$$
\begin{array}{lll}
1. & \text{Bob} \rightarrow \text{Alice}: & \mathcal{E}_{K_A}(M, Bob, N_B); \\
2. & \text{Alice} \rightarrow \text{Bob}: & N_B; \\
3. & \text{Bob} & \left\{ \begin{array}{ll} \text{accepts} & \text{if the returned nonce is correct} \\ \text{rejects} & \text{otherwise.} \end{array} \right.
\end{array} \quad (11.4.8)
$$

Here $\mathcal{E}_{K_A}$ denotes a public-key encryption algorithm under Alice's public key. In these two variations, Bob validates Alice's lively correspondence by encrypting a

---

[e]As in Footnote d, [151] mistakenly specifies Text2 in the cleartext part of Text1, and so $B$ may not be able to check the CCF.

freshness identifier and testing if she can perform timely decryption. We shall use *encryption-then-decryption* (of freshness identifier) to refer to these mechanisms.

While performing encryption-then-decryption of freshness identifier does provide a means for validating the lively correspondence of an intended communication partner, such a mechanism is not desirable for constructing authentication protocols. In such a mechanism Alice can be used as a decryption oracle (see §7.8.2.1 and 8.9 for the meaning of an oracle service) and inadvertently disclose confidential information. For example, Malice may record a ciphertext chunk from a confidential conversation between Alice and Bob, and insert it in a protocol which uses an encryption-then-decryption mechanism; then Alice may be tricked into disclosing the confidential conversation. Recall our convention for honest principals (in §11.3): Alice may misinterpret a message as a nonce and therefore return the "nonce" by faithfully following the "protocol instruction."

The undesirability of encryption-then-decryption mechanisms has also been manifested by the fact that the ISO/IEC standardization process has not been considered to standardize such a mechanism. That is part of the reason why we name mechanisms in (11.4.7) and (11.4.8) as non-standard ones.

However, many authentication protocols have been designed to use an encryption-then-decryption mechanism. We will analyze several such protocols in §17.2; there we shall identify as the use of the non-standard mechanisms is the main cause of the security flaws in those protocols.

## 11.4.2 Mutual Authentication

The basic mechanisms for message freshness or principal-liveness introduced so far achieve so-called "unilateral authentication" which means that only one of the two protocol participants is authenticated. In **mutual authentication**, both communicating entities are authenticated to each other.

ISO and IEC have standardized a number of mechanisms for mutual authentication. A signature based mechanism named "ISO Public Key Three-Pass Mutual Authentication Protocol" [150] is specified in Prot 11.1. We choose to specify this mechanism in order to expose a common misunderstanding on mutual authentication.

One might want to consider that mutual authentication is simply twice unilateral authentication; that is, mutual authentication could be achieved by applying one of the basic unilateral authentication protocols in §11.4.1 twice in the opposite directions. However, this is not generally true!

A subtle relationship between mutual authentication and unilateral authentication was not clearly understood in an early stage of the ISO/IEC standardization process for Prot 11.1. In several early standardization drafts for Prot 11.1 [145, 132],

---

**Protocol 11.1:** ISO Public Key Three-Pass Mutual Authentication Protocol

PREMISE:  A has public key certificate $\text{Cert}_A$;
                  B has public key certificate $\text{Cert}_B$;

GOAL:       They achieve mutual authentication.

1. $B \to A : R_B$;

2. $A \to B : \text{Cert}_A, \text{Token}AB$;

3. $B \to A : \text{Cert}_B, \text{Token}BA$.
      Here
      $\text{Token}AB = R_A \parallel R_B \parallel B \parallel \text{sig}_A(R_A \parallel R_B \parallel B)$;
      $\text{Token}BA = R_B \parallel R_A \parallel A \parallel \text{sig}_B(R_B \parallel R_A \parallel A)$.

($*$ optional text fields are omitted. $*$)

---

$\text{Token}BA$ was slightly different from that in the current version:

$$\text{Token}BA = R'_B \parallel R_A \parallel A \parallel \text{sig}_B(R'_B \parallel R_A \parallel A).$$

The early draft intentionally disallowed $B$ to reuse his challenge nonce $R_B$ in order to avoid him signing a string which is partly defined, and fully known in advance, by $A$. Apart from this reasonable consideration, $\text{Token}BA$ in the early drafts was a syntactic and symmetric mirror image of $\text{Token}AB$. This version survived through a few revisions of ISO/IEC 9798-3, until an attack was discovered by the Canadian member body of ISO [145]. The attack is hence widely known as the "Canadian Attack." The attack is due to Wiener (see §12.9 of [200]). In addition to the ISO documentation, Diffie, van Oorschot and Wiener discuss the attack in [100]. We shall therefore also call the attack Wiener's attack.

### 11.4.2.1  Wiener's Attack (the Canadian Attack)

Wiener's attack on an early draft for "ISO Public Key Three-Pass Mutual Authentication Protocol" is given in Attack 11.1 (recall our notation agreed in §2.6.2 for describing Malice sending and intercepting messages in a masquerading manner).

After the discovery of Wiener's attack, the ISO/IEC 9798 series for standard-

---

**Attack 11.1:** Wiener's Attack on ISO Public Key Three-Pass Mutual Authentication Protocol

PREMISE:   In addition to that of Prot 11.1,
     Malice has public key certificate $\text{Cert}_M$;

1. $\text{Malice}(\text{“}B\text{”}) \to A : R_B$

2. $A \to \text{Malice}(\text{“}B\text{”}) : \text{Cert}_A, R_A \parallel R_B \parallel B \parallel \text{sig}_A(R_A \parallel R_B \parallel B)$

   1'. $\text{Malice}(\text{“}A\text{”}) \to B : R_A$

   2'. $B \to \text{Malice}(\text{“}A\text{”}) : \text{Cert}_B, R'_B \parallel R_A \parallel A \parallel \text{sig}_B(R'_B \parallel R_A \parallel A)$

3. $\text{Malice}(\text{“}B\text{”}) \to A : \text{Cert}_B, R'_B \parallel R_A \parallel A \parallel \text{sig}_B(R'_B \parallel R_A \parallel A)$

CONSEQUENCE:
$A$ thinks that it is $B$ who has initiated the run and accepts $B$'s identity; but $B$ did not initiate the run, and is still awaiting for terminating a run started by Malice(“$A$”).

---

ization of authentication protocols start to take a cautious approach to mutual authentication. If TokenAB appears in a unilateral authentication protocol, then in a mutual authentication protocol which is augmented from the unilateral version, the matching counterpart TokenBA for mutual authentication will have a context-sensitive link to TokenAB; this link is usually made via reusing a freshness identifier used in the same (i.e., current) run.

In the current version of "ISO Public Key Three-Pass Mutual Authentication Protocol" (i.e., Prot 11.1 which has been fixed from the early version vulnerable to Wiener's attack), $A$ is explicitly instructed to maintain the state regarding $B$'s nonce $R_B$ until the current run terminates.

## 11.4.3   Authentication Involving Trusted Third Party

In the basic constructions of authentication protocols introduced in this chapter so far, we have assumed that the two protocol participants either already share a secure channel (in the cases of the constructions using symmetric cryptographic techniques), or one knows the public key of the other (in the cases of the constructions using asymmetric cryptographic techniques). So we may say that these protocol constructions are for use by principals who already know each other. Then why do they still want to run an authentication protocol? One simple answer is that they want to refresh the secure channel between them by reconfirming a lively correspondence between them.

Another answer, a better one, is that these basic protocol constructions actually form building blocks for authentication protocols which are for a more general and standard mode of communications in an open system environment.

The standard mode of communications in an open system is that principals "interact then forget." An open system is too large for a principal to maintain the state information about its communications with other principals in the system. If two principals, who may be unknown to each other, want to conduct secure communications, they will first establish a secure channel. In modern cryptography, a secure communication channel is underpinned by a cryptographic key. Therefore, the two principals who wish to establish a secure channel between them should run an authentication protocol which has a sub-task of establishing an authenticated key. Such a protocol is called an authenticated key establishment protocol. Upon completion of a session of secure communication which is underpinned by the key established, the two principals will promptly throw the channel away. Here, "throw the channel away" means that a principal forgets the key underpinning that channel and will never reuse it anymore. That is why a secure channel established as an output of a run of an authenticated key establishment protocol is often called a session channel and the output key underpinning the channel is called a **session key**.

The standard architecture for principals to run authentication and key establishment protocols in an open system is to use a centralized authentication service from a **trusted third party** or a TTP. Such a TTP service may be an online one, or an offline one. In the next chapter we shall introduce the authentication frameworks for authentication services provided by an offline TTP.

In authentication services provided by an online TTP, the TTP has a long-term relationship with a large number of subjects in the system or in a subsystem. Authentication and/or authenticated key establishment protocols under the online TTP architecture are so designed that they are built upon the basic protocol constructions in §11.4.1 and §11.4.2 where one of the two "already known to each other" principals is the TTP, and the other is a subject. Cryptographic operation performed by the TTP can imply or introduce a proper cryptographic operation performed by a subject. With the help from the TTP, a secure channel between any two subjects can be established even if the two principals may not know each other at all. In Chapter 2 we have already seen a number of such protocols, where we name the TTP Trent.

The ISO/IEC standards for authentication protocols (the 9798 series) have two standard constructions involving an online trusted third party [149]. One of them is named "ISO Four-Pass Authentication Protocol" and the other, "ISO Five-Pass Authentication Protocol." These two protocols achieve mutual entity authentication and authenticated session key establishment. We shall, however, not specify these two protocols here for two reasons.

First, these protocols are built upon applying the basic protocol constructions we have introduced in §11.4.1 and §11.4.2, and therefore, in terms of providing design principles, they will not offer us anything new or positive in terms of conducting our further study of the topic. On the contrary, they contain a prominent feature of standardization which we do not wish to introduce in a textbook: many optional fields which obscure the simple ideas behind the protocols.

Secondly, they already have a "normal size" of authentication protocols, and should no longer be considered as building blocks for constructing authentication protocols for higher-level applications. Moreover, they actually contain some undesirable features such as a sequence number maintained by the protocol participants (including TTP, i.e., stateful TTP!). Therefore, these two protocols must not be considered as model protocol constructions for any future protocol designers! On the contrary again, great care should be taken if either of these two protocols is to be applied in real applications.

We shall look at an entity authentication protocol involving TTP. However, this protocol is an insecure one: it is vulnerable to several kinds of attacks which we will expose in a later section.

### 11.4.3.1 The Woo-Lam Protocol

The protocol is due to Woo and Lam [303] and hence we name it the Woo-Lam Protocol. The protocol is specified in Prot 11.2.

By choosing to introduce the Woo-Lam Protocol, we do *not* recommend it as a model protocol. On the contrary, not only is this protocol fatally flawed in several ways, although it has several different repaired versions which are all still flawed, it also contains undesirable design features we should expose, criticize and identify as one fundamental reason for the discovered flaws in it. So we think that the Woo-Lam Protocol serves a useful role in our study of the difficult matter of designing correct authentication protocols.

The goal of this protocol is for Alice to authenticate herself to Bob even though the two principals do not know each other initially.

Initially, since Alice and Bob do not know each other, Alice's cryptographic capability can only be shown to Trent: she encrypts Bob's nonce $N_B$ using her long term key shared with Trent (step 3). Trent, as TTP, will honestly follow the protocol and decrypt the ciphertext formed by Alice (after receiving the message in step 4). Finally, when Bob sees his fresh nonce retrieved from the cipher chunk from Trent, he can conclude: Trent's honest cryptographic operation is only possible after

---

**Protocol 11.2:** The Woo-Lam Protocol

PREMISE:    Alice and Trent share a symmetric key $K_{AT}$,
            Bob and Trent share a symmetric key $K_{BT}$;

GOAL:       Alice authenticates herself to Bob
            even though Bob does not know her.


1. Alice $\rightarrow$ Bob: *Alice*;

2. Bob $\rightarrow$ Alice: $N_B$;

3. Alice $\rightarrow$ Bob: $\{N_B\}_{K_{AT}}$;

4. Bob $\rightarrow$ Trent: $\{Alice, \{N_B\}_{K_{AT}}\}_{K_{BT}}$;

5. Trent $\rightarrow$ Bob: $\{N_B\}_{K_{BT}}$;

6. Bob decrypts the cipher chunk using $K_{BT}$, and accepts if the decryption returns his nonce correctly; he rejects otherwise.

---

Alice's cryptographic operation, and both of these operations are on his nonce which he has deemed fresh; thus, Alice's identity and her liveness have been demonstrated and confirmed.

On the one hand, the Woo-Lam Protocol can be viewed as being built upon applying a standard protocol construction which we have introduced and recommended in §11.4.1.1. For example, message lines 2 and 3 are compatible with mechanism (11.4.1); the same mechanism is also applied in message lines 3 and 4.

We shall defer the revelation of several security flaws in the Woo-Lam Protocol to §11.7. In addition, this protocol has a deeper undesirable design feature which we believe to be responsible for its security flaws. However, we shall further defer our analysis and criticism of that undesirable feature to §17.2.1 where we investigate formal approaches to developing correct authentication protocols.

# 11.5  Password-based Authentication

Because it is easily memorable by the human brain, **password-based authentication** is widely applied in the "user-host" mode of remotely accessed computer systems. In this type of authentication, a user and a host share a password which is essentially a long-term but rather small-size symmetric key.

So a user $U$ who wishes to use the service of a host $H$ must first be initialized by $H$ and issued a password. $H$ keeps an archive of all users' passwords. Each entry of the archive is a pair $(\mathrm{ID}_U, P_U)$ where $\mathrm{ID}_U$ is the identity of $U$, and $P_U$ is the password of $U$. A straightforward password-based protocol for $U$ to access $H$ can be as follows:

1. $U \rightarrow H : \mathrm{ID}_U$;

2. $H \rightarrow U :$ "Password";

3. $U \rightarrow H : P_U$;

4. $H$ finds entry $(\mathrm{ID}_U, P_U)$ from its archive;

   Access is granted if $P_U$ received matches the archive.

We should note that this protocol does not actually achieve any sense of entity authentication, not even a unilateral authentication from $U$ to $H$. This is because no part of the protocol involves a freshness identifier for identifying lively correspondence of $U$. Nevertheless, the term "password authentication" began to be used in the early 1970s when a user accessed a mainframe host from a dumb terminal and the communication link between the host and the terminal was a dedicated line and was not attackable. Under such a setting of devices and communications, the above protocol does provide unilateral entity authentication from $U$ to $H$.

However, under a remote and open network communication setting, because no principal in the password protocol performs any cryptographic operation, this protocol has two serious problems.

The first problem is the vulnerability of the password file kept in $H$. The stored password file in $H$ may be read by Malice (now Malice is an insider who can even be a system administrator). With the password file, Malice obtains all rights of all users; he can gain access to $H$ by impersonating a user and cause undetectable damage to the impersonated user or even to the whole system. Obviously, causing damage under a user's name lowers the risk of Malice being detected.

The second problem with the simple password-based remote access protocol is that a password travels from $U$ to $H$ in cleartext and therefore it can be eavesdropped by Malice. This attack is called **online password eavesdropping**.

## 11.5.1   Needham's Password Protocol and its Realization in the UNIX Operating System

Needham initiates an astonishingly simple and effective method to overcome the secure storage of passwords in a host (see "Acknowledgements" in [106], see also [134]). The host $H$ should use a one-way function to encode the passwords, that

---

**Protocol 11.3:** Needham's Password Authentication Protocol

PREMISE:   User $U$ and Host $H$ have setup $U$'s password entry
$(\text{ID}_U, f(P_U))$ where $f$ is a one-way function;
$U$ memorizes password $P_U$;

GOAL:       $U$ logs in $H$ using her/his password.

1. $U \rightarrow H : \text{ID}_U$;

2. $H \rightarrow U :$ "Input Password:";

3. $U \rightarrow H : P_U$;

4. $H$ applies $f$ on $P_U$, finds entry $(\text{ID}_U, f(P_U))$ form its archive;

Access is granted if the computed $f(P_U)$ matches the archived.

---

is, the entry $(\text{ID}_U, P_U)$ should be replaced with $(\text{ID}_U, f(P_U))$ where $f$ is a one-way function which is extremely difficult to invert. The simple "password protocol" given above should also be modified to one shown in Prot 11.3.

Prot 11.3 is realized as the password authentication scheme for the UNIX[f] operating system. In this realization, the function $f$ is realized using the DES encryption algorithm (§7.6). The system at the host $H$ stores in a password file a user's identity (UID) and a ciphertext generated from a cryptographic transformation of the string of 64 zeros (as input) where the transformation is the DES encryption which uses the user's password $P_U$ as the encryption key. In order to prevent the use of off-the-shelf high-speed DES hardware to crack passwords, the transformation $f(P_U)$ is actually not a pure encryption in the DES. Instead, it repeats 25 successive rounds of the DES encryption in conjunction with a varying method called "bit-swapping permutation." The "bit-swapping permutation" is on the output ciphertext block from each round. In each round, certain bits in the ciphertext block output from the DES encryption are swapped according to a 12-bit random number called **salt** which is also stored in the password file. The ciphertext block after the "bit-swapping permutation" is then used as the input to the next round of the DES encryption. For details of the scheme, see [208].

In this way, the transformation $f(P_U)$ using the DES function can be considered as a keyed and parameterized one-way hashing of the constant string $0^{64}$ where the key is $P_U$ and the parameter is the salt. With the involvement of the salt, a password entry stored in the password file in $H$ should be viewed as $(\text{ID}_U, salt, f(P_U, salt))$,

---

[f] UNIX is a trademark of Bell Laboratories.

although for clarity in exposition, we shall still use $f(P_U)$ in place of $f(P_U, salt)$.

Now in the UNIX realization of Needham's Password Protocol, stealing $f(P_U)$ from $H$ will no longer provide Malice with an easy way to attack the system. First, $f(P_U)$ cannot be used in Prot 11.3 because using it will cause $H$ to compute $f(f(P_U))$ and fail the test. Secondly, it is computationally infeasible to invert the one-way function $f$, especially considering the transformation involves 25 rounds of "bit-swapping permutation." So if the users choose their passwords properly so that a password cannot be guessed easily, then it will be very difficult for Malice to find $P_U$ from $f(P_U)$. (We shall discuss the password guessing problem in §11.5.3.)

Although confidentiality of the password file becomes less of a concern, the data-integrity of the file must be maintained. Still, the protocol is vulnerable to online password eavesdropping attack. A one-time password scheme is proposed to tackle this attack. Let us now describe it.

## 11.5.2    A One-time Password Scheme (and a Flawed Modification)

Lamport proposes a simple idea to thwart online password eavesdropping [176]. The technique can be considered as a one-time password scheme. Here "one-time" means that the passwords transmitted from a given $U$ to $H$ do not repeat, however they are computationally related one another. Now, a password eavesdropped from a protocol run is no good for further use, and hence the password eavesdropping problem is successfully prevented.

In the user initialization time, a password entry of $U$ is set to $(\mathrm{ID}_U, f^n(P_U))$ where

$$f^n(P_U) \stackrel{\text{def}}{=} \underbrace{f(\cdots (f(P_U)) \cdots)}_{n}$$

for a large integer $n$. The user $U$ still memorizes $P_U$ as in the case of the Password Authentication Protocol.

When $U$ and $H$ engages in the first run of password authentication, upon prompted by "Password" (message line 2 in the Password Authentication Protocol), a computing device of $U$, such as a client platform or a calculator, will ask $U$ to key in $P_U$, and will then compute $f^{n-1}(P_U)$ by repeatedly applying $f$ $n-1$ times. This can be efficiently done even for a large $n$ (e.g., $n = 1000$). The result will be sent to $H$ as in message line 3 in the Password Authentication Protocol.

Upon receipt of $f^{n-1}(P_U)$, $H$ will apply $f$ once on the received password to obtain $f^n(P_U)$ and then performs the correctness test as in step 4 in the Password Authentication Protocol. If the test passes, it assumes that the received value is $f^{n-1}(P_U)$ and must have been computed from $P_U$ which was set-up in the user initialization, and hence it must be $U$ at the other end of the communication. So $U$ is allowed to enter the system. In addition, $H$ will update $U$'s password entry:

replace $f^n(P_U)$ with $f^{n-1}(P_U)$.

In the next run of the protocol, $U$ (whose computing device) and $H$ will be in the state of using $f^{n-2}(P_U)$ with respect to $f^{n-1}(P_U)$, as in the previous case of using $f^{n-1}(P_U)$ with respect to $f^n(P_U)$. The protocol is hence a stateful one on a counter number descending from $n$ to 1. When the counter number reaches 1, $U$ and $H$ have to reset a new password.

The method requires $U$ and $H$ to be synchronous for the password state: when $H$ is in state of using $f^i(P_U)$ then $U$ must be in state of sending $f^{i-1}(P_U)$. This synchronization can be lost if the communication link is "unreliable" or when the system "crashes." Notice that "unreliability" or a "crash" can be the working of Malice!

Lamport consider a simple method to reestablish synchronization if it is lost [176]. The method is essentially to have the system to "jump forward:" if $H$'s state is $f^j(P_U)$ while $U$'s state is $f^k(P_U)$ with $j \neq k + 1$, then synchronization is lost. The system should "jump forward" to a state $f^i(P_U)$ for $H$ and $f^{i-1}(P_U)$ for $U$ where $i \leq \min(j, k)$. It is clear that this way of resynchronization requires mutually authenticated communications between $H$ and $U$, however, no detail for this necessity is given in Lamport's short technical note.

Lamport's password-based remote access scheme has been modified and implemented into a "one-time password" system named **S/KEY**[g] [136]. The S/KEY modification attempts to overcome the "unreliable communication" problem by $H$ maintaining a counter number $c$ for $U$. In the user initialization time $H$ stores $U$'s password entry $(\text{ID}_U, f^c(P_U), c)$ where $c$ is initialized to $n$. Prot 11.4 specifies the S/KEY scheme.

Clearly, in Prot 11.4, $U$ and $H$ will no longer lose synchronization and thereby unreliable communication link will no longer be a problem.

Unfortunately, the S/KEY modification to Lamport's original technique is a dangerous one. We notice that a password-based remote access protocol achieves, at best, an identification of $U$ to $H$. Thus, the counter number sent from $H$ can actually be one from Malice, or one modified by him. The reader may consider how Malice should, e.g., modify the counter number and how to follow up an attack. The reader is encouraged to attack the S/KEY Protocol before reading §11.7.2.

One may want to argue: "the S/KEY Protocol cannot be more dangerous than Needham's Password Authentication Protocol (Prot 11.3) which transmits passwords in cleartext!" We should however notice that Needham's Password Authentication Protocol never claims security for preventing an online password eavesdropping attack. The S/KEY Protocol is designed to have this claim, which unfortunately does not stand.

---

[g]S/KEY is a trademark of Bellcore.

---

**Protocol 11.4:** The S/KEY Protocol

PREMISE:  User $U$ and Host $H$ have setup $U$'s initial password entry
$(\text{ID}_U, f^n(P_U), n)$ where $f$ is a cryptographic hash function;
$U$ memorizes password $P_U$;
The current password entry of $U$ in $H$ is
$(\text{ID}_U, f^c(P_U), c)$ for $1 \le c \le n$.

GOAL:  $U$ authenticates to $H$ without transmitting $P_U$ in cleartext.

1. $U \to H : \text{ID}_U$;

2. $H \to U : c$, "Input Password:";

3. $U \to H : Q = f^{c-1}(P_U)$;

4. $H$ finds entry $(\text{ID}_U, f^c(P_U), c)$ from its archive;

   Access is granted if $f(Q) = f^c(P_U)$, and $U$'s password entry is updated
   to $(\text{ID}_U, Q, c - 1)$.

---

## 11.5.3 Add Your Own Salt: Encrypted Key Exchange (EKE)

Most password-based systems advise users to choose their passwords such that a
password should have eight keyboard (ASCII) characters. A password of this length
is memorable by most users without writing down. Since an ASCII character is
represented by a byte (8 bits), an eight-character password can be translated to a
64-bit string. A space of 64-bit strings has $2^{64}$ elements and is therefore comfortably
large. So it seems that an 8-key-board-character password should resist guessing
and even automated searching attacks mounted by a non-dedicated attacker.

However, the "64-bit" password is not a true story. Although the information
rate of the full set of ASCII characters is not substantially below 8 bits/character
(review §3.8 for information rate of a language), people usually do not choose their
passwords using random characters in the ASCII table. In contrast, they choose
bad passwords that are easily memorable. A typical bad password is a dictionary
word, or a person's name, all in lower case, maybe trailed by a digit or two. Shannon
estimated that the rate of English is in the range of 1.0 to 1.5 bits/character ([267],
this estimate is based on English words of all lower case letters, see §3.8). Thus,
in fact, the space of 8-character passwords should be much much smaller than $2^{64}$,
and may be significantly much smaller if many passwords in the space are bad ones
(lower case alphabetic, person's names, etc.). The smaller password space permits

an **offline dictionary attack**. In such an attack, Malice uses $f(P_U)$ to search through a dictionary of bad passwords for the matching $P_U$. Because the attack is mounted offline, it can be automated and can be fast. We should notice that Lamport's one-time password scheme does not provide protection against offline dictionary attacks either: Malice can eavesdrop the current state value $i$ and $f^i(P_U)$ and hence can conduct the dictionary search.

Bellovin and Merritt propose an attractive protocol for achieving secure password based authentication. Their protocol is named **encrypted key exchange (EKE)** [30]. The EKE Protocol protects the password against not only online eavesdropping, but also offline dictionary attacks. The technique used in the EKE scheme is essentially **probabilistic encryption**. In Chapter 14 we shall study general techniques for probabilistic encryption. Here, the reader may consider the trick as "adding your own salt" to a password.

Unlike in the password based protocols (Prot 11.3 or Prot 11.4) where $H$ only possesses a one-way image of $U$'s password, in the EKE Protocol $U$ and $H$ share a password $P_U$. The shared password will be used as a symmetric cryptographic key, though, as we have mentioned, this symmetric key is chosen from a rather small space.

The EKE Protocol is specified in Prot 11.5.

The ingenuity of the EKE Protocol is in the first two steps. In step 1, the cipher chunk $P_U(\mathcal{E}_U)$ is a result of encrypting a piece of one-time and random information $\mathcal{E}_U$ under the shared password $P_U$. In step 2, the content which is doubly encrypted in the cipher chunk $P_U(\mathcal{E}_U(K))$ is another one-time and random number: a session key $K$. Since $P_U$ is human-brain memorable and hence is small, the random strings $\mathcal{E}_U$ and $K$ must have larger sizes than that of $P_U$. So the two cipher chunks in message lines 1 and 2 can hide $P_U$ in such a way that $P_U$ is statistically independent from these two cipher chunks.

We must emphasize that it is the one-time randomness of $\mathcal{E}_U$ that plays the "adding you own salt" trick. Should the "public key" be not one-time, the unique functionality of the EKE Protocol would have failed completely: it would even be possible to facilitate Malice to search the password $P_U$ using the weakness of a textbook public-key encryption algorithm (see, e.g., a "meet-in-the-middle" attack in §8.9).

If the nonces $N_U$, $N_H$ encrypted in message lines 3, 4 and 5 are generated at random and have adequately large sizes (i.e, larger than that of the session key $K$), then they further hide the session key $K$ in the same fashion as the password $P_U$ is hidden in the first two messages. Thus, $P_U$ remains statistically independent from any messages passed in the EKE Protocol.

The statistical independence of the password $P_U$ from the messages passed in a protocol run means that the password is hidden from an eavesdropper in an information-theoretically secure sense (see §7.5). So a passive eavesdropper can no

**Protocol 11.5:** Encrypted Key Exchange (EKE)

PREMISE:   User $U$ and Host $H$ share a password $P_U$;
The system has agreed on a symmetric encryption algorithm,
$K()$ denotes symmetric encryption keyed by $K$;
$U$ and $H$ have also agreed on an asymmetric encryption scheme,
$\mathcal{E}_U$ denotes asymmetric encryption under $U$'s key.

GOAL:       $U$ and $H$ achieve mutual entity authentication,
they also agree on a shared secret key.

1. $U$ generates a random "public" key $\mathcal{E}_U$, and sends to $H$:

$$U, P_U(\mathcal{E}_U);$$

( $*$ the "public" key is in fact not public, it is the encryption key of an asymmetric encryption algorithm $*$ )

2. $H$ decrypts the cipher chunk using $P_U$ and retrieves $\mathcal{E}_U$;
$H$ generates random symmetric key $K$, and sends to $U$:

$$P_U(\mathcal{E}_U(K));$$

3. $U$ decrypts the doubly encrypted cipher chunk and obtains $K$;
$U$ generates a nonce $N_U$, and sends to $H$:

$$K(N_U);$$

4. $H$ decrypts the cipher chunk using $K$, generates a nonce $N_H$, and sends to $U$:
$$K(N_U, N_H);$$

5. $U$ decrypts the cipher chunk using $K$, and return to $H$:

$$K(N_H);$$

6. If the challenge-response in steps 3, 4, 5 is successful, logging-in is granted and the parties proceed further secure communication using the shared key $K$.

longer mount an offline dictionary attack on $P_U$ using the protocol messages. The only possible other ways to attack the protocol are either to try to guess $P_U$ directly, or to mount an active attack by modifying protocol messages. The guessing attack is an uninteresting one, it can never be prevented, however fortunately, it can never be effective. An active attack, on the other hand, will be detected with a high probability by an honest protocol participant, and will cause a run being promptly abandoned.

The encryption of a random public key in step 1 by $U$, and that of a random session key in step 2 by $H$, are what we have referred to as "add your own salt" to the password $P_U$. The ever changing "salt" keeps an attacker out of step. Therefore, the first two message lines in the EKE Protocol provide an ingenious technical novelty. The message lines 3, 4 and 5 form a conventional challenge-response-based mutual authentication protocol. Indeed they can be replaced by a suitable mutual protocol construction based on a shared symmetric key.

The EKE Protocol is very suitable for being realized using the Diffie-Hellman key exchange mechanism. Let $\alpha$ generate a group of order larger than $2^{64} > 2^{|P_U|}$. Then in step 1, $U$'s computing device picks at random $x \in (0, 2^{64})$ and computes $\mathcal{E}_U = \alpha^x$, and in step 2, $H$ picks at random $y \in (0, 2^{64})$ and computes $\mathcal{E}_U(K) = \alpha^y$. The agreed session key between $U$ and $H$ will be $K = \alpha^{xy}$. Now, each party has its own contribution to the agreed session key. In this realization, the group generator $\alpha$ can be agreed between $U$ and $H$ in public: $U$ sends to $H$ the group description (which includes the group generator $\alpha$) in a pre-negotiation step.

Notice that we have only required that $\alpha$ generates a group of order larger than $2^{64}$. This is a very small number as a lower bound for a group order for use by an asymmetric cryptographic system. So the protocol can be very efficient. The small group order renders easy ways to compute discrete logarithm, and hence to solve the computational Diffie-Hellman problem. However, without $\alpha^x$, $\alpha^y$, $\alpha^{xy}$, the ease of solving Diffie-Hellman problem is of no help for finding the password: $P_U$ remains statistically independent in a space of size $2^{64}$. Likewise, for sufficiently large and random nonces encrypted in message lines 3, 4, and 5, the session key $K$ shall remain independent in the group of an order larger than $2^{64}$. Thus, offline dictionary attacks or online key guessing remain difficult.

In essence, the random "salt" added to a password "amplifies" the size of the password space from that of a dictionary to that of the random asymmetric key. This is the trick behind the EKE Protocol.

## 11.6 Authenticated Key Exchange Based on Asymmetric Cryptography

We say that a protocol establishes a shared session key via a **key transport** mechanism if the protocol outputs a shared key which comes from one of the protocol participants. We say that a protocol establishes a shared session key via a **key exchange** (or **key agreement**) mechanism if a run of the protocol outputs a shared key which is a function of all protocol participants' random input. The advantage of key exchange over key transport is that each of the key-sharing parties can have its own control, hence a high confidence, on the quality of the key output.

Apart from the Diffie-Hellman realized EKE protocol, the basic authentication techniques introduced so far, if involving key establishment, are all key transport mechanisms. Now let us introduce a key exchange mechanism.

Key exchange can be achieved by generating a key as the output of a pseudo-random function or a one-way hash function where the key-sharing parties have their own inputs to the function. The most commonly used method is the great discovery of Diffie and Hellman: Diffie-Hellman Key Exchange, which we have considered as a one-way function (see Remark 8.1.3 in §8.4). We have specified Diffie-Hellman Key Exchange in Prot 8.1. This mechanism achieves agreement on a key between two remote principals without using encryption.

Prot 8.1 is the basic version of Diffie-Hellman Key Exchange which achieves unauthenticated key agreement. We have seen a **man-in-the-middle attack** in Attack 8.1 in which Malice shares one key with Alice and another with Bob and hence can relay the "confidential" communications between Alice and Bob. A proper use of Diffie-Hellman Key Exchange must be a variation of Prot 8.1. The simplest variation is a two-party protocol in which Alice knows for sure that $g^b$ is Bob's public key:

$$1. \text{ Alice } \rightarrow \text{ Bob: } Alice, g^a \qquad (11.6.1)$$

where number $a$ is picked at random by Alice from a suitably large integer interval.

After sending the message in (11.6.1), Alice knows that $g^{ab}$ is a key exclusively shared with Bob since for anybody other than herself and Bob, to find $g^{ab}$ is to solve the computational Diffie-Hellman problem (CDH problem, see Definition 8.1 in §8.4) which is assumed computationally infeasible. Since Alice has picked her exponent at random which is new, the agreed key is fresh and this means that the key is authenticated to Alice. However, upon receipt of $g^a$, Bob cannot know with whom he shares the key $g^{ab}$ or whether the key is fresh. Therefore, this simple variation achieves unilateral authenticated key agreement.

Applying various mechanisms introduced so far, it is not difficult to augment mechanism (11.6.1) to one which allows the agreed key to be mutually authenticated. For example, Alice may digitally sign $g^a$ with her identity and a timestamp.

Let us introduce here a well-known authenticated key exchange protocol which is a variation of Diffie-Hellman Key Exchange.

## 11.6.1 The Station-to-Station Protocol

The **Station-to-Station (STS) Protocol** is proposed by Diffie et al. [100].

In the STS Protocol, Alice and Bob have agreed on using a large finite abelian group which is generated by a common element $\alpha$. System-wide users can use a common generator $\alpha$. The reader may review §8.4.1 for cautions to setting up the shared group to be used in the STS Protocol.

Alice and Bob also have their respective public key certificates:

$$\text{Cert}_A = \text{sig}_{CA}(Alice, P_A, \text{desc}\,\langle\alpha\rangle)$$

$$\text{Cert}_B = \text{sig}_{CA}(Bob, P_B, \text{desc}\,\langle\alpha\rangle)$$

where $CA$ is a certification authority (see Chapter 13), $P_A$ and $P_B$ are the public keys of Alice and Bob, respectively, and desc $\langle\alpha\rangle$ is the description of the shared group generated by $\alpha$. In addition, the two parties have also agreed on using a symmetric-key encryption algorithm, which we shall use the notation given in Definition 7.1 (in §7.2). The encryption algorithm can also be agreed upon for system-wide users.

The STS Protocol is specified in Prot 11.6.

It is intended that the STS Protocol should have the following four security properties (several of them are only true if a minor flaw in the protocol is fixed):

**Mutual Entity Authentication**    However this property actually does not hold according to the rigorous definition for authentication given by the authors of the STS Protocol. In [100], Diffie et al. make two mistakes in this respect. We shall discuss them in §11.6.2 and §11.6.3, respectively.

**Mutually Authenticated Key Agreement**    Key agreement is obvious from the Diffie-Hellman key exchange protocol; the freshness of the agreed key is guaranteed if each party has picked her/his random exponent properly; the exclusive sharing of the agreed key is implied by both parties' digital signature on their key agreement material. However, pulling together all these features does not actually result in mutually authenticated key agreement: the property will only hold if a minor flaw in the protocol is fixed.

**Mutual Key Confirmation**    Upon termination of a run, both parties have seen that the other party has used the agreed key to encrypt the key agreement material. Again, the correct mutual key confirmation depends on the correct mutual authentication which only holds if a minor flaw in the protocol is fixed.

**Perfect Forward Secrecy (PFS)**    This is an attractive property of a key establishment protocol which means that if a long-term private key used in a key establishment protocol is compromised at a point in time, the security of any session established earlier than that point will not be effected [135, 100]. The PFS property holds for a key establishment protocol where a session key is properly agreed using the Diffie-Hellman key exchange mechanism. Here in the case of the STS protocol, the long-term keys are the private keys of Alice

**Protocol 11.6:** The Station-to-Station (STS) Protocol

PREMISE:   Alice has her public-key certificate $\text{Cert}_A$,
              Bob has his public-key certificate $\text{Cert}_B$,
              the system-wide users share a large finite abelian group desc $\langle \alpha \rangle$,
              and they agree on a symmetric encryption algorithm $\mathcal{E}$;

GOAL:        Alice and Bob achieves mutual authentication
              and mutually authenticated key agreement.

1. Alice picks a random large integer $x$, and sends to Bob:

$$\alpha^x;$$

2. Bob picks a random large integer $y$, and sends to Alice:

$$\alpha^y, \text{Cert}_B, \mathcal{E}_K(\text{sig}_B(\alpha^y, \alpha^x));$$

3. Alice sends to Bob:

$$\text{Cert}_A, \mathcal{E}_K(\text{sig}_A(\alpha^x, \alpha^y)).$$

Here $K = \alpha^{xy} = \alpha^{yx}$.

WARNING:
This protocol is flawed in a minor way; to be analysed in §11.6.3.

and Bob. Since each session key agreed in a run of the protocol is a one-way function of two ephemeral secrets which will be securely disposed of upon termination of the run, compromise of either of the signing long-term keys cannot have any effect on the secrecy of the previously agreed session keys.

**Anonymity (Deniability)** If the public-key certificates are encrypted inside the respective cipher chunks, then the messages communicated in a run of the protocol will not be revealed to any third party who are involved in the message exchanges. However we should notice that addressing information transmitted in a lower-layer communication protocol may disclose the identities of the protocol participants. Therefore, precisely speaking, "anonymity" should be rephrased to a kind of "deniability" which means that a network monitor cannot prove that a given protocol transcript takes place between two specific principals. Because the STS Protocol is one of the bases for the Internet Key Exchange (IKE) protocol suite for Internet Security [137, 160, 227], this property is a feature in the IKE. We shall study IKE (and this feature) in the next chapter (§12.2).

The STS Protocol, although the version specified in Prot 11.6 is flawed in a very minor way, is an important and influential work in the area of authentication and authenticated key-exchange protocols. It is one of the bases for "Internet Key Exchange (IKE) Protocol" [137, 227] which is an industrial standard authentication protocol for Internet security. We will study IKE in §12.2 and see the influence of the STS Protocol on it.

The paper [100] contains two flaws: a serious one in a simplified version of the STS Protocol for an "authentication only" usage; a minor one in the STS Protocol proper. If a widely recognized protocol design principle is followed (that principle was documented and became widely acknowledged after the publication of [100]), then both flaws disappear. Let us now look at these flaws. Our study of these flaws shall lead to that widely recognized protocol design principle.

## 11.6.2  A Flaw in a Simplified STS Protocol

In order to argue the mutual authentication property, Diffie et al. simplify the STS Protocol into one they name "Authentication-only" STS Protocol (§5.3 of [100]). They claim that the "simplified protocol is essentially the same as the three-way authentication protocol" proposed by ISO. The "ISO protocol" they referred to is in fact what we named (after ISO/IEC's name) the "ISO Public Key Three-Pass Mutual Authentication Protocol" (Prot 11.1 with Wiener's attack having been fixed, see §11.4.2).

The simplified "Authentication-only" STS Protocol is specified in Prot 11.7.

However, Prot 11.7 has an important difference from the ISO Protocol. In this simplified STS Protocol, the signed messages do not contain the identities of the protocol participants, while in the ISO Protocol the signed messages contain the identities. The simplified STS Protocol suffers a "certificate-signature-replacement attack" which is demonstrated in Attack 11.2.

In this attack, Malice, who is a legitimate user of the system and hence has a public-key certificate, waits for Alice to initiate a run. Upon occurrence of such an opportunity, he starts to talk to Bob by impersonating Alice and using her nonce. Upon receipt of Bob's reply, Malice replaces Bob's certificate and signature with his own copies, respectively. Doing so can successfully persuade Alice to sign Bob's nonce, which in turn allows Malice to cheat Bob successfully. This is a perfect attack because neither Alice nor Bob can discover anything wrong.

Notice that in this attack, Malice is not passive in the whole attacking run

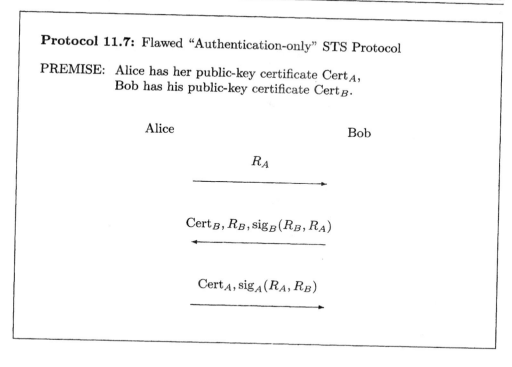

**Protocol 11.7:** Flawed "Authentication-only" STS Protocol

PREMISE:   Alice has her public-key certificate $Cert_A$,
            Bob has his public-key certificate $Cert_B$.

Alice                                                    Bob

$$R_A$$
$$\longrightarrow$$

$$Cert_B, R_B, sig_B(R_B, R_A)$$
$$\longleftarrow$$

$$Cert_A, sig_A(R_A, R_B)$$
$$\longrightarrow$$

orchestrated by him: he signs Bob's nonce and hence successfully persuades Alice to sign Bob's nonce so that he can fool Bob completely. Should Malice be passive, i.e., behave like a wire, then Bob would have never received Alice's signature on his nonce, and thereby would not have been cheated.

This "certificate-signature-replacement attack" does not apply to the STS Protocol because the encryption used in the full version of the protocol prevents Malice from replacing Bob's signature. The attack does not apply to the ISO Protocol (Prot 11.1) either because there, Malice's identity will appear in the message signed by Alice, and hence that message cannot be passed to Bob to fool him.

It is interesting to point out that, in their paper (§5.1 of [100]) Diffie et al. do discuss a similar "certificate-signature-replacement attack" on a dismissed simplification of the STS Protocol where the encryption is removed. That attack has not been tried on the "Authentication-only" STS Protocol, perhaps because the latter looks very similar to the fixed version of the ISO Protocol. The same paper (§6 of [100]) demonstrates Wiener's attack on the flawed version of the ISO Protocol, which is obviously different from the "certificate-signature-replacement attack" (the reader may confirm that Wiener's attack on the flawed version of the ISO Protocol does not apply to the "Authentication-only" STS Protocol). From these entanglements we are witnessing the error-prone nature of authentication protocols.

**Attack 11.2:** An Attack on the "Authentication-only" STS Protocol

PREMISE:   In addition to that in Prot 11.7,
            Malice has his public key certificate $\text{Cert}_M$.
            (* so Malice is also a normal user in the system *)

(* Malice faces Alice using his true identity, but he faces Bob by masquerading as Alice: *)

Alice                              Malice       $\rightarrow$ I'm "Alice" $\rightarrow$     Bob

$$R_A \qquad\qquad\qquad R_A$$

$$\longrightarrow \qquad\qquad \longrightarrow$$

$$\text{Cert}_M, R_B, \text{sig}_M(R_B, R_A) \qquad \text{Cert}_B, R_B, \text{sig}_B(R_B, R_A)$$

$$\longleftarrow \qquad\qquad \longleftarrow$$

$$\text{Cert}_A, \text{sig}_A(R_A, R_B) \qquad\qquad \text{Cert}_A, \text{sig}_A(R_A, R_B)$$

$$\longrightarrow \qquad\qquad \longrightarrow$$

CONSEQUENCE:
Bob thinks he has been talking with Alice while she thinks to have been talking with Malice.

---

Including the identity of the intended verifier inside a signature does indeed constitute a method to fix the flaw. Of course, we do not suggest that adding identity is the only way to fix this flaw. In some applications (e.g., "Internet Key Exchange (IKE) Protocol," see §12.2.3), identities of the protocol participants are desirably omitted in order to obtain a privacy property (see §12.2.4). A novel way of fixing such flaws while keeping the desired privacy property can be devised by using a novel cryptographic primitive, which we shall introduce in a later chapter.

## 11.6.3   A Minor Flaw of the STS Protocol

Lowe discovers a minor attack on the STS Protocol [181]. Before presenting Lowe's attack, let us review a rigorous definition for authentication given by the authors of the STS Protocol.

In [100], Diffie et al. define a secure run of an authentication protocol using the notion of "matching records of runs." Let each protocol participant record messages received during a run. A "matching records of a run" means that the messages originated by one participant must appear in the record of the other participant in the same order of sequence as the messages are sent, and vice versa. Then an insecure run of an authentication protocol (Definition 1 of [100]) is one:

> if any party involved in the run, say Alice, executes the protocol faithfully, accepts the identity of another party, and the following condition holds: at the time that Alice accepts the other party's identity, the other party's record of the partial or full run does not match Alice's record.

Under this definition for an insecure run of an authentication protocol, what is demonstrated in Attack 11.3 qualifies a legitimate attack on the STS Protocol, even though the damage it can cause is very limited.

Lowe's attack is a minor one in the following two senses:

i) In the run part between Alice and Malice, although Malice is successful in fooling Alice, he does not know the shared session key and hence cannot fool Alice any further after the run.

ii) In the run part between Malice and Bob, Malice cannot complete the run, and so this part is not a successful attack.

We however think Lowe's attack qualifies a legitimate attack also for two reasons:

I) Alice accepts the identity of Bob as a result of Malice simply copying bit-by-bit all of Bob's message to Alice. However, in Bob's end, since he sees the communication partner as Malice while he signs Alice's random challenge, his recorded messages do not match those of Alice. Therefore, the attack meets the "insecure run" criterion defined by the STS authors, i.e., mutual authentication actually fails. Of course, as the notion of entity authentication is quite hard to capture precisely, and as the area of study has been developing through mistakes, a verdict of an attack given on the basis of a quite old definition (i.e., that of an "insecure run" given by Diffie et al. [100]) may not be sufficiently convincing. Today, one may well question whether that early definition is correct at all. However, a better question should be: "Will this 'attack' be a concern in practice today?" This is answered in (II).

II) Malice successfully fools Alice into believing a normal run with Bob. Her subsequent requests or preparation for secure communications with Bob will be denied without any explanation since Bob thinks he has never been in communication with Alice. Also, nobody will notify Alice of any abnormality. We

**Attack 11.3:** Lowe's Attack on the STS Protocol (a Minor Flaw)

(∗ Malice faces Bob using his true identity, but he faces Alice by masquerading as Bob: ∗)

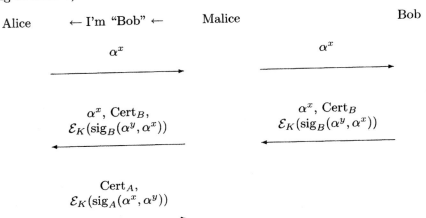

Alice     ← I'm "Bob" ←     Malice                     Bob

CONSEQUENCE:
Alice is fooled perfectly and thinks she has been talking and sharing a session key with Bob, while Bob thinks he has been talking with Malice in an incomplete run. Alice will never be notified of any abnormality, and her subsequent requests or preparation for secure communications with Bob will be denied without any explanation.

should compare this consequence with one resulted from a much less interesting "attack" in which Malice is passive except for cutting the final message from Alice to Bob without letting Bob receive it. In this less interesting "attack," due to the expected matching records, Bob may notify Alice the missed final message. Regarding whether Lowe's attack is a concern in practice today, we may consider that if Alice is in a centralized server's situation, and is under a distributed attack (i.e., is under a mass attack launched by Malice's team distributed over the network), lack of notification from end-users (i.e., from many Bobs) is indeed a concern: the server will reserve resources for many end-users and its capacity to serve the end-users can be drastically powered down. We should particularly notice that in Lowe's attack, Malice and his friends do not use any cryptographic credentials (certificates). So this attack costs them very little. This is again very different from a conventional denial-of-service attack in which Malice and his friends have to talk to Alice in their true names (i.e., with certificates).

For the reason explained in (II), we shall name Lowe's attack a **perfect denial of service attack** against Alice: the attackers succeed using other parties' cryptographic credentials.

This attack can be avoided if the protocol is modified into one which follows a correct and well recognized protocol design principle proposed by Abadi and Needham [1]:

> If the identity of a principal is essential to the meaning of a message, it is prudent to mention the principal's name explicitly in the message.

Indeed, the signed messages in the STS Protocol should include the identities of both protocol participants! This way, the message from and signed by Bob will contain "Malice" so that Malice cannot forward it to Alice in Bob's name, i.e., Malice can no longer fool Alice. Moreover, if the simplified "Authentication-only" STS Protocol is simplified from this identities-in-signature version, then it will not suffer the "certificate-signature-replacement attack" either since now the simplified version is essentially the ISO Protocol (Prot 11.1).

As we have mentioned earlier, the STS Protocol is one of the bases for the "Internet Key Exchange (IKE) Protocol" [137, 160, 227]. As a result, we shall see in §12.2 that the "perfect denial of service attack" will also apply to a couple of modes in IKE.

Finally, we should recap a point we have made in §11.6.2: adding identity of a signature verifier is not the only way to prevent this attack. For example, using a **designated verifier signature** can achieve a better fix while without adding the identity. Such a fix will be a topic in a later chapter.

# 11.7 Typical Attacks on Authentication Protocols

In §2.3 we have agreed that Malice (perhaps by co-working with his friends distributed over an open communication network) is able to eavesdrop, intercept, alter and inject messages in the open communication network, and is good at doing so by impersonating other principals. Viewing from a high layer (the application layer) of communications, Malice's capabilities for mounting these attacks seem like magic: how can Malice be so powerful?

However, viewing from a lower-layer (the network layer) communication protocol, it actually does not require very sophisticated techniques for Malice to mount these attacks. We shall see the technical knowhow for mounting such attacks on a lower-layer communication protocol in §12.2 where we shall also see how communications take place in the network layer. For the time being, let us just accept that Malice has magic-like capabilities. Then, a flawed authentication protocol may permit Malice to mount various types of attacks.

While it is impossible for us to know all the protocol attacking techniques Malice may use (since he will constantly devise new techniques), knowing several typical ones will provide us with insight into how to develop stronger protocols avoiding these attacks. In this section, let us look at several well-known protocol attacking techniques in Malice's portfolio. We should notice that, although we classify these attacking techniques into separate types, Malice may actually apply them in a combined way: a bit of this and a bit of that, until he can end up with a workable attack.

Before we go ahead, we should emphasize the following important point:

**Remark 11.3:** *A successful attack on an authentication or authenticated key establishment protocol usually does not refer to breaking a cryptographic algorithm, e.g., via a complexity theoretic-based cryptanalysis technique. Instead, it usually refers to Malice's unauthorized and undetected acquisition of a cryptographic credential or nullification of a cryptographic service without breaking a cryptographic algorithm. Of course, this is due to an error in protocol design, not one in the cryptographic algorithm.* □

## 11.7.1  Message Replay Attack

In a message replay attack, Malice has previously recorded an old message from a previous run of a protocol and now replays the recorded message in a new run of the protocol. Since the goal of an authentication protocol is to establish lively correspondence of communication parties and the goal is generally achieved via exchanging fresh messages between/among communication partners, replay of old messages in an authentication protocol violates the goal of authentication.

In §2.6.4.2 we have seen an example of message replay attack on the Needham-Schroeder Symmetric-key Authentication protocol (Attack 2.2). Notice that there (review the last paragraph of §2.6.4.2) we have only considered one danger of that message replay attack: the replayed message encrypts an old session key which is assumed vulnerable (Malice may have discovered its value, maybe because it has been discarded by a careless principal, or maybe due to other vulnerabilities of a session key that we have discussed in §2.5).

Another consequence, probably a more serious one, of that attack should be referred to as authentication failure, i.e., absence of a lively correspondence between the two communication partners. Indeed, for that attack to work (review Attack 2.2) Malice does not have to wait for an opportunity that Alice starts a run of the protocol with Bob; he can just start his attack by jumping to message line 3 and replaying the recorded messages, as long as he knows the old session key $K'$:

3.   Malice("Alice") $\rightarrow$ Bob: $\{K', \; Alice\}_{K_{BT}}$;

4.   Bob $\rightarrow$ Malice("Alice"): $\{I'm \; Bob! \; N_B\}_{K'}$;

5.   Malice("Alice") $\rightarrow$ Bob: $\{I'm \; Alice! \; N_B - 1\}_{K'}$.

Now Bob thinks Alice is communicating with him, while in fact Alice is not even online at all.

Message replay is a classic attack on authentication and authenticated key establishment protocols. It seems that we have already established a good awareness of message-replay attacks. This can be evidently seen from our ubiquitous use of freshness identifiers (nonces, timestamps) in the basic and standard protocol constructions introduced in §11.4. However, a good awareness does not necessarily mean that we must also be good at preventing such attacks. One subtlety of authentication protocols is that mistakes can be made and repeatedly made even when the designers know the errors very well in a different context. Let us look at the following case which shows another form of message replay attack.

In [295], Varadharajan et al. present a number of "proxy protocols" by which a principal passes on its trust in another principal to others who trust the former. In one protocol, Bob, a client, shares the key $K_{BT}$ with Trent, an authentication server. Bob has generated a timestamp $T_B$ and wants a key $K_{BS}$ to communicate with another server $S$. Then $S$ constructs $\{T_B + 1\}_{K_{BS}}$, and sends:

5.   $S \rightarrow$ Bob: $S, B, \{T_B + 1\}_{K_{BS}}, \{K_{BS}\}_{K_{BT}}$.

The authors reason:

> Having obtained $K_{BS}$, Bob is able to verify using $T_B$ that $S$ has replied to a fresh message, so that the session key is indeed fresh.

However, although a freshness identifier is cryptographically integrated with $K_{BS}$, Bob can obtain no assurance that $K_{BS}$ is fresh. All that he can deduce is that $K_{BS}$ has been used recently, but it may be an old, or even compromised key.

So we remark:

**Remark 11.4:** *Sometimes, a cryptographic integration between a freshness identifier and a message may only indicate the fresh action of the integration, not the freshness of the message being integrated.*   $\square$

## 11.7.2   Man-in-the-Middle Attack

Man-in-the-middle attack in the spirit of the well-known "chess grandmaster problem"[h] is generally applicable in a communication protocol where mutual authentication is absent. In such an attack, Malice is able to pass a difficult question asked by one protocol participant to another participant for an answer, and then passes the answer (maybe after a simple processing) back to the asking party, and/or vice versa.

In §2.6.6.3 and §8.3.1, we have seen two cases of man-in-the-middle attack, one on the Needham-Schroeder Public-key Authentication Protocol, one on the unauthenticated Diffie-Hellman key exchange protocol.

A man-in-the-middle attack on the S/KEY Protocol (Prot 11.4, attack shown in Attack 11.4) shows another good example on how Malice can gain a cryptographic credential without breaking the cryptographic algorithm used in the scheme.

The cryptographic hash function $f$ used in the S/KEY scheme can be very strong so that it is computationally infeasible to invert; also the user $U$ can have chosen the password $P_U$ properly so that an offline dictionary attack aiming at finding $P_U$ from $f^c(P_U)$ does not apply (review §11.5.3 for offline dictionary attack). However, the protocol fails miserably on an active attack which is demonstrated in Attack 11.4.

The attack 11.4 works because in the S/KEY Protocol, messages from $H$ are not authenticated to $U$.

The countermeasure for man-in-the-middle attack is to provide data-origin authentication service in both directions of message exchanges.

## 11.7.3   Parallel Session Attack

In a parallel session attack, two or more runs of a protocol are executed concurrently under Malice's orchestration. The concurrent runs make the answer to a difficult question in one run available to Malice so that he can use the answer in another run.

An early attack on the Woo-Lam Protocol (Prot 11.2) discovered by Abadi and Needham [1] illustrates a parallel session attack. The attack is shown in Attack 11.5.

This attack should work if Bob is willing to talk to Alice and Malice at roughly the same time. Then Malice can block messages flowing to Alice. In messages 1 and 1', Bob is asked to respond two runs, one with Malice and one with "Alice." In messages 2 and 2', Bob responds with two different nonce challenges, of course both will be received by Malice (one of them, $N_B$, will be received via interception).

---

[h] A novice who engages in two simultaneous chess games with two distinct grandmasters, playing Black in one game and White in the other, can take his opponents' moves in each game and use them in the other to guarantee himself either two draws or a win and a loss, and thereby unfairly have his chess rating improved.

---

**Attack 11.4:** An Attack on the S/KEY Protocol

(∗ notations in the attack are the same as those in Prot 11.4 ∗)

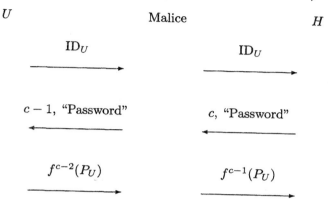

$U$           Malice         $H$

$\text{ID}_U$             $\text{ID}_U$

$c - 1$, "Password"      $c$, "Password"

$f^{c-2}(P_U)$          $f^{c-1}(P_U)$

CONSEQUENCE:
Malice has in his possession $f^{c-2}(P_U)$ which he can use for logging-in in the name of $U$ in the next session.

---

Malice throws away $N_B'$ which is meant for him to use, but uses the intercepted $N_B$ which is intended for Alice to use. So in messages 3 and 3' Bob receives $\{N_B\}_{K_{MT}}$. Notice that the two ciphertext chunks received in messages 3 and 3' may or may not be identical, this depends on the encryption algorithm details (see Chapters 14 and 15). At any rate, Bob should simply follow the protocol instruction in messages 4 and 4': he just encrypts them and sends them to Trent. Notice that even if the two cipher chunks received by Bob in messages 3 and 3' are identical (when the encryption algorithm is deterministic, a less likely case nowadays in applications of encryption algorithms), Bob should not be able to notice it since the cipher chunk is not recognizable by Bob as it is not a message for Bob to process. Not to process a "foreign ciphertext" is consistent with our convention for the behavior of honest principals (see §11.3): Bob is not anticipating an attack and cannot recognize ciphertext chunks which are not meant for him to decrypt. We know such a behavior is stupid, but we have agreed as convention that Bob should be so "stupid." Now in messages 5 and 5', one of the cipher chunks Bob receiving from Trent will have the nonce $N_B$ correctly returned, which will deceive Bob to accept "the run with Alice," but Alice is not online at all; the other cipher chunk will be decrypted to

**Attack 11.5:** A Parallel-Session Attack on the Woo-Lam Protocol

PREMISE:   In addition to that of Prot 11.2,
              Malice and Trent share long term key $K_{MT}$.
              ($*$ so Malice is also a normal user in the system $*$)

1. Malice("Alice") $\rightarrow$ Bob: *Alice*;

1'. Malice $\rightarrow$ Bob: *Malice*;

2. Bob $\rightarrow$ Malice("Alice"): $N_B$;

2'. Bob $\rightarrow$ Malice: $N'_B$;

3. Malice("Alice") $\rightarrow$ Bob: $\{N_B\}_{K_{MT}}$;

3'. Malice $\rightarrow$ Bob: $\{N_B\}_{K_{MT}}$;

4. Bob $\rightarrow$ Trent: $\{Alice, \{N_B\}_{K_{MT}}\}_{K_{BT}}$;

4'. Bob $\rightarrow$ Trent: $\{Malice, \{N_B\}_{K_{MT}}\}_{K_{BT}}$;

5. Trent $\rightarrow$ Bob: $\{$"garbage"$\}_{K_{BT}}$;
   ($*$ "garbage" is the result of Trent decrypting $\{N_B\}_{K_{MT}}$ using $K_{AT}$ $*$)

5'. Trent $\rightarrow$ Bob: $\{N_B\}_{K_{BT}}$;

6. Bob rejects the run with Malice;
   ($*$ since decryption returns "garbage" rather than nonce $N'_B$ $*$)

6'. Bob accepts "the run with Alice," but it is a run with Malice;
   ($*$ since decryption returns $N_B$ correctly $*$)

CONSEQUENCE:
Bob believes that Alice is corresponding to him in a run while in fact Alice
has not participated in the run at all.

"garbage" because it is a result of Trent decrypting $\{N_B\}_{K_{MT}}$ using $K_{AT}$. The result, Bob rejects the run with Malice, but accepts the run "with Alice."

In a parallel session attack, the sequence of the two parallelled sessions are not important. For example, if Bob receives message 3' before receiving message 3, the attack works the same way. Bob can know who has sent which of these two messages from the addressing information in the network layer and we will see this clearly in §12.2.

Abadi and Needham suggest a fix for the Woo-Lam Protocol which we shall see in a moment. They also inform Woo and Lam about the attack in Attack 11.5 [1]. The latter authors propose a series of fixes [304] which includes the fix suggested by Abadi and Needham (called $\Pi^3$ in [304]) and several more aggressive fixes. The most aggressive fix is called $\Pi^f$: adding the identities of the both subjects, i.e., *Alice* and *Bob*, inside all cipher chunks. They claim that their fixes are secure. Unfortunately, none of them is (and hence the fix suggested by Abadi and Needham is also flawed). Each of their fixes can be attacked in an attack type which we shall describe now.

## 11.7.4    Reflection Attack

In a reflection attack, when an honest principal sends to an intended communication partner a message for the latter to perform a cryptographic process, Malice intercepts the message and simply sends it back to the message originator. Notice that such a reflected message is not a case of "message bounced back:" Malice has manipulated the identity and address information which is processed by a lower-layer communication protocol so that the originator will not notice that the reflected message is actually one "invented here." We shall see the technical know-how in §12.2.

In such an attack, Malice tries to deceive the message originator into believing that the reflected message is expected by the originator from an intended communication partner, either as a response to, or as a challenge for, the originator. If Malice is successful, the message originator either accepts an "answer" to a question which was in fact asked and answered by the originator itself, or provides Malice with an oracle service which Malice needs but cannot provide to himself.

After having discovered the parallel-session attack (Attack 11.5) on the original Woo-Lam Protocol (Prot 11.2), Abadi and Needham suggested a fix [1]: the last message sent from Trent to Bob in Prot 11.2 should contain the identity of Alice:

$$5. \text{ Trent } \rightarrow \text{ Bob: } \{Alice, N_B\}_{K_{BT}} \tag{11.7.1}$$

This fix indeed removes the parallel-session attack in Attack 11.5 since now if Malice still attacks that way then the following will occur:

$$5. \text{ Trent } \rightarrow \text{ Bob: } \{Malice, N_B\}_{K_{BT}}$$

while Bob is expecting (11.7.1), and hence detects the attack.

**Attack 11.6:** A Reflection Attack on a "Fixed" Version of the Woo-Lam Protocol

PREMISE:  Same as that of Prot 11.2;

1.  Malice("Alice") $\rightarrow$ Bob: *Alice*;

2.  Bob $\rightarrow$ Malice("Alice"): $N_B$;

3.  Malice("Alice") $\rightarrow$ Bob: $N_B$;

4.  Bob $\rightarrow$ Malice("Trent"): $\{Alice, Bob, N_B\}_{K_{BT}}$;

5.  Malice("Trent") $\rightarrow$ Bob: $\{Alice, Bob, N_B\}_{K_{BT}}$;

6.  Bob accepts.

CONSEQUENCE:
Bob believes that Alice is alive in a protocol run, however in fact Alice has not participated in the run at all.

However, while having the identities of the protocol participants explicitly specified in a protocol is definitely an important and prudent principle for developing secure authentication protocols (an issue to be addressed in a different attacking type in §11.7.7), it is only one of many things which need to be considered. Often, one countermeasure prevents one attack but introduces another. The fixed version of Abadi and Needham [1] for the Woo-Lam Protocol is still insecure. Their fixed version of the Woo-Lam Protocol suffers a reflection attack which is given in Attack 11.6 (the attack is due to Clark and Jacob [78]).

Here, Malice mounts reflection attack twice: message 3 is a reflection of message 2, and message 5 is that of message 4. This attack works under an assumption that, in messages 3 and 5, Bob receives messages and cannot detect anything wrong. This assumption holds perfectly for both cases according to our agreed convention for the behavior of honest principals (§11.3). First, the random chunk Bob receives in message 3 is actually Bob's nonce sent out in message 2; however, Bob can only treat it as an unrecognizable foreign cipher chunk; to follow the protocol instruction is all that he can and should do. Again, the cipher chunk Bob receives in message 5 is actually one created by himself and sent out in message 4; however, Bob is stateless with respect to the message pair 4 and 5. This also follows our convention on stateless principal agreed in §11.3). Therefore Bob cannot detect the attack.

A series of fixes for the Woo-Lam Protocol proposed by Woo and Lam in [304] are also flawed in a similar way: they all suffer various ways of reflection attack. For the most aggressive fix, $\Pi^f$ in which the identities of both user principals will be included in each ciphertext, reflection attack will still work if Bob is not sensitive about the size of a foreign cipher chunk. This is of course a reasonable assumption due to our agreement on the "stupidity" of honest principals.

A more fundamental reason for the Woo-Lam Protocol and its various fixed versions being flawed will be investigated in §17.2.1 where we take formal approaches to developing correct authentication protocols. A correct approach to the specification of authentication protocols will be proposed in §17.2.2. The correct approach will lead to a general fix for the Woo-Lam Protocol and for many other protocols, too. We shall see in §17.2.3.2 that the Woo-Lam Protocol under the general fix (Prot 17.2) will no longer suffer any of the attacks we have demonstrated so far.

## 11.7.5  Interleaving Attack

In an interleaving attack, two or more runs of a protocol are executed in an overlapping fashion under Malice's orchestration. In such an attack, Malice may compose a message and sends it out to a principal in one run, from which he expects to receive an answer; the answer may be useful for another principal in another run, and in the latter run, the answer obtained from the former run may further stimulate the latter principal to answer a question which in turn be further used in the first run, and so on.

Some authors, e.g., [35], consider that interleaving attack is a collective name for the previous two attacking types, i.e., parallel-session attack and reflection attack. We view these attacking types different by thinking that an interleaving attack is more sophisticated than reflection and parallel-session attacks. In order to mount a successful interleaving attack, Malice must exploit a sequentially dependent relation among messages in different runs.

Wiener's attack (Attack 11.1) on an early draft of the "ISO Public Key Three-Pass Mutual Authentication Protocol," which we have seen in §11.4.2, is a good example of interleaving attack. In that attack, Malice initiates a protocol run with $A$ by masquerading as $B$ (message line 1); upon receipt $A$'s response (message line 2), Malice initiates a new run with $B$ by masquerading as $A$ (message line 1'); $B$'s response (message line 2') provides Malice with the answer that $A$ is waiting for, and thus, Malice can return to and complete the run with $A$. In comparison with the parallel-session attack (e.g., Attack 11.5), an interleaving attack is very sensitive to the sequence of the message exchanges.

Related to Wiener's attack, the "certificate-signature-replacement attack" on the "Authentication-only" STS Protocol (Attack 11.2) is another perfect interleaving attack. Also, Lowe's attack on the Needham-Schroeder Public-key Authentication

Protocol (Attack 2.3) is an interleaving attack.

Usually, a failure in mutual authentication can make an interleaving attack possible.

## 11.7.6   Attack Due to Type Flaw

In a type flaw attack, Malice exploits a fact we agreed upon in §11.3 regarding an honest principal's inability to associate a message or a message component with its semantic meaning (review Remark 11.1 and Example 11.1 in §11.3).

Typical type flaws include a principal being tricked to misinterpret a nonce, a timestamp or an identity into a key, etc. Misinterpretations are likely to occur when a protocol is poorly designed in that the type information of message components are not explicit. Let us use a protocol proposed by Neuman and Stubblebine [216] to exemplify a type flaw attack [287, 70]. First, here is the protocol:

1. Alice → Bob: $A, N_A$;

2. Bob → Trent: $B, \{A, N_A, T_B\}_{K_{BT}}, N_B$;

3. Trent → Alice: $\{B, N_A, K_{AB}, T_B\}_{K_{AT}}, \{A, K_{AB}, T_B\}_{K_{BT}}, N_B$;

4. Alice → Bob: $\{A, K_{AB}, T_B\}_{K_{BT}}, \{N_B\}_{K_{AB}}$.

This protocol intends to let Alice and Bob achieve mutual authentication and authenticated key establishment by using a trusted service from Trent. If a nonce and a key are random numbers of the same size, then this protocol permits Malice to mount a type-flaw attack:

1. Malice("Alice") → Bob: $A, N_A$;

2. Bob → Malice("Trent"): $B, \{A, N_A, T_B\}_{K_{BT}}, N_B$;

3. none;

4. Malice("Alice") → Bob: $\{A, N_A, T_B\}_{K_{BT}}, \{N_B\}_{N_A}$.

In this attack, Malice uses the nonce $N_A$ in place of the session key $K_{AB}$ to be established, and Bob can be tricked to accept it if he cannot tell the type difference. Indeed, there is no good mechanism to prevent Bob from being fooled.

A type flaw is usually implementation dependent. If a protocol specification does not provide sufficiently explicit type information for the variables appearing in the protocol, then type flaw can be very common in implementation. Boyd [55] exemplified the problem using the Otway-Rees Authentication Protocol [228] where he discussed the importance for avoiding hidden assumptions in cryptographic protocols.

## 11.7.7  Attack Due to Name Omission

In authentication protocols often the names relevant for a message can be deduced from other data parts in the context, and from what encryption keys have been applied. However, when this information cannot be deduced, name omission is a blunder with serious consequences.

It seems that experts in the fields (reputable authors in cryptography, computer security and protocol design) are ready to make a name-omission blunder. Perhaps this is because of their desire to obtain an elegant protocol which should contain little redundancy. The two attacks on two versions of the STS Protocol, which we have studied in §11.6.2 and §11.6.3, respectively, are such vivid examples. Here is another.

Denning and Sacco proposed a protocol as a public-key alternative to their fix of the Needham-Schroeder Symmetric-key Authentication Protocol [95]. The protocol of Denning and Sacco is as follows:

1. Alice $\rightarrow$ Trent: $A, B$;

2. Trent $\rightarrow$ Alice: $\text{Cert}_A, \text{Cert}_B$;

3. Alice $\rightarrow$ Bob: $\text{Cert}_A, \text{Cert}_B, \{\text{sig}_A(K_{AB}, T_A)\}_{K_B}$.

In this protocol, the third message is encrypted for both secrecy and authenticity. When Bob receives the message from Alice, he sees that the session key $K_{AB}$ should be exclusively shared between Alice and him because he sees Alice's signature and the use of his public key.

Unfortunately, nothing in this protocol guarantees such an exclusive-key sharing property. Abadi and Needham discovered a simple but rather shocking attack [1] in which Bob, after receiving the message from Alice, can fool another principal to believe this "property:"

3'. Bob("Alice") $\rightarrow$ Charlie: $\text{Cert}_A, \text{Cert}_C, \{\text{sig}_A(K_{AB}, T_A)\}_{K_C}$.

Charlie will believe that the message is from Alice, and may subsequently send a confidential message to Alice encrypted under the session key $K_{AB}$. Alas, Bob can read it!

The intended meaning of message line 3 is: "At time $T_A$, Alice says that $K_{AB}$ is a good key for communication between Alice and Bob." The obvious way to specify this in this protocol should be:

3. Alice $\rightarrow$ Bob: $\text{Cert}_A, \text{Cert}_B, \{\text{sig}_A(A, B, K_{AB}, T_A)\}_{K_B}$.

Making explicit the identities of participants in authentication protocols, especially making them explicit inside the scope of a cryptographic operation, must have been "common sense" for protocol designers. However, we have witnessed that it is not rare for experienced protocol designers to neglect "common sense." Abadi and Needham have documented this "common sense" as one of the prudent principles for authentication protocol design [1]. We should quote here again this prudent principle for protocol design:

> If the identity of a principal is essential to the meaning of a message, it
> is prudent to mention the principal's name explicitly in the message.

Our reemphasis of this prudent principle is not redundant: in §12.2 we shall further see name-omission blunders in the *current* version of the IKE Protocol for Internet security [137], even after many years of the protocol's development by a committee of highly experienced computer security experts.

## 11.7.8  Attack Due to Misuse of Cryptographic Services

We should mention finally a very common protocol design flaw: misuse of cryptographic services.

Misuse of cryptographic services means that a cryptographic algorithm used in a protocol provides an incorrect protection so that the needed protection is absent. This type of flaw can lead to various attacks. Here are two of the most common ones:

i) Attacks due to absence of data-integrity protection. We will demonstrate an attack on a flawed protocol to illustrate the importance of data-integrity protection. Many more attacking examples of this type on public-key cryptographic schemes will be shown in Chapter 14 where we study the notion of security against adaptively active attackers. We shall further study this type of protocol failure in depth in §17.2 where we study a topic of formal approaches to authentication protocols analysis.

ii) Confidentiality failure due to absence of "semantic security" protection. In this type of protocol (and cryptosystem) failure, Malice can extract some partial information about a secret message encrypted in a ciphertext and hence achieves his attacking agenda without fully breaking an encryption algorithm in terms of a "all-or-nothing" quality of confidentiality (see Property 8.2 in §8.2). We shall study the notion of semantic security in Chapter 14 and show many such attacks there. There and in Chapter 15 we shall also study cryptographic techniques which offer semantic security.

These two common misuses of cryptographic services frequently appear in the literature of authentication protocols. Apparently, the misuses indicate that those protocol designers were not aware of the general danger of "textbook crypto."

Now let us demonstrate a flaw due to missing of integrity service. The flawed protocol is a variation of the Otway-Rees Protocol [228]. We have derived the variation by following a suggestion in [62]. The variation is specified in Prot 11.8.

---

**Protocol 11.8:** A Minor Variation of the Otway-Rees Protocol

PREMISE:  Alice and Trent share key $K_{AT}$;
Bob and Trent share key $K_{BT}$;

GOAL:  Alice and Bob authenticate to each other;
they also establish a new and shared session key $K_{AB}$.

1. Alice $\rightarrow$ Bob : $M, Alice, Bob, \{N_A, M, Alice, Bob\}_{K_{AT}}$;

2. Bob $\rightarrow$ Trent : $M, Alice, Bob, \{N_A, M, Alice, Bob\}_{K_{AT}}$,

$$\{N_B\}_{K_{BT}}, \{M, Alice, Bob\}_{K_{BT}};$$

3. Trent $\rightarrow$ Bob : $M, \{N_A, K_{AB}\}_{K_{AT}}, \{N_B, K_{AB}\}_{K_{BT}}$;

4. Bob $\rightarrow$ Alice : $M, \{N_A, K_{AB}\}_{K_{AT}}$.

($*$ $M$ is called a run identifier for Alice and Bob to keep tracking the run between them $*$)

---

Prot 11.8 applies the rather standard technique of using an online authentication server (Trent) to achieve mutual authentication and authenticated session establishment between two user principals. Let us consider Bob's view on a protocol run (Alice's view can be considered likewise). Bob can conclude that the session received in step 3 is fresh from the cryptographic integration between the key and his nonce. He should also be able to conclude that the session key is shared with Alice. This is implied by the cryptographic integration between the run identifier $M$ and the two principals' identities; the integration has been created by Bob himself and has been verified by Trent.

The variation differs from the original Otway-Rees Protocol only very slightly: in step 2 of the variation, Bob's encrypted messages (encrypted under the key $K_{AT}$) are in two separate cipher chunks, one encrypts his nonce $N_B$, the other encrypts other message components. In the original Otway-Rees Protocol, the nonce and the rest of the message components are encrypted (more precisely, they are specified to be encrypted) inside one cipher chunk: $\{N_B, M, Alice, Bob\}_{K_{BT}}$.

It is interesting to point out that for some implementors, this variation may not qualify as a variation at all: encryption of a long message is always implemented in a plural number of blocks whether or not the specification uses one chunk or two chunks. This is an important point and we shall return to clarify it at the end of our discussion of this type of protocol failure.

This minor variation is actually a much less aggressive version of modification to the original protocol than that suggested in [62]. There it is considered that Bob's nonce needn't be a secret, and hence Bob can send it in cleartext. Indeed, if the freshness identifier has been sent in cleartext in step 2, Bob can of course still use $N_B$ returned in step 3 to identify the freshness of the session key $K_{AB}$. We, however, insist on using encryption in step 2 in order to expose our point more clearly.

Prot 11.8 is fatally flawed. Attack 11.7 shows an attack. This attack was discovered by Boyd and Mao [56].

In this attack, Malice begins with masquerading as Alice to initiate a run with Bob. He then intercepts the message from Bob to Trent (step 2); he changes Alice's identity into his own, does not touch Bob's first cipher chunk (no need for him to know the encrypted nonce) and replaces Bob's second cipher chunk $\{M, Alice, Bob\}_{K_{BT}}$ with an old chunk $\{M, Malice, Bob\}_{K_{BT}}$ which he has recorded from a previous normal run of the protocol between himself and Bob. After sending the modified messages to Trent by masquerading as Bob (step 2'), everything will go fine with Trent and Bob: Trent thinks that the two client-users requesting authentication service are Malice and Bob, while Bob thinks that the run is between Alice and himself. Alas, Bob will use the established session key which he thinks to share with Alice but in fact with Malice, and will disclose to Malice the confidential messages which should be sent to Alice!

This attack reveals an important point: to protect the freshness identifier $N_B$ in terms of confidentiality is to provide a wrong cryptographic service! The correct service is data integrity which must be provided to integrate the nonce and the principals identities. $N_B$ can indeed be sent in clear if a proper integrity protection is in place. Without integrity protection, encryption of $N_B$ is missing the point!

We have mentioned that for some implementors, Prot 11.8 will not be viewed as a variation from the original Otway-Rees Protocol. This is true indeed because, encryption of a long message is always implemented in a plural number of blocks. If in an implementation, a plural number of ciphertext blocks are not integrated with one another cryptographically, then both protocols will be implemented into the same code, and hence one cannot be a "variation" of the other.

In the usual and standard implementation of block ciphers, a sequence of separate ciphertext blocks are cryptographically chained one another. The cipher-block-chaining (CBC, see §7.8.2) mode of operation is the most likely case. We should

**Attack 11.7:** An Attack on the Minor Variation of the Otway-Rees Protocol

PREMISE:   In addition to that in Prot 11.8,
Malice and Trent share key $K_{MT}$.
(* so Malice is also a normal user in the system *)

1. Malice("Alice") $\rightarrow$ Bob: $M, Alice, Bob, \{N_M, M, Malice, Bob\}_{K_{MT}}$;

2. Bob $\rightarrow$ Malice("Trent"): $M, Alice, Bob, \{N_M, M, Malice, Bob\}_{K_{MT}}$,

$$\{N_B\}_{K_{BT}}, \{M, Alice, Bob\}_{K_{BT}};$$

2'. Malice("Bob") $\rightarrow$ Trent: $M, Malice, Bob, \{N_M, M, Malice, Bob\}_{K_{MT}}$,

$$\{N_B\}_{K_{BT}}, \{M, Malice, Bob\}_{K_{BT}};$$

(* where $\{M, Malice, Bob\}_{K_{BT}}$ is an old cipher chunk which Malice preserves from a previous normal run between himself and Bob. *)

3. Trent $\rightarrow$ Bob: $M, \{N_M, K_{MB}\}_{K_{MT}}, \{N_B, K_{MB}\}_{K_{BT}}$;

4 Bob $\rightarrow$ Malice("Alice"): $M, \{N_M, K_{MB}\}_{K_{MT}}$.

CONSEQUENCE:
Bob believes that he has been talking to Alice and shares a session key with her. However, in fact he has been talking to Malice and shares the session key with the latter.

notice that in the CBC mode, the cryptographically chained cipher blocks are actually not protected in terms of data integrity service, as in contrast to a common and wrong belief. Without integrity protection, some of the chained blocks can be modified without having the modification detected during decryption time. We shall show how CBC misses the point of providing data-integrity protection in §17.2.1.2.

## Not the End of the List

It is still possible to further name several other ways to attack authentication protocols, such as "side channel attack" (we shall see such an attack on the TLS/SSL

Protocol in §12.5.4 and in that case the side-channel attack is a "timing analysis attack"), "implementation dependent attack," "binding attack," and "encapsulation attack" (see §4 of [78]) or "misplaced trust in server attack" (see §12.9.1 of [200]), etc. Because some of these types of attacks have certain overlapping parts with some of the types we have listed, also because, even including them, we still cannot exhaust all possible types of attacks, we should therefore stop our listing here.

The readiness for authentication protocols to contain security flaws, even under the great care of experts in the fields, have urged researchers to consider systematic approaches to design and analysis of authentication protocols. In Chapter 17 we shall study several topics on formal methods for design and analysis of authentication protocols.

## 11.8    A Brief Literature Note

Authentication is a big subject in cryptographic protocols. We recommend a few important literature references in this subject.

- A logic of authentication by Burrows, Abadi and Needham [62]. This seminal paper is essential reading. Most security protocol papers reference it. It is a good source of many early authentication protocols and an early exposure of many security flaws with them.

- A survey on various ways cryptographic protocols fails by Moore [206, 207]. This is an important paper. It is a good introduction to various cryptographic failures which are not a result of any inherent weakness in the cryptographic algorithms themselves, rather it is because the way in which they are used requires that they provide certain cryptographic services which they do not in fact provide.

- Prudent engineering practice for cryptographic protocols summarized by Abadi and Needham [1]. This paper sets out eleven heuristic principles which intend to guide protocol designers to develop good protocols. The principles form an engineering account of protocol development, serving a menu for protocol designers: "have I checked this sort of attack?" An excellent piece of work and will prove of considerable use for protocol designers.

- A survey of authentication protocol literature written by Clark and Jacob [78]. This document includes a library of a large number of authentication and key-establishment protocols. Many of the protocols in the library are accompanied by attacks. The document also has a comprehensive and well annotated literature survey. This is an essential reading for protocol developers. A Web site called "Security Protocols Open Repository" (SPORE) has been setup as the further development of the document of Clark and Jacob. The Web address for SPORE is http://www.lsv.ens-cachan.fr/spore/

- A forthcoming book of Boyd and Mathuria entitled *"Protocols for Key Establishment and Authentication"* (Information Security and Cryptography Series, Publisher: Springer, ISBN: 3-540-43107-1). This book is the first comprehensive and integrated treatment of authentication key-establishment protocols. For key-establishment protocols which include the basic protocols using symmetric and asymmetric cryptographic techniques, group-oriented, conference-key, and password-based protocols, this book takes an exhaustive approach to their description, explanation and reporting of the known flaws. The book allows researchers and practitioners to quickly access a protocol for their needs and become aware of existing protocols which have been broken in the literature. As well as a clear and uniform presentation of the protocols this book includes a description of all the main attack types and classifies most protocols in terms of their properties and resource requirements. It also includes tutorial material suitable for graduate students.

## 11.9    Chapter Summary

Our study of authentication in this chapter covers a wide range of topics in the subject with indepth discussions. The range includes basic concepts (data-origin, entity, authenticated-key-establishment, unilateral, mutual, liveness), good constructions of authentication protocols (recommended by the international standards), standard protocols, several interesting and useful protocols (e.g., one-time password, EKE, STS) and a taxonomy of attacks.

As an active academic research topic, authentication protocols is an important but also rather a pre-mature subject in the area of cryptographic protocols. Our coverage of the subject in this chapter is by no means comprehensive. We therefore have listed a brief literature note for the readers who will be interested in a further study of the subject in an academic research direction. For these readers, a later chapter in this book (Chapter 17 on formal analysis methodologies of authentication protocols) is also material for further study.

Authentication protocols have importance in real world applications. This chapter has touched a few aspects of applications. Let us turn to the real world applications of authentication protocols in the next chapter.

## Exercises

11.1  Describe the difference for the following security services: data integrity, message authentication, entity authentication.

11.2  What is a freshness identifier?

11.3  Does the recency of a cryptographic action performed by a principal necessarily imply the freshness of a message sent by the principal?

11.4 After the decryption of a ciphertext (e.g., formed by the AES-CBC encryption) Alice sees a valid freshness identifier (e.g., a nonce she has just sent out). Can she conclude the freshness of the ciphertext message?

11.5 Why is the data integrity of an encrypted protocol message important for the message's secrecy?

11.6 In §11.4 we have introduced the most basic constructions of authentication protocols. In these constructions, what is the essential difference between the standard constructions and the non-standard ones?

11.7 Identify a non-standard construction in the Woo-Lam Protocol (Prot 11.2).

Hint: observe a security service used in the interaction between Bob and Trent in message lines 4 and 5, and compare the construction with that in (11.4.7).

11.8 What is common in the following three attacks? (i) Wiener's attack on the flawed version of the ISO Protocol (Attack 11.1), (ii) the "certificate-signature-replacement attack" on the "Authentication-only" STS Protocol (Attack 11.2) and (iii) Lowe's attack on the Needham-Schroeder Public-key Authentication Protocol (Attack 2.3).

11.9 Inside computers every ASCII character is represented by 8 bits. Why usually does a password of 8 ASCII characters contain information quantity which is less than that measured by 64 bits?

11.10 What is a salt in a password-based authentication protocol? What is the role of a salt?

11.11 In the password authentication protocol for the UNIX operating system (see §11.5.1 and Prot 11.3), the cryptographic transformation $f(P_U)$ is generated using the DES encryption function. Does the protocol apply the DES decryption function? Discuss an important difference between this transformation and that in the non-standard authentication mechanism (11.4.7).

11.12 The S/KEY Protocol (Prot 11.4) uses essentially the same cryptographic transformation as the UNIX password authentication protocol (Prot 11.3) does. Why do we say that the former is flawed while the latter is not?

11.13 The EKE Protocol (Prot 11.5) uses asymmetric cryptographic techniques. Is it a public-key based authentication protocol?

11.14 We have shown a flaw in the "Authentication-only" STS Protocol (Attack 11.2). Revise the protocol to remove the flaw.

11.15 In §11.6.3 we have reasoned that signing the intended verifier's identity provides a fix for the minor flaw in the STS Protocol (the minor flaw is demonstrated in Attack 11.3). However, such a fix damages the anonymity (deniability) property of the protocol. Provide a different fix which does not involve signing identities.

Hint: the two parties actually have not combined the shared session key with the intended identities; that was why we did not consider that the agreed session key has been mutually confirmed, see our discussions on the intended properties of the protocol in §11.6.1.

# Chapter 12

# AUTHENTICATION PROTOCOLS — THE REAL WORLD

## 12.1 Introduction

Our study of authentication protocols in the preceding chapter has an academic focus: we have studied good (and standard) constructions for authentication protocols, introduced a few important authentication protocols and techniques selected from the literature, and conducted a systematic examination of various "academic attacks" on authentication protocols. However, we have touched little on the application aspect. Undoubtedly, real world applications of authentication protocols must have real world problems to solve, some of which are very challenging.

In this chapter, let us face some authentication problems in the real world. We shall introduce and discuss a number of authentication protocols which have been proposed for, and some already widely used in, various important applications in the real world. All of the protocols to be introduced in this chapter are de facto or industrial standards.

The first real world protocol we shall study is the Internet Key Exchange Protocol (IKE) [137, 160] which is the authentication mechanism for the IETF (Internet Engineering Task Force) standard for Internet Security (IPSec). This protocol suite (a system) contains authentication and authenticated key exchange protocols which operate at a low layer of communications called the network layer. Our study shall let us see how communications take place at the network layer, understand how various attacks demonstrated in the previous chapter can be based on various ways for Malice to manipulate addressing information handled by the network layer protocol, and realize that security offered at the network layer can be very effective in thwarting those attacks. We shall also see that a challenging problem in IKE is for the protocol suite to offer an optional privacy feature which is desirable at the network layer of communications in order not to cause privacy damage to applications in higher layers of communications.

Next, we shall introduce the Secure Shell (SSH) Protocol [306, 309, 310, 307, 308]. This is a public-key based authentication protocol suite for secure access of remote computer resource (secure remote login) from an untrusted machine (i.e., from an untrusted client machine to a remote server host). It is a de facto standard for secure remote login computer resources in an open systems environment and is already widely used in the global range. SSH is a client-server protocol. Its server part mainly runs on machines which use UNIX[a], or its popular variant, Linux, operating systems (this is true especially on the server side); its client part further covers other operating systems such as Windows, etc. A challenging problem for this protocol is to enable a security service in a harmonic manner: insecure systems are already in wide use, secure solutions should be added on with the least interruption to the insecure systems which are already in operation (backward compatibility).

Next, we shall introduce another important and already-in-wide-use authentication protocol system: the Kerberos Authentication Protocol [204, 170]. This is the network authentication basis for another popular operating system: Windows 2000. This operating system is in wide use in an enterprise environment where a user is entitled to enterprise-wide distributed services while unable to keep many different cryptographic credentials for using the different servers (it is unrealistic for a user to memorize many different passwords and is uneconomic for a user to manage many smartcards). We shall see that Kerberos' "single-signon" authentication architecture finds a good application in such an environment.

Finally, we shall overview the Secure Socket Layer (SSL) Protocol [138], or the Transport Layer Security (TLS) Protocol named by the Internet-wide industrial standards community IETF. At the time of writing, this protocol qualifies as the most-widely-used public-key based authentication technique: it is nowadays an integral part in every WorldWideWeb browser and Web server, though in most cases its use is limited to unilateral authentication only (a server authenticates to a client). This is an authentication protocol for a typical client-server environment setting. Although the idea behind the protocol is extremely simple (this is the simplest protocol of the four real-world authentication protocols to be introduced in this chapter), we shall see from this case that a real-world realization of any simple authentication protocol is never a simple job.

## 12.1.1  Chapter Outline

IPSec and the IKE Protocol will be introduced in §12.2. The SSH Protocol will be introduced in §12.3. An enterprise single-signon scenario suitable for using the Windows 2000 operating system will be discussed in §12.4, and then the Kerberos Protocol, the network authentication basis for this operating system, will be de-

---

[a] UNIX is a trademark of Bell Laboratories.

scribed. Finally we overview the SSL (TLS) Protocol in §12.5.

# 12.2 Authentication Protocols for Internet Security

We have been introducing various cryptographic techniques for protecting messages transmitted through open networks. The techniques introduced so far in this book all provide protections at a high communication layer or the application layer. A protection at the application layer means that only the content part of a message is protected whereas the addressing part, regarded as low-layer information, is not.

However, for securing communications over the Internet, protection provided at a low layer of communication which covers the addressing information as well as the content can be very effective. This is because, as we have witnessed in §11.7, manipulation of a message's addressing information is the main source of tricks available to Malice for mounting various attacks.

In this section we shall first look at how messages are processed by a low-layer communication protocol. There, we shall realize how Malice could materialize his tricks due to absence of security in that protocol. We shall then study a suite of authentication protocols proposed by a standards body for Internet security. That suite of protocols is collectively named the **Internet Key Exchange (IKE)**; they are intended to protect messages in the low-layer communication protocol using authentication techniques we have studied in the preceding chapter. We shall analyze a couple of important "modes" in IKE and reveal some vulnerabilities they have. We shall also report some critical comments and concerns on IKE from the research community.

## 12.2.1 Communications at the Internet Protocol Layer

The Internet is an enormous open network of computers and devices called "nodes." Each node is assigned a unique network address so that messages sent to and from the node have this address attached. A protocol which processes the transmission of messages using the network address is called the **Internet Protocol** (IP for short) and hence, the unique network address of a node is called the IP address of the node. According to the ISO's "Open Systems Interconnection (ISO-OSI) Seven-layer Reference Model" (e.g., pages 416–417 of [229] or §1.5.1 of [161]), the IP works at "layer 3" (also called the network layer or the IP layer). Many communication protocols including many authentication protocols which are invoked by end-users work at "layer 7" (also called the application layer). This is another reason why we have called the IP a "low-layer" communication protocol and the other protocols "high-layer" ones.

Communications at the IP layer take the form of "IP packets." Fig 12.1 illustrates an IP packet which has no cryptographic protection. The first three fields of an IP packet have apparent meanings. The fourth field, "Upper-layer Fields"

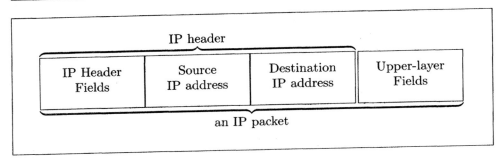

**Figure 12.1.** An Unprotected IP Packet

contains two things: (i) the specification of the protocol which runs in the immediate upper layer and processes the IP packet (e.g., "transmission control protocol" TCP), and (ii) data which are transmitted by the IP packet.

Let us use electronic mail communication to exemplify Internet communications which are organized in IP packets. We begin with considering an insecure case where IP packets has no cryptographic protection. Let James_Bond@007.654.321 and Miss_Moneypenny@123.456.700 be two e-mail addresses. Here, James_Bond and Miss_Moneypenny are users' identities, each is called an "endpoint identity," 007.654.321 and 123.456.700 are two IP addresses[b]; for example, the former can be the IP address of a palm-top multi-purpose device, while the latter can be the IP address of an office computer. An e-mail sent from Miss_Moneypenny@123.456.700 to James_Bond@007.654.321 viewed at the IP layer can be

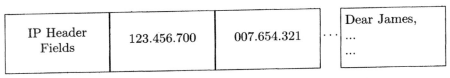

For exposition clarity, we have only presented the data field in "Upper-layer fields" and omitted the processing protocol specification (the omitted protocol specification in this case is "SMTP" which stands for simple mail transfer protocol [166]). Notice that the two endpoint identities will appear in some "IP header fields," and hence when James_Bond receives the e-mail, he may know who has sent it and may be able to reply.

These two parties may wish to conduct confidential communications by applying end-to-end encryption, using either a shared key or public keys. Since an end-to-end encryption operates in the application-layer protocol, only the message content in the fourth box in the "IP packet" will be encrypted. If the IP they use offers no security, then the data fields in "IP header" are not protected. Modification of data

---

[b]Often an IP address is mapped to a "domain name" for ease of memory; for instance, 007.654.321 may be mapped to the following "domain name:" spy1.mi.five.gb.

in these fields forms the main source of tricks behind the attacks which we have listed in §11.7. Let us now see how.

## 12.2.2   Internet Protocol Security (IPSec)

The Internet Engineering Task Force (IETF) has been in a series of standardization processes for IP security widely known as **IPSec** [165, 163]. Briefly speaking, IPSec is to add cryptographic protection to "IP header" which consists of the first three boxes in an IP packet (see Fig 12.1). IPSec stipulates a mandatory authentication protection for "IP header" and an optional confidentiality protection for the endpoint-identity information which is in some "IP header fields."

We should notice that, in absence of security at the IP layer, it is the unprotected transmission of "IP header" that may permit Malice to mount various attacks on Internet communications such as spoofing (masquerading), sniffing (eavesdropping) and session hijacking (combination of spoofing and sniffing while taking over a legitimate party's communication session). For example, if Malice intercepts an IP packet originated from James_Bond@007.654.321, copies "Source IP address" to "Destination IP address," and sends it out, the packet will go back to James_Bond@007.654.321. If this modification is undetected due to lack of security means at the IP layer, then the modification can essentially cause a "reflection attack" which we have seen in §11.7.4. Moreover, if Malice also forges a "Source IP address" and an endpoint identity (say "Miss_Moneypenny"), then James_Bond@007.654.321 may be fooled to believe that the message came from the forged sender. This is exactly the attack scenario which we have denoted at the application layer by

$$\text{Malice}(\text{"Miss\_Moneypenny"}) \to \text{James\_Bond: ...}$$

Virtually all attacks which we have seen in §11.7 require Malice to perform some manipulations on the IP-address and endpoint-identity information in an "IP header." Security protection offered at the IP layer can therefore effectively prevent such attacks since now any message manipulation in "IP header" can be detected. In general, security at the IP layer can provide a wide protection on all applications at higher layers.

Moreover, for traffic between two **firewalls**[c], because each firewall is a node which shields many nodes "inside" or "behind" it, an IP-layer protection can cause encryption on the IP address of any node "inside" the firewall. This means that unauthorized penetration through a firewall can be prevented via cryptographic means which is a very strong form of protection. Without security offered at the

---

[c]A firewall is a special-purpose computer which connects a cluster of protected computers and devices to the Internet so that accessing the protected computers and devices from the Internet requires knowing some identity and IP address information.

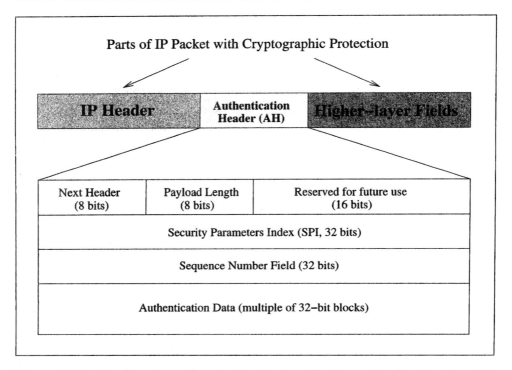

**Figure 12.2.** The Structure of an Authentication Header and its Position in an IP Packet

IP layer, the firewall technique uses much weaker form of "secrets" such as IP addresses, machine names and user names, etc., and so penetration is much easier.

It has been widely agreed that offering security at the IP layer is a wise thing to do.

### 12.2.2.1   Authentication Protection in IPSec

The Internet Protocol (IP) has evolved from version 4 (IPv4) to version 6 (IPv6). The data structure for IPv6 is a multiple of 32-bit data blocks called datagrams. In IPv6 with IPSec protection, an IP packet (Fig 12.2, cf. Fig 12.1) has an additional field called "**Authentication Header**" (**AH**). The position for the AH in an IP packet is in between "IP header" and the "Upper-layer fields." AH can have a variant length but must be a multiple of 32-bit datagrams which are organized into several subfields which contain data for providing cryptographic protection on the IP packet.

Authentication (in fact, data integrity with origin identification) is a mandatory service for IPSec. The protection is achieved by data provided in two subfields in an AH. One of the subfield is named "**Security Parameters Index**" (**SPI**). This subfield is an arbitrary 32-bit value which specifies (uniquely identifies) the cryptographic algorithms used for the authentication service for this IP packet. The other subfield is named "Authentication Data" which contains the authentication data generated by the message sender for the message receiver to conduct data-integrity verification (hence the data is also called Integrity Check Value, ICV). The receiver of the IP packet can use the algorithm uniquely identified in SPI and a secret key to regenerate "Authentication Data" and compare with that received. The secret key used will be discussed in §12.2.3.

The subfield named "Sequence Number" can be used against replay of IP packets. Other subfields in the first datagram of an AH with names "Next Header", "Payload Length" and "Reserved for future use" do not have security meanings and therefore their explanations are omitted here.

### 12.2.2.2 Confidentiality Protection in IPSec

Confidentiality (encryption) is an optional service for IPSec. To achieve this, a multiple of 32-bit datagrams named "**Encapsulating Security Payload**" (**ESP**) [164] is specified and allocated in an IP packet. An ESP can follow an AH as the second shaded field in Fig 12.2 ("Upper-layer fields"). The format of an ESP is shown in Fig 12.3.

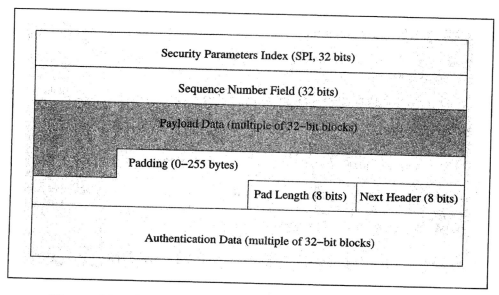

**Figure 12.3.** The Structure of an Encapsulating Security Payload

The first subfield is "Security Parameters Index (SPI)" which now specifies (i.e., uniquely identifies) the encryption algorithm. The second subfield "Sequence Number" has the same meaning as that in an AH (see §12.2.2.1). The third subfield "Payload Data" has a variable length which is the ciphertext of the confidential data. Since an IP (v6) packet must have a length as a multiple of 32 bits, the plaintext "Payload Data" of variable length must be padded, and the paddings are given in "Padding". The Padding bytes are initialized with a series of (unsigned, 1-byte) integer values. The first padding byte appended to the plaintext is numbered 1, with subsequent padding bytes making up a monotonically increasing sequence:

$$\text{`01'} \parallel \text{`02'} \parallel \cdots \parallel \text{`xy'}$$

where 'xy' is the hexadecimal value such that $\text{`01'} \leq \text{xy} \leq \text{`FF'}$. Therefore, the maximum number of the padding bytes is $\text{`FF'} = 255_{(10)}$. The length of the padding bytes is stated in "Padding Length". Finally, "Authentication Data" has the same meaning as that in an AH.

The reader should notice the difference between "Authentication Data" in an ESP and that in an AH. In an ESP, this data is for providing a data integrity protection on the ciphertext in the ESP packet (i.e., the fields in ESP packet minus the subfield "Authentication Data") and is optional [164], while in an AH, "Authentication Data" is for providing a data integrity protection on an IP packet and is mandatory.

The optional inclusion of "Authentication Data" in ESP is in fact a mistake. We shall discuss this mistake in §12.2.5.

### 12.2.2.3  Security Association

Central to IPSec is a notion called **"Security Association"** (SA). An SA is uniquely identified by triple

$$(\text{SPI, "IP Destination Address," "Service Identifier"})$$

where "Service Identifier" identifies either Authentication or ESP.

In essence, IPSec can be considered as AH + ESP. For two nodes to communicate under IPSec protection, they need to negotiate mandatorily one SA (for authentication) or optionally two SAs (for authentication and confidentiality) and the secret cryptographic keys to be shared between the two nodes in order for them to compute the cryptographic protections. The negotiation is achieved using the **Internet Key Exchange Protocol** which we shall now introduce.

## 12.2.3  The Internet Key Exchange (IKE) Protocol

With the added "Authentication Header" (HA) and "Encapsulating Security Payload" (ESP), IPSec accommodates cryptographic protections on an IP packet. However, two nodes in communication must first agree on SAs (which contains cryptographic keys, algorithms, parameters) in order to enable the protections. This is achieved using the **Internet Key Exchange (IKE) Protocol** [137, 160]. IKE is the current IETF standard of authenticated key exchange protocol for IPSec.

IKE is a suite of authentication and authenticated key exchange protocols. Each protocol in the suite is a hybrid one which uses part of "Oakley" (the Oakley Key Determination Protocol [227]), part of "SKEME" (a Versatile Secure Key Exchange Mechanism for Internet [174]) and part of "ISAKMP" (the Internet Security Association and Key Management Protocol [189]).

Oakley describes a series of key exchanges – called "modes" – and gives details of the services provided by each (e.g., perfect forward secrecy for session keys, endpoint identity hiding, and mutual authentication). SKEME describes an authenticated key exchange technique which supports deniability of connections between communication partners (due to using shared key, a feature adopted in IKE and IKE v2, to be discussed in a moment) and quick key refreshment. ISAKMP provides a common framework for two communication parties to achieve authentication and authenticated key exchange, to negotiate and agree on various security attributes, cryptographic algorithms, security parameters, authentication mechanisms, etc., which are collectively called "Security Associations (SAs)." However ISAKMP does not define any specific key exchange technique so that it can support many different key exchange techniques.

As a hybrid protocol of these works, IKE can be thought of as a suite of two-party protocols, featuring authenticated session key exchange, most of them in the suite using the Diffie-Hellman key exchange mechanism, having many options for the two participants to negotiate and agree upon in an on-line fashion.

The IKE Protocol consists of two phases, called "Phase 1" and "Phase 2," respectively.

Phase 1 assumes that each of the two parties involved in a key exchange has an identity of which each party knows. Associated with that identity is some sort of cryptographic capability which can be shown to the other party. This capability might be enabled by a pre-shared secret key for a symmetric cryptosystem, or by a private key matching a reliable copy of a public key for a public-key cryptosystem. Phase 1 attempts to achieve mutual authentication[d] based on showing that cryptographic capability, and establishes a shared session key which is used in the current run of Phase 1, can be used to protect Phase 2 exchanges if they are needed, or can be further used to secure higher-level communications as an output from the IKE phases of exchanges.

A multiple number of Phase 2 exchanges may take place after a Phase 1 exchange between the same pair of entities involved in Phase 1. Phase 2 is often referred to as

---

[d]We shall see in a moment that some modes in IKE Phase 1 fail to achieve mutual authentication in that an entity may be fooled perfectly to believe sharing a session key with an intended party, whereas actually sharing it with another party.

"Quick Mode." It relies on the shared session key agreed in Phase 1. The reason for having a multiple number of Phase 2 exchanges is that they allow the users to set up multiple connections with different security properties, such as "integrity-only," "confidentiality-only," "encryption with a short key" or "encryption with a strong key."

To see a flavor of IKE, let us focus our attention only on a couple of IKE Phase 1 modes.

### 12.2.3.1  IKE Phase 1

There are eight variants for the IKE Phase 1. This is because there are three types of keys (pre-shared symmetric key, public key for encryption, and public key for signature verification), and in addition there are two versions of protocols based on public encryption keys, one of which is intended to replace the other, but the first must still be documented for backward compatibility. Thus there are actually four types of keys (pre-shared symmetric key, old-style public encryption key, new-style public encryption key, and public signature-verification key). For each key type there are two types of Phase 1 exchanges: a "main mode" and an "aggressive mode."

Each main mode has six messages exchanges; 3 messages sent from an initiator ($I$ for short) to a responder ($R$ for short), 3 sent from $R$ to $I$. A main mode is mandatory in IKE, that is, two users cannot run an aggressive mode without running a main mode first.

Each aggressive mode has only three messages; $I$ initiates a message, $R$ responds one, then $I$ sends a final message to terminate a run. An aggressive mode is optional, that is, it can be omitted.

For IKE Phase 1, we shall only describe and analyze "signature based modes." Other modes generally use an encryption-then-decryption of freshness identifier mechanism for achieving authentication; we have labeled such a mechanism non-standard (see §11.4.1.5) which we will further criticize in §17.2.

### 12.2.3.2  Signature-based IKE Phase 1 Main Mode

Signature-based IKE Phase 1 Main Mode (also named "Authenticated with Signatures," §5.1 of [137]) is specified in Prot 12.1. This mode is born under the influence of several protocols, however, its real root can be traced back to two protocols: the STS Protocol (Prot 11.6), and a protocol proposed by Krawczyk [173] named SIGMA Protocol (we shall discuss SIGMA design in §12.2.4).

In the first pair of messages exchange $I$ sends to $R$ HDR$_I$ and SA$_I$, and $R$ responds with HDR$_R$ and SA$_R$. The header messages HDR$_I$ and HDR$_R$ include "cookies" $C_I$ and $C_R$; the former is for $R$ to keep the run (session) state information for $I$, and vice versa for the latter. Of the two Security Associations, SA$_I$ specifies

**Protocol 12.1:** Signature-based IKE Phase 1 Main Mode

1. $I \to R$: $\text{HDR}_I$, $\text{SA}_I$;

2. $R \to I$: $\text{HDR}_R$, $\text{SA}_R$;

3. $I \to R$: $\text{HDR}_I$, $g^x$, $N_I$;

4. $R \to I$: $\text{HDR}_R$, $g^y$, $N_R$;

5. $I \to R$: $\text{HDR}_I$, $\{\text{ID}_I, \text{Cert}_I, \text{Sig}_I\}_{g^{xy}}$;

6. $R \to I$: $\text{HDR}_R$, $\{\text{ID}_R, \text{Cert}_R, \text{Sig}_R\}_{g^{xy}}$.

Notation (∗ for ease of exposition, we omitted some minute details. Our omission will not effect the functionality of the protocol, in particular, it will not effect an attack we shall describe in a moment. ∗)

$I$, $R$: An initiator and a responder, respectively.

$\text{HDR}_I$, $\text{HDR}_R$: Message headers of $I$ and $R$, respectively. These data contain $C_I$, $C_R$ which are "cookies"[a] of $I$ and $R$, respectively, which are for keeping the session state information for these two entities.

$\text{SA}_I$, $\text{SA}_R$: Security Associations of $I$ and $R$, respectively. The two entities use $\text{SA}_I$, $\text{SA}_R$ to negotiate parameters to be used in the current run of the protocol; negotiable things include: encryption algorithms, signature algorithms, pseudo-random functions for hashing messages to be signed, etc. $I$ may propose multiple options, whereas $R$ must reply with only one choice.

$g^x$, $g^y$: Diffie-Hellman key agreement material of $I$ and $R$, respectively.

$\text{ID}_I$, $\text{ID}_R$: Endpoint identities of $I$ and $R$, respectively.

$N_I$, $N_R$: Nonces of $I$ and $R$, respectively.

$\text{Sig}_I$, $\text{Sig}_R$: Signature created by $I$ and $R$, respectively. The signed messages are $M_I$ and $M_R$, respectively, where

$$M_I = \text{prf}_1(\text{prf}_2(N_I|N_R|g^{xy})|g^x|g^y|C_I|C_R|\text{SA}_I|\text{ID}_I)$$

$$M_R = \text{prf}_1(\text{prf}_2(N_I|N_R|g^{xy})|g^y|g^x|C_R|C_I|\text{SA}_R|\text{ID}_R)$$

where $\text{prf}_1$ and $\text{prf}_2$ are pseudo-random functions agreed in SAs.

---

[a]A "cookie" is a text-only string that gets entered into a remote host system's memory or saved to file there for the purpose of keeping the state information for a client-server communication session.

a list of security attributes that $I$ would like to use; $SA_R$ specifies ones chosen by $R$.

The second pair of messages consists of the Diffie-Hellman key exchange material.

In message 5 and 6, the algorithms for encryption, signature and pseudo-random functions for hashing messages to be signed are the ones agreed in the SAs.

Signature-based IKE Phase 1 Main Mode has some similarity to the STS Protocol (Prot 11.6). However, two significant differences can be spotted:

i) The STS Protocol leaves the certificates outside of the encryptions, whereas here the certificates are inside the encryptions. Encryption of the certificates allows an anonymity feature which we have discussed when we introduced the STS Protocol (§11.6.1). This is possible and a useful feature for $I$ and/or $R$ being endpoints inside firewalls.

ii) Signatures in the STS Protocol do not involve the agreed session key, whereas here a signed message is input to a pseudo-random function prf which also takes in the agreed session key $g^{xy}$ as the seed. Hence in this mode, the signatures are exclusively verifiable by the parties who have agreed the shared session key.

### 12.2.3.3  Authentication Failure in Signature-based IKE Phase 1 Main Mode

Similar to the situation in the STS Protocol, a signed message in this mode of IKE only links to the endpoint identity of the signer, and not also to that of the intended communication partner. The lack of this specific explicitness also makes this mode suffer from an authentication-failure flaw similar to Lowe's attack on the STS Protocol (Attack 11.3). The flaw is illustrated in Example 12.1. Meadows has shown a similar flaw for this mode of IKE [197].

With this flaw, Malice can successfully fool $R$ into believing that $I$ has initiated and completed a run with it. However in fact $I$ did not do so. Notice that $R$ is fooled perfectly in the following two senses: first, it accepts a wrong communication partner and believes to have shared a key with the wrong partner, and second, nobody will ever report to $R$ anything abnormal. So Attack 12.1 indeed demonstrates an authentication failure.

The authentication-failure attack can also be called a "denial of service attack" for a good reason. In IKE, after a successful Phase 1 exchange, a server in the position of $R$ will keep the current state with $I$ so that they may use the agreed session key for further engagement in a multiple number of Phase 2 exchanges. However, after the attack run shown in Attack 12.1, $I$ will never come to $R$ and hence, $R$ may keep the state, allocate resource with $I$ and wait for $I$ to come back for further exchanges. If Malice mounts this attack in a distributed manner, using a

**Attack 12.1:** Authentication Failure in Signature-based IKE Phase 1 Main Mode

(∗ Malice faces $I$ using his true identity, but he faces $R$ by masquerading as $I$: ∗)

1. $I \rightarrow$ Malice: $HDR_I$, $SA_I$;

     1' Malice("$I$") $\rightarrow R$: $HDR_I$, $SA_I$;

     2' $R \rightarrow$ Malice("$I$"): $HDR_R$, $SA_R$;

2. Malice $\rightarrow I$: $HDR_R$, $SA_R$;

3. $I \rightarrow$ Malice: $HDR_I$, $g^x$, $N_I$;

     3' Malice("$I$") $\rightarrow R$: $HDR_I$, $g^x$, $N_I$;

     4' $R \rightarrow$ Malice("$I$"): $HDR_R$, $g^y$, $N_R$;

4. Malice $\rightarrow I$: $HDR_R$, $g^y$, $N_R$;

5. $I \rightarrow$ Malice: $HDR_I$, $\{ID_I,\ Cert_I,\ Sig_I\}_{g^{xy}}$;

     5' Malice("$I$") $\rightarrow R$: $HDR_I$, $\{ID_I,\ Cert_I,\ Sig_I\}_{g^{xy}}$;

     6' $R \rightarrow$ Malice("$I$"): $HDR_R$, $\{ID_R,\ Cert_R,\ Sig_R\}_{g^{xy}}$;

6. Dropped.

CONSEQUENCE:
$R$ is fooled perfectly and thinks it has been talking and sharing a session key with $I$, while $I$ thinks it has been talking with Malice in an incomplete run. $R$ will never be notified of any abnormality and may either be denied a service from $I$; it enters a state awaiting a service request from $I$ (perhaps only drops the state upon "timeout").

large team of his friends over the Internet to target a single server at the same time, then the server's capacity to serve other honest nodes can be drastically reduced or even nullified. Notice that this attack does not demand sophisticated manipulation nor complex computation from Malice and his distributed friends, and hence the distributed denial of service attack can be very effective.

This attack works because a signed message in the protocol only contains the identity of the signer, and so it can be used to fool a principal who is not the intended communication partner of the signer. If both endpoint identities of the intended principals are included in a signed message, then the message becomes specific to these two principals, and hence cannot be used for any other purpose.

We have witnessed again the generality of attacks due to name omission.

### 12.2.3.4   Signature-based IKE Phase 1 Aggressive Mode

Signature-based IKE Phase 1 Aggressive Mode is a cut-down simplification from Main Mode: it does not use encryption and has three message exchanges instead of six. Using the same notation as that in Main Mode (Prot 12.1), this mode is specified as follows:

1. $I \rightarrow R$: $\text{HDR}_I$, $\text{SA}_I$, $g^x$, $N_I$, $\text{ID}_I$

2. $R \rightarrow I$: $\text{HDR}_R$, $\text{SA}_R$, $g^y$, $N_R$, $\text{ID}_R$, $\text{Cert}_R$, $\text{Sig}_R$

3. $I \rightarrow R$: $\text{HDR}_R$, $\text{Cert}_I$, $\text{Sig}_I$

At first glance, this mode is very similar to "Authentication-only STS Protocol" (Prot 11.7) due to omission of encryption. A closer look exposes a difference: in "Authentication-only STS Protocol," signed messages do not involve the session key, whereas here, a signed message is input to pseudo-random function prf which also takes in the agreed session key $g^{xy}$ as the seed. So in this mode, the signatures are exclusively verifiable by the principals who hold the agreed session key. This difference prevents the "certificate-signature-replacement attack" (Attack 11.2) from being applied to this mode.

However, this mode fails to achieve mutual authentication in a different way. A similar "denial of service attack" applies to this mode. It is essentially Lowe's attack on the STS Protocol (see Attack 11.3). Now it is $I$ who can be fooled perfectly in believing that it has been talking and sharing a session key with $R$, whereas $R$ does not agree so. We shall leave the concrete construction of the attack as an exercise for the reader (Ex 12.6).

We should further notice that if the signature scheme used in this mode features message recovery, then Malice can gain more. For example, from a signed message Malice can obtain $\text{prf}_2(N_I|N_R|g^{xy})$ and so he can use this material to create his own signature using his own certificate and identity. Thus he can mount a "certificate-signature-replacement attack" which we have seen in Attack 11.2 against the "Authentication-only STS Protocol." Such an attack is a perfect one because both interleaved runs which Malice orchestrates in between $I$ and $R$ will terminate successfully and so neither of the two honest entities can find anything wrong. Notice that some signature schemes do feature message recovery (e.g., [222] which is even standardized [152]). Therefore, it is not impossible for the two communication partners to have negotiated to use a signature scheme with message recovery feature. In §12.2.5, we shall discuss the IKE's feature of supporting flexible options.

Without using encryption or MAC, the IKE's Aggressive Mode cannot have a "plausible deniability feature" which we shall discuss in §12.2.4. When this feature is not needed, a fix for the authentication-failure flaw is standard: both two endpoint identities of the intended principals should be included inside the both signatures so that the signed messages are unusable in any context other than this mode between the intended principals.

Methods for fixing authentication failure while keeping a deniability feature will be discussed in §12.2.4.

### 12.2.3.5 Other Security Analysis on IPSec and IKE

Several researchers have conducted security analysis work on IKE.

Meadows, using her NRL Protocol Analyzer (an automated exhaustive flaw checker, to study in §17.5.2 [196, 195]), has discovered that the Quick Mode (an IKE Phase 2 exchange) is vulnerable to a reflection attack [197].

Ferguson and Schneier conduct a comprehensive cryptographic evaluation for IPSec [109].

Bellovin makes an analysis on a serious problem with IPSec: an option for an IPSec mode in which ciphertext messages are not protected in terms of data integrity [28]. We have seen through an attacking example and now know that confidentiality without integrity completely misses the point (§11.7.8). We shall further see in later chapters (Chapters 14 – 17) that most encryption algorithms cannot provide proper confidentiality protection if the ciphertext messages they output are not also protected in terms of data integrity. However, this dangerous option seems to remain unnoticed by the IPSec community (see below), maybe due to the high system complexity in the specifications for IPSec.

## 12.2.4 A Plausible Deniability Feature in IKE

At the time of writing, IKE Version 2 (IKEv2) specification has been published [160]. IKEv2 unites the many different "modes" of "Phase 1 Exchanges" of IKE into a single IKEv2 "Phase 1 Exchange." However, the current specification [160] limits the protocol to using digital signatures as the basis for authentication (see Section 5.8 of [160]). Boyd, Mao and Paterson demonstrate that IKEv2 "Phase 1 Exchange" suffers essentially the same weakness of IKE shown in Attack 12.1 [57].

A feature which is adopted as an option in IKEv2 is called "plausible deniability" [141] of communications by an entity who may have been involved in a connection with a communication partner. This feature, which originates from the SIGMA protocol construction of Krawczyk (SIGMA stands for "Sign and MAc", see an explanation in [173]), and Canetti and Krawczyk [68], permits an entity to deny "plausibly" the existence of a connection with a communication partner. Offering such a denying-of-a-connection feature at the IP layer is desirable because it permits various fancy privacy services, such as anonymity, to be offered at the higher layers with uncompromised quality. A privacy damage caused at the IP layer can cause irreparable privacy damage at the application layer. For example, an identity connected to an IP address, if not deniable, certainly nullifies an anonymous quality offered by a fancy cryptographic protocol running at the application level.

The "plausible deniability" feature in the SIGMA design can be described by following two message lines in the position of message lines 5 and 6 in Prot 12.1:

$$I \rightarrow R : s, \text{ID}_I, \text{Sig}_I(\text{"1"}, s, g^x, g^y), \text{MAC}(g^{xy}, \text{"1"}, s, \text{ID}_I)$$

$$R \rightarrow I : s, \text{ID}_R, \text{Sig}_R(\text{"0"}, s, g^y, g^x), \text{MAC}(g^{xy}, \text{"0"}, s, \text{ID}_R)$$

Here ($s$ is session identifier) both parties can verify the respective signatures and then use the shared session key to verify the respective MACs, and hence are convinced that the other end is the intended communication partner. Now, if they dispose of the session key then they cannot later prove to a third party that there was a connection between them.

It is not difficult to see that this construction contains the authentication-failure flaw demonstrated in Attack 12.1. Canetti and Krawczyk did anticipate a less interesting form of attack in which Malice simply prevents the final message from reaching $I$. They suggested a method for preventing this "cutting-final-message attack" by adding a final acknowledgement message from $I$ to $R$ (see Remark 2 in [68]). Since now $R$ (who is normally in the server's position) receives the final message, the "cutting-final-message attack" will be detected by $R$ and hence upon occurrence of the attack, $R$ should reset the state and release the resources. In this way, the protocol is less vulnerable to a denial of service attack. The final acknowledgement may have a useful side effect of preventing the authentication-failure flaw (depending on the cryptographic formulation of the acknowledgement message). But clearly this method of fixing the protocol is not particularly desirable, since it involves additional traffic and protocol complexity.

Since a deniability feature is useful, we should keep it while fixing the authentication failure flaw. We suggest augmenting the SIGMA design into the following two lines:

$$I \rightarrow R : s, \text{ID}_I, \text{Sig}_I(\text{"1"}, s, g^x, g^y), \text{MAC}(g^{xy}, \text{"1"}, s, \text{ID}_I, \text{ID}_R)$$

$$R \rightarrow I : s, \text{ID}_R, \text{Sig}_R(\text{"0"}, s, g^y, g^x), \text{MAC}(g^{xy}, \text{"0"}, s, \text{ID}_R, \text{ID}_I)$$

Namely, the two principals should still not explicitly sign their identities and so to retain the "plausible deniability" feature, however, they should *explicitly* verify both intended identities inside the MACs.

Notice that this denying-of-a-connection feature is not high quality because a party (call it a "traitor") who keeps the session key $g^{xy}$ can later still show to a third party the evidence that a named (authenticated) entity has been involved in this connection. This is clearly possible since the traitor can use exactly the same verification operations it has used when the two parties were in the authentication connection. That is why the deniability must be prefixed by the modifier "plausible."

In §13.3.5 we will introduce a new and practical cryptographic primitive which can provide a deniable authentication service in an absolute sense.

## 12.2.5  Critiques on IPSec and IKE

The most prominent criticism of IPSec and IKE is of their intensive system complexity and lack of clarity. They contain too many options and too much flexibility. There are often many ways of doing the same or similar things. Kaufman has a calculation on the number of cryptographic negotiations in IKE: 1 MUST, 806,399 MAY [159]. The high system complexity relates to an extreme obscurity in the system specification. The obscurity is actually not a good thing: it may easily confuse expert reviewers and blind them from seeing security weaknesses, or may mislead implementors and cause them to code flawed implementations.

Ferguson and Schneier regard the high-degree system complexity as a typical "committee effect" [109]. They argue that "committees are notorious for adding features, options, and additional flexibility to satisfy various factions within the committee." Indeed, if a committee effect, i.e., the additional system complexity, is seriously detrimental to a normal (functional) standard (as we sometimes experience), then it shall have a devastating effect on a security standard.

A serious problem with the high-degree flexibility and numerous options is not just an extreme difficulty for reviewers to understand the system behavior, nor just a ready possibility for implementors to code incorrect system, but that some specified options may themselves be dangerous. In §12.2.3.4, we have depicted an optional scenario for Malice to mount a perfect interleaving attack on IKE's Signature-based Aggressive Mode, by choosing a signature scheme with message recovery property. Let us now see another example of such dangers.

The example of danger is manifested by an excerpt from an interpretation paper entitled "Understanding the IPSec Protocol Suite" [12]. That paper, published in March 2000, provides explanations on IPSec and IKE at various levels, from a general concept for network security to some detailed features of IPSec and IKE. The following excerpt (from page 6 of [12]) explains an optional feature for "Authentication within the encapsulating security payload (ESP)" (an ESP is a ciphertext chunk which encrypts some confidential data transmitted in an IP packet, see §12.2.2.2):

> The ESP authentication field, an optional field in the ESP, contains something called an integrity check value (ICV) — essentially a digital signature computed over the remaining part of the ESP (minus the authentication field itself). It varies in length depending on the authentication algorithm used. It may also be omitted entirely, if authentication services are not selected for the ESP.

In this explanation, we can see an option to omit the entire data-integrity protection for a ciphertext. We have seen in §11.7.8 and shall further see in a few later chapters that encryption without integrity ("authentication" in the excerpt) is generally dangerous, and most encryption algorithms cannot provide proper confidentiality protection without a proper data-integrity protection. Thus, a security problem in IPSec which Bellovin identified and criticized in 1996 (see the final paragraph of §12.2.3.5) is retained and explained as a feature four years later (the IPSec explanation paper was published in March 2000)! We believe that it is the high complexity of the IPSec specifications that contributes to the hiding of this dangerous error.

Aiello et al. [10] criticize IKE for its high (system design) complexities in computation and communication. They consider that protocols in IKE are vulnerable to denial of service attacks: Malice and his friends distributed over the Internet can just initiate numerous requests for connections, which include numerous stateful "cookies" for a server to maintain. They proposed a protocol named "Just Fast Keying" (JFK) and suggest that JFK be the successor of IKE. Blaze disclosed one reason why their protocol should be named JFK [40]:

> We decided this was an American-centric pun on the name Ike, which was the nickname of President Eisenhower, who had the slogan "I like Ike." We don't like IKE, so we'd like to see a successor to IKE. We call our protocol JFK, which we claim stands for "Just Fast Keying," but is also the initials of a president who succeeded Eisenhower for some amount of time. We're hoping not to ever discuss the protocol in Dallas. If there's ever an IETF in Dallas again[e], we're not going to mention our protocol at all there.

## 12.3   The Secure Shell (SSH) Remote Login Protocol

The Secure Shell (SSH) [306, 309, 310, 307, 308] is a public-key based authentication protocol suite which enables a user to securely login onto a remote server host

---

[e]The 34th IETF was held in Dallas, Texas in December 1995.

machine from a client machine through an insecure network, to securely execute commands in the remote host, and to securely move files from one host to another. The protocol is a de facto industrial standard and is in wide use for server machines which run UNIX or Linux operating systems. The client part of the protocol can work for platforms running any operating systems. The reason for the protocol to work mainly for UNIX (Linux) servers is because of these operating systems' open architecture of supporting interactive command sessions for remote users.

The basic idea of the SSH Protocol is for the user on a client machine to download a public key of a remote server, and to establish a secure channel between the client and the server using the downloaded public key and some cryptographic credential of the user. Now imagine the case of the user's credential being a password: then the password can be encrypted under the server's public key and transmitted to the server. This is already a stride of improvement in security from the simple password authentication protocol we have seen in the preceding chapter.

## 12.3.1   The SSH Architecture

The SSH protocol runs between two untrusted computers over an insecure communications network. One is called the remote server (host), the other is called the client from which a user logs on to the server by using the SSH protocol.

The SSH protocol suite consists of three major components:

- The SSH Transport Layer Protocol [310] provides server authentication to a client. This protocol is public-key based. The premise of (i.e., input to) this protocol for the server part is a public key pair called "host key" and for the client part is the public host key. The output from this protocol is a unilaterally authenticated secure channel (in terms of confidentiality and data integrity) *from the server to the client*. This protocol will typically be run over a TCP (Transport Control Protocol) and (Internet Protocol) connection, but might also be used on top of any other reliable data stream.

- The SSH User Authentication Protocol [307]. This protocol runs over the unilateral authentication channel established by the SSH Transport Layer Protocol. It supports various unilateral authentication protocols to achieve entity authentication *from a client-side user to the server*. For this direction of authentication to be possible, the remote server must have a priori knowledge about the user's cryptographic credential, i.e., the user must be a known one to the server. These protocols can be public-key based or password based. For example, it includes the simple password based authentication protocol (Prot 11.3). The output from an execution of a protocol in this suite, in conjunction with that from the SSH Transport Layer Protocol, is a mutually authenticated secure channel between the server and a given user in the client side.

- The SSH Connection Protocol [308]. This protocol runs over the mutually authenticated secure channel established by above two protocols. It materializes an encrypted communication channel and tunnels it into several secure logical channels which can be used for a wide range of secure communication purposes. It uses standard methods for providing interactive shell sessions.

Clearly, the SSH Connection Protocol is not an authentication protocol and is outside the interest of this book, and the SSH User Authentication Protocol suite can be considered as a collection of applications of standard (unilateral) authentication protocols which we have introduced in Chapter 11 (however notice a point to be discussed in §12.3.4). Thus, we only need to introduce the SSH Transport Layer Protocol.

## 12.3.2   The SSH Transport Layer Protocol

In the new version of the SSH Protocol [309, 310], the SSH Transport Layer Protocol applies the Diffie-Hellman key exchange protocol and achieves unilateral authentication from the server to the client by the server signing its key exchange material.

### 12.3.2.1   Server's Host Keys Pairs

Each server host has a pair of host public-private keys. A host may have multiple pairs of host keys for supporting multiple different algorithms. If a server host has key pairs at all, it must have at least one key pair using each required public-key algorithm. The current Internet-Draft [309] stipulates the default required public-key algorithm be the DSS (Digital Signature Standard, 10.4.8.2). The default public-key algorithm for the current version in use ([306] in the time of writing) is the RSA signature (§10.4.2).

The server host (private, public) keys are used during key exchange: the server uses its private key to sign its key exchange material; the client uses the server's host public key to verify that it is really talking to the correct server. For this to be possible, the client must have a priori knowledge of the server's host public key.

SSH supports two different trust models on the server's host public key:

- The client has a local database that associates each server host name with the corresponding public part of the host key. This method requires no centrally administered infrastructure (called public-key infrastructure, to be introduced in Chapter 13), and hence no trusted third party's coordination. The downside is that the database for (server-name, host-public-key) association may become burdensome for the user to maintain. We shall exemplify a realistic method (§12.3.2.2) for a remote user to obtain an authenticated copy of the host public key.

- The (server-name, host-public-key) association is certified by some trusted certification authority (CA) using the technique to be introduced in Chapter 13. The client only needs to know the public key of the CA, and can verify the validity of all host public keys certified by the CA.

The second alternative eases the key maintenance problem, since ideally only a single CA's public key needs to be securely stored on the client (security here means data integrity). On the other hand, each host public key must be appropriately certified by a CA before authentication is possible. Also, a lot of trust is placed on the central infrastructure.

As there is no widely deployed public-key infrastructure (PKI, Chapter 13) available on the Internet yet, the first trust model, as an option, makes the protocol much more usable during the transition time until a PKI emerges, while still providing a much higher level of security than that offered by older solutions (such as the UNIX session commands: `rlogin`, `rsh`, `rftp`, etc.).

### 12.3.2.2   Realistic Methods for Authenticating a Server's Host Public Key

A workable method for a user to have an authenticated copy of the server's host public key is for the user to bring with her/him a copy of the server's host public key and put it in the client machine before running the key exchange protocol. For example, when the user is traveling, (s)he can bring with her/him a floppy diskette which contains the server's host public key. In the current working version of the SSH Protocol [306] with the client machine running UNIX or Linux operating systems, the server's host public key used by a client machine is put in a file named `$HOME/.ssh/known_hosts`. The user should physically secure the server's host public key (e.g., in a floppy diskette the user takes while traveling) in terms of data integrity while traveling. In the case of client machine running a Windows operating system (e.g., , the server's host public key may only exists in the internal memory of the client machine and in this case the public key is downloaded in real time from the server (of course, via an insecure link) with a "fingerprint" (see the next paragraph) of the public key displayed to the user.

Another realistic method for a user to have an authenticated copy of the server's host public key downloaded via an insecure link is to use voice authentication over the telephone. First, the server's host public key is downloaded by the user in the client machine via an insecure communication link. A hexadecimal "fingerprint" of the host public key will be displayed to the user. This "fingerprint" is

$$\text{"fingerprint"}(\text{host key}) = H(\text{host key})$$

where $H$ is an agreed cryptographic hash function, such as SHA-1. In the SHA-1 case, the whole "fingerprint" has 160 bits and can therefore be read over the phone as 40 hexadecimal characters. So the user can make a phone call to the site of the remote server and check the "fingerprint" with the security administrator of the server to see if the copy computed by the client machine is identical to that read by the security administrator. In this way, the user at the client side and the security administrator at the remote server side use their voices to authenticate the correctness of the host public key. We assume that the user and the security administrator recognize each other's voices.

These means are not secure in a foolproof sense, but are practically secure and workable to a quite good degree. They are useful today when PKI is not ready over the Internet.

### 12.3.2.3   The Key Exchange Protocol

A key exchange connection is always initiated by the client side. The server listens on a specific port waiting for connections. Many clients may connect to the same server machine.

The new version of the SSH Protocol [309, 310] applies Diffie-Hellman key exchange protocol (§8.3) to achieve session key agreement. In the description of the protocol we use the following notation:

- $C$: the client;

- $S$: the server;

- $p$: a large safe prime;

- $g$: a generator for a subgroup $G_q$ of $GF(p)$;

- $q$: the order of the subgroup $G_q$;

- $V_C$, $V_S$: $C$'s and $S$'s protocol versions, respectively;

- $K_S$: $S$'s public host key;

- $I_C$, $I_S$: $C$'s and $S$'s "Key Exchange Initial Message" which have been exchanged before this part begins.

The key exchange protocol is as follows:

1. $C$ generates a random number $x$ $(1 < x < q)$ and computes

$$e \leftarrow g^x \pmod{p};$$

   $C$ sends $e$ to $S$;

2. $S$ generates a random number $y$ $(0 < y < q)$ and computes

$$f \leftarrow g^y \pmod{p};$$

$S$ receives $e$; it computes

$$K \leftarrow e^y \pmod{p},$$

$$H \leftarrow hash(V_C \parallel V_S \parallel I_C \parallel I_S \parallel K_S \parallel e \parallel f \parallel K),$$

$$s \leftarrow \mathrm{Sig}_S(H).$$

$S$ sends $K_S \parallel f \parallel s$ to $C$;

3. $C$ verifies that $K_S$ really is the host key for $S$ (using any suitable methods, e.g. a certificate or a trusted local database or the method described in §12.3.2.2);

$C$ then computes

$$K \leftarrow f^x \pmod{p},$$

$$H \leftarrow hash(V_C \parallel V_S \parallel I_C \parallel I_S \parallel K_S \parallel e \parallel f \parallel K),$$

and verifies the signature $s$ on $H$; $C$ accepts the key exchange if the verification passes.

After the key exchange, the communications between the two parties will be encrypted using the agreed session key $K$. The two parties turn to execute the SSH User Authentication Protocol [307] which may be any one of the known unilateral authentication technique. After that, the user on the client can request a service using the SSH Connection Protocol [308].

## 12.3.3 The SSH Strategy

One of the goals of the SSH Protocol is to improve security on the Internet in a progressive manner. The permission for the client to use "any suitable methods" (e.g., those given in §12.3.2.2) to verify authenticity of the server's public key clearly demonstrates SSH's strategy of quick deployment and supporting backward compatibility.

At the stage way before a public-key infrastructure is ready over the Internet, the improved security from SSH needn't be a very strong one, but is much stronger and than without. The easy to use and quick to deploy solution is a great value of SSH and is the reason why the technique has been popularly implemented and widely used in cases where the servers are UNIX or Linux platforms.

From this real-world application of authentication techniques we also see that public-key cryptography forms a vital enabler for the easy solution. The server's host key in the untrusted environment (e.g., in the client or in the route from the server to the client) only exists in public-key form, and so the management of this important key material becomes much easier. The problem will become immensely complicated if the protocol is based on secret-key cryptographic techniques.

### 12.3.4  Warnings

Finally, we should point out warning for a user to handle with care her/his cryptographic credential which is used by the SSH User Authentication Protocol. This credential, which can be public-key-based, password-based, or a secure-hardware-token-based, will be used by the protocol part running on the client machine which is considered part of the untrusted environment.

In the current working version of the SSH Protocol [306], a public-key-based user cryptographic credential (i.e., the private key matching the user's public key) is encrypted under the user's password and the resultant ciphertext is stored in a file on the client machine where the file is named $HOME/.ssh/identity (in the case of client machine running UNIX or Linux operating systems). This file is read at protocol execution time by the client part of the protocol which prompts the user to input password. Naturally, the user should make sure that the protocol part running on the client machine is a genuine one. To minimize the risk of the private key being searched by an off-line attacker (its algorithm which inputs the user's public key and searches the matching private key by searching through passwords), the user should also delete the encrypted private key file $HOME/.ssh/identity from the client machine after use.

A secure-hardware-token-based mechanism should be the most secure means for the user side credential. This mechanism in the user side uses a small hardware token of handheld size or a keyring size. The token has a window displaying a number of several digits which keep changing in synchronization with the server host and is customized to an individual user by a password shared with the server host. Of course, since the password is small, the user should securely keep in physical possession of the token and report its loss immediately.

## 12.4  The Kerberos Protocol and its Realization in Windows 2000

Let Alice be an employee of a multi national company. She may be provided with various kinds of information resources and services. For example, from her "home server," Alice gets the usual computer network services (i.e., WorldWideWeb, e-mail, etc.); on a "project server," Alice and her team members will be the exclusive users and the owners of the data related to their work; on an "human resource server," Alice may manage her HR related issues, e.g., managing how much percentage of her next month's salary should be invested for company share purchase; if Alice is a manager, she may need to update her subordinates' performance review records on an HR database; from an "intellectual property server," Alice (as an inventor) may be working on her current patent filing; on an "expenses server," Alice shall often make expense claims after her business trips. It is not difficult to imagine more examples of services.

In an enterprise environment, a user (an employee or a customer) is usually entitled to use enterprise-wide distributed information services. These services are usually maintained by various business units in the enterprise. As a result, the various information servers can operate in different geographical locations (even around the globe). Speaking in terms of network organization, these servers are in different **network domains**. For secure use of these services (all examples we have listed in the previous paragraph involve seriously sensitive information), a user needs various credentials for her/him to be authenticated before a service can be granted. However, it would be unrealistic and uneconomic to require a user to maintain several different cryptographic credentials, whether in terms of memorizing various passwords, or in terms of holding a number of smartcards.

A suitable network authentication solution for this environment is the Kerberos Authentication Protocol [204, 170]. The basic idea is to use a trusted third party to introduce a user to a service by issuing a shared session key between the user and the server. This idea is due to Needham and Schroeder [215] and is illustrated in the Needham-Schroeder Authentication Protocol (Prot 2.4). As the original Needham-Schroeder protocol is flawed (see §2.6.4.2), Kerberos uses essentially a timestamp version of the Needham-Schroeder protocol.

Now consider that Alice in Prot 2.4 is in the position of a user who shares a long-term secret key with a trusted third party (Trent in that protocol). Also consider that Bob in that protocol is in the position of a server who also shares a long-term secret key with the trusted third party. When Alice wants to use Bob's service, she can initiate a protocol run with Trent and ask Trent for a cryptographic credential good for accessing Bob's service. Trent can provide a ("ticket granting") service by issuing a session key to be shared between Alice and Bob, and securely delivers the session key inside two "tickets" encrypted under the long-term secret keys which Trent shares with Alice and with Bob, respectively. That's the idea.

Windows 2000, an important operating system now widely used in an enterprise network environment, uses the Kerberos Authentication Protocol (based on Version 5 [170]), as its network authentication basis.

Kerberos is created by Project Athena at the Massachusetts Institute of Technology (MIT) as a solution to network security problems. MIT has developed the Kerberos Version 5 as a free software (with source code available) which can be downloaded from MIT's Web site <http://web.mit.edu/kerberos/www/>. However, due to the exportation control on cryptographic products regulated by the government of the United States of America, at the time of writing, this distribution of Kerberos executables is only available to the citizens of the USA located in the USA, or to Canadian citizens located in Canada.

The Kerberos Protocol Version 5 is slightly more complex than the Needham-Schroeder Authentication Protocol (the timestamp-fixed version). Let us now introduce Kerberos Protocol Version 5.

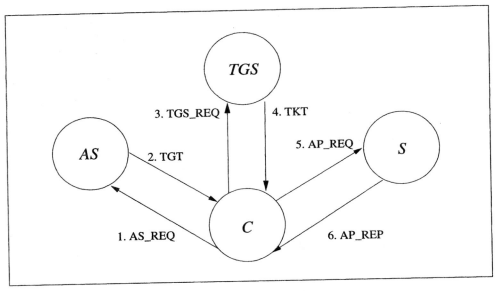

**Figure 12.4.** Kerberos Exchanges

## 12.4.1  A Single-signon Architecture

The Kerberos Authentication Protocol consists of a suite of three sub-protocols called exchanges[f]. These three exchanges are:

1. The Authentication Service Exchange (AS Exchange): it runs between a "client" $C$ and an "authentication server" $AS$.

2. The Ticket-Granting Service Exchange (TGS Exchange): it runs between $C$ and a "ticket granting server" $TGS$ after the AS Exchange.

3. The Client/Server Authentication Application Exchange (AP Exchange): it runs between $C$ and an "application server" $S$ after the TGS Exchange.

Each of these three exchanges is a two-message exchange protocol. These exchanges have the sequential dependent relation listed above which can be illustrated as a three-headed creature[g] in Fig 12.4.

Kerberos has five principals who operate in these three exchanges and these principals have the following roles:

---

[f]The suite contains a much bigger number of auxiliary sub-protocols for various specialized tasks, such as password changing, ticket renewal, error handling, etc., however, we shall only describe the three main protocols which provide authentication functions.

[g]The name Kerberos comes from Greek mythology; it is the three-headed dog that guarded the entrance to Hades.

- $U$: a User (a human being) whose actions in the protocols are always performed by her/his client process; so $U$ only appears in the protocols as a message. Each user memorizes a password as her/his **single-signon** credential for using the Kerberos system.

- $C$: a Client (a process) which makes use of a network service on behalf of a user. In an AS Exchange, in which $C$ is initiated by $U$, $C$ will need $U$'s Kerberos system credential. This user credential is given to $C$ as it prompting $U$ to key-in her/his password.

- $S$: an application Server (a process) which provides an application resource to a network client $C$. In an AP Exchange, it receives an "application request" (AP_REQ) from $C$. It responds with "application reply" (AP_REP) which may entitle $C$ an application service.

  An AP_REQ contains $C$'s credential called a "ticket" (TKT) which in turn contains an application session key $K_{C,S}$ temporarily shared between $C$ and $S$.

- KDC: Key Distribution Center. KDC is a collective name for the following two authentication servers:

  - $AS$: an Authentication Server. In an AS Exchange, it receives a plaintext "authentication service request" (AS_REQ) from a client $C$. It responds with a "ticket granting ticket" (TGT) which can later be used by $C$ in a subsequent TGS Exchange.

    Initially, $AS$ shares a password with each user it serves. A shared password is set up via a single-signon means outside the Kerberos system.

    A TGT supplied to a client $C$ as the result of an AS Exchange has two parts. One part is for $C$ to use and is encrypted under a key derived from a user's single-signon password. The other part is for a "ticket granting server" (to be described in the $TGS$ item below) to use and is encrypted under a long-term key shared between $AS$ and the latter. Both parts of a TGT contain a ticket session key $K_{C,TGS}$ to be shared between $C$ and a "ticket granting server."

  - $TGS$: a Ticket Granting Server. In a TGS Exchange it receives a "ticket granting request" (TGS_REQ) (which contains a "ticket-granting ticket" TGT) from a client $C$. It responds with a "ticket" (TKT) which entitles $C$ to use in a subsequent AP Exchange with an application server $S$.

    Similar to a TGT, a TKT has two parts. One part is for a client $C$ to use and is encrypted under a ticket session key $K_{C,TGS}$ (which has been distributed to $C$ and $TGS$ in TGT). The other part is for an application server $S$ to use and is encrypted under key $K_{S,TGS}$ which is a long-term key shared between $S$ and $TGS$.

Both parts of a TKT contain a new application session key $K_{C,S}$ to be shared between $C$ and $S$. The application session key is the cryptographic credential for $C$ to run a subsequent AP Exchange with $S$ to get an application service from $S$.

### 12.4.1.1  Why is KDC Divided into two Sub-servers $AS$ and $TGS$?

We shall see in a moment that the roles of $AS$ and $TGS$ are actually very similar: both are collectively referred to as a key distribution center (KDC).

The reason to divide KDC into two similar roles is the consideration that the system may be used in a very large network "realm" in which application servers belonging to different network domains should be organized as subordinators of different $TGS$'s in different domains. Therefore, even though a fixed user $U$ only has a fixed single-signon $AS$, (s)he can be served by a plural number of $TGS$'s and consequently by even a larger number of application servers.

## 12.4.2  The Kerberos Exchanges

Now let us describe each of the three Kerberos exchanges. For ease of exposition of the main idea in the Kerberos Authentication Protocol, we shall only present mandatory protocol messages. For the full description of all protocol message details which include an enormous volume of optional messages, the interested reader should study [170].

### 12.4.2.1  The Authentication Service Exchange

The AS Exchange concerns only $C$ and $AS$:

1. AS_REQ    $C \rightarrow AS : U, TGS, \text{Life\_time1}, N_1$

2. TGT      $AS \rightarrow C : U, T_{C,TGS}, TGT_C$

where

$$T_{C,TGS} = \{U, C, TGS, K_{C,TGS}, \text{Time\_start}, \text{Time\_expire}\}_{K_{AS,TGS}},$$

$$TGT_C = \{TGS, K_{C,TGS}, \text{Time\_start}, \text{Time\_expire}, N_1\}_{K_U}.$$

Message 1 is invoked by the user $U$. The client $C$ informs the authentication server $AS$ using the plaintext AS_REQ messages that it wishes to communicate on behalf of the user $U$ with the ticket granting server $TGS$. A lifetime Life_time1 (bookkeeping information) and a nonce $N_1$ (freshness identifier) are also included in the request.

In response, the authentication server $AS$ generates a new ticket session key $K_{C,TGS}$ for sharing between $C$ and $TGS$; it then encrypts the ticket session key inside a ticket granting ticket TGT and sends it back to $C$ as message 2.

The part of TGT for $TGS$ is $T_{C,TGS}$ and is encrypted using the long-term key $K_{AS,TGS}$ shared between itself and $TGS$, the part of TGT for $C$ is $T_C$ and is encrypted under the user's password $K_U$.

Upon receipt of message 2, $C$ can decrypt $T_C$ (it has prompted $U$ for inputting the password $K_U$). If everything passes validation (be careful about the validation, to discuss in §12.4.3), then $C$ accepts the ticket session key $K_{C,TGS}$ and the ticket $T_{C,TGS}$. $C$ now has a valid "ticket granting ticket" for use with $TGS$.

A warning on proper decryption of a Kerberos ticket will be discussed in §12.4.3.

### 12.4.2.2   The Ticket-granting Service Exchange

The TGS Exchange has a format similar to that of the AS Exchange, except that the client's request message, TGS_REQ, now contains an **authenticator** trailing after the plaintext request message.

3. TGS_REQ    $C \rightarrow TGS : S, \text{Life\_time2}, N_2, T_{C,TGS}, A_{C,TGS}$

4. TKT        $TGS \rightarrow C : U, T_{C,S}, TKT_C$

where

$$T_{C,S} = \{U, C, S, K_{C,S}, \text{Time\_start}, \text{Time\_expire}\}_{K_{S,TGS}},$$

$$TKT_C = \{S, K_{C,S}, \text{Time\_start}, \text{Time\_expire}, N_2\}_{K_{C,TGS}},$$

$$A_{C,TGS} = \{C, \text{Client\_time}\}_{K_{C,TGS}}.$$

The functionalities of this pair of exchange and actions of principals can be explained analogously to those for the AS Exchange. The only additional item worth explaining is $A_{C,TGS}$. This is an authenticator. The use of an authenticator is to show the ticket granting server $TGS$ that the client $C$ has used the ticket session key $K_{C,TGS}$ in Client_time. $TGS$ should check its local host time to confirm that the difference between Client_time and its local time is within an allowable range.

A warning on a Kerberos authenticator is discussed in §12.4.3.

### 12.4.2.3   The Application Service Exchange

Finally, in the AP Exchange a client $C$ uses the newly obtained application session key $K_{C,S}$ and the ticket $T_{C,S}$ to obtain an application service from an application server $S$.

5. AP_REQ    $C \to S : T_{C,S}, A_{C,S}$

6. AP_REP    $S \to C : A_{S,C}$

where

$$A_{C,S} = \{C, \text{Client\_time1}\}_{K_{C,S}},$$
$$A_{S,C} = \{\text{Client\_time1}\}_{K_{C,S}}.$$

The meaning of this pair of exchange is straightforward.

As we have warned in the descriptions of the previous two exchanges, we shall pay attention to the warnings below.

### 12.4.3  Warnings

We must discuss two warnings in Kerberos exchanges.

The first one is about careful validation of a Kerberos ciphertext in a decryption time.

When a principal decrypts a ticket, it should validate the decryption. From the structure of a Kerberos ticket, the validation obviously include steps for checking the freshness identifiers and the correctness of the intended identities. However, what is not so obvious is the need of verifying data-integrity of a ciphertext. The importance of the data-integrity verification has been illustrated by several examples in the previous chapter (e.g., §11.7.8), and will be further investigated in §17.2.1.

This warning applies to all encryption in Kerberos exchanges.

The second warning is about "authenticator."

Although the name "authenticator" and its position and usage (trailing a ticket) may suggest that it plays the role of a message authentication code (MAC, see §10.3) for providing a data-integrity protection on the ticket it trails (e.g., $A_{C,TGS}$ with respect to $T_{C,TGS}$), this imagined "protection" is actually absent.

Not only must the needed integrity protection on the ticket be supplied by a proper mechanism (e.g., by a MAC), but also notice: using encryption to create an authenticator is using a wrong cryptographic service. In order to prevent an adversary from modifying a Client_time in an authenticator, the cipher block of an authenticator itself needs data-integrity protection!

This warning applies to all authenticators in Kerberos.

## 12.5  SSL and TLS

An important authentication protocol, mainly for WorldWideWeb (Web for short) security, is the Secure Sockets Layer Protocol (SSL) [138, 112]. The term "sockets" refers to standard communication channels linking peer processes on network devices (e.g., on client/server machines). A sockets-layer protocol runs under the application-layer protocols such as the Hypertext Transfer Protocol (HTTP), Lightweight Directory Access Protocol (LDAP), or Internet Messaging Access Protocol (IMAP), and above the network layer protocols such as Transport Control Protocol (TCP) and Internet Protocol (IP). When the sockets-layer communications are secured (e.g., in confidentiality and data integrity), communications in all application-layer protocols will be secured in the same manner.

SSL is a commonly used protocol for managing the security of a message transmission on the Internet. The protocol is originally developed by Netscape Communications Corporation as an integral part of its Web browser (client-side software) and Web server. It is later accepted by Microsoft and other Internet client/server developers as well, and evolves into the de facto standard for Web security until it further evolves into the Transport Layer Security (TLS) [96]. The latter is an Internet standard for Web security developed by the industrial standardization body Internet Engineering Task Force (IETF).

TLS is based on SSL and is not drastically different from SSL. However, since TLS succeeds SSL as Internet standard for Web security, we shall from now on comply with the standards track and only use the term TLS in our description of the Web security protocol.

## 12.5.1  TLS Architecture Overview

TLS is composed of two layered protocols: the **TLS Record Protocol** and the **TLS Handshake Protocol**. The latter is on top of the former.

The TLS Record Protocol provides secure encapsulation of the communication channel for use by higher layer application protocols. This protocol runs on top of the TCP and IP layers and provides a reliable session connection. It takes messages to be transmitted, fragments the data into manageable blocks, optionally compresses the data, applies a MAC (HMAC, see §10.3.2) for data-integrity, encrypts (symmetric algorithm) for confidentiality, and transmits the result to the peer communicant. At the receiving end, it receives cipher data blocks, decrypts them, verifies the MAC, optionally decompressed, reassembles the blocks and delivers the result to higher level application processes.

The keys for symmetric encryption and for HMAC are generated uniquely for each session connection and are based on a secret negotiated by the TLS Handshake Protocol.

The TLS Handshake Protocol allows the server and client to authenticate each other, negotiate cryptographic algorithms, agree on cryptographic keys and thereby establish a secure session connection for the TLS Record Protocol to process secure communications for higher level application protocols.

From this TLS architecture description it is clear that the TLS Record Protocol is not an authentication protocol, although it is a protocol for achieving secure communications. We therefore should only introduce the TLS Handshake Protocol.

## 12.5.2  TLS Handshake Protocol

The TLS Handshake Protocol can be considered as a stateful process running on the client and server machines. A stateful connection is called a "session" in which the communication peers perform the following steps:

- They exchange hello messages to agree on algorithms, exchange random values, and check for session resumption.

- They exchange the necessary cryptographic parameters to allow the client and server to agree on a secret (called "master secret").

- They exchange certificates and cryptographic information to allow the client and server to authenticate themselves to one another.

- They generate session secrets from the master secret by exchanging random values.

- They verify that their peer has calculated the same security parameters to confirm that the handshake has been completed without having been tampered with by an attacker.

- The established secure channel is passed on to the TLS Record Protocol for processing higher level application communications.

These steps are realized by four message exchanges which we describe below. In order to achieve a better exposition of the protocol idea we shall only describe a simplified version of the TLS Handshake Protocol by omitting some optional elements. In the protocol description, $C$ denotes the client (i.e., the client-side Web browser), $S$ denotes the Web server. If a message is trailed with $*$, this message is optional.

1. $C \rightarrow S$ :  ClientHello;

2. $S \rightarrow C$ :  ServerHello,
   ServerCertificate$*$,
   ServerKeyExchange$*$,
   CertificateRequest$*$,
   ServerHelloDone;

3. $C \rightarrow S$ :  ClientCertificate$*$,

ClientKeyExchange,
CertificateVerify∗,
ClientFinished;

4. $S \rightarrow C$ :   ServerFinished.

This protocol can be executed with all the optional messages and the Client-KeyExchange message omitted. This is the case when the client wants to resume an existing session.

Now let us provide an overview level explain on the messages exchanged in the TLS Handshake Protocol.

### 12.5.2.1   Hello Message Exchange

The client starts the session connection by sending a ClientHello message to which the server must respond with a ServerHello message, or else the connection will fail. These two messages establish the following fields: "protocol_version," "random," "session_id," "cipher_suites," and "compression_methods."

The field "protocol_version" is for backward compatibility use: the server and client may use this field to inform their peer of the version of the protocol it is using.

The field "random" contains random numbers (nonces as freshness identifiers) which are generated by the both sides and are exchanged. It also contains the local time of the each communicant.

The field "session_id" identifies the current session connection. When the client wishes to start a new session connection, ClientHello.session_id should be empty. In this case, the server generates a new session_id, uses this new value in the field ServerHello.session_id, and caches the session_id in its local memory. If Client-Hello.session_id is non-empty (when the client wants to resume an existing session), the server should try to find the session_id from its local cache, and resume the identified session.

A point of noticing is the field "cipher_suites." ClientHello.cipher_suites is a list of the cryptographic options supported in the client side machine, sorted with the client's first preference first. A wide range of public-key and symmetric cryptographic algorithms, digital signature schemes, MAC schemes and hash functions can be proposed by the client. The server selects a single scheme for each necessary cryptographic operation, and informs the client in ServerHello.cipher_suites.

### 12.5.2.2   Server's Certificate and Key-exchange Material

After the hello message exchange, the server may optionally send its certificate, if it is to be authenticated. The ServerCertificate message, if non-empty, is a list of X.509.v3 certificates (see § 13.2). An X.509 certificate contains sufficient information about the name and the public key of the certificate owner and that about the issuing certification authority (see Example 13.1). Sending a list of certificates permits the client to choose one with the public key algorithm supported at the client's machine.

Subsequent to ServerCertificate is ServerKeyExchange. It contains the server's public key material matching the certificate list in ServerCertificate. The material for Diffie-Hellman key agreement will be included here which is the tuple $(p, g, g^y)$ where $p$ is a prime modulus, $g$ is a generator modulo $p$ of a large group and $y$ is an integer cached in the server's local memory (linked to "session_id").

The server who provides non-anonymous services may further request a certificate from the client using the CertificateRequest message, if that is appropriate to its selection of the public-key algorithm from ClientHello.cipher_suite.

Now the server will send the ServerHelloDone message, indicating that the hello-message phase of the handshake is complete. The server will then wait for a client response.

### 12.5.2.3 Client Response

If the server has sent the CertificateRequest message, the client must send either the ClientCertificate message or the NoCertificate alert.

The ClientKeyExchange message is now sent. The content of this message will depend on the public key algorithm agreed between the ClientHello and ServerHello messages.

In the case of the client's KeyExchangeAlgorithm being RSA, the client generates a "master_secret" (a 48-byte number) and encrypts it under the server's certified RSA public key (obtained from the ServerCertificate).

If the client has sent a certificate and the client has the signing ability, then a digitally-signed CertificateVerify message will be sent for the server to explicitly verify the client's certificate.

### 12.5.2.4 Finished Message Exchange

The client now sends the ClientFinished message which includes a keyed HMAC (keyed under the "master_secret") to allow the server to confirm the proper hand-shake executed at the client side.

In response, the server will send its own ServerFinished message which also includes a keyed HMAC to allow the client to confirm the proper handshake executed at the server side.

At this point, the handshake is complete and the client and server may begin to exchange application layer data.

## 12.5.3 A Typical Run of the TLS Handshake Protocol

Let us complete our description of the TLS Protocol by exemplifying a typical run of the Handshake Protocol. The execution example is illustrated in Prot 12.2.

---

**Protocol 12.2:** A Typical Run of the TLS Handshake Protocol.

1. $C \rightarrow S$ : ClientHello.protocol_version = "TLS Version 1.0",
   ClientHello.random = $T_C, N_C$,
   ClientHello.session_id = "NULL",
   ClientHello.crypto_suite = "RSA: encryption, SHA-1: HMAC",
   ClientHello.compression_method = "NULL";

2. $S \rightarrow C$ : ServerHello.protocol_version = "TLS Version 1.0",
   ServerHello.random = $T_S, N_S$,
   ServerHello.session_id = "xyz123",
   ServerHello.crypto_suite = "RSA: encryption, SHA-1: HMAC",
   ServerHello.compression_method = "NULL",
   ServerCertificate = point_to(server's certificate),
   ServerHelloDone;

3. $C \rightarrow S$ : ClientKeyExchange = point_to(RSA_Encryption(master_secret)),
   ClientFinished = SHA-1(master_secret $\| C \|, N_C, N_S, ...$);

4. $S \rightarrow C$ : ServerFinished = SHA-1(master_secret $\| S \|, N_S, N_C, ...$).

---

In this execution of the TLS Handshake Protocol, the client chooses to be anonymous and so is not authenticated to the server, the client chooses to use RSA for encryption, SHA-1 for computing HMACs. As a result, the server unilaterally authenticates itself to the client. The output from the execution is a unilaterally authenticated channel from the server to the client.

This execution shows a typical example of using the TLS Protocol in a Web-based electronic commerce application, for example, buying a book from an on-line bookseller. The output channel assures the client that only the authenticated server will receive its instructions on book purchase which may include confidential information such as its user's bankcard details, the book title, and the delivery address.

## 12.5.4  A Side Channel Attack on a TLS Application

In **side channel attacks** Malice tries to find some subliminal information which a principal disclose inadvertently. A **timing analysis attack** is a special case of side channel attacks. In this special case, Malice observes and analyzes the time behavior of a principal in responding to his challenge in order to discover a secret. The first published side-channel and timing-analysis attack is that of Kocher [169] which is best applied on a system performing modulo exponentiation (e.g., signing or decrypting in RSA, ephemeral-key exponentiation in ElGamal family signature scheme of in Diffie-Hellman key exchange). The attack aims to discover the secret exponent. Modulo exponentiation uses the square-and-multiply technique and proceeds bit-by-bit on the exponent (see Alg 4.3). The operation performs, for each bit 1 in the exponent, squaring and multiplication while for each bit 0, squaring only. The attack is to detect the time difference between these two cases. A successful detection means to extract the secret exponent bit by bit.

Recently, Canvel et al. [69] discover a side channel (via timing analysis) attacking technique against a protocol case: a TLS/SSL protected link between a server and a client. A typical target of this attack is a user's password for accessing an e-mail (IMAP) server. In this case, the targeted password is sent from a client machine to an e-mail server and the communications between the client and the server is protected by a TLS link. The link is encrypted using a strong session key as a result of a TLS protocol run (e.g., that illustrated in Prot 12.2). The session encryption uses a strong block cipher (e.g., triple DES) in the CBC mode of operation (see §7.8.2).

The timing analysis attack utilizes Vaudenay's "bomb oracle attack" on the standard CBC padding scheme [296] which we have studied in §7.8.2.1. Let us recap that attack briefly here. Let $C$ be a CBC ciphertext block which encrypts a password and is recorded by Malice. In Vaudenay's attack on the standard CBC plaintext padding scheme, Malice sends to a decryption oracle

$$r, C$$

where $r$ is some random data block(s). Malice then waits for the decryption oracle's response, either "correct padding" or "incorrect padding". The "correct padding" response reveals the final plaintext byte encrypted under $C$ (in the case of $C$ encrypting a password, this byte reveals the final character of the password). Now we are technically ready to describe the timing analysis attack against the TLS link.

Now Malice sends to the e-mail server $r, C$, pretending that he is the owner of the targeted password encrypted in $C$ and is accessing e-mail. The server, upon receipt of $r, C$, will perform CBC decryption and check the validity of the padding. If the padding is correct (with probability close to $2^{-8}$, see §7.8.2.1), it will further check data integrity by recalculating a MAC (message authentication code, review the data integrity mechanism using MAC in §10.3.3). If a padding error is detected, then there is no need to perform the data-integrity checking (i.e., no further recalculation of the MAC). An error in either cases will be sent back to the client machine, of course, encrypted under the strong TLS session key.

It seems that Malice, who does not know the strong session key, cannot get an oracle service, that is, the e-mail server who sends error messages encrypted, is not a decryption oracle.

However, for random $r$, if the CBC padding is correct, then in an overwhelming probability the data integrity checking will fail. Therefore, the e-mail server under attack actually only responds in one of the following two ways:

i) Sending back $\{$ "invalid padding" $\}_K$, with probability $\approx 1 - 2^{-8}$, or

ii) Sending back $\{$ "invalid MAC" $\}_K$, with probability $\approx 2^{-8}$.

The case (ii) implies "valid padding" from which Malice obtains the final plaintext byte under $C$.

Now the timing attack kicks in! For a sufficiently large $r$ (a few blocks), in case (ii) the server has to recalculate a lengthy CBC MAC while in case (i) no such calculation is performed. On a fairly standard implementation of the server, Canvel et al. [69] detect consistent difference in the server's response time and the difference is in terms of a few milliseconds. Thus, under timing analysis, the server acts, indeed, as a decryption oracle. Notice that the error-handling procedure, usually necessary in applications, means that the decryption oracle never explodes; it is a reliable oracle!

By changing $r$ craftily (without changing $C$), Malice can discover the whole password byte-by-byte backward. The method of changing $r$ is left as an exercise for the reader (a hint is given in Ex 12.12). If $C$ encrypts a password of 8 bytes, the extraction of the whole password can be done in $8 \times 2^8 = 2048$ trials which are pretended e-mail accessing loging-in sessions.

This is an extraordinary attack, although it works better on (or is probably confined to) the case of local area network (LAN) where the client and the server are in the same LAN so that the difference in time delay can be detected more accurately. This attack manifests that oracle services can be generally available, sometimes via side channels. From this attack we also know that error messages in cryptographic protocols need to be handled with care.

A possible fix for this attack in this specific application is that the server should take a random elapse of "sleep" before responding an error message.

## 12.6  Chapter Summary

In this chapter we have introduced four authentication protocols (systems and standards) for real world applications. They are: IKE as the IETF authentication standard for IPSec, SSH as the de facto authentication standard for remote secure shell interaction sessions, Kerberos as the industrial standard for Windows-based operating systems for an enterprise computer and information resource environment, and TLS (SSL) as the de facto standard for the Web security.

Although in our description of each protocol suite (system), we have taken a great deal of simplification, still, our descriptions show enough engineering complexities. These complexities are due to real-world necessities such as algorithm and parameter negotiation, compatibility for use by a wide range of systems, backward compatibility, easy to use, etc. In the case IPSec and IKE, the need of supporting a general quality of confidentiality also contributed to the high system complexity. From our study in this chapter we know that for any real-world application of authentication protocols, we are not only facing a number of security problems, but also facing a great deal of system engineering problems. The latter problems, if not dealt with due care, can cause serious consequences in security.

We have also seen that the extreme error-prone nature of authentication protocols inevitably appears in the versions for real world applications. For this reason, we have still not completed our topic on authentication protocols for this book. We will return to this important topic in Chapter 17 on formal analysis techniques.

# Exercises

12.1 In absence of IPSec protection for IP communications, by what means can Malice manipulate messages transmitted over the Internet (e.g., masquerade as a message originator, reroute a message, etc.)?

12.2 What role does an "authentication header" (AH) play in an IPSec enabled IP packet?

12.3 What is the relationship between IPSec and IKE?

12.4 In which two ways can an IP packet be cryptographically protected?

12.5 In Ex 11.15 we have considered a fix of the minor flaw in the STS protocol without damaging its anonymity (deniability) property. Provide a similar fix for the minor flaw in the IKE Signature-based Phase 1 Main Mode without damaging its "plausible deniability" property.

12.6 Demonstrate a "perfect denial service attack" on Signature-based IKE Phase 1 Aggressive Mode in §12.2.3.4.

Hint: such an attack is similar to one in Attack 11.3.

12.7 Both the encrypted key exchange (EKE) protocol (Prot 11.5) and the SSH protocol encrypt passwords using asymmetric encryption algorithms. However, there is an essential difference between them. What is the difference?

12.8 How can a server in the SSH protocol be practically authenticated to a user on a client?

12.9 Why in the general setting of the Kerberos protocol should each client face three different kinds of servers?

12.10 Why is the Kerberos protocol suitably used in an enterprise environment? Is it suitable for a cross-enterprise (open systems) environment?

12.11 The TLS (SSL) protocols have been widely used in the Web-based electronic commerce applications. However, are these protocols naturally suitable in such applications? If not, why?

Hint: these protocols do not support authorization of payments with the non-repudiation service.

12.12 In §12.5.4 we have introduced a timing attack technique for extracting the final byte in the plaintext message encrypted in a CBC ciphertext block which uses the standard CBC plaintext padding scheme. How are further bytes extracted?

Hint: review the standard CBC plaintext padding scheme in §7.8.2.1; to extract the-last-but-one byte after successful extraction of the last byte, you should consider the following event of "valid padding": the two final bytes ("two padding bytes") are '02' || '02'; now modify the final byte of $r$ to maximize the probability for this event to occur.

# Chapter 13

# AUTHENTICATION FRAMEWORK FOR PUBLIC-KEY CRYPTOGRAPHY

## 13.1 Introduction

In the usual sense of public-key cryptography, a key generation procedure invariantly contains the following step:

$$\text{public-key} = F(\text{private-key}). \tag{13.1.1}$$

Here, $F$ is some efficient and one-way function which maps from the private key space to the public-key space. Due to the one-way property of the function $F$ (a good mixing-transformation), public-key computed from private-key always contains a part which looks random.

With every public key containing a random-looking part, it is obviously necessary that a principal's public key be associated with the principal's identity information in a verifiable and trustworthy way. Clearly, to send a confidential message encrypted under a public key, the sender must make sure that the random-looking public key used really belongs to the intended recipient. Likewise, to establish the origin of a message using a digital signature scheme, the verifier must make sure that the public key used for the signature verification really belongs to the claimed signer.

In general, to use public-key cryptography in real-world applications, we need a mechanism which enables a ready verification of the association between a public key and a principal's identity. Such a mechanism is usually realized in an authentication framework: it enables the owner of a public key to authenticate toward the system.

## 13.1.1   Chapter Outline

In the rest of this chapter we will introduce two different ways to establish an authentication framework for public-key cryptography: one is called **public key certification infrastructure** (**PKI**) (§13.2), and the other, **identity-based public-key cryptography** (§13.3).

# 13.2   Directory-Based Authentication Framework

For a pair of principals who communicate frequently, it need not be difficult for them to securely identify the other party's public key: they can exchange their public keys initially in a physically secure manner, e.g., in a face-to-face meeting, and then store the keys by a secure means. However, this "simple" **key-management** method does not scale up well. In the general setting for an open communications system, communications take place between principals who may have never met before; also in most cases a communication may take place between a pair of principals *once* only. The "simple" key-management method will require each principal to manage an unrealistically huge number of public keys. Moreover, such a method does not really make use of the advantages of public-key cryptography.

In §2.4 we have seen an online service offered by a trusted principal for the management of secret keys. The service is a combination of sub-services such as key registration, authentication and name-directory. To use the key-management service, every principal should first establish a one-to-one and long-term relationship with a trusted server principal (authentication server) by sharing a long-term secret key with the latter. When two (end-user) principals need to conduct a secure communication between them, they can engage in an authentication protocol run together with the authentication server to establish a secure communication channel between them. Thus, each end-user principal only need to manage a single secret key shared with the authentication server. The key-management and authentication service introduced in Chapter 2 is for authentication protocols based on secret-key cryptosystems (even though in §2.6.6 we discussed the Needham-Schroeder public-key authentication protocol, the authentication service in that protocol still uses an online trusted third party, essentially in a secret-key style).

The secret-key management service can naturally be extended to the management of public keys. Here the key-management service is called **public-key certification service**, and a trusted server is called a **certification authority** (**CA**). A CA is a special principal who is well-known and trusted directly by the principals in the domain it serves, and can also be known and trusted in a bigger domain through an indirect way (we shall discuss more about "trust" in a moment). For each end-user within the domain of a CA, the CA will issue a **public-key certificate** for certifying the user's public key material. A public-key certificate is a structured data record with a number of data entries which include a uniquely identifiable identity of the holder and her/his public key parameter. A certificate is digitally signed by the issuing CA. Thus the CA's signature of a certificate provides a cryptographic binding between the holder's identity and her/his public key. A principal, after having verified the certificate of another principal, should believe the validity of the binding if she/he trusts the CA in that the CA has issued the certificate only after having properly identified the holder. In this way, the verification principal establishes a secure **key channel** which is directed from the certified public key toward her/him (in fact, toward the system). Kohnfelder first uses the name "public key certificate" [171].

A public-key channel based on a certification service is often called a directory-based channel, as we have illustrated in Figures 7.1 and 10.1. The certification service is thus also often called a directory service.

Notice that, in comparison with the "trust" required by an authentication server for secret-key based authentication protocols (see §2.4), the "trust" required by a CA is much weaker. Here, the security service provided is message authentication, which can be provided without need of handling any secret (since verifying a CA's signature of a certificate only involves using the CA's public key). Without the need of handling any secret, the service can be provided off-line, that is, a CA need not be engaged in a protocol run with the end-user principals. An important feature of an off-line service is that it can scale up to deal with a very large system. Obviously, a CA's public key used for verifying the certificates that the CA has issued can itself, in turn, be certified by another CA, and so on.

The data entries in a certificate should include the identity information and the public key information of the issuing CA. They should also include some additional information, such as the description on the algorithm to be used for verifying the issuing CA's signature and that to be used by the public key certified, the valid period, condition of the use, etc. Semi-formally, a public-key certificate may be defined as in Example 13.1.

## Example 13.1: Public-key Certificate

```
certificate ::=
   {
     issuer name;
     issuer information;
     subject name;
     subject information;
     validity period;
   }
issuer information ::=
   {
     issuer public key;
     signature algorithm identifier;
```

```
      hash function identifier
   }
subject information ::=
   {
     subject public key;
     public key algorithm identifier
   }
validity period ::=
   {
     start date;
     finish date
   }
```

□

## 13.2.1  Certificate Issuance

In the issuance of a certificate, a CA should validate the identity of a principal who requests a certificate. The validation should of course involve some physical (i.e., non-cryptographic) means of identification, as we usually have to conduct in some business interaction (e.g., in the opening of a bank account). The principal should also prove that she/he knows the private component of the public key to be certified. The proof can either be in the form of a user creating a signature of a challenge message, which is verifiable using the public key, or be in the form of a zero-knowledge proof protocol between the user and the CA, with the public key as the common input. Some applications requires the private component of a public key to have certain structure. In such applications, a zero-knowledge protocol can be designed to enable a proof of the needed structure. We shall see in later chapter a few zero-knowledge protocols for proof of the structure of a secret.

## 13.2.2  Certificate Revocation

Occasionally, it may be necessary to revoke a certificate. Compromise of a user's private key or a change of user information are two examples of this situation.

In the case of the directory-based certification framework, the root CA should maintain a hot list of the revoked certificates. The hot list may be available on-line. Alternatively, the root CA may issue a "$\Delta$-revocation list" throughout the system, which only contains newly revoked certificates. The system-wide users can update their local copies of the certificate revocation list whenever they receive a $\Delta$-revocation list.

A revocation of a certificate should be timestamped by the revocation CA. Signatures of a principal issued prior to the date of her/his certificate's revocation should be considered as still valid (according to application) even if the date of the signature verification is later than the date of the certificate's revocation.

### 13.2.3  Examples of Public-key Authentication Framework

Now let us see several examples of directory-based public-key authentication framework.

#### 13.2.3.1  X.509 Public-key Certification Framework

The standard public-key certification framework, called the X.509 [154] certification infrastructure, scales up in a tree hierarchy, called a **directory information tree** (**DIT**). In such a tree hierarchy, each node represents a principal whose public-key certificate is issued by its immediate parent node. The leaf nodes are end-user principals. The non-leaf nodes are CAs at various levels and domains; for example, a country level CA has industry, education and government organization domains; each of these domains has many sub-domains, e.g, the education domain has various university sub-domains. The root node is called the **root CA** which is a well-known principal in the whole system. The root CA should certify its own public key. Since each CA is potentially capable of serving a large domain (of CAs or end-users), the depths of a DIT need not be a large number. Two end-user principals can establish a secure communication channel by finding upward in the DIT a CA who is the nearest common ancestor node of them.

#### 13.2.3.2  PGP "Web of Trust"

Another public-key certification framework which has a large number of amateur users is called a PGP "web of trust" or "key-ring" (PGP stands for "Pretty Good Privacy" which is a secure e-mail software developed by Zimmermann [314]). This authentication model scales up in an unhierarchical manner. In the PGP "web of trust," any individual can be a "CA" for any other principals in the system by signing their "key certificates" which is simply a pair ⟨name, key⟩. Evidently, the signing relationship forms a web structure. Any single "CA" in the web is not well trusted or not trusted at all. The theory is that with enough such signatures, the association ⟨name, key⟩ could be trusted because not all of these signers would be corrupt. Thus, when Alice wants to establish the authenticity of Bob's key, she should request to see a number of Bob's "key certificates." If some of the issuing "CAs" of these certificates are "known" by Alice "to some extent," then she gains a certain level of authenticity about Bob's public key. Alice can demand Bob to provide more "certificates" until she is satisfied with the level of the trust.

### 13.2.3.3   Simple Public Key Infrastructure (SPKI)

The X.509 public-key certification framework can be viewed as a global online telephone book. Each individual user occupies an entry in it and therefore the entry subject name in each user's certificate (see Example 13.1) must be a globally distinguished name. Such an authentication framework seems quite adequate for the early years of applications of public-key cryptography: secure communications in terms of confidentiality (i.e., against eavesdropping): the recipient of a confidential message should be uniquely identified together with her/his key.

Since the 1990's, applications of public key became much wider to include electronic commerce, remote access and actions (see a list of applications in the Preface). Ellison et al. consider that for the newly emerged applications, a globally distinguished name with a key bound to it becomes inadequate [104]. What an application needs to do, when given a public key certificate, is to answer the question of whether the remote key holder is permitted some access, or some authorized action. That application must make a decision. The data needed for that decision is almost never the spelling of a key holder's name. Instead, the application needs to know if the key holder is authorized for some access. This should be the primary job of a public-key certificate.

Ellison et al. also consider that the original X.500 plan is unlikely ever to come to fruition. Collections of directory entries (such as employee lists, customer lists, contact lists, etc.) are considered valuable or even confidential by those owning the lists and are not likely to be released to the world in the form of an X.500 directory sub-tree. For an extreme example, they imagine the CIA adding its directory of agents to a world-wide X.500 pool, how can this be possible? The X.500 idea of a distinguished name (a single, globally unique name that everyone could use when referring to an entity) is also not likely to occur. That idea requires a single, global naming discipline and there are too many entities already in the business of defining names not under a single discipline. Legacy therefore militates against such an idea.

Ellison et al. propose a directory-based public-key certification framework named **SPKI** (which stands for "**Simple Public Key Infrastructure**") [104]. It is also a tree-structured framework, similar to an X.509 key certification framework. However, its naming convention includes a person's usual name and a hash of the public key value. For example:

```
(name (hash sha1 |TLCgPLF1GTzgUbcaYLW8kGTEnUk=|) jim therese)
```

is the proper SPKI name for the person whose usual name is "Jim Therese." Here, the use of the SHA-1 hash of a public key makes the SPKI name globally uniquely identifiable, even though there may be many "Jim Thereses."

This naming method is suggested by Rivest and Lampson in **SDSI** [247] (which stands for "**A Simple Distributed Security Infrastructure**"). SDSI features localization naming rules. These features also aim to make a decentralized authentication and authorization framework. Thus, a SPKI name is also called a SDSI name.

SPKI also considers "authorization" and "delegation" entries which carry authorization and delegation information. A piece of authorization information can be an authorization description which is bound to a public key. Thus, a certificate can directly show to an application whether or not the requester is authorized to perform an action. The delegation information describes the requester's power to delegate authorization to another person. We may say that SPKI extends X.509 authentication framework to one with authorization and delegation features. At the heart of the authorization scheme of SPKI is the use of LISP-like[a] S-expressions proposed by Rivest [246]. As an example, the S-expression

```
(object document (attributes (name *.doc) (loc Belgium))
        (op read) (principals (users OrgEU)))
```

might express the authorization of all users in `OrgEU` to read objects of type `document` which have names postfixed `doc` and are located in Belgium.

PolicyMaker [41] is another proposal which considers authorization and policy issues in an authentication framework. PolicyMaker features the descriptions of certificate holder's role and the role-based policy.

### 13.2.4   Protocols Associated with X.509 Public-key Authentication Infrastructure

There are several protocols for processing practical necessities in the X.509 Public-key Authentication Infrastructure. They are:

- Certificate Management Protocol (CMP) [7, 210]. This protocol supports online interactions between Public Key Infrastructure (PKI) components. For example, a management protocol might be used between a Certification Authority (CA) and a client system with which a key pair is associated, or between two CAs that issue cross-certificates for each other. These interactions are needed when, e.g., an entity (either end-entity or CA) is required to prove the possession of a private key upon its request for key certification or key update.

- Online Certificate Status Protocol (OCSP) [209]. This protocol enables applications to determine the (revocation) state of an identified certificate. OCSP

---

[a]LISP: a programming language.

may be used to satisfy some of the operational requirements of providing more timely revocation information than is possible with CRLs and may also be used to obtain additional status information. An OCSP client issues a status request to an OCSP responder and suspends acceptance of the certificate in question until the responder provides a response.

- Internet X.509 Public Key Infrastructure Time Stamp Protocols [6]. This protocol consists of a request sent to a Time Stamping Authority (TSA) and of the response that is returned. It also establishes several security-relevant requirements for TSA operation, with regards to processing requests to generate responses. Non-repudiation services require the ability to establish the existence of data before specified times. This protocol may be used as a building block to support such services.

- Internet X.509 Public Key Infrastructure Operational Protocols: FTP and HTTP [142]. This is a specification of protocol conventions for PKI to use the File Transfer Protocol (FTP) and the Hypertext Transfer Protocol (HTTP) to obtain certificates and certificate revocation lists (CRLs) from PKI repositories.

These protocols are developed as standards under the IETF standardization body "the Public-Key Infrastructure X.509 Working Group" (the PKIX Working Group). We shall not described the details of these protocols. Interested readers should visit the PKIX Working Group's web page:

$$\text{http://www.ietf.org/html.charters/pkix-charter.html}$$

where documents describing these protocols (the references cited above) can be downloaded.

## 13.3  Non-Directory Based Public-key Authentication Framework

The key generation procedure in (13.1.1) in the usual sense of public-key cryptography renders all public keys random. Consequently, it is necessary to associate a public key with the identity information of its owner in an authentic manner. We have seen that such an association can be realized by a public-key authentication framework: a tree-like hierarchical public-key certification infrastructure (e.g., X.509 certification framework, see §13.2.3). However, to establish and maintain a tree hierarchy, PKI incur a non-trivial level of system complexity and cost. It has long been desired that the standard public-key authentication framework be simplified.

It is reasonable to think that, if public keys are not random-looking, then the system complexity and the cost for establishing and maintaining the public-key authentication framework may be reduced. Imagine, if a public key of a principal is self-evidently associated with the principal's identity information such as name, affiliation information plus electronic and postal mail addresses, then in essence there is no need to authenticate a public key. Indeed, our postal mail systems work properly this way.

Shamir pioneers a public-key cryptosystem in an unusual sense [262]. It enables a great-deal of reduction in the system complexity for key authentication: in essence to one similar to that of a postal mail system. In his unusual public-key cryptosystem, the key generation procedure has the following step

$$\text{private-key} = F(\text{master-key}, \text{public-key}).\tag{13.3.1}$$

This key generation step takes the opposite direction to the key generation step for the usual sense of public-key cryptosystems, see (13.1.1). Of course, in order for a so-computed private-key to be kept secret, the computation must not be public: it is restricted to a privileged principal (a trusted authority, TA). TA possesses exclusively the secret key master-key in order to be able to perform the computation in (13.3.1). Now that public-key is an input to the key generation procedure, any bit string can be public-key! Since using identity information as a public key can greatly reduce the complexity of public-key authentication, Shamir suggested that the public keys in his novel public-key cryptosystem be chosen as users' identities and thus he named his scheme **identity-based public-key cryptography**.

It is obvious that the key generation procedure in (13.3.1) is a service offered by TA to system wide users. The service is essentially an authentication one: the private key that TA creates for a principal in connection to her/his ID as public key provides the key owner with a credential for her/his ID-based public key to be recognized and used by other users in the system. Before creating a private key for a principal, TA should conduct a thorough checking of the identity information of the principal. This checking should include some physical (i.e., non-cryptographic) means of identification. Also, TA has to be satisfied that the identity information supplied by the principal can uniquely pinpoint the principal. A similar identification checking is necessary before a CA issues a public-key certificate to a principal (see §13.2.1).

Now that users' private keys are generated by TA, they have to trust TA absolutely, completely and unconditionally: namely, they must not feel uncomfortable with the situation that TA can read all of their private communications or forge all of their signatures. Therefore, ID-based cryptography should only be suitable for applications where an unconditional trust is acceptable to the users. In an organization environment in which the employer has the complete ownership of the information communicated to and from the employees; then the employer can play the role of TA. It is however possible that TA represents a plural number entities who collectively computes (13.3.1) for a user. Privacy intrusion then must be done collectively by these entities. This collective basis of trust is more acceptable. We will see such a technique in §13.3.7.1.

With a principal's uniquely identifiable identity being directly used as her/his public key, during the use of an ID-based public-key cryptosystem there is no need for the user to establish a key channel; namely, the "key channels" in Figures 7.1 and 10.1 are no longer needed. Moreover, $ke$ in Figures 7.1 and $kv$ in Fig 10.1 can be replaced with a string of a piece of self-evident information, for example, a globally distinguishable identity.

## 13.3.1  Shamir's ID-Based Signature Scheme

In Shamir's ID-based signature scheme there are four algorithms:

- Setup: this algorithm is operated by TA (from now on let us call TA Trent) to generate global system parameters and master-key.

- User-key-generate: this algorithm (also operated by Trent), inputting master-key and an arbitrary bit string id $\in \{0,1\}^*$, outputs private-key which corresponds to id; this is an instantiation of (13.3.1).

- Sign: a signature generation algorithm; inputting a message and the signer's private key, it outputs a signature.

- Verify: a signature verification algorithm; inputting a message-signature pair and id, it outputs True or False.

Alg 13.1 specifies Shamir's ID-based signature scheme.

We now show that the system specified in Alg 13.1 is indeed a signature scheme.

A True case in a signature verification shows that Alice has in her possession of both $\text{ID} \cdot t^{h(t\|M)}$ and its *unique* $e$-th root modulo $N$ (which is $s$, and the uniqueness is guaranteed by the fact $\gcd(e, \phi(N)) = 1$).

The construction of $\text{ID} \cdot t^{h(t\|M)}$ need not be a difficult job. For example, one can choose a random $t$, construct $h(t \| M)$, then compute $t^{h(t\|M)}$ (mod $N$) and lastly multiply ID to the result. However, because the value so constructed is *recognizable* due to the involvement of a cryptographic hash function in the construction, it should be difficult to extract the $e$-th root of a so-constructed value. It is therefore assumed that Alice should have in her possession of the $e$-th root of ID, which is her private key issued by Trent, and should have used the private key in the construction of the signature pair.

However we have not provided a formal and strong argument for the unforgeability of Shamir's ID-based signature scheme. Because the difficulty of signature forgery is related to that of constructing $\text{ID} \cdot t^{h(t\|M)}$ (mod $N$) and finding its $e$-th root modulo $N$, the difficulty must certainly be related to the details of the hash function used (in addition to the RSA problem). Similar to the situation of providing security proofs for other digital signature schemes, a rigorous argument on

**Algorithm 13.1:** Shamir's Identity-based Signature Scheme

**Setup of System Parameters**
Trent sets up:

1. $N$: the product of two large primes;

2. $e$: an integer satisfying $\gcd(e, \phi(N)) = 1$;
   (* $(N, e)$ are public parameters for using by the system-wide users *)

3. $d$: an integer satisfying $ed \equiv 1 \pmod{\phi(N)}$;
   (* $d$ is Trent's master-key *)

4. $h : \{0, 1\}^* \mapsto \mathbb{Z}_{\phi(N)}$;
   (* $h$ is a strong one-way hash function *)

Trent keeps $d$ as the system private key (master-key), and publicizes the system parameters $(N, e, h)$.

**User Key Generation**
Let ID denote user Alice's uniquely identifiable identity. Having performed physical identification of Alice and made sure the uniqueness of ID, Trent's key generation service is

$$g \leftarrow \mathsf{ID}^d \pmod{N}.$$

**Signature Generation**
To sign a message $M \in \{0, 1\}^*$, Alice chooses $r \in_U \mathbb{Z}_N^*$, and computes

$$t \leftarrow r^e \pmod{N},$$
$$s \leftarrow g \cdot r^{h(t \,\|\, M)} \pmod{N}.$$

The signature is the pair $(s, t)$.

**Signature Verification**
Given the message $M$ and the signature $(s, t)$, Bob uses Alice's identity ID to verify the signature as follows:

$$\mathsf{Verify}(\mathsf{ID}, s, t, M) = \mathsf{True} \ \text{ if } \ s^e \equiv \mathsf{ID} \cdot t^{h(t \,\|\, M)} \pmod{N}.$$

the security for Shamir's ID-based signature scheme requires a formal model of the behavior of the hash function $h$. Such a model will be given in a later chapter.

## 13.3.2  What Exactly does ID-Based Cryptography Offer?

In public-key cryptography in the usual sense, for Bob to verify a signature of Alice using her public key, Bob should also verify, separately, the authenticity of Alice's public-key, e.g., by verifying her key certificate (which links Alice's public key with her identity). Namely, Bob should make sure that the key channel from and to Alice has been properly established (see Fig 10.1).

It is interesting to realize that in an ID-based signature scheme, there is no need for Bob to perform a separate verification for the proper establishment of a key channel. Here, a True case in a signature verification shows Bob two things at the same time:

- the signature has been created by Alice using her private key which is behind her ID; and

- her ID has been certified by Trent, and it is the result of Trent's certification of her ID that has enabled Alice to create the signature.

Being able to simultaneously verify these two things in one go is a nice feature offered by an ID-based signature scheme. Being able to avoid transmitting a certificate from the signer to the verifier also saves the communication bandwidth. This feature also brands the ID-based cryptography with another name: **non-interactive public key cryptography**. We will see in a moment that the non-interaction property will make better sense in an ID-based encryption system.

Finally we must recap and remember that Trent can forge any user's signature! Therefore, Shamir's ID-based signature scheme is not suitable for applications in an open system environment. Rather, it is more suitable for those in a closed system in which Trent has legitimate ownership of all information in the whole system. This is unfortunately a very restrictive setting.

A challenging open problem is to design an ID-based signature scheme which is free from this restrictive setting. Another open problem is to design an ID-based signature scheme which features non-interactive key revocation. Key revocation is necessary when a user's private key is compromised.

It seems that without having these two open problems solved, an ID-based signature scheme will have rather limited applications. We shall see in the remainder of this chapter that one of these two problems, free from the need for an absolute trust on Trent, can be solved for an ID-based encryption scheme.

## 13.3.3  Self-certified Public Keys

Let $(s, P)$ be a pair of secret and public keys, respectively. A public-key authentication framework is to provide a key pair with a guarantee $G$ which links $P$ to an identity $I$.

In a directory-based public-key authentication framework (e.g., X.509 which we have seen in Example 13.1), the guarantee $G$ takes the form of a digital signature of the pair $(I, P)$, which is computed and delivered by a certification authority CA. The authentication framework is organized by items of four distinct attributes: $(s, I, P, G)$. Three of them, $(I, P, G)$, are public and should be available in a public directory. When a principal needs an authenticated copy of $I$'s public key, it gets the public triple $(I, P, G)$, checks $G$ using CA's public key, and afterwards makes use of $P$ to authenticate this user.

In identity-based authentication framework (e.g., Shamir's scheme in §13.3.1), the public key is nothing but the identity $I$. So $P = I$ and the authentication framework is organized by items of two attributes: $(s, I)$. As we have seen in §13.3.1, when a principal needs to authenticate $I$'s public key $I$, it has to verify a signature; a **True** answer confirms the authenticity of the public key $I$. Therefore, the guarantee is nothing but the secret key itself, i.e., $G = s$.

Girault proposes a scheme for public-key authentication framework which is intermediate between a certificate-based scheme and identity-based one [124, 123]. In Girault's scheme, the guarantee is equal to public key, i.e., $G = P$, which therefore may be said self-certified, and each user has three attributes: $(s, P, I)$. In Girault's scheme, a user's private key can be chosen by the user.

### 13.3.3.1  Girault's Scheme

Girault's scheme still needs a trusted authority TA (let it be Trent), who sets up the system parameter and helps an individual user to set up her/his key attribute.

### 13.3.3.2  System Key Material

Trent generates an RSA key material as follows:

1. a public modulus $N = PQ$ where $P, Q$ are large primes of roughly equal size, e.g., $|P| = |Q| = 512$;

2. a public exponent $e$ co-prime to $\phi(N) = (P-1)(Q-1)$;

3. a secret exponent $d$ satisfying $ed \equiv 1 \pmod{\phi(N)}$;

4. a public element $g \in \mathbb{Z}_N^*$ which has the maximum multiplicative order modulo $N$; to compute $g$, Trent can find $g_P$ as a generator modulo $P$ and $g_Q$ as

a generator modulo $Q$, and can then construct $g$ by applying the Chinese Remainder Theorem (Theorem 6.7 in §6.2.3).

Trent publicizes the system public key material $(N, e, g)$, and keeps the system secret key material $d$ securely.

### 13.3.3.3   User Key Material

Alice randomly chooses a secret key $s_A$ which is a 160-bit integer, computes

$$v \leftarrow g^{-s_A} \pmod{N}$$

and gives $v$ to Trent. Then she proves to Trent that she knows $s_A$ without revealing it, by using a simple protocol to be described in §13.3.3.4. Alice also sends her identity $I_A$ to Trent.

Trent creates Alice's public key as the raw RSA signature of the value $v - I_A$:

$$P_A \leftarrow (v - I_A)^d \pmod{N}.$$

Trent sends $P_A$ to Alice as part of her public key. So the following equation holds:

$$I_A \equiv P_A^e - v \pmod{N}. \tag{13.3.2}$$

At first sight, in this key setup, because both $P_A$ and $v$ are random elements in $\mathbb{Z}_N^*$, so it seems that making equation (13.3.2) is not a difficult job. For example, Alice can pick $P_A$ at random, computes $v$ using $P_A^e$ and $I_A$ using (13.3.2). However, if $v$ is computed this way, then Alice should not be able to know its discrete logarithm to the base $g$ modulo $N$.

It is Alice's capability to demonstrate her possession of the discrete logarithm of $v$ to the base $g$ modulo $N$, i.e., the value $-s_A$, that will provide the guarantee that $P_A$ has been issued by Trent. The simplest way to achieve this demonstration is by using a variation of the Diffie-Hellman key exchange protocol to be described in §13.3.3.4.

### 13.3.3.4   Key Exchange Protocol

Let $(s_A, P_A, I_A)$ be Alice's public key material, and $(s_B, P_B, I_B)$ be Bob's public key material. They can simply exchange an authenticated key by agreeing:

$$K_{AB} \equiv (P_A^e + I_A)^{s_B} \equiv (P_B^e + I_B)^{s_A} \equiv g^{-s_A s_B} \pmod{N}.$$

In this key agreement, Alice computes $(P_B^e + I_B)^{s_A} \pmod{N}$ and Bob computes $(P_A^e + I_A)^{s_B} \pmod{N}$. Therefore it is indeed the Diffie-Hellman key agreement protocol. If the two parties can agree on the same key, then they know that the other end has proved her/his identity.

Girault also proposes an identity-based identification protocol and an identity-based signature scheme which is in the ElGamal signature scheme [124].

### 13.3.3.5   Discussions

The self-certified public keys of Girault share one feature of Shamir's identity-based scheme: free from verifying an additional key certificate issued by a trusted third party to a key owner. The verification is implicit and is done at the same time of verifying the key owner's cryptographic capability.

However, the verifier needs a separate public key in addition to an identity, i.e., $P$ in addition to $I$, and the former cannot be derived from the latter by the verifier. This means that the verifier has to ask for the key owner to send the public key over before using it. This is an additional step of communication. Therefore, Girault's self-certified public keys cannot be considered as *non-interactive* public key cryptography (review our discussion on this point in §13.3.2). This is a drawback of self-certified public keys.

## 13.3.4   Identity-Based Public-key Cryptosystems from Pairings on "Weak" Elliptic Curves

Shamir's original ID-based public-key cryptosystem is a digital signature scheme. He also conjectures the existence of ID-based encryption systems. After Shamir's posing of the problem in 1984, several ID-based cryptosystems have been proposed [253, 52, 79, 143, 193, 291, 289].

Sakai, Ohgishi and Kasahara [253] and Joux [156] independently pioneer the idea of utilizing a special property of a **pairing-mapping** function which works on an abelian group formed by points on an elliptic curve (see §5.5). The work of Sakai et al. [253] is a marvelous application of a previous cryptanalysis result (to explain in §13.3.4.1) which make Shamir's conjecture a practical reality. Independently, the work of Joux [156] uses the same technique to achieve another fascinating application: one-round three-party Diffie-Hellman key sharing (Joux names it "tripartite Diffie-Hellman").

The independent applications of the pairing technique by Sakai et al. [253] and by Joux [156] not only achieve things which previously no one knew how to do, more meaningfully, they turn a previous cryptanalysis result of Menezes, Okamoto and Vanstone [199] (a negative result about elliptic curves) into positive applications. Their seminal works gave rise to a resurgence of interest in identity-based cryptography after the year 2000.

The special property utilized by Sakai et al. [253] and by Joux [156] is the following. In a "weak" elliptic curve group in which a "pairing-mapping" can be efficiently computed, the **decisional Diffie-Hellman problem** (DDH problem) is easy while its computational counterpart remains difficult. Let us first study the "weak" family of elliptic curves and the related easy DDH problem. After this we will then introduce these two pairing based key agreement schemes.

### 13.3.4.1   A "Weak" Class of Elliptic Curves

Menezes, Okamoto and Vanstone [199] show that for a special class of elliptic curves defined over finite fields, there exists an efficient algorithm to "map-in-pair" two points on a curve (over a finite field) to an element in the underlying field. The special class of curves are called **supersingular curves**; they satisfy that $t$ in (5.5.6) is divisible by the characteristic of the underlying field. As in §5.5, we remain to confine our description to the easy case of fields with characteristic greater than 3.

Let $E(\mathbb{F}_q)$ be such a curve ($q$ is a prime power). For some large prime number $\alpha|\#E(\mathbb{F}_q)$ ($\alpha$ and $q$ co-prime to each other), we know from Lagrange's Theorem (Corollary 5.2) that the group $E(\mathbb{F}_q)$ contains order-$\alpha$ points (those $P$ satisfying $[\alpha]P = \mathcal{O}$, if necessary review §5.5). Moreover, the group $E(\mathbb{F}_{q^\ell})$ (notice, the underlying field is an extension $\mathbb{F}_{q^\ell}$ of $\mathbb{F}_q$ for some integer $\ell$, i.e., the $(x, y)$ coordinates of a curve point are elements in $\mathbb{F}_{q^\ell}$, if necessary, review §5.4 for the notion of field extension) is non-cyclic and contains disjoint subgroups of order-$\alpha$ points. That is, in the group $E(\mathbb{F}_{q^\ell})$ there are order-$\alpha$ points $P$, $Q$ satisfying $P \notin \langle Q \rangle$ and $Q \notin \langle P \rangle$. Since such points satisfy $P \neq [u]Q$ and $Q \neq [v]P$ for all integers $u, v$, we also say that they are "linearly independent". It can be shown that two linearly independent order-$\alpha$ points form a basis to generate all order-$\alpha$ points on $E(\mathbb{F}_{q^\ell})$.

For this prime $\alpha$, the extended field $\mathbb{F}_{q^\ell}$, as a multiplicative group of non-zero elements, also has the order-$\alpha$ subgroup. Notice the use of the article "the" here: this subgroup is unique (recall Theorem 5.11, the multiplicative group of non-zero elements of $\mathbb{F}_{q^\ell}$ is cyclic, and Theorem 5.2.(2) for the uniqueness).

It is known that there is an onto, operation-preserving and efficiently computable mapping from all the pairs of order-$\alpha$ points on the curve $E(\mathbb{F}_{q^\ell})$ to the order-$\alpha$ subgroup of $\mathbb{F}_{q^\ell}$. The **Weil pairing** provides such a mapping. Menezes, Okamoto and Vanstone [199] show that for $E(\mathbb{F}_q)$ being supersingular the Weil pairing mapping can be constructed for the case of a small field extension: $\ell \leq 6$. In fact, it is very easy to construct the mapping for the case of $\ell = 2$. The smallness of the field extension is very important! We shall return to this point in a moment.

The Weil pairing takes two order-$\alpha$ points on $E(\mathbb{F}_{q^\ell})$ to an element in the order-$\alpha$ subgroup of $\mathbb{F}_{q^\ell}$. Let $P$, $Q$ be points in order-$\alpha$ subgroups of $E(\mathbb{F}_{q^\ell})$. We denote the Weil pairing

$$e_\alpha(P, Q).$$

In this denotation, the subscript $\alpha$ explicitly specifies that $P$, $Q$ are points in order-$\alpha$ subgroups. Notice that these points may be in a same subgroup (this includes the cases $P = \mathcal{O}$ and/or $Q = \mathcal{O}$) and hence are linearly dependent, or in different order-$\alpha$ subgroups and hence are linearly independent.

The Weil pairing satisfies the following properties:

**Property 13.1: The Weil Pairing Properties** *Let $\alpha$ be a prime number, $P, Q, R$ be points in order-$\alpha$ subgroups of $E(\mathbb{F}_{q^\ell})$. The Weil pairing $e_\alpha$ has the following properties:*

**Identity** *for all $P$:*

$$e_\alpha(P, P) = 1.$$

**Bilinearity** *for all $P, Q, R$:*

$$e_\alpha(P + Q, R) = e_\alpha(P, R)e_\alpha(Q, R), \quad e_\alpha(R, P + Q) = e_\alpha(R, P)e_\alpha(R, Q).$$

**Non-degeneracy** *for $P$ and $Q$ being linearly independent (i.e., in different order-$\alpha$ subgroups):*

$$e_\alpha(P, Q) \neq 1, \quad e_\alpha(Q, P) \neq 1.$$

**Practical Efficiency** *for all $P, Q$, $e_\alpha(P, Q)$ and $e_\alpha(Q, P)$ are practically efficiently computable.*

Notice that by bilinearity we have

$$e_\alpha([n]P, Q) = e_\alpha(P, Q)^n = e_\alpha(P, [n]Q).$$

Further by non-degeneracy we know that, as long as $P$ and $Q$ are linearly independent and $\alpha \nmid n$, this pairing-mapped result is not the multiplicative identity (unity) of $\mathbb{F}_{q^\ell}$ and so the pairing-mapping is not uninteresting. Since in the non-degeneracy case the mapped result is a non-unity element in the prime order ($\alpha$) subgroup, it is an $\alpha$-th root of the unity in $\mathbb{F}_{q^\ell}$.

These properties of the Weil pairing enable a profound reduction, called the **MOV reduction**, from the difficulty of the elliptic curve discrete logarithm problem (ECDLP, defined in §5.5.3) to that of the discrete logarithm problem in finite fields. To apply the MOV reduction to the ECDLP on given pair of order-$\alpha$ points $(P, [n]P)$, we can compute the Weil pairings $\xi = e_\alpha(P, X)$ and $\eta = e_\alpha([n]P, X)$ for some $X$ which is linearly independent from $P$. Now notice

$$\eta = e_\alpha([n]P, X) = e_\alpha(P, X)^n = \xi^n. \tag{13.3.3}$$

Since $P$ and $X$ are linearly independent, by non-degeneracy $e_\alpha(P, X) \neq 1$, and so the pair $(\xi, \eta)$ in $\mathbb{F}_{q^\ell}$ provides a discrete logarithm problem in the finite field. We know that for the latter problem there is a subexponential solver with the time complexity expressed as sub_exp($q^\ell$) (using $q^\ell$ in place of $q$ in the complexity expression (8.4.2)). Recall that we have discussed earlier, that for supersingular curves, $\ell \leq 6$. Therefore, the MOV reduction is a drastic one: it reduces a widely believed exponential problem: $O(\sqrt{\alpha}) \approx O(\sqrt{q})$ into a subexponential one: sub_exp($q^\ell$) with $\ell$ not exceeding 6 (often $\ell = 2$).

Considering that the progress of the hardware computing technology will cause $q$ to grow its size, then the parameter of a supersingular curve has to grow in the way of that of a finite field. In other words, the advantage of using elliptic curve in cryptography is gone. Therefore, after the cryptanalysis work of Menezes, Okamoto and Vanstone [199], it becomes a widely agreed convention that supersingular elliptic curves should be excluded from cryptographic use. They are weak curves.

Then why have we used the quoted form of "weak" in the title of this subsection? These curves have a newly discovered useful property which sends a shock wave to the research community. Let us first describe the decisional form of the Diffie-Hellman problem.

### 13.3.4.2  Decisional Diffie-Hellman Problem

In Definition 8.1 (in §8.4) we have introduced the CDH problem (the computational version of the Diffie-Hellman problem). The decisional version of the problem is given below in Definition 13.1.

**Definition 13.1: Decisional Diffie-Hellman Problem (DDH Problem)**

INPUT        desc($G$): the description of an abelian group $G$;
             $(g, g^a, g^b, g^c) \in G^4$ where $g$ is a generator of the group $G$;

OUTPUT    YES   if $ab \equiv c \pmod{\#G}$.

The DDH problem can not be harder than the CDH problem. If there exists a CDH problem solver (such an assumed solver is usually called an oracle), then on inputting $(g, g^a, g^b, g^c)$, the oracle can find $g^{ab}$ from the first three elements in the input, and thus can answer the DDH problem by checking whether or not the output from the CDH oracle is equal to $g^c$.

However, in the *general case* of abelian groups we do not know for sure anything more than this relation between these two problems. Moreover, we do not know any efficient algorithm to solve the DDH problem. The difficulty of answering the DDH problem has rendered the problem a standard and widely accepted intractability assumption (to be described in Assumption 14.2) for underlying the security of many cryptographic systems, e.g., [21, 59, 85, 211, 285].

Now for the special case of supersingular elliptic curves, we know the following newly discovered fact: the DDH problem is easy. This is identified by Joux and Nguyen [157]. Before we explain the fact, we need to translate the problem (and the CDH, DL problems) into the additive form, since the elliptic curve groups are written additively.

## The Discrete Logarithm (DL) Problem in $(G, +)$

INPUT        Two elements $P, Q \in G$ with $P$ being a group generator;

OUTPUT    Integer $a$ such that $Q = aP$.

## The Computational Diffie-Hellman (CDH) Problem in $(G, +)$

INPUT        Three elements $P, aP, bP \in G$ with $P$ being a group generator;

OUTPUT    Element $(ab)P \in G$.

## The Decisional Diffie-Hellman (DDH) Problem in $(G, +)$

INPUT        Four elements $P, aP, bP, cP \in G$ with $P$ being a group generator;

OUTPUT    YES   iff   $c \equiv ab \pmod{\#G}$.

### 13.3.4.3   "Weak" Curves Enable Easy Decisional Diffie-Hellman Problem

The identity property of the Weil pairing (see Property 13.1) is somewhat awkward. It means that for $P, Q$ being points in the same order-$\alpha$ subgroup (i.e., they are linearly dependent and so $Q = [a]P$ for some integer $a$), pairing $e_\alpha(P, Q) = e_\alpha(P, P)^a = 1^a = 1$. In order to obtain a non-degenerated mapped result, we must work on linearly independent points. This is often cumbersome and forms a big limitation for the Weil pairing to be directly used in positive cryptographic applications.

Verheul [298] engineers a what he names "distortion map" method. A distortion map is a modification on the coordinates of a curve point. Denote by $\Phi(P)$ this modification. For $P$ being a point in $E(\mathbb{F}_{q^\ell})$, $\Phi(P)$ is still a point in $E(\mathbb{F}_{q^\ell})$ of the same order as long as $P$ has an order greater than 3. A usual treatment is to have the modification done in the "ground field" $\mathbb{F}_q$; that is, choose $P \in E(\mathbb{F}_q)$ and have the modification done on the coordinate(s) of $P$ so that $\Phi(P) \in E(\mathbb{F}_{q^\ell})$ results. This usual treatment guarantees that $P$ and $\Phi(P)$ are linearly independent. This is because the $(x, y)$ coordinates of $P$ and those of $\Phi(P)$ are now in different fields, while point multiplications $[u]P, [v]\Phi(P)$ using integers (see §5.5.2) can never take these co-ordinates cross fields (i.e., $[u]P \in E(\mathbb{F}_q)$ and $[v]\Phi(P) \in E(\mathbb{F}_{q^\ell})$ for all integers $u$ and $v$).

Under a distortion map, the Weil pairing is modified to

$$e(P, P) = e_\alpha(P, \Phi(P)).$$

Clearly now, $e(P, P) \neq 1$ since $P$ and $\Phi(P)$ are linearly independent. Moreover, for $P, Q$ in the same order-$\alpha$ group, we further have the following symmetric property for the modified Weil pairing:

$$e(P, Q) = e(P, [n]P) = e(P, P)^n = e([n]P, P) = e(Q, P). \qquad (13.3.4)$$

Now let $G_1$ denote an order-$\alpha$ subgroup of $E(\mathbb{F}_{q^\ell})$ (in fact, for simplicity, we can always confine $G_1 \subset E(\mathbb{F}_q)$), and let $G_2$ denote the order-$\alpha$ subgroup (multiplicative) of $\mathbb{F}_{q^\ell}$. Due to the operation-preserving property given by bilinearity of the Weil pairing we know that the modified Weil pairing is actually an isomorphism between $G_1$ and $G_2$.

Consider the DDH problem in group $G_1$. To answer whether a quadruple $(P, [a]P, [b]P, [c]P)$ is a DH quadruple, we compute pairings $\xi = e(P, [c]P)$ and $\eta = e([a]P, [b]P)$. Noticing

$$\xi = e(P, P)^c, \quad \eta = e(P, P)^{ab},$$

and $e(P, P) \neq 1_{G_2}$, therefore the quadruple is DH one if and only if $\xi = \eta$, i.e., if and only if $ab \equiv c \pmod{\#G_1}$. With the practical efficiency property of the modified Weil pairing, this decisional question can be efficiently answered.

This important observation made by Joux and Nguyen [157] enables many interesting new cryptographic usages of supersingular elliptic curves. The ID-based cryptography is a prominent one of them. These new usages are based on a fact and an intractability assumption which we have discussed so far, which are summarized here:

## Fact (The DDH Problem is easy)

The DDH problem in supersingular elliptic curve group can be efficiently answered using the Weil pairing algorithm.

## Assumption (CDH, DL Problems remain hard)

The CDH problem (and hence the DL problem) in supersingular elliptic curve groups remains hard by a suitable choice on the size of of an elliptic curve. For a curve $E(\mathbb{F}_q)$, the difficulty can be expressed as sub_exp$(q^\ell)$ for $\ell \leq 6$.

In the assumption "CDH, DL problems remain hard," the complexity expression sub_exp$(q^\ell)$ follows the effect of the MOV reduction and the subexponential algorithm for solving the discrete logarithm in finite fields. Thus, we now have to use an enlarged security parameter (the size of the curve) for a supersingular curve in comparison with the general curves. The enlarged security parameter should be one such that sub_exp$(q^\ell)$ is an infeasible quantity. So, in order to make use of the newly discovered mathematical property in supersingular elliptic curves (the positive applications to be presented in §13.3.5–§13.3.7), we choose to sacrifice the efficiency which is the original advantage of elliptic curves over finite fields.

There are two kinds of pairing techniques: the Weil pairing which we have discussed, and the Tate pairing. The latter is more efficient. The details of the pairing algorithms are out of the scope of this book. The interested reader may study them from [52, 118]. In the remainder of this chapter we will always use the modified Weil pairing.

## 13.3.5   ID-based Non-interactive Key Sharing System of Sakai, Ohgishi and Kasahara

Like Shamir's ID-based signature scheme, the key sharing system of Sakai et al. [253] (**SOK key sharing system**) also needs a trusted authority TA (let it be named Trent) to operate a key setup center.

The SOK key sharing system has the following three components:

- **System Parameters Setup**   Trent runs this algorithm to set up global system parameters and master-key;

- **User Key Generation**   Trent runs this algorithm; on inputting master-key and an arbitrary bit string id $\in \{0,1\}^*$, this algorithm outputs private-key which corresponds to id; this is an instantiation of (13.3.1);

- **Key-Sharing-Scheme**   Two end-users run this scheme in a non-interactive manner; for each end-user, the scheme takes in as input the private key of the end-user and the public key (id) of the intended communication partner; the scheme outputs a secret key shared between the two end-users.

These three components are realized by the following steps.

**System Parameters Setup**

Trent sets up the system parameters before opening a key generation center to offer the key generation service. In the generation of the system parameters, Trent performs:

1. Generate two groups $(G_1, +)$, $(G_2, \cdot)$ of prime order $p$ and the modified Weil pairing[b] $e : (G_1, +)^2 \mapsto (G_2, \cdot)$. Choose an arbitrary generator $P \in G_1$;

2. Pick $\ell \in_U \mathbb{Z}_p$ and set $P_{pub} \leftarrow [\ell]P$; $\ell$ is in the position of master-key;

3. Choose a cryptographically strong hash function $f : \{0,1\}^* \mapsto G_1$; this hash function is for mapping a user's id to an element in $G_1$.

---

[b]The original SOK key sharing system uses the (unmodified) Weil pairing, and is less convenient to use than the version presented here.

Trent publishes the system parameters and their descriptions

$$(\mathrm{desc}(G_1), \mathrm{desc}(G_2), e, P, P_{pub}, f),$$

and keeps $\ell$ as the system private key. Since Trent is assumed to be the system-wide well-known principal, the published system parameters will also be well-known by all users in the system (for example, maybe these parameters will be hardwired into every application that uses this scheme).

Notice that the secrecy of the master key $\ell$ is protected by the difficulty of the DLP in $G_1$.

Trent now opens the key generation center.

### User Key Generation

Let $\mathsf{ID}_A$ denote user Alice's uniquely identifiable identity. We assume that $\mathsf{ID}_A$ contains a sufficient quantity of redundancy such that it is impossible for any other user in the system to also have $\mathsf{ID}_A$ as her/his identity. Having performed physical identification of Alice and made sure of the uniqueness of $\mathsf{ID}_A$, Trent's key generation service is as follows:

1. Compute $P_{\mathsf{ID}_A} \leftarrow f(\mathsf{ID}_A)$, this is an element in $G_1$, and is Alice's ID-based public key;

2. Set Alice's private key $S_{\mathsf{ID}_A}$ as $S_{\mathsf{ID}_A} \leftarrow [\ell]P_{\mathsf{ID}_A}$.

Notice that as a hashed value, $P_{\mathsf{ID}_A}$ should look random. However, with $\mathsf{ID}_A$ containing sufficient recognizable (redundant) information and being the pre-image of $P_{\mathsf{ID}_A}$ under the cryptographic hash function $f$, $P_{\mathsf{ID}_A}$ is a *recognizable* element. Therefore, there is essentially no difference to view $\mathsf{ID}_A$ as Alice's public key, or to view $P_{\mathsf{ID}_A}$ as Alice's public key.

We should also notice that Alice's private key is protected by the difficulty of the CDH problem in $G_1$; this is because $P_{\mathsf{ID}_A}$ must be generated by $P$ (a generator element of $G_1$) and so we can denote it by $P_{\mathsf{ID}_A} = [a]P$ for some $a < p$; then from $P, P_{pub}(= [\ell]P), P_{\mathsf{ID}_A}(= [a]P)$, to find

$$S_{\mathsf{ID}_A} = [\ell]P_{\mathsf{ID}_A} = [\ell a]P$$

is clearly a CDH problem in $G_1$.

### Key-Sharing-Scheme

For users Alice and Bob, $\mathsf{ID}_A$ and $\mathsf{ID}_B$ are their ID information which is known to them one another. Therefore, the respective public keys $P_A = f(\mathsf{ID}_A)$ and $P_B = f(\mathsf{ID}_B)$ are known to them one another, too.

Alice can generate a shared key $K_{AB} \in (G_2, \cdot)$ by computing

$$K_{AB} \leftarrow e(S_{\mathsf{ID}_A}, P_{\mathsf{ID}_B}).$$

Bob can generate a shared key $K_{BA} \in (G_2, \cdot)$ by computing

$$K_{BA} \leftarrow e(S_{\mathsf{ID}_B}, P_{\mathsf{ID}_A}).$$

Noticing the bilinear property of the pairing (Property 13.1), we have

$$K_{AB} = e(S_{\mathsf{ID}_A}, P_{\mathsf{ID}_B}) = e([\ell]P_{\mathsf{ID}_A}, P_{\mathsf{ID}_B}) = e(P_{\mathsf{ID}_A}, P_{\mathsf{ID}_B})^\ell.$$

Similarly,

$$K_{BA} = e(P_{\mathsf{ID}_B}, P_{\mathsf{ID}_A})^\ell.$$

Due to the symmetric property (13.3.4) of the modified Weil pairing, we have

$$K_{AB} = K_{BA}.$$

So Alice and Bob can indeed share a secret even without interaction with one another.

For a party other than Alice, Bob and Trent, to find $K_{AB}$ from the public data $(P, P_{\mathsf{ID}_A}, P_{\mathsf{ID}_B}, P_{pub})$ is a problem called **bilinear Diffie-Hellman problem** [52]. It is essentially a CDH problem.

When Bob receives a message which is authenticated using $K_{AB}$, he knows exactly that Alice is the author of the message as long as himself has not authored it. However, Alice, while showing the authorship to the *designated verifier* Bob, can deny her involvement in the communication in front of a third party since Bob has the same cryptographic capability to have constructed the message. One may consider a scenario that Alice and Bob are spies. When they contact, they must authenticate themselves to one another. However, Alice, as a double agent, may be worrying that Bob is a double agent too. Therefore, an authentication scheme for spies must have an absolutely deniable authentication property. The SOK key sharing system has precisely such a feature. It is a public-key based system, that is, the authentication needn't be based on an online trusted third party (like the one based on shared secret which we have introduced in Chapter 2).

A more serious application scenario for the SOK key sharing system can be for the Internet Key Exchange Protocol (IKE, introduced in the preceding chapter). The IKE Protocol has an authentication mode which has a "plausible deniability" feature (see §12.2.4). The absolute deniability feature of the key sharing system of Sakai et al. can provide an obviously better solution while keeping the protocol public-key based.

## 13.3.6 Tripartite Diffie-Hellman Key Agreement of Joux

Joux [156] applies the pairing technique and achieves key agreement among three parties in an astonishingly simple way. He names his protocol "tripartite Diffie-Hellman". Again, Joux's original protocol works in the Weil pairing (i.e., not modified by the distortion map technique) and hence is less convenient for a real application use (the users have to construct linearly independent points). We introduce here a simplified version using the modified Weil pairing.

Let Alice constructs her key agreement material $P_A$ by computing

$$P_A \leftarrow [a]P$$

where $P \in G_1$ is an order-$\alpha$ (prime) point on supersingular elliptic curve, $a < \alpha$ is an integer. Similarly, let the respective key agreement material of Bob and Charlie be

$$P_B \leftarrow [b]P, \quad P_C \leftarrow [c]P$$

for some integers $b < \alpha$, $c < \alpha$. The integers $a, b, c$ are the secret keys of these parties, respectively.

The three parties exchange $P_A$, $P_B$ and $P_C$, e.g., each announce the key agreement material on a public directory. Once this is done, they share the following key:

$$e(P_B, P_C)^a = e(P_A, P_C)^b = e(P_A, P_B)^c = e(P, P)^{abc}.$$

Alice computes the shared key by exponentiating the first pairing, Bob does the second, and Charlie, the third.

Without using the pairing technique, tripartite Diffie-Hellman key agreement cannot be achieved with a single round.

Of course, as in the original Diffie-Hellman key exchange protocol, this scheme does not have the authentication property and hence is vulnerable to man-in-the-middle attack.

## 13.3.7  ID-Based Cryptosystem of Boneh and Franklin

Since a shared key can be established between two principals by only using their identities, encryption is also possible by only using identities. Boneh and Franklin [52] apply the pairing technique and achieve the first practical (and formally provably secure) ID-based public key cryptosystem which fully satisfies Shamir's call for ID-based public-key cryptosystems.

There are four algorithms in the ID-based cryptosystem of Boneh and Franklin.

- **System Parameters Setup**  Trent runs this algorithm to generate global system parameters and master-key;

- **User Key Generate**  Trent runs this algorithm; on inputting master-key and an arbitrary bit string id $\in \{0, 1\}^*$, the algorithm outputs private-key which corresponds to id; this is an instantiation of (13.3.1);

- **Encryption**  This is a probabilistic algorithm; it encrypts a message under the public key id;

- **Decryption** This algorithm inputs a ciphertext and **private-key**, and returns the corresponding plaintext.

Alg 13.2 specifies the identity-based cryptosystem of Boneh and Franklin.

We now show that the system specified in Alg 13.2 is indeed a cryptosystem. Observe

$$e(d_{\mathsf{ID}}, U) = e([s]Q_{\mathsf{ID}}, [r]P) = e(Q_{\mathsf{ID}}, [r]P)^s = e(Q_{\mathsf{ID}}, [rs]P) = e(Q_{\mathsf{ID}}, [r]P_{pub}) = g_{\mathsf{ID}}.$$

Therefore, the value which Alice puts inside the hash function $H$ in the decryption time is in fact $g_{\mathsf{ID}}$, i.e., the same value which Bob has put inside the hash function $H$ in the encryption time. Then

$$V \oplus H(e(d_{\mathsf{ID}}, U)) = M \oplus H(g_{\mathsf{ID}}) \oplus H(g_{\mathsf{ID}}) = M$$

since bitwise-XOR-ing is self inverting.

Boneh and Franklin also provide a formal proof of security for their ID-based encryption scheme. The security notion is a strong one: adaptive chosen-ciphertext attack. The direct use of a hash function in the ElGamal style of encryption means that the proof is based on a so-called "random oracle model". Because we will study formal and strong notion of security and the random oracle model in Part V, we shall not introduce their proof of security technique here.

### 13.3.7.1 Extension to an Open System's Version

We must notice that Trent can decrypt every ciphertext message sent to every principal in the system! Therefore, the basic scheme of Boneh and Franklin is not suitable for applications in an open system. However, their basic scheme can be extended to one which is suitable for applications in an open system environment. We describe here an extension method which is a simplified variation of the method discussed in the paper of Boneh and Franklin.

The basic idea is to, of course, use multiple TAs. However, doing so will be interesting only if it won't cause a blowup in the number of the individual user's ID, nor in the size of the ciphertext. Here is one way to do it. We describe the case of two TAs. It is trivial to extend to many TAs.

**System Parameters Setup** Let parameters $(G_1, G_2, e, n, P, F, H)$ be identical to those defined in §13.3.7. Let further

$$P_1 \leftarrow [s_1]P,$$

$$P_2 \leftarrow [s_2]P$$

such that the tuple

$$(P, P_1, P_2)$$

**Algorithm 13.2:** The Identity-Based Cryptosystem of Boneh and Franklin

**System Parameters Setup** (performed by Trent)

1. Generate two groups $(G_1, +)$, $(G_2, \cdot)$ of prime order $p$ and a mapping-in-pair $e : (G_1, +)^2 \mapsto (G_2, \cdot)$. Choose an arbitrary generator $P \in G_1$.

2. Pick $s \in_U \mathbb{Z}_p$ and set $P_{pub} \leftarrow [s]P$; $s$ is in the position of **master-key**.

3. Choose a cryptographically strong hash function $F : \{0,1\}^* \mapsto G_1$; this hash function is for mapping a user's id to an element in $G_1$.

4. Choose a cryptographically strong hash function $H : G_2 \mapsto \{0,1\}^n$; this hash function determines that $\mathcal{M}$ (the plaintext message space) is $\{0,1\}^n$.

Trent keeps $s$ as the system private key (**master-key**), and publicizes the system parameters and their descriptions

$$(G_1, G_2, e, n, P, P_{pub}, F, H),$$

**User Key Generation**

Let ID denote user Alice's uniquely identifiable identity. Having performed physical identification of Alice and made sure the uniqueness of ID, Trent's key generation service is as follows:

1. Compute $Q_{\mathsf{ID}} \leftarrow F(\mathsf{ID})$, this is an element in $G_1$, and is Alice's ID-based public key;

2. Set Alice's private key $d_{\mathsf{ID}}$ as $d_{\mathsf{ID}} \leftarrow [s]Q_{\mathsf{ID}}$.

**Encryption**

To send confidential messages to Alice, Bob first obtains the system parameters $(G_1, G_2, e, n, P, P_{pub}, F, H)$. Using these parameters, Bob then computes

$$Q_{\mathsf{ID}} = F(\mathsf{ID}).$$

Let the message be blocked into $n$-bit blocks. Then to encrypt $M \in \{0,1\}^n$, Bob picks $r \in_U \mathbb{Z}_p$ and computes

$$g_{\mathsf{ID}} \leftarrow e(Q_{\mathsf{ID}}, [r]P_{pub}) \in G_2,$$
$$C \leftarrow ([r]P, \ M \oplus H(g_{\mathsf{ID}})).$$

The ciphertext is $C = ([r]P, \ M \oplus H(g_{\mathsf{ID}}))$.

**Decryption**

Let $C = (U, V) \in \mathcal{C}$ be a ciphertext encrypted using Alice's public key ID. To decrypt $C$ using her private key $d_{\mathsf{ID}} \in G_1$, Alice computes

$$V \oplus H(e(d_{\mathsf{ID}}, U)).$$

is in the position of

$$(P, P_{pub})$$

in §13.3.7, that is, $s_1$ and $s_2$ are the two master keys of TA$_1$ and TA$_2$, respectively.

Thus, $(G_1, G_2, e, n, P, P_1, P_2, F, H)$ is the system-wide public parameters. These parameters can be "hardwired" into applications.

**User Key Generation**   Let ID denote user Alice's uniquely identifiable identity. For $i = 1, 2$, the key generation service provided by TA$_i$ is as follows:

1. Compute $Q_{ID} \leftarrow F(ID)$, this is an element in $G_1$, and is Alice's unique ID-based public key;

2. Set Alice's private key as $d_{ID}^{(i)} \leftarrow [s_i]Q_{ID}$.

Alice's private key is the sum:

$$d_{ID} \leftarrow d_{ID}^{(1)} + d_{ID}^{(2)}.$$

If the two TAs do not collude, then this private key is not known to them.

Notice that Alice has a single public key: ID.

**Encryption**   To send confidential messages to Alice, Bob first obtains the system parameters $(G_1, G_2, e, n, P, P_1, P_2, F, H)$. Using these parameters, Bob then computes

$$Q_{ID} = F(ID).$$

Let the message be blocked into $n$-bit blocks. Then to encrypt $M \in \{0, 1\}^n$, Bob picks $r \in_U \mathbb{Z}_p$ and computes

$$g_{ID} \leftarrow e(Q_{ID}, [r](P_1 + P_2)),$$

$$C \leftarrow ([r]P, \ M \oplus H(g_{ID})).$$

The ciphertext is $C$. Thus, the ciphertext is a pair comprising of a point in $G_1$ and a block in $\{0, 1\}^n$. Namely, $\mathcal{C}$ (the ciphertext space) is $G_1 \times \{0, 1\}^n$.

**Decryption**   Let $C = (U, V) \in \mathcal{C}$ be a ciphertext encrypted using Alice's public key ID. To decrypt $C$ using her private key $d_{ID} \in G_1$, Alice computes

$$V \oplus H(e(d_{ID}, U)).$$

Notice that

$$
\begin{aligned}
e(\,d_{\mathsf{ID}}, U\,) &= e(\,[s_1]Q_{\mathsf{ID}} + [s_2]Q_{\mathsf{ID}}, [r]P\,) \\
&= e(\,[s_1]Q_{\mathsf{ID}}, [r]P\,)e(\,[s_2]Q_{\mathsf{ID}}, [r]P\,) \\
&= e(\,Q_{\mathsf{ID}}, [rs_1]P\,)e(\,Q_{\mathsf{ID}}, [rs_2]P\,) \\
&= e(\,Q_{\mathsf{ID}}, [r](P_1 + P_2)\,) \\
&= g_{\mathsf{ID}}.
\end{aligned}
$$

So Alice has recovered $g_{\mathsf{ID}}$ and hence is able to decrypt:

$$
V \oplus H(e(d_{\mathsf{ID}}, U)) = M \oplus H(g_{\mathsf{ID}}) \oplus H(g_{\mathsf{ID}}) = M
$$

since bitwise-XOR-ing is self inverting.

### Discussions

- Compared with the single TA case, computations for encryption and decryption doubled. But there is no increase in the number of Alice's ID, or the size of ciphertext.

- While colluding TAs can do the decryption too, not any single of them can. When more TAs are used, confidence of no corruption becomes evident. It is easy to see that increasing the number of TAs, the number of Alice's ID and the size of the ciphertext remains unchanged. However, the computations in encryption and in decryption increase linearly proportional to the number of TAs.

- With several TAs are used, performing decryption of an end user's ciphertext requires the full collusion of all TAs. If we trust that at least one of the TAs is honestly trustworthy, then eavesdropping by TAs is prevented. Thus, this extended IBE scheme is suitable for applications in an open system environment.

## 13.3.8  Non-interaction Property:  Authentication Without Key Channel

When Bob is to send a confidential message to Alice using a cryptographic technique in the usual sense, he should first establish a key channel from him to her (see Fig 7.1). In public-key cryptography in the usual sense, a key channel can be directory-based: for example, based on the sender verifying the public-key certificate of the recipient. Thus, the sender should first make a request to the recipient for obtaining her/his public-key certificate. Considering applications in an open system in which principals cannot memorize a link between a public key and its owner, it is necessary for the sender and recipient to have some interaction(s) in order to establish a key channel before sending a confidential message encrypted under the public key of the recipient.

It is interesting to realize that in an ID-based public-key cryptosystem, the notion of key-channel establishment is not only unnecessary, but in fact is impossible! Even if Bob does make a request for Alice to send her ID-based public key, there will be *no way* for Bob to verify whether the ID received from her is indeed her public key. All Bob needs to do is to treat the acquired ID as a valid public key of Alice and goes ahead to use it to encrypt the message. If in the end Alice is able to decrypt the ciphertext sent by Bob, then her ID is indeed her public key. Thus, as long as each ID is precise in terms of uniquely pinpointing an individual (this has to be made sure by TA, or TAs), then there is no need for the sender to be in an interaction with the recipient before using an ID-based encryption algorithm for sending confidential messages. This is why an ID-based public-key cryptosystem is also called non-interactive public key cryptosystem.

The non-interaction feature of an ID-based cryptographic scheme is most prominently evident in the case of the SOK key sharing system (see §13.3.5). Once Alice and Bob have registered their respective ID-based public keys, they already share a secure key channel without even engaging in any communication: the shared channel is underpinned by the two private keys. There is no need to run a protocol between Alice and Bob while a shared secure channel has been established! We should contrast this non-interaction case of shared key agreement with the key exchange protocol using Girault's self-certified public keys which we have seen in §13.3.3.4. That protocol cannot be non-interactive because the two participants must exchange their public keys before they can establish a shared key.

The impossibility to directly confirm that a public key belongs to a principal, i.e., the absence of a publicly verifiable key certificate, will enable an interesting application of ID-based public-key cryptography: "spy problem." We shall see this application in a latter chapter after we have introduced **zero-knowledge protocols**.

## 13.3.9  Two Open Questions for Identity-based Public-key Cryptography

First, let us review the user-key generation procedure

$$\mathsf{private\text{-}key} = F(\mathsf{master\text{-}key}, \mathsf{public\text{-}key}).$$

In this method for user private key extraction, a user submits public-key of the user's choice. The threat model is that the user can be potentially malicious, however TA must simply serve this computation unconditionally and hand private-key back to the user.

Notice that in order for the cryptosystem being an ID-based, i.e., being non-interactive or without a certificate, the function $F$ must be **deterministic**. Thus, the procedure for user-key generation has no any random input. In other words, each user's **private-key** is a deterministic image of **master-key**. This computation is in general considered as potentially a dangerous one (in terms of cryptanalysis against **master-key**). The danger has become well understood after the well-known critique of Goldwasser-Micali on the deterministic trapdoor function model of Diffie-Hellman [127], and has been widely avoided in the standard applications of public-key cryptography (e.g., by TA adding his random input).

ID-based public-key cryptography with probabilistic **private-key** is thus an interesting thing to pursue. This is the first open question.

The second and a challenging open problem is to design an ID-based cryptosystem which features non-interactive identity revocation. Identity revocation necessary if an end-user's private key is compromised.

## 13.4   Chapter Summary

In this chapter we have introduced several techniques for realizing authentication framework for public-key cryptography. These techniques include a directory-based certification framework using hierarchically organized certification authorities, a "web-of-trust"-based non-hierarchical authentication framework, and an identity-based technique in which a public key can be non-random and so self-authenticated.

Recent progress in identity-based public-key cryptography not only provides practical and convenient ways of authenticating (recognizing) public keys, but also opens some new kinds of authentication services: public-key based authentication without using a certificate. A certificate-free authentication framework has some interesting and useful properties. In a later chapter, we will see a very good use of a certificate-free authentication service.

## Exercises

13.1  Why must a public key generated from a private key in (13.1.1) be certified?

13.2  What is $F$ in (13.1.1) for the cases of RSA, Rabin and ElGamal public-key cryptographic systems, respectively?

13.3  Does a revocation of a public key certificate necessarily invalidate a digital signature issued before the revocation?

13.4  If a private key is generated from a public key, as in the case (13.3.1), why is there no need to certify the public key?

13.5  Why is an ID-based cryptography also called non-interactive public-key cryptography?

13.6 Is Girault's self-certified public-key cryptosystem a non-interactive one?

13.7 In the key exchange protocol of Girault's self-certified public-key cryptosystem (§13.3.3.4), a protocol participant can deny an involvement in a protocol run. Why?

13.8 Why must a supersingular elliptic curve for cryptographic use have a significantly larger security parameter than that of a non-supersingular one?

13.9 Unlike the Diffie-Hellman key agreement protocol (Prot 8.1), the key exchange protocol of Girault's self-certified public-key cryptosystem (§13.3.3.4) and the SOK key sharing system (§13.3.5) do not suffer man-in-the-middle attack. Why?

13.10 From (13.3.4) we know that the modified Weil pairing is symmetric. Can the original Weil pairing be symmetric for two linearly independent points?

Hint: apply bilinearity and identity to $e_\alpha(P + X, P + X)$.

13.11 If we view the SOK key sharing system (§13.3.5) as a non-interactive version of the Diffie-Hellman key exchange protocol, then the ID-based cryptosystem of Boneh and Franklin (Algorithm 13.2) can be viewed as non-interactive version of which interactive version of the cryptosystem?

Hint: usual public-key cryptosystems are interactive, i.e., a sender must first fetch the public key of the intended receiver before a ciphertext can be created and sent.

# Part V

# FORMAL APPROACHES TO SECURITY ESTABLISHMENT

Systems' complexity, in particular, that due to communications among systems and system components, has been the main cause of failures that are introduced into computing and communications systems. Cryptographic systems (algorithms and protocols), which are usually complex systems, are open to a further cause of failures: attacks. While ordinary computing and communications systems work in a friendly environment (a user will try carefully not to input or send invalid data to a program or to a communication partner in order to avoid system crash), cryptographic systems work in a hostile environment. In addition to possible failures in an ordinary way, cryptographic systems may also fail due to deliberate abnormal use. They are subject to various attacks which can be mounted not only by an external attacker who may interact with the system without being invited, but also by a legitimate user (an attacker from inside). Often cryptographic systems, even developed by experts, are vulnerable to failures. The long hidden flaws in Needham-Schroeder protocols are a well-known lesson on unreliability of security experts (see Chapter 2).

Formal methodologies for systems analysis involve systematic procedures for the analysis task. The systematic procedures base their foundations squarely on mathematics in order to preserve rigorousness and generality in the modeling and construction of complex systems and in the observation and reasoning of their behavior. These procedures either develop systems in a systematic manner so that the desired system properties are evidently demonstrable, or examine systems via systematic search so that errors in systems are uncovered. The error-prone nature of cryptographic systems has raised a wide consensus for these systems to be developed and/or analyzed by formal methodologies.

This part contains four chapters on topics of formal approaches to the development and the analysis of cryptographic systems. Chapter 14 introduces formal definitions of strong (i.e., fit-for-application) security notions for public-key cryptography. It takes a progressive approach to reaching the fit-for-application security notion from a textbook one. Chapter 15 introduces and explains two important and practical public-key cryptosystems with their fit-for-application security established using the notion defined in Chapter 16 introduces a fit-for-application security notion for digital signatures and describes techniques for arguing security for several signature schemes under the strong security notion introduced. In Chapter 17 we will return to the topic of authentication protocols: we introduce various formal analysis techniques for authentication protocols correctness.

# Chapter 14

# FORMAL AND STRONG SECURITY DEFINITIONS FOR PUBLIC-KEY CRYPTOSYSTEMS

## 14.1  Introduction

Secrecy is at the heart of cryptography. Let us now reconsider security notions for public-key encryption algorithms. We shall later see that the confidentiality-oriented security notions established in this chapter will have a wider generality for basing other kinds of security services.

So far we have confined ourselves to a very weak confidentiality notion for public-key cryptosystems. The notion is described in Property 8.2 (in §8.2): we only face a passive attacker and such an attacker may break a target cryptosystem only in the "all-or-nothing" sense. This is a typical textbook crypto security notion. It is useless for real applications.

In reality, however, attackers are most likely active ones while retaining their passive ability of eavesdropping: they may modify a ciphertext or calculate a plaintext in some unspecified ways and send the result to an unwitting user to get *oracle services* (see §7.8.2.1 and §8.9 for the meaning of oracle services). Therefore, a security notion which only deals with passive attackers is not strong enough. We need to anticipate Malice, our active and clever attacker (review §2.3 for the power of Malice).

Moreover, in many applications, plaintext messages may contain *apriori* information which can be guessed easily. For example, such *apriori* information can be a value from a known range of salaries, a candidate's name from several known candidates in a voting protocol, one of several possible instructions, or even one-bit information about a plaintext (e.g., a BUY/SELL instruction to a stock broker, or HEADS/TAILS in a remote "Coin Flipping" protocol see Prot 1.1). To guess such information about a plaintext encrypted under a one-way-trapdoor based public-key encryption algorithm, Malice can simply re-encrypt the guessed plaintext and see if the result matches the target ciphertext. Therefore, a confidentiality notion in the "all-or-nothing" sense cannot be sufficiently strong.

To anticipate attacks of various degrees of severity we need various more stringent security notions. In order to establish more stringent security notions, the first step is to *formalize* the problems properly. In the area of cryptographic systems with formally provable security, various attack games have been proposed to model and capture various attack scenarios. Such games are played between Malice and an oracle. The rule of the game allows Malice to obtain cryptographic assistance provided by the oracle, virtually on Malice's demand. We can view that such assistance provides a kind of "cryptanalysis training course" to Malice. A cryptosystem is regarded as secure against the formal model of an attack game if, even given adequate "cryptanalysis training course," Malice cannot succeed with satisfaction.

The second aspect of the formal treatment on security is a rigorous measure on Malice's satisfaction. In the area of formally provable security for cryptographic systems, security of a cryptographic system concerns a quantitative relation which links the security of the cryptosystem to some intractable problem in the theory of computational complexity. A standard technique for establishing a high degree of confidence in security is to express and translate the satisfaction level of Malice against a target cryptographic system into some values which measure *how fast* and *how often* it takes for one to solve some reputable intractable problems in the theory of computational complexity. Such a translation is an efficient mathematical transformation, or a sequence of such transformations, leading from the alleged successful attack to a solution to a reputable intractable problem. Since we are highly confident about *how slow* and *how infrequent* it is for us to solve the latter problems, we will also have a definite (high) confidence about Malice's *dissatisfaction* with the alleged attack on the target cryptosystem.

Due to the diversity of the attack scenarios and the use of several intractable problems as the computational basis for security, the area of cryptographic systems with formally provable security has adopted a language with plenty of jargon. With this jargon we can describe various security properties and requirements with convenience and precision. Here are a few examples of security statements:

- Cryptosystem $X$ is *semantically secure* against a passive eavesdropper of unbounded computing resource, but is *malleable* under *chosen-ciphertext attack* in which the attacker only has to work at *lunchtime* with a low-end device such as a handheld calculator.

- Digital signature scheme $Y$ is secure in terms of unforgeability of signature under *adaptive chosen-message attack*. Formal proof of its security *reduces* a successful forgery to solving the discrete logarithm problem. The reduction is under a *random oracle model* in which the forger can be *forked* with a non-negligible probability.

- Signcryption scheme $Z$ is secure in terms of *indistinguishability* of encryption under *adaptive chosen-ciphertext attack* and unforgeability of signature under adaptive chosen-message attack, regardless of whether the attacker works at lunchtime, at *midnight* or in the *small hours*. Formal proofs of these security qualities are with respect to the integer factorization problem.

- Electronic auction protocol $\Pi$ is secure for the bidders in terms of *deniability* of their participation in a protocol run and for the winner in terms of indistinguishability of its identity. Formal proofs of these security qualities are with respect to a *standard intractability assumption*: the decisional Diffie-Hellman problem.

In our study of formally provable security in this and the next three chapters, the jargon appearing in these security statements will be defined or explained. Security statements such as those listed here will become much more meaningful after our study.

### 14.1.1   Chapter Outline

We begin in §14.2 with an introduction to the main theme of this chapter: formal treatment on security which involves formal modeling of attack scenarios and precise measuring of the consequences. The formal treatment will show clearly the inadequacy of the "all-or-nothing" based security notion we have introduced in Chapter 8. A strengthened security notion, "semantic security," which means hiding any partial information about a message, will be introduced in §14.3. The inadequacy of semantic security will be exposed in §14.4. The exposure leads to several further steps of strengthening security notions: "chosen ciphertext security," "adaptive chosen-ciphertext security," and "non-malleability." These strengthened security notions and their relations will be studied in §14.5.

## 14.2   A Formal Treatment for Security

Speaking at a very abstract level, "formally provable security" for a cryptographic system is an affirmative *measure* of the system's strength in resisting an attack. Secure systems are those in which Malice cannot do something bad *too often* or *fast enough*. Thus, the measure involves establishing success probabilities and computational cost.

To provide a concrete view of such a measure let us look at an "attack game" played between Malice and an "oracle" who models an innocent user of a cryptographic system in which the user should be inevitably in interactions with Malice.

This game provides a formal treatment of a computational view of what we mean by security; it also makes a first step in our process of strengthening the security notion for cryptosystems (from what has so far been confined in Property 8.2 in §8.2).

Let Malice be the attacker and let $\mathcal{O}$ denote an oracle in our game of attack. In the context of confidentiality, the target of Malice is a cryptosystem. Thus, "something bad" means that the game results in a breach of confidentiality regarding the target cryptosystem.

Let us use Definition 7.1 in §7.2 to provide the syntactic notation for the target cryptosystem which has an encryption algorithm $\mathcal{E}$, plaintext space $\mathcal{M}$ and ciphertext space $\mathcal{C}$. Nevertheless, we should make an important point here: the encryption algorithm $\mathcal{E}$ is now probabilistic, that is, it has an internal random operation which has certain probability distribution and will cause the ciphertext output as a random variable of this distribution. For example, if a plaintext message is encrypted under an encryption key twice, the two resultant ciphertexts will be different with an overwhelming probability (due to the encryption algorithm's 1-1 mapping property).

Prot 14.1 specifies an attack game.

In the attack game $\mathcal{O}$ challenges Malice to answer the following question:

From which of the two ensembles (experiments) $\mathcal{E}_{ke}(m_0)$, $\mathcal{E}_{ke}(m_1)$
comes the challenge ciphertext $c^*$?

We consider that Malice is a probabilistic polynomial-time distinguisher defined in Definition 4.14 (in §4.7). This is not only because $\mathcal{O}$'s output is probabilistic, but also because Malice is *polynomially bounded* and therefore may wish to use a probabilistic polynomial-time (PPT) algorithm if he thinks such algorithms may be more efficient than deterministic ones (this is usually true as we have witnessed many times in Chapter 4). Denote by Adv the advantage of Malice for making a distinction. By Definition 4.14, Adv should be the difference between Malice's probabilistic distinguishing of the ensembles $\mathcal{E}_{ke}(m_0)$ and $\mathcal{E}_{ke}(m_1)$:

$$\text{Adv} = | \text{Prob}[\, 0 \leftarrow \text{Malice}(c^* = \mathcal{E}_{ke}(m_0))\,] - \text{Prob}[\, 0 \leftarrow \text{Malice}(c^* = \mathcal{E}_{ke}(m_1))\,] |. \tag{14.2.1}$$

The probability space should include the probabilistic choices made by $\mathcal{O}$, Malice and the internal random operation of the encryption algorithm. Also notice that Malice's answer is based not solely on the challenge ciphertext $c^*$, but also on the two chosen plaintext messages $(m_0, m_1)$. Only because so, can his answer be regarded as an "educated guess." However, for clarity in exposition, we have omitted $(m_0, m_1)$ from Malice's input.

We must notice that there is an additional clue for Malice to "improve" his educated guess: $\mathcal{O}$ tosses a fair coin. The advantage formulation (14.2.1) does not

**Protocol 14.1:** Indistinguishable Chosen-plaintext Attack

PREMISE

i) Malice and an oracle $\mathcal{O}$ have agreed on a target cryptosystem $\mathcal{E}$ of plaintext message space $\mathcal{M}$ and ciphertext message space $\mathcal{C}$;

ii) $\mathcal{O}$ has fixed an encryption key $ke$ for $\mathcal{E}$.

1. Malice chooses distinct messages $m_0, m_1 \in \mathcal{M}$ and sends them to $\mathcal{O}$;

   (∗ the messages $m_0$, $m_1$ are called **chosen plaintext** messages. Malice has so far been in a **"find-stage"** for preparing $m_0$, $m_1$; he should of course prepare them in such a way that he hopes the encryption of them is easily recognizable ∗)

2. If these two messages are not the same length, $\mathcal{O}$ will pad the shorter one into the same length of the other;

   (∗ e.g., using a dummy string $0^d$ where $d$ is the difference between the message lengths ∗)

   $\mathcal{O}$ tosses a fair coin $b \in_U \{0, 1\}$ and performs the following encryption operation

   $$c^* = \begin{cases} \mathcal{E}_{ke}(m_0) & \text{if } b = 0 \\ \mathcal{E}_{ke}(m_1) & \text{if } b = 1 \end{cases}$$

   $\mathcal{O}$ sends $c^* \in \mathcal{C}$ to Malice;

   (∗ the ciphertext message $c^*$ is called a *challenge ciphertext*. As convention in the area of provable security, a ciphertext with a "∗" superscript is always considered as a challenge ciphertext ∗)

   (∗ remember, $c^*$ is a random variable of two random input values: fair coin $b$ and an internal random operation of $\mathcal{E}$ ∗)

3. Upon receipt of $c^*$, Malice must answer either 0 or 1 as his working out of $\mathcal{O}$'s coin tossing.

   (∗ Malice is now in a **"guess-stage"** for an educated guess of $\mathcal{O}$'s coin tossing; an answer other than 0 or 1 is not allowed ∗)

explicitly express how Malice could have used this clue, though *implicitly* we know that each probability term in (14.2.1) can never exceed $\frac{1}{2}$ since, e.g., the event "$c^* = \mathcal{E}_{ke}(m_0)$," can only occur with probability $\frac{1}{2}$. We should explicitly express Malice's use of this clue in his advantage formulation. Applying the conditional probability (Definition 3.3 in §3.4.1) while noticing the equal probability of $\frac{1}{2}$ for both cases of $\mathcal{O}$'s coin-tossing, (14.2.1) can be rewritten to

$$
\text{Adv} \;=\; \big|\; \tfrac{1}{2}\text{Prob}[\,0 \leftarrow \text{Malice}(c^*)\,|\,c^* = \mathcal{E}_{ke}(m_0)\,] - \tfrac{1}{2}\text{Prob}[\,0 \leftarrow \text{Malice}(c^*)\,|\,c^* = \mathcal{E}_{ke}(m_1)\,]\;\big|. \tag{14.2.2}
$$

By rule of the game, Malice is not allowed to answer other than 0 or 1, and hence the event of a wrong (correct) answer is complementary to that of a correct (wrong) answer. So applying Property 5 of probability (§3.3), we have

$$
\text{Adv} \;=\; \big|\; \tfrac{1}{2}\text{Prob}[\,0 \leftarrow \text{Malice}(c^*)\,|\,c^* = \mathcal{E}_{ke}(m_0)\,] - \tfrac{1}{2}(1 - \text{Prob}[\,0 \leftarrow \text{Malice}(c^*)\,|\,c^* = \mathcal{E}_{ke}(m_0)\,])\;\big|,
$$

that is,

$$
\text{Prob}[\,0 \leftarrow \text{Malice}(c^*)\,|\,c^* = \mathcal{E}_{ke}(m_0)\,] = \frac{1}{2} \pm \text{Adv}. \tag{14.2.3}
$$

The formulation (14.2.3) is often used to express an algorithmic advantage on top of that for a sheer guessing of fair coin tossing (probability $\frac{1}{2}$). So if $\text{Adv} = 0$, then Malice's probabilistic answer will be exactly the distribution of tossing a fair coin. Of course, we should not be too cynical about Malice's algorithmic advantage and should generously consider (i) $\text{Adv} > 0$ and (ii) the positive sign prefixing Adv. Clearly, (14.2.3) will also hold if all appearances of 0 in it are replaced with 1.

From (14.2.3) we can also see that Malice's advantage can never exceed $\frac{1}{2}$ since a probability value cannot be outside the interval $[0,1]$. Indeed, given that $\mathcal{O}$ has exactly $\frac{1}{2}$ probability to have encrypted either of the two plaintexts, Adv formulated in (14.2.1) as the probability difference for *joint* events can never exceed $\frac{1}{2}$. The reader might be wondering what (14.2.3) would look like if $\mathcal{O}$ tosses a *biased* coin, say one with $\frac{1}{4}$ probability to encrypt the plaintext query $m_0$ and $\frac{3}{4}$ probability to encrypt $m_1$. Hint: replace $\frac{1}{2}$ in (14.2.2) with respective biased probability values and see how (14.2.3) will change. We will then realize that it *is* possible for Malice's advantage to exceed $\frac{1}{2}$, *provided* that $\mathcal{O}$ tosses a biased coin.

We say that the target cryptosystem is secure against the attack game in Prot 14.1 if $\mathcal{E}_{ke}(m_0)$ is indistinguishable from $\mathcal{E}_{ke}(m_1)$. According to Definition 4.15 (in §4.7), this means there should exist no PPT distinguisher for any $\text{Adv} > 0$ as a non-negligible quantity. Equivalently, for any Malice successfully to make a distinction, his Adv must be a negligible quantity. Here "negligible" is measured with respect to a security parameter of the target encryption scheme which is usually the size of the key material. We can consider Adv for any polynomially bounded Malice (i.e., any PPT algorithm) as a slow-growing function of Malice's computational resources.

Here "slow-growing" means that even if Malice adds his computational resources in a tremendous manner, Adv will only grow in a marginal manner so that Malice cannot be very happy about his "advantage." This is exactly what we meant when we mentioned in the beginning of this chapter that Malice cannot do something bad too often or fast enough.

Since our argument has followed exactly Definition 4.15 for **polynomial indistinguishable ensembles**, the new security notion we have just established can be named **polynomial indistinguishability of encryption**. Moreover, because the indistinguishability is between the two plaintexts chosen by Malice, the precise name for this new notion is **security against polynomially indistinguishable chosen-plaintext attack**. It is usually shorten to **IND-CPA security**.

Now that in the IND-CPA attack game in Prot 14.1, Malice has freedom to choose plaintext messages, and is only required to answer sheer one-bit information about the chosen plaintexts: "Is the encrypted plaintext $m_0$ or $m_1$?" the difficulty for Malice to break the target cryptosystem is drastically reduced from that to break the cryptosystem in the "all-or-nothing" sense of security (defined in Property 8.2.(i) in §8.2). Indeed, all textbook public-key encryption algorithms (see §8.14 for the meaning of textbook crypto) we have introduced so far are insecure under IND-CPA. It is easy to see this for the RSA and Rabin cryptosystems since they are deterministic and thereby allow Malice to pinpoint $m_0$ or $m_1$ by re-encryption. We shall further see in §14.3.5 that the ElGamal cryptosystem specified in Alg 8.3, which provides a probabilistic encryption algorithm, is no longer secure under IND-CPA too.

With the difficulty of an attack being reduced, the security requirement for cryptosystems should be strengthened. To reduce the difficulty for Malice to attack cryptosystems, or speaking equivalently, to strengthen the security notion for cryptosystems, and to do so with formal rigorousness, is the main topic for this chapter.

## 14.3   Semantic Security — the Debut of Provable Security

The IND-CPA security notion which we have just defined is originally introduced by Goldwasser and Micali [127]. They use **semantic security** to name this security notion. This notion means that a ciphertext does not leak any useful information about the plaintext (if we may consider that the length of the plaintext is not a piece of useful information) to any attacker whose computational power is polynomially bounded. They observed that, in many applications, messages may contain certain *apriori* information which can be useful for an attack. For example, a ciphertext may only encrypt a simple instruction such as "BUY" or "SELL," or one of the identities of a handful of known candidates who are being voted on. Goldwasser and Micali point out that public-key cryptosystems which are based on direct applications of one-way trapdoor functions are in general very weak for hiding such messages. We shall see that their critique does apply to each of the public-key cryptosystems which we have introduced in Chapter 8.

The need for this rather strong security notion is very real. The failure of a mental poker protocol provides a good illustration on the weakness of public-key cryptosystems as direct applications of one-way trapdoor functions. Let us first review the mental poker protocol of Shamir, Rivest and Adleman [263].

## 14.3.1  The SRA Mental Poker Protocol

Alice lives in New York and Bob lives in London. They have never met, but they wish to play poker across the Atlantic. The same authors of the RSA cryptosystems made this possible: Shamir, Rivest and Adleman propose a protocol called "SRA mental poker" [263].

Mental poker is played like ordinary poker, however the cards are encoded into messages so that the card game can be played in communications. In order to play a poker game, Alice and Bob should first deal the cards fairly. Here "fair" means the following four requirements:

i) The deal must distribute all possible hands with equal probability (i.e., uniform distribution) and should not allow the same card to appear in two hands simultaneously.

ii) Alice and Bob must know the cards in their own hand, but neither can have any information about the other's hand.

iii) Both Alice and Bob must be viewed as potential cheaters who cannot be relied upon to follow the rules of the protocol.

iv) Alice and Bob should both be able to verify that a preceding game has been fairly played.

The idea behind the SRA mental poker is to make use of a cipher with the commutative property. In such a cipher, a message can be doubly encrypted by Alice and Bob using their respective secret keys and the resultant ciphertext must also be doubly decrypted by both of them. Let

$$C = E_X(M) \quad \text{and} \quad M = D_X(C)$$

denote the encryption and decryption algorithms performed by principal $X$. The commutative property of the cipher is that the following equations hold for any message $M$ in its plaintext space:

$$\begin{aligned} M &= D_A(D_B(E_A(E_B(M)))) \\ &= D_B(D_A(E_B(E_A(M)))) \end{aligned} \tag{14.3.1}$$

That is, the plaintext message can be correctly retrieved even though the sequence of the double decryption can be independent from that of the double encryption.

For simplicity while without loss of generality, let us suppose that Alice and Bob decide to play a game of one-card hand using a deck of three cards. Prot 14.2 specifies a method for a fair deal of hands. The generalization to the case of a deck having any number of cards is, however maybe tedious, straightforward.

---

**Protocol 14.2:** A Fair Deal Protocol for the SRA Mental Poker Game

PREMISE:

> Alice and Bob have agreed on a commutative cipher with the properties in (14.3.1) and they have picked their own secret encryption keys;
>
> They have agree on a deck of three cards $M_1$, $M_2$, $M_3$.

GOAL:

> They achieve a fair deal of a one-card hand for each party satisfying the fairness properties (i)-(iv).

1.  Alice encrypts the three cards as $C_i = E_A(M_i)$ for $i = 1, 2, 3$; she sends to Bob these three ciphertexts in a random order;

    (∗ sending the encrypted cards in a random order models shuffling of the deck ∗)

2.  Bob picks at random one ciphertext; denoting it by $C$, he doubly encrypts $C$ as $CC = E_B(C)$; he also picks at random another ciphertext, denoting it by $C'$; he sends $CC$, $C'$ to Alice;

    (∗ $CC$ determines Bob's hand; $C'$ determines Alice's hand; the other encrypted card is discarded ∗)

3.  Alice decrypts both $CC$ and $C'$; the decryption of $C'$ is her hand; the decryption of $CC$, denoting it by $C''$, is returned to Bob;

4.  Bob decrypts $C''$ and thereby obtains his hand.

    (∗ they can now play their mental poker game ∗)

---

## 14.3.2   A Security Analysis Based on Textbook Security

For the time being let us suppose that the cryptosystem used in Prot 14.2 is sufficiently strong in both single and double encryption operations. By saying that a cryptosystem is "sufficiently strong," we mean that, given a plaintext (respectively, a ciphertext) without giving the correct encryption key (respectively, decryption key), a polynomially bounded attacker cannot create a valid ciphertext from the given plaintext (respectively, cannot retrieve the plaintext from the given ciphertext). This is an "all-or-nothing" sense of secrecy given in Property 8.2.(i) which we have agreed for textbook crypto algorithms (in §8.2). Under this notion of security we can now provide a security analysis for Prot 14.2 with respect to the fairness properties (i)-(iv).

After a run of Prot 14.2:

- Alice and Bob each obtains a hand of a card in $\{M_1, M_2, M_3\}$ with equal probability (i.e., uniform in this set); this is because Alice has shuffled the deck in Step 1. Notice that it is Alice's interest to shuffle the deck in uniformly random to prevent Bob from having an advantage in choosing his hand. So fairness property (i) is satisfied.

- Each of the two parties knows her/his own hand after double decryption, but does not know the hand of the other party since neither of them knows the discarded card. So fairness property (ii) is satisfied.

- It is obvious that the protocol does not rely on any party to be honest. So fairness property (iii) is satisfied.

Fairness property (iv) depends on whether or not the cryptosystems used in the protocol permits a honest verification after a poker game. Shamir et al. suggest to use a variation of the RSA cryptosystem (see §8.5) where the two parties keep both of their encryption and decryption exponents secret before a poker game finishes, and they disclose these exponents to the other party for checking their honest conduct after a game finishes.

Let $N$ be the shared RSA modulus. In this variation, Alice and Bob know the factorization of $N$. Let $(e_A, d_A)$ be Alice's encryption and decryption exponents, and $(e_B, d_B)$ be Bob's encryption and decryption exponents. Knowing the factorization of $N$ permits Alice (respectively, Bob) to compute $d_A$ from $e_A$ (respectively, $d_B$ from $e_B$). They do so by solving the congruence

$$e_X d_X \equiv 1 \pmod{\phi(N)} \tag{14.3.2}$$

(where $X$ means $A$ or $B$). Then for principal $X$ we have

$$E_X(M) = M^{e_X} \pmod{N}$$

$$D_X(C) = C^{d_X} \pmod{N}.$$

Since the RSA group is commutative, it is trivial to see the holding of (14.3.1). Before finishing a game, both parties keep their encryption and decryption exponents secret. Thus, no one can create a valid ciphertext which has been created by the other party; this prevents a party from testing which card has been encrypted under which ciphertext. Also, neither can decrypt a ciphertext which has been created by the other party. Thus, indeed, the cryptosystem is "sufficiently strong" as we have required it to be.

It is now clear that after a game finishes, both parties can disclose their encryption and decryption exponents to the other party and thereby they can check that the encryption, double encryption and decryption have all been correctly performed. Thus, fairness property (iv) is satisfied.

In our analysis we have used a rather inadequate and unreasonable notion of security: a "sufficiently strong" cryptosystem means an attacker's inability to create a valid ciphertext from a given plaintext without the correct encryption key, or to decrypt a ciphertext without the correct decryption key. The inadequacy and unreasonability of this security notion now become apparent. Lipton [180] observes that Prot 14.2 fails if it uses the variation of the RSA cryptosystem suggested by the original authors of the mental poker game. The failure is due to the cryptosystem's inability to hide certain *apriori* information in plaintext messages. Here, the *apriori* information is the quadratic residuosity. Review §6.5, a number $a$ is a quadratic residue modulo $n$ if $\gcd(a, N) = 1$ and there exists $x < N$ such that

$$x^2 \equiv a \pmod{N}.$$

Notice that because $\phi(N)$ is even, the encryption exponent $e$ and the decryption exponent $d$ which satisfy congruence (14.3.2) must both be odd. Consequently, a plaintext $M$ is a quadratic residue modulo $N$, i.e., $M \in \mathrm{QR}_N$ if and only if the corresponding ciphertext $C \in \mathrm{QR}_N$, since

$$C \equiv M^e \equiv (x^2)^e \equiv (x^e)^2 \pmod{N},$$

for some $x < N$. That is, the RSA encryption cannot change the quadratic residuosity of the plaintext message. Further review §6.5, we know that with the factorization of $N$, deciding $C \in \mathrm{QR}_N$ can be easily done: first having $C$ modulo each prime factor of $N$, then evaluating Legendre symbol of the results using Alg 6.2.

Therefore, if some plaintext card(s) is (are) in $\mathrm{QR}_N$ and others (the other) are (is) not, then a party who knows Lipton's trick will have an unfair advantage in a game: (s)he will know exactly which of the cards will never be encrypted, whether under single encryption or double.

We conclude that the SRA mental poker protocol is not secure. To state our conclusion with the formal precision, we say that it is not secure against the IND-CPA model specified in Protocol (Game) 14.1.

### 14.3.3   Probabilistic Encryption of Goldwasser and Micali

It is possible to fix Prot 14.2 against Lipton's attack. For example, forcing all cards to be chosen from $QR_N$ provides a specific fix. However, Goldwasser and Micali envision a need for a general fix of a much bigger problem: the need for a stronger security notion: semantic security. They describe their notion of semantic security in Property 14.1.

**Property 14.1: Semantic Security** *Whatever is efficiently computable about the plaintext given the ciphertext, is also efficiently computable without the ciphertext.*

They proposed a **probabilistic encryption** scheme which possesses this property. Let us name this scheme the GM cryptosystem. The GM cryptosystem encrypts the entire message bit by bit, where the difficulty of finding an encrypted single bit from a ciphertext $c$ is that of deciding whether $c \in QR_N$ or $c \in J_N(1) \setminus QR_N$, where $J_N(1) = \{\, x \mid x \in \mathbb{Z}_N^*,\ \left(\dfrac{x}{N}\right) = 1 \,\}$.

The GM cryptosystem is specified in Alg 14.1.

We now show that the system specified in Alg 14.1 is indeed a cryptosystem, i.e., Alice's decryption procedure will actually return the same plaintext message that Bob has encrypted.

Observing the encryption algorithm it is easy to see that the plaintext bit 0 is encrypted to a ciphertext in $QR_N$.

For the plaintext bit 1, the corresponding ciphertext is $c = yx^2$. Noticing $\left(\dfrac{y}{p}\right) = \left(\dfrac{y}{q}\right) = -1$, we have (due to the multiplication property of Legendre symbol, see Theorem 6.16 in §6.5.2):

$$\left(\frac{c}{p}\right) = \left(\frac{yx^2}{p}\right) = \left(\frac{y}{p}\right)\left(\frac{x^2}{p}\right) = (-1) \times 1 = -1$$

and

$$\left(\frac{c}{q}\right) = \left(\frac{yx^2}{q}\right) = \left(\frac{y}{q}\right)\left(\frac{x^2}{q}\right) = (-1) \times 1 = -1$$

and therefore

$$\left(\frac{c}{N}\right) = \left(\frac{c}{p}\right)\left(\frac{c}{q}\right) = (-1) \times (-1) = 1.$$

That is, the plaintext 1 is encrypted to a ciphertext in $J_N(1) \setminus QR_N$.

The decryption algorithm works properly because knowing $p$, $q$, Alice can decide whether $c_i \in QR_N$ or $c_i \in J_N(1) \setminus QR_N$, respectively, and hence can retrieve the plaintext bit by bit correctly.

It is not difficult to see that encryption of an $\ell$-bit message $b$ takes $O_B(\ell(\log_2 N)^2)$ bit operations; this is the time complexity for encryption. The encryption algorithm

**Algorithm 14.1:** The Probabilistic Cryptosystem of Goldwasser and Micali

**Key Setup**

To set up a user's key material, user Alice performs the following steps:

1) choose two random prime numbers $p$ and $q$ such that $|p| = |q| = k$

   (* e.g., using Alg 4.7 with input $1^k$ *)

2) compute $N = pq$;

3) pick a random integer $y$ satisfying $\left(\dfrac{y}{p}\right) = \left(\dfrac{y}{q}\right) = -1$

   (* thus $y \in J(N) \setminus QR_N$ *)

4) publicize $(N, y)$ as her public key material, and keep $(p, q)$ as her private key.

**Encryption**

To send a binary string $m = b_1 b_2 \cdots b_\ell$ to Alice, Bob performs:

```
for ( i = 1, 2, ..., ℓ )
    {
        x ←U Z*N;
        if (bi == 0)  ci ← x² (mod N)
        else ci ← yx² (mod N)
    }
```

Bob sends to Alice: $E_N(m) \leftarrow (c_1, c_2, \ldots, c_\ell)$.

**Decryption**

Upon receipt an $\ell$-tuple ciphertext $(c_1, c_2, \ldots, c_\ell)$, Alice performs:

```
for ( i = 1, 2, ..., ℓ )
    {
        if (ci ∈ QRN) bi ← 0
        else bi ← 1;
    }
set m ← (b1, b2, ..., bℓ).
```

has a message expansion ratio of $\log_2 N$: one bit of plaintext is expanded into $\log_2 N$ bits of ciphertext.

Since computing Legendre symbol mod $p$ and mod $q$ with $|p| = |q| = k$ can be done in $O_B(k^2)$ bit operations (review the discussion after Alg 6.2 on careful realization of the Jacobi-symbol algorithm), decryption of $(c_1, c_2, \ldots, c_\ell)$ requires $O_B(\ell(\log_2 N)^2)$ bit operations. This is the time complexity for decryption.

The "bit-by-bit" fashion of encryption means that the GM cryptosystem is highly inefficient.

## 14.3.4 The Security of the GM Cryptosystem

The encryption algorithm of the GM cryptosystem can be considered as an error-free randomized algorithm: the random operations in the encryption algorithm can introduce no any error into the ciphertext but achieve the following important function:

> Distributing the plaintext bit 0 uniformly (that is, correctly) over $\mathrm{QR}_N$ and the plaintext bit 1 uniformly over $\mathrm{J}_N(1) \setminus \mathrm{QR}_N$.

Both distributions are uniform. This is because, for the plaintext bit 0, squaring maps from $\mathbb{Z}_N^*$ onto $\mathrm{QR}_N$, and for the plaintext bit 1, multiplying-$y$ to an element in $\mathrm{QR}_N$ is a permutation from $\mathrm{QR}_N$ onto $\mathrm{J}_N(1) \setminus \mathrm{QR}_N$. Thus, picking $x \in_U \mathbb{Z}_N^*$ in the encryption algorithm means picking either a uniform element in $\mathrm{QR}_N$ if the plaintext bit is 0, or a uniform element in $\mathrm{J}_N(1) \setminus \mathrm{QR}_N$ if the plaintext bit is 1.

To express it formally, we say that the difficulty of the GM cryptosystem is that of deciding the quadratic residuosity problem (QR) problem which is formally specified in Definition 6.2 (in §6.5.1). The QR problem is a well-known hard problem in number theory (review the discussion we provided §6.5.1 after Definition 6.2). We have the following assumption on its intractability.

**Assumption 14.1: Quadratic Residuosity Assumption (QR Assumption)**
*Let $\mathcal{IG}$ be an integer instance generator that on input $1^k$, runs in time polynomial in $k$, and outputs a 2k-bit modulus $N = pq$ where $p$ and $q$ are each a k-bit uniformly random odd prime.*

*We say that $\mathcal{IG}$ satisfies the quadratic residuosity (QR) assumption if for all sufficiently large $k$ and for $N \leftarrow \mathcal{IG}(1^k)$, ensembles $\mathrm{QR}_N$ and $\mathrm{J}_N(1) \setminus QR_N$ are polynomially indistinguishable where the concept of polynomial indistinguishability is given in Definition 4.14 in §4.7.*

It is clear that the availability of the public key $N$ places an upper bound for the difficulty of the QR problem since it suffices for an attacker to factor $N$ and then apply the GM decryption algorithm to solve the QR problem. Therefore, the

GM cryptosystem assumes that the attacker is polynomially bounded. That is why semantic security for encryption algorithms is also called **polynomial indistinguishability of encryptions.**

If the QR assumption truly holds, then we can consider that, viewed by a polynomially bounded attacker, the GM encryption algorithm distributes a plaintext bit uniformly over the ciphertext space $J_N(1)$. The uniform distribution of the ciphertext means that an attempt for such an attacker to guess the plaintext from the corresponding ciphertext is a completely senseless thing to do. This is exactly what Goldwasser and Micali mean by expressing their notion of semantic security in the form of Property 14.1.

We can re-express the notion of semantic security as in Definition 14.1.

**Definition 14.1: Semantic Security, Security for Indistinguishable Chosen-plaintext Attack (IND-CPA Security)** *A cryptosystem with a security parameter $k$ is said to be semantically secure (IND-CPA secure) if after the attack game in Prot 14.1 being played with any polynomially bounded attacker, the advantage Adv formulated in (14.2.3) is a negligible quantity in $k$ for all sufficiently large $k$.*

We have the following result for the security of the GM cryptosystem.

**Theorem 14.1:** *Let $k$ be the size of the two prime factors of an RSA modulus $N$. The GM cryptosystem with security parameter $k$ is semantically secure (IND-CPA secure) if and only if the QR assumption holds.*  □

## 14.3.5  A Semantically Secure Version of the ElGamal Cryptosystem

Similar to the case of the RSA cryptosystem, the ElGamal cryptosystem specified in Alg 8.3 does not hide the quadratic residuosity of the plaintext. This is because in that algorithm we have set the public parameters $(g, p)$ such that $g$ generates the whole group $\mathbb{Z}_p^*$. In such a parameter setting, the quadratic residuosity of a plaintext can be related to that of the corresponding ciphertext. This is shown in Example 14.1.

**Example 14.1:** Let the oracle $\mathcal{O}$ setup $(p, g, y)$ as the public key material for the ElGamal cryptosystem specified in Alg 8.3. Then due to Euler's criterion (Theorem 6.13 in §6.5.1), $g \in \mathrm{QNR}_p$ (i.e., $g$ is a quadratic non-residue modulo $p$).

Let Malice be an IND-CPA attacker. He should submit a message $m_0 \in \mathrm{QR}_p$ and $m_1 \in \mathrm{QNR}_p$ (applying Alg 6.2, it is easy for Malice to prepare $m_0$ and $m_1$ to satisfy these two conditions). Let $(c_1^*, c_2^*)$ be the pair of challenge ciphertext returned from $\mathcal{O}$; we have

$$c_2^* = \begin{cases} y^k m_0 \pmod{p} & 50\% \text{ probability,} \\ y^k m_1 \pmod{p} & 50\% \text{ probability.} \end{cases}$$

Now, Malice can pinpoint the plaintext by deciding the quadratic residuosity of $y$, $c_1^*$ and $c_2^*$. There are a few cases to consider.

Let us first consider $y \in QR_p$. This case is very easy. The plaintext is $m_0$ if and only if $c_2^* \in QR_p$. This is due to the the multiplicative property of Legendre symbol given in Theorem 6.16.(ii) (in §6.5.2).

The case $y \in QNR_p$ has two sub-cases which are also very easy. The first sub-case of $c_1^* \in QR_p$ will cause $y^k \in QR_p$ (because now $k$ is even), and thereby the decision is identical to that in the previous paragraph. The reader may complete the second sub-case of $c_1^* \in QNR_p$ by noticing that now $k$ is odd.    □

As usual, having seen where the problem is, it is relatively easy to fix it. If we restrict the cryptosystem to working in $QR_p$, then the attack in Example 14.1 will no longer work. Alg 14.2 specifies a fix.

---

**Algorithm 14.2:** A Semantically Secure Version of the ElGamal Cryptosystem

**Public Parameter Setup**

Let $G$ be an abelian group with the following description:

1. find a random prime number $q$ with $|q| = k$;

2. test primality of $p = 2q + 1$, if $p$ is not prime, go to 1;

3. pick a random generator $h \in \mathbb{Z}_p^*$; set $g = h^2 \pmod{p}$;

4. let $desc(G)$ be such that $G = \langle g \rangle$;

   (∗ the group generated from $g$, see Definition 5.10 in §5.2.3 ∗)

5. let $(p, g)$ be the public parameters for the ElGamal cryptosystem;

6. let $G$ be the plaintext message space.

(∗ the rest part is the same as that of Alg 8.3 ∗)

---

First of all we should notice that Alg 14.2 will terminate because there are plenty of prime numbers $p$ such that $(p-1)/2$ is also prime (7, 11, 23, 39, 47 are several examples). Such a prime is called a **safe prime**.

Next, by Fermat's Little Theorem, $\text{ord}_p(g) = q$ which is a large prime; therefore, the group $G = \langle g \rangle$ has a large order. This is a necessary requirement for the DL assumption to hold (Assumption 8.2).

Moreover, by Euler's Criterion (Theorem 6.13 in §6.5.1) we know $g \in \text{QR}_p$ and therefore $G = \text{QR}_p$ (the reader may answer why by noticing Theorem 5.2 in §5.2.3). So for chosen plaintexts $m_0, m_1 \in \text{QR}_p$, the numbers $g, y, c_1^*, c_2^*$ are all quadratic residues modulo $p$. Consequently, the quadratic-residuosity attack demonstrated in Example 14.1 will no longer work since now all cases of quadratic residuosity testing will output the YES answer.

The stipulation of the plaintext space being $G = \text{QR}_p$ can cause no trouble for message encoding (in encryption time) and decoding (in decryption time). For example, for any message $m < p$, if $m \in \text{QR}_p$, then we are done; if $m \notin \text{QR}_p$, then $-m = p - m \in G$. This is because from

$$(-1)^{(p-1)/2} = (-1)^q = (-1)^{\text{odd number}} = -1 \ (\text{mod } p),$$

we have

$$(-m)^{(p-1)/2} = (-1)^{(p-1)/2} m^{(p-1)/2} = (-1)(-1) = 1 \ (\text{mod } p)$$

and therefore $-m \in \text{QR}_p = G$ after Euler's Criterion.

For the fixed version of the ElGamal cryptosystem, Malice now faces a different decisional problem. Upon receipt of the challenge ciphertext $(c_1^*, c_2^*)$ after having submitted $m_0, m_1$ for encryption, he can compute from $c_2^*$:

$$c_2^*/m_0 = \begin{cases} y^k \equiv g^{xk} \ (\text{mod } p) & 50\% \text{ probability,} \\ y^k(m_1/m_0) \ (\text{mod } p) & 50\% \text{ probability.} \end{cases}$$

Notice that in the first case, the tuple

$$(g, y, c_1^*, c_2^*/m_0) = (g, g^x, g^k, g^{xk}) \ (\text{mod } p)$$

is a Diffie-Hellman tuple, while in the second case it is not. So Malice should ask himself:

$$\text{Is } (g, y, c_1^*, c_2^*/m_0) \ (\text{mod } p) \text{ a DH tuple?}$$

or

$$\text{Is } (g, y, c_1^*, c_2^*/m_1) \ (\text{mod } p) \text{ a DH tuple?}$$

That is, the IND-CPA game actually challenges Malice to answer the DDH Question in $G$ (see Definition 13.1 in §13.3.4.3).

If Malice can answer the DDH Question in $G$ correctly, then given the challenge ciphertext pair he can of course pinpoint the plaintext, i.e., the coin tossing of $\mathcal{O}$, correctly. Conversely, because $(g, y, c_1^*, c_2^*/m_0) \ (\text{mod } p)$ and $(g, y, c_1^*, c_2^*/m_1) \ (\text{mod } p)$ are random tuples generated by $g$, so if he can pinpoint the plaintext correctly then he can answer the DDH Question in $G = \langle g \rangle$ correctly. So IND-CPA security for the ElGamal cryptosystem using the public parameters in Alg 14.2 is precisely the difficulty for answering the DDH Question in $G$ (Theorem 14.2).

In the *general case* of abelian groups (which includes $G$ defined in Alg 14.2) we do not know any efficient algorithm to answer the DDH Question. The difficulty has rendered the DDH Question a standard and widely accepted intractability. The reader is referred to Boneh's survey article [48] for further study of this problem.

**Assumption 14.2: Decisional Diffie-Hellman Assumption in finite fields (DDH Assumption)**  *Let $\mathcal{IG}$ be a group instance generator that on input $1^k$, runs in time polynomial in $k$, and outputs (i) $\mathrm{desc}(G)$ (the description of an abelian group $G$ of a finite field) with $|\#G| = k$, (ii) a group generator $g \in G$.*

*We say that $\mathcal{IG}$ satisfies the decisional Diffie-Hellman (DDH) assumption if for all sufficiently large $k$ and for $(\mathrm{desc}(G), g) \leftarrow \mathcal{IG}(1^k)$, ensembles $(g, g^a, g^b, g^{ab})$ and $(g, g^a, g^b, g^c)$ are polynomially indistinguishable where the concept of polynomial indistinguishability is given in Definition 4.14 (in §4.7).*

We must notice that the DDH assumption is only considered on groups of finite fields, rather than in general abelian groups, since the DDH problem is easy in groups of points on supersingular elliptic curves (review §13.3.4.3).

We have established the following result for the fixed version of the ElGamal cryptosystem.

**Theorem 14.2:**  *The ElGamal cryptosystem using the public parameters in Alg 14.2 is IND-CPA secure if and only if the DDH assumption holds.*  □

## 14.3.6  Semantically Secure Cryptosystems Based on Rabin Bits

After the work of Goldwasser and Micali in cryptosystems with semantic security, several public-key encryption schemes with semantic security and form improvements to the GM cryptosystem have been proposed by several authors. These include, Blum and Micali [47], Yao [305] and an efficient scheme by Blum and Goldwasser [46].

The main idea in these improvements is the notion of a CSPRB generator (see the previous subsection). Such a generator is a program which takes as input a $k$-bit random seed and produces as output a $k^t$-bit number, where $t > 1$ is fixed. The output produced by a CSPRB generator is of high quality in the following sense: if the $k$-bit seed is totally unknown, then the output $k^t$-bit number cannot be distinguished from truly random number of the same length by any statistical test which runs in polynomial in $k$ time.

Now, to encrypt an $\ell$-bit message $m$, the sender sends the exclusive-or of $m$ with an $\ell$-bit output string $pr$ of a CSPRB generator on a $k$-bit input seed $s$ along with a public-key encryption of $s$, that is

$$(c_1, c_2) = (\mathcal{E}_{pk}(s), \ m \oplus ps). \tag{14.3.3}$$

The legitimate recipient (i.e., the owner of the public key $pk$) can decrypt $c_1$ and obtain the seed $s$. This will enable the recipient to regenerate the $\ell$-bit pseudo-random bit string $ps$ from the CSPRB generator, and thereby to retrieve $m$ from $c_2$ by the exclusive-or operation.

A CSPRB-generator-based encryption scheme has much improved efficiency over the "bit-by-bit" fashion of encryption. An $\ell$-bit plaintext message is now expanded to an $(\ell + k)$-bit ciphertext message instead of $\ell k$-bit as in the case of the "bit-by-bit" fashion of encryption. The improved time and space complexities are similar to those of the textbook encryption schemes such as RSA, Rabin and ElGamal.

### 14.3.6.1 Semantic Security of a CSPRB-based Encryption Scheme

If the seed $s$ is a uniformly random $k$-bit string and if the block-based deterministic encryption algorithm $\mathcal{E}_{pk}$ (with security parameter $k$) forms a permutation over its message space, then the first ciphertext block $c_1$ in (14.3.3) is permuted from a uniformly random number and hence itself is uniformly random. Thus, it can provide no *apriori* nor *aposteriori* information about the plaintext for an attacker to exploit.

The RSA encryption algorithm is a permutation over its message space. The Rabin encryption algorithm can be constructed into a permutation in $\mathrm{QR}_N$ if $N$ is a Blum integer; this has been shown in Theorem 6.18(iv) (in §6.7). So these encryption algorithms are good candidates for $\mathcal{E}_{pk}$.

Further because of the strength of the CSPRB generator, the pseudo-random string $ps$ generated from it using the seed $s$ plays the role of the internal random operation of the encryption scheme. Consequently, the exclusive-or between $m$ and $ps$ provides a semantically secure encryption of $m$.

In the case of the efficient CSPRB-generator-based encryption scheme by Blum and Goldwasser (the **BG cryptosystem**, [46]), $c_1$ in (14.3.3) is $s^{2^i} \pmod{N}$ where $i = \left\lfloor \frac{\log_2 m}{\log_2 \log_2 N} \right\rfloor + 1$; and the pseudo-random bit string $ps$ is generated from $s$ using the BBS pseudo-random generator (9.3.1) in a block-by-block fashion: each block is the $\log_2 \log_2 N$ least significant bits of an element which is the $2^j$-th power of $s$ modulo $N$ ($j = 1, 2, \ldots, i - 1$). Notice that the first element in the ciphertext pair is essentially a Rabin encryption of $s$.

Since the problem of extracting the simultaneous $\log_2 \log_2 N$ least significant bits of a plaintext from a Rabin ciphertext is equivalent to factoring $N$ (review Remark 9.1 in §9.3.1), the semantic security of the BG cryptosystem can be quantified to being equivalent to factoring the modulus $N$.

## 14.4    Inadequacy of Semantic Security

The notion of the IND-CPA security (semantic security) introduced in Definition 14.1 (and in Property 14.1) captures the intuition that any polynomially bounded attacker should not be able to obtain any *apriori* information about a plaintext message given its encryption. However, this guarantee of plaintext secrecy is only valid when the attacker is passive when facing a ciphertext, i.e., all the attacker does about a ciphertext is eavesdrop.

In §8.6 and §8.14 we have pointed out that many public-key cryptosystems are particularly vulnerable to a so-called **chosen-ciphertext attack** (CCA and CCA2, see Definition 8.3 in §8.6). In CCA and CCA2, an attacker (now he is Malice) may get decryption assistance, that is, he may be in a certain level of control of a "decryption box" and so may have some ciphertext of his choice to be decrypted for him even though he does not have possession of the decryption key. We have treated such an assistance as a "cryptanalysis training course" provided to Malice in order to ease his attack job. These modes of attacks, in particular CCA2, are realistic in many applications of public-key cryptography. For example, some protocols may require a principal to perform decryption operation on a random challenge to form a challenge-response mechanism. For another example, a receiver of an encrypted e-mail may reveal the plaintext message in subsequent public discussions.

The particular vulnerability to CCA or CCA2 shared by many public-key cryptosystems is due to the generally nice algebraic properties that underlie these cryptosystems. Malice may explore these nice properties and make up a ciphertext via some clever calculations. If Malice is given decryption assistance, his clever calculations on the chosen ciphertext based on the nice algebraic properties of the target public-key cryptosystem may allow him to obtain messages which should otherwise not be available to him.

In Example 8.8 we have seen a vulnerability of the ElGamal cryptosystem to CCA2. That attack is obviously applicable to the fixed version of the cryptosystem with IND-CPA security, too. The same-style CCA2 attacks are obviously applicable to any IND-CPA secure scheme based on a CSPRB generator (in §14.3.6); in such attacks, $c_2$ in (14.3.3) is replaced with $c_2' = r \oplus c_2$ where $r$ is an $\ell$-bit random string and plays the same (blinding) role of the random number $r$ in Example 8.8.

Example 14.2 shows the vulnerability of the GM cryptosystem to CCA2.

**Example 14.2:** Let Malice be in a conditional control of Alice's GM decryption box. The condition is quite "reasonable:" if the decryption result of a ciphertext submitted by Malice looks random, then Alice should return the plaintext to Malice.

Let ciphertext $C = (c_1, c_2, \ldots, c_\ell)$ encrypt plaintext $B = (b_1, b_2, \ldots, b_\ell)$ which is from a confidential communication between Alice and someone else (not with Malice!). However, Malice has eavesdropped $C$ and he wants to know $B$. He now sends to Alice the following "cleverly calculated ciphertext:"

$$C' = (yc_1, yc_2, \ldots, yc_\ell) \pmod{N}. \qquad (14.4.1)$$

In this attack, Malice is making use of the following nice algebraic property:

$$ab \pmod{N} \in \mathrm{QR}_N \text{ iff } \begin{cases} a \in \mathrm{QR}_N & \text{and} \quad b \in \mathrm{QR}_N \\ a \in \mathrm{J}_N(1) \setminus \mathrm{QR}_N & \text{and} \quad b \in \mathrm{J}_N(1) \setminus \mathrm{QR}_N. \end{cases}$$

This property is a direct result of Euler's criterion (see Theorem 6.13 in §6.5.1).

Thus, because $y \in \mathrm{J}_N(1) \setminus \mathrm{QR}_N$, we can view $y$ to encrypt the bit 1. Then the "multiplying-$y$" attack in (14.4.1) causes flipping of the bit $b_i$ for $i = 1, 2, \ldots, \ell$, that is, the decryption result by Alice will be

$$B' = (b_1', b_2', \ldots, b_\ell'),$$

where $b_i'$ denotes the complementary of the bit $b_i$ for $i = 1, 2, \ldots, \ell$.

This decryption result should look random for Alice. So Alice returns $B'$ back to Malice. Alas, Malice finds $B$!

Malice can also make $B'$ *uniformly* random (not just "look random") by using the "multiplier" $Y = (y_1, y_2, \ldots, y_\ell)$ instead of $(y, y, \ldots, y)$, where $Y$ is a GM encryption, under Alice's public key, of a uniformly random $\ell$-bit tuple $Z = (z_1, z_2, \ldots, z_\ell) \in_U \{0, 1\}^\ell$. It is easy to check

$$B = (b_1' \oplus z_1, b_2' \oplus z_2, \ldots, b_\ell' \oplus z_\ell). \qquad \square$$

In this attack, Alice has provided Malice with an "oracle service" for decryption assistance. Notice that the oracle service need not be an explicit one. Example 14.3 shows that without replying Malice's cipher query need not necessarily be a good strategy.

**Example 14.3:** Suppose that now Alice will no longer return random-looking decryption result back to Malice. For the encrypted message $(c_1, c_2, \ldots, c_\ell)$ (e.g., sent from Bob to Alice), Malice can still find the plaintext bit by bit.

For instance, in order to find whether $c_1$ encrypts 0 or 1, Malice can send to Alice an encrypted question for her to answer (e.g., a question for a YES/NO answer). Malice can encrypt the first half of the question in the usual way, but encrypts the second half of the question using $c_1$ in place of $y$ in Alg 14.1.

If $c_1 \in \mathrm{QR}_N$, then Alice will only decrypt the first half of the question correctly. The decryption of the rest of the question will be all zeros. So she will ask Malice why he only sends an uncompleted sentence. Then Malice knows $c_1$ encrypts 0. On the other hand, if Alice can answer the question correctly, then Malice knows that $c_1$ is a non-residue and hence encrypts 1.

Notice that in this way of attack, Malice can even digitally sign all of his messages to Alice to assure her the full and real authorship of these messages. Malice cannot be accused of any wrong doing!    □

From these two ways of active attacks we realize that the GM cryptosystem is hopelessly weak against an active attacker. In fact, the security notion in IND-CPA is hopelessly weak.

## 14.5  Beyond Semantic Security

Lifting security notion from the "all-or-nothing" secure (Property 8.2 in §8.2) to IND-CPA secure (Definition 14.1) forms a first step in our process of strengthening security notions.

In §14.4 we have seen that a security notion in the IND-CPA sense is not good enough for applications where a user may be tricked into providing an oracle serv in the decryption mode. Indeed, in applications of cryptographic systems, it will be impractical to require an innocent user to keep vigilant all the time and not to provide an oracle service in the decryption mode. Therefore, stronger security notions are needed.

The next step in our process of strengthening security notions is to consider an attack model called **indistinguishable chosen-ciphertext attack (IND-CCA)**. In this attack model, we will further ease the difficulty for Malice to break the target cryptosystems: in addition to the encryption assistance provided in the CPA game (in Prot 14.1), we will further allow Malice to obtain a conditional assistance in the decryption mode. A formal treatment of the IND-CCA model is based on a game due to Naor and Yung [212]. The game is named **"lunchtime attack"** or **"indifferent chosen-ciphertext attack."**

### 14.5.1  Security Against Chosen-ciphertext Attack

A lunchtime attack describes a real-life scenario of Malice who, in the absence of other employees of an organization (e.g., during lunchtime), queries the decryption mechanism of the organization, in hope that the interactions with the decryption box may provide him with a kind of "cryptanalysis training course" which may make him more experienced in a future cryptanalysis of the organization's cryptosystem. Due to the short duration of lunchtime, Malice does not have enough time to prepare his ciphertext queries so that they are related to the answers of the decryption box in some function. Therefore, all ciphers he queries during lunchtime are ones which he had prepared before lunchtime.

This real-life scenario can also be modeled by a game of attack. The game will be played by the same players in the IND-CPA attack game (Prot 14.1): Malice who may be a disgruntled employee of an organization, and an oracle $\mathcal{O}$ who is now

**Protocol 14.3:** "Lunchtime Attack" (Non-adaptive Indistinguishable Chosen-ciphertext Attack)

PREMISE

i) As in Prot 14.1, Malice and oracle $\mathcal{O}$ have agreed on a target cryptosystem $\mathcal{E}$ for which $\mathcal{O}$ has fixed an encryption key;

ii) Malice has prepared some ciphertext messages, before lunchtime.

1. Malice sends to $\mathcal{O}$ a prepared ciphertext message $c \in \mathcal{C}$;

2. $\mathcal{O}$ decrypts $c$ and returns the decryption result back to Malice;

   (∗ the ciphertext $c$ is called a **chosen ciphertext** or an **indifferent chosen-ciphertext**; it is considered that to return the decryption result back to Malice is to provide him with a "cryptanalysis training course;" Malice can ask for this "training course" to repeat as many times as he wishes; he may want to consider to use a program to speed up the "training sessions" since lunchtime is short ∗)

3. Upon satisfaction of the "decryption training course," Malice now asks $\mathcal{O}$ to play the CPA game in Prot 14.1;

   (∗ in this instantiation of the CPA game, the chosen plaintext messages $m_0$ and $m_1$ are called **adaptive chosen-plaintext** messages; that is, these two messages can be some functions of the entire history of the "decryption training course" provided in Steps 1 and 2; therefore, Malice's "find-stage" starts right at the beginning of this protocol and ends upon his receipt of the challenge ciphertext $c^* \in \mathcal{C}$, which encrypts, equally likely, one of his two chosen plaintext messages $m_0, m_1 \in \mathcal{M}$ ∗)

   (∗ we reasonably assume that Malice can compute adaptive chosen-plaintext messages even in the short lunchtime since working on plaintext should be relatively easier than working on ciphertext ∗)

   (∗ by now, "lunchtime" is over; so Malice should answer either 0 or 1 as his educated guess on $\mathcal{O}$'s coin tossing in the CPA game; however, even the game is over, Malice remains in "guess-stage" until he answers ∗)

the decryption (and encryption) mechanism of the organization. We shall name the game a **indistinguishable chosen-ciphertext attack (IND-CCA)**. The new game is specified in Prot 14.3.

At first glance, one may argue that the lunchtime attack game does not model a realistic attack scenario. Who will be so nice and so naive to play the role of a decryption box and answer Malice's decryption queries? We should answer this question in three different considerations.

- In many applications of cryptosystems (in particular, in cryptographic protocols), it is often the case that a user (a participant of a protocol) is required, upon receipt of a challenge message, to perform a decryption operation using her private key and then send the decryption result back. This is the so-called challenge-response mechanism (see Chapter 2 and Chapter 11).

- We may have to accept a fact of life: many users are just hopelessly naive and cannot be required or educated to maintain a high degree of vigilance in anticipation of any trick launched by bad guys. In fact, it will not be wrong for us to say that stronger cryptosystems and security notions are developed exactly for naive users.

- Malice can embed decryption queries inside normal and innocent looking communications, and in so doing he may get implicit answers to his queries. Examples 9.2 and 14.3 provide vivid active attacks which are very innocent looking. It can be very difficult to differentiate such attacks and legitimate secure communications. Not to answer any questions (encrypted questions or answers) does not constitute a good solution to active attacks but a self-denial from the benefit of the secure communication technology.

- Malice can even exploit a subliminal channel such as that in the timing attack we have seen in §12.5.4 which answers Malice's questions in terms of difference in time delays.

The correct attitude toward Malice is to face him straight on and provide him the "cryptanalysis training course" on his demand. The training course can be in encryption or in decryption, at a whole data-block level or at a single bit level. Our strategy is to design strong cryptosystems such that the "cryptanalysis training course" even supplied on demand won't help Malice to break a target cryptosystem!

Following the same reasoning in §14.2 for deriving Malice's advantage for breaking the target cryptosystem in the CPA game (Prot 14.1), we can analogously derive Malice's advantage in the lunchtime attack game. The formulation of the advantage is very similar to (14.2.3), except that we should now add the entire history of the chosen ciphertext cryptanalysis training course to the input of Malice. Let Hist-CCA denote this history. Malice's advantage is:

$$\text{Prob}[\, 1 \leftarrow \text{Malice}(c^*, m_0, m_1, \text{Hist-CCA}) \mid c^* = \mathcal{E}_{ke}(m_1) \,] = \frac{1}{2} + \text{Adv}. \qquad (14.5.1)$$

To this end we reach a new security notion which is strengthened from the IND-CPA security notion.

**Definition 14.2: Security for Indistinguishable Chosen-ciphertext Attack (IND-CCA Security)** *A cryptosystem with a security parameter $k$ is said to be secure against an indistinguishable chosen-ciphertext attack (IND-CCA secure) if after the attack game in Prot 14.3 being played with any polynomially bounded attacker, the advantage* Adv *formulated in (14.5.1) is a negligible quantity in $k$.*

Since in a lunchtime attack, the decryption assistance (or "cryptanalysis training course") for Malice is provided on top of the IND-CPA game in Prot 14.1, the new attack game must have reduced the difficulty of Malice's cryptanalysis task from that of the IND-CPA game. We should therefore expect that some cryptosystems which are IND-CPA secure will no longer be IND-CCA secure.

None of the IND-CPA secure cryptosystems which we have introduced in this chapter has been proven IND-CCA secure. Alas, among them, there is a demonstrably *insecure* one! This is the efficient CSPRB-generator-based cryptosystem of Blum and Goldwasser, which we have introduced in §14.3.6.

**Example 14.4:** To attack the BG cryptosystem in lunchtime attack, Malice should make a chosen-ciphertext query $(c, m)$ where $c$ is a chosen quadratic residue modulo $N$, and $|m| = \lfloor \log_2 \log_2 N \rfloor$. Observing the BG cryptosystem described in §14.3.6, we know that the response to Malice will be the following decryption result

$$m \oplus \text{ "} \lfloor \log_2 \log_2 N \rfloor \text{ least significant bits of a square root of } c \text{ modulo } N\text{".}$$

Bit-wise XOR-ing $m$ to the reply, Malice obtains $\lfloor \log_2 \log_2 N \rfloor$ least significant bits of a square root modulo $N$ of $c$. Remember that $c$ is a chosen quadratic residue modulo $N$. Review Remark 9.1 (in §9.3.1), providing Malice with $\lfloor \log_2 \log_2 N \rfloor$ least significant bits of a square root of $c$ will entitle him to factor $N$ in probabilistic polynomial-time!  $\square$

Example 14.4 shows that it is indeed the very cryptanalysis training course provided to Malice that empowers him to break the cryptosystem. The consequence is so severe and thorough that it is not a mere disclosure of one ciphertext, but the total destruction of the cryptosystem.

We also realize that the precise basis for the BG cryptosystem to be IND-CPA secure is also the very exact cause for the cryptosystem to be insecure against IND-CCA. This is analogous to the case for the Rabin cryptosystem under the "all-or-nothing" sense of security (see Theorem 8.2 in §8.11).

Naor and Yung propose a cryptosystem which is provably secure against IND-CCA [212]. In that cryptosystem, a plaintext message is encrypted in a bit-by-bit fashion into two ciphertext messages under two different public keys. The encryption algorithm includes a **non-interactive zero-knowledge** (NIZK) proof procedure which enables the sender of a plaintext message to prove that the two ciphertext messages do encrypt the same plaintext bit under the respective public keys (consider the encryption algorithm forms an NP problem with the plaintext and random input to the algorithm as the witness to the NP problem, see discussion in §4.8.1). This proof will be verified in the decryption time (e.g., by $\mathcal{O}$ in the lunchtime attack game). Passing of the verification procedure in the decryption time implies that the plaintext encrypted under the pair of ciphertext messages is already known to the sender (e.g., known to Malice in the lunchtime attack game). So serving Malice in "lunchtime" will not provide him with any new knowledge for easing his cryptanalysis job. Due to a rather high cost of realizing a NIZK proof (verification) for an encryption (decryption) algorithm and the bit-by-bit fashion of encryption and decryption, the cryptosystem of Naor and Yung [212] is not intended for practical use.

Lunchtime attack is a quite restrictive attack model in that, the decryption assistance provided to Malice is only available in a short period of time. It is as if the decryption box would be switched off permanently after "lunchtime," or Malice would not strike back anymore, not even at "lunchtime" tomorrow. This is not a reasonable or realistic scenario. In reality, naive users will remain permanently naive, and Malice will definitely strike back, probably even as soon as the afternoon tea-break time! Therefore the security notion in IND-CCA is, again, not strong enough. We need a still stronger security notion.

## 14.5.2  Security Against Adaptive Chosen-ciphertext Attack

A further step in our process of strengthening security notions is to consider an attack model called **indistinguishable adaptive chosen-ciphertext attack (IND-CCA2)**. Rackoff and Simon originally propose this stronger attack model [243].

In this attack model, we will further ease the difficulty for Malice to attack cryptosystems from that in lunchtime attack. In the lunchtime attack game (see Prot 14.3), the decryption assistance (or "cryptanalysis training course") is conditional in that the assistance will be stopped upon Malice's submission of the pair of the adaptive chosen-plaintext messages; that is, a lunchtime attack stops upon termination of the IND-CPA game (i.e., Prot 14.1), and from then on the decryption assistance will become permanently unavailable.

In the new attack model we remove this unrealistic condition of a short-period availability of decryption assistance which is somewhat artificially placed in lunchtime attack. Now the decryption assistance for Malice will be permanently available before and after a lunchtime attack. We can imagine this attack scenario as a prolonged lunchtime attack. For this reason, we shall name this new attack model **small-hours attack**. This name describes a real-life scenario that Malice, again as a disgruntled employee of an organization, stays up all night to play with the decryption mechanism of the organization. Notice that the small-hours attack is different from a so-called **midnight attack** which often appears in the literature as another name for lunchtime attack; perhaps as in lunchtime attack, it is considered that the security guards of an organization should have meals rather punctually around midnight.

Since now Malice has plenty of time to go unnoticed, he will of course play the decryption box in a more sophisticated and more interesting way. In addition to what he can do in lunchtime (in fact at midnight), i.e., adaptively choose plaintext queries using information gathered from the "decryption training course" and subsequently obtain a corresponding challenge ciphertext, now Malice can also submit *adaptive chosen-ciphertext messages after* he receives the challenge ciphertext. Therefore, the adaptive chosen-ciphertext messages can somehow be related to the challenge ciphertext of which the corresponding plaintext is chosen by him. Of course, the decryption box is intelligent enough not to decrypt the exact challenge ciphertext for Malice! This is the only restriction, and is of course a reasonable one. Without this restriction, Malice can simply ask the decryption box to decrypt the challenge ciphertext for him, and we will not have an interesting game to play! The decryption box is also dummy enough so that it will decrypt a ciphertext which can be related to the the challenge ciphertext in any straightforward way! Any minute change of the challenge ciphertext, such as multiplying 2, or adding 1, will guarantee a decryption service!

Our description on the new attack model is specified in Prot 14.4.

Again, following the same reasoning in §14.2 for deriving Malice's advantage for breaking the target cryptosystem in the IND-CPA game (Prot 14.1), we can analogously derive Malice's advantage to break the target cryptosystem in the small-hours attack game. The formulation of the advantage is again very similar to (14.2.3), except that we should now add to Malice's input the entire history of the two cryptanalysis training courses, one for the pre-challenge CCA, and one for the post-challenge CCA or "extended CCA." Let Hist-CCA2 denote this whole history. Malice's advantage is:

$$\text{Prob}[\,1 \leftarrow \text{Malice}(c^*, m_0, m_1, \text{Hist-CCA2}) \mid c^* = \mathcal{E}_{ke}(m_1)\,] = \frac{1}{2} + \text{Adv}. \quad (14.5.2)$$

To this end we reach a new security notion which is further strengthened from the IND-CCA security notion.

**Definition 14.3: Security for Indistinguishable Adaptive Chosen-ciphertext Attack (IND-CCA2 Security)** *A cryptosystem with a security parameter k is said to be secure against an indistinguishable adaptive chosen-ciphertext attack (IND-CCA2 secure) if after the attack game in Prot 14.4 being played with any polynomially bounded attacker, the advantage Adv formulated in (14.5.2) is a negligible quantity in k.*

---

**Protocol 14.4:** "Small-hours    Attack"    (Indistinguishable    Adaptive
Chosen-ciphertext Attack)

PREMISE

　　As in Prot 14.1, Malice and oracle $\mathcal{O}$ have agreed on a target cryptosystem $\mathcal{E}$ for which $\mathcal{O}$ has fixed an encryption key.

1. Malice and $\mathcal{O}$ play the lunchtime attack game in Prot 14.3;

   (∗ in this instantiation of the lunchtime attack game Malice's "find-stage" is the same as that in Prot 14.3, which ends upon his receipt of the challenge ciphertext $c^* \in \mathcal{C}$, which encrypts, equally likely, one of his two chosen plaintext messages $m_0, m_1 \in \mathcal{M}$; however, in this instantiation, Malice is allowed to extend his "guess-stage;" the extended "guess-stage" is as follows ∗)

2. Malice further computes ciphertext $c' \in \mathcal{C}$ and submits it to $\mathcal{O}$ for decryption;

   (∗ the ciphertext $c'$ is called an **adaptive chosen-ciphertext** or **post-challenge chosen ciphertext**; in contrast, the chosen ciphertext in the lunchtime attack game (Prot 14.3) is also called **pre-challenge chosen ciphertext**; step 2 is considered to serve Malice a "decryption training course" *extended* from that of the lunchtime attack game; Malice can ask for the "extended training course" to repeat as many times as he wishes ∗)

   (∗ it is stipulated that $c' \neq c^*$, namely, Malice is not allowed to send the challenge ciphertext back for decryption ∗)

3. Upon satisfaction of the "extended decryption training course," Malice must now answer either 0 or 1 as his educated guess on $\mathcal{O}$'s coin tossing.

---

We summarize the various IND attack games introduced so far in Fig 14.1.

Since in the small-hours attack game, the "extended" decryption assistance (or, the "extended cryptanalysis training course") is provided after the lunchtime attack game in Prot 14.1, the new attack game must have further reduced the difficulty for Malice to break the target cryptosystem from that in a lunchtime attack. We should therefore expect that some cryptosystems which are IND-CCA secure will no longer be IND-CCA2 secure. In fact, except for the RSA-OAEP which we have specified in Alg 10.6, none of the other cryptosystems introduced so far in this

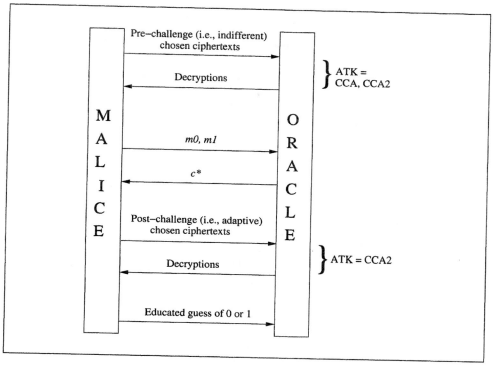

**Figure 14.1.** Summary of the Indistinguishable Active Attack Games

book is provably IND-CCA2 secure. We have demonstrated plenty of examples of cryptosystems which are CCA2 insecure, i.e., in "all-or-nothing" sense, and hence they are also IND-CCA2 insecure (see Examples 8.4, 8.6, 8.8, 9.2, 14.2, 14.3).

After having introduced the notion of IND-CCA2 security, Rackoff and Simon proposed IND-CCA2 secure cryptosystems which are also based on NIZK proof. However, they considered the case of an NIZK proof with a *specific prover*. In their IND-CCA2 secure cryptosystems, not only the receiver has public-private key pair, the sender has such a key pair too. Moreover, the sender's public key is certified by a public-key certification infrastructure (see the techniques in §13.2). The sender will use not only the receiver's public key to encrypt a message as usual, but also his own private key in the construction of a NIZK proof so that the receiver of the ciphertext can verify the proof using the sender's public key. Passing of the NIZK verification implies that it is the specific sender (prover) who has created the plaintext, and hence, returning the plaintext back to the sender will not provide him any information useful for breaking the target cryptosystem. The IND-CCA2 secure cryptosystems of Rackoff and Simon also operate in the bit-by-bit fashion.

## 14.5.3   Non-Malleable Cryptography

**Non-malleable (NM) cryptography** [101] strengthens security notions for public-key cryptography in the computational direction. NM is an important requirement that it should not be easy for Malice to modify a plaintext message in a meaningfully controllable manner via modifying the corresponding ciphertext. Dolev et al. describe the importance of this requirement very well using a contract bidding example.

Suppose that construction companies are invited by a municipal government to a bid for constructing a new elementary school. The government, which actively progresses its electronic operations, advertises its public key $E$ to be used for encrypting bids, and opens an e-mail address `e-gov@bid.for.it.gov` for receiving the encrypted bits. Company A places its bid of \$1,500,000 by sending $\mathcal{E}(1,500,000)$ to the `e-gov@bid.for.it.gov`. However, the e-mail is intercepted by Malice, the head of CheapSub, a one-man company specializing selling sub-contracts to some cheap builders. If the encryption algorithm used by the e-government is malleable, then Malice may somehow transform $\mathcal{E}(1,500,000)$ into $\mathcal{E}(15,000,000)$. In so doing, Malice's own bid would have a much better chance of winning.

The simplest example of a malleable encryption algorithm is the one-time pad. In Part III we have also seen that all the basic and popular public-key encryption functions are easily malleable.

Unlike in the various cases of attacks on indistinguishability (IND) security where attack problems are decisional ones, a malleability attack is a computational problem. The problem is described in Prot 14.5.

In this malleability attack, because the goal of Malice, given a challenge ciphertext $c^*$, is not to learn something about the target plaintext $\alpha$, he need not know $\alpha$ at all. However, for his attack to be successful, Malice must output a "meaningful" relation $R$ to relate the decryptions of $c^*$ and $c'$.

Malice's success is also expressed in terms of an advantage. In [101], the authors use the idea of zero-knowledge simulation[a] to express this advantage. First, Malice, who is again a PPT algorithm, is given $c^* = \mathcal{E}_{pk}(\alpha)$ and outputs $(\mathcal{E}_{pk}(\beta), R)$ with certain probability. Secondly, a *simulator*, who we denote by ZK-Sim and is a PPT algorithm, is *not* given $c^*$ but will also output a ciphertext $\bar{c}$ with certain probability. (ZK-Sim even ignores the encryption algorithm and the public key!) Malice's advantage in mounting a malleability attack is the following probability difference:

$$\text{NM-Adv} \;=\; \begin{aligned} &\text{Prob}\left[(\mathrm{E}_{pk}(\beta), R) \leftarrow \text{Malice}(\mathrm{E}_{pk}(\alpha), pk, \text{desc}(\mathbf{v}))\right] - \\ &\text{Prob}\left[(\bar{c}, R) \leftarrow \text{ZK-Sim}\right]. \end{aligned} \qquad (14.5.3)$$

The cryptosystem $\mathcal{E}_{pk}()$ with a security parameter $k$ is said to be non-malleable

---

[a]In a later chapter we shall study topics of zero-knowledge proof and polynomial-time simulation of such proofs.

---

**Protocol 14.5:** Malleability Attack in Chosen-plaintext Mode

PREMISE

> As in Prot 14.1, Malice and oracle $\mathcal{O}$ have agreed on a target cryptosystem $\mathcal{E}$ for which $\mathcal{O}$ has fixed an encryption key $pk$.

Malice and $\mathcal{O}$ play the following game:

1. Malice sends to $\mathcal{O}$: $\mathbf{v}, \mathrm{desc}(\mathbf{v})$, where $\mathbf{v}$ is a vector containing a plural number of plaintexts, $\mathrm{desc}(\mathbf{v})$ is a description on the distribution of the plaintexts in $\mathbf{v}$;

2. $\mathcal{O}$ creates a valid challenge ciphertext $c^* = \mathcal{E}_{pk}(\alpha)$ where $\alpha$ is created following the distribution of the plaintexts in $\mathbf{v}$; $\mathcal{O}$ sends $c^*$ to Malice;

3. Upon receipt of $c^*$, Malice must output a "meaningful" PPT-computable relation $R$ and another valid ciphertext $c' = \mathcal{E}_{pk}(\beta)$ such that $R(\alpha, \beta) = 1$ holds.

---

if, for all PPT computable relation $R$ and for all PPT attackers (i.e., Malice and the like), NM-Adv is a negligible function in $k$. In [101], this security notion is called **"semantic security with respect to relations under chosen-plaintext attack."** We therefore name it **NM-CPA**. NM-CPA intuitively captures the following desirable security quality.

**Property 14.2: NM-CPA Security**  *Given a ciphertext from an NM-CPA secure cryptosystem, Malice's advantage to mount a malleability attack on the cryptosystem does not increase in any PPT discernible way from that to "mount the attack" (i.e., to simulate an attack) without the ciphertext.*

While providing a ciphertext should not ease an attack problem, providing "cryptanalysis training courses" should! Analogous to the cases of IND-CCA and IND-CCA2, a malleability attack can also be eased in the lunchtime attack mode and in the small-hours attack mode. In a malleability attack eased in the lunchtime attack mode, Malice can send plural number of chosen ciphertexts to $\mathcal{O}$ for decryption, but this service will terminate upon Malice requests to receive the challenge ciphertext $c^*$. In a malleability attack eased in the small-hours attack mode, the decryption service does not terminate after the challenge ciphertext $c^*$ has been sent to Malice. Of course, as we have stipulated in the small-hours attack game, Malice is not allowed to send $c^*$ back to $\mathcal{O}$ for decryption service.

Consequently, we have **NM-CCA** and **NM-CCA2** security notions.

Due to these problems' computational nature, we shall not include here a rigorously formal treatment for NM-security notions. The inquisitive reader is referred to [101] for details. It is quite reasonable to anticipate that a formalization of NM notions will involve some complexities which need not be involved in the IND-security notions. For example, unlike in the case of a decisional-problem where we do not need to take care of the size of a plaintext message space (there it can even be as small as 2, e.g., as in the GM cryptosystem), a formalization of NM notion must stipulate that the plaintext message space be sufficiently large so that the computation of the relation $R$ will not degenerate into a trivial problem.

In [20], the authors provide slightly different formalizations for NM security notions which are based on attack games similar to those we have introduced for various IND attacks. The reader may find that the treatment in [20] is easier to access as a result of their similarity to the games we have introduced for IND security notions.

Nevertheless, our description on NM security notions does suffice us to capture the idea of NM-security notions with adequate precision. Immediately we can see that most textbook encryption algorithms which are results of direct applications of one-way trapdoor functions are easily malleable. As we have seen in Chapter 9, all common one-way (trapdoor) functions underlying popular public-key cryptography can be inverted by making use of some partial information oracles (e.g., "parity oracle" or "half-order oracle"); the principle of these inverting methods is exactly malleability attacks mounted on the unknown plaintext messages. For example, for the RSA case of $c = m^e \pmod{N}$, Malice knows that the unknown plaintext $m$ can be doubled if he multiplies $c$ with $2^e \pmod{N}$.

Dolev et al. proposed a public-key encryption scheme which is provable NM-CCA2 secure [101]. The scheme uses a plural number of public/private key pairs, and encrypts a plaintext message in bit-by-bit manner. The encryption of each plaintext bit also contains an NIZK proof.

## 14.5.4   Relations between Non-Malleability and Indistinguishability

The non-malleable security notions are undoubtedly very important. However, due to these problems' computational nature, formal treatment for non-malleable security notions turns out being rather complex. Consequently, designing a cryptosystem and establishing that it has non-malleable security is rather a difficult job.

Fortunately, researchers have established a number of important relations between non-malleable security notions and indistinguishable security notions. Moreover, under CCA2, the most useful security notion, non-malleability is found equivalent to indistinguishability. Since formal treatment for IND-CCA2 has been well established, we can achieve provable security in the NM-CCA2 mode by proving security under the IND-CCA2 notion.

Formal proof for relations between security notions can be achieved by constructing a **polynomial-time reduction algorithm**. In the context of relating attacks on cryptosystems, such a reduction (algorithm) "reduces" a target attacking problem (call it "Target Attack") to another attack (call it "Source Attack"). If a successfully constructed reduction is a PPT algorithm, then "Target Attack" can be successfully mounted based on the successful mounting of "Source Attack," and the cost for mounting "Target Attack" is bounded by a polynomial in that for mounting "Source Attack."

Since an attack on a cryptosystem is always based on some appropriate assumptions and requirements (e.g., for an CCA2 attacker to work properly, the attacker should be entitled to pre-challenge and post-challenge cryptanalysis training courses), a reduction algorithm must satisfy an attacker about these necessary assumptions and environmental requirements. Often we will use a special agent, who we name **Simon Simulator**, to conduct a reduction. Simon will satisfy an attacker of all the assumptions and the entitled requirements by simulating the attacker's working environment.

Sometimes, Simon himself will become a successful attacker for "Target Attack" as a result of the fact that he has been taught by the attacker for "Source Attack" after having interacted with the attacker. In such a reduction, Simon will be "orchestrating" two attack games in between an attacker and an encryption/decryption oracle. One the one hand, Simon plays the "Source Attack" game with an attacker by simulating the environment for "Source Attack" (i.e., by masquerading as an encryption/decryption oracle to face the attacker). On the other hand, Simon plays the "Target Attack" game with an encryption/decryption oracle, and now he is an attacker. In such a situation, we can consider that the attacker for "Source Attack" is teaching Simon to mount "Target Attack." Figures 14.2 and 14.3 illustrate such a orchestration conducted by Simon.

Now we are ready to state and prove some useful relations.

### 14.5.4.1 Non-malleability Implying Indistinguishability

Let ATK denotes CPA, CCA or CCA2. we can show that if a public-key cryptosystem is NM-ATK secure then it must be IND-ATK secure.

**Theorem 14.3:** *If a public-key cryptosystem is NM-ATK secure then it is also IND-ATK secure,*

**Proof** We can prove the theorem by showing that if a public-key cryptosystem $\mathcal{E}_{pk}$ is IND-ATK insecure then it must be NM-ATK insecure.

Suppose $\mathcal{E}_{pk}$ is IND-ATK insecure. Then we have a PPT attacker $\mathcal{A}$ who can break $\mathcal{E}_{pk}$ in the IND-ATK mode with a non-negligible advantage $\mathrm{Adv}(\mathcal{A})$. We let Simon Simulator conduct a reduction by using $\mathcal{A}$ to break $\mathcal{E}_{pk}$ in the NM-ATK mode.

Simon is in orchestration between two attack games. One game is in the IND-ATK mode (i.e., any of the Protocols 14.1, 14.3, or 14.4) in which Simon plays the role of $\mathcal{O}$ in interaction with $\mathcal{A}$ who is in the position of Malice. The other game is the NM-ATK mode (i.e., the ATK version of Prot 14.5) in which Simon plays the role of Malice in interaction with an encryption oracle (and decryption oracle if ATK $\in$ {CCA, CCA2}) $\mathcal{O}$. Fig 14.2 illustrates the reduction for the most general case of ATK = CCA2. Some of the interactions can be omitted in the other two cases of ATK.

Notice that in the malleability-ATK game (i.e., the right-hand side interactions in Fig 14.2), the description on the distribution of the chosen plaintexts is uniform; therefore $\mathcal{O}$ will have to encrypt a random choice of the chosen plaintexts.

The "educated guess" from $\mathcal{A}$ is $b \in \{0, 1\}$. Simon then has freedom to output $c' = \mathcal{E}_{pk}(m_b + 1)$ and the relation $R(x, y) = 1$ if and only if $y = x + 1$ for all $x$ in the plaintext space. Clearly, with $\mathcal{A}$ being PPT, Simon can output this correct malleability result also in polynomial time.

Since $\mathcal{A}$ answers $b$ with advantage $\mathrm{Adv}(\mathcal{A})$, we have

$$\text{NM-Adv(Simon)} = \mathrm{Adv}(\mathcal{A}) - \mathrm{Prob}\left[(\bar{c}, R) \leftarrow \text{ZK-Sim}\right].$$

Notice that ZK-Sim does not have access to the challenge ciphertext $c^*$ and hence does not have the use of $\mathcal{A}$; so for the simulated output ciphertext $\bar{c}$ to correspond a plaintext satisfying $R$, $\mathrm{Prob}\left[(\bar{c}, R) \leftarrow \text{ZK-Sim}\right]$ must be negligible. Hence, NM-Adv(Simon) is non-negligible as desired.                                    $\square$

Recall that we have demonstrated numerous attacks in various IND-ATK modes on various cryptosystems. By Theorem 14.3, these cryptosystems are also insecure in the respective NM-ATK modes.

It is known that there exist cryptosystems which are IND-CPA (respectively, IND-CCA) secure, but are not NM-CPA (respectively, NM-CCA) secure. These cases can be found in [20].

Among the relations among NM and IND security notions which have been investigated in [20], the following relation is the most important one.

### 14.5.4.2  Indistinguishability Implying Non-malleability Under Adaptive Chosen-ciphertext Attack

For the case of ATK = CCA2, the converse of the statement in Theorem 14.3 is also true.

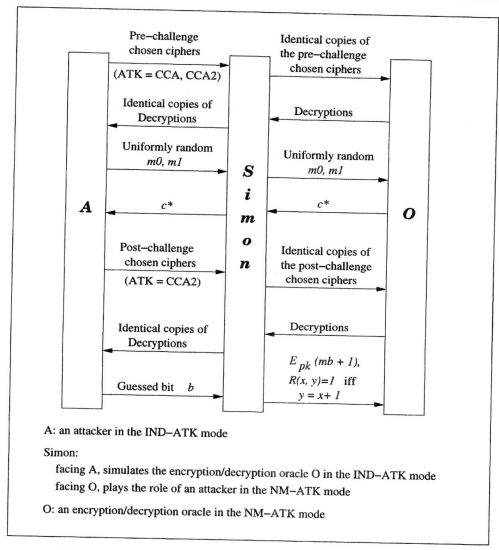

**Figure 14.2.** Reduction from an NM-attack to an IND-attack

**Theorem 14.4:** *A public-key cryptosystem is NM-CCA2 secure if and only if it is IND-CCA2 secure.*

**Proof** Since in Theorem 14.3 we have established NM-CCA2 $\Longrightarrow$ IND-CCA2, we only need to establish the opposite case: IND-CCA2 $\Longrightarrow$ NM-CCA2. We can show that if a public-key cryptosystem $\mathcal{E}_{pk}$ is NM-CCA2 insecure then it must be

IND-CCA2 insecure.

Suppose $\mathcal{E}_{pk}$ is NM-CCA2 insecure. Then we have a PPT attacker $\mathcal{A}$ who can break $\mathcal{E}_{pk}$ in NM-CCA2 with a non-negligible advantage $\mathrm{Adv}(\mathcal{A})$. We let Simon Simulator conduct a reduction by using $\mathcal{A}$ to break $\mathcal{E}_{pk}$ in the IND-CCA2 mode.

Fig 14.3 illustrates the reduction orchestrated by Simon. Notice that the reduction is possible exactly because the ciphertext $c'$ output by the malleability attacker $\mathcal{A}$ is different from the challenge ciphertext $c^*$, and therefore the orchestrater of the two games, Simon who plays the role of Malice in the IND-CCA2 game, can send $c'$ to $\mathcal{O}$ for decryption a post-challenge chosen ciphertext. With the decryption result, Simon can verify the relation between the plaintexts (the relation has been given by $\mathcal{A}$) and thereby determines the challenge bit $b$.

Clearly, since $\mathcal{A}$ is PPT, the two games orchestrated by Simon will terminate in polynomial time, and the advantage of Simon is non-negligible since the advantage of $\mathcal{A}$ is non-negligible. $\qquad\square$

Fig 14.4 summarize the known relations among the security notions we have introduced so far. We have not demonstrated the non-implication cases (those separated by $\nrightarrow$). The interested reader may study [20] for details.

Theorem 14.4 tells us that in the context of public-key encryption schemes, we only need to consider IND-CCA2 notion which is easier to handle than NM-CCA2 notion is. Also, due to the equivalence relation between IND-CCA2 and NM-CCA2, it is now generally agreed that IND-CCA2 is *the* right definition of security for public key encryption algorithms for general use.

In the next chapter we shall introduce two practically efficient public-key cryptosystems which are provable IND-CCA2 secure.

# 14.6   Chapter Summary

In this chapter we have taken a step-wise approach to introducing progressively stronger security notions for public-key cryptosystems.

We started with a protocol which uses a typical textbook encryption algorithm and seeing its weakness and unsuitability for applications. We then introduced a first-step strengthened security notion: semantic security or indistinguishable encryption under passive attack. Weaknesses of semantic security were exposed, followed by further steps of strengthening steps. We finally reached the strongest security notion for public-key cryptosystems: indistinguishable encryption under adaptive chosen-ciphertext attack (IND-CCA2) which we consider as a fit-for-application security notion. Finally, we considered the security notion for public-key encryption against a different attacking scenario: non-malleability, and relate the notions of IND-CCA2 and non-malleability.

Nowadays, IND-CCA2 is the standard and fit-for-application security notion

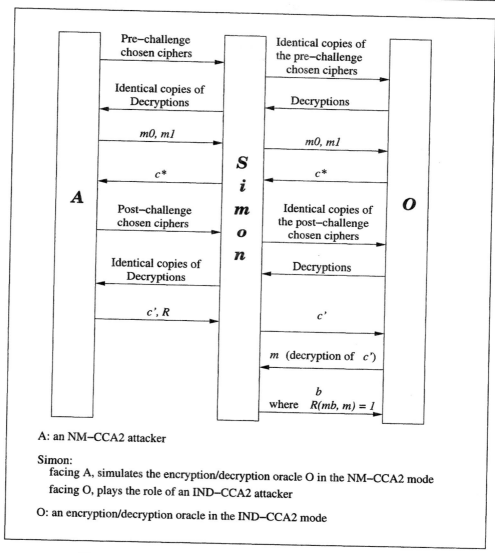

Figure 14.3. Reduction from IND-CCA2 to NM-CCA2

for public-key cryptosystems. All new public-key encryption schemes for general purpose applications ought to have this security quality. In the next chapter we shall introduce practical public-key cryptosystems which are formally provably secure under the IND-CCA2 attacking mode.

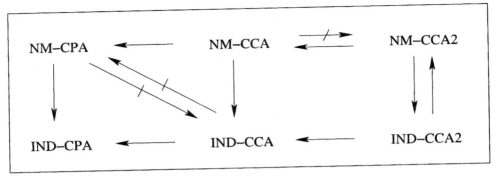

**Figure 14.4.** Relations Among Security Notions for Public-key Cryptosystems

## Exercises

14.1 Can the textbook RSA encryption hide the sign of Jacobi symbol of the plaintext message?

14.2 Can the textbook RSA (Rabin) encryption be secure to encrypt, e.g., a salary figure? How about the textbook ElGamal if, e.g., the salary figure is not in $\langle g \rangle$?

14.3 If, in a chosen-plaintext attack game (Prot 14.1), $\mathcal{O}$ flips a biased coin with $2/3$ probability for HEADS appearance, derive Malice's advantage formula which corresponds to (14.2.3).

14.4 For a public-key encryption algorithm, does Malice need to play the chosen-plaintext attack game?

14.5 What is semantic security? Is it a security notion against (i) a passive and polynomially bounded attacker, (ii) a passive and polynomially unbounded attacker, and (iii) an active (and polynomially bounded) attacker?

14.6 Semantic security means to hide all partial information about plaintext messages. Why is it still not strong enough for real-world applications?

14.7 If the Rabin encryption scheme (Alg 8.2) is attacked under a lunchtime attack (Prot 14.3), what can an attacker achieve?

Hint: in a lunchtime attack an attacker can *adaptively* choose plaintext messages and get decryption assistance.

14.8 Cryptanalysis training courses (encryption, decryption assistances) are very effective for providing Malice with measures to break all textbook cryptographic algorithms. Why should we generally (and generously) grant Malice such assistances?

14.9 What is the IND-CCA2 security notion? What kind of attacks does it counter?

14.10 Discuss the importance of the equivalence relation between the security notions IND-CCA2 and NM-CCA2.

Hint: consider the difficulty of using the NM security formulations.

14.11 If, in a small-hours attack game (Prot 14.4), Malice only submits ciphertexts which he constructs using the prescribed encryption scheme, show that the game degenerates to a lunchtime one. Why can't the game further degenerate to an IND-CPA one?

# Chapter 15

# PROVABLY SECURE AND EFFICIENT PUBLIC-KEY CRYPTOSYSTEMS

## 15.1 Introduction

In the preceding chapter we have seen that early solutions to IND-CCA2 (equivalently, NM-CCA2) secure public-key cryptosystems have generally rested on applications of non-interactive zero-knowledge (NIZK) proof techniques. Such a proof shows a receiver of a ciphertext that the creator of the ciphertext already knows the corresponding plaintext because what is proved is the following NP membership[a] statement:

> "The ciphertext $c$ is in language $L$ defined by encryption algorithm $\mathcal{E}$ under public key $pk$, and the creator of $c$ has in its possession an auxiliary input (i.e., a witness of an NP problem) for the membership proof."

Here "auxiliary input" for the membership proof consists of the corresponding plaintext and perhaps plus a random input to the encryption algorithm $\mathcal{E}$ (the random input is necessary if the encryption scheme needs to be semantically secure). If the verification of such a proof outputs "Accept." the receiver, who may be required or tricked to provide a decryption service, can then be sure that even if the creator of the ciphertext $c$ is Malice (the bad guy), to return the corresponding plaintext to him is only to return to him something he already knows, and hence to do so will not help him in any way should he try to attack the target cryptosystem.

---

[a]We shall study the relation between NP membership statement and zero-knowledge proof in Chapter 18.

While this is a sound idea, it is quite an expensive one. The general method for realizing NIZK proof is for the prover (here, the creator of a ciphertext) and the verifier (here, a receiver of that message) to share a *mutually trusted* random string. This demand is way beyond what an encryption scheme should ask for. If we consider that eliminating the need for two parties to share secret information before secure communication constitutes the most important advantage of public-key cryptography[b], then provable security for public-key encryption schemes should not be built at the expense of regressing back to sharing mutually trusted information between communication parties!

In fact, what provable security should achieve is an affirmative measure to ensure that Malice should not be able to do something bad *too often* or *fast enough*. So provable security can be established as long as we can establish the success probabilities and computational cost for Malice to succeed in an attack. In the context of achieving a provably secure encryption, to ask for a guarantee that Malice must know the corresponding plaintext of a ciphertext is to ask for too mu  and NIZK proof is unnecessary and overkill. In fact, none of the previous public-key encryption schemes which are provably IND-CCA2 secure based on applying NIZK proof techniques is sufficiently efficient for practical use.

Many practically efficient and provably secure public-key encryption and digital signature schemes have been proposed. These schemes are mainly results of enhancing popular textbook public-key algorithms or digital signature schemes using a message integrity checking mechanism. Here, by textbook public-key algorithms (see §8.14), we mean those which are direct applications of some one-way trapdoor functions such as the RSA, Rabin and ElGamal functions. A message integrity checking mechanism allows us to establish the success probabilities and the computational costs for Malice to mount a successful attack on the enhanced scheme.

The cost for using a scheme enhanced this way is at the level of a small constant multiple of that for using the underlying textbook public-key encryption algorithm.

## 15.1.1  Chapter Outline

In this chapter we shall introduce two well-known public-key encryption schemes which are provably secure against IND-CCA2 and are practically efficient. They are the **Optimal Asymmetric Encryption Padding (OAEP)** [25, 272, 116] (§15.2) and the **Cramer-Shoup public-key cryptosystem** [85] (§15.3). We shall then conduct an overview on a family of so-called **hybrid cryptosystems** which are a combination of public-key and secret-key encryption algorithms, are provably secure against IND-CCA2 and are practically efficient (§15.4). We shall end this chapter with a literature review of practical and provably secure public-key cryptosystems (§15.5).

---

[b]We have witnessed ways of secure communication even without need for two parties to share public information, see §13.3.

# 15.2 The Optimal Asymmetric Encryption Padding

The Optimal Asymmetric Encryption Padding (OAEP) is invented by Bellare and Rogaway [25]. This is a **randomized message padding technique** and is an easily invertible transformation from a plaintext message space to the domain of a **one-way trapdoor permutation (OWTP)**. The RSA and Rabin functions are the two best-known OWTP[c]. The transformation uses two cryptographic hash functions and takes as the input a plaintext message, a random number and a string of zeros as added redundancy for message recognizability. Fig 15.1 depicts the transformation in picture. Detailed instructions for using the RSA-OAEP scheme (i.e., the OWTP is instantiated under the RSA function) have been specified in Alg 10.6. We should notice that for the case of the RSA-OAEP specified in Alg 10.6, due to our added testing step in the encryption procedure, the padding result $s \parallel t$ as an integer is always less than the RSA modulus $N$.

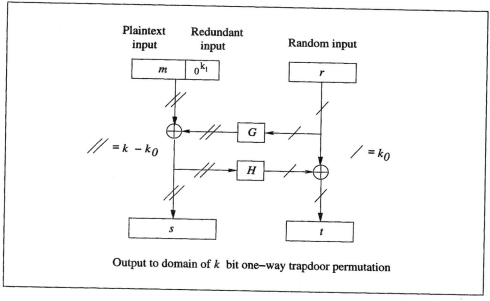

**Figure 15.1.** Optimal Asymmetric Encryption Padding (OAEP)

An OAEP based public-key encryption scheme can be viewed as a sequentially combined transformation:

$$\text{Plaintext} \stackrel{\text{OAEP}}{\longmapsto} \text{Domain of OWTP} \stackrel{\text{OWTP}}{\longmapsto} \text{Ciphertext.} \qquad (15.2.1)$$

---

[c]See §14.3.6.1 for why and how a recommended way of using the Rabin encryption algorithm forms OWTP.

Let us now provide three explanations on the central idea behind this combined transformation.

**Mixing of Different Algebraic Structures**   As we have discussed in §8.6, usually a mathematical function underlying a textbook public-key algorithm has very well-behaving and public algebraic properties. These algebraic properties are from an underlying algebraic structure in which the OWTP is defined (e.g., axioms of a group or a field provide very nice algebraic properties, see Definitions 5.1 and 5.13 in Chapter 5). A large number of attacks on textbook public-key encryption algorithms we have shown so far (including those on some semantically secure schemes, e.g., the GM cryptosystem, Alg 14.1 which is attacked in Examples 14.2 and 14.3) have invariantly shown a general technique for Malice to attack textbook encryption algorithms: manipulating a ciphertext such that the corresponding plaintext can be modified in a controlled way thanks to the nicely-behaving algebraic properties of the OWTP.

Rather differently, the OAEP transformation is constructed by networking cryptographic hash functions with a well-known symmetric crypto-algorithmic structure. Indeed, as shown in Fig 15.2 (compare with Fig 7.2), the OAEP construction can be viewed as a two-round Feistel cipher, with the first round using a hash function $G$ and the second round using a hash function $H$ in places of an "s-box function" for a Feistel cipher; though here the two "s-box functions" are not keyed, and the two "half blocks" can have different sizes.

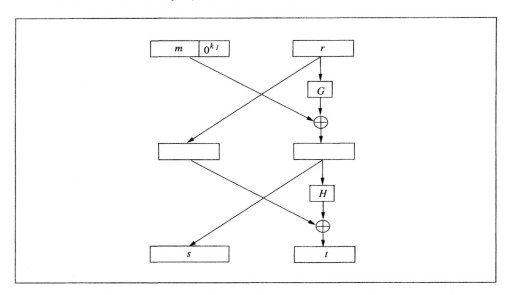

**Figure 15.2.** OAEP as a Two-round Feistel Cipher

These two kinds of structures, i.e., the structures of the OWTPs underlying popular public-key cryptosystems and the Feistel-cipher structure of OAEP, have vastly different algebraic properties. For a rough judgement we can apparently see that a former structure has block-wise algebraic properties in a large-order space while the latter structure has bit-wise (i.e., in an order-2 space) algebraic properties. We should therefore have a good hope that the combined transformation (15.2.1) should cause a tremendous difficulty for Malice to modify a plaintext in a controlled way via manipulating the corresponding ciphertext.

**Plaintext Randomization**   As we have studied in Chapter 9, if the plaintext message input to a basic and textbook public-key cryptographic function has a random distribution, then the function provides a strong protection in hiding the plaintext information, even down to the level of an individual bit. A padding scheme like OAEP has a random input value which adds randomness to the distribution of the padding result, that is, it makes the input to the OWTP to have more random distribution. Thus, to sequentially combine the randomized padding scheme with the OWTP, we hope to be able to make use of the strong bit-security of the public-key cryptographic primitive function which we have seen in Chapter 9.

**Data Integrity Protection**   We have witnessed many times that a main drawback shared by textbook crypto algorithms is an extreme vulnerability to active attacks. The invertible function (the RSA decryption and the Feistel network) and the added redundancy $0^{k_1}$ provides the decryption end with a mechanism to check data integrity (data integrity from Malice, see §10.5). So active attacks are prevented.

These three observations should make a good sense if the randomized padding output does have a good random distribution over the input message space of the OWTP.

Formal proof for an OAEP encryption scheme is based on a powerful technique called **random oracle model**. Such a proof assumes that hash functions used in the construction of OAEP behave as completely random functions, usually called **random oracles** (review §10.3.1.2 for the behavior of a random oracle). Under the random oracle assumption, i.e., when the hash functions used in the padding scheme are random oracles, then the padding output, i.e., the input to the OWTP, should indeed have a uniform distribution. Therefore, it's intuitively promising that we could establish a proof to lead to the result similar to what we have obtained in Chapter 9.

Precisely, a random-oracle-model (ROM) based proof for an OAEP-OWTP encryption scheme aims to construct an efficient transformation (called a reduction) which translates an advantage for an alleged attack on the OAEP-OWTP encryption scheme to a similar (up to polynomially different) advantage for inverting the

OWTP used in the scheme. For example, for the OWTP being the RSA function, the inversion actually solves the RSA problem or breaks the RSA assumption (Definition 8.4, Assumption 8.3 in §8.7). Since it is widely believed that there exists no efficient algorithm for inverting the OWTP, the efficient reduction transformation is considered to lead to a contradiction. Therefore, the proof so constructed is called **reduction to contradiction**.

## 15.2.1  Random Oracle Model for Security Proof

In §10.3.1.2 we have introduced the notion of **random oracle**. A random oracle is a powerful and imaginary function which is deterministic and efficient and has uniform output values.

Bellare and Rogaway make use of these random oracle properties for proving that an OAEP encryption scheme is secure [25]. Their model for security proof is called **random oracle model (ROM)** [23].

In an ROM-based technique for security proof, not only random oracles are used (i.e., not only are they assumed to exist), but also a special agent, Simon Simulator whom we have met in §14.5.4, shall be able to, somehow, *simulate* the behavior of *everybody's* (including Malice's) random oracles. So whenever someone wants to apply a random oracle, say $G$, to a value, say $a$, (s)he shall unwittingly make a so-called **random oracle query** to Simon; one does this by submitting $a$ to, and subsequently receiving a query result $G(a)$ from, Simon. Simon shall always honestly comply with any query order and duly return a good query result back.

As long as everybody obeys the rule of making random oracle queries only from Simon, then Simon can easily simulate the random oracle behavior with perfect precision. Let us now explain how Simon could simulate the behavior of a random oracle.

For oracle $G$ for example, Simon shall maintain a $G$-list which contains all the pairs $(a, G(a))$ such that $a$ has been queried in the entire history of $G$. The simulation job is rather mundane: for each query $a$, Simon shall check whether or not $a$ is already in the list; if it is, he shall just return $G(a)$ as the query result (that's why *deterministic*); otherwise, he shall invent a new value for $G(a)$ at uniformly random in the range of $G$, return this new value as the query result (that's why *uniform*) and archive the new pair $(a, G(a))$ in the list. Simon could build his list so that the pairs are sorted by the first element. There is no need to apply a sorting algorithm because each list is initialized to empty at the beginning, and grow as queries arrive. For each query, a search through a sorted list of $N$ elements can be done in $\log N$ time (see Alg 4.4), i.e., in PPT in the size of the elements (and that's why *efficient*).

To this end, we have constructively obtained the statement in Lemma 15.1.

**Lemma 15.1:** *A random oracle can be simulated perfectly in PPT.*     □

For a public-key encryption scheme using random oracles (e.g., OWTP-OAEP), this way to simulate random oracles enables Simon to construct a 1-1 mapping relation between plaintexts and ciphertexts (e.g., in the case of OWTP-OAEP in (15.2.1), mapping from left-hand side to right-hand side). Now if an attacker, say Malice, constructs a *valid* chosen ciphertext $c$ using an OWTP $f$, then as long as Malice has used Simon's random oracle services (which he is forced to use) in the construction of $c$, Simon shall be able to "decrypt" $c$ even though he does not have in his possession of the trapdoor information for inverting $f$. This is merely because Simon has the plaintext-ciphertext pair in his list simulated random oracles. Indeed, the "plaintext" must have been in some of his lists as long as the ciphertext is valid.

Therefore, in addition to having simulated random oracles, Simon can *also simulate* a decryption oracle[d], i.e., $\mathcal{O}$ in Prot 14.3 or Prot 14.4. This is another reason why we have named our special agent Simon Simulator. The simulated "decryption" capability enables Simon to offer a proper "cryptanalysis training course" to Malice in IND-ATK games (ATK stands for any of CPA, CCA or CCA2).

If the "training course" is provided at the precise quality (i.e., the simulated "training course" is accurate) then Malice, as a successful attacker, must end up with a non-negligible advantage in short enough time (PPT) to break the encryption scheme (i.e., in the IND-ATK case, he ends up relating one of the two chosen plaintexts to the challenge ciphertext). Then Simon who has in his possession the random oracles shall also end up with a successful inversion of the cryptographic function at the point of the challenge ciphertext: the pair (plaintext, challenge-ciphertext) can be found in one of his simulated random oracle lists. We shall see details of this "trick" for the case of OWTP-OAEP in §15.2.3.1. In the next chapter we shall also see this "trick" for the case of ROM-based security proofs for some digital signature schemes.

This does constitute a valid argument, however, only in a world with random oracles!

Nevertheless, due to the good approximation of the random oracle behavior from cryptographic hash functions, this argument provides a convincing heuristic insight for an OAEP enhanced encryption scheme being secure in the real world. Even though we know that it is only an unproven assumption that a cryptographic hash function emulates a random oracle behavior in a PPT indiscernible manner, this assumption has now been widely accepted and used in practice. After all, each of the reputable OWTPs underlying a popular public-key cryptosystem is an unproven but widely accepted assumption.

Goldreich considers (in "§6.2 Oded's Conclusions" of [66]) that an ROM-based technique for security proof is a useful test-bed; cryptographic schemes which do not perform well on the test-bed (i.e., cannot pass the sanity check) should be dumped.

---

[d]The reader must not confuse a "decryption oracle" with a "random oracle," they are totally different things. The former can be real, e.g., a naive user tricked by Malice to provide a decryption service, while the latter is an imaginary function.

It is widely agreed that designing a cryptographic scheme so that it is argued secure in the ROM is a good engineering principle.

In the real world, if hash functions (or pseudo-random functions) used in a cryptographic scheme or protocol have no "obvious" flaw, then a security proof for such a scheme or protocol using their idealized version can be considered as valid, in particular if the goal of the proof is up to the unproven assumption of polynomial time indistinguishability. Such a proof of security is called a security proof based on the ROM.

Let us now describe an ROM-based security proof for an OWTP-OAEP encryption scheme. In the next chapter we will also see ROM-based security proofs for some digital signature schemes.

## 15.2.2  RSA-OAEP

In the case of **RSA-OAEP**, the OWTP is the RSA encryption function. We notice that in the remaining part of this chapter, all instances of RSA-OAEP apply to Rabin-OAEP where the OWTP is the permutation realization of the Rabin encryption function (see §14.3.6.1 for how to realize the Rabin encryption function into a OWTP).

Since the RSA-OAEP encryption scheme involves two hash function evaluations followed by an application of the RSA function (see Alg 10.6), and since hash function can be efficiently evaluated, the scheme is very efficient, almost as efficient as the textbook RSA. This scheme also has a very high bandwidth for message recovery. If we consider using an RSA modulus of the standard length of 2048 bits (the reason why 2048 bits is a standard length for the RSA-OAEP encryption scheme will be explained in §15.2.5), and consider $k_0 = k_1 = 160$ (so that $2^{-k_0}$ and $2^{-k_1}$ are negligibly small), then the plaintext massage can have a length $|M| = |N| - k_0 - k_1 = 2048 - 320 = 1728$, that is, the plaintext message encrypted inside the RSA-OAEP scheme can have a length up to 84% of the length of the modulus.

These practically important features have been widely recognized by the practitioners so that the scheme has been accepted as the RSA encryption standard under industrial and international standardization organizations (PKCS#1, IEEE P1363). It has also been chosen to use in the well-known Internet electronic commerce protocol SET [261].

So, RSA-OAEP is a very successful public-key encryption scheme. However, for its provable security, success is a son of failure.

If the reader only wants to know how to encrypt in RSA with a fit-for-application security, then the RSA-OAEP scheme specified in Alg 10.6 has provided adequate "know-how" information and the reader can thereby proceed to §15.3. The text between here and §15.3 is "know-why" material: it answers why the RSA-OAEP scheme has a fit-for-application security. We will try to provide the answer in an intuitive manner and discuss some important issues related to the proof of security.

## 15.2.3   A Twist in the Security Proof for RSA-OAEP

The original ROM-based proof for $f$-OAEP [25] tried to relate an attack on the $f$-OAEP scheme in the IND-CCA2 mode to the problem of inverting the OWTP $f$ without using the trapdoor information of $f$. Recently, Shoup has made an ingenious observation and revealed a flaw in that proof [272]. Moreover, he points out that for $f$ being a general case of OWTP, it is unlikely that an ROM-based proof exists for that $f$-OAEP is secure against IND-CCA2. Fortunately and very quickly, the danger for us losing a very successful public-key encryption algorithm standard was over! A closer observation is made by Fujisaki et al. [116] and they find a way to rescue OAEP for $f$ being the RSA function.

Let us now review this dramatic matter. We shall start with studying the original security argument attempted by Bellare and Rogaway. We then describe Shoup's observation of a flaw in that argument. Finally we shall see the rescue work of Fujisaki et al. (Shoup also works out a special case for the same rescue, and we shall see that as well).

### 15.2.3.1   A Reduction Based on Random Oracle Model

Suppose that an attacker $\mathcal{A}$, who is a PPT algorithm, can have a non-negligible advantage to break an $f$-OAEP scheme in the IND-CCA2 mode. Let us construct an algorithm which will enable our special agent, Simon Simulator, to make use of the IND-CCA2 attacker $\mathcal{A}$ to invert the OWTP $f$, also with a non-negligible advantage. This algorithm must be efficient (i.e., a PPT one). Thus, Simon efficiently "reduces" his task of inverting $f$ to $\mathcal{A}$'s capability of attacking the $f$-OAEP scheme. The algorithm used by Simon is therefore called a **polynomial-time reduction**. Since both $\mathcal{A}$ and the reduction run by Simon are polynomial time, inversion of $f$ as the combination of $\mathcal{A}$ and the reduction conducted by Simon then also runs in polynomial time. It is the belief that inversion of $f$ cannot be done in PPT that should refute the existence of the alleged IND-CCA2 attacker $\mathcal{A}$ on $f$-OAEP (however, we should be careful about an issue which we shall discuss in §15.2.5). A security proof in this style, in addition to the name "reduction to contradiction," is also called a **reductionist proof**.

Let us now describe the reduction.

Let Simon be given (the description of) an OWTP $f$ and a uniformly random point $c^*$ in the range of $f$. Simon wants to uncover $f^{-1}(c^*)$ by using $\mathcal{A}$ as an IND-CCA2 attacker. We must notice the importance of the randomness of $c^*$: if $c^*$ is not random, then Simon's result cannot be a useful algorithm.

### Top-level Description of the Reduction Algorithm

Fig 15.3 provides a visual aid for the reduction we will be describing now. The picture shows that Simon has taken over all the communication links of $\mathcal{A}$ to and from the external world so that $\mathcal{A}$ can interact only with Simon.

- Simon starts by sending (the description of) the $f$-OAEP encryption algorithm to $\mathcal{A}$.

- Simon shall play with $\mathcal{A}$ an IND-CA2 attack game (i.e., they run Prot 14.4). In this game, Simon shall impersonate the decryption oracle $\mathcal{O}$ as if he has in his possession a valid decryption box. The impersonation is via simulation. We shall see that in ROM, Simon can indeed do so without $\mathcal{A}$ detecting anything wrong.

- Simon shall also provide $\mathcal{A}$ with simulated services for the random oracles $G$ and $H$ used in OAEP (see Fig 15.1). So as we have stipulated in §15.2.1, whenever $\mathcal{A}$ wants to apply $G$ and/or $H$ (e.g., when it wants to prepare a chosen ciphertext in a proper way during the game play), it shall actually make queries to Simon and subsequently gets the respective query results back from Simon.

It is vitally important that the simulations provided by Simon must be accurate so that $\mathcal{A}$ cannot feel anything wrong in its communications with the outside world. Only under a precise simulation can $\mathcal{A}$ be educated properly by Simon and thereby release its attacking capacity fully. The IND-CCA2 attacking game played between Simon and $\mathcal{A}$ is as follows.

i) In $\mathcal{A}$'s "find stage," Simon shall receive from $\mathcal{A}$ indifferent chosen-ciphertexts for decryption (i.e., those in a lunchtime attack). $\mathcal{A}$ has freedom to construct these ciphertexts in any way it wishes; but if it does want to construct them properly, e.g., via applying the random oracles, then its queries must go to Simon (as illustrated in Fig 15.3, Simon has taken over all $\mathcal{A}$'s communication channels to and from the external world). The ways for Simon to simulate these random oracles will be described in a moment.

ii) Since Simon receives from $\mathcal{A}$ chosen ciphertexts for decryption, Simon shall answer them to $\mathcal{A}$ by simulating the decryption box (oracle $\mathcal{O}$). Details for Simon to simulate $\mathcal{O}$ shall also be given in a moment.

iii) $\mathcal{A}$ shall end its "find stage" by submitting to Simon a pair of chosen plaintexts $m_0, m_1$. Upon receipt of them, Simon shall flip a fair coin $b \in_U \{0, 1\}$, and send to $\mathcal{A}$ the "challenge ciphertext" $c^*$ as a *simulated* $f$-OAEP encryption of $m_b$. Here, Simon pretends as if $c^*$ encrypts $m_b$.

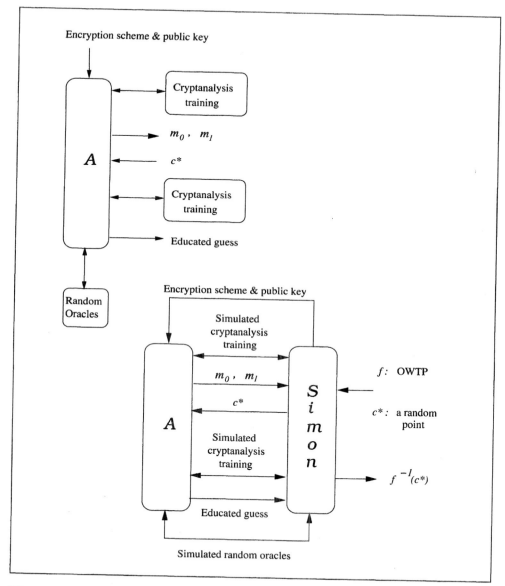

**Figure 15.3.** Reduction from Inversion of a One-way Trapdoor Function $f$ to an Attack on the $f$-OAEP Scheme

iv) Now $\mathcal{A}$ is in its "guess stage." So it may submit further adaptive chosen-ciphertexts for its "extended cryptanalysis training course." Simon shall serve as in (ii). In case $\mathcal{A}$ makes random oracle queries in its proper construction of the adaptive chosen-ciphertexts, Simon shall serve as in (i).

Eventually, $\mathcal{A}$ should output its educated guess on the bit $b$. This is the end of the attacking game.

As we have agreed and emphasized many times, $\mathcal{A}$ should not submit the "challenge ciphertext" $c^*$ for decryption. Were $c^*$ submitted, it would be impossible for Simon to provide a simulated decryption since this is the very ciphertext that Simon needs $\mathcal{A}$'s help to decrypt.

**Simulation of Random Oracles.** Simon shall simulate the two random oracles $G$ and $H$ used in the OAEP transformation. In the simulation, Simon maintains two lists, called his $G$-list and his $H$-list, both are initially set to empty:

$G$-oracle   Suppose $\mathcal{A}$ makes $G$-query $g$. Simon shall first search his $G$-list trying to find $g$. If $g$ is found in the list, Simon shall provide $G(g)$ to $\mathcal{A}$. Otherwise, $g$ is fresh; then Simon picks at uniformly random a string $G(g)$ of length $k_0$, provides $G(g)$ to $\mathcal{A}$ and adds the new pair $(g, G(g))$ to $G$-list.

If the query occurs in $\mathcal{A}$'s "guess stage," then Simon shall try to invert $f$ at the point $c^*$. What he should do is: for each $(g, G(g)) \in G$-list and each $(h, H(h)) \in H$-list, Simon builds $w = h \parallel (g \oplus H(h))$ and checks whether $c^* = f(w)$. If this holds for some so-constructed string, then $f^{-1}(c^*)$ has been found.

$H$-oracle   Suppose $\mathcal{A}$ makes $H$-query $h$. Simon shall first search his $H$-list trying to find $h$. If $h$ is found in the list, Simon shall provide $H(h)$ to $\mathcal{A}$. Otherwise, $h$ is fresh; then Simon picks at uniformly random a string $H(h)$ of length $k - k_0$, provides $H(h)$ to $\mathcal{A}$ and adds the new pair $(h, H(h))$ to $H$-list.

If the query occurs in $\mathcal{A}$'s "guess stage," then Simon shall try to invert $f$ at the point $c^*$ as in the case of $G$-oracle.

**Simulation of the Decryption Oracle.** Simon shall simulate the decryption box (oracle $\mathcal{O}$). His simulation steps are: upon receipt of ciphertext $c$ from $\mathcal{A}$ for decryption, Simon looks at each query-answer $(g, G(g)) \in G$-list and $(h, H(h)) \in H$-list; for each pair taken from both lists, Simon computes

$$w = h \parallel (g \oplus H(h)),$$

$$v = G(g) \oplus h,$$

and checks

$$c \stackrel{?}{=} f(w)$$

and

Does $v$ have $k_1$ trailing zeros?

if the both checking steps yield "YES," Simon shall return the most significant $n = k - k_0 - k_1$ bits of $v$ to $\mathcal{A}$. Otherwise, Simon shall return REJECT to $\mathcal{A}$.

Because $\mathcal{A}$ is polynomially bounded, the number of random oracle queries and that of decryption requests made by $\mathcal{A}$ are also polynomially bounded. Hence, Simon can run the simulated game in polynomial time.

### 15.2.3.2 Accuracy of the Simulation

As we have mentioned, for $\mathcal{A}$ to work properly, the accuracy of the simulations is vitally important (is everything)!

First of all, as we have established in Lemma 15.1, the two random oracles have been perfectly simulated.

Now let us examine the accuracy of Simon's simulation of the decryption box.

Let Simon be given a chosen ciphertext $c$ (either a pre-challenge one or a post-challenge one, i.e., either an indifferently chosen one or an adaptively chosen one). Simon's simulation for the decryption box is in fact very accurate. Let

$$s \parallel t = f^{-1}(c), \tag{15.2.2}$$

$$r = t \oplus H(s), \tag{15.2.3}$$

$$m \parallel 0^{k_1} = s \oplus G(r) \tag{15.2.4}$$

be the values which are defined by $c$ should $c$ be a valid ciphertext. Below, whenever we say "the correct value," we mean the value processed by a real decryption oracle $\mathcal{O}$ should $c$ be sent to $\mathcal{O}$.

If the correct $s$ defined by $c$ in (15.2.2) has not been queried for random oracle $H$, then the correct $H(s)$ is missing. So in each $G$-query, we can only have probability at the level of $2^{-k_0}$ for $r$ defined in (15.2.3) being correct. So like the missing correct value $s$ being queried for $H$, the correct value $r$ is also missing from being queried for $G$ (except for probability at the level of $2^{-k_0}$). Consequently, as in (15.2.4), value $s \oplus G(r)$ can have probability $2^{-k_1}$ to have $k_1$ trailing zeros since this requires $s$ and $G(r)$ to have their $k_1$ least significant bits identical bit by bit, but the former is missing, and the latter is uniformly random. Notice that in this analysis we have already also considered the case for the correct $r$ having not been queried for $G$: rejection is correct except for an error probability of $2^{-k_1}$.

In summary, we can conclude the following result regarding the simulated decryption of a chosen ciphertext $c$:

- If both $s$ and $r$ have been queried for the respective random oracles, then the simulated decryption can correctly construct $f^{-1}(c)$ and thereby further decrypt $c$ in the usual way.

- If *either s and/or r* has not been queried for the respective random oracles, then it is correct for the simulated decryption to return REJECT except for an error probability at the level of $2^{-k_0} + 2^{-k_1}$.

Notice that in the case of *either s and/or r* having not been queried for the respective random oracles, the error probability bound holds in a *statistical* sense: namely, the probability bound holds as long as $\mathcal{A}$ has not made the necessary random oracle query regardless of how powerful $\mathcal{A}$ may be.

At this point we can confirm that our argument so far has already shown that $f$-OAEP is provably secure against IND-CCA (i.e., lunchtime attack or indifferent chosen-ciphertext attack). This is because in an IND-CCA attack game the decryption box only works in the "find stage," and we have established that in that stage, the simulated decryption works accurately except for a minute error probability.

We should explicitly emphasize that our argument is solely based on the one-way-ness of $f$.

### 15.2.3.3  Incompleteness

Shoup observes that the original OAEP security argument (for IND-CCA2 security) contains a flaw [272]. Before we go ahead to explain it, let us make it very clear that the OAEP construction is *not* flawed. It is the formal proof described in §15.2.3.2 that has not gone through completely for IND-CCA2 security. A short way to state the incompleteness can be as follows:

> The simulated decryption performed by Simon is statistically precise as long as $s^*$ defined by the challenge ciphertext $c^*$ in (15.2.5) is not queried for random oracle $H$, but the statistical precision falls apart as soon as $s^*$ is queried. However, the possibility of $s^*$ being queried was not considered in the security argument in §15.2.3.2.

In order to explain the incompleteness, let us consider various values defined by the challenge ciphertext $c^*$. Let

$$s^* \parallel t^* = f^{-1}(c^*), \tag{15.2.5}$$

$$r^* = t^* \oplus H(s^*), \tag{15.2.6}$$

$$m_b \parallel 0^{k_1} = s^* \oplus G(r^*). \tag{15.2.7}$$

The three values $(s^*, r^*, m_b)$ are defined by the challenge ciphertext $c^*$ where $b$ is the coin tossing result performed by Simon.

Let us now imagine that $s^*$ is queried for random oracle $H$. Of course, in statistics this must be remotely unlikely in $\mathcal{A}$'s "find stage" since at that point in time it has not yet been given the challenge ciphertext $c^*$. This is why we have concluded at the end of §15.2.3.2 that the argument there does provide a *valid* proof for $f$-OAEP being secure in the IND-CCA mode. However, it may be *possible* for $\mathcal{A}$ to query $s^*$ in its "guess stage" when it has been given the challenge ciphertext $c^*$.

What is the probability for $\mathcal{A}$ to query $s^*$ in its "guess stage?" Well, we do not know for sure. All we definitely know is that: given $\mathcal{A}$ being allegedly powerful, there is no way for us to deny a possibility for it to query $s^*$ in its "guess stage." Otherwise, why should we have assumed $\mathcal{A}$ being able to guess the bit $b$ in first place? (Nevertheless, the conditional probability bound for $s^*$ having been queried, given that $\mathcal{A}$ answers correctly, can be estimated; the result is non-negligible. We shall provide an estimate in §15.2.3.4.)

As long as $\mathcal{A}$ can query $s^*$, it can find discrepancy in the simulated attack game. Here is an easy way for us to imagine the discrepancy. For $r^*$ fixed by (15.2.6), $\mathcal{A}$ may further query $r^*$. The uniformly random $G(r^*)$ returned back will mean little chance for $G(r^*) \oplus s^*$ to meet either chosen plaintexts. So at this moment $\mathcal{A}$ shall shout: "Stop fooling around!" $\mathcal{A}$ should shout so because it has spotted that the " hallenge ciphertext" $c^*$ has nothing to do with any of its chosen plaintexts.

Of course, this "easy" way of finding discrepancy would "cost" $\mathcal{A}$ too much: it would have already disclosed both $s^*$ and $t^* = r^* \oplus H(s^*)$ to Simon and hence would have already helped Simon to invert $f$ at the point $c^* = f(s^* \parallel t^*)$!

Shoup has a better exploitation of this problem. He observes that for some $f$ as an OWTP, $\mathcal{A}$'s ability to query $s^*$ given $c^*$ suffices it to construct a valid ciphertext without querying $r^*$ for random oracle $G$ (in fact, without ever querying $G$ at all in the entire history of the attack game). Moreover, because the valid ciphertext so constructed is a malleability result of another valid ciphertext, this $f$-OAEP scheme is NM-CCA2 insecure, and by Theorem 14.4 (in §14.5.4.2), it is also IND-CCA2 insecure. However, the reduction technique described in §15.2.3.1 shall not help Simon to invert $f$ since Simon's $G$-list can even be empty (i.e., $\mathcal{A}$ has never queried anything for random oracle $G$)!

Shoup constructs a $k$-bit OWTP $f$ for a counterexample. He supposes this permutation is "xor-malleable:" given $f(w_1)$, $w_2$, one can construct $f(w_1 \oplus w_2)$ with a significant advantage. Notice that this is not an unreasonable assumption. In the security proof for an $f$-OAEP scheme described in §15.2.3.1 we have only required $f$ to be one-way and have never required it to be non-malleable. After all, as we have seen in the previous chapter, OWTPs underlying popular textbook public-key encryption algorithms are generally malleable, and the general malleability is the very reason for us to enhance a textbook public-key scheme with the OAEP technique.

To make the exposition clearer, let this $f$ not hide the $k - k_0$ most significant bits at all. Then this $f$ can be written as:

$$f(s \parallel t) = s \parallel f_0(t)$$

where $f_0$ is a "xor-malleable" $(k - k_0)$-bit OWTP, i.e., given $f_0(t_1)$, $t_2$, one can construct $f_0(t_1 \oplus t_2)$ with a significant advantage. This $f$ is still an OWTP with one-way-ness quantified by the security parameter $k_0$.

Now consider $f$-OAEP encryption scheme instantiated under this $f$. Remember that for $c^*$ being the challenge ciphertext, values $s^*$, $t^*$, $r^*$ and $(m_b \parallel 0^{k_1})$ correspond to $c^*$ under this $f$-OAEP scheme.

Since $\mathcal{A}$ is a black box, we have freedom to describe how he should construct a valid ciphertext out of modifying another valid ciphertext. Upon receipt of the challenge ciphertext $c^*$, $\mathcal{A}$ decomposes $c^*$ as $c^* = s^* \parallel f_0(t^*)$. It then chooses an arbitrary, non-zero message $\Delta \in \{0,1\}^{k-k_0-k_1}$, and computes:

$$s = s^* \oplus (\Delta \parallel 0^{k_1}), \quad v = f_0(t^* \oplus H(s^*) \oplus H(s)), \quad c = s \parallel v.$$

Clearly, in order to construct the new ciphertext $c$ from the challenge ciphertext $c^*$ $\mathcal{A}$ only needs to query $s^*$ and $s$ for $H$.

Let us now confirm that $c$ is a valid $f$-OAEP encryption of $m_b \oplus \Delta$ as long as $c^*$ is a valid $f$-OAEP encryption of $m_b$. From $t = t^* \oplus H(s^*) \oplus H(s)$, we have

$$r = H(s) \oplus t = t^* \oplus H(s^*) = r^* \qquad (15.2.8)$$

Clearly, (15.2.8) holds even though $\mathcal{A}$ has not queried $r = r^*$ for $G$ (he may not even know $r^*$ because it may not know $t^*$).

Had this game been played between $\mathcal{A}$ and the real decryption oracle $\mathcal{O}$, then $\mathcal{O}$ would retrieve $r$ properly by computing

$$f^{-1}(c) = s \parallel t,$$

$$r = H(s) \oplus t.$$

But noticing (15.2.8), $\mathcal{O}$ would have actually retrieved $r^*$. So $\mathcal{O}$ would further apply hash function $G$, and would compute

$$G(r) \oplus s = G(r^*) \oplus s^* \oplus (\Delta \parallel 0^{k_1}) = (m_b \oplus \Delta) \parallel 0^{k_1}.$$

Upon seeing the trailing $k_1$ zeros, $\mathcal{O}$ would return $m_b \oplus \Delta$ as the correct decryption of $c$. From the returned plaintext $m_b \oplus \Delta$, $\mathcal{A}$ can easily extract $m_b$ and hence break this $f$-OAEP in the IND-CCA2 mode.

However, for this game being played in the reduction between $\mathcal{A}$ and Simon, because Simon's $G$-list is empty, Simon shall promptly return REJECT. Now, $\mathcal{A}$ will definitely shout very loudly:

"STOP FOOLING AROUND!"

### 15.2.3.4  Probability for $\mathcal{A}$ to have Queried $s^*$ in its "Guess Stage"

We have left out a small detail regarding the incompleteness of the original proof of Bellare-Rogaway: the conditional probability for $\mathcal{A}$ to have queried $s^*$ in its "guess stage" given that it can answer the challenge bit correctly. Because this part has involved probability estimation, it may be skipped without causing any trouble in understanding how the security proof for RSA-OAEP works. (In fact, the probability estimation is quite elementary; we will state all rule applications by referring to their origins in Chapter 3).

To start with, we suppose that $\mathcal{A}$ somehow has advantage Adv to guess the challenge bit $b$ correctly after he has had enough adaptive chosen-ciphertext training.

During the training, Simon may mistakenly reject a valid ciphertext in a decryption query. This is a bad event because it shows $\mathcal{A}$ a low quality of the training course. So let this event be denoted DBad. In §15.2.3.2 our examination on Simon's simulated decryption procedure has concluded that the simulated decryption is accurate or a high-quality one: the probability for inaccuracy is at the level $2^{-k_0} + 2^{-k_1}$. So we have

$$\text{Prob}\,[\text{DBad}] \approx 2^{-k_0} + 2^{-k_1} \tag{15.2.9}$$

Let further AskG (respectively, AskH) denote the event that $r^*$ (respectively, the event $s^*$) has ended up in $G$-list (respectively, in $H$-list). These two events are also undesirable because they disclose to $\mathcal{A}$ information for it to discover that the challenge ciphertext $c^*$ actually has nothing to do with its "chosen plaintexts" $m_0$, $m_1$. Therefore, let us also call them bad events. Define the event Bad as

$$\text{Bad} = \text{AskG} \cup \text{AskH} \cup \text{DBad}.$$

Now, let $\mathcal{A}$ wins denote the event that $\mathcal{A}$ makes a correct guess of the challenge bit $b$. It is clear that in absence of the event Bad, due to the uniform randomness of the values which the random oracles can have, the challenge bit $b$ is independent from the challenge ciphertext $c^*$. Thus we have

$$\text{Prob}\,[\mathcal{A}\,\text{wins} \mid \overline{\text{Bad}}] = \frac{1}{2}. \tag{15.2.10}$$

Applying conditional probability (Definition 3.3 in §3.4.1) we can re-express (15.2.10) into

$$\text{Prob}\,[\mathcal{A}\,\text{wins} \mid \overline{\text{Bad}}] = \frac{\text{Prob}\,[\mathcal{A}\,\text{wins} \cap \overline{\text{Bad}}]}{\text{Prob}\,[\overline{\text{Bad}}]} = \frac{1}{2}$$

or

$$\text{Prob}\,[\mathcal{A}\,\text{wins} \cap \overline{\text{Bad}}] = \frac{1}{2} \cdot (1 - \text{Prob}\,[\text{Bad}]). \tag{15.2.11}$$

We should notice that in the event $\overline{\text{Bad}}$ (i.e., in absence of Bad), the simulated random oracles and the simulated decryption box work perfectly and are identical to these true functions. So $\mathcal{A}$'s attacking advantage should be fully released, and we have

$$\text{Prob}\,[\mathcal{A}\,\text{wins}] = \frac{1}{2} + \text{Adv}. \tag{15.2.12}$$

On the other hand (see the law of total probability, Theorem 3.1 in §3.4.3),

$$\text{Prob}\,[\mathcal{A}\,\text{wins}] = \text{Prob}\,[\mathcal{A}\,\text{wins} \cap \overline{\text{Bad}}] + \text{Prob}\,[\mathcal{A}\,\text{wins} \cap \text{Bad}]. \tag{15.2.13}$$

If we conjunct (15.2.12) and (15.2.13), we have

$$\text{Prob}\,[\mathcal{A}\,\text{wins} \cap \overline{\text{Bad}}] + \text{Prob}\,[\mathcal{A}\,\text{wins} \cap \text{Bad}] = \frac{1}{2} + \text{Adv}$$

or

$$\text{Prob}\,[\mathcal{A}\,\text{wins} \cap \overline{\text{Bad}}] + \text{Prob}\,[\text{Bad}] \geq \frac{1}{2} + \text{Adv} \tag{15.2.14}$$

Noticing (15.2.11), the inequality (15.2.14) becomes

$$\frac{1}{2} \cdot (1 - \text{Prob}\,[\text{Bad}]) + \text{Prob}\,[\text{Bad}] \geq \frac{1}{2} + \text{Adv},$$

that is

$$\text{Prob}\,[\text{Bad}] \geq \text{Adv}. \tag{15.2.15}$$

Since $\text{Bad} = \text{AskG} \cup \text{AskH} \cup \text{DBad}$, we have

$$\text{Prob}\,[\text{Bad}] \;\leq\; \text{Prob}\,[\text{AskG} \cup \text{AskH}] + \text{Prob}\,[\text{DBad}] \tag{15.2.16}$$
$$= \text{Prob}\,[\text{AskH}] + \text{Prob}\,[\text{AskG} \cap \overline{\text{AskH}}] + \text{Prob}\,[\text{DBad}] \tag{15.2.17}$$
$$\leq \text{Prob}\,[\text{AskH}] + \text{Prob}\,[\text{AskG} \mid \overline{\text{AskH}}] + \text{Prob}\,[\text{DBad}] \tag{15.2.18}$$

where (15.2.16) is due to Probability Addition Rule 1, (15.2.17) is due to Example 3.3, and finally (15.2.18) follows the definition for conditional probability and the fact that a probability value is always less than 1.

Finally, we notice that the uniform randomness of the $H$ oracle, the conditional event $\text{AskG} | \overline{\text{AskH}}$ (i.e., given that $s^*$ has not been queried, $r^*$ has been queried) can only occur with probability $2^{-k_0}$. We have also known from (15.2.9) that probability for DBad is also at the level of $2^{-k_0} + 2^{-k_1}$. The inequalities (15.2.15—15.2.18) conclude

$$\text{Prob}\,[\text{AskH}] \geq \text{Adv} - (2^{-k_0+1} + 2^{-k_1}).$$

Therefore, if Adv is non-negligible in $k$, so is $\text{Prob}\,[\text{AskH}]$.

To this end, we can clearly see that if an attacker is capable of breaking, in IND-CCA2 mode, the RSA-OAEP implemented by random oracles, then the attacker is capable of partially inverting the RSA function: finding $s^*$ with a similar advantage. **Partial inversion** of the RSA function can actually lead to full inversion. Let us now see how this is possible.

## 15.2.4   Rescue Work for RSA-OAEP

The mathematics in §15.2.3.4 actually plays an important role in the rescue work for RSA-OAEP. However, the initial rescue attempt did not rely on it.

### 15.2.4.1   Shoup's Initial Attempt

Fortunately, the malleability property of the RSA function is not so similar to that of a Feistel cipher which bases the OAEP transformation (review Fig 15.2 and our discussion there on the difference in algebraic properties between these two structures). Ironically, the significant difference in algebraic properties (or in malleability properties) between these two structures enabled Shoup to prove that the RSA-OAEP is IND-CCA2 secure provided the RSA encryption exponent is extremely small: for $N$ being the RSA modulus, his proof requires

$$k_0 \leq (\log_2 N)/e. \tag{15.2.19}$$

Let us see why.

Recall that our analysis has concluded that if $s^*$, which is defined by the challenge ciphertext $c^*$ in (15.2.5), is not queried for oracle $H$, then the reduction is statistically correct. The only case for the reduction being incorrect is when $s^*$ is queried for $H$. For this case, we have not considered how Simon should act.

Shoup observes that with $s^*$ being a $(k - k_0)$-bit string in Simon's $H$-list, Simon can solve the following equation for the RSA problem:

$$(X + 2^{k_0} I(s^*))^e \equiv c \pmod{N} \tag{15.2.20}$$

where $I(x)$ is the integer value for the string $x$. This equation is solvable in time polynomial in the size of $N$ using Coppersmith's algorithm [83] provided $X < N^{1/e}$. With $X$ being a quantity at the level of $2^{k_0}$ and with the restriction in (15.2.19), the condition $X < N^{1/e}$ is met.

Thus, upon being given a ciphertext $c$ for decryption service, Simon should, upon failure to decrypt $c$ using the method specified in §15.2.3.1, try to solve (15.2.20) for $X$ using each element in his $H$-list. If all of these attempts fail, Simon should reject $c$. Otherwise, the solution is $X = I(t^*)$; knowing $s^*$ and $t^*$, Simon should decrypt $c$ in the usual way.

Therefore, for this case of the RSA-OAEP, i.e., for the encryption exponent $e$ satisfying (15.2.20), querying $s^*$ for $H$ has already helped Simon to invert $c^*$. The question is: what is the magnitude of $e$ satisfying (15.2.20)? For the standard security parameter settings for the RSA-OAEP, we have $N > 2^{1024}$, and $k_0 = 160$ (in order for $2^{-k_0}$ being negligible), and so $e \leq \frac{1024}{160} = 6.4$. So for the standard security parameter settings, $e = 3$ or $e = 5$ are the only possible cases for encryption exponents ($e$ must be co-prime to $\phi(N)$ which is even). Although using such small exponents we can reach provable security for the RSA-OAEP, it is widely recognized after Coppersmith's work, that one should not use such small exponents for RSA encryption.

Because the standard security parameter setting for $k_0$ is already close to the lower bound and that for the size of $N$ cannot be increased dramatically, there is little hope to use this reduction method for any larger $e$.

### 15.2.4.2  Full Rescue by Fujisaki et al.

Fortunately again, soon after Shoup's analysis, Fujisaki et al. [116] made a further observation and found a way to invert the RSA function for the general case of the encryption exponent.

For the case of the RSA-OAEP, disclosing to Simon $s^*$ as a significantly large chunk of the pre-image of $c^*$ has actually already disclosed too much. Because $s^*$ has $k - k_0$ bits and because $k > 2k_0$, more than half the bits (the most significant bits) of the pre-image of $c^*$ are disclosed. Given such a large chunk of the pre-image, Fujisaki et al. applied a brilliant lattice technique which can solve for $T = I(t^*)$ from the equation

$$(2^{k_0} I(s^*) + T)^e \equiv c^* \pmod{N} \tag{15.2.21}$$

for arbitrarily large $e$. Recall that given a one-bit RSA oracle ("RSA parity oracle," review §9.2), we have studied an algorithm (Alg 9.1) which applies the one-bit oracle $\log_2 N$ times to invert the RSA function. Exactly the same principle applies here: $\mathcal{A}$ is in fact an "RSA half-or-greater-block oracle" since $s^*$ has more than half the bits of the pre-image of $c^*$. Using the algorithm of Fujisaki et al, Simon can apply $\mathcal{A}$ twice to obtain two related blocks (half-or-greater-block) of partial pre-image information. These two blocks can be used in the formula (15.2.21) for solving two unknown integers which are smaller than $\sqrt{N}$. One of these smaller integers is $T(t^*)$, and hence, Simon has inverted the RSA function.

Since Simon has to apply $\mathcal{A}$ twice, he should play with $\mathcal{A}$ twice the reduction-via-attack game: once feeding $\mathcal{A}$ with $c^*$, and once feeding $\mathcal{A}$ with $\bar{c}^* = c^* \alpha^e \pmod{N}$ for a random $\alpha \in \mathbb{Z}_N^*$. The respective $s^*$ and $\bar{s}^*$ will be in his $H$-list and his $\bar{H}$-list, respectively. Let $q = \max(\#(H\text{-list}), \#(\bar{H}\text{-list}))$. From these two lists Simon will deal with no more than $q^2$ pairs $(t, \bar{t})$. One of these pairs will enable Simon to make two correct equations in the formula (15.2.21) and thereby to invert the RSA function, unless he has chosen a bad $\alpha$ which has a small probability (negligible when $k \gg 2k_0$ which is the case in the RSA-OAEP). Because solving two cases of (15.2.21) can be done in time $O_B((\log_2 N)^3)$, Simon can invert the RSA function in time

$$2\tau + q^2 \times O_B((\log_2 N)^3), \tag{15.2.22}$$

where $\tau$ is time bound for $\mathcal{A}$ to perform the IND-CCA2 attack on the RSA-OAEP.

The RSA-OAEP has other two variations for the padding parameter settings. They are PKCS#1 versions 2 and higher [232] and SET [261]. In these variations, the known data chunk $s^*$ is positioned in different places in the plaintext chunk. Due to the sufficiently large size of $s^*$ (considerably larger than the half-block size), root-extraction can easily be done by at most twice running of $\mathcal{A}$. So a variation of the technique of Fujisaki et al. will still apply to these variations.

In this way, the RSA-OAEP, and the variations, remain provably secure in the IND-CCA2 mode.

We should notice that the lattice method solving the partial unknown from (15.2.21) works thanks to the multiplicative property of the RSA function. It is a bit of irony that one of the very functionality of the RSA-OAEP is to destroy the multiplicative property of the RSA function (considered to be undesirable), while the security proof requires the property.

Finally, we point out that the same result applies to the Rabin-OAEP. Therefore inverting the Rabin function, i.e., extracting a square root modulo $N$, at an arbitrary point implies factoring $N$. This can be done by Simon applying Theorem 6.17.(iii) (in §6.6.2): picking a random value $x$ and setting $c^*$ as raw Rabin encryption of $x$. The security result for the Rabin-OAEP is better than that for the RSA-OAEP since factorization is a weaker assumption that the RSA assumption.

## 15.2.5  Tightness of "Reduction to Contradiction" for RSA-OAEP

The RSA-OAEP scheme is very efficient. However, the "reduction to contradiction" should not be considered so. Let us now explain this issue.

The expression (15.2.22) shows the time needed by Simon Simulator to apply $\mathcal{A}$ twice to invert the RSA function at an arbitrary point. The expression has a quadratic term $q^2$ where $q$ is the number of RO queries to $H$ that $\mathcal{A}$ is entitled to make in each instance of it being used by Simon.

Notice that an RO idealizes a hash function which can be evaluated very efficiently. For a dedicated attacker, we ought to reasonably entitle it to make, say $2^{50}$, hash function evaluations. Thus, it is reasonable to consider $q \approx 2^{50}$. Consequently, the quadratic term $q^2$ in (15.2.22) means that Simon's time to invert the RSA problem is

$$2^{100} \cdot O_B((\log_2 N)^3).$$

Now review §4.6 for the state of the factorization art, (4.6.1) is the expression for factoring $N$ using the Number Field Sieve (NFS) method. For the usual size of $|N| = 1024$, (4.6.1) provides a value at the level of $2^{86}$. Thus, a contradiction given by $2^{100} \cdot O_B((\log_2 N)^3)$ is not a meaningful one at all since using the NFS method, Simon can invert the RSA function based on a 1024-bit modulus at a far lower cost without using $\mathcal{A}$. Thus, the "reduction to contradiction" proof is not a valid one for the case of a 1024-bit RSA modulus.

Since 1024-bit RSA moduli are currently regarded within the safe margin for many secure applications, the invalidity of the security proof for the RSA-OAEP exposes the dissatisfaction of the reduction as a degree-2 polynomial.

The "reduction-to-contradiction" proof is valid for much larger RSA moduli; for example, it is valid in a marginal way for an 2048-bit modulus for which (4.6.1) will produce a $2^{116}$-level value.

## 15.2.6    A Critique on the Random Oracle Model

Canetti, Goldreich and Halevi hold a rather negative view on the ROM-based security proofs [65, 66]. They demonstrate that there exists signature and encryption schemes which are provably secure under the ROM, but cannot have secure realizations in the real world implementation. Their basic idea is to devise nasty schemes. Such a scheme usually behaves properly as a signature scheme or an encryption scheme. However, upon holding of a certain condition (basically, when non-randomness is sensed), the scheme becomes nasty and outputs the private signing key it is it a signature scheme, or the plaintext message if it is an encryption scheme.

Clearly, when we prove security for this nasty scheme under ROM, since the plaintext to be signed or encrypted is assumed uniformly random (of course purely owing to the ROM trick), the proof will go through. However, in the real world with practical applications, since there is no uniformly random plaintext, any real-world implementation is clearly insecure.

Their steps to create such nasty schemes are rather involved. The more interested reader is referred to [66].

However, after elegant and convincing scientific argument, it is interesting to find that the three authors reach rather different conclusions in terms of disagreements on the usefulness of the random oracle methodology. They decide to present their disagreements in the most controversial form by having three separate conclusions, one from each author.

Canetti's conclusion (§6.1 of [66]) exposes the most critical view of the three. He considers that the random oracle model is a bad abstraction and leads to the loss of reductions to hard problems (i.e., it nullifies the elegant idea of "reduction to contradiction"). He further considers that to identify any useful, special-purpose properties of random oracle can be alternative directions of research.

Goldreich's conclusion (§6.2 of [66]) is the mildest among the three. He considers the problem with the ROM as incompleteness: it may fail to rule out insecure designs due to some flaws in the implementation of random oracles. He therefore recommends that in currently published work, proofs of security under the ROM should not be included (we interpret this as: these proofs should not be considered as real proofs). However, he has a rather optimistic bottom-line: the model has its value in playing the role of a test-bed for conducting the sanity check for cryptographic schemes. He further hopes that in the future the model may show more value to be recommended.

Halevi's conclusion (§6.3 of [66]) involves an event of seemingly non-negligible probability. He regards that the current success of this methodology is due to pure luck: "all the current schemes that are proven secure in the random oracle model happen to be secure also in the real world for no reason." His bottom line: today's standards should be around the schemes with proof in the ROM rather than be around those without. After all, this is rather an optimistic bottom line.

### 15.2.7    The Author's View on the Value of the Random Oracle Model

The author of this book has his own view on the value of the ROM-based security proof. In order to be objective about the content we have studied so far in this chapter, let me confine my observation to the case of the RSA-OAEP encryption scheme.

The ROM-based security proof for the RSA-OAEP essentially reveals the following fact:

> If the padding scheme is a truly random function, then the padding result output from OAEP is a "plaintext" in an ideal world: it has a uniformly random distribution in the plaintext space of the RSA function. Thus, our investigation on the strength of the RSA function being used in the ideal world in §9.2 concludes that the easiest way to break the IND-CCA2 security is to solve the RSA problem first and then to do what the decryption algorithm does.

Thus, the ROM-based proof suggests that for a real world padding-based encryption scheme which uses real world hash functions rather than ROs, the most vulnerable point to mount an attack is the hash functions used in the scheme. In order to reach a high confidence about a padding based encryption scheme, we should pay much attention on the design of hash function and its inputting randomness.

From this point of view. we consider that an ROM-based technique for security proof manifests its importance in that it suggests where to focus the attention for careful design.

## 15.3    The Cramer-Shoup Public-key Cryptosystem

Another well-known provably IND-CCA2-secure and practically efficient public-key cryptosystem is the **Cramer-Shoup public-key cryptosystem** [85], named after its inventors Cramer and Shoup.

## 15.3.1     Provable Security Under Standard Intractability Assumptions

We have just seen the general methodology for formally provable security: to "reduce" an alleged attack on a cryptographic scheme to a solution to a reputably hard problem (i.e., to make use of an allegedly successful attacker as a black box to solve a reputably hard problem). We desire such a "reduction to contradiction" proof to have the following two important properties.

**Property 15.1:** Desirable Properties for "Reduction to Contradiction"

   i) The reduction should be efficient; ideally, an allegedly successful attacker for a cryptographic scheme should be able to solve a hard problem underlying the scheme in an effort similar to that for mounting the attack.

   ii) The intractability assumptions which are required for a scheme being secure should be as weak as possible; ideally, for a public-key encryption scheme based on an one-way trapdoor function (OWTF, notice: OWTP is a special case of OWTF), the only assumption for the scheme to become provably secure should be the intractability of the one-way trapdoor function.

Property 15.1.(i) has a practical importance: an inefficient reduction, even if it is in polynomial time, may provide no practical relation at all between an attack and a solution to a hard problem. For example, if a reduction relation is a polynomial of degree 8 where the security parameter is the usual case of 1024, then the time complexity for the reduction is at the level of $1024^8 = 2^{80}$. Under such a reduction, while an attacker may enjoy an efficient attack which breaks a scheme as fast as $10^{-6}$ second, the reduction using this attacker will only solve a hard problem in 38 billion years! Such provable security is not only certainly useless, but also may not constitute any *contradiction* for qualifying a mathematical proof: known methods for solving the reputably hard problem may well be far less costly than the figure given by the reduction! In fact, as we have seen in §15.2.5, even a reduction measured by a degree-2 polynomial can already be regarded as invalid for applications using a quite standard size of security parameters.

One may think that the desired Property 15.1.(ii) is less practically important since it seems merely to go with a general principle in mathematical proof: if weakening of assumptions does not restrict the derivation of a proof then a proof should only be based on the weakened assumptions. While pursuing a beautiful proof is certainly an important part of the motivation, the importance of Property 15.1.(ii) is more on the practical side. The importance of Property 15.1.(ii) is especially true in the design of cryptographic systems; weaker assumptions are easier to satisfy using more practical and available cryptographic constructions, and consequently, cryptographic systems using weaker assumptions provide a higher security confidence than those using stronger assumptions.

We have seen that the ROM-based proof for RSA-OAEP does not satisfy Property 15.1.(i) to the ideal extent in that the reduction is not tight enough for standard size of RSA moduli. Moreover, the ROM-based proof for RSA-OAEP does meet Property 15.1.(ii) very well. This is because the proof not only needs the intractability of the RSA function (the RSA assumption, Assumption 8.3), it also needs a very much stronger assumption: hash functions used in the OAEP construction should have the random oracle property. We say that this assumption is very strong, in fact, it is unreasonably strong: as we have discussed in §10.3.1.2 that there exists no random oracle in the real world; consequently, this assumption is mathematically unsatisfiable. Indeed, speaking in practical terms, what we can obtain from the proof of the RSA-OAEP is that we must use high quality hash functions in the construction of the RSA-OAEP scheme. Unfortunately, this is not an absolute confidence which a mathematical proof should provide.

A formal proof of security for a public-key cryptosystem relying solely on the intractability of the underlying OWTP of the cryptosystem is said to be a proof under **standard intractability assumption(s).**. Such a proof establishes security in the real world: it proves that a cryptosystem cannot be broken without breaking the underlying intractability assumption(s).

There are a number of provably secure (in the IND-CCA2 mode) cryptosystems based on standard intractability assumptions, the NM-CCA2 (equivalent to IND-CCA2) secure scheme of Dolev et al. [101] is an example. However, as we have discussed in §14.5.3, the need for using NIZK proof in that scheme makes it unattractive for practical applications.

The Cramer-Shoup public-key cryptosystem [85] is the first public-key cryptosystem which is practically efficient and provably IND-CCA2 secure under a standard intractability assumption. We shall also see that the scheme has a tight "reduction to contradiction" proof of security: a linear reduction. So the Cramer-Shoup public-key encryption scheme meets the two desirable properties in Property 15.1 to the ideal quality.

Let us now introduce the Cramer-Shoup scheme.

## 15.3.2   The Cramer-Shoup Scheme

The Cramer-Shoup public-key encryption scheme is a CCA2 enhancement of the semantically secure ElGamal encryption scheme (see §14.3.5). As in the case of the semantically secure ElGamal encryption scheme, the standard intractability assumption underlying the security of the Cramer-Shoup scheme is the decisional Diffie-Hellman (DDH) assumption. The reader may like to review Definition 13.1 in §13.3.4.3 for the DDH problem, and Assumption 14.2 in §14.3.5 for the DDH assumption.

The Cramer-Shoup cryptosystem is specified in Alg 15.1.

---

**Algorithm 15.1:** The Cramer-Shoup Public-key Cryptosystem

**Key Parameters**
Let $G$ be an abelian group of a large prime order $q$. The plaintext space is $G$;
($*$ we assume there exists an encoding scheme to code any plaintext as a bit string into $G$ and decode it back; given $\text{desc}(G)$, such an encoding scheme can be easily realized, see, e.g., §14.3.5 $*$)

To set up a user's key material, user Alice performs the following steps:

1. pick two random elements $g_1, g_2 \in_U G$;

2. pick five random integers $x_1, x_2, y_1, y_2, z \in_U [0, q)$;

3. compute $\quad c \leftarrow g_1^{x_1} g_2^{x_2}, \quad d \leftarrow g_1^{y_1} g_2^{y_2}, \quad h \leftarrow g_1^z$;

4. choose a cryptographic hash function $H : G^3 \mapsto [0, q)$;

5. publicizes $(g_1, g_2, c, d, h, H)$ as public key, keeps $(x_1, x_2, y_1, y_2, z)$ as private key.

**Encryption**
To send a confidential message $m \in G$ to Alice, the sender Bob picks random integer $r \in_U [0, q)$ and computes

$$u_1 \leftarrow g_1^r, \quad u_2 \leftarrow g_2^r, \quad e \leftarrow h^r m, \quad \alpha \leftarrow H(u_1, u_2, e), \quad v \leftarrow c^r d^{r\alpha}.$$

The ciphertext is $(u_1, u_2, e, v)$.

**Decryption**
To decrypt ciphertext $(u_1, u_2, e, v)$, Alice performs the following steps:

1. $\alpha \leftarrow H(u_1, u_2, e)$;

2. output $\begin{cases} m \leftarrow e/u_1^z & \text{if } u_1^{x_1+y_1\alpha} u_2^{x_2+y_2\alpha} = v \\ \text{REJECT} & \text{otherwise} \end{cases}$

It is easy to see that part of the ciphertext $(u_1, e)$ is exactly the ciphertext pair of the semantically secure ElGamal cryptosystem. By Theorem 14.2 (in §14.3.5), we already know that the Cramer-Shoup scheme is IND-CPA secure under the DDH assumption.

Like any CCA2-secure encryption scheme, the decryption procedure has a data-integrity validating step in the decryption procedure. Suppose that the ciphertext has not been altered en route to Alice. Then we have

$$u_1^{x_1+y_1\alpha}u_2^{x_2+y_2\alpha} = (u_1^{x_1}u_2^{x_2})(u_1^{y_1\alpha}u_2^{y_2\alpha}) = (g_1^{rx_1}g_2^{rx_2})(g_1^{ry_1\alpha}g_2^{ry_2\alpha}) = c^r d^{r\alpha} = v.$$

Upon passing this data-integrity validating step, the rest of the decryption procedure follows that of the semantically secure ElGamal cryptosystem. Later we shall see that this data-integrity validating step is very effective: it virtually stops any hope of constructing a valid ciphertext without using the specified encryption procedure.

A reader might want to ask the following question:

"Why is the security of the scheme based solely on the DDH assumption? Since the data-integrity validating step uses a hash function $H$, why is the scheme's security not also based on some hash function property, e.g., the random oracle property?"

Of course, the hash function used in the scheme must not be a weak one. However, we should notice that the security service used in the data-integrity validating step is solely the one-way-ness of the hash function. There is no need to use the random oracle property. For example, hash function $H(x)$ can be implemented by $g^x$ in the same group $G$, and thereby we will only use the one-way-ness of the discrete logarithm (DL) problem (see Definition 8.2 in §8.4). The associated intractability assumption is the discrete logarithm (DL) assumption (see Assumption 8.2 in §8.4) which is not only standard, but also is weaker than the DDH assumption in the same group; that is, if we use the DDH assumption in $G$, the DL assumption must also be in place in $G$. It is from this point of view, we say that the security of the scheme can be solely based on the DDH assumption. In contrast, as we have witnessed in Shoup's attack on an $f$-OAEP (§15.2.3.3), a security proof for $f$-OAEP cannot solely be based on the one-way-ness property, be it that of the hash functions used in the OAEP construction, or that of the underlying intractability.

### 15.3.2.1 The Performance

At first glance, it appears that the Cramer-Shoup cryptosystem is associated with much larger keys and many more exponentiations in comparison with the ElGamal cryptosystem. However, a closer examination will reveal that the difference is not so substantial.

A public key of the scheme consists of five elements in $G$, increased from a two-element public key in the case of ElGamal. The size of a ciphertext is a quadruple in $G$, doubling the size of that of ElGamal. Encryption requires "five" (but in fact, four, see in a moment) exponentiations, increased from two exponentiations in the case of ElGamal. Decryption requires "three" (in fact two) exponentiations, increased from one exponentiation in the case of ElGamal.

Now let us explain why encryption (decryption) only needs four (two) exponentiations instead of five (three) of them as obviously specified in the scheme. This is because the product of two exponentiations in the formulation of $g^x h^y$ can be computed at the cost of a single exponentiation. Alg 15.2 specifies this method. It is easy to see that the algorithm terminates in $\max(|x|, |y|)$ steps of the well-known "square-and-multiply" operation and outputs the correct result. Notice that this algorithm and in fact throughout our introduction to the Cramer-Shoup scheme, we have been omitting the presentation of the group operation. Indeed, $G$ can be any abelian group in which the DDH assumption holds.

After our examination on the performance of the Cramer-Shoup cryptosystem, we can conclude: in both communication bandwidth and computation, the overhead of the Cramer-Shoup cryptosystem is roughly twice that of the ElGamal cryptosystem.

### 15.3.3  Proof of Security

If the reader only wants to know how to encrypt in Cramer-Shoup with a fit-for-application security, then Alg 15.1 has provided adequate "know-how" information and the reader can thereby proceed to §15.4. The text between here and §15.4 is "know-why" material: it answers why the Cramer-Shoup cryptosystem has a fit-for-application security. We will try to provide the answer in an intuitive manner.

The reader who decides to follow our "know-why" route should be relieved to know that there is no need of any advanced mathematical knowledge in order to understand the technique for the proof of security for the Cramer-Shoup cryptosystem. A very basic understanding of the group theory which we have introduced in §5.2 plus an elementary knowledge of linear algebra (we shall state the fact when it is used) will suffice.

Proof of security for the Cramer-Shoup cryptosystem follows the "reduction to contradiction" methodology for formally provable security: "reducing" a hard problem supported by the underlying intractability assumption to an alleged IND-CCA2 attack. In the Cramer-Shoup cryptosystem, the hard problem is the following one:

> Let $G$ be a group of a prime order $q$, and let $(g_1, g_2, u_1, u_2) \in G^4$ be an arbitrary quadruple with $g_1 \neq 1$, $g_2 \neq 1$. Answer the question: Is $(g_1, g_2, u_1, u_2)$ a Diffie-Hellman quadruple? That is, whether or not

**Algorithm 15.2:** Product of Exponentiations

INPUT    $g, h \in A$, where $A$ is an algebraic structure;
$x, y$: integers in interval $(0, \#A)$;
$\text{Exp}(u, z)$: single exponentiation which returns $u^z$;
(* e.g., using Alg 4.3 for Exp *)

OUTPUT    $g^x h^y$.

1. if ( $|x| > |y|$ )

   {

   $u \leftarrow \text{Exp}(g,\ x \ (\text{mod } 2^{|x|-|y|}))$;

   (* exponentiation uses the least $|x| - |y|$ significant bits of $x$ *)

   $x \leftarrow x \div 2^{|x|-|y|}$ (* "$\div$:" division in integers; the operation chops the lease significant $|x| - |y|$ bits off $x$, and hence now $|x| = |y|$ *)

   }

2. if ( $|y| > |x|$ )

   {

   $u \leftarrow \text{Exp}(h,\ y \ (\text{mod } 2^{|y|-|x|}))$;

   $y \leftarrow y \div 2^{|y|-|x|}$

   }

3. $v \leftarrow gh$; (* below this line $|x| = |y|$ *)

4. while ( $x \neq 0$ ) do

   {

   (a) $u \leftarrow u^2$;

   (b) if ( $x \ (\text{mod } 2) == 1 \wedge y \ (\text{mod } 2) == 1$ ) $u \leftarrow uv$;

   (c) if ( $x \ (\text{mod } 2) == 1 \wedge y \ (\text{mod } 2) == 0$ ) $u \leftarrow ug$;

   (d) if ( $x \ (\text{mod } 2) == 0 \wedge y \ (\text{mod } 2) == 1$ ) $u \leftarrow uh$;

   (e) $x \leftarrow x \div 2$; $y \leftarrow y \div 2$; (* throw away the least significant bit *)

   }

5. return( $u$ ).

   (* total number of "square-and-multiply:" $\max(|x|, |y|)$ *)

existing integers $a, b \in [0, q)$ such that

$$g_2 = g_1^a, \quad u_1 = g_1^b, \quad u_2 = g_1^{ab}? \tag{15.3.1}$$

Since $G$ is of prime a order, $g_1 \neq 1$ is a generator of $G$ (Corollary 5.3) and hence there always exists integers $a, b \in [0, q)$ to satisfy the first two equations in (15.3.1). That is why we have only put the question mark of the third equation. It is routine to check that holding of the three equations in (15.3.1) is equivalent to

$$\log_{g_1} u_1 = \log_{g_2} u_2 \pmod{q}.$$

By the Decisional Diffie-Hellman assumption (Assumption 14.2), this question is a hard problem for the general case of an abelian group.

### 15.3.3.1    A Top-level Description for the Security Proof Technique

Suppose there exists an attacker $\mathcal{A}$ who can break the Cramer-Shoup cryptosystem in the IND-CCA2 mode with a non-negligible advantage. We shall construct an efficient reduction algorithm to enable our special agent, Simon Simulator, to answer a Decisional Diffie-Hellman question.

The input to Simon is an *arbitrary* quadruple $(g_1, g_2, u_1, u_2) \in G^4$ where $g_1 \neq 1$ and $g_2 \neq 1$. This quadruple may be a Diffie-Hellman quadruple, if this is the case we denote $(g_1, g_2, u_1, u_2) \in \mathbf{D}$; or it may not be a Diffie-Hellman quadruple, if this is the case we denote $(g_1, g_2, u_1, u_2) \notin \mathbf{D}$.

Using the input values, Simon can construct a public key $PK = (g_1, g_2, c, d, h, H)$ for $\mathcal{A}$ to use, and during the IND-CCA2 attack game played with $\mathcal{A}$, Simon can also, upon $\mathcal{A}$'s request, construct a challenge ciphertext $C^* = (u_1, u_2, e, v)$ which encrypts a chosen plaintext $m_b \in_U \{m_0, m_1\}$ ($m_0, m_1$ are chosen by $\mathcal{A}$, but the bit $b$ is hidden from $\mathcal{A}$).

The challenge ciphertext $C^*$ has the following two properties:

i) If $(g_1, g_2, u_2, u_2) \in \mathbf{D}$, then $C^*$ is a valid Cramer-Shoup ciphertext which encrypts $m_b$ under the public key $PK$. We shall see the validity of $C^*$ in §15.3.3.3 and §15.3.3.4. Also, whether using the given public key or not, $\mathcal{A}$ can get cryptanalysis training courses which will be precisely simulated by Simon. We shall see the exact precision of the simulated cryptanalysis training courses in §15.3.3.5. So in this case, Simon asks $\mathcal{A}$ to release its attacking advantage to the full capacity.

ii) If $(g_1, g_2, u_2, u_2) \notin \mathbf{D}$, then the challenge ciphertext $C^*$ encrypts $m_b$ in Shannon's information-theoretical security sense (i.e., perfect encryption, see §7.5), that is, the ciphertext will be uniformly distributed in the entire ciphertext space. We shall see Shannon's perfect encryption in §15.3.3.4. Moreover, we shall also see in §15.3.3.5 that the quality of Shannon's perfect encryption cannot be compromised by the cryptanalysis training courses delivered to $\mathcal{A}$. So in this case, $\mathcal{A}$ cannot have any advantage whatsoever!

It is the difference in the respective advantages in these two cases that makes $\mathcal{A}$ a good teacher for Simon to answer the Decisional Diffie-Hellman question.

Let us now construct a "reduction to contradiction."

### 15.3.3.2    The Reduction

The reduction involves the following steps:

1. On input $(g_1, g_2, u_1, u_2) \in G^4$, Simon will construct a public key for the Cramer-Shoup cryptosystem, and send this public key to $\mathcal{A}$; the method for the public key construction will be described in §15.3.3.3.

2. Simon will provide $\mathcal{A}$ with needed pre-challenge cryptanalysis training course; the method for Simon to simulate $\mathcal{O}$'s decryption procedure will be described in §15.3.3.5.

3. Simon will receive from $\mathcal{A}$ a pair of chosen plaintext $m_0, m_1$, will flip a fair coin $b \in_U \{0, 1\}$, and will encrypt $m_b$ to construct a challenge ciphertext $C^*$ and will send $C^*$ to $\mathcal{A}$; the method for Simon to simulate $\mathcal{O}$'s encryption procedure will be described in §15.3.3.5.

4. Simon will continue providing $\mathcal{A}$ with needed post-challenge cryptanalysis training course by simulating $\mathcal{O}$'s decryption procedure.

5. Simon will finally receive from $\mathcal{A}$ an educated guess on the bit $b$; upon this time, Simon will be able to answer the question whether $(g_1, g_2, u_1, u_2) \in \mathbf{D}$ or $(g_1, g_2, u_1, u_2) \notin \mathbf{D}$.

Fig 15.4 provides an illustration of the reduction. It is an attacking game played between the IND-CCA2 attacker $\mathcal{A}$ and Simon Simulator. Simon has taken over all communication links of $\mathcal{A}$ so that $\mathcal{A}$ can interact only with Simon. For Simon, the attacking game is a simulated one, however, as we shall see that because the simulation is perfect in quality, $\mathcal{A}$ cannot discern the simulation from a real attack.

### 15.3.3.3    Public Key Construction

Using the input quadruple $(g_1, g_2, u_1, u_2) \in G^4$, Simon constructs public-key as follows: he picks

$$x_1, x_2, y_1, y_2, z_1, z_2 \in_U [0, q)$$

and computes

$$c \leftarrow g_1^{x_1} g_2^{x_2}, \quad d \leftarrow g_1^{y_1} g_2^{y_2}, \quad h \leftarrow g_1^{z_1} g_2^{z_2}. \tag{15.3.2}$$

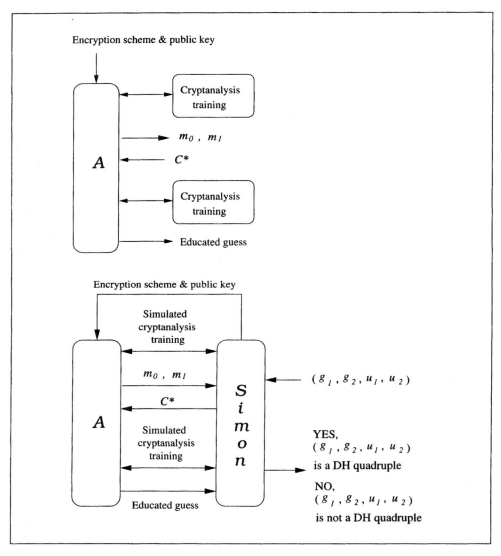

**Figure 15.4.** Reduction from the DDH Problem to an Attack on the Cramer-Shoup Cryptosystem

Simon also chooses a cryptographic hash function $H$. The public key for $\mathcal{A}$ to use is

$$(g_1, g_2, c, d, h, H).$$

The private key that Simon will use is

$$(x_1, x_2, y_1, y_2, z_1, z_2).$$

The reader may have already noticed that part of the public key, namely the $h$ component, is different from that specified in Alg 15.1. Let us explain that this is not a problem. We first show that the $h$ component of the public key constructed by Simon is perfectly valid.

For $h = g_1^{z_1} g_2^{z_2}$ with $g_1 \neq 1$, we note that $g_1$ is a generator of $G$ (Corollary 5.3) and hence $g_2 = g_1^w$ for some $w \in [0, q)$; thus

$$h = g_1^{z_1 + wz_2} = g_1^z \tag{15.3.3}$$

for $z \equiv z_1 + wz_2 \pmod{q}$. So, indeed, $h$ follows exactly the key-setup procedure in Alg 15.1.

The reader might still have the following concern:

"Since Simon does not know $w = \log_{g_1} g_2 \pmod{q}$, how can he later use $z \equiv z_1 + wz_2 \pmod{q}$ in the decryption procedure?"

In §15.3.3.5 we shall see that for any ciphertext which is valid with respect to the public key, Simon can indeed correctly use $z \equiv z_1 + wz_2 \pmod{q}$ as the "normal version" of the decryption exponent even he does not have possession of $z$.

### 15.3.3.4    Simulation of the Encryption Procedure

Upon receipt of two chosen plaintext messages $m_0, m_1$ from $\mathcal{A}$, Simon tosses an unbiased coin $b \in_U \{0, 1\}$, and encrypts $m_b$ as follows:

$$e = u_1^{z_1} u_2^{z_2} m_b, \quad \alpha = H(u_1, u_2, e), \quad v = u_1^{x_1 + y_1 \alpha} u_2^{x_2 + y_2 \alpha}.$$

The challenge ciphertext $C^*$ is $(u_1, u_2, e, v)$.

The reader may have noticed again that this encryption procedure is different from the normal encryption procedure where $e$ should be computed as

$$e = h^r m_b$$

for some $r \in [0, q)$.

However, this should cause no problem at all. Instead, the difference is vitally important for the proof of security. Let us explain the crux by considering the following two cases:

i) $(g_1, g_2, u_1, u_2) \in \mathbf{D}$. In this case, because there exists $r \in [0, q)$ such that $u_1 = g_1^r$, $u_2 = g_2^r$, we have

$$u_1^{z_1} u_2^{z_2} = (g_1^r)^{z_1} (g_2^r)^{z_2} = (g_1^{z_1} g_2^{z_2})^r = h^r.$$

So the simulated encryption is exactly a valid Cramer-Shoup encryption under the given public key. This is exactly what we desire for as in this case we want $\mathcal{A}$ to show its attacking advantage in the full capacity.

ii) $(g_1, g_2, u_1, u_2) \notin \mathbf{D}$. In this case, there exists integers $r_1, r_2 \in [0, q)$ with $r_1 \neq r_2 \pmod{q}$, $u_1 = g_1^{r_1}$ and $u_2 = g_2^{r_2}$. Since $g_1 \neq 1$ is a generator of $G$, there exists $\log_{g_1} g_2$, $\log_{g_1} h$, $\log_{g_1}(e/m_0)$, and $\log_{g_1}(e/m_1)$.

To make our exposition clearer, we may consider that $\mathcal{A}$ is now (i.e., in this case only) computationally unbounded. Given $e$ in the challenge ciphertext $C^*$, with its unbounded computational power, $\mathcal{A}$ can see the following two linear equation systems on two unknown integers $(z_1, z_2)$:

$$\begin{pmatrix} 1 & \log_{g_1} g_2 \\ r_1 & r_2 \log_{g_1} g_2 \end{pmatrix} \begin{pmatrix} z_1 \\ z_2 \end{pmatrix} = \begin{pmatrix} \log_{g_1} h \\ \log_{g_1}(e/m_0) \end{pmatrix} \pmod{q} \qquad (15.3.4)$$

$$\begin{pmatrix} 1 & \log_{g_1} g_2 \\ r_1 & r_2 \log_{g_1} g_2 \end{pmatrix} \begin{pmatrix} z_1 \\ z_2 \end{pmatrix} = \begin{pmatrix} \log_{g_1} h \\ \log_{g_1}(e/m_1) \end{pmatrix} \pmod{q}. \qquad (15.3.5)$$

With $(g_1, g_2, u_1, u_2) \notin \mathbf{D}$, we have $r_1 \neq r_2 \pmod{q}$; also notice $\log_{g_1} g_2 \neq 0 \pmod{q}$ (since $g_2 \neq 1$). So the left-hand side matrix is of the full rank, 2, and so both systems have a unique integer solution for the pair $(z_1, z_2)$. There is no way for $\mathcal{A}$ to verify which of the two cases is the correct one. Thus, even computationally unbounded, $\mathcal{A}$ can have absolutely no idea whether $m_0$ or $m_1$ is encrypted under $C^*$. So for this case, $C^*$ encrypts $m_b$ in Shannon's information-theoretical security sense, and so $\mathcal{A}$ can have no advantage whatsoever!

We must point out that, so far, the exact Cramer-Shoup encryption in case (i), or Shannon's information-theoretically secure encryption in case (ii) are only true up to the CPA mode. That is, the qualities of the respective cases of the simulated encryption hold if $\mathcal{A}$ is passive. Our attacker is not so feeble! Remember, $\mathcal{A}$ entitles cryptanalysis training courses even after receipt of the challenge ciphertext. For example, if in case (ii) $\mathcal{A}$ can obtain a third linear system in addition to (15.3.4) and (15.3.5), maybe as a result of the CCA2 training course, then we can no longer claim Shannon's information-theoretical security of the encryption.

We shall see in the next section how the qualities of the two cases of the simulated encryption will be maintained throughout the cryptanalysis training courses which an IND-CCA2 attacker enjoys.

### 15.3.3.5 Simulation of the Decryption Procedure

Upon receipt of a ciphertext $C = (U_1, U_2, E, V)$ from $\mathcal{A}$, Simon will first conduct the data-integrity validating procedure specified in Alg 15.1. If the test yields YES, then the ciphertext is deemed valid. Simon then computes

$$m = E/(U_1^{z_1} U_2^{z_2}),\tag{15.3.6}$$

and returns $m$ to $\mathcal{A}$ as the decryption result. If the test yields NO, then the ciphertext is deemed invalid and Simon will return REJECT as the decryption result.

We will state and prove in a moment Theorem 15.1 which claims that a valid ciphertext $C = (U_1, U_2, E, V)$ implies $(g_1, g_2, U_1, U_2) \in \mathbf{D}$ with probability $1 - \frac{1}{q}$. So there exists $R \in [0, q)$ such that $U_1 = g_1^R$, $U_2 = g_2^R$. Thus,

$$U_1^{z_1} U_2^{z_2} = g_1^{Rz_1} g_2^{Rz_2} = (g_1^{z_1} g_2^{z_2})^R = h^R.\tag{15.3.7}$$

Thus we see that the simulated decryption performed by Simon in (15.3.6) is correct, except for a negligible probability $\frac{1}{q}$. This clarifies the doubt we have left over at the end of §15.3.3.3 on how Simon can properly decrypt without "the normal version" of the private exponent $z \equiv z_1 + z_2 \log_{g_1} g_2 \pmod{q}$.

Simon's ability to conduct correct decryption for valid ciphertexts permits Simon to offer $\mathcal{A}$ proper cryptanalysis training courses which $\mathcal{A}$ entitles as an IND-CCA2 attacker.

We now show that the cryptanalysis training courses will not compromise the perfect qualities for the challenge ciphertext hiding $m_b$, which we have established in §15.3.3.4.

For any valid ciphertext submitted by $\mathcal{A}$, the returned decryption result will only confirm $\mathcal{A}$ (15.3.7) in which the integer pair $(z_1, z_2)$ is defined by $(U_1, U_2, h^R)$ *exactly* the same way as the pair is defined by the public key components $(g_1, g_2, h)$ in the third equation in (15.3.2). So no information about $z_1, z_2$ in addition to what has already been shown in the public key can be obtained by $\mathcal{A}$. Therefore, if $\mathcal{A}$ submits valid ciphertexts, then the cryptanalysis training courses are useless for it.

In order not to waste the precious cryptanalysis training opportunity, $\mathcal{A}$ must submit ciphertexts such that for $C = (U_1, U_2, E, V)$, it holds $(g_1, g_2, U_1, U_2) \notin \mathbf{D}$. If such a ciphertext passes Simon's validating step, then a numerical decryption result will be returned to $\mathcal{A}$ and this decryption result might relate to the challenge ciphertext in some way which may only be known to $\mathcal{A}$. Since it is supposed that $\mathcal{A}$ is very clever, we can never be sure, in the case of $(g_1, g_2, U_1, U_2) \notin \mathbf{D}$, how the returned decryption result may relate to the challenge ciphertext. Should $\mathcal{A}$ be confirmed of a hidden relation, then we could no longer claim that the encryption of $m_b$ is exactly under the Cramer-Shoup scheme for case (i), or is information-theoretically secure for case (ii), as we have established in §15.3.3.4 under the CPA mode.

Fortunately, if $\mathcal{A}$ somehow manages to come up with a ciphertext $(U_1, U_2, E, V)$ such that $(g_1, g_2, U_1, U_2) \notin \mathbf{D}$, it will be promptly replied with REJECT. This is due to Theorem 15.1 which we shall state and prove in a very short moment. As we shall see, the rejection probability is at least $1 - \frac{1}{q}$. Notice that in the remaining probability of $\frac{1}{q}$, there is no need for $\mathcal{A}$ to obtain any clue from Simon by taking the trouble to submit a ciphertext; $\mathcal{A}$ can always help itself to guess anything in $G$ correctly with probability $\frac{1}{q}$ since $G$ is only of size $q$.

Thus, $\mathcal{A}$ cannot use its "cleverness" by submitting bad ciphertexts and hoping not to be rejected.

The probability for constructing a bad ciphertext and escaping rejection can be established as follows.

**Theorem 15.1:** *Let $(g_1, g_2, c, d, h, H)$ be a public key for the Cramer-Shoup encryption scheme in a group $G$ of a prime order $q$, where $g_1 \neq 1$ and $g_2 \neq 1$. If $(g_1, g_2, U_1, U_2) \notin \mathbf{D}$, then the successful probability for solving the following problem is bounded by $\frac{1}{q}$ regardless of what algorithm is used:*

Input:   *public key* $(g_1, g_2, c, d, h, H)$, $(U_1, U_2, E) \in G^3$;
Output: $V \in G$: $(U_1, U_2, E, V)$ *is a valid ciphertext deemed by the key owner.*

**Remark 15.1:** *We have simplified the problem of creating a valid ciphertext as to output the fourth component $V$ from a given triple $(U_1, U_2, E)$ and the public key. Treating $V$ as an input component and outputting any one of the first three ciphertext components is essentially the same problem, however since $V$ is not input to the hash function $H$, outputting $V$ makes the simplest case.*  $\square$

**Proof** To construct a valid ciphertext from the input values, an algorithm has to output $V \in G$ satisfying

$$U_1^{x_1 + y_1 \alpha} U_2^{x_2 + y_2 \alpha} = V \tag{15.3.8}$$

where $x_1, y_1, x_2, y_2$ is the private key of the owner of the input public key and $\alpha = H(U_1, U_2, E)$.

Since $G$ is of prime order $q$, $g_1 \neq 1$ is a generator of $G$ (Corollary 5.3). So we can denote $r_1 = \log_{g_1} U_1$, $r_2 = \log_{g_2} U_2$, $w = \log_{g_1} g_2$; there also exists $\log_{g_1} c$, $\log_{g_1} d$ and $\log_{g_1} V$ for any $V \in G$. Combining (15.3.8) with the construction of the public-key components $c$ and $d$ (which have been implicitly verified during the key setup time), we have the following linear system

$$\begin{pmatrix} 1 & 0 & w & 0 \\ 0 & 1 & 0 & w \\ r_1 & r_1 \alpha & w r_2 & w r_2 \alpha \end{pmatrix} \begin{pmatrix} x_1 \\ y_1 \\ x_2 \\ y_2 \end{pmatrix} = \begin{pmatrix} \log_{g_1} c \\ \log_{g_1} d \\ \log_{g_1} V \end{pmatrix} \pmod{q}. \tag{15.3.9}$$

Applying Gaussian elimination, the matrix in (15.3.9) is equivalent to

$$
\begin{pmatrix}
1 & 0 & w & 0 \\
0 & 1 & 0 & w \\
0 & 0 & w(r_2 - r_1) & w\alpha(r_2 - r_1)
\end{pmatrix}
\pmod{q}.
\qquad (15.3.10)
$$

With $(g_1, g_2, U_1, U_2) \notin \mathbf{D}$, we have $r_1 \neq r_2 \pmod{q}$; also notice $w \neq 0 \pmod{q}$ (since $g_2 \neq 1$ is also a generator of $G$). So the matrix in (15.3.10) is of the full rank, 3, i.e., the three row vectors are linearly independent. By a simple fact in linear algebra, for any $V \in G$, system (15.3.9) has (non-unique) solutions for $(x_1, y_1, x_2, y_2) \pmod{q}$.

Thus, we have proved that for the input values satisfying the theorem condition, all $q$ elements in $G$ are valid candidates for $V$, i.e., for the input values, every $V \in G$ makes $(U_1, U_2, E, V)$ a valid ciphertext. However, for the key owner, among these $q$ possibilities, there is only one single $V \in G$ satisfying her/his choice of the private key components $(x_1, y_1, x_2, y_2)$. (We should clarify that, even though for any fixed $V \in G$, the integer solutions from system (15.3.9) are not unique, however, it is very clear that any fixed integer tuple $(x_1, y_1, x_2, y_2)$ can only be mapped to a single $V \in G$.) Hence the successful probability for the problem in the theorem statement is established. □

We have, to this end, completed the security proof for the Cramer-Shoup cryptosystem.

It is easy to observe that the "reduction to contradiction" in this proof is a linear function: $\mathcal{A}$'s capability to attack the cryptosystem is identically translated to its capability to distinguish whether or not a given quadruple is in $\mathbf{D}$. We therefore say that the reductionist proof for the security of the Cramer-Shoup scheme has a tight reduction.

## 15.4   An Overview of Provably Secure Hybrid Cryptosystems

In §8.15 we have introduced hybrid cryptosystems mainly under efficiency considerations. Hybrid cryptosystems also form a general solution to IND-CCA2 secure and practical public-key encryption. In this section let us conduct an overview of a series of hybrid encryption schemes. As the number of these schemes is not small, we cannot include security proofs; interested readers may study the original papers for details.

A ciphertext output from a hybrid cryptosystem has two components: a **key encapsulation mechanism (KEM)** and a **data encapsulation mechanism (DEM)**. This KEM-DEM pair ciphertext can be written as

$$
\text{KEM} \parallel \text{DEM} = \mathcal{E}_{pk}^{\text{asym}}(K) \parallel \mathcal{E}_K^{\text{sym}}(\text{Payload\_Message}).
$$

Upon receipt of this pair, the receiver should decrypt the KEM block using her/his private key to obtain the ephemeral symmetric key $K$, and then using this key to decrypt the DEM block to retrieve Payload_Message.

If KEM is output from a provably IND-CCA2 secure asymmetric encryption scheme, then the IND property of the DEM block is then a natural result of the randomness of the ephemeral key. It is not difficult conceive that a KEM-DEM structured hybrid cryptosystem can be IND-CCA2 secure. Indeed, Hybrid schemes in a KEM-DEM structure should be regarded as the most natural approach to public-key encryption with IND-CCA2 security and practical efficiency.

We regard hybrid schemes as the most natural ones because they can encrypt messages of any length at a low overhead. In applications, data have varied lengths and in most situations have lengths larger than a length fixed by a security parameter in a public-key cryptosystem, e.g., $n$ in the case of the RSA-OAEP or $\log_2(\#G)$ in the case of the Cramer-Shoup. Because public-key cryptosystems have a much higher overhead than those of a symmetric cryptosystem, it is very likely that in applications a provably secure public-key encryption scheme, such as the RSA-OAEP and the Cramer-Shoup, is only used to form a KEM block in a hybrid scheme, while the encryption of data is done in a series of DEM blocks.

Hybrid encryption schemes include several KEM-DEM schemes proposed by Shoup [273], a scheme named FO proposed by Fujisaki and Okamoto [115], a scheme named HD-RSA proposed by Pointcheval [234], a scheme named DHAES proposed by Abdalla, Bellare and Rogaway [4], a variation of the Cramer-Shoup scheme proposed by Shoup [271], and a scheme named REACT proposed by Okamoto and Pointcheval [225].

The scheme of Fujisaki and Okamoto takes the following formulation:

$$\mathcal{E}_{pk}^{\text{hybrid}}(m) = \text{KEM} \parallel \text{DEM} = \mathcal{E}_{pk}^{\text{asym}}(\sigma, H(\sigma, m)) \parallel \mathcal{E}_{G(\sigma)}^{\text{sym}}(m),$$

where $G, H$ are hash functions. In this scheme, the decryption result from the KEM block is pair $\sigma, H(\sigma, m)$. The recipient uses $\sigma$ to "seed" the hash function $G$ to obtain a symmetric key $G(\sigma)$; then using it to decrypt the DEM block; finally, the recipient can verify the correctness of the decryption by re-evaluation $H(\sigma, m)$. So this scheme allows the recipient to detect whether the ciphertext has been modified or corrupted en route. The detection of ciphertext alteration is the main technical enabler for a cryptosystem being secure against active attackers.

The HD-RSA scheme of Pointcheval is based on an intractability problem named **dependent RSA** [235]: given an RSA ciphertext $A = r^e \pmod{N}$, find $B = (r+1)^e \pmod{N}$. This problem is apparently hard if one cannot find the $e$-th root of $A$ modulo the composite $N$ (the RSA problem). Then, the KEM block of the HD-RSA scheme is simply $A = r^e \pmod{N}$ for a random $r \in \mathbb{Z}_N^*$. The recipient as the owner of $N$ can of course extract $r$ from $A$ and then construct $B$. The scheme uses $K = G(B)$ as the symmetric key for the DEM block, as in the hybrid scheme of Shoup and that of Fujisaki-Okamoto.

The DHAES scheme of Abdalla, Bellare and Rogaway [4] is a hybrid scheme where the DEM block also attaches a message authentication code (MAC, see §10.3) as a means for data integrity validation. The two symmetric keys (one for the DEM block and one for the MAC block) are derived from a hash function formulation: $H(g^u, g^{uv})$ where $g^u$ is the KEM block and $g^v$ is the recipient's public key. Clearly, the owner of the public key $g^v$ can operate the private key $v$ on the KEM block $g^u$ to obtain $g^{uv}$, and thereby reconstruct $H(g^u, g^{uv})$ for further derivation of the two symmetric keys. Without using the private key $v$, the task of decryption seems to be something similar to solving the computational Diffie-Hellman problem (Definition 8.1). The problem for finding $H(g^u, g^{uv})$ given $g^u$, $g^v$ is called **hash Diffie-Hellman (HDH) problem**.

In DHAES, it is interesting to notice that if $g^{uv}$ is directly used as an encryption multiplier as in the cases of the ElGamal and Cramer-Shoup schemes, then semantical security will be based on a decisional problem: deciding whether or not $(g, g^u, g^v, g^{uv}(= e/m_b))$ is a Diffie-Hellman quadruple. Now in this hybrid scheme, the use of hash function prevents the easy access to the fourth element in the quadruple, and so the decisional problem seems to have been weakened to a computational problem. Remember, it is desirable to underlie security with intractability assumptions which are as weak as possible. The reader may do an exercise to show that the HDH problem lies in between the CDH problem (Definition 8.1 in §8.4) and the DDH problem (Definition 13.1 in §13.3.4.3). Of course, we must notice that the "weakening of assumption" from the DDH problem to the HDH problem is not unconditional: it needs some (hidden from our brief description) assumption on the hash function used. Unfortunately, the hidden assumption should be something very close to a random oracle one.

Shoup's hybrid scheme [271] is a "weakening of assumption" version for the Cramer-Shoup scheme. In the original Cramer-Shoup scheme (Alg 15.1), encryption of message $m$ takes the ElGamal formulation: $h^r m$. In the "weakening of assumption" version in [271], $h^r$ is hidden under a hash function $H(...; h^r)$ to stop the easy testing of the DDH problem. The hashed value $H(...; h^r)$ will be used to derive symmetric keys for encoding the DEM block and a data integrity validating mechanism. Shoup uses "hedging with hash" to name his version of "weakening of assumption."

## 15.5 Literature Notes on Practical and Provably Secure Public-key Cryptosystems

Damgård originates the work on practical public-key cryptosystems with security resilience to active attackers [89]: thwarting active attackers by including a data-integrity validating procedure in public-key cryptosystems. The method has since then become a general strategy for designing cryptosystems with provable security against active attackers. However Damgård's schemes (there are two schemes in his original work) are demonstrably insecure in the CCA2 mode (see, e.g., [313]).

Zheng and Seberry propose practical encryption and digital signature schemes which aim to be secure in the CCA2 mode [313, 312]. The general idea in their scheme is to enhance one-way function based textbook public-key schemes (ElGamal based) using hash functions. This is an important idea which is later developed to the random oracle model for provable security which we have studied in §15.2. The security proof in the IND-CCA2 mode provided in [312] is based on a non-standard assumption called "sole-samplability of spaces induced by functions" (together with the computational Diffie-Hellman assumption). Soldera discovered that one of the schemes of Zheng and Seberry is actually IND-CCA2 insecure [282, 283].

In the case of RSA based randomized padding schemes, upon discovery of the incompleteness in the security proof for the RSA-OAEP (§15.2.3.3), Shoup proposes a modification to OAEP called OAEP+ [272] and obtains security proof which is a tighter reduction than that of the security proof for the RSA-OAEP obtained by Fujisaki et al. [116]. The reduction becomes tighter because Simon's advantage to invert the RSA function is linearly related to Malice's advantage to break the cryptosystem. However, because Simon's time to invert the RSA function is still a quadratic function of the number of RO queries which Malice is entitled to make, and hence the reduction remains inefficient (review the similar case for the RSA-OAEP in §15.2.5). Boneh also proposes modifications to OAEP, named Simple-OAEP (SAEP) and Simple-OAEP+ (SAEP+) [50]. However, these schemes have a low bandwidth of message recovery (we will discuss the problem of low bandwidth of message recovery with some randomized padding schemes in §16.4.4.2). Recently, Coron et al. [84] show that another randomized padding scheme for RSA, named Probabilistic Signature Scheme with message Recovery (PSS-R, originally proposed by Bellare and Rogaway [27], details see the next chapter) can also be used for encryption. Essentially, these authors insightfully realize that, with the use of hash functions, data-integrity validation in a padding scheme needn't be based on introducing additional redundancy such as a string of zeros as in the case of the RSA-OAEP. We will see this scheme in the next chapter. Like SAEP and SAEP+, PSS-R has a low bandwidth of message recovery when it is used for RSA encryption (see §16.4.4.2).

Like the RSA-OAEP scheme, the randomized padding schemes mentioned in the preceding paragraph all are provably secure in the IND-CCA2 mode under the ROM. However, because provable IND-CCA2 security for the RSA-OAEP has been re-established (§15.2.4), because the RSA-OAEP has long been the RSA encryption standard, and most importantly, because OAEP turns out to have the highest bandwidth for message recovery, it is not clear whether these new modifications can gain a similar momentum as the RSA-OAEP has obtained as the standard for RSA encryption.

Padding techniques for OWTP can result in optimally efficient schemes. However, OWTP is actually a very rare function. RSA and Rabin (over quadratic residues) are probably the only OWTPs among common public-key cryptographic functions. Moreover, the random oracle model based security proof (or argument) for padding schemes have so far fail to derive a tight "reduction to contradiction." Some researchers consider to devise provably secure schemes for general one-way function based public-key cryptographic functions with more tight reductions for provably security. Some authors devise schemes which extend padding based schemes from OWTP to general one-way trapdoor functions. Many public-key cryptographic functions are not permutations (e.g., the ElGamal function is not a permutation). Therefore such extensions are useful. Fujisaki and Okamoto [114] and Pointcheval [236] propose two such generalized schemes. However, these generalized schemes are not optimally efficient: re-encryption is required in the decryption time as the means to detect errors. Since decryption is often operated in a slow device, such as smart cards, decryption-heavy schemes should be avoided.

Of course, a number of hybrid cryptosystems form a family of provably IND-CCA2 secure and practical public-key encryption schemes. Detailed literature notes of this family have been overviewed in §15.4.

Finally, we should remind the reader that for practical public-key encryption schemes, the data-integrity validating mechanism used in the provably IND-CCA2 secure encryption schemes only provides a security service which we have termed "data integrity without source identification," or "integrity from Malice" (review §10.5). In most applications in the real world, this notion of security service is inadequate. The common approach to achieving source identification in public-key cryptography is to use digital signatures.

Recently, a novel public-key cryptographic primitive named **signcryption** has emerged. A signcryption scheme combines encryption and signature in one go. The motivation of the combination is to achieve efficient public-key encryption at the same time to offer additional security services important for electronic commerce applications: message source identification and non-repudiation. As this new cryptographic primitive appeared after the wide spreading of the notion of provable security for public-key cryptosystems (originated in 1997 by Zheng [311]), researchers have the readiness to apply the provable security strategy in the design of signcryption schemes. We shall study a provably secure and practical signcryption scheme in the next chapter.

# 15.6 Chapter Summary

In this chapter we have described with detailed explanations two important public-key cryptosystems which not only have formally established fit-for-application security, i.e., provably secure under the IND-CCA2 attacking mode, but also are practically efficient: their efficiency is similar to their textbook counterparts. The encryption schemes from this chapter stride from previous bit-by-bit based solutions (e.g., those described in the preceding chapter), and hence are practical public-key encryption schemes.

The reader may consider that in a public-key cryptosystem which has data integrity verification step in the decryption time, a ciphertext encrypts a message which is "digitally signed" by the sender using the public key of the receiver. The "signature" scheme has a message recovery feature and therefore the receiver can retrieve the plaintext and verifies the "signature" using her/his private key. This thought is technically correct. The only reason we have used quotes "digitally signed," "signature," is because the "signer" can be anybody and therefore the cryptographic transformation does not provide a signature in the usual sense. Nevertheless, it is the difficulty to forge a "signature" without using the given procedure and the given public key that effectively stops an adaptive chosen-ciphertext attack. This is the main reason for such an encryption scheme (and the two practical cryptosystems introduced in this chapter) secure in CCA2 sense.

In the course of security proof for these cryptosystems, we also introduce and explain several important concepts: random oracle model for security proof (with its limitation discussed), formal proof via reduction to contradiction, and tightness of such a reduction.

We also conducted an overview on various hybrid encryption schemes which combine symmetric and asymmetric encryption techniques and achieve practical public-key cryptosystems.

Finally we provided a literature note to review the development of the subject.

## Exercises

15.1 What is the role of the random input in the RSA-OAEP algorithm? What is the role of the constant string $0^{k_1}$ in the same algorithm?

15.2 The bandwidth of an encryption algorithm is the size the plaintext it can encrypt over the value of the security parameter. Let an instantiation of the RSA-OAEP use 2048 as the security parameter and 160 as the size of the random input. What is the bandwidth of this instantiation of the RSA-OAEP?

15.3 What is the random oracle model for security proof?

15.4 What are the limitations of the random-oracle-model-based security proof?

15.5 Why must the simulation of an RO in §15.2.1 be built from a sorted list which is initially empty?

15.6 What is a "contradiction" in "reduction to contradiction" in a security proof for cryptosystems with security based on a computational complexity problem?

15.7 Why must the challenge ciphertext in a reductionist proof be random?

15.8 In the proof of security for the RSA-OAEP, why must Simon run the attacker more than once?

15.9 Why is a 1024-bit modulus for the RSA-OAEP regarded too small even though such a modulus resists the current factorization technology?

15.10 The Cramer-Shoup cryptosystem also uses a hash function. Does the security proof for the cryptosystem require this function to have a random oracle behavior?

15.11 Suppose that the Cramer-Shoup cryptosystem is modified into one which encrypts as

$$e \leftarrow h^r + m$$

(and hence decryption performs subtraction), and all other parts remain unchanged. Show that the modified scheme is CCA2 secure, i.e., any active attack can be detected. Is it IND-CCA2 secure?

15.12 Why is the cost for computing $g^x h^y \pmod{p}$ measured as that of one modulo exponentiation?

15.13 Extend Alg 15.2 to the case of $f^x g^y h^z \pmod{p}$.

15.14 What is a hybrid cryptosystem?

15.15 In applications, confidential data usually have sizes much larger than, while a symmetric encryption key have sizes much less than, a security parameter of a public-key cryptosystem. For secure transmission of such data, which of the following algorithms will you choose? (i) RSA, (ii) AES, (iii) RSA-OAEP, (iv) ElGamal, (v) Cramer-Shoup, or (vi) a hybrid cryptosystem.

# Chapter 16

# STRONG AND PROVABLE SECURITY FOR DIGITAL SIGNATURES

## 16.1 Introduction

Although in our definition for digital signature schemes (Definition 10.2 in §10.4) we stipulate an "overwhelming" probability for $\mathsf{Verify}_{pk}(m, s) = \mathsf{False}$ if $(m, s)$ is a forged message-signature pair created without using the prescribed signing procedure, we have not conducted any investigation on how overwhelming the probability should be for any signature scheme introduced in Chapter 10. Also, as we have discussed in §10.4.9, the textbook security notion of digital signatures, i.e., difficulty of forging a signature "from scratch," is too weak to be fit for applications. Therefore, security arguments for signature schemes in Chapter 10, if we have conducted any there, are too informal to provide an adequate level of confidence and too weak to be useful in practice. The real reason for having considered informal and weak security arguments in Chapter 10 is because then we were not technically ready for conducting a formal and strong security argument.

After having studied in the two preceding chapters formal methodologies for security proof for public-key encryption schemes, which include strong security notions (e.g., IND-CCA2), the "reduction-to-contradiction" philosophy, the random oracle and standard models for security proof, we are now technically ready to further study formal security analysis methodologies for digital signature schemes. Analogous to the case of enhanced security analysis for public-key encryption schemes, the following two issues will be covered in our study of enhanced security analysis for digital signature schemes:

- **Difficulty for signature forgery against the most general way of attacking digital signature schemes** The most general attack on digital signatures is **adaptive chosen-message attack**. An adaptive attacker has

in its possession the public key of a target user, and can use the user as
an **oracle signing service** provider (meaning given in §8.2) for signing any
messages of its choice. It can then adapt its queries according to the message-
signature pairs it has collected. We can consider this way of attack as the
attacker obtaining a training course from the targeted signer for forging signatures. The task for the attacker, after querying sufficiently many adaptively
chosen messages and getting respective signatures, i.e., after sufficient training, is to output a *new* message-signature pair which is valid with respect to
the targeted user's public key. Here, "new" means a message which has never
been previously signed by the user.

- **Security argument with formal evidence establishment**   This is to
  conduct a "reduction to contradiction" style of demonstration to establish security. Such a reduction of a secure signature scheme is an efficient transformation which shows that any successful forgery algorithm (e.g., under adaptive
  attack) can be used as a "blackbox" for solving a reputably hard problem in
  computational complexity. Here "contradiction" is because of a wide belief
  that there exists no efficient algorithm to solve the reputably hard problem.

Goldwasser, Micali and Rivest make systematic considerations on these two
issues for digital signatures in their seminal work published in [129]. They also realize a signature scheme which is probably invulnerable to (existentially) adaptive
chosen-message attack. That scheme uses a notion of "claw-free" permutation pairs:
informally, these are permutations $f_0$ and $f_1$ over a common domain for which it
is computationally infeasible to find a triple $(x, y, z)$ such that $f_0(x) = f_1(y) = z$.
Goldwasser et al. realize their "claw-free" permutation pairs using the integer factorization problem (see [129] for details). That signature scheme has an advantage
that it can sign any random string without adding to the string any recognizable
redundancy, e.g., without using hash functions for message formatting. However,
that scheme signs a message in a bit-by-bit manner and hence is regarded as not
ideally suitable for applications. However, the work of Goldwasser et al. [129] lays
the important foundation for the strong (i.e., fit-for-application) security notion for
digital signature schemes.

## 16.1.1   Chapter Outline

In §16.2 we introduce the strongest security notion for digital signature schemes. In
§16.3 we conduct a formal reductionist security proof for ElGamal-family signature
schemes. In §16.4 we introduce fit-for-application signature schemes which are based
on randomized padding techniques and one-way trapdoor permutations (mainly,
RSA and Rabin functions). In §16.5 we study signcryption schemes and their fit-
for-application security.

# 16.2 Strong Security Notion for Digital Signatures

We provide here necessary definitions to be used in this chapter.

First, a digital signature scheme is denoted by (Gen, Sign, Verify) and these elements are defined in Definition 10.2 (in §10.4). However, because of the general uses of cryptographic hash functions in digital signatures we have witnessed in Chapter 10 (there the usage was mostly to prevent an existential forgery), in this chapter we shall consider that Sign and Verify of a signature scheme use one or more strong hash functions. By a strong hash function we mean that, when we argue security for a signature scheme, we will formally model such a hash function used in the scheme to have the random oracle behavior described in §10.3.1.2. Indeed, all security arguments to be provided in this chapter are given under the random oracle model for security proof (review §15.2.1).

Now we provide an asymptotic definition for the game of adaptive chosen-message attack on a digital signature scheme which uses hash function(s).

**Definition 16.1: Adaptive Chosen-message Attack** *Let $k$ be a positive integer. An adaptive forger against a signature scheme* (Gen, Sign, Verify) *is a (probabilistic) polynomial-time (in $k$) algorithm. It takes as input a public key $pk$, where $(pk, sk) \leftarrow_U$* Gen$(1^k)$, *and tries to forge signatures with respect to $pk$. The forger is allowed to request, and obtain, signatures of messages of its choice. This is modeled by allowing the forger to access to the signing and hash algorithms, both polynomial (in $k$) times.*

*The forger is said to $(t(k), Adv(k))$-break the signature scheme if in time $t(k)$ with probability $Adv(k)$ it outputs a valid forgery – namely, a message-signature pair $(m, s)$ such that* Verify$_{pk}(m, s) =$ True *where $m$ is a recognizable message according the hash functions used in the scheme but is not one which has been input to* Sign *earlier by the signer. Here $t(k)$ is a polynomial, and $Adv(k)$, a significant quantity, in $k$.*

For the meaning of a significant quantity (function), review §4.6.

We have simplified the definition without stating two expressions which are for the number of times the forger makes signing and hash queries. These omitted expressions are both polynomials in $k$: since the forger is a polynomial-time (in $k$) algorithm, it can only make polynomially many (in $k$) signing and hash queries.

**Definition 16.2: Secure Signature Scheme** *Signature scheme* (Gen, Sign, Verify) *is said $(t(k), Adv(k))$-secure if there exists no forger who $(t(k), Adv(k))$-breaks the scheme for all sufficiently large $k$.*

The use of Definition 16.2 will be in a contradiction manner. Assume that a given signature scheme is $(t(k), Adv(k))$-breakable where $t(k)$ is a polynomial and

$Adv(k)$, a significant function, in $k$. A reduction transformation will be constructed which can translate $t(k)$ to $t'(k)$ and $Adv(k)$ to $Adv'(k)$ so that an underlying hard problem becomes $(t'(k), Adv'(k))$-breakable. If the reduction is efficient enough, then $t'(k)$ will be small enough and $Adv'(k)$ will be sufficiently close to $Adv(k)$ and will therefore also be significant enough. Consequently, it is widely known to be untrue that the underlying hard problem can be $(t'(k), Adv'(k))$-breakable. In this way we reach a contradiction and complete a security proof. The reader may review §15.2.5 for the meaning of an efficient reduction and the importance for a reduction to be as efficient as possible.

Similar to the cases of the "reduction-to-contradiction" techniques for public-key encryption schemes which we have studied in the preceding chapter, reductions for proving signature schemes in this chapter will also be conducted by a special agent named Simon Simulator. Simon will be playing the role of a targeted signer in interaction with the forger by issuing signatures of messages of the forger's choice. This is done via simulation of a signing oracle. In order for the forger to release its full capacity for signature forgery, the simulated signing oracle must behave indistinguishably from a true signer. Since the forger is polynomially bounded, it suffices for us to use the polynomial-time indistinguishability notion which follows Definition 4.15 (in §4.7).

In the rest of this chapter we name a forger Malice, who is an active attacker.

## 16.3 Strong and Provable Security for ElGamal-family Signatures

For a long period of time (1985–1996) after the birth of the ElGamal signature scheme (§10.4.6) and the family of such signatures (e.g., Schnorr §10.4.8.1 and DSS §10.4.8.2), it was widely believed that the difficulty of forging such a signature should somehow be related to solving the discrete logarithm in a large subgroup of a finite field. However, no formal evidence (formal proof) was ever established until 1996.

Pointcheval and Stern succeed demonstrating affirmative evidence for relating the difficulty of signature forgery under a signature scheme in the ElGamal-family signatures to that of computing discrete logarithm [237]. They do so by making use of a powerful tool: the random oracle model (ROM) for proof of security [23]. The reader may review §15.2.1 to refresh the general idea of using ROM for security proof (there, ROM-based proofs are for public-key encryption schemes). The ROM-based technique of Pointcheval and Stern is an insightful instantiation of the general ROM-based security proof technique to proving security for the ElGamal-family signatures.

## 16.3.1 Triplet ElGamal-family Signatures

Let us now introduce a typical version of the ElGamal-family signature schemes which can be provably unforgeable under ROM. A scheme in this version takes as input a signing key $sk$, a public key $pk$ and a message $M$ which is a bit string, and outputs a signature of $M$ as a triplet $(r, e, s)$. Here

- $r$ is called a **commitment**; it commits an ephemeral integer $\ell$ called a **committal** which is independent of such values used in all previous signatures; the usual form for constructing a commitment is $r = g^\ell \pmod{p}$ where $g$ and $p$ are part of the public parameters of the signature scheme;

- $e = H(M, r)$ where $H()$ is a cryptographic hash function; and

- $s$ is called a signature; it is a linear function of the commitment $r$, the committal $\ell$, the message $M$, the hash function $H()$ and the private signing key $sk$.

Let us name such a signature scheme a **triplet signature scheme**.

The original ElGamal signature scheme given in Alg 10.3 is not a triplet signature scheme because it does not use a hash function and does not resist an existential forgery (not to further consider adaptive chosen-message attack). However, the version which uses a hash function and thereby becomes existential-forgery resistant, i.e., the variation which we have described in §10.4.7.2, is a triplet version.

The Schnorr signature scheme (Alg 10.4) is also a triplet one. A signature of a message $M$ produced by the signing algorithm of the Schnorr signature scheme is $(r, e, s)$ where $e = H(M, r)$ for some hash function $H()$, although in the Schnorr scheme there is no need to send the value $r$ to the verifier since the value can be computed as $g^s y^e$.

Let us now introduce the reduction technique of Pointcheval and Stern for proving unforgeability for a triplet signature scheme. It is called a **forking reduction technique**.

## 16.3.2 Forking Reduction Technique

We have shown in §10.4.7.1 that a violation for the one-time use of an ephemeral key (committal $\ell$ or equivalently commitment $r$) in a signature scheme in triplet ElGamal-family signatures will lead to uncovering of the signing private key. The uncovering of a signing private key is an efficient solution to a hard problem: extraction of the discrete logarithm of an element (a public key) in group modulo a large prime.

A reductionist security proof for triplet ElGamal-family signature schemes makes use of this commitment replay technique to uncover the signing private key. A successful forger for such a signature scheme can be reduced, with a similar cost, to an extractor for the signing private key. Since the latter problem, extraction of the discrete logarithm of an element (a public key) in group modulo a large prime, is reputably hard (Assumption 8.2 in §8.4), the alleged successful signature forgery should also be similarly hard, where the similarity between the two efforts depends on the efficiency of the reduction.

In the ROM-based reductionist security proof for a triplet ElGamal signature scheme, the hash function is idealised by a random function called "random oracle" (RO) which has the behavior specified in §10.3.1.2. Under the ROM, all ROs are simulated by Simon Simulator. In addition, Simon will also simulate the signing procedure and so answer Malice's signature queries. Thus, Simon can provide Malice with the necessary training course which Malice is entitled to in order to prepare him well in his signature forgery task. If Malice is indeed a successful forger, then he should be educatable, and will output a forged message-signature pair with a non-negligible probability. Simon will use the forged signature to solve a hard problem, which in the case of a triplet ElGamal signature scheme, is the discrete logarithm problem in a finite field. Fig 16.1 illustrates a reduction technique in which Simon makes use of Malice to solve a hard problem.

In our description of the reduction technique of Pointcheval and Stern, which we will be giving in the next two sections, we will try to provide as much intuition as possible. As a result, our probability estimation result does not take the exact formula given by Pointcheval and Stern although our measurement follows the same logic of reasoning as theirs. In terms of the reduction tightness, our result is an upper bound in comparison to that obtained by Pointcheval and Stern. Nevertheless, our upper bound suffices to produce a reasonably meaningful contradiction for a large security parameter. The reader with a more investigative appetite is referred to [238] to study their more involved probability measurement.

### 16.3.2.1 Unforgeability under Non-adaptive Attack

Let us first consider the case of the unforgeability property of triplet ElGamal signature schemes under non-adaptive attack.

Let $(\mathsf{Gen}(1^k), \mathsf{Sign}, \mathsf{Verify})$ be an instance of the *triplet version* of the ElGamal signature scheme (i.e., the triplet version of Alg 10.3) where the prime $p$ satisfies that there exists a $k$-bit prime $q$ dividing $p - 1$ and $(p - 1)/q$ has no large prime factors.

Suppose that Malice is a successful forger against $(\mathsf{Gen}(1^k), \mathsf{Sign}, \mathsf{Verify})$. Let Simon Simulator wrap all communication channels from and to Malice as illustrated in Fig 16.1. However, under the non-adaptive attack scenario, there is no "simulated signing training" in the interaction between Malice and Simon since Malice never requests a signature.

Simon will pick a random element $y \in \mathbb{Z}_p^*$. His goal is to uncover the discrete

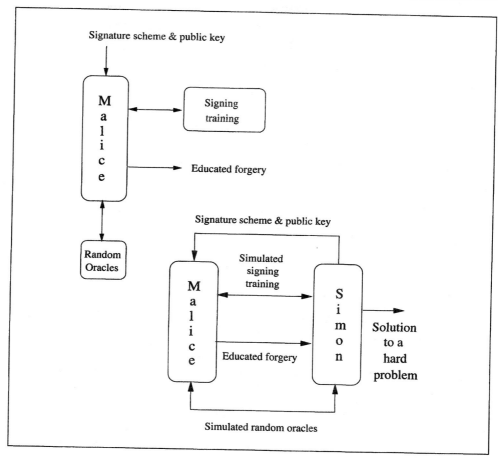

**Figure 16.1.** Reduction from a Signature Forgery to Solving a Hard Problem

logarithm of $y$ to the generator base $g$ modulo $p$, i.e., to uncover integer $x$ satisfying $y \equiv g^x \pmod{p}$. Simon will use Malice as a blackbox in such a way that Malice's successful forgery of a new signature on a chosen message will provide Simon enough information to uncover the discrete logarithm. We hope that by now the reader has become instinctively aware of the need for the input problem (i.e., $y$) to be arbitrary: otherwise, the reduction will not be a useful algorithm.

Let Malice's successful probability for signature forgery be $Adv(k)$ which is a significant quantity in $k$ and let his time spent on signature forgery be $t(k)$ which is a polynomial in $k$. We shall find out Simon's successful probability $Adv'(k)$ for discrete logarithm extraction and his time $t'(k)$ for doing the job. Of course we will relate $(t'(k), Adv'(k))$ to $(t(k), Adv(k))$.

### First Lot of Runs of Malice

Now Simon runs Malice $1/Adv(k)$ times. Since Malice is a successful forger, after having been satisfied of a condition (to be given in a moment), he will output, with probability 1 (since he has been run $1/Adv(k)$ times) a valid signature $(r, e, s)$ of message $M$ under the scheme (Gen, Sign, Verify). That is,

$$e = H(M, r),$$

$$y^r r^s \equiv g^e \pmod{p},$$

where $|e| = k$.

The condition of which Simon must satisfy Malice is that the latter should be entitled to some number of evaluations of the RO function $H$. Under the ROM, as illustrated in Fig 16.1, Malice has to make RO-queries to Simon. Simon's response is via the simulation of the RO: he simulates $H$ by maintaining an $H$-list of sorted elements $((M_i, r_i), e_i)$ (e.g., sorted by $M_i$) where $(M_i, r_i)$ are queries and $e_i$ are random answers.

Since Malice is polynomially bounded, he can only make $n = q_H$ RO queries where $q_H$ is polynomially (in $k$) bounded. Let

$$Q_1 = (M_1, r_1), Q_2 = (M_2, r_2), \ldots, Q_n = (M_n, r_i) \tag{16.3.1}$$

be $n$ distinct RO queries from Malice. Let

$$R_1 = e_1, R_2 = e_2, \ldots, R_n = e_n$$

be the $n$ answers from Simon. Since $|H| = k$, Simon's answers are uniformly random in the set $\{1, 2, 3, \ldots, 2^k\}$.

Due to the uniform randomness of Simon's answers, when Malice outputs a valid forgery $(r, e, s)$ on $M$, he must have queried $(M, r)$ and obtained the answer $e = H(M, r)$. That is, it must be the case that $(M, r) = (M_i, r_i)$ and for some $i \in [1, n]$. The probability for $(M, r)$ not having been queried is $2^{-k}$ (i.e., Malice has guessed Simon's uniformly random answer $R_i = e_i$ correctly without making a query to Simon). Considering the quantity $2^{-k}$ being negligible, we know that $((M, r), e)$ are in Simon's $H$-list.

Let us recap an important point which we must bear in mind: without making an RO-query to Simon and without using Simon's answer, Malice cannot be successful except for a minute probability value $2^{-k}$ which is negligible. With this observation, we can imagine as if Malice has been "forced" to forge a signature on one of the $n$ messages in (16.3.1).

### Second Lot of Runs of Malice to Achieve a Successful Forking

Now Malice is re-run another $1/Adv(k)$ times under exactly the same condition. That is, he will make exactly the same $n$ queries in (16.3.1). However, this time Simon will reset his $n$ answers at uniformly random.

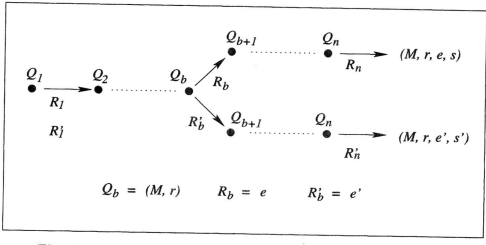

**Figure 16.2.** Successful Forking Answers to Random Oracle Queries

We must notice that since the reset answers still follow the uniform distribution in the set $\{1, 2, 3, \ldots, 2^k\}$, these answers remain being the correct ones since they have the correct distribution. (This point will be further explained in Remark 16.1 in a moment.)

After having been fed the second lot of $n$ correct answers, Malice must again fully release his forgery capacity and output, with probability 1, a new forgery $(r', e', s')$ on $M'$. Again, as we have discussed in the first lot of runs of Malice, $(M', r')$ must be a $Q_j$ in (16.3.1) for some $j \in [1, n]$ except for a minute probability value $2^{-k}$.

An event of "successful forking of Malice's RO queries," which is illustrated in Fig 16.2, occurs when in the two lots of runs of Malice the two forged message-signature pairs $(M, (r, e, s))$ and $(M', (r', e', s'))$ satisfy $(M, r) = (M', r')$. Notice that in each lot of runs of Malice, he can forge a signature for $(M_i, r_i)$ where $i \in_U [1, n]$ is uniformly random and needn't be fixed. Applying the birthday paradox (see §3.6), we know that the probability for this event to occur (i.e., $i = j = b$) is roughly $1/\sqrt{n}$. Notice: this is different from the case of fixing $i$ in the second lot of runs, which will result in the probability for successful forking (at the fixed point $i$) to be $1/n$.

Recall that $n$ is polynomially bounded, so $1/\sqrt{n}$ is a non-negligible quantity. That is, with the non-negligible probability value $1/\sqrt{n}$, Simon obtains two valid forgeries $(r, e, s)$ and $(r, e', s')$. Further notice that because in the second run Simon has reset his answers at uniformly random, we must have $e' \neq e \pmod{q}$ with the overwhelming probability value $1 - 2^{-k}$.

With a successful forking, Simon will be able to extract the targeted discrete logarithm value. Let us see how this is done.

### Extraction of Discrete Logarithm

From the two valid forgeries Simon can compute

$$y^r r^s = g^e \pmod{p},$$

$$y^r r^{s'} = g^{e'} \pmod{p}.$$

Since $g$ is a generator element modulo $p$, we can write $r = g^\ell \pmod{p}$ for some integer $\ell < p - 1$. Also notice $y = g^x \pmod{p}$, we have

$$xr + \ell s = e \pmod{q},$$

$$xr + \ell s' = e' \pmod{q}.$$

Since $e' \neq e \pmod{q}$ necessarily implies $s' \neq s \pmod{q}$, we have

$$\ell = \frac{e - e'}{s - s'} \pmod{q}.$$

Finally, if $q|r$, then the reduction fails. This condition satisfies that for mounting Bleichenbacher's attacks [42] on the ElGamal signature scheme which we have warned as the first warning in §10.4.7.1. However, while Bleichenbacher's attacks are enabled by malicious choice of public key parameters, for randomly chosen public key instance, the event $q|r$ obviously has the negligible probability value of $1/q$, and so we do not need to care if Malice may be successful in forging signatures $(M, \xi q, H(M, \xi q), s)$ for some integer $\xi$ since these successful forgeries form a negligible fraction of valid signatures. Thus, with an overwhelming probability: $r$ is relatively prime to $q$ and hence Simon can extract $x \pmod{q}$ as

$$x = \frac{e - \ell s}{r} \pmod{q}.$$

Recall that $(p-1)/q$ has no large prime factors, $x \pmod{p-1}$ can easily be further extracted.

Since the numbers $r, e, e'$ are in Simon's two RO lists, and $s, s'$ are Malice's output, Simon can indeed use the described method to extract the discrete logarithm of $y$ to the base $g$ modulo $p$. In this method Simon uses Malice as a blackbox: he does not care nor investigate how Malice's technology works; but as long as Malice's technology works, so does Simon's.

### Reduction Result

To this end we have obtained the following reduction results:

i) Simon's advantage for extracting discrete logarithm is

$$Adv'(k) \approx \frac{1}{\sqrt{q_H}}.$$

since $q_H$ is polynomially (in $k$) bounded, the value $Adv'(k)$ is non-negligible in $k$.

ii) Simon's time cost is roughly

$$t' \approx \frac{2(t + q_H)}{Adv(k)}$$

where $t$ is Malice's time for forging a signature. We will discuss in §16.3.2.3 the efficiency of this reduction algorithm.

The theoretic basis for this ROM-based reduction proof is called **forking lemma** [237].

**Remark 16.1:** *The forking reduction technique works because Simon Simulator resets the RO answers so that one set of questions from Malice are answered with two completely independent sets of answers. It seems that Malice is very stupid for not having detected the changed answers to the same set of questions. No, Malice is still very clever as a successful forger. We should consider that Malice is a probabilistic algorithm whose sole functionality is to output a valid forgery whenever the algorithm is working in a correct environment and has been responded to with RO answers of the* correct *distribution. We must not think that the probabilistic algorithm may have any additional functionality, such as that the algorithm may be conscious like a human being and may thereby be able to detect whether or not somebody in the communication environment is fooling around. In fact, by responding to Malice with correctly distributed answers, Simon is* not *fooling him at all.* □

### 16.3.2.2   Unforgeability under Adaptive Chosen-message Attack

Now let us consider the case of unforgeability under adaptive chosen-message attack.

The reduction technique will be essentially the same as that in the case of non-adaptive attack. However, now Malice is also allowed to make signing queries ($q_s$ of them), in addition to making RO queries. Hence Simon Simulator must, in addition to responding to RO queries, also respond the signing queries with answers which can pass Malice's verification steps using $\mathsf{Verify}_{pk}$. Simon must do so even though he does not have possession of the signing key. The signing is the very piece of information he is trying to obtain with the help of Malice! Simon's procedure for signing is done via simulation.

Therefore here it suffices for us to show that under the ROM, Simon can indeed satisfy Malice's signing queries with the perfect quality.

Since the signing algorithm uses a hash function which is modeled by an RO, under the ROM, for each signing query $M$, Simon will choose a new element $r < p$ and make the RO query $(M, r)$ on behalf of Malice and then returns both the RO answer and the signing answer to Malice. The generation of a new $r$ by Simon for each signing query follows exactly the signing procedure; Simon should never reuse any $r$ which has been used previously.

Here is precisely what Simon should do. For signing query $M$, Simon picks random integers $u$, $v$ less than $p - 1$, and sets

$$r \leftarrow g^u y^v \pmod{p};$$

$$s \leftarrow -rv^{-1} \pmod{p - 1};$$

$$e \leftarrow -ruv^{-1} \pmod{p - 1}.$$

Simon returns $e$ as the RO answer to the RO query $(M, r)$, and returns $(r, e, s)$ as the signature of $M$ (i.e., as the signing answer to the signing query $M$). The reader may verify that the returned signature is indeed valid. In fact, this simulated signing algorithm is exactly the one with which we generated an existential forgery in §10.4.7.2; there we have verified the validity of such an existential forgery.

Under the ROM, this simulated signature has the identical distribution as one issued by the signing algorithm which uses an RO in place of the hash function $H$. That is why Malice cannot discern any abnormality. Thus, the "simulated signing training" provided by Simon (see Fig 16.1) is a high quality one, and thereby Malice can be satisfied with the signature responses, in addition to being satisfied with the RO responses. His forgery capacity should be fully released and the same reduction used in §16.3.2.1 should also lead to a contradiction as desired.

Now we are done. Theorem 16.1 summarizes the security result we have obtained.

**Theorem 16.1:** *Let* $(\mathsf{Gen}(1^k), \mathsf{Sign}, \mathsf{Verify})$ *be an instance in triplet ElGamal-family signature schemes where the prime* $p$ *satisfies that there exists a $k$-bit prime $q$ dividing* $p - 1$ *and* $(p - 1)/q$ *has no large prime factors. If an adaptive chosen-message forger can break the scheme in time* $t(k)$ *with advantage* $Adv(k)$, *then the discrete logarithm problem modulo* $p$ *can be solved in time* $t'(k)$ *with advantage* $Adv'(k)$ *where*

$$t'(k) \approx \frac{2 \cdot (t(k) + q_H \cdot \tau) + O_B(q_s \cdot k^3)}{Adv(k)},$$

$$Adv'(k) \approx \frac{1}{\sqrt{q_H}},$$

*where* $q_s$ *and* $q_H$ *are the numbers of signing and $H$ oracle queries, respectively, and* $\tau$ *is time for answering an $H$ query.* $\square$

In this result, $k^3$ is the number of bit operations for computing exponentiation modulo a $k$-bit integer (we have derived the cubic time-complexity expression for modulo exponentiation in §4.3.2.6).

### 16.3.2.3    Discussions

- We have again witnessed the power of the ROM for security proof. Here is a fact revealed by the ROM-based security proof for triplet ElGamal-family signature schemes: if the signing algorithm is a truly random function, then the easiest way to forge a signature is to solve the discrete logarithm first and then do as a true signer does. This is compatible to the bit-security investigation result which we have conducted in Chapter 9.

  Thus, an ROM-based proof suggests that for a real world signature scheme which uses real world hash functions rather than ROs, the most vulnerable point to mount an attack is probably the hash functions used in the scheme, unless an attacker considers that attacking the hash functions is harder than solving the discrete logarithm problem. We therefore consider that the ROM-based technique for security proof manifests its importance in that it suggests where to focus the attention for a careful design.

- We have seen that Simon's advantage to solve discrete logarithm problem is $\frac{1}{\sqrt{q_H}}$ where $q_H$ is the number of RO queries to $H$ that Malice is entitled to make. In order for Simon to achieve a constant advantage to solve discrete logarithm problem, the reduction should run $\sqrt{q_H}$. This will further increase Simon's time to

$$\sqrt{q_H} \cdot \frac{2 \cdot (t + q_H \cdot \tau) + O_B(q_s \cdot (\log p)^3)}{Adv}.$$

If we consider that a hash function can be evaluated efficiently, it is therefore reasonable to grant a dedicated forger to evaluate $2^{50}$ hash functions (same as our instantiation in §15.2.5). Therefore in the reduction proof we ought to permit Malice to make $2^{50}$ RO queries, that is, $q_H = 2^{50}$ is a reasonable setting. Under this reasonable setting, we consider the dominant cost part of $q_H^{3/2}$ in Simon's time, and obtain

$$O(\frac{2^{75}}{Adv})$$

as Simon's time for solving the discrete logarithm problem. This time cost indicates that our reduction is not very efficient. The resultant contradiction is not a very meaningful one for $p$ being a 1024-bit prime especially if $Adv$ is small. It is however reasonably meaningful for $p$ being a 2048-bit prime.

Although the reduction does not have ideal efficiency, nevertheless, the ROM-based forking reduction technique of Pointcheval and Stern provides the first reductionist security proof for triplet ElGamal-family signature schemes.

- It is rather ironic to see that the proof for unforgeability against adaptive chosen-message attack, which is the strongest notion of security for digital signatures, is made possible only because the signature scheme has an inherent weakness of being existentially forgeable. However, this irony is different from the one in the case of "Shoup's initial attempt" in §15.2.4.1 for proving security for the RSA-OAEP scheme where he suggests using 3 as the public exponent for RSA encryption. The inherent "weakness" of the existential forgery property of digital signature schemes based on one-way trapdoor functions is not an essential weakness (it is a property), while the RSA encryption using public exponent 3 is a real weakness. The irony here is more anologous to the one we have seen in §15.2.4.2: the multiplicative property of the RSA function playing a role in proving security for the RSA-OAEP by enabling the lattice-based method for solving partial unknown from (15.2.21).

- Although the Digital Signature Standard (DSS, see §10.4.8.2) is not a triplet signature scheme (the hash function takes as input the message bit string only, rather than the message and the commitment value), there is no essential technical difficulty in proving the same unforgeability quality for the DSS under the ROM. The formality can go through if we assume that Simon is able to document all messages which have been RO queried and signing queried in the entire history with respect to a given key pair. In this way, queries of old messages can be responded with the old answers. Perhaps, the successful ROM-based proof of the triplet ElGamal signature schemes suggests that the DSS should be modified into a triplet version, that is, the commitment value should also be hashed.

- Pointcheval and Stern [237] also provided a security proof for the signature scheme of Fiat and Shamir [110] due to the fact that the scheme of Fiat and Shamir is essentially a triplet signature scheme. That signature scheme is modified from a zero-knowledge identification scheme which we shall introduce in a later chapter.

## 16.3.3    Heavy-Row Reduction Technique

There is a different reduction technique for the proof of unforgeability for triplet ElGamal-family signature schemes. The technique is called **heavy row** and is invented by Feige, Fiat and Shamir [107] for proving a soundness property for a zero-knowledge identification scheme of Fiat and Shamir [110] (we will study the soundness property of a zero-knowledge protocol in §18.2.2). Since that identification protocol can easily be turned to a triplet signature scheme of Fiat and Shamir (though not in the ElGamal family), the heavy-row technique trivially applies to triplet ElGamal-family signature schemes. This fact is eventually documented in [224]. Now let us provide a brief description of the heavy-row reduction technique for proving security for triplet ElGamal-family signature schemes.

In the heavy-row reduction technique, we also assume that Malice has advantage *Adv* to forge a signature. Then Simon will run Malice a lot of times proportional to $1/Adv$ (exactly $3/Adv$ times).

Now let us imagine a gigantic binary matrix H of $q$ rows and $q$ columns. The $q$ rows corresponds all possible random choices of the first element in a triplet ElGamal signature scheme. The $q$ columns corresponds all possible random choices of the second element in this signature scheme. An entry of $h_{i,j}$ in H is 1 if $(i,j,s)$ is a valid signature, and is 0 otherwise. A row is said to be heavy if it contains has at least two 1's.

An extremely simple but crucially important fact with this matrix is:

**Lemma 16.1: Heavy-row Lemma** *The probability for 1's in* H *and in heavy rows is at least* 1/2.

This is simply because heavy rows have more 1's than other rows.

Since Malice is a successful forger against the triplet signature scheme with advantage $Adv$, we know that there are $Adv \cdot q^2$ 1's in H. Running Malice $1/Adv$ times, Malice ought to output a correct forgery $(i,j,s)$. By Heavy-row Lemma, with probability at least $1/2$, $i$ is a heavy row. Now run Malice another $2/Adv$ times, sticking to the commitment $i$, Malice will successfully forge another valid signature $(i,j',s')$ where $j' \neq j$.

We already know that these two forged signatures achieve the extraction the needed discrete logarithm value, i.e., lead to a contradiction as desired.

In our description of the heavy-row technique we have focused our attention explaining the intuition of the idea. As a result we have omitted the application of a birthday-paradox effect which can lead to an enlargement the probability values. For the precise reduction formulations of the heavy-row technique which makes use of the birthday-paradox effect, the reader is referred to [224].

## 16.4    Fit-for-application Ways for Signing in RSA and Rabin

The RSA and Rabin functions are one-way trapdoor permutations (OWTP, review §14.3.6.1 for why and how a recommended way of using the Rabin function forms OWTP). As a result, the textbook-version signature schemes based on these functions (the textbook RSA signature scheme §10.4.2 and the textbook Rabin signature scheme §10.4.4) are deterministic algorithms. This means that for a given key pair $(sk,pk)$ and a given message $M$, the signature of $M$ output from the signing algorithm is uniquely determined by $(sk,pk)$ and $M$.

In cryptography, determinism is an undesirable property. In the case of the textbook Rabin signature scheme, the determinism is also the cause of a devastating attack on the scheme which we have shown in §10.4.5: adaptive chosen-message attack permits Malice to obtain two different square roots of a chosen message and thereby factor the modulus. Therefore, fit-for-application versions of the RSA and Rabin signatures must be probabilistic schemes.

### 16.4.1   Signatures with Randomized Padding

Bellare and Rogaway initiate the work of signing with RSA and Rabin in a probabilistic method [27]. They name their method **probabilistic signature scheme (PSS)**. It is a randomized padding-based scheme for the RSA (and Rabin) function. For ease of wording, below we only mention the case of RSA.

Like the OAEP padding scheme (see Fig 15.1 for a picture of the padding scheme), the PSS padding scheme is also constructed from hash functions and is essentially in the same spirit as the OAEP scheme. In the case of the RSA-OAEP scheme for encryption, the encryption procedure is a transformation which uses the one-way part of the RSA function. In the case of the RSA-PSS signature scheme, the signing procedure is a transformation which uses the trapdoor part of the RSA function since now the private key is available to the signer.

Now let us specify the RSA-PSS scheme, an important fit-for-application digital signature scheme.

### 16.4.2   The Probabilistic Signature Scheme — PSS

We shall only specify the algorithm for the RSA case; the Rabin case is analogous.

Fig 16.3 illustrates a picture of the PSS padding. The signature scheme is specified in Alg 16.1.

The signing and verifying algorithms make use of two hash functions. The first, $H$, called the compressor, maps as $H : \{0,1\}^* \mapsto \{0,1\}^{k_1}$ and the second, $G$, called the generator, maps as $G : \{0,1\}^{k_1} \mapsto \{0,1\}^{k-k_1-1}$. In the analysis of security, these hash functions are modeled by ROs.

What is the role of the leading 0? From the lengths of the hash functions and the random input, we know that the padding result has $k-1$ bits. Thus, prefixing the padding result with 0 produces a $k$-bit string, and when interpreted as an integer, will be less than $N$. This is necessary in order for the modulo exponentiation to be conducted correctly. An alternative way for making sure that the padding result is less than $N$ while saving one-bit bandwidth is to make the padding result an exactly $k$-bit string and to have the signer perform trial-and-error tests. This method has been included in our specification of the RSA-OAEP padding in Alg 10.6 which is a minor step of correction from the original algorithm given in [25].

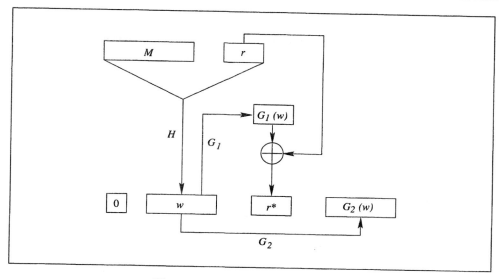

**Figure 16.3.** The PSS Padding

### 16.4.2.1  Proof of Security

Formal evidence for unforgeability of signature under the RSA-PSS scheme can be shown using an ROM-based reduction technique and is given in [27]. The formal evidence is again derived from reduction to contradiction: a successful forgery can lead to an inversion of the RSA function which is a well-known hard problem. The construction of the reduction is very similar to that for an RSA padding algorithm as an encryption scheme (e.g., that for RSA-OAEP which we have studied in §15.2).

Specifically, the reduction for RSA-PSS security proof will also transform a successful signature forgery into a partial inversion of the RSA function as we have seen in §15.2.3.4 in the case of the reductionist proof for RSA-OAEP (there, a successful IND-CCA2 attack leads to discovery of $s^*$, which is a partial $e$-th root of the challenge ciphertext $c^*$). Nevertheless, the signature case turns out to be easier than the encryption case: partial inversion of the RSA function can directly lead to the full inversion without having to rerun Malice as in the encryption case. This is due to the computational nature of a signature forgery: in a successful signature forgery, Malice has to provide Simon a pair of message, signature, and this pair can be verified using the one-way function (here the RSA function). In contrast, in a successful IND-CCA2 attack, Malice provides Simon much less information, merely a one-bit guessing, and so there is no one-way function available for Simon to relate the guessed plaintext to the challenge ciphertext. The resultant inversion is just a partial one. Thus, in the encryption case, the reduction resorts to a rerun of Malice by shifting the position of the partial inversion in order to obtain the full inversion

---

**Algorithm 16.1:** The Probabilistic Signature Scheme (PSS)

**Key Parameters**
Let $(N, e, d, G, H, k_0, k_1) \leftarrow_U \mathsf{Gen}(1^k)$ where: $(N, e, d)$ are RSA key material with $(N, e)$ public and $d = e^{-1} \pmod{\phi(N)}$ private; $k = |N| = k_0 + k_1$ with $2^{-k_0}$ and $2^{-k_1}$ being negligible quantities; $G$, $H$ are hash functions satisfying

$$G : \{0,1\}^{k_1} \mapsto \{0,1\}^{k-k_1-1}, \quad H : \{0,1\}^* \mapsto \{0,1\}^{k_1}.$$

($*$ the output bit string from $G$ is split into two sub-bit-strings, one is denoted by $G_1$ and has the first (i.e., the most significant) $k_0$ bits, the other is denoted by $G_2$ and has the remaining $k - k_1 - k_0 - 1$ bits $*$)

**Signature Generation**

$\mathsf{SignPSS}(M, d, N) =$
$\quad r \leftarrow_U \{0,1\}^{k_0}; \; w \leftarrow H(M \parallel r); \; r^* \leftarrow G_1(w) \oplus r;$
$\quad y \leftarrow 0 \parallel w \parallel r^* \parallel G_2(w);$
$\quad \mathsf{return}(y^d \pmod{N}).$

**Signature Verification**

$\mathsf{VerifyPSS}(M, U, e, N) =$
$\quad y \leftarrow U^e \pmod{N};$
$\quad \text{Parse } y \text{ as } b \parallel w \parallel r^* \parallel \gamma;$
$\quad (* \text{ That is, let } b \text{ be the first bit of } y,$
$\quad\quad w, \text{ the next } k_1 \text{ bits},$
$\quad\quad r^*, \text{ the next } k_0 \text{ bits},$
$\quad\quad \text{and } \gamma, \text{ the remaining bits } *)$
$\quad r \leftarrow r^* \oplus G_1(w);$
$\quad \text{if } (\; H(M \parallel r) = w \;\wedge\; G_2(w) = \gamma \;\wedge\; b = 0 \;) \; \mathsf{return}(\mathsf{True})$
$\quad \text{else } \mathsf{return}(\mathsf{False}).$

---

of the function.

A direct result of the full inversion in one go in the security proof for the RSA-PSS signature scheme is an efficient reduction: Malice's advantage for signature forgery, $Adv$, is tightly translated to Simon's advantage, $Adv'$; that is, $Adv' \approx Adv$. Bellare and Rogaway name the tight reduction result the **exact security** for their RSA padding based signature scheme.

Due to the conceptual similarity between security proof for the RSA-PSS signature scheme and that for the RSA-OAEP encryption scheme, also due to a nontrivial degree of detailedness in the presentation of the reduction, we shall not describe the reduction proof here. The more investigative reader is referred to [27] for details.

### 16.4.3    PSS-R: Signing with Message Recovery

From the fact that the RSA-OAEP encryption scheme permits a private key owner to recover an encrypted message, we can think the issue in the opposite direction: a padding based signature scheme with message recovery can also permit *everybody*, as long as having in possession of the correct public key, to recover a signed message. This is exactly what the RSA-**PSS-R** scheme does: Probabilistic Signature Scheme *with message Recovery*. Bellare and Rogaway provide the PSS-R padding scheme for RSA and Rabin [27].

We shall introduce a slight variation to the original PSS-R padding scheme of Bellare and Rogaway. The variation is due to Coron et al. [84]. The reason for us to choose to introduce the variation of Coron et al. is because the latter authors prove that their variation is not only secure for signature usage when the signature is created using the trapdoor part of the RSA function, but also secure for encryption usage when the ciphertext is created using the one-way part of the RSA function. Here secure for the signature usage is in terms of unforgeability under adaptive chosen-message attack, while that for the encryption usage is under the IND-CCA2 mode.

### 16.4.4    Universal PSS-R Padding for Signature and Encryption

Fig 16.4 illustrates two pictures of the PSS-R padding; one for the original version of Bellare and Rogaway [27], and the other for the variation of Coron et al. [84]. The universal padding scheme for signature and encryption is specified in Alg 16.2.

In this universal RSA-padding scheme, the signing and encryption procedure will be called PSS-R-Padding. It takes as input a message $M \in \{0,1\}^{k-k_1-k_0}$, an RSA exponent and an RSA modulus; the RSA exponent is $d$ for signature generation, and $e$ for encryption. Notice that unlike the PSS signature scheme where the message can have an unlimited length, now the message must have a limited length: $k - k_1 - k_0$. The procedure for signature verification and decryption with ciphertext integrity verification will be called PSS-R-UnPadding. It takes as input a number $U < N$ and RSA key material and its output is in $\{\text{True}, \text{False}\} \cup \{0,1\}^{k-k_1-k_0}$; in the case of the first part of the output being True, the remaining bit string from the output is the message recovered; otherwise, the remaining part of the output is a null string Null.

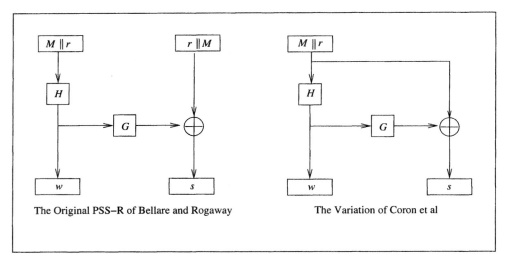

**Figure 16.4.** The PSS-R Padding

## 16.4.4.1  Proof of Security

Proofs of security properties for RSA-PSS-R encryption and signature schemes are conceptually the same to (i) in the case of encryption, that for RSA-OAEP, and (ii) in the case of signature, that for RSA-PSS. Again, due to the conceptual similarity and the non-trivial degree of detailedness, we shall not include the reductions here. The reader is referred to [84] for details.

## 16.4.4.2  Discussions

- In PSS-R-Padding, in order to guarantee that the padding result as an integer is less than $N$, we conduct a trial-and-error test. The probability for repeating the test $i$ times is $2^{-i}$. Alternatively, the leading-0 technique used in the PSS padding scheme can also be used here.

- When PSS-R-Padding is used for encryption, integrity verification of the ciphertext validity is done via checking the hash function value. This method is different from the case of the OAEP padding scheme: checking a string of 0's as recovered redundancy.

- The ROM-based IND-CCA2 security analysis for the encryption case of the RSA PSS-R-Padding scheme is essentially the same as that we have conducted for the RSA-OAEP scheme: via reduction to a partial inversion of the RSA function where $w$ is uncovered; that is, if Malice is successful in breaking the scheme with advantage $Adv$, then in the attacking game run with Simon Simulator, Malice must have queried the RO $G$ with an advantage similar to

**Algorithm 16.2:** The Universal RSA-Padding Scheme for Signature and Encryption

**Key Parameters**

Let $(N, e, d, G, H, k_0, k_1) \leftarrow_U \mathsf{Gen}(1^k)$ where: $(N, e, d)$ are RSA key material with $(N, e)$ public and $d = e^{-1} \pmod{\phi(N)}$ private; $k = |N| = k_0 + k_1$ with $2^{-k_0}$ and $2^{-k_1}$ being negligible quantities; $G, H$ are hash functions satisfying

$$G : \{0,1\}^{k_1} \mapsto \{0,1\}^{k-k_1-1}, \quad H : \{0,1\}^{k-k_1-1} \mapsto \{0,1\}^{k_1}.$$

**Signature Generation or Message Encryption**

PSS-R-Padding$(M, x, N) =$
    1. $r \leftarrow_U \{0,1\}^{k_0}$; $w \leftarrow H(M \parallel r)$; $s \leftarrow G(w) \oplus (M \parallel r)$; $y \leftarrow (w \parallel s)$;
    2. if ( $y \geq N$ ) go to 1;
    3. return($y^x \pmod{N}$).

**Signature Verification or Decryption with Ciphertext Validation**

PSS-R-UnPadding$(U, x, N) =$
    $y \leftarrow U^x \pmod{N}$;
    Parse $y$ as $w \parallel s$;
    (* i.e., let $w$ be the first $k_1$ bits, $s$, the remaining $k - k_1$ bits *)
    Parse $G(w) \oplus s$ as $M \parallel r$;
    (* i.e., let $M$ be the first $k - k_1 - k_0$ bits, $r$, the remaining $k_0$ bits *)
    if ( $H(M \parallel r) = w$ ) return(True $\parallel M$ )
    else return(False $\parallel$ Null).

*Adv.* Since a run of the attacker only causes a partial inversion, the reduction has to run the attacker more than once in order to obtain enough information for inverting the function fully. As we have seen in §15.2.4, in order to make the reduction leading to a meaningful contradiction, the reduction should run Malice no more than twice (so that the reduction is a polynomial of degree 2).

Even in the case of running Malice the minimum number: twice, the reduction is already far from tight. The reader may review §15.2.5 to see the consequence of the non-tightness of the reduction. In order to reach a meaningful contradiction, the non-tight reduction stipulates that the RSA modulus for the RSA-PSS-R encryption scheme should be at least a 2048-bit one.

- The need of the minimum of twice running Malice requires the padding scheme to satisfy $|w| > \frac{|N|}{2}$. Consequently, $|M \parallel r| \leq \frac{|N|}{2}$. Therefore, the RSA-PSS-R padding scheme for encryption has a rather low bandwidth for message recovery: the size of the recovered message must be below half the size of the modulus. In the typical key setting of $k = |N| = 2048$ and $k_0 = 160$, we can obtain as maximum $|M| = \frac{|N|}{2} - k_0 = 1024 - 160 = 862$, that is, $|M|$ is only up to 42% of $|N|$.

- As we have discussed in §16.4.2.1 for the case of the RSA-PSS signature scheme, the ROM-based security proof for the RSA-PSS-R signature scheme (unforgeability against adaptive chosen-message attack) has a tight reduction. This is because a successful forgery of a signature can lead to full inversion of the RSA function in one go. Thus, unlike security proof for the encryption case discussed in the preceding paragraph, security proof for the signature case does not require the condition $|w| > \frac{|N|}{2}$. We consider that it suffices for $k_0$, $k_1$ to have sizes with $2^{-k_0}$, $2^{-k_1}$ being negligible against a guessing attack for which $k_0 = k_1 = 160$ suffices. Thus, $|M| = k - k_1 - k_0$ can be rather large. Instantiating the typical case of $k = |N| = 2048$ and $k_0 = k_1 = 160$, we can obtain $|M| = 2048 - 320 = 1728$, that is, $|M|$ can be up to 84% of $|N|$.

## 16.5   Signcryption

To avoid forgery and ensure confidentiality of the contents of a letter, it has been a common practice that the author of the letter should sign and then seal the letter in an envelope, before handing it over to a deliverer. This common practice in secure communications applies to digital signature and data encryption, often separately and straightforwardly: signing a message and then encrypting the result at the sending end; decrypting the ciphertext and verifying the signature at the receiving end.

Signature and encryption consume machine cycles, and also introduce expanded bits to a message. The cost of a cryptographic operation on a message is typically measured in the message expansion rate and the computational time spent by the both the sender and the recipient. With the straightforward signature-then-encryption procedure, the cost for delivering a message in an authenticated and confidential way is essentially the sum of the cost for digital signature and that for encryption. Often this is not an economical way to do the job.

**Signcryption** is a public key primitive to achieve the combined functionality of digital signature and encryption in an efficient manner. It therefore offers the three frequently used security services: confidentiality, authenticity and non-repudiation. Since these services are frequently required simultaneously, Zheng proposes signcryption [311] as a means to offer them in a more efficient manner than that a straightforward composition of digital signature scheme and encryption scheme.

# 16.5.1  Zheng's Signcryption Scheme

Zheng proposes two very similar signcryption schemes, named SCS1 and SCS2, respectively [311]. They apply two very similar signature schemes in the ElGamal family, named SDSS1 and SDSS2, respectively.

Recall §16.3.1, in a triplet ElGamal signature $(r, e, s)$, the commitment $r$ is usually computed by $r = g^k \pmod{p}$ where $g$ and $p$ are part of the public key material, and the committal $k$ is a integer independent to such values used in all previous signatures. Further recall that in the Schnorr signature scheme (Alg 10.4), which is a triplet ElGamal scheme, there is no need for the signer to send the commitment to the receiver; the way that the signature is generated permits the receiver to recover the commitment by computing $r = g^s y^e \pmod{p}$.

Thus, if a message sender (as a signer of the message) computes the commitment in a special way so that it is only recoverable by an intended receiver (e.g., computed using the receiver's public key), then the commitment value can be used as (or can seed) a symmetric key shared between the sender and the receiver and so symmetric encryption can be applied for providing message confidentiality.

This is more or less what all Zheng's signcryption schemes are about: using the recoverable commitment value of a triplet signature scheme in the ElGamal-family signatures as the symmetric key to achieve symmetric encryption of the message while the triplet signature scheme serves the signature. From this brief and abstract description, we can already write a signcrypted message as a triplet $(c, e, s)$, here $c$ is a ciphertext output from a symmetric encryption algorithm, $(e, s)$ is the second and third elements in a triplet signature; the first element of the triplet signature scheme (which is conventionally denoted by $r$) is recoverable only by an intended message receiver.

Due to the similarity between SCS1 and SCS2, we shall only provide the specification of SCS1, which is given in Alg 16.3. For ease of exposition, our specification follows the conventional notation for specifying triplet ElGamal signature schemes, except that we use $K$ in place of $r$ (the commitment value of a triplet ElGamal signature scheme) to indicate that this value is used as a symmetric key.

We now show that the system specified in Alg 16.3 is both a cryptosystem and a signature scheme, i.e., (i) Bob's decryption procedure will actually return the same plaintext message that Alice has signcrypted; and (ii) Alice has signed the message.

To show (i), it suffices to show that Bob can recover $K = g_B^u \pmod{p}$ as Alice has encoded. Bob's recovery procedure is

$$K = (g^e y_A)^{s x_B} \equiv (g^{x_B})^{se} (g^{x_A x_B})^s \equiv y_B^{s(e + x_A)} \equiv y_B^u \pmod{p}.$$

Thus, indeed, Bob recovers $K$ as Alice has encoded. Using $K_1$ split from $K$, Bob can of course decrypt the ciphertext $c$ and retrieve the message $M$.

To show (ii), we notice that with $K = g_B^u \pmod{p}$ being recovered, $(K_2, e, s)$

**Algorithm 16.3:** Zheng's Signcryption Scheme SCS1

**Setup of System Parameters**
A trusted authority performs the following steps:

1. Setup system parameters $(p, q, g, H)$;

   (∗ these parameters are the same as those for Schnorr signature scheme (Alg 10.4) ∗)

2. In addition, setup a symmetric encryption algorithm $\mathcal{E}$;

   (∗ for example, AES is a good candidate for $\mathcal{E}$ ∗)

The parameters $(p, q, g, H, \mathcal{E})$ are publicized for use by system-wide users.

**Setup of a Principal's Public/Private Key**
User Alice picks a random number $x_A \in_U \mathbb{Z}_q$ and computes

$$y_A \leftarrow g^{x_A} \pmod{p}.$$

Alice's public-key material is $(p, q, g, y_A, H, \mathcal{E})$; her private key is $x_A$.

**Signcryption**
To send to Bob $M$ in signcryption, Alice performs:

1. Pick $u$ randomly from $[1, q]$, computes $K \leftarrow y_B^u \pmod{p}$. Split $K$ into $K_1$ and $K_2$ of appropriate lengths;

2. $e \leftarrow H(K_2, M)$;

3. $s \leftarrow u(e + x_A)^{-1} \pmod{q}$;

4. $c \leftarrow \mathcal{E}_{K_1}(M)$;

5. Send to Bob the signcrypted text $(c, e, s)$.

**Unsigncryption**
Upon receipt of the signcrypted text $(c, e, s)$ from Alice, Bob performs:

1. Recover $K$ from $e, s, g, p, y_A$ and $x_B$: $K \leftarrow (g^e y_A)^{s x_B} \pmod{p}$;

2. Split $K$ into $K_1$ and $K_2$;

3. $M \leftarrow \mathcal{D}_{K_1}(c)$;

4. Accept $M$ as a valid message originated from Alice only if $e = H(K_2, M)$.

forms a triplet ElGamal signature on the retrieved message $M$. Therefore the system in Alg 16.3 is indeed a signature scheme.

### 16.5.1.1   Discussions

- **Efficiency**   The SCS1 scheme is very efficient both in computation and in communication bandwidth. In computation, to signcrypt, the sender performs one modulo exponentiation, one hashing and one symmetric encryption; to unsigncrypt, the receiver performs a similar amount of computation if the exponentiation expression $(g^e y_A)^{s x_B}$ is rewritten to $g^{e s x_B} y_A^{s x_B}$ and computed using Alg 15.2. In communication bandwidth, considering that the symmetric encryption of a message does not cause data expansion, then a signcrypt text can be sent in $2|q|$ bits plus the bits of the message being signcrypted. This is the same bandwidth for transmitting a signature (with the signed message) in the ElGamal-family signatures. Moreover, the use of a symmetric cipher algorithm makes the scheme suitable for sending bulk volume of data efficiently (e.g., using a block cipher with the CBC mode of operation, see §7.8.2). In essence, SCS1 can be viewed as a hybrid public-key encryption scheme which we have overviewed in §15.4.

- **Security**   For unforgeability of signature, Zheng conducts a reasonable argument for his schemes. Since we have seen that the SCS1 scheme is essentially a triplet ElGamal signature with a recoverable commitment, unforgeability of signature under adaptive chosen-message attack should be straightforward by following the ROM-based proof for a triplet ElGamal signature schemes proposed by Pointcheval and Stern [237] (we have studied the technique in §16.3). However, for confidentiality of message, due to the involvement of a symmetric encryption algorithm, Zheng has not given a reductionist proof on the IND-CCA2 security for his signcryption schemes. Perhaps, here is the reason for a non-trivial hurdle for constructing a reductionist proof for the IND-CCA2 security: only the intended receiver is able to recover the commitment value $K$, under adaptive chosen-ciphertext attack.

- **Non-repudiation**   Non-repudiation, i.e., a principal cannot deny the authorship of a message, is an important security service for many applications, e.g., electronic commerce. Digital signatures provide this service because a signature of a message is verifiable universally; when two parties dispute regarding a message-signature pair, a third party can be called upon to make an arbitration. In the case of signcryption, if a signature cannot be made universally verifiable, then the non-repudiation service will have a cost. This is the case for Zheng's signcryption schemes. Here, verification of a (triplet) signature requires recovery of the commitment value $K$ and the recovery needs to use the receiver's private key. So a third party's arbitration cannot be straightforwardly done. Zheng suggests that upon dispute between the receiver (Bob) and the sender (Alice), then Bob can conduct a zero-knowledge proof with an arbitrator to show that he has in his possession of Alice's signature. No zero-knowledge proof protocol is given. Although it should not be difficult to devise such a protocol, it is a pain to have to turn a simple verification procedure into an interactive protocol. This is the most serious drawback of Zheng's signcryption schemes.

## 16.5.2   Two Birds One Stone: Signcryption using RSA

Malone-Lee and Mao propose a signcryption scheme named "two birds one stone" (TBOS) [184] (the name will be explained in a moment). The TBOS signcryption scheme is realized in RSA. They provide reductionist proofs of strong security properties for message confidentiality and signature unforgeability. Both proofs, although ROM-based, are under the assumption that inverting the RSA function is hard.

The TBOS signcryption scheme is very simple and can indeed be simply described. It "double-wraps" a message in RSA signing and encryption functions: a sender (e.g., Alice) first signs a message by "wrapping" it inside the trapdoor part of her own RSA function, and then encrypts the signature by further "wrapping" it inside the one-way part of the RSA function of an intended receiver (Bob). Thus, if we denote by $(N_A, e_A), (N_A, d_A)$ Alice's RSA public, private key material, and by $(N_B, e_B), (N_B, d_B)$ that of Bob's, a TBOS signcrypted message $M$ should be a "double wrapped" like this:

$$[M^{d_A} \ (\text{mod} \ N_A)]^{d_B} \ (\text{mod} \ N_B).$$

Although the idea is conceptually very simple, for textbook RSA, this way of "double wrapping" won't work in general. This is because Alice's RSA modulus may be larger than Bob's, and hence an "inner wrapping" result, as an integer, may already be larger than the modulus to be used for an "outer wrapping."

Nevertheless, we have seen that a fit-for-application RSA scheme, whether encryption or signature, only "wraps" a message after the message has been processed with a randomized padding scheme. For such an RSA scheme, system-wide users should use moduli of the same size since the sending and receiving ends should agree upon a padding and unpadding scheme.

With system-wide users using moduli of the same size, "double wrapping" will work nicely. If an "inner wrapping" result exceeds the modulus for an "outer wrapping," then the sender simply "chops" one bit off (e.g., the most significant bit) from the "inner wrapping" result. With one bit "chopped off," the remaining integer must be less than the "outer wrapping" modulus (to show this in a moment) and hence direct "wrapping" can be conducted. Remember that the receiving end of such an RSA ciphertext will have to conduct ciphertext integrity verification;

the verification step will allow the receiver to use trial-and-error test to put the "chopped-off" bit back. That's the idea.

So now for $|N_A| = |N_B| = k$. Let $\text{Padding}(M, r) \in \{0,1\}^k$ denote a randomized padding of message $M$ with random input $r$. Then a message $M$ signcrypted under the TBOS signcryption scheme sent from Alice to Bob looks like a "double wrapping" as follows:

$$[\text{Padding}(M, r)^{d_A} \ (\text{mod } N_A)]^{d_B} \ (\text{mod } N_B).$$

After this abstract description of the TBOS signcryption scheme, we can already see three nice features of the scheme:

- It produces compact ciphertexts: a signcrypt text has the same size of an RSA ciphertext without a signature, or the same size of an RSA signature without encryption. This is why the scheme is named "two birds one stone" (after an English phrase: "to kill two birds with one stone"). This property is very attractive in many electronic commerce applications where a short message (such as a credit card number for a payment authorization) needs to be sent over the Internet with confidentiality protection as well as non-repudiation for payment authorization. In these applications, the TBOS is able to produce one short cryptogram. Not only does this achieve efficiency, but it also helps to reduce the engineering complexity of an e-commerce protocol.

- It offers non-repudiation in a very straightforward manner: the receiver, Bob, after "unwrapping" a signcrypt text, and maybe after fixing the "chopped-off bit" back, has an RSA signature of the sender Alice in the usual formulation: $\text{Padding}(M, r)^{d_A} \ (\text{mod } N_A)$. Any third party can verify the signature in the usual way.

- Security proofs for the TBOS scheme can be established by following those for the fit-for-application RSA padding schemes and are given in a reductionist manner. Although the proofs are ROM based, the reductionist proofs otherwise only rely on a reputably hard problem (the RSA problem and assumption, Definition 8.4, Assumption 8.3 in §8.7); this is very desirable.

Now let us explain that proper unsigncryption on Bob's end can always be properly conducted. This is obviously true if $N_A < N_B$. For the case $N_A > N_B$, with roughly $1/2$ probability, we have

$$\sigma = \text{Padding}(M, r)^{d_A} \ (\text{mod } N_A) > N_B.$$

However, since $|N_A| = |N_B| = k$, we have

$$\sigma < N_A < 2^k$$

and therefore, let

$$\sigma' \leftarrow \sigma - 2^{k-1}$$

i.e., $\sigma'$ is $\sigma$ with the most significant bit "chopped off," then

$$\sigma' < 2^{k-1} < N_B.$$

That is, Bob can recover $\sigma'$ properly. Thereafter, Bob's verification step will guide Bob whether or not to fix the "chopped bit" back.

### 16.5.2.1  RSA-TBOS

The RSA-TBOS scheme of Malone-Lee and Mao [184] applies the PSS-R padding scheme (§16.4.4). The signcryption scheme is specified in Alg 16.4.

The point of step 6 in signcryption is to ensure that $c' < N_B$. If $c'$ initially fails this test then we have $N_A > c' > N_B$. Since both $N_A$ and $N_B$ have $k$-bits we infer that $c'$ also has $k$-bits and so the assignment $c' \leftarrow c' - 2^{k-1}$ is equivalent to removing the most significant bit of $c'$. This gives us $c' < N_B$ as required.

Note that this step may cause an additional step in unsigncryption. In particular it may be necessary to perform $c'^{e_A} \pmod{N_A}$ twice (the two $c'$'s will differ by $2^{k-1}$). It would have been possible to define an alternative scheme under which the trial-and-error occurs in the signcryption stage. This would mean repeating steps 1-5 in signcryption with different values of $r$ until $c' < N_B$ was is obtained.

Non-repudiation is very simple for RSA-TBOS. The receiver of a signcryption follows the unsigncryption procedure up until stage 2, $c'$ may then be given to a third party who can verify its validity.

Although the TBOS signcryption scheme has many attractive features (we have listed before the specification of the algorithm), we should notice a drawback it inheres from the application of the RSA-PSS-R padding scheme: it has a rather low message bandwidth for message recovery. The reader should review our discussion on this point for the RSA-PSS-R encryption scheme (in §16.4.4.2).

### 16.5.2.2  Proof of Security

Malone-Lee and Mao provide formal reductionist proofs of strong security properties for the TBOS signcryption scheme [184]. They also include a description of the security model for signcryption. The strong security properties are: message confidentiality under the IND-CCA2 model, and signature unforgeability under the chosen-message attack.

Due to the essential similarity of these proofs to those we have conducted in §15.2 for RSA-OAEP, and due to the non-trivial degree of detailedness, we should omit presenting the reductions here. The reader with a more investigative appetite should check [184] for details.

**Algorithm 16.4:** Two Birds One Stone: RSA-TBOS Signcryption Scheme

**Key Parameters**

Let $k$ be an even positive integer. Let sender Alice's (respectively, receiver Bob's) RSA public and private key material be $(N_A, e_A), (N_A, d_A)$ (respectively $(N_B, e_B), (N_B, d_B)$), satisfying $|N_A| = |N_B| = k$.

Let $G$ and $H$ be two hash functions satisfying

$$H : \{0,1\}^{n+k_0} \mapsto \{0,1\}^{k_1} \text{ and } G : \{0,1\}^{k_1} \mapsto \{0,1\}^{n+k_0},$$

where $k = n + k_0 + k_1$ with $2^{-k_0}$ and $2^{-k_1}$ being negligible quantities.

**Signcryption**

When Alice signcrypts a message $M \in \{0,1\}^n$ for Bob, she performs:

1. $r \leftarrow_U \{0,1\}^{k_0}$

2. $\omega \leftarrow H(M \parallel r)$

3. $s \leftarrow G(\omega) \oplus (M \parallel r)$

4. If $s \parallel \omega > N_A$ goto 1

5. $c' \leftarrow (s \parallel \omega)^{d_A} \pmod{N_A}$

6. If $c' > N_B$, $c' \leftarrow c' - 2^{k-1}$

7. $c \leftarrow c'^{e_B} \pmod{N_B}$

8. Send $c$ to Bob

**Unsigncryption**

When Bob unsigncrypts a cryptogram $c$ from Alice, he performs:

1. $c' \leftarrow c^{d_B} \pmod{N_B}$

2. If $c' > N_A$, reject

3. $\mu \leftarrow c'^{e_A} \pmod{N_A}$

4. Parse $\mu$ as $s \parallel \omega$

5. $M \parallel r \leftarrow G(\omega) \oplus s$

6. If $H(M \parallel r) = \omega$, return $M$

7. $c' \leftarrow c' + 2^{k-1}$

8. If $c' > N_A$, reject

9. $\mu \leftarrow c'^{e_A} \pmod{N_A}$

10. Parse $\mu$ as $s \parallel \omega$

11. $M \parallel r \leftarrow G(\omega) \oplus s$

12. If $\omega \neq H(M \parallel r)$, reject

13. Return $M$

Nevertheless, even without describing the reduction details, we can still reach an informal and abstract level of understanding of why a provably secure encryption padding scheme, when used with the trapdoor direction of the RSA function, can form a secure signature scheme. Clearly, we need to argue for the case of signature unforgeability under a chosen-message attack scenario. Let us try to reach this understanding using the OAEP padding with which we are already familiar.

Let us recall the case of the RSA-OAEP reduction proof against an attack in the IND-CCA2 mode (given in §15.2). There, we have estimated that if Malice does not comply with the prescribed encryption procedure, then the probability for him to be able to submit a valid *ciphertext* is statistically negligible, regardless of whatever algorithm Malice may use (recall that Malice is a blackbox) and regardless of the fact that he may construct ciphertexts in an adaptive manner (i.e., under an adaptive chosen-ciphertext decryption training scenario).

This fact can be mechanically translated to a proof of unforgeability of signatures for a randomized padding signature scheme: without using the prescribed signing procedure (due to missing of the signing exponent), the probability of Malice forging a valid message-signature pair (which is in the position of a valid plaintext-ciphertext pair constructed without using the prescribed encryption procedure) is statistically negligible, even under an adaptive chosen-message training scenario.

Of course, however intuitively convincing, we must emphasize that this description is not a formal proof of security for an RSA padding based signature scheme because it does not follow our established formal approach of "reduction to contradiction." The interested reader should check the reductionist proof in [184].

## 16.6  Chapter Summary

In this chapter we began by providing a strong security notion for digital signatures: signature unforgeability under an adaptive chosen-message attack. This is an attack mode for signature schemes counterparting to the IND-CCA2 mode for public-key encryption schemes. The basic idea shared by the two modes is that in these attacks, Malice is entitled to cryptanalysis training. A cryptographic system is strong and resistant to attack even giving Malice the cryptanalysis training, even as much of it as he wishes (provided he is polynomially bounded and so the number of interactions in a training session is polynomially bounded).

Then we studied two important families of "fit-for-application" signature schemes. The first family is triplet ElGamal-family signature schemes, and the second family is randomized padding schemes applied to one-way trapdoor permutations, such as the RSA and Rabin functions.

We then proceeded to establish formal evidence of strong security for the signature schemes in both families.

For the first family, we studied an ROM-based reductionist proof technique which works on the principle that there is a non-negligible probability for successful "forked answers to forger's questions." That is, a set of questions from the forger can be answered with two sets of completely different answers, yet both are correct in terms of having the correct random distribution (the uniform distribution). Since the forger whose questions are forked is an unconscious probabilistic algorithm, the correct distribution is all that it is after. Therefore, although questions are responded to with forked answers, the forked forger is not fooled, and it will thereby proceed to help the reduction algorithm to solve a difficult problem: the discrete logarithm problem. We have also described an alternative proof approach for this family: the heavy-row model. Although both proof approaches are rigorously formal, as we have analyzed, the reduction algorithms are not very efficient. Consequently, a proof is only meaningful for rather large security parameters.

For the second family, signature schemes are constructed from sequential combination of randomized paddings for one-way trapdoor permutations. An ROM-based reductionist proof is similar to that for the public-key encryption schemes from randomized paddings for one-way trapdoor permutations which we have studied in the preceding chapter. Nevertheless, now for the signature case, a successful attack (signature forgery under the adaptive chosen message attack) can lead to the full inversion of the one-way function in a direct manner. The resulting reduction proof for the randomized padding-based signature schemes is thus a tight one, that is, the attacker's ability for signature forgery can be fully translated to one for inverting the hard function (i.e. the underlying one-way trapdoor function). This is called an exact security property.

Finally, we have also studied signcryption schemes as efficient and useful cryptographic primitives. Likewise the other cases of fit-for-application encryption and signature schemes introduced in this book, the signcryption schemes introduced here are also based on the two popular cryptographic underlying problems: the discrete logarithm problem and integer factorization problem.

## Exercises

16.1 What is the "fit-for-application" security notion for digital signatures?

16.2 Given that Malice is a bad guy, why should we still grant him the entitlement to obtaining signatures on messages of his choice and even to obtaining them as many as he wishes?

16.3 In the ROM-based forking-lemma proof of security for triplet ElGamal signatures, Simon runs Malice twice and answers his same set of RO queries with two sets of independent responses. Should we consider that Malice is fooled by Simon in the second run?

16.4 Discuss the usefulness of the existential forgeability of a triplet ElGamal signature in the security proof for the scheme.

16.5 Using the PSS to sign the same message twice, what is the probability for the algorithm to output the same signature value?

16.6 In Ex 15.2 we have defined the bandwidth of an encryption scheme. The bandwidth of a digital signature scheme with message recovery is similarly defined. With the same security parameter setting as in Ex 15.2, what is the bandwidth of using the Universal RSA-Padding scheme (Alg 16.2) for (i) signing, (ii) encryption?

16.7 Why are the two bandwidth results in the preceding problem different?

16.8 Discuss the difference between the non-repudiation properties served by Zheng's signcryption scheme and by the TBOS signcryption scheme.

16.9 Our argument on the unforgeability of the TBOS signcryption scheme (in §16.5.2.2) is a convincing one, however is not a formal security proof. Why?

Hint: is the argument a reductionist one?

# Chapter 17

# FORMAL METHODS
# FOR AUTHENTICATION
# PROTOCOLS ANALYSIS

## 17.1  Introduction

In Chapter 11 we have witnessed the fact that authentication and authenticated key establishment protocols (in this chapter we shall often use authentication protocols to refer to both kinds) are notoriously error prone. These protocols can be flawed in very subtle ways. How to develop authentication protocols so that they are secure is a serious research topic pursed by researchers with different backgrounds; some are cryptographers and mathematicians, others are theoretic computer scientists. It is widely agreed by these researchers that formal approaches should be taken to the analysis of authentication protocols.

Formal approaches are a natural extension to informal ones. Formal can mean many things, ranging over notions such as methodical, mechanical, rule and/or tool supported methods. A formal method usually supports a symbolic system or a description language for modeling and specifying a system's behavior so that the behavior can be captured (i.e., comprehended) and reasoned about by applying logical and mathematical methods in a rigorous manner. Sometimes, a formal method is an expert system which captures human experience or even tries to model human ingenuity. A common characteristic of formal methods is that they take a systematic, sometime an exhaustive, approach to a problem. Therefore, formal methods are particularly suitable for the analysis of complex systems.

In the areas of formal analysis of authentication protocols, we can identify two distinct approaches. One can be referred to as formal reasoning about holding of some desirable, or secure properties; the other can be referred to as systematic search for some undesirable, or dangerous, properties.

In the first approach, a protocol to be analyzed must be very carefully chosen or designed so that it is already believed or likely to be correct. The analysis tries to establish that the protocol is indeed correct with respect to a set of desirable properties which have also been carefully formalized. Because of the carefully chosen protocols to be analyzed, a formal proof is often specially tailored to the target protocol and may hence need to have much human ingenuity involvement, although the proof methodology can be more general. This approach further branches to two schools: a computational school and a symbolic manipulation school. In the former, security properties are defined and measured in terms of probability, and a proof of security or protocol correctness is a mathematician's demonstration of holding of a theorem; the proof often involves a reductionist transformation to a well-accepted complexity-theoretic assumption (see Chapters 14 and 15 for the case of provably secure public-key encryption schemes). In the latter school, which consists of theoretic computer scientists in formal methods area, security properties are expressed as a set of abstract symbols which can be manipulated, sometimes by a formal logic system, sometimes by an mechanical tool called a theorem prover, toward a YES/NO result.

The second approach considers that an authentication protocol, however carefully chosen or designed, or even having gone through a formal proof of correctness (i.e., as a result of the first approach), can still contain error. This is because "proof of correctness" can only demonstrate that a protocol satisfies a set of *specified* desirable properties; it is still possible that a provably secure protocol can fail if a failure has not been considered in the "proof of security " process. Therefore, in this approach, analysis is in terms of systematic, or exhaustive, search for errors. Formalization of a protocol involves expressing of the protocol into a (finite) state system which is often composed from sub-state systems of protocol parts run by different principals (including "Malice's part"). An error can be described in general terms, e.g., in the case of secrecy of a message, a bad state can be that the message ends up in Malice's set of knowledge; or in the case of entity authentication, a bad state can be that a wrong identity ends up in the set of accepted identities of an honest principal. This approach has a close relation with the area of formal analysis of complex systems in theoretic computer science, and hence often applies well developed automatic analysis tools developed there.

In this chapter we shall study these approaches to formal analysis of authentication protocols.

## 17.1.1   Chapter Outline

The technical part of the chapter starts with formalization of protocol specifications; in §17.2 we shall study a refinement approach to authentication protocols specification. After the specification topic, we shall concentrate on analysis techniques. In §17.3 we shall introduce a proof technique based on a computational model for protocol correctness where a proof is in terms of a mathematician's demonstration of holding of a theorem. In §17.4 we shall introduce techniques for arguing protocol security by manipulation of abstract symbols; a logical approach and a theorem proving approach will be introduced there. In §17.5 we shall introduce formal analysis techniques which model a protocol as a finite-state system and search for system errors. Finally, in §17.6 we shall provide a brief discussion on a recent work to bridge a gap between security under a computational view and that under a symbolic view.

# 17.2   Toward Formal Specification of Authentication Protocols

Let us begin the technical part of this chapter by providing evidence of a need for a more formalized specification means for authentication protocols. Specification should be an indispensable component in any formal methods for the analysis of complex systems. In the case of complex systems being authentication protocols, we consider that the area of study needs a more precise description of the use of cryptographic transformations.

As we have seen in Chapters 2 and 11, many authentication protocols are designed solely using encryption, and for this reason, a widely agreed notation for expressing the use of encryption in these protocols is $\{M\}_K$. This notation denotes a piece of ciphertext: its sender must perform encryption to create it while its receiver has to perform decryption in order to extract $M$ from it. It is the demonstration of these cryptographic capabilities to the communication partners that prove a principal holding of a secret key and hence prove the holder's identity.

Thus, it seems that the idea of authentication achieved by using encryption is simple enough; there should not be much subtlety here.

However in fact, the simple idea of achieving authentication using cryptographic transformation is often misused. The misuse is responsible for many protocol flaws. In this section, we shall first identify a popular misuse of encryption in authentication protocols; then we shall propose an authentication protocol design method based on a refined specification on the use of cryptographic transformations.

## 17.2.1   Imprecision of Encryption-decryption Approach for Authentication

In §11.4.1.5 we have listed two "non-standard" mechanisms for construction authentication protocols using encryption. In those mechanisms, a sender generates ciphertext $\{M\}_K$ and sends it to an intended receiver; the correct receiver has a secret key to perform decryption, and subsequently can return to the sender a message component extracted from the ciphertext. The returned message component, often containing a freshness identifier, proves to the sender a lively correspondence of the receiver. This achieves authentication of the receiver to the sender.

Let us name these (non-standard) mechanisms the "authentication via encryption-decryption" approach.

An often unpronounced security service which implicitly plays the role in the encryption-decryption approach is *confidentiality*, which must be realized using a reversible cryptographic transformation. However, in many cases of authentication protocols where this approach is used, the needed security service is actually *not* confidentiality, but *data integrity*, which is better realized using some one-way (i.e., non reversible) transformations. That is why we have labeled such cases *misuse* of cryptographic transformations.

When a misuse of cryptographic transformations takes place, there are two undesirable consequences. Let us now discuss them in detail.

### 17.2.1.1   Harmful

In a challenge-response mechanism for verifying message freshness, the encryption-decryption approach assists an adversary to use a principal to provide an *oracle decryption service* (see §7.8.2.1 and §8.9). Such a service may grant an unentitled cryptographic operation to Malice who otherwise cannot perform himself as he does not have in his possession of the correct cryptographic key.

Oracle decryption service provides a major source of tricks for Malice to manipulate protocol messages and defeat the goal of authentication. Lowe's attack on the Needham-Schroeder Public-key Authentication Protocol (Attack 2.3) shows exactly such a trick: in the attacking step 1-7, Malice uses Alice's oracle decryption service to decrypt Bob's nonce $N_B$ for him, and is subsequently able to talk to Bob by masquerading as Alice.

Oracle decryption services also provide Malice with valuable information usable for cryptanalysis, e.g., in chosen-plaintext or chosen-ciphertext attacks. We have seen such tricks in numerous attacking examples in Chapter 14.

The correct cryptographic transformation in a challenge-response based mechanism for a receiver to show a cryptographic credential (possessing the correct key) is for her/him to perform a one-way transformation. In the case of using symmetric cryptographic technique, mechanism 11.4.2 is a more desirable one. If the freshness identifier must be kept secret, then mechanism 11.4.1 can be used, however, in that case, Bob should still apply an data-integrity service to protect his ciphertext (reason to be given in §17.2.1.2), which should in fact be achieved using a one-way transformation, that is, the ciphertext in mechanism 11.4.1 still needs a protection based on mechanism 11.4.2. In the case of using asymmetric techniques, mechanism 11.4.3 is standard.

Of course mechanisms 11.4.1 and 11.4.2 also enable the challenger to use the responder to provide an oracle service for creating plaintext-ciphertext pairs:

$$N, \mathcal{E}_K(\ldots, N),$$

$$N, \text{MDC}(K, \ldots, N),$$

where $N$ is a freshness identifier of the challenger's choice. Nevertheless, considering $N$ being non-secret, providing such a pair can cause far less problem than providing a decryption service.

Moreover, in the second case, the "oracle encryption service" is in fact not in place. Any one-way cryptographic transformation for realizing an MDC has a data compression property (see, e.g., §10.3.1 and §10.3.3 for the data compression property in hash-function based and block-cipher based MDC). The data compression property renders loss of information and that's why the transformation becomes irreversible. The loss of information makes the resultant challenge/response pair unusable in a different context: their usage is fixed as in the context of mechanism 11.4.2; using them in any other context will cause a detectable error.

### 17.2.1.2   Insufficient

In general, a ciphertext encrypting a confidential message should itself be protected in terms of data integrity. In absence of a data-integrity protection, it seems impossible to prevent an active adversary from manipulating the encrypted messages and defeating the goal of a protocol if the ciphertext is an important protocol message.

Let us now look at this issue using the Needham-Schroeder Symmetric-key Authentication Protocol (the fixed version due to Denning and Sacco, see §2.6.5.1). We assume that the encryption algorithm used in the protocol provides a strong confidentiality protection for any message component inside a ciphertext. However, for the purpose of exposing our point, we shall stipulate that the encryption algorithm does *not* provide any protection in terms of data integrity. This stipulation is not unreasonable. In fact, any encryption algorithm which is not designed to also provide a data-integrity protection can have this feature if the plaintext message contains a sufficient quantity of randomness so that the plaintext extracted from decryption is unrecognizable.

For instance, we may reasonably assume that the encryption algorithm is the AES (§7.7) with the CBC mode of operation (§7.8.2). The reader may extend our attack to other symmetric encryption algorithms, for example, the one-time pad encryption. We should notice that, regardless of what encryption algorithm is to be used, our attack will not make use any weakness in the algorithm's quality of confidentiality service.

Let us examine the first two steps of the Needham-Schroeder Symmetric-key Authentication Protocol.

1. Alice $\rightarrow$ Trent: *Alice, Bob*, $N_A$;

2. Trent $\rightarrow$ Alice: $\{N_A, K, Bob, Y\}_{K_{AT}}$;

where $Y = \{Alice,\ K,\ T\}_{K_{BT}}$.

Let
$$P_1, P_2, \ldots, P_\ell$$
denote the plaintext message blocks for the plaintext message string

$$N_A, K, Bob, Y.$$

In order for the protocol to suit the needs for general applications, we should reasonably assume that the size of the session key $K$ should be no smaller than the size of one ciphertext block. This is a reasonable assumption since a session key should contain sufficiently many information bits (e.g., for secure keying a block cipher or seeding a stream cipher). The nonce $N_A$ should also be sufficiently large to prevent prediction. Since the nonce $N_A$ starts in $P_1$, our assumption on the size of the session key will naturally deduce that the whole plaintext block $P_2$ will be used solely for containing the session key, or may be $P_2$ only contains part of the session key.

Notice that although we have related $P_2$ to $K$, this is purely for clarity in the exposition; if the session key $K$ is very large, then it may occupy a number of plaintext blocks starting from $P_2$. Of course, Malice will know the size of the session key $K$. Yes, our attack does require Malice to know the size of the plaintext messages and the implementation details. After all, these should not be secret.

Let
$$IV, C_1, C_2, \ldots, C_\ell$$
denote the AES-CBC ciphertext blocks corresponding the plaintext blocks $P_1$, $P_2$, ..., $P_\ell$ (review the CBC mode of operation in §7.8.2). Let further

$$IV', C_1', C_2', \ldots, C_\ell'$$

be the ciphertext blocks of a previous run of the same protocol between the same pair of principals. Of course, Malice had recorded the old ciphertext blocks.

To attack the protocol in a new run, Malice should intercept the new ciphertext blocks flowing from Trent to Alice:

2. Trent $\rightarrow$ Malice("Alice"): $IV, C_1, C_2, C_3 \ldots, C_\ell$;

Malice should now replace these blocks in the following way:

2. Malice("Trent") $\rightarrow$ Alice: $IV, C_1, C_2', C_3' \ldots, C_\ell'$;

That is, Malice should replace the last $\ell - 1$ ciphertext blocks in the current run with the respective old blocks which he had recorded from an old run of the protocol, and let the manipulated chain of blocks go to Alice as if they were coming from Trent.

The CBC decryption by Alice will return $N_A$ in good order since the decryption result is a function of $IV$ and $C_1$. It will return (see **"CBC Decryption"** in §7.8.2)

$$\hat{K} = D_{K_{AT}}(C_2') \oplus C_1 = K' \oplus C_1' \oplus C_1$$

as the "new" session key (or the first block of the "new" session key). Here $K'$ is the old session key (or the first block of it) which was distributed in the recorded old run of the protocol. Alice's decryption of the subsequent ciphertext blocks will return the rest of the $\ell - 1$ plaintext blocks identical to those she had obtained in the old run of the protocol.

Since $K'$ is the old session key, we should not exclude a possibility that Malice may have somehow acquired the old session key already (maybe because Alice or Bob had accidentally disclosed it). Thus, Malice can use $\hat{K}$ (or maybe a value which is the concatenation of $\hat{K}$ with the rest blocks of $K'$, if the size of a session key is longer than one block) to talk to Alice by masquerading as Bob.

From this attack we see that, regardless of what Alice may infer from her correct extraction of her freshness identifier $N_A$, no any other plaintext message returned from Alice's decryption operation should be regarded as fresh!

There can be numerous ways to implement the encryption-decryption approach in this protocol, each of them may thwart this specific attack, but may be subject to a different attack, as long as the implementation details are not secret to Malice.

Several authentication protocols in two early draft international standard documents [146, 147] follow the wrong idea of CBC realization of encryption providing data-integrity service (general guideline for these protocols using CBC is documented in [148, 144]), and of course, these protocols are fatally flawed [186, 187] as we have demonstrated in this section.

We believe that the correct solution to securing this protocol is to have the ciphertext blocks protected under a proper data-integrity service; for example, by applying the message authentication techniques which we have introduced in §10.3.2 and §10.3.3 (manipulation detection code technique). Such a technique essentially is a based on one-way transformation, rather than the encryption-decryption approach.

To this end, we have clearly demonstrated that in the case of authentication protocols applying symmetric cryptographic techniques, the encryption-decryption approach is insufficient for securing authentication protocols.

In authentication using asymmetric cryptographic techniques, the encryption-decryption approach is also insufficient. The Needham-Schroeder Public-key Authentication Protocol (Prot 2.5) is an example of this approach. Lowe's attack on that protocol (Attack 2.3) provides a clear evidence of the insufficiency. We will see later (§17.2.3.3) that a one-way transformation approach for specifying that protocol will provide a sound fix to that protocol with respect to thwarting Lowe's attack.

## 17.2.2   A Refined Specification for Authentication Protocols

In order to specify authentication protocols so that the precisely needed crypto-graphic services are expressed, Boyd and Mao propose to specify authentication protocols in a more complete manner [188]. They take a refinement approach which uses two notations to express the use of cryptographic transformations. Here the two notations are described:

- $\{M\}_K$ denotes a result of an encryption of the message $M$ using the key $K$. The security service provided on $M$ is confidentiality: $M$ may only be ex-tracted by a principal who is in possession of $K^{-1}$ which is the decryption key matching $K$. Notice that the message output from the decryption procedure may *not* be recognizable by the holder of $K^{-1}$.

- $[M]_K$ denotes a result of a one-way transformation of the message $M$ using the key $K$. The security service provided on $M$ is data integrity with *mes-sage source identification* which should use the techniques we have studied in Chapter 10. The message $M$ in $[M]_K$ is not a secret and may be visible from $[M]_K$ even without performing any cryptographic operation. A principal who has possession of $K^{-1}$ which is the verification key matching $K$ can verify the data-integrity correctness of $[M]_K$ and identify the message source. The ver-ification procedure outputs YES or NO: in the YES case, $[M]_K$ is deemed to have the correct data integrity and $M$ is deemed to be a recognizable mes-sage from the identified source; in the NO case, $[M]_K$ is deemed to have an incorrect data integrity and $M$ is deemed to be unrecognizable.

  In practice, $[M]_K$ can be realized by a pair $(M, \mathrm{prf}_K(M))$ where $\mathrm{prf}_K$ de-notes a keyed pseudo-random function (e.g., a message authentication code in cipher-block-chaining mode of operation, CBC-MAC, see §10.3.3, or a keyed cryptographic hash function, HMAC, see §10.3.2) for the case of symmetric technique realization, or a digital signature algorithm for the case of asym-metric technique realization. These are practically efficient realizations.

The refined notations unifies symmetric and asymmetric cryptographic tech-niques. In the former case, $K$ and $K^{-1}$ are the same, whereas in the latter case, they are the matching key pair in a public-key cryptographic algorithm.

We should emphasize that the transformation $[M]_K$ not only serves data in-tegrity, but also *message source identification*. If the verification of $[M]_K$ returns YES, then even though the message $M$ may not contain any information about its source, the verifier can identify the correct source based on the verification key in use.

Recently, the importance of coupling ciphertexts (confidentiality service) with data-integrity service becomes more widely adopted. We have seen the idea's general applications in public-key cryptography in Chapter 15. In the security community,

---

**Protocol 17.1:** The Needham-Schroeder Symmetric-key Authentication Protocol in Refined Specification

PREMISE and GOAL:   Same as in Prot 2.4.

1. Alice → Trent : $Alice, Bob, N_A$;

2. Trent → Alice : $[\{K\}_{K_{AT}}, N_A, Alice, Bob]_{K_{AT}}$;
$$[\{K\}_{K_{BT}}, T, Alice, Bob]_{K_{BT}};$$

3. Alice → Bob : $[\{K\}_{K_{BT}}, T, Alice, Bob]_{K_{BT}}$;

4. Bob → Alice : $[N_B]_K$;

5. Alice → Bob : $[N_B - 1]_K$.

---

Aiello et al. [11] use the following notation for refinement of security services:

$$\{M\}_{K_1}^{K_2}.$$

In this notation, the message $M$ is encrypted using key $K_1$, as well as protected in data-integrity where the verification key is $K_2$.

## 17.2.3   Examples of Refined Specification for Authentication Protocols

Now let us provide a few examples of authentication protocols specified using the refined notation.

### 17.2.3.1   The Needham-Schroeder Symmetric-key Authentication Protocol

The first example is the Needham-Schroeder Symmetric-key Authentication Protocol, which is specified in Prot 17.1.

In the refined specification of the Needham-Schroeder Symmetric-key Authentication Protocol, the need for data integrity service is made explicit. If the messages which Alice and Bob receive from Trent and those between them have not been altered in the transmission, then both parties can be sure, after seeing YES output from data-integrity verification, that the session key $K$ has a correct cryptographic association with their identities and their respective freshness identifiers. These assure them the correctness of the key sharing parties and the freshness of the session key. It is clear that any unauthorized alteration of the message, such as that we have seen in §17.2.1.2, will be detected.

From this refined specification of the protocol we can see that the confidentiality service is provided at the minimum level: only the session key $K$ is protected in that way. Given the random nature of a key, the minimum use of confidentiality service is desirable because it limits (minimizes) the amount of information disclosure which may be useful for cryptanalysis.

### 17.2.3.2  The Woo-Lam Protocol

The second example of a refined protocol specification is that for the Woo-Lam Protocol. The refined specification is given in Prot 17.2 (cf. Prot 11.2). This example will reveal the effectiveness of using the refined specification to achieve avoiding various attacks. The reasons behind the attacks we have seen on this protocol will become apparent: incorrect cryptographic services implied by the imprecision of the widely agreed notation for expressing the use of encryption in authentication protocols.

---

**Protocol 17.2:** The Woo-Lam Protocol in Refined Specification

PREMISE and GOAL: Same as in Prot 11.2;

CONVENTION:
  Abort run if any one-way transformation verification returns NO.

1. Alice → Bob: $Alice$;

2. Bob → Alice: $N_B$;

3. Alice → Bob: $[N_B]_{K_{AT}}$;

4. Bob → Trent: $[Alice, N_B, [N_B]_{K_{AT}}]_{K_{BT}}$;

   (∗ note: Bob includes $N_B$ in his part of the one-way transformation since *himself* is the source of this freshness identifier ∗)

5. Trent → Bob: $[N_B]_{K_{BT}}$;

6. Bob accepts if the integrity verification of $[N_B]_{K_{BT}}$ returns YES, and rejects otherwise.

---

We notice that since no message in the Woo-Lam Protocol (Prot 11.2) is secret, there is no need for providing confidentiality protection on any protocol message. The only needed cryptographic protection in the protocol is data integrity with source identification. Therefore in the refined specification of the protocol we only specify one-way transformation.

Now let us reason that none of the attacks on the original Woo-Lam Protocol or on various "fixes" which we have seen in §11.7 can be applicable to the protocol's refined version.

First, the parallel-session attack demonstrated in Attack 11.5 will no longer work. To see this, let Malice sends to Bob $[N_B]_{K_{MT}}$ in two parallel steps 3 and 3':

3. Malice("Alice") $\rightarrow$ Bob: $[N_B]_{K_{MT}}$

3'. Malice $\rightarrow$ Bob: $[N_B]_{K_{MT}}$

Let us assume that Bob remains inauspicious: he does not check these messages (since they are not meant for him to perform any checking), and simply proceeds to send out two messages in two parallel steps 4 and 4':

4. Bob $\rightarrow$ Trent: $[Alice, N_B, [N_B]_{K_{MT}}]_{K_{BT}}$

4'. Bob $\rightarrow$ Trent: $[Malice, N_B', [N_B]_{K_{MT}}]_{K_{BT}}$

However, Trent will detect two errors in these two steps. The first error occurs on the verification of the message in step 4: Trent uses $K_{AT}$ to verify $[N_B]_{K_{MT}}$ and this of course returns NO, and so the run with step 4 will be aborted. The second error occurs on the verification of the message in step 4': Trent finds that the two one-way transformations use different nonces, and hence this run will have to be aborted too (otherwise, which of the two nonces Trent should return to Bob?)

Finally, it is trivial to see that the reflection attack in Attack 11.6 will no longer work on the refined specification too. This is because, if Malice reflects message line 4 in message line 5, the verification step performed by Bob in step 6 will certainly return NO.

Now it is clear that the fundamental reason for the original Woo-Lam Protocol being flawed is its misuse of cryptographic services.

### 17.2.3.3   The Needham-Schroeder Public-key Authentication protocol

Finally, let us look at the refined protocol specification example on a public-key application: the Needham-Schroeder Public-key Authentication Protocol.

Following our discussion in §2.6.6.3, the Needham-Schroeder Public-key Authentication Protocol can be presented in three steps of message transitions. This simplified version is specified in Prot 17.3.

---

**Protocol 17.3:** The Needham-Schroeder Public-key Authentication Protocol

PREMISE and GOAL:    Same as in Prot 2.5.

    1. Alice $\rightarrow$ Bob : $\{N_A,\ Alice\}_{K_B}$;

    2. Bob $\rightarrow$ Alice : $\{N_A,\ N_B\}_{K_A}$;

    3. Alice $\rightarrow$ Bob : $\{N_B\}_{K_B}$.

---

**Protocol 17.4:** The Needham-Schroeder Public-key Authentication Protocol in Refined Specification

PREMISE and GOAL:    Same as in Prot 2.5.

    1. Alice $\rightarrow$ Bob : $\{[\,N_A, Alice\,]_{K_A}\}_{K_B}$;

    2. Bob $\rightarrow$ Alice : $\{N_A, [\,N_B\,]_{K_B}\}_{K_A}$;

    3. Alice $\rightarrow$ Bob : $\{[\,N_B\,]_{K_A}\}_{K_B}$.

---

Here, $\{\ldots\}_{K_A}$ and $\{\ldots\}_{K_B}$ denote the encryption using Alice's and Bob's public keys, respectively, and so, they can only be decrypted by Alice and Bob, respectively. Thus, upon receipt of message line 2, Alice should believe that only Bob can have decrypted message line 1 and subsequently returned her nonce $N_A$. Likewise, upon receipt of message line 3, Bob should believe that only Alice can have decrypted message line 2 and subsequently returned his nonce $N_B$. Thus, it is rather reasonable to expect that, upon termination of a run, both parties should have achieved lively identification of the other party and shared the two nonces.

However, Lowe's attack in Attack 2.3 refutes this "reasonable" belief. Now, after our convincing arguments in §17.2.1 against the imprecision of achieving authentication via encryption-decryption approach, we are able to review Lowe's attack on the original protocol from a new angle: it is the missing of the correct cryptographic service that has been the cause of the attack. The attack will disappear if the protocol is specified in a refined precision. Prot 17.4 specifies one case.

---

**Protocol 17.5:** Another Refined Specification of the Needham-Schroeder Public-key Authentication Protocol

PREMISE and GOAL:   Same as in Prot 2.5.


1. Alice → Bob : $[\{N_A\}_{K_B}, Alice]_{K_A}$;

2. Bob → Alice : $[\{N_A, N_B\}_{K_A}]_{K_B}$;

3. Alice → Bob : $[\{N_B\}_{K_B}]_{K_A}$.

---

In the refined specification, $[N_A, Alice]_{K_A}$ denotes a message of which the verification of data integrity (and message source identification) should use Alice's public key $K_A$. Hence, the transformation $[N_A, Alice]_{K_A}$ can be Alice's signature. So the message in step 1 is Alice's nonce, signed by Alice then encrypted under Bob's public key. Likewise, the message in step 2 can be one signed by Bob and then encrypted under Alice's public key.

Because the second message is signed by Bob, Lowe's attack in Attack 2.3 can no longer work on the protocol in the refined version. Malice can initiate a run with Bob by masquerading as Alice using Alice's signature (Alice has sent her signature to Malice, and he can decrypt to retrieve the signature and re-encrypt it using Bob's public key), however, now Malice cannot forward Bob's response to Alice as he did in the attack on the original protocol since then Alice will detect an error when she tries to verify Malice's signature.

Although in §2.6.6.4 we have suggested a fix for Lowe's attack on the Needham-Schroeder Public-key Authentication Protocol by adding identities of the intended communication partner in the encrypted message, we now know that the fix is not necessarily correct. Indeed, if the encryption algorithm is malleable (see §14.5.3), then there is no guarantee for the decrypting principal to be sure about the correctness of the identity revealed from decryption. Clearly, the correct fix is to use correct cryptographic services, and the refined protocol specification helps to identify and specify the correct services.

The Needham-Schroeder Public-key Authentication Protocol can also be refined in a different version, encryption-then-sign, as specified in Prot 17.5.

Again, Lowe's attack on the original protocol won't work on Prot 17.5: now Malice cannot even initiate a masquerading run with Bob.

## 17.3 A Computational View of Correct Protocols — the Bellare-Rogaway Model

In Chapters 14 and 15 we have been familiar with the idea of provable security under a computational model which originates from the seminal work of Goldwasser and Micali [127]. There, a security property (one of several confidentiality qualities) is argued under a given attacking scenario (one of several attacking games each of which models, with sufficient generality and precision, one of several typical behaviors of a real-world attacker against public-key encryption schemes). A proof of security for public-key encryption schemes with respect to an alleged attack involves to demonstrate an efficient transformation (called a polynomial-time reduction) leading from the alleged attack to a major breakthrough to a well-believed hard problem in computational complexity. It is the wide belief on the unlikelihood of the major breakthrough that should refute the existence of the alleged attack, that is, a proof is given by contradiction.

Therefore, a formal proof of security under the computational model consists of the following three steps:

i) Formal modeling of the behavior of protocol participants and that of an attacker: the modeling is usually given in the form of an attacking game played between the attacker and the target.

ii) Formal definition of security goal: success for the attacker in the attacking game is formulated here, usually in terms of (a non-negligible) probability and (affordable) time complexity formulations.

iii) Formal demonstration of a polynomial-time reduction, leading from an alleged attack on a given target to an unlikely breakthrough in the theory of computational complexity; the formal demonstration of the reduction is a mathematician's proof which shows holding of a theorem.

Bellare and Rogaway are the first researchers who initiate a computational-model approach to proof of security for authentication and authenticated key establishment protocols [24]. In their seminal work, they model attacks on authentication and authenticated key establishment protocols, design several simple protocols (entity authentication and authenticated key agreement) and then conduct proofs that their protocols are correct. Their proof leads from an alleged successful attack on a protocol to the collapse of pseudo-randomness, i.e., the output of a pseudo-random function can be distinguished from that of a truly random function by a polynomial-time distinguisher; in other words, the existence of pseudo-random functions is denied.

The reader may now like to review our discussions in §4.7 leading to Assumptions 4.1 and 4.2. These assumptions are the foundations for modern cryptography.

They imply that the result of the reduction should either be false or a major breakthrough in the foundations for modern cryptography. As the former is more likely the case, the reduction derives a contradiction as desired.

We shall only introduce the simplest case in the initial work of Bellare and Rogaway: proof of security for a two-party entity authentication protocol based on shared symmetric key [24]. Nevertheless, this simple case suffices us to view the working principle of the computational model for proof of protocol correctness.

Our introduction to the original work of Bellare and Rogaway on authentication protocols follows the three steps in the computational model for provable security. In §17.3.1 we formally model the behavior of protocol participants and that of Malice. In §17.3.2 we provide a formal definition on the security goal of mutual entity authentication. In §17.3.3 we demonstrate a proof by reduction to contradiction for a mutual entity authentication protocol.

## 17.3.1 Formal Modeling of the Behavior of Principals

The protocols considered in [24] are two-party ones. Each of the two participants of a protocol has its part as a piece of efficiently executable code with input and output values. A protocol is composed by the communications between these two parts on the input and output values. However we should notice that "communications" here may go through Malice and may be subject to his manipulation of the communicated values.

Thus, we use two steps to describe an abstract protocol: first, an efficiently executable function owned by a protocol participant; and secondly, the composition via communications.

### 17.3.1.1 Formalization of the Protocol Part Owned by an Honest Participant

Formally, this part of an abstract protocol is specified by a polynomial-time function $\Pi$ on the following input values:

$1^k$: The security parameter — $k \in \mathbb{N}$ (review §4.4.6 and Definition 4.7 for the reason why we write $k$ in the unary representation).

$i$: The identity of the principal who owns this part of the protocol; let us call this principal "the owner;" $i \in I$ where $I$ is a set of principals who share the same long-lived key.

$j$: The identity of the intended communication partner of the owner; $j \in I$.

$K$: The long-lived symmetric key (i.e., the secret input) of the owner; in our case of two-party protocols based on shared symmetric key, $K$ is also the long-lived key for $j$.

*conv:*    Conversation so far — *conv* is a bit string; this string grows with the protocol runs; new string is concatenated to it.

*r:*    The random input of the owner — the reader may consider $r$ as a nonce created by the owner.

Since $\Pi(1^k, i, j, K, conv, r)$ runs in polynomial-time in the size of its input values (notice that $1^k$ is of size $k$), we may consider $K$, $r$ of size $k$, and $i$, $j$, *conv* of size polynomial in $k$.

An execution of $\Pi(1^k, i, j, K, conv, r)$ will yield three values:

*m:*    The next message to send out — $m \in \{0,1\}^* \cup \{\text{"no message output"}\}$; this is the public message to be transmitted over the open network to the intended communication partner.

$\delta$:    The decision for the owner — $\delta \in \{\text{Accept, Reject, No-decision}\}$; the owner decides whether to accept or reject or remain undecided regarding the claimed identity of the intended communication partner; an acceptance decision usually does not occur until the end of the protocol run, although a rejection decision may occur at any time. Once a decision other than "No-decision" is reached, the value of $\delta$ will no longer change.

$\alpha$:    The private output to the owner — $\alpha \in \{0,1\}^* \cup \{\text{"no private output"}\}$; the reader may consider that an agreed session key as a result of an acceptance run is a private output to the owner.

From this formal modeling of a protocol part, we can see that Bellare and Rogaway model entity authentication protocols using important protocol ingredients: cryptographic operations, participants' identities, freshness identifiers, and the conversed messages (review §11.4 for the meanings of these protocol ingredients).

We sometimes use $\Pi(1^k, I)$ to denote an abstract protocol for the entities in set $I$.

For any given pair $i, j \in I$ (i.e., for two principals who share a long-lived symmetric key) and for $s \in \mathbb{N}$, we denote by $\Pi_{i,j}^s$ to mean player $i$ attempting to authenticate player $j$ in a session which $i$ considers as labeled by $s$. This attempt may be initiated by $i$, or may be a response to a message from the intended communication peer $j$. In fact, we shall generally (and conveniently) treat that this attempt is always a response to an *oracle query* made by Malice. This generalization is formulated by formalization of communications.

### 17.3.1.2 Formalization of Communications

Bellare and Rogaway follow the communication model of Dolev and Yao [102] (see §2.3): Malice, the attacker, controls the entire communication network.

Given Malice's network observation capability which we have been familiar with in Chapters 2 and 11, Malice can observe a series of $\Pi_{i,j}^s$, $\Pi_{j,i}^t$ for any given pair $i, j \in I$ (i.e., who share a long-lived symmetric key) even if the executions of these functions are not the making of himself. However, as an active attacker, Malice can do much more than passive observation. He can conduct as many *sessions* as he pleases among the honest principals, and he can persuade a principal (e.g., $i$) to start a protocol run as if it is run with another honest principal (e.g., $j$).

For the reason that Malice is a powerful active attacker, we conveniently let Malice own $\Pi_{i,j}^s$, $\Pi_{j,i}^t$ as *oracles* in a black-box style (for $i, j \in I$, $s, t \in \mathbb{N}$). This means, Malice can query $\Pi_{i,j}^s$ by supplying $i$ with input values $(i, j, s, conv)$, and he can query $\Pi_{j,i}^t$ likewise. When Malice queries oracle $\Pi_{i,j}^s$ using input $(i, j, s, conv)$, $i$ will add to Malice's input its own secret input $K$ and its random input $r$, and so $\Pi^s(1^k, i, j, K, conv, r)$ can be executed. After the execution, $i$ will send out an output message $m$ (if there is one), or "no message output," and the decision $\delta$, and will keep the private output $\alpha$ to itself. The outbound output results will of course be obtained by Malice, and so he may proceed his attack further.

Under the Dolev-Yao threat model of communications, before an oracle reaches the "Accept" decision, it always considers that any query it receives is from Malice.

Without loss of generality, it is harmless to consider that there always exists a particularly friendly kind of attacker, called a "benign adversary," who restricts its action to choosing a pair of oracles $\Pi_{i,j}^s$ and $\Pi_{j,i}^t$ and then faithfully conveying each flow from one oracle to the other, with $\Pi_{i,j}^s$ beginning first. In other words, the first query a benign adversary makes is $(i, j, s, \text{``"})$ (where "" denotes an empty string), generating response $m_1^{(i)}$; the second query he makes is $(j, i, t, m_1^{(i)})$, generating response $m_1^{(j)}$; and so forth, until both oracles reach the "Accept" decision and terminate. Therefore, a benign adversary behaves just like a wire linking between $i$ and $j$. We shall later see that for a provably secure protocol, Malice's behavior, if he wishes to have the targeted principals to output the "Accept" decision, will be restricted to that of a benign adversary.

In a particular execution of a protocol, Malice's $t$-th query to an oracle is said to occur at time $\tau = \tau_t \in \mathbb{R}$. For $t < u$, we demand that $\tau_t < \tau_u$.

## 17.3.2 The Goal of Mutual Authentication: Matching Conversations

Bellare and Rogaway define a notion of **matching conversations** (notice the plural form) as the security goal of mutual entity authentication.

A conversation of oracle $\Pi_{i,j}^s$ is a sequence of timely ordered messages which $\Pi_{i,j}^s$ has sent out (respectively, received), and as consequent responses, received (respectively, sent out). Let $\tau_1 < \tau_2 < \cdots < \tau_R$ (for some positive integer $R$) be a time sequence recorded by $\Pi_{i,j}^s$ when it converses. The conversation can be denoted by the following sequence:

$$conv = (\tau_1, m_1, m_1'), (\tau_2, m_2, m_2'), \ldots, (\tau_R, m_R, m_R').$$

This sequence encodes that at time $\tau_1$ oracle $\Pi_{i,j}^s$ was asked $m_1$ and responded with $m_1'$; and then, at some later time $\tau_2 > \tau_1$, the oracle was asked $m_2$, and responded with $m_2'$; and so on, until, finally, at time $\tau_R$ it was asked $m_R$, and responded with $m_R'$.

We should remind the reader that under the Dolev-Yao threat model of communications, oracle $\Pi_{i,j}^s$ should assume that this conversation has been between it and Malice, unless at time $\tau_R$ it has reached "Accept" decision. It is convenient to treat as if all conversations are started by Malice. So if $m_1 = $ "", then we call $\Pi_{i,j}^s$ an initiator oracle, otherwise, we call it a responder oracle.

Let

$$conv = (\tau_0, \text{""}, m_1), (\tau_2, m_1', m_2), (\tau_4, m_2', m_3), \ldots, (\tau_{2t-2}, m_{t-1}', m_t)$$

be a conversation of oracle $\Pi_{i,j}^s$. We say that oracle $\Pi_{j,i}^t$ has a conversation $conv'$ which matches $conv$ if there exists time sequence $\tau_0 < \tau_1 < \tau_2 < \cdots < \tau_R$ and

$$conv' = (\tau_1, m_1, m_1'), (\tau_3, m_2, m_2'), (\tau_5, m_3, m_3'), \ldots, (\tau_{2t-1}, m_t, m_t'),$$

where $m_t' = $ "no message output". These two conversations are called matching conversations.

Given a protocol $\Pi$, if $\Pi_{i,j}^s$ and $\Pi_{j,i}^t$ both always have matching conversations whenever they are allowed to complete a protocol run (again, we remind that, before reaching the "Accept" decision, each of the oracles thinks it has been running with Malice), then it is clear that Malice has not been able to mount any attack more harmful than being a benign adversary, i.e., acting honestly just like a wire.

Now we are ready to formally pronounce what a secure mutual entity authentication protocol is.

**Definition 17.1:** *We say that $\Pi(1^k, \{A, B\})$ is a secure mutual authentication protocol between A and B if the following statement holds except for a negligible probability in k: oracles $\Pi_{A,B}^s$ and $\Pi_{B,A}^t$ both reach the "Accept" decision if and only if they have matching conversations.*

When we prove that a protocol is secure using this definition, it is trivial to see that the existence of matching conversations implies acceptance by both oracles since an oracle accepts upon completing its part of the (matching) conversations.

---

**Protocol 17.6:** $MAP1$

PREMISE:    Alice $(A)$ and Bob $(B)$ share a secret symmetric key $K$ of size $k$;
$R_A$ is Alice's nonce, $R_B$ is Bob's nonce, both are of size $k$;
$[x]_K$ denotes pair $(x, \mathrm{prf}_K(x))$ where $x \in \{0,1\}^*$ and
$\mathrm{prf}_K : \{0,1\}^* \mapsto \{0,1\}^k$ is a pseudo-random function keyed by $K$.

$A$                                                        $B$

$$A \| R_A$$

$\longrightarrow$

$$[B \| A \| R_A \| R_B]_K$$

$\longleftarrow$

$$[A \| R_B]_K$$

$\longrightarrow$

---

The other direction is the non-trivial step: acceptance by both parties implies the existence of matching conversations. Consequently, the goal for Malice in an attack on a protocol is to have both oracles to accept while they do not have matching conversations. Therefore the following definition is more relevant and will be used in our proof of protocol security:

**Definition 17.2:** *We say that* $\Pi(1^k, \{A, B\})$ *is a secure mutual authentication protocol between* $A$ *and* $B$ *if Malice cannot win with a non-negligible probability in* $k$. *Here Malice wins if* $\Pi_{A,B}^s$ *and* $\Pi_{B,A}^t$ *both reach the "Accept" decision while they do not have matching conversations.*

## 17.3.3    Protocol $MAP1$ and its Proof of Security

Bellare and Rogaway demonstrate their formal proof technique by providing a simple mutual entity authentication protocol named $MAP1$ (standing for "mutual authentication protocol one") and conducting its proof of security. $MAP1$ is specified in Prot 17.6.

In this protocol, Alice begins by sending Bob $A \| R_A$ where $R_A$ is her random nonce of length $k$. Bob responds by making up a nonce challenge $R_B$ of length $k$ and sending back $[B\|A\|R_A\|R_B]_K$. Alice checks whether this message is of the right form and is correctly labeled as coming from Bob. If it is, Alice sends Bob the message $[A\|R_B]_K$ and accepts. Bob then checks whether the final message is of the right form and is correctly labeled as coming from Alice, and, if it is, he accepts.

If Alice and Bob are interfaced with a benign adversary, then with $\tau_0 < \tau_1 < \tau_2 < \tau_3$, Alice will accept with the following conversation:

$$conv_A = (\tau_0, \text{``''}, A\|R_A), (\tau_2, [B\|A\|R_A\|R_B]_K, [A\|R_B]_K);$$

and Bob will accept with the following conversation

$$conv_B = (\tau_1, A\|R_A, [B\|A\|R_A\|R_B]_K), (\tau_3, [A\|R_B]_K, \text{``no message output''}).$$

Clearly, $conv_A$ and $conv_B$ are two matching conversations.

To prove that $MAP1$ is secure when Alice and Bob are interfaced with any kind of polynomially bounded attacker (i.e., Malice), Bellare and Rogaway consider two experiments. In the first experiment, $\text{prf}_K$ in $MAP1$ is a truly random function, that is, $MAP1^s_{A,B}$ and $MAP1^t_{B,A}$ somehow share the function $\text{prf}_K$; when they apply it to a given input $x$, the result $\text{prf}_K(x)$ is a bit string uniformly distributed in $\{0,1\}^k$. Of course, we must admit that there exists no real-world method to implement such a shared function. In the second experiment, $MAP1$ is realized by a pseudo-random function family just as what happens in the real world.

Now that in the first experiment, since $\text{prf}_K(x)$ is a $k$-bit uniform string, when $MAP1^s_{A,B}$ sees the conversation $conv_A$, it sees that the uniformly random string $[B\|A\|R_A\|R_B]_K$ is computed using $R_A$ invented by itself; it can therefore conclude that the probability for this bit string not having been computed by its intended peer (in other words, having been computed by Malice) is at the level of $2^{-k}$. This level of the probability value should hold regardless how Malice acts, benign or malicious. Consequently, it can conclude that its intended peer has a conversation which is prefixed by $(\tau_1, A\|R_A, [B\|A\|R_A\|R_B]_K)$. This essentially shows to $MAP1^s_{A,B}$ that there exists a conversation matching $conv_A$ and this conversation has been computed by the intended peer in an overwhelming probability (in $k$).

Likewise, when $MAP1^t_{B,A}$ sees $conv_B$, it can conclude that a conversation matching $conv_B$ must have been produced by its intended peer except for a probability at the level of $2^{-k}$.

So if $MAP1$ is realized by a truly random and shared function, then Malice cannot win except for a negligible probability in $k$ (review Definition 17.2 for the meaning of "Malice wins").

The remaining part of the proof is an argument by contradiction.

Suppose that in the second experiment, Malice wins in a non-negligible probability (in $k$). We can construct a polynomial-time test $T$ which distinguishes random functions from pseudo-random functions. $T$ receives a function $g : \{0,1\}^* \mapsto \{0,1\}^k$ which is chosen according to the following experiment:

flip a coin $C$;

if $C =$ "HEADS" let $g$ be a random function

else pick $K$ at random and let $g = \mathrm{prf}_K$.

$T$'s job is to predict $C$ with some advantage non-negligible in $k$. $T$'s strategy is to run Malice on $MAP1$ which is realized by $g$.

If Malice wins (note that $T$ can tell whether or not Malice wins since $T$ has in its possession both oracles $MAP1_{A,B}^s$ and $MAP1_{B,A}^t$, and hence can see their conversations), then $T$ predicts $C =$ "HEADS" (i.e., $g$ is a pseudo-random function), else $T$ predicts $C =$ "TAILS" ($g$ is truly random). Thus we see that $T$'s advantage to make a distinction between a $k$-bit-output random function and a $k$-bit-output pseudo-random function is similar to Malice's advantage to win, i.e., non-negligible in $k$. This contradicts to the common belief that there exists no polynomial-time (in $k$) distinguisher to make such a distinction (see Assumption 4.2).

In practice, the pseudo-random function $\mathrm{prf}_K$ can be practically realized by a message authentication code in cipher-block-chaining mode of operation (CBC-MAC, see §10.3.3) or by a keyed cryptographic hash function (HMAC, see §10.3.2). These are practically efficient realizations.

## 17.3.4   Further Work in Computational Model for Protocols Correctness

In their seminal paper [24], Bellare and Rogaway also consider the correctness for authenticated session key establishment (session key transport) protocols (also for the two-party case). For those protocols, "Malice wins" means either a win under Definition 17.2, or a successful guess of the session key. Since the transported key is encrypted under the shared long-lived key, successful guessing of the key is similarly hard as making distinction between a pseudo-random function and a truly random function.

Later, Bellare and Rogaway extend their initial work to the three-party case: also simple protocols using a trusted third party as an authentication server [26].

Several other authors develop and explore the same approach further: e.g., [38] on key transport protocols, [37, 39] on key agreement protocols, [22, 58] on password-based protocols, [19, 67] on key exchange protocols and design to be correct protocols, and [68] on the Internet Key Exchange (IKE) protocols.

## 17.3.5   Discussion

With the rigorous formulation of matching conversations, Bellare and Rogaway provide a useful formalization for protocol security. Immediately we can see that in order for a principal to reach a meaningful conversation, some silly protocol flaws (design features) which cause reflection attacks (see §11.7.4) and type flaws (see §11.7.6) can be easily eliminated from protocol design. Also, the mathematical analysis can require, to certain extent, a protocol designer or analyzer to consider using correct or more precise cryptographic services, and so protocol flaws due to misuse of cryptographic services (see §11.7.8) will become less frequent.

It is clear that this proof technique should be working together with protocol design. It guides protocol design, and it only works on correctly designed protocols.

We should remark a limitation in this approach. Definition 17.1, and hence Definition 17.2, do not consider the case of acceptance by one oracle when two ora  s do not have matching conversations. In this case, these definitions do not ju  e whether or not a protocol is secure since we only have one acceptance. However, because the the acceptance oracle actually reaches a wrong decision, the protocol should actually be deemed insecure.

Perhaps the wrong decision in this case needn't be a concern at all. For any secure protocol, Malice can always cut the final message and thereby prevent the oracle which should otherwise receive the final message from reaching an acceptance decision. Clearly, such a non-acceptance by one oracle should not turn the protocol into an insecure one. However, we should remind ourselves that there exists non-trivial authentication failures (i.e., not a result of the non-interesting "dropping the final message attack") which cannot be handled by Definitions 17.1 and 17.2. The authentication-failure flaw in the IKE Protocol (Prot 12.1) which we demonstrated in Attack 12.1 is just such an example.

Due to the nature of communication, provable security for authentication protocols is a considerably harder problem than provable security for a cryptographic algorithm. The approach of Bellare and Rogaway sets out a correct direction. Further work extending their initial promising result is currently an active research topic.

## 17.4   A Symbolic Manipulation View of Correct Protocols

A symbolic manipulation view of correct authentication protocols is based on formal methods research results conducted by theoretic computer scientists. Under this view, security properties are expressed as a set of abstract symbols which can be manipulated, sometimes by a formal logic system, sometimes by an mechanical tool called a theorem prover, toward a YES/NO result.

## 17.4.1   Theorem Proving

A theorem proving approach can be described as follows:

- A set of algebraic or logical formulae are defined for use in system behavior description or in statement construction, where statements can be premises (known formulae) or consequences (formulae to be derived);

- A set of axioms are postulated for allowing algebraic or logical ways to derive new formulae from known ones;

- Desired behavior or properties of a system being analyzed are specified as a set of theorems that need to be proved;

- A proof of a theorem is conducted by using premises and applying axioms or proved theorems to reach desired consequences.

Sometimes, the proof process in a theorem proving approach can be mechanized if there are certain rules for applying axioms or theorems. The proof tool is then called a (mechanical) theorem prover. Applying *term rewriting rules* to rewrite a formula to a *normal form* is a standard example for mechanizing a proof. For instance, it is well-known that any boolean expression can be mechanically rewritten to a "conjunctive normal form" (CNF). However, in most cases, a mechanical theorem prover produces long and tedious proofs. It is also a well-known phenomenon that the length of a mechanical proof can be a non-polynomially bounded quantity in the size of the formula being reasoned about (review §4.6 for the meaning of a non-polynomial bounded quantity).

Although a mechanical theorem prover tends to produce impractically large proofs, a theorem proving approach is, nevertheless, capable of dealing with a system whose behavioral description cannot be represented by a finite structure (e.g., a system has an infinite state space). An induction proof of an integer-based mathematical statement is such an example. However, a short-cut proof usually requires the involvement of human ingenuity.

A necessary property in an algebraic-based theorem proving approach is that the axiom system must preserve a so-called **congruence** property. This is a generalization of the congruence relation over integers (defined in §4.3.2.5) to an arbitrary algebraic structure. A binary relation $R$ over an algebraic structure is said to be a congruence if for every dyadic operation $\circ$ of the structure, whenever

$$R(x, u) \text{ and } R(y, v)$$

then

$$R(x \circ y, u \circ v).$$

The congruence property is also referred to as the substitution property or substitutability. With substitutability, a system component can be substituted by another one of a related behavior while the desired system behavior can be consistently maintained according to the relation between the substituted components. A theorem proving system will not be regarded as a sound system if it does not preserve substitutability. Therefore, substitutability is also referred to as the *soundness* property of a theorem proving system. An unsound "theorem proving" should be useless because it is capable of producing an inconsistent statement, for example, a nonsense statement "$1 = 2$."

The *completeness* property of a theorem proving system refers to a sufficiency status of its axiom system with respect to a notion of "semantic validity." Basically, if a theorem proving system is complete, then any semantically valid statement must be provable, that is, there must exist a sequence of axioms applications which demonstrates *syntactically* the validity of the statement. The completeness property is desirable but is generally missing from a mechanical theorem prover.

A theorem proving approach aims to demonstrate some desired properties of a system, rather than to find errors in a system. This is because usually an undesirable property cannot be formulated into a theorem. Nevertheless, failure to demonstrate a desired property by a theorem proving system may often result in some insightful ideas leading to a revelation of a hidden error.

Authentication protocols are extremely error-prone systems. In general, it is difficult to come up with a secure protocol in the first place and then to demonstrate its security using a theorem proving approach. Therefore, a theorem proving approach is less useful than one which is capable of finding flaws directly.

## 17.4.2    A Logic of Authentication

One of the first attempts at formalizing the notion of protocol correctness is the "Logic of Authentication" proposed by Burrows, Abadi and Needham, named the BAN logic [62]. The BAN logic can be viewed as taking the theorem proving approach. It provides a set of logical formulae to model the basic actions of protocol participants and the meanings of the basic protocol components in an intuitive manner:

- a principal **sees** a message;

- a principal **utters** a message;

- a principal **believes** or **provides jurisdiction over** the truth of a logical statement;

- two (or more) principals **share** a secret (message);

- message encryption;

- message freshness;

- conjunction of logical statements;

- a good shared key: it has never been discovered by Malice and it is fresh.

Its axiom system is also postulated on the basis of intuition. For example, the following rule (named "nonce verification") captures the freshness requirement in message authentication precisely:

$$\frac{P \text{ believes fresh}(X) \;\wedge\; P \text{ believes } (Q \text{ said } X)}{P \text{ believes } (Q \text{ believes } X)} \qquad (17.4.1)$$

Here $Q$ believe $X$ in the consequence should be interpreted to mean that principal $Q$ uttered message $X$ *recently*. This axiom should be interpreted as saying: if principal $P$ believes that message $X$ is fresh and that principal $Q$ said $X$, then he should believe that $Q$ has said $X$ *recently*.

A protocol analysis in the BAN logic starts by formulating a set of premises which are protocol assumptions. Next, the protocol messages are "idealized." This is a process to transform protocol messages into logical formulae. Then, axioms are applied on the logical formulae with an aim of establishing a desired property such as a good-key statement.

As a theorem proving approach, the BAN logic does not have a mechanism for directly finding a flaw in a protocol. However, we should notice that one can conduct a reasoning process in a backward manner: starting from the desired goal and applying the axioms to workout a necessary set of premises. Therefore, the BAN logic has been very successful in uncovering implicit assumptions that were missing from protocol specifications but are actually necessary in order for the statement of the desired goal to hold true. A missing assumption can often lead to a discovery of a flaw. A number of flaws in a number of authentication protocols have been uncovered in the seminal work [62]. However, flaw-finding in this way depends highly on the (human) analyzer's experience, insight or even luck.

The procedure for protocol idealization can be an error-prone process. Protocols in the literature are typically specified as a sequence of principals sending/receiving messages. Use of the BAN logic requires that the analyzer translate a protocol into formulae about the message transmitted between principals, so that axioms can be applied. For example, if Trent sends a message containing the key $K_{AB}$, then the message sending step might need to be converted into

$$T \text{ said } A \xleftrightarrow{K_{AB}} B$$

and this means that the key $K_{AB}$ is a good key for communication between Alice and Bob. This idealization step seems to be a quite straightforward. However, protocol idealization is actually a subtle job. Mao observes that the BAN logic provided a context-free procedure for protocol idealization [185]. For example, the idealization step we have illustrated above is done without considering the context of the protocol. This is in fact a dangerous simplification. Mao argues that the protocol idealization in the BAN logic must be a context-sensitive process.

Another drawback in the original proposal of the BAN logic is its lack of a formal definition for an underlying semantics upon which the soundness of the axiom systems is based. As a result, the logic as a theorem proving system may be considered unsound. As another result, some axioms even lack a meaningful type; for example, in the nonce-verification rule listed in (17.4.1), $Q$ believes $X$ has a type error for most cases of $X$ (a nonce): $X$ is normally not a logical formula even after idealization. (We have made a necessary correction in our interpretation of the meaning of the nonce-verification rule.)

Attempts for providing the underlying semantics and arguing the soundness for the BAN logic have been made [3, 288].

Notable extensions to the BAN logic include the GNY logic of Gong, Needham and Yahalom [133], an extension of van Oorschot [294] and Kailar's accountability logic [158].

The GNY logic extension includes the notion of recognizability which is ba    l on specifying the type information of protocol messages so as to prevent type flaws, and the notion of a message being possessed by a principal as a result of inventing or recognizing the messages.

The extension of van Oorschot is to facilitate examination of public-key based authenticated key establishment protocols. The extended logic is used to analyze three Diffie-Hellman based key agreement protocols which includes the STS Protocol (Prot 11.6 which we have examined in §11.6.1).

In Kailar's extension, Kailar convincingly argued that in e-commerce applications, it is accountability and not belief that is important, and provides a syntax which allows such properties to be expressed and a set of proof rules for verifying them. Similar to the BAN logic, these three extensions lack a formal semantic model for the soundness of these logics.

Nevertheless, the BAN logic is undoubtedly an important seminal work. It has inspired the start of formal approaches to the analysis of authentication protocols.

# 17.5 Formal Analysis Techniques: State System Exploration

Another popular approach to formal analysis of complex systems' behavior models a complex system into a (finite) state system. Properties of a state system can be expressed by some state satisfaction relations. The analysis of the behavior of a system usually involves a state space exploration to check whether or not certain properties will or will not be satisfied. The methodology is usually called **model checking**.

In general, model checking can be a methodology for guarding against certain undesirable properties so that they never occur, or one for making sure that certain desirable properties do eventually occur. The former kind of checking is usually considered for *safety* of a system; while the latter kind of checking is for *liveness* of a system.

It is seems that checking in the safety direction is more relevant for model checking technique to be applied to the analysis of authentication protocols.

## 17.5.1   Model Checking

A model checking approach can be described as follows (we will use some concrete examples in our description):

- The operational behavior of a *finite state* system is modeled by a finite state transition system which can make state transitions by interacting with its environment on a set of events; such a system is called a "labeled transition system" (LTS).

  - For example, our single-tape Turing machine Div3 given in Example 4.1 is an LTS which can make state transitions by scanning a bit string on its input tape.

- Each state of an LTS is interpreted mechanically into (or assigned with) a logical formula.

  - For example, each state of the machine Div3 can be interpreted into a propositional logic statement in $\{0, 1, 2\}$, each stating: "the bit string scanned so far represents an integer congruent to 0, 1, or 2 modulo 3," respectively.

- A system property which is the target of an analysis is also explicitly interpreted into a logical formula.

  - For example, a target statement for the machine Div3 can be "an accepted bit string is an integer divisible by 3."

- An LTS is symbolically executed; a symbolic execution produces a "trace"

$$\pi = f_0 e_1 f_1 e_2 \ldots e_n f_n$$

where $f_0, \ldots, f_n$ are logical formulae and $e_1, \ldots, e_n$ are events.

  - For example, all bit strings in all traces accepted by the machine Div3 forms the language DIV3.

- A mechanical procedure can check whether or not a target formula is satisfiable by any formula in any trace; here satisfiability means that the target formula is a logical consequence of a formula in a trace.

    – For example, for the machine Div3, it is mechanically checkable that any terminating trace satisfies the target formula "an accepted bit string represents an integer divisible by 3."

We should notice that, unlike in the case of theorem proving where a theorem must be an assertion of a desired goal of a system, in model checking, a target formula can model an *undesirable* property of the system as well as a desirable one. For example,

"Malice knows the newly distributed session key $K$"

is a formula modeling an undesirable property for a key distribution protocol specified to run by other principals. In the case of a target formula modeling an undesirable property, the result of a satisfiable checking produces a trace which provides an explicit description of a system error. Therefore, a model checking approach can work in the mode for finding an error in a system.

We should emphasize that checking for flaws will be the main working mode for a model checking technique applied to the analysis of authentication protocols.

### 17.5.1.1  System Composition in Model Checking

When we design a complex system it is usually easier to build it up from simpler components.

For example, if we want to design a Turing machine which accepts bit strings divisible by 6 (let's denote the machine by Div6), a simple method for us to do the job can be to design a machine which accepts even numbers (let's denote such a machine by Div2) and Div3 (which has been given in Example 4.1) and then to compose the latter two machines by a "conjunctive composition." It is quite possible that designing Div2 and Div3 is easier than designing Div6 from scratch.

In this conjunctive composition, Div2 and Div3 scan their respective input tapes with the identical content, and the two machines are concurrently synchronized, namely, they make every move at the same time. Let the composed machine accept an input if and only if both component machines accept the input. Now it is obvious that this composition method does arrive at a correct Div6 (a concrete realization of such a "conjunctive composition" will be exemplified in §17.5.3).

For a more convincing example, a "disjunctive composition" of Div2 and Div3 will produce a machine to accept strings divisible by 2 *or* by 3, i.e., it accepts any number in the following sequence:

$$0, 2, 3, 4, 6, 8, 9, 10, 12, 14, 15, \ldots.$$

Here, "disjunctive composition" means that the composed machine should terminate with acceptance whenever either Div2 or Div3 does. Clearly, designing a machine with this rather awkward behavior, if not using our composition method, can be rather an awkward job too.

The task for finding flaws in authentication protocols via a model checking approach can also be simplified by a system composition method.

In fact, the problem for finding flaws from an authentication protocol is a process of examining a system which is always larger than the system which represents the specified part of the protocol. A protocol specification, at best, only describes how legitimate protocol participants should act. A successful attack, however, will always describe the behavior of a larger system in which Malice lives "in harmony" with (some of) the legitimate participants (i.e., Malice successfully cheats a principal or uncovers a secret without being detected).

Therefore, in a model checking approach to authentication protocols analysis, not only will the legitimate participants' roles specified in a protocol be modeled, but also will some typical behavior of Malice be modeled (we will see later how to model the typical behavior of Malice). Each of these modeled component parts is an LTS. They will be composed into a larger LTS which is then checked. A composition operation in a model checking tool often models asynchronous communications between system components. Here, "asynchronous" means that the composed system may make a move as a result of one of the component subsystem making a move. This models the situation that Malice's moves may be independent from those of the honest protocol participants.

In the very beginning of our introduction to the model checking approach we have emphasized that such an approach is suitable to deal with a finite state systems. Indeed, a model checking technique can only deal with systems which can be modeled into a finite state LTS. In authentication protocols analysis, this limitation requires that Malice is a computationally bounded principal: actions which relate to unbounded computational power will not be considered.

Model checking methods frequently face a "state explosion" problem: a system maps to a large LTS of too many states so that the computing resources cannot cope with it. This is problem can be particularly acute when the system being analyzed is a large software or hardware system. Such a system tends to be modeled by a huge state space. Fortunately, under the reasonable assumption that Malice is computationally bounded, most authentication protocols can be modeled by rather small LTSs. Therefore, model checking techniques are particularly suitable for the analysis of authentication protocols.

Now let us provide a brief introduction to two model checking techniques for authentication protocols analysis.

## 17.5.2   The NRL Protocol Analyzer

Meadows developed a PROLOG-based protocol checking tool named the NRL Protocol Analyzer, where "NRL" stands for Naval Research Laboratory of the United States of America [196].

Like other methodologies for authentication protocols analysis, the NRL Protocol Analyzer is also based on the Dolev and Yao threat model of communications [102] (see §2.3). So Malice is able to observe all message traffic over the network, intercept, read, modify or destroy messages, perform transformation operations on the intercepted messages (such as encryption or decryption, as long as he has in his possession of the correct keys), and send his messages to other principals by masquerading as some principal. However, Malice's computational capability is polynomially bounded, therefore there is set of "words" that Malice does not know for granted at the beginning of a protocol run, and these words should remain unknown to him after an execution of the protocol if the protocol is secure. This set of words can be secret messages or cryptographic keys for which a protocol is meant to protect. Let us call this set of words "forbidden words."

In addition to being a model checking method, the NRL also has the flavor of a term-rewriting system. It uses a modified version of the Dolev-Yao thread model which is called "term-rewriting Dolev-Yao model." We can think of Malice as manipulating a term-rewriting system. If the goal of Malice is to find out a forbidden word, then the problem of proving a protocol secure becomes a word problem in a term-rewriting system: forbidden words should remain forbidden. Equivalently, the problem of showing a protocol insecure becomes to establish a term-rewriting sequence which demonstrates that some "forbidden words" can become available to Malice.

In the NRL Protocol Analyzer, a protocol is modeled by a "global" finite-state system. The global state system is composed of a few "local" state systems together with some state information for Malice. Each local state system describes an honest principal who participates in the protocol. This way of building up the system behavior follows the standard methodology for constructing a complex system from easier-comprehensible components (see §17.5.1.1).

Malice's involvement in the global state system models how he can generate his knowledge as a result of a protocol execution. Malice's goal is to generate a "forbidden word," maybe via his involvement in the global state system which models his attempt to cause honest principals to reach certain states that are incompatible with the aimed function of the protocol. Such a state is called an "insecure state." If a protocol contains a flaw, then an insecure state should be reachable. Under the term-rewriting model, reaching an insecure state is equivalent to establishing a term-rewriting sequence which demonstrates that some words which should not be available to Malice (i.e., "forbidden words") can become available to him.

In the NRL Protocol Analyzer a set of state transition rules are defined. A transition rule can be "fired" when some conditions hold and after "firing" of a rule some consequence will occur:

Before a rule can be fired:

- Malice must be assigned some words;
- the related local states must be associated with some values;

After a rule is fired:

- some words will be output by an honest principal (and hence learned by Malice);
- the related local states will be associated with some new values.

The words involved in these rules obey a set of term-rewriting rules. Typically, there are three rules used to capture the notion of equality and the fact that encryption and decryption are inverse functions. These rules are:

$$\text{encrypt}(X, \text{decrypt}(X, Y)) \to Y$$

$$\text{decrypt}(X, \text{encrypt}(X, Y)) \to Y$$

$$\text{id\_check}(X, X) \to \text{YES}$$

To perform an analysis, the user of the NRL Protocol Analyzer queries it by presenting it with a description of a state in terms of words known by Malice (i.e., a description of an insecure state). The NRL Protocol Analyzer then searches backward in an attempt to find the initial state of the global state system. This is accomplished naturally in PROLOG by attempting to unify the current state against the right hand side of a term-rewriting rule and thus reducing from the left hand side what the state description for the previous state must be. If the initial state is found, then the system is indeed insecure; otherwise an attempt is made to prove that the insecure state is unreachable by showing that any state that leads to this particular state is also unreachable. This kind of search often leads to an infinite trace where in order for Malice to learn a word A, he must learn word B, and in order to learn word B, he must learn word C, and so on. The Analyzer includes certain features that allow the user to prove lemmas about the unreachable of classes of states. Eventually, the goal is to reduce the state space to one small enough to be examined by exhaustive search to determine whether or not an attack on the protocol is possible.

We should notice that the main algorithm used in the NRL Protocol Analyzer answers a state reachability problem. It is well known that such algorithms are not guaranteed to terminate. Therefore a limit is placed on the number of recursive calls allowed for some of the checking routines. Using the tool seems to require quite a high level of user expertise in accurately coding the transition rules for a protocol and in specifying insecure state. The tool also has an inherent limitation on being particularly applicable to protocols for key establishment.

The NRL Protocol Analyzer has been used to analyze a number of authentication protocols and has successfully found or demonstrated known flaws in some of them. These protocols include the Needham-Schroeder Public-key Authentication Protocol (Prot 2.5) [195] (for the analysis of this protocol Meadows provided a comparison between the analysis using the NRL Protocol Analyzer and Lowe's analysis using the model checker FDR in [183]), a "selective broadcast protocol" of Simmons [194, 276], the Tatebayashi-Matsuzaki-Newman protocol [162], the Internet Key Exchange protocol (IKE, see §12.2.3, a reflection attack is found in the signature based "Phase 2" exchange protocol) [137, 197] and the Secure Electronic Transaction protocols (SET) [261, 198].

## 17.5.3    The CSP Approach

CSP stands for *Communicating Sequential Processes*  and is mainly the work of Hoare [139]. The name was later changed to TCSP (Theoretical CSP) [61] after a renovation on its semantics. Finally in [140], TCSP was renamed back to CSP.

CSP belongs to a family of systems named **process algebra**. It follows an algebraic approach to the construction of an abstract computational structure (see Chapter 5). An an algebra, CSP is a language of *terms* upon which a few *operations* are defined. These operations obey a "Closure Axiom" which means that the CSP terms form a closure upon these operations (review Definitions 5.1, 5.12 and 5.13 in Chapter 5). Each operation is associated with an operational semantics to provide the meaning for the term constructed. We will see the basic CSP operations and terms in a moment.

### 17.5.3.1    Actions and Events

In CSP, a system is modeled in terms of the actions that it can perform. An action is a finite sequence of events occurring sequentially, which includes a sequence of zero length which models "doing nothing." The set of all possible events (fixed at the beginning of the analysis) is called the alphabet of a process and is denoted $\Sigma$. Thus, for any action $a$, we have $a \in \Sigma^*$. An example of alphabet for several processes to be given in a moment is $\Sigma = \{0, 1\}$, and an example of an action which can be performed by these processes is a bit string of certain property (to be clear in a moment).

In the case of CSP modeling protocols or communication systems, an action can be an atomic message, or a sequence of messages. If $M$ and $N$ are sequence of messages, then $M.N$ is also a sequence of message. Sometimes we can omit the symbol "." from a sequence of messages without causing trouble in understanding.

- $STOP$ ("inaction:" do nothing);

- $a \rightarrow P$ ("prefix:" perform action $a$ and then behave like $P$);

- $P \ \square \ Q$ ("deterministic choice:" behave like $P$ or $Q$ reactively according to external action occurred in the environment);

- $P \sqcap Q$ ("nondeterministic choice:" behave like $P$ or $Q$ with no clear reason, perhaps due to the weather);

- $/a$ ("concealment:" pay no attention to action $a$);

- $\mu X.P(x)$ ("recursion:" iterate the behavior of $P$ with $X$ being a variable, meaning: $\mu X.P(x) \stackrel{\text{def}}{=} P(\mu X.P(x))$);

- $P \parallel Q$ ("concurrency:" $P$ and $Q$ communicate evolve together when *both* can perform the *same* action);

- $P \ \vertiii\ Q$ ("interleaving:" $P$ and $Q$ are composed without communication, meaning: they do not have to perform the same action).

**Figure 17.1.** The CSP Language

## 17.5.3.2  Processes

Processes are the components of systems. They are the entities that are described using CSP, and they are described in terms of the possible actions that they may engage in. Fig 17.1 lists the most basic CSP processes and their associated operational semantics.

The basic operations in Fig 17.1 are the basic building blocks for constructing a CSP process to model and describe the behavior of a finite state system. With these building blocks and the associated operational semantics, the CSP language is powerful enough to describe a complex system finite-state system.

For example, our Turing machine Div3 given in Example 4.1, which is a finite-state system, can be re-specified concisely by a CSP process which is given in Example 17.1. This CSP specification only uses "prefix," "deterministic choice" and "recursion" operations.

**Example 17.1:** CSP Specification of Div3

$$\text{Div3} \stackrel{\text{def}}{=} S_0;$$
$$S_0 \stackrel{\text{def}}{=} (0 \to S_0) \,\square\, (1 \to S_1) \,\square\, (\{\} \to STOP);$$
$$S_1 \stackrel{\text{def}}{=} (0 \to S_2) \,\square\, (1 \to S_0);$$
$$S_2 \stackrel{\text{def}}{=} (0 \to S_1) \,\square\, (1 \to S_2)$$

$\square$

The process Div3 is defined from a number of sub-processes in a recursive manner. All the sub-processes, except $STOP$, react on events in $\Sigma = \{0, 1\}$;[a] $STOP$ reacts on nothing to mean termination. It is easy to verify that Div3 has the following behavior:

$$\text{Div3} = a \to STOP \quad \text{for all } a \in \text{DIV3} \cup \{\}$$

where for the meaning of the language DIV3, see Example 4.1.

### 17.5.3.3  Traces

The semantics of a process $P$ is defined as the set of sequences of events, denoted $traces(P)$, that it may possibly perform. Examples of traces include $\{\}$ (the empty trace) and 1001 (a possible trace of Div3).

An operation "." is defined on two sets of traces $T$, $T'$ as follows:

$$T.T' = \{tr.tr' | tr \in T \wedge tr' \in T'\}$$

where the concatenated sequence $tr.tr'$ has been defined in §17.5.3.1.

### 17.5.3.4  Analyzing Processes

A process $P$ satisfies a language (e.g., a specification) $L$ if all of its traces are part of $L$:
$$P \,\textbf{sat}\, L \Leftrightarrow traces(P) \subseteq L.$$

A process $P$ refines a process $Q$ if $traces(P) \subseteq traces(Q)$. This means that if $Q$ satisfies $L$ (i.e., $Q \,\textbf{sat}\, L$) then $P$ will also satisfies it.

---

[a]In fact, recall our stipulation in §17.5.3.1 on eliding an atomic action $\{e\}$ into to $e$; these subprocesses, except $STOP$, react on atomic action $\{0\}$ and $\{1\}$ in $\Sigma^*$; $S_0$ also reacts on the empty action $\{\}$ which leads Div3 to termination.

For example, Div3 **sat** DIV3 $\cup$ {} since $traces(\text{Div3})$ = DIV3 $\cup$ {}. Moreover, Div3 refines a process which performs all bit strings. Also, we naturally have that $STOP$ refines Div3 ($STOP$ refines any process). In a moment, we shall see a non-trivial process which refines Div3.

Model-checking techniques allow the refinement relation to be checked mechanically for finite-state processes using the tool named Failures Divergences Refinement [250] (FDR, a product of Formal Systems (Europe) Ltd; for details, visit their web site http://www.fsel.com/index.html).

### 17.5.3.5   System Composition in CSP

In §17.5.1.1 we have argued that system composition plays a crucially important role in a model checking technique. In CSP, system composition is achieved in a mechanical manner by applying "concurrency" and "interleaving" operations (these two operations together form CSP's system composition operation).

We provide here an example to show the power of CSP's composition operation. In §17.5.1.1 we have suggested a method to realize Div6, a machine accepting bit strings which are integers divisible by 6. That method considers Div6 as joint running of Div2 and Div3, which accepts a string when both sub-machines do. Although the method is not complex, it is only an abstract idea and does not provide a concrete construction for Div6.

Now, if we have constructed Div2 and Div3 in CSP, then Div6 can be built *mechanically* by composing the CSP specifications of Div2 and Div3, and the result is a concrete CSP specification for Div6. First, Div2 is simple enough to construct directly, and is given in Example 17.2.

**Example 17.2:** CSP Specification of Div2

$$\text{Div2} \stackrel{\text{def}}{=} R_0;$$
$$R_0 \stackrel{\text{def}}{=} (0 \rightarrow R_0) \,\square\, (1 \rightarrow R_1) \,\square\, (\{\} \rightarrow STOP);$$
$$R_1 \stackrel{\text{def}}{=} (0 \rightarrow R_0) \,\square\, (1 \rightarrow R_1).$$

$\square$

Now, the mechanical composition of Div6 is achieved by applying CSP's "concurrency" operation, and is given in Example 17.3.

**Example 17.3:** CSP Composition Construction of Div6

$$\text{Div6} \stackrel{\text{def}}{=} \text{Div2} \,\|\, \text{Div3} = R_0 \| S_0;$$
$$R_0 \| S_0 \stackrel{\text{def}}{=} (0 \rightarrow R_0 \| S_0) \,\square\, (1 \rightarrow R_1 \| S_1) \,\square\, (\{\} \rightarrow STOP \| STOP);$$

$$R_1 \| S_1 \stackrel{\text{def}}{=} (0 \to R_0 \| S_2) \; \Box \; (1 \to R_1 \| S_0);$$

$$R_0 \| S_2 \stackrel{\text{def}}{=} (0 \to R_0 \| S_1) \; \Box \; (1 \to R_1 \| S_2);$$

$$R_1 \| S_0 \stackrel{\text{def}}{=} (0 \to R_0 \| S_0) \; \Box \; (1 \to R_1 \| S_1);$$

$$R_0 \| S_1 \stackrel{\text{def}}{=} (0 \to R_0 \| S_2) \; \Box \; (1 \to R_1 \| S_0);$$

$$R_1 \| S_2 \stackrel{\text{def}}{=} (0 \to R_0 \| S_1) \; \Box \; (1 \to R_1 \| S_2);$$

$$STOP \| STOP \; = \; STOP.$$

$\Box$

In Example 17.3,

$$STOP \| STOP \; = \; STOP$$

is a CSP axiom named "absorption axiom" (absorption for $\|$), which is obviously true since both sides of the equation can perform nothing.

The mechanically composed version of Div6 does realize the machine correctly (the reader may test it with several numerical examples, though such tests do not form a proof for the correctness). The mechanical model checker FDR will be able to confirm that Div6 refines Div3, and it refines Div2. These two confirmations should constitute a proof that Div6 is indeed a correct realization of the aimed machine.

We can also mechanically construct a machine from Div2 and Div3, which accepts integer strings divisible by 2 or 3. This mechanical composition can be achieved by (i) applying "interleaving" operation where "interleaving" is switched to "concurrency" whenever two terms being composed can perform the same action, and (ii) by applying the following "deadlock axiom" in CSP:

$$STOP \,\|\, P \; = \; STOP \,\|\, P \; = \; P \,\|\, STOP \; = \; P \,\|\, STOP \; = \; STOP.$$

The resultant machine will be rather big (will have many states) and therefore we shall not explicitly provide its specification.

### 17.5.3.6 Analysis of Security Protocols

The usefulness of the composition operation in CSP makes the CSP particularly suitable for modeling and describing the behavior of concurrency and communication systems. It is this feature of CSP that has inspired some researchers to argue for its suitability for formal analysis of authentication protocols [251, 255, 252]. In addition, there exists a model checker tool FDR [250] which is tailored to check CSP processes for refinement relations. Lowe applied the FDR model checker and successfully uncovered a previously unknown error in the Needham-Schroeder Public-key Authentication Protocol [183].

Let $I$ be an initial set of available information. Then

- If $m \in I$ then $I \vdash m$

- If $I \vdash m$ and $I \subseteq I'$ then $I' \vdash m$

- If $I \vdash m_1$ and $I \vdash m_2$ then $I \vdash (m_1, m_2)$ (paring)

- If $I \vdash (m_1, m_2)$ then $I \vdash m_1$ and $I \vdash m_2$ (projection)

- If $I \vdash m$ and $I \vdash K \in \mathcal{K}$ then $I \vdash \{m\}_K$ (encryption)

- If $I \vdash \{m\}_K$ and $I \vdash K^{-1} \in \mathcal{K}$ then $I \vdash m$ (decryption)

**Figure 17.2.** The CSP Entailment Axioms

When analysing the property of confidentiality of messages, an "entailment" relation $I \vdash m$ captures how a piece of information can be derived from available information. Fig 17.2 specifies the entailment axioms for information derivation.

For example, we have

$$(\{\{K_1\}_{K_2}\}_{K_3}, K_3) \vdash K_3$$

and

$$(\{\{K_1\}_{K_2}\}_{K_3}, K_3) \vdash \{K_1\}_{K_2}$$

but not

$$(\{\{K_1\}_{K_2}\}_{K_3}, K_3) \vdash K_1 \quad \text{(false)}.$$

The entailment axioms intuitively model how Malice derives information. When Malice is trying to defeat the (confidentiality) goal of a protocol, he can use an initial set of information he has in his possession and some protocol messages which have been sent to the network. By the way of information derivation, $I$ is in principle an infinite set. However, in reality, given a protocol, we can always limit $I$ to a finite set of "interesting" information. Moreover, researchers have taken advantage of the fact that there is no need to actually construct $I$. It suffices to check $m \in I$ for some finite number of messages.

In summary, in the CSP approach, the use of a mechanical tool is an important element for analysis of system behavior. The mechanical tool applies a set of intuitively defined rules. For example, in system construction, a composition tool can build a larger system from composing smaller components by applying the semantic rules given in Fig 17.1; in process refinement checking, a tool can check trace relations by applying definition for refinement (see §17.5.3.4), and in information derivation, a tool can apply the entailment axioms in Fig 17.2).

The syntax of CSP, in particular the fact that it involves communications among system components, is rather unsuitable for being comfortably comprehended by humans, although it can cause no trouble when being dealt with by a mechanical checker. (We should notice that our mechanical construction of Div6 in Example 17.3 using CSP's composition operation is *succinct* because it does not involve any communications *between* the Div2 and Div3; these two components concurrently communicate with the environment which need not be specified.)

Since authentication protocols involve communications among several principals, it is far from straightforward to present the CSP model for authentication protocols to most readers of this book who are not specialists in the formal methods areas. The interested reader is referred to a textbook by Ryan and Schneider [252].

## 17.6    Reconciling Two Views of Formal Techniques for Security

Since Chapter 14, we have been seeing two distinct views of formal reasoning about security.

One view, named the computational view, which we have introduced in Chapter 14 and revisited in §17.3, is based on a detailed computational model. Let us take security for encryption (i.e., confidentiality) for example. The computational view considers confidentiality as the difficulty of distinguishing plaintexts, that is, an attacker, given two plaintexts and a ciphertext which encrypts one of the former, cannot decide which of the two plaintexts has been encrypted. Reasoning about security is usually conducted by constructing a "reduction to contradiction" style of proof where the "contradiction" is an efficient solution to a widely believed difficult problem in the area of computational complexity.

The other view, named symbolic view, which we have introduced in §17.4 and §17.5, relies on simple but effective formal language approaches. Let us, again, take security for encryption for example. The symbolic view considers confidentiality as the difficulty of finding plaintext by mechanical application of the entailment axioms in Fig 17.2. The mechanical application of the axioms can be based either on theorem proving techniques or on state system exploration techniques.

These two views come from two mostly separate communities. An uncomfortable gap between them and, indeed, between the two communities, has long been noticed. The symbolic view is desirably simple, however, sometime may mislead researchers to reach a wrong view due to oversimplification. For example, it is sometimes seen under the symbolic view that signing and encryption under the same pair of private-public key pair "cancel each other" while in fact few public-key cryptographic algorithms, even textbook versions, do so. More often, the symbolic view of encryption is viewed as a deterministic function which may easily mislead security engineers to realize them by applying some textbook encryption algorithms.

Abadi and Rogaway dutifully start a work for bridging the gap [2]. They consider that connections between the symbolic view and the computational view should ultimately benefit one another. They elaborate

- These connections should strengthen the foundations for formal cryptology, and help in elucidating implicit assumptions and gaps in formal methods. They should confirm or improve the relevance of formal proofs about a protocol to concrete instantiations of the protocol, making explicit requirements on the implementations of cryptographic operations.

- Methods for high-level reasoning seem necessary for computational cryptology as it treats increasingly complex systems. Symbolic approaches suggest such high-level reasoning principles, and even permit automated proofs. In addition, some symbolic approaches capture naive but powerful intuitions about cryptography; a link with those intuitions should increase the appeal and accessibility of computational cryptology.

The initial gap bridging work of Abadi and Rogaway provides a computational justification for the symbolic treatment of encryption. The basic idea of their work is to show that these two views are "almost homomorphic." First, under the computational view, two indistinguishable ciphertexts are considered equivalent. Secondly, under the symbolic view, two ciphertexts which cannot be deemed meaningful using the entailment axioms are considered equivalent. They establish that equivalent ciphertexts under the symbolic view necessarily implies that they are indistinguishable under the computational view. In this way, the computational view of security can be considered as a sound formal basis underpinning security in the symbolic view.

The initial gap bridging work of Abadi and Rogaway also provides insight for conducting further work for formal treatments of security for other cryptographic primitives such as signatures, hash functions, authentication or authenticated key distribution protocols.

## 17.7    Chapter Summary

In this chapter we returned to the practically important subject of authentication protocols. However, our study here was on formal techniques for their correctness.

We began by arguing the need for a refined method for protocol specification. We identified that the imprecision of the widely used protocol specification method is responsible for the common pitfalls of misusing cryptographic services in authentication protocols. We then proposed a refine specification method and presented a few refined protocols to show the effectiveness of the refined method proposed.

We then introduced formal protocol analysis methodologies, both under a computational view of proving protocol correctness and under a symbolic manipulation view of model checking for protocol errors.

As both views have their advantages and limitations, we provided a discussion on a recent move for finding relations and reconciling conflict between between the two views.

Formal analysis of authentication protocols is still a topic in an early stage of research and investigation. The material covered in this chapter inevitably has this feature too.

# Exercises

17.1 The cipher-block chaining (CBC) mode of operation is widely used with block ciphers for producing randomized ciphertexts. Does it provide confidentiality service under the "fit-for-application" security notion?

Hint: does the CBC mode of operation thwart an active attack?

17.2 In Chapter 2 we conducted a series of steps of attacking-and-fixing authentication protocols. Did our process there end up with any secure protocol? If not, why?

17.3 Use the refined protocol specification method to re-specify various exchanges of Kerberos (in §12.4.2). Provide the correct specifications for "authenticators."

Hint: review §12.4.3.

17.4 Misuse of cryptographic services is a common mistake in the design of authentication protocols and authenticated key exchange protocols. What is the most common form of the misuse?

17.5 The Bellare-Rogaway model for proving the correctness of authentication protocols is based on a "reduction-to-contradiction" approach. What "contradiction" does such a reduction lead to?

17.6 Can the Bellare-Rogaway model for proving the correctness of authentication protocols be applied to arbitrary authentication protocols?

17.7 Apply CSP "interleaving composition" to construct a CSP process which accepts integer strings divisible by 2 or 3.

Hint: review §17.5.3.5; one should use the CSP tool to do this as the resulting process is rather large.

# Part VI

# CRYPTOGRAPHIC PROTOCOLS

Nowadays, more and more commerce activities, business transactions and government services are taking place and being offered over the Internet, in particular, via WorldWideWeb-based tools. Many of these applications require security services. Shopping, billing, banking, administration of job or university applications, and tax assessments are a few such examples. For these applications, authentication, confidentiality and non-repudiation are the most commonly needed security services. These services can be adequately offered by some simple cryptographic protocols, such as TLS (SSL, which we have introduced in Chapter 12).

However, there are many "fancier things" which can also be conducted on-line while the security services they need cannot be met by a simple protocol such as TLS. For example: micro-payments (how to keep transactions at a very low cost), electronic cash (how to offer spenders' anonymity while preventing extortion), auctions (how to separate the winning bid from the losing ones without opening the seals), voting (how to keep voters' anonymity and immunity from coercion), fair exchange (how to preserve fairness in spite of the participants' resource difference), timestamping and notarization (how to maintain a legally binding effect even when the underlying mechanism, e.g., a signature scheme used, breaks down in the future), timed key recovery (is a secret recoverable after exactly $t$ multiplications).

"Fancier" security services are in general offered by "fancier" cryptographic protocols. This part contains two chapters. In Chapter 18 we introduce a class of cryptographic protocols called zero-knowledge protocols which forms a kernel technique underlying "fancier" services: proving a claimed property without disclosing a secret. In Chapter 19, we will conclude our work in this book by providing a concrete realization of our first protocol "Coin Flipping Over Telephone" (Prot 1.1). That realization provides a very strong solution to remote coin flipping where a strong and mutually trusted string of random bits is needed, yet the solution is a practical one in that the protocol uses widely available cryptographic techniques and achieves an efficiency similar to ordinary use of public-key cryptography.

# Chapter 18

# ZERO-KNOWLEDGE PROTOCOLS

## 18.1  Introduction

A basic problem in cryptography is a two-party interactive game in which one party (called the prover) *proves* to the other party (called the verifier) that a predicate of a statement holds true without letting the latter learn how to conduct the proof as the former does. Here, the verifier on its own cannot verify the predicate due to the lack of some information which is available to the prover. The game has a general name of **interactive proof (IP)** protocol (system). We can consider a proof conducted by an IP protocol as *"proof in the dark."* The phrase "in the dark" has two meanings: first, a verifier, after having been convinced the validity of what is proved, cannot have learned the knowledge possessed by the prover in order to conduct the proof; secondly, after the protocol terminates, any other third party cannot see any meaningful thing which has taken place between the prover and the verifier.

With a bold imagination, a statement which needs a proof "in the dark" can be an affirmative answer to a famous open question in mathematics (e.g., the Goldbach Conjecture[a]). In this case, a prover who may worry a possibility that, were the knowhow technique demonstrated "in the open" to a reviewer, the latter may steal or rob her/his credibility, can conduct the proof "in the dark" by convincing the latter (now the verifier in the IP protocol) the affirmative answer without providing any additional information about the knowhow.

In many real applications, there are many more serious reasons for conducting proofs "in the dark." Proof of identity as a means of authentication is a common application of IP protocols. Unlike the conventional way of authentication, e.g., by a subject issuing a digital signature, here a prover as the subject being authenticated does not want the communication transcripts for authentication to be visible by

---

[a]Every even integer greater than 2 can be represented as the sum of two primes.

any third party other than the intended verifier, and hence authentication must be conducted "in the dark." Another common case of using IP protocols is to prove that a piece of hidden information has a certain structure; this is necessary in some security applications (e.g., in an auction application) in which a hidden number (a bid) must be in a valid range in order for the application to provide a fancy service (e.g., demonstrating $x > y$ without opening $\mathcal{E}_k(x)$, $\mathcal{E}_k(y)$ which are sealed bids).

For IP protocols we are always concerned with two important questions:

**Question I** How much information does a verifier gain during the course of an interactive proof?

**Question II** How few interactions are needed for a prover to convince a verifier?

The ideal answer to Question I is *none*, or *zero* amount. An IP protocol with this quality is called a **zero-knowledge (ZK)** protocol. Question II has importance not only in practical application of IP protocols, but also in the theory of computational complexity since a quantitative answer to this problem for a given class of problems can mean discovery of a new lower bound of complexity.

In this chapter we shall study ZK protocols. Our study is a systematic introduction to various notions on the subject (including answering the above two questions). These notions are very important, however, many of them are based on background material which has been established and accumulated in many years of research papers but is not available in most textbooks in cryptography. In order to achieve a concrete understanding of them, we shall use many concrete protocols to exemplify these notions when they are introduced. We believe that this way of studying ZK protocols will ease the access to the subject.

### 18.1.1  Chapter Outline

§18.2 introduces the basic concepts of IP system. §18.3 introduces various ZK properties of IP protocols. §18.4 differentiates the notion of ZK proof from that of ZK argument. §18.5 studies error-probability characterization of two-sided-error protocols. §18.6 studies the round-efficiency problem. Finally, §18.7 introduces the notion of non-interactive ZK protocols.

## 18.2  Basic Definitions

Zero-knowledge protocols not only have a great application value in applied cryptography, the subject within the framework of IP protocols has been developed as an important branch in the theory of computational complexity. As a result, it has a rich set of definitions. We should introduce some of the notions which are relevant to applied cryptography.

## 18.2.1   Model of Computation

For the time being let us detach ourselves from Questions I and II without concerning ourselves with the points of information disclosure and practical efficiency.

We introduce the model of computation of an **interactive proof system** which is defined by Goldwasser, Micali and Rackoff [128]. A basic model of an interactive proof protocol can be denoted by $(P, V)$ where $P$ is a **prover** and $V$, a **verifier**. In the general case, the protocol $(P, V)$ is for proving a language membership statement where the language is over $\{0, 1\}^*$. We will provide a general meaning for the language in §18.2.2 and narrow it down to a special meaning of cryptographic interest in §18.2.3.

Let $L$ be a language over $\{0, 1\}^*$. For a membership instance $x \in L$, $P$ and $V$ must share the input $x$ which is therefore called **common input**. The proof instance is denoted by $(P, V)(x)$. These two parties are linked by a communication channel, through which they conduct an interaction to exchange a sequence of information denoted by

$$a_1, b_1, a_2, b_2, \ldots, a_\ell, b_\ell. \tag{18.2.1}$$

This sequence of information exchange is called a **proof transcript**. The proof transcript interleaves data transmitted by $P$, which we shall name **prover's transcript**, and those by $V$, which we shall name **verifier's transcript**. Here, not only the length $\ell$ of the proof transcript, but also that of each element exchanged in the transcript, i.e., $|a_i|$, $|b_i|$ (for $i = 1, 2, \ldots, \ell$), are bounded by a polynomial in $|x|$. The proof instance $(P, V)(x)$ must terminate in time polynomial in $|x|$.

Upon completion of the interaction in time bounded by a polynomial in $|x|$, the output of the protocol should have the following type

$$(P, V)(x) \in \{\mathsf{Accept}, \mathsf{Reject}\}.$$

These two output values mean $V$'s acceptance or rejection of $P$'s claim $x \in L$, respectively. Because $(P, V)$ is a probabilistic system, for each $x$, the output value $(P, V)(x)$ is a random variable of the common input $x$, a **private input** value of $P$, and some **random input** values of $P$ and $V$. Moreover, the elements in a proof transcript (18.2.1) are also such random variables.

Since $(P, V)$ is a game between two parties, it is natural to expect that each party will try to gain an advantage which may be more than that to which it is entitled. On the one hand, the prover $P$ should have an interest to make $(P, V)(x) = \mathsf{Accept}$ as much as possible even when in fact $x \notin L$. A prover having this behavior (strategy) is called a **cheating prover** and is usually denoted by $\tilde{P}$. On the other hand, the verifier $V$ should have an interest to discover some information about $P$'s private input from the interaction. A verifier having this behavior (strategy) is called a **dishonest verifier** and is usually denoted by $\tilde{V}$.

## 18.2.2    Formal Definition of Interactive Proof Protocols

Now we are ready to provide the formal definition for interactive proof system.

**Definition 18.1:** *Let $L$ be a language over $\{0,1\}^*$. We say that an IP protocol $(P,V)$ is an interactive proof system for $L$ if*

$$\mathrm{Prob}\left[(P,V)(x) = \mathsf{Accept} \mid x \in L\right] \geq \epsilon, \tag{18.2.2}$$

*and*

$$\mathrm{Prob}\left[(\tilde{P},V)(x) = \mathsf{Accept} \mid x \notin L\right] \leq \delta. \tag{18.2.3}$$

*where $\epsilon$ and $\delta$ are constants satisfying*

$$\epsilon \in (\frac{1}{2}, 1], \qquad \delta \in [0, \frac{1}{2}). \tag{18.2.4}$$

*The probability space is the all input values to $(P,V)$ and all random input values of $P$ and $V$.*

The probability expression in (18.2.2) characterizes a notion of **completeness** for $(P,V)$. The probability bound $\epsilon$ is called **completeness probability** of $(P,V)$. This means that if $x \in L$, then $V$ will accept with probability *at least* $\epsilon$.

The probability expression in (18.2.3) characterizes a notion of **soundness** for $(\tilde{P},V)$. The probability bound $\delta$ is called **soundness probability** of $(\tilde{P},V)$. This means that if $x \notin L$, then $V$ will accept with probability *at most* $\delta$.

Comparing Definition 18.1 with Definition 4.5 (in §4.4) in which the complexity class $\mathcal{PP}$ has the error probability characterizations in (4.4.1), (4.4.2) and (4.4.3), we obtain the following result:

**Theorem 18.1:** $\mathcal{IP} = \mathcal{PP}$ *where $\mathcal{IP}$ is the class of all languages whose membership questions can be answered by IP protocols.*  $\square$

Moreover, from our study in §4.4.1 we know that the completeness (respectively, soundness) probability bound can be enlarged (resp., reduced) to arbitrarily closing to 1 (resp., 0) by sequentially and independently repeating $(P,V)$ polynomially many times (in the size of the common input) and by $V$ taking "majority election" to reach an acceptance/rejection decision.

Now let us review all the notions introduced so far by looking at a concrete example of IP protocol: Prot 18.1.

**Example 18.1:** In Prot 18.1, Alice is a *prover* and Bob is a *verifier*. The *common input* to (Alice, Bob) is $X = f(z)$ where $f$ is a one-way and homomorphic function over $\mathbb{Z}_n$ stated in Prot 18.1. The *membership claim* made by Alice is that $X \in$

---

**Protocol 18.1:** An Interactive Proof Protocol for Subgroup Membership
(∗ see Remark 18.1 regarding the name of this protocol ∗)

COMMON INPUT:
  i) $f$: a one-way function over $\mathbb{Z}_n$ satisfying the homomorphic condition:

$$\forall x, y \in \mathbb{Z}_n : f(x + y) = f(x) \cdot f(y);$$

  ii) $X = f(z)$ for some $z \in \mathbb{Z}_n$;

PRIVATE INPUT of Alice: $z < n$;

OUTPUT TO Bob: Membership $X \in \langle f(1) \rangle$, i.e., $X$ is generated by $f(1)$.

Repeat the following steps $m$ times:

  1. Alice picks $k \in_U \mathbb{Z}_n$, computes Commit $\leftarrow f(k)$ and sends Commit to Bob;

  2. Bob picks Challenge $\in_U \{0, 1\}$ and sends it to Alice;

  3. Alice computes Response $\leftarrow \begin{cases} k & \text{if Challenge} = 0 \\ k + z \ (\text{mod } n) & \text{if Challenge} = 1 \end{cases}$
     She sends Response to Bob;

  4. Bob checks $f(\text{Response}) \overset{?}{=} \begin{cases} \text{Commit} & \text{if Challenge} = 0 \\ \text{Commit } X & \text{if Challenge} = 1 \end{cases}$
     he rejects and aborts the protocol if the checking shows error;

Bob accepts.

---

$\{ f(x) \mid x \in \mathbb{Z}_n \}$. This is in fact the subgroup membership $X \in \langle f(1) \rangle$ since $X = f(1)^z$ (see Remark 18.1 for a general condition for this problem to be hard for Bob). Alice's *private input* is $z \in \mathbb{Z}_n$ as the pre-image of $X$ under the one-way and homomorphic function $f$.

In the protocol the two parties interact $m$ times and produce the following *proof transcript*:

$$\text{Commit}_1, \text{Challenge}_1, \text{Response}_1, \ldots, \text{Commit}_m, \text{Challenge}_m, \text{Response}_m.$$

The protocol *outputs* Accept if every checking conducted by Bob passes, and Reject otherwise.

This protocol is *complete*. That is, if Alice does have in her possession of the pre-image $z$ and follows the protocol instruction, then Bob will always accept.

**Completeness**

Indeed, the *completeness probability* expression (18.2.2) is met by $\epsilon = 1$ since Alice's response always satisfies Bob's verification step:

$$f(\textsf{Response}) = \begin{cases} \textsf{Commit} & \text{if } \textsf{Challenge} = 0 \\ \textsf{Commit } X & \text{if } \textsf{Challenge} = 1 \end{cases}$$

for either cases of his random choice of $\textsf{Challenge} \in_U \{0, 1\}$.

This protocol is *sound*.

**Soundness**

We need to find the *soundness probability* $\delta$.

Bob's checking step (Step 4) depends on his random choice of $\textsf{Challenge}$ which takes place after Alice has sent $\textsf{Commit}$. The consistent passing of Bob's verification shows him the following two cases:

**Case** $\textsf{Challenge} = 0$:   Bob sees that Alice knows pre-image($\textsf{Commit}$);

**Case** $\textsf{Challenge} = 1$:   Bob sees

$$\text{pre-image}(X) = \textsf{Response} - \text{pre-image}(\textsf{Commit}) \pmod{n}.$$

Since Alice cannot anticipate Bob's random choice of the challenge bit after she has sent out the commitment, in the case $\textsf{Challenge} = 1$, she should also know pre-image($\textsf{Commit}$) and hence should know pre-image($X$) too.

If Alice does not know pre-image($X$), then she has to cheat by guessing the random challenge bit *before* sending out the commitment. In her cheating "proof," the commitment can be computed as follows:

- choosing at random $\textsf{Response} \in_U \mathbb{Z}_n$;

- guessing $\textsf{Challenge}$;

- computing "commitment" $\textsf{Commit} \leftarrow \begin{cases} f(\textsf{Response}) & \text{if } \textsf{Challenge} = 0 \\ f(\textsf{Response})/X & \text{if } \textsf{Challenge} = 1 \end{cases}$

Clearly, in this cheating "proof," Bob will have $1/2$ odds to reject each iteration of the interaction. Therefore, we have $\delta = 1/2$ as the *soundness* error probability (i.e., for Alice having survived successful cheating). If $m$ iterations result in no rejection, then probability for Alice's successful cheating should be bounded by $2^{-m}$. Bob will be sufficiently confident that Alice cannot survive successful cheating if $m$ is sufficiently large, i.e., $2^{-m}$ is sufficiently small. For example, $m = 100$ provides a sufficiently high confidence for Bob to prevent Alice's cheating. Therefore, Alice's proof is valid upon Bob's acceptance.

Later (in §18.3.1 and Example 18.2) we shall further investigate a property of *perfect zero-knowledge-ness*: if the function $f$ is indeed one-way, then Bob, as polynomially bounded verifier, cannot find any information about Alice's private input. □

**Remark 18.1:** *By homomorphism, $f(x) = f(1)^x$ for all $x \in \mathbb{Z}_n$. Therefore Prot 18.1 is also (in fact, more often) called a protocol for Alice to prove her possession of the discrete logarithm of $X$ to the base $f(1)$. We have chosen to name the protocol "subgroup membership proof" because the membership problem is a more general one tackled by IP protocols. When using this (more general and appropriate) name, we should emphasize the general case of $\mathrm{ord}[f(1)]$ being a proper and secret divisor of $n$, i.e., the general case where $f(1)$ does not generate a group of $n$ elements. In this general case, Bob cannot directly verify the subgroup membership without Alice's help.* □

Remark 18.1 actually states that deciding subgroup membership is in general a hard problem. We should provide some further elaborations on the difficulty. Notice that although the set

$$ L_n = \{ f(x) = f(1)^x \mid x \in \mathbb{Z}_n \} $$

is a cyclic group (since it is generated by $f(1)$, see §5.2.3), Bob cannot easily decide $\#L_n \overset{?}{=} n$. He will need to factor $n$ down to individual primes in order to answer this question (i.e., to see if $f(1)$ is a primitive root or an $n$th root of 1, see Theorem 5.11 in §5.4.4). Only for the case of $\#L_n = n$ can Bob answer YES to the subgroup membership problem in Prot 18.1 without actually running the protocol with Alice (since then $f(1)$ must generate all $n$ elements in $L_n$). The difficulty for subgroup membership decision then rests on that for factoring $n$ of a large magnitude. Therefore, for Prot 18.1 to tackle subgroup membership problem, the integer $n$ must be a sufficiently large composite. For this reason, we stipulate $\log n$ as the security parameter for Prot 18.1.

In §18.3.1.1 we will see a special case of common input parameter setting which will degeneralize Prot 18.1 into the special case for proving possession of discrete logarithm.

## 18.2.3 A Complexity Theoretic Result

The material to be given here (in the scope of §18.2.3) may be skipped without causing any trouble for understanding other notions of ZK protocols to be introduced in the rest of this chapter.

We now derive a fact in the theory of computational complexity. The fact is stated in (4.5.1). In Chapter 4 we were not able to provide an evidence for this fact. Now we are.

In *applied cryptography*, we shall only be interested in IP protocols which answer membership questions for a subclass languages of $\mathcal{IP}$. For any $L$ in the subclass, the membership question $x \overset{?}{\in} L$ have the following two characterizations:

i) It is not known whether there exists a polynomial-time (in $|x|$) algorithm, deterministic or probabilistic, to answer the question. Otherwise, there is no role for $P$ to play in $(P, V)$ since $V$ alone can answer the question.

ii) The question can be answered by a polynomial-time (in $|x|$) algorithm if the algorithm has in its possession of a witness for the question.

Recall our classification for the complexity class $\mathcal{NP}$ (§4.5): we can see that (i) and (ii) characterize the class $\mathcal{NP}$. Precisely, they characterize NP problems which have sparse witnesses. Since $\mathcal{IP} = \mathcal{PP}$ (Theorem 18.1), we have

$$\mathcal{NP} \subseteq \mathcal{PP}.$$

Therefore for any language $L \in \mathcal{NP}$, there exists an IP protocol $(P, V)$ for $L$, that is, for any $x \in L$, $(P, V)(x) = \mathsf{Accept}$ terminates in time polynomial in $|x|$.

In fact, this property has been demonstrated in a *constructive* manner by several authors. They construct ZK (IP) protocols for some NPC languages (Definition 4.11 in §4.5.1), e.g., Graph 3-Colourability by Goldreich, Micali and Wigderson [126], and Boolean Express Satisfiability by Chaum [72]. Once a ZK protocol $(P, V)$ for an NPC language $L$ has been constructed, it is clear that membership $y \in L'$ for $L'$ being an *arbitrary* NP language can be proved in ZK in the following two steps:

1. $P$ reduces $y \in L'$ to $x \in L$ where $L$ is an NPC language (e.g., $x$ is an instance of Graph 3-Colourability or one of Boolean Express Satisfiability. Since $P$ knows $y \in L'$, this reduction transformation can be performed by $P$ in time polynomial in the size of $y$. $P$ encrypts the transformation and sends the ciphertext to $V$.

2. $P$ conducts a ZK proof for $V$ to verify the correct encryption of the polynomial reduction transformation. We shall provide a convincing explanation in §18.4.2 that ZK proof of correct encryption of a string can be easily done if the encryption is in Goldwasser-Micali probabilistic encryption scheme (Alg 14.1).

Clearly, these two steps combining the concrete ZK protocol construction for proving membership $x \in L$ do constitute a valid ZK proof for $y \in L'$. Notice that the method does not put any restriction of the NP language $L'$ other than its membership in $\mathcal{NP}$.

Also clearly, such a general proof method for membership in an arbitrary NP language cannot have an efficiency for practical use. In §18.6 we shall stipulate that a practically efficient ZK (and IP) protocol should have the number of interactions bounded by a linear function in a security parameter. A general proof method can hardly have its number of interactions be bounded by a linear polynomial, since at the moment we do not know any linear reduction method to transform an NP problem to an NPC one. Any known reduction is a polynomial of a very high degree. That is why we say that ZK proof for membership in an arbitrary NP language is only a theoretic result, albeit an important one. It provides a *constructive* evidence for $\mathcal{NP} \subseteq \mathcal{PP}$.

Equation $\mathcal{NP} = \mathcal{PP}$ is an open question in the theory of computational complexity.

# 18.3   Zero-knowledge Properties

Let us now consider the case of Question I (in §18.1) being answered ideally: $(P, V)$ is a ZK protocol, that is, *zero* amount or *no* information whatsoever about $P$'s private input is disclosed to $\tilde{V}$ (or $V$) after an execution of the protocol, except the validity of $P$'s claim.

In order for $(P, V)$ to achieve this quality, we must restrict the computational power of $V$ (and $\tilde{V}$) so that it is bounded by a polynomial in the size of the common input. Clearly, without this restriction we needn't talk about zero knowledge since $V$ of an unbounded computational resource can help itself to find $P$'s private input hidden behind the common input.

In several sections to follow we shall identify several qualities of ZK-ness:

- perfect ZK (§18.3.1),

- honest-verifier ZK (§18.3.2),

- computational ZK (§18.3.3), and

- statistical ZK (18.3.4).

## 18.3.1   Perfect Zero-knowledge

Let $(P, V)$ be an IP protocol for a language $L$. For any $x \in L$, a proof run $(P, V)(x)$ not only outputs Accept, but also produces a proof transcript which interleaves the prover's transcript and the verifier's transcript. The elements in the proof transcript are random variables of all input values including the random input to $(P, V)$.

Clearly, should $(P, V)(x)$ disclose any information about $P$'s private input, then it can only be the case that it is the proof transcript that has been responsible for the information leakage.

However, if the random variables in the proof transcript are *uniformly random* in their respective probability spaces and are independent of the common input, then it is quite senseless to allege that they can be responsible for any information leakage. We can consider that in such a situation (i.e., when the proof transcript is uniformly random and independent of the common input), the prover speaks to the verifier in a language which contains *no redundancy*, or contains the *highest possible entropy* (see Properties of Entropy in §3.7.1). Therefore, *no matter how clever* (or how powerful) the verifier can be, it cannot learn anything conveyed by this language, even if it spends very very long time to learn the language!

Now let us show that Prot 18.1 is perfect ZK.

**Example 18.2:** Review Prot 18.1. A proof transcript produced from a proof run of (Alice, Bob)$(X)$ is

$$\mathsf{Commit}_1, \mathsf{Challenge}_1, \mathsf{Response}_1, \ldots, \mathsf{Commit}_m, \mathsf{Challenge}_m, \mathsf{Response}_m,$$

where (for $i = 1, 2, \ldots, m$)

- $\mathsf{Commit}_i = f(k_i)$ with $k_i \in_U \mathbb{Z}_n$;

  clearly, since Alice chooses uniform $k_i$, $\mathsf{Commit}_i$ must also be uniform in the range space of the function $f$ and is independent of the common input $X$;

- $\mathsf{Challenge}_i \in \{0, 1\}$;

  Bob should pick the challenge bit uniformly, but we needn't demand him to do so, see $\mathsf{Response}$ below;

- $\mathsf{Response}_i = k_i + z\,\mathsf{Challenge}_i \pmod{n}$;

  clearly, due to the uniformity of $k_i$, $\mathsf{Response}_i$ must be uniform in $\mathbb{Z}_n$ for either cases of $\mathsf{Challenge}_i \in \{0, 1\}$ (even if $\mathsf{Challenge}_i$ is non-uniform) and is independent of the common input $X$.

Therefore the data sent from Alice in a run of Prot 18.1 are uniform. They can tell Bob no information whatsoever about Alice's private input. This protocol is a perfect ZK protocol.                                                                  □

From this example we also see that the elements in Alice's transcript are uniform regardless of how Bob chooses his random challenge bits. In other words, Bob can have no strategy to make an influence on the distribution of Alice's transcript. Therefore, Prot 18.1 is perfect ZK even if Bob is dishonest.

For a perfect ZK protocol, we do not have to run the protocol in order to obtain a proof transcript. Such a transcript (which is merely a string) can be produced via random coin flipping in time polynomial in the length of the transcript. Definition 18.2 captures this important notion of perfect ZK-ness.

**Definition 18.2:** *An IP protocol $(P, V)$ for $L$ is said to be perfect zero-knowledge if for any $x \in L$, a proof transcript of $(P, V)(x)$ can be produced by a polynomial-time (in the size of the input) algorithm $\mathcal{EQ}(x)$ with the same probability distributions.*

Conventionally, the efficient algorithm $\mathcal{EQ}$ is named a **simulator** for a ZK protocol, which produces a simulation of a proof transcript. However, in the case of $(P, V)$ being perfect ZK, we do not want to name $\mathcal{EQ}$ a simulator. It is exactly an **equator**.

### 18.3.1.1   Schnorr's Identification Protocol

In Prot 18.1, Bob uses bit challenges. This results in a large soundness error probability value $\delta = 1/2$. Therefore the protocol has to repeat $m$ times in order to reduce the error probability to $2^{-m}$. Typically, $m = 100$ is required to achieve a high confidence against Alice's cheating. The necessity for a large number of interactions means a poor performance both in communication and in computation.

Under certain conditions for setting the security parameter in the common input, it is possible to reduce the soundness error probability value and hence to reduce the number of interactions. The condition is: the verifier Bob should know the factorization of $n$. The reason why this condition is needed will be revealed in §18.6.1. A special case for Bob knowing the factorization of $n$ is $n$ being a prime number. Let us now see a concrete protocol using this case of parameter setting. The protocol is **Schnorr's Identification Protocol** which is proposed by Schnorr [258] for a real-world (smartcard-based) identification application.

Schnorr's Identification Protocol is a special case of Prot 18.1 where the function $f(x)$ is realized by $g^{-x} \pmod{p}$ in the finite field $\mathbb{F}_p$ where the subgroup $\langle g \rangle$ is of a prime order $q | p - 1$. It is easy to see that $g^{-x} \pmod{p}$ is homomorphic. Moreover, for sufficiently large primes $p$ and $q$, e.g., $|p| = 1024$, $|q| = 160$, $g^{-x} \pmod{p}$ is also one-way due to the DL assumption (Assumption 8.2 in §8.4).

In this parameter setting, Schnorr's Identification Protocol, which we specify in Prot 18.2, permits Bob to use slightly enlarged challenges up to $\log_2 \log_2 p$ bits.

**Remark 18.2:** *With the prime $q | p - 1$ given publicly, Schnorr's Identification Protocol is no longer one for answering subgroup membership question. Now Bob himself alone can answer question $y \in \langle g \rangle$ without need of Alice's help by checking: $y^q \equiv g^q \equiv 1 \pmod{p}$. Therefore, Schnorr's Identification Protocol is for proving a more specific problem: Alice has in her possession of the discrete logarithm of $y$ to the base $g$, as her cryptographic credential.* □

Now let us investigate security properties of Schnorr's Identification Protocol.

---

**Protocol 18.2:** Schnorr's Identification Protocol

COMMON INPUT:

   $p, q$: two primes satisfying $q|p - 1$;
   (∗ typical size setting: $|p| = 1024$, $|q| = 160$ ∗)
   $g$: $\text{ord}_p(g) = q$;
   $y$: $y = g^{-a} \pmod{p}$;
   (∗ tuple $(p, q, g, y)$ is Alice's public-key material, certified by an CA ∗)

PRIVATE INPUT of Alice: $a < q$;

OUTPUT TO Bob: Alice knows some $a \in \mathbb{Z}_q$ such that $y \equiv g^{-a} \pmod{p}$.

Repeating the following steps $\log_2 \log_2 p$ times:

1. Alice picks $k \in_U \mathbb{Z}_q$ and computes $\mathsf{Commit} \leftarrow g^k \pmod{p}$;
   she sends $\mathsf{Commit}$ to Bob;

2. Bob picks $\mathsf{Challenge} \in_U \{0, 1\}^{\log_2 \log_2 p}$;
   he sends $\mathsf{Challenge}$ to Alice;

3. Alice computes $\mathsf{Response} \leftarrow k + a\,\mathsf{Challenge} \pmod{q}$;
   She sends $\mathsf{Response}$ to Bob;

4. Bob checks $\mathsf{Commit} \equiv g^{\mathsf{Response}} y^{\mathsf{Challenge}} \pmod{p}$;
   he rejects and aborts if the checking shows error;

Bob accepts.

(∗ Bob's computation of $g^{\mathsf{Response}} y^{\mathsf{Challenge}} \pmod{p}$ should apply Alg 15.2 and so the cost is similar to computing single modulo exponentiation ∗)

---

### 18.3.1.2   Security Properties of Schnorr's Identification Protocol

**Completeness**

Trivially preserved. In fact, $\epsilon = 1$ can be obtained. This is left for the reader as an exercise (Ex 18.7).

**Soundness**

Suppose Alice is a cheater, i.e., she does not have the correct discrete logarithm value. For $\mathsf{Commit}$ she sent in an iteration, Bob, after picking $\mathsf{Challenge} \in_U$

$\{0,1\}^{\log_2 \log_2 p}$, is waiting for

$$\mathsf{Response} = \log_g[\mathsf{Commit}\ y^{\mathsf{Challenge}}\ (\bmod\ p)]\ (\bmod\ q).$$

This equation shows that, for fixed Commit and $y$, there will be $\log_2 p$ distinct values for Response which correspond to $\log_2 p$ distinct values for Challenge, respectively. Given the small magnitude of $\log_2 p$, the best strategy for computing the correct response from Commit $y^{\mathsf{Challenge}}$ $(\bmod\ p)$ is to guess Challenge before fixing Commit as follows:

1. picking $\mathsf{Response} \in_U \mathbb{Z}_q$;

2. guessing $\mathsf{Challenge} \in_U \{0,1\}^{\log_2 \log_2 p}$;

3. computing $\mathsf{Commit} \leftarrow g^{\mathsf{Response}} y^{\mathsf{Challenge}}\ (\bmod\ p)$.

Clearly, the soundness probability for correct guessing is $1/\log_2 p$ per iteration, that is, we have found $\delta = 1/\log_2 p$ as the soundness error probability for a single round of message interactions.

The reduced soundness error probability for a single round of message exchange in Schnorr's Identification Protocol means an improved performance from that of Prot 18.1. This is because, for Prot 18.1 running $m$ iterations to achieve a negligibly small soundness error probability $\delta = 2^{-m}$, Schnorr's Identification Protocol only needs

$$\ell = \frac{m}{\log_2 \log_2 p}$$

rounds of iterations while maintaining the soundness error probability unchanged from that of Prot 18.1 using $m$ rounds of interactions.

For $p \approx 2^{1024}$ and $m = 100$, we have $\ell = 100/10 = 10$. That is, the enlarged challenge reduces the number of interactions from that of Prot 18.1 by 10 fold while keeping the same low soundness error probability.

**Perfect ZK-ness**

For common input $y$, we can construct a polynomial-time (in $|p|$) equator $\mathcal{EQ}(y)$ as follows:

1. $\mathcal{EQ}$ initializes Transcript as an empty string;

2. For $i = 1, 2, \ldots, \log_2 \log_2 p$:

   (a) $\mathcal{EQ}$ picks $\mathsf{Response}_i \in_U \langle g \rangle$;

   (b) $\mathcal{EQ}$ picks $\mathsf{Challenge}_i \in_U \{0,1\}^{\log_2 \log_2 p}$;

   (c) $\mathcal{EQ}$ computes $\mathsf{Commit}_i \leftarrow g^{\mathsf{Response}_i} y^{\mathsf{Challenge}_i}\ (\bmod\ p)$;

   (d) $\mathsf{Transcript} \leftarrow \mathsf{Transcript} \parallel \mathsf{Commit}_i, \mathsf{Challenge}_i, \mathsf{Response}_i,$

Clearly, Transcript can be produced in polynomial time, and the elements in it have distributions which are the same as those in a real proof transcript.

From our analysis of Schnorr's Identification Protocol we see that enlarging challenge size reduces the number of interactions while maintaining the soundness error probability unchanged. Then why have we confined the size enlargement to a rather strange and small value $\log_2 \log_2 p$?

Enlarging challenge size not only improves performance (a positive result), in §18.3.2 we will further see that this also has a negative consequence. Be careful, size matters!

## 18.3.2    Honest-Verifier Zero-knowledge

At first glance of Schnorr's Identification Protocol, it is not very clear why we have restricted the size for the challenge bits to the case $|\mathsf{Challenge}| = \log_2 \log_2 p$. It seems that if we use $|\mathsf{Challenge}| = \log_2 p$, then the protocol will become even more efficient: it only needs one interaction to achieve the same low soundness probability ($\delta \approx 1/p$) against Alice cheating. Moreover, it seems that the equator $\mathcal{EQ}$ can be constructed in the same way for Schnorr's Identification Protocol; again, now $\mathcal{EQ}$ only needs one single "loop" to produce Transcript which contains uniformly distributed elements.

However, there is a subtlety for the problem. Let us examine it now.

### 18.3.2.1    What a Dishonest Verifier Can Do

Let $\tilde{\mathsf{Bob}}$ be a **dishonest verifier**, that is, he does not follow protocol instructions and always tries to trick Alice to disclose some information which may be useful for him. Suppose that $\tilde{\mathsf{Bob}}$ is allowed to pick a large Challenge so that $2^{\mathsf{Challenge}}$ is a non-polynomially bounded quantity. Then he may devise a trick to force Alice to produce a transcript which is inequatable (i.e., cannot be equated) or unsimulatable in polynomial time. If $\tilde{\mathsf{Bob}}$ can do this, then by Definition 18.2, the protocol can no longer be perfect ZK.

Let us examine the issue by slightly modifying Schnorr's Identification Protocol which allows $\tilde{\mathsf{Bob}}$ to choose $\mathsf{Challenge} \in \mathbb{Z}_q$, i.e., amplifying the challenge space from $\{0,1\}^{\log_2 \log_2 p}$ to $\mathbb{Z}_q$. Here is what $\tilde{\mathsf{Bob}}$ should do in this modified Schnorr's Identification Protocol.

Upon receipt of Commit, he applies a suitable pseudo-random function prf with the large output space $\mathbb{Z}_q$ to create his Challenge as:

$$\mathsf{Challenge} \leftarrow \mathrm{prf}(\text{"Meaningful transcript, signed Alice"} \parallel \mathsf{Commit}).$$

So created Challenge is pseudo-random (i.e., not truly random). We shall see in a moment the full meaning of the string "Meaningful transcript, signed Alice."

Poor Alice, due to the general indistinguishability between pseudo-randomness and true randomness (Assumption 4.2), she can have no way to recognize the pseudo-randomness of Challenge, and will have to follow the protocol instruction by sending back Response $= k + a$ Challenge (mod $q$).

Remember that Alice's answer satisfies

$$\text{Commit} = g^{\text{Response}} y^{\text{Challenge}} \pmod{p}, \tag{18.3.1}$$

since this is exactly the verification procedure conducted by B̃ob. Therefore, Alice has helped B̃ob to have constructed the following equation

$$\text{Challenge} = \text{prf}(\text{``Meaningful transcript, signed Alice''}$$
$$\| \, g^{\text{Response}} y^{\text{Challenge}} \pmod{p}). \tag{18.3.2}$$

Viewed by a third party, (18.3.2) means either of the following two cases:

i) the equation was constructed by Alice using her private input, and hence Alice discloses the fact that she has been in interaction with, and fooled by, B̃ob, or

ii) B̃ob has successfully broken the pseudo-random function prf of the large output space $\mathbb{Z}_q$, because he has constructed equation

$$\text{Challenge} = \text{prf}(\cdots y^{\text{Challenge}}).$$

This is a well-known hard problem because prf is assumed one-way.

Given that B̃ob is polynomially bounded, the third party will of course believe that (i) is the case. Poor Alice, in the proof transcript (Commit, Challenge, Response) satisfying (18.3.1) and (18.3.2), the pair (Commit, Response) is precisely a signature of message "Meaningful transcript, signed Alice" under Schnorr's signature scheme (check Alg 10.4 with prf $= H$)! Since only Alice could have issued the signature (recall, in §16.3.2 we have proved the signature scheme's strong security against forgery under adaptive chosen-message attack), the third party has made a correct judgement!

A small consolation for Alice is that the information disclosure caused by B̃ob is not a too disastrous one (though this assertion has to be based on applications really). As we have analyzed in §7.5.2, if Alice picks $k \in_U \mathbb{Z}_q$ independent from all previous instances, then

$$\text{Response} = k + a \, \text{Challenge} \pmod{q}$$

forms a one-time pad (shift cipher) encryption of Alice's private input $a$, which provides information-theoretic quality of security. This means that the proof transcript still does not disclose to B̃ob or a third party any information about Alice's private input $a$.

However, as an interactive proof degenerates to a signature which needn't be issued in an interactive way, the security service offered by an interactive proof is lost: now any third party can verify the proof result. This means that now showing knowledge is no longer conducted "in the dark," it is conducted "in the open." That is why the variant protocol (i.e., Schnorr's Identification Protocol using a large challenge) is no longer ZK any more!

In general, if Schnorr's Identification Protocol uses large challenge in $\mathbb{Z}_q$, then the protocol has a **honest-verifier zero-knowledge** property. In an honest-verifier ZK protocol, if the verifier honestly follows the protocol instruction, then the protocol is perfect ZK. This is because, if the verifier picks a truly random challenge, then the proof transcript can be equated efficiently.

For an honest-verifier ZK protocol $(P, V)$, if the behavior of $V$ is fixed into a confined manner so that it cannot force $P$ to produce an inequatable or unsimulatable transcript, then $(P, \tilde{V})$ can still be a perfect ZK protocol. In §18.3.2.3 we will see that limiting the size of the challenge bits is a solution. There are ways to impose behavioral confinement on $V$, e.g.,

- forcing $V$ to demonstrate its honesty in choosing random challenge is a solution; in §18.6.2 we will introduce an extremely efficient perfect ZK proof protocol which uses this idea;

- providing $V$ with an entitlement to simulate a "proof," and hence a dishonest verifier can only show its dishonesty if it tries to trick the prover; in §18.7.1 we will see another extremely efficient protocol which uses this idea.

### 18.3.2.2   The Fiat-Shamir Heuristic

Fiat and Shamir suggest a general method for transforming a secure honest-verifier ZK protocol into a digital signature scheme [110]. The method uses exactly the same attacking technique of a dishonest verifier which we have seen in §18.3.2.1. In general, let (Commit, Challenge, Response) denote the transcript of an honest-verifier ZK protocol, then the transforming method uses a suitable hash function $H$ to construct a digital signature of message $M \in \{0,1\}^*$ as

$$\text{Challenge} \leftarrow H(M \parallel \text{Commit}).$$

This general method is called the **Fiat-Shamir heuristic**.

It is easy to see that a triplet ElGamal-family signature scheme (§16.3.1) is a special case of signature schemes generated from the Fiat-Shamir heuristic. In fact, the formal security proof technique on the strong unforgeability of triplet ElGamal-family signature schemes (studied in §16.3.2) applies to any signature scheme which is converted from an honest-verifier ZK protocol by applying the Fiat-Shamir heuristic.

A claim hidden behind a one-way function (e.g., membership, or **witness hiding** claim) which is verified like verification of digital signature due to the fact that Fiat-Shamir heuristic is clearly publicly verifiable, i.e., it is not a "proof in the dark." Often, a claim shown in this style is called **proof-of-knowledge**. Because of the strong security result (unforgeability against adaptive chosen-message attack) which we have established in §16.3.2, proof-of-knowledge remains being a quality and useful way for demonstrating a claim hidden behind a one-way function.

In some applications, such as proof that a secret has a required structure, "proof in the dark" is not an essential security requirement (i.e., a prover does not feel a need to deny participation in an interaction). In such applications, proof-of-knowledge is a very useful and adequate notion.

### 18.3.2.3   Returning to Perfect Zero-knowledge

Now let us consider the case of Schnorr's Identification Protocol (note, not the variation using large challenge bits) being run with the dishonest verifier Bob, in which he tries to fool Alice to issue a signature under Schnorr's signature scheme.

However now for any pseudo-random function prf of output size $\log_2 \log_2 p$ bits, equation (18.3.2) can be *efficiently made up* by anybody, that is, a proof transcript can be efficiently equated. Let us see how to do this and how efficiently this can be done.

Let $\mathcal{EQ}$ be an equator. All $\mathcal{EQ}$ has to do is to pick at random Response $\in_U \mathbb{Z}_q$, and test if (18.3.2) holds for a fixed Challenge $\in \{0, 1\}^{\log_2 \log_2 p}$. If the test fails, $\mathcal{EQ}$ simply tries another Response $\in_U \mathbb{Z}_q$. The trial-and-error test will be successful before the output space of prf of $\log_2 \log_2 p$ bits is exhausted. Since prf only has length $\log_2 \log_2 p$, its output space can be exhausted within $\log_2 p$ steps, that is, in time polynomial (linear) in the size of $p$.

Once the equation is found, $\mathcal{EQ}$ can set Commit using (18.3.1). Thus,

$$\text{Transcript} = \text{Commit, Challenge, Response}$$

is an equated "proof transcript" imitating a single round of interaction, and is produced in time polynomial in the size of $p$ (i.e., in $\log p$). This equated "proof transcript" satisfies

$$\text{Challenge} = \text{prf}(\text{"Meaningful transcript, signed Alice"} \parallel \text{Commit})$$

and

$$\text{Commit} \equiv g^{\text{Response}} \, y^{\text{Challenge}} \pmod{p}.$$

However, it is *not* a meaningful transcript at all and as we have seen, it *needn't* be issued by Alice!

To this end, we know that for challenge bits in a ZK protocol, size does matter!

## 18.3.3    Computational Zero-knowledge

We have seen that in order to demonstrate that an IP protocol $(P, \tilde{V})$ is perfect ZK, we must construct an equator: it can efficiently generate a "proof" transcript which has the same probability distribution as that produced by $(P, \tilde{V})$. This requirement can be relaxed for an IP protocol which is **computational zero-knowledge**.

**Definition 18.3:** *An IP protocol $(P, V)$ for L is said to be computational ZK if for any $x \in L$, a proof transcript of $(P, V)(x)$ can be simulated by a polynomial-time (in the size of the input) algorithm $\mathcal{S}(x)$ with probability distributions which are polynomially indistinguishable from that of the proof transcript.*

In this definition, the notion of polynomial indistinguishability is defined in Definition 4.15.

To see a computational ZK protocol, let us modify Prot 18.1 in another way. In this modification, the one-way and homomorphic function $f$ is defined over a space of an unknown magnitude, that is, now $n$ in $\mathbb{Z}_n$ is a secret integer for both $P$ and $V$. It is possible to construct $f$ over a secret domain. Here is a concrete construction.

### 18.3.3.1    A Construction of One-way and Homomorphic Function $f(x)$

Let $P$ and $V$ agree on a random and very large odd composite integer $N$ such that no one knows the factorization of $N$. This is easy if both parties input their own randomness in the agreement of $N$, however, we shall omit the details for doing this. They can similarly agree on a random element $a < N$ so that $\gcd(a, N) = 1$.

Since $N$ is large and random, with an overwhelming probability $N$ has a large prime factor $p$ unknown to both $P$ and $V$, and moreover, $p - 1$ should have a large prime factor $q$, also unknown to both $P$ and $V$. We should omit the investigation on how "overwhelming" the probability should be, but remind the reader that for a random and large composite $N$, the existence of such large primes $p$ and $q$ is the exact reason why a large and random odd composite is hard to factor (the reader can find some insights about this by reviewing §8.8).

Also, since both $N$, $a$ are randomly agreed upon, with an overwhelming probability, the multiplicative order $\mathrm{ord}_N(a)$ is a larger and secret integer. We are sure of this "overwhelming:" the probability for $q | \mathrm{ord}_N(a)$ is at least $1 - 1/q$ because for any prime $q | \phi(N)$, in $\mathbb{Z}_N^*$ there can be at most $1/q$ fraction of elements whose orders are co-prime to $q$.

Now $P$ and $V$ "define"

$$f(x) \stackrel{\text{def}}{=} a^x \pmod{N} \tag{18.3.3}$$

for any integer $x \in \mathbb{Z}_N$. Notice that we have quoted "define" here because the domain of this function cannot be $\mathbb{Z}_N$, instead, it is $\mathbb{Z}_{\mathrm{ord}_N(a)}$: namely, for any

$x \in \mathbb{Z}_N$, it always holds

$$f(x) = f(x \;(\mathrm{mod}\; \mathrm{ord}_N(a))).$$

In other words, the input to $f$ is always from the space $\mathbb{Z}_{\mathrm{ord}_N(a)}$ which is smaller than $\mathbb{Z}_N$.

Still, it is easy to see that $f(x)$ is homomorphic and one-way. The homomorphism is trivially observed as

$$f(x + y) = a^{x+y} = a^x \cdot a^y \;(\mathrm{mod}\; N).$$

The one-way property is based on that of the discrete logarithm problem modulo $p$ (recall, an unknown large prime $p|N$): finding $x$ from $f(x) = f(1)^x \;(\mathrm{mod}\; N)$ is necessarily harder than finding $x \;(\mathrm{mod}\; p - 1)$ from $f(1)^x \;(\mathrm{mod}\; p)$, while function $f(1)^x \;(\mathrm{mod}\; p)$ is one-way due to the discrete logarithm assumption (Assumption 8.2).

### 18.3.3.2 A Computational Zero-knowledge Protocol

Using $f(x)$ constructed in §18.3.3.1, we can construct a computational ZK protocol.

**Example 18.3:** Let $(\mathrm{Alice}, \tilde{\mathrm{Bob}})$ be a variation of Prot 18.1 using the one-way and homomorphic function $f(x)$ constructed in §18.3.3.1, i.e., $f(x)$ is defined in (18.3.3).

Now that Alice no longer knows $n = \mathrm{ord}_N(a)$, she can no longer sample random numbers in $\mathbb{Z}_{\mathrm{ord}_N(a)}$ with the uniform distribution. In order for Alice to still be able to conduct a proof (i.e., to preserve the completeness property), protocol instructions for Alice have to be slightly adjusted, e.g., as follows (let $z < N$ be Alice's private input):

1. Alice picks $k \in_U \mathbb{Z}_{N^2-z}$, computes Commit $\leftarrow f(k)$ and sends it to Bob;

2. Bob ... (∗ no change ∗)

3. Alice computes Response $\leftarrow \begin{cases} k & \text{if Challenge} = 0 \\ k + z & \text{if Challenge} = 1 \end{cases}$

   She sends Response to Bob;

4. Bob ... (∗ no change ∗)

In this modification, instructions for Bob are unchanged. However, instructions for Alice have two changes. In Step 1, the random value $k$ is sampled from $\mathbb{Z}_{N^2-z}$. We will explain in a moment why she has to pick $k$ from this rather peculiar space. In Step 3 (in case of Challenge $= 1$), she computes Response ($\leftarrow k + z$) using addition in the integer space $\mathbb{Z}$, i.e., without conducting modulo reduction. Now she can no longer compute the modulo reduction since she does not have the modulus $n = \text{ord}_N(a)$ for the operation.

The completeness and soundness properties of this modification can be reasoned analogously to those we have conducted in Example 18.1.

However, now we can no longer show that this variation is perfect ZK, because now we can no longer construct an efficient equator to produce a "proof" transcript which has the same distribution as that produced by $(\text{Alice}, \tilde{\text{Bob}})(X)$.

Indeed, a usual simulation technique will produce a transcript of a different distribution. In such a simulation, a simulator $\mathcal{S}$ performs the following steps:

1. $\mathcal{S}$ picks Response $\in_U \mathbb{Z}_{N^2}$;

2. $\mathcal{S}$ picks Challenge $\in_U \{0, 1\}$;

3. $\mathcal{S}$ computes Commit $\leftarrow f(\text{Response})/X^{\text{Challenge}} \pmod{N}$.

Clearly, (in the case of Challenge $= 1$) while Response in the proof transcript is uniform in the interval $[z, N^2)$, that in this simulated transcript is uniform in the interval $[0, N^2)$. They have *distinct* distributions. Without $z$, $\mathcal{S}$ just cannot equate Alice's behavior!

Nevertheless, the variation $(\text{Alice}, \tilde{\text{Bob}})$ is computational ZK. This is because the two distributions $x \in_U [z, N^2)$ and $y \in_U [0, N^2)$ are computational indistinguishable for $z < N$. From

$$\text{Prob}\left[y \leq z < N \mid y \in_U [0, N^2)\right] < \frac{N}{N^2} = \frac{1}{N}, \tag{18.3.4}$$

we have

$$\left|\text{Prob}\left[\text{Response} \in_U [z, N^2)\right] - \text{Prob}\left[\text{Response} \in_U [0, N^2)\right]\right| < \frac{1}{N}.$$

Following Definition 4.15 (in §4.7), Response in the proof transcript and that in the simulated transcript are computationally indistinguishable. Thereby, we have constructed a polynomial-time simulator $\mathcal{S}$, or $(\text{Alice}, \tilde{\text{Bob}})$ is computational ZK by Definition 18.3.                                                        □

Now we can explain why Alice has to pick committal $k$ from the rather peculiar space $\mathbb{Z}_{N^2-z}$.

First, the $-z$ part in $N^2 - z$ is necessary or else Response may end up to be larger than $N^2$ due to addition without modulo reduction. If that happens, the protocol can by no means to be labelled ZK in any sense!

Secondly, the $N^2$ part in $N^2 - z$ is in order to obtain the probability bound (18.3.4) and hence the protocol can achieve the computational ZK quality. In fact,

$N^2$ is unnecessarily too large. Computational ZK can be achieved by using $N^{1+\alpha}$ for any constant $\alpha > 0$. The reader is encouraged to confirm this (hint: observe that in the right-hand side of (18.3.4) $\frac{1}{N}$ should be replaced with $\frac{1}{N^\alpha}$).

In real-world applications of ZK protocols (e.g., Schnorr's Identification Protocol), most one-way functions are realized by available public-key cryptographic techniques (e.g., as in the case of $f(x)$ being realized in §18.3.3.1, or in Schnorr's Identification Protocol). Therefore computational ZK is the most important and adequate (i.e., fit-for-application) notion in ZK (and IP) protocols.

### 18.3.4   Statistical Zero-knowledge

Goldwasser, Micali and Rackoff [128] also introduce a notion of **statistical zero-knowledge**. An IP protocol is statistical ZK if there exists an efficient simulator to simulate a proof transcript to a precision which cannot be differentiated by any statistical distinguisher. A statistical distinguisher is similar to a polynomial distinguisher defined in Definition 4.14 except that its running time needn't be polynomially bounded. From this difference we know that a statistical ZK protocol has a more stringent ZK quality than a computational one.

As a matter of fact, the computational ZK protocol (Alice, B̃ob) in Example 18.3 is statistical ZK. This is because, (18.3.4) states that the following event occurs with probability less than a negligible quantity $1/N$:

> **Response** in a simulated transcript is less than $z$.

Thus, with probability at least $(N-1)/N$, **Response** in both transcripts are larger than $z$ and are both uniform. They cannot be differentiated by any distinguisher even if it runs forever!

Conceptually, statistical ZK and computational ZK have no essential difference. Nevertheless, since the former is a more stringent security notion, in real applications, it is more desirable to establish that a protocol is statistical ZK if a protocol designer is able to do so.

## 18.4   Proof or Argument?

We have reasoned *explicitly* that in order for an IP protocol $(P, V)$ to have ZK properties (any of the four ZK notions introduced so far), the computing power for $V$ and $\tilde{V}$ must be bounded by a polynomial in the size of the common input. However, so far we have not been very explicit about the computing power of $P$ or $\tilde{P}$.

## 18.4.1   Zero-knowledge Argument

A careful reader may have noticed that for all ZK protocols we have introduced so far, we actually require $P$ or $\tilde{P}$ to have a polynomially bounded computing power. Indeed, when we reason the soundness property for these protocols, we have always begun with saying "if $P$ (or $\tilde{P}$) does not know the pre-image of $X$ ...."

For a language in $\mathcal{IP} = \mathcal{PP}$, this "if ..." actually implies that $P$ (or $\tilde{P}$) is polynomially bounded. If we say that an unbounded $P$ is one who can extract the pre-image under the one-way function $f$, then none of the soundness reasonings for these protocols is valid. Clearly, for any Challenge, an unbounded $P$ or $\tilde{P}$ can extract Response as

$$\text{Response} \leftarrow \text{pre-image}(\text{Commit } X^{\text{Challenge}}).$$

For this way of pre-image extraction by an unbounded algorithm, we can never estimate the soundness probability $\delta$ for (18.2.3). In each case of our soundness reasoning conducted for the protocols introduced so far, the value $\delta$ has always been obtained under the (implicit) assumption that $P$ (and $\tilde{P}$) are bounded.

If a ZK protocol $(P, V)$ for a language $L$ requires $P$ (and $\tilde{P}$) to have a polynomially (in the size of the input) bounded computing power, then $(P, V)$ is called a **zero-knowledge argument protocol**. Usually, the requirement is needed in order to establish the soundness for the protocol. An argument is not as rigorous as a proof and in particular, it fails to make a good sense when $P$ is an unbounded entity.

Thus, we have so far seen perfect, honest-verifier, computational and statistical ZK *argument* protocols. Also, Schnorr's Identification Protocol is a ZK argument protocol. We have actually not met any **zero-knowledge proof protocol** yet.

Before we go ahead and describe ZK proof protocols, we should clarify one important point very clearly. In most real-world applications, i.e., in the usual cases of securing information using the complexity-theoretic based modern cryptographic techniques, principals of a secure system (including a prover of a ZK protocol) will most likely have their computational resource polynomially bounded, and hence they cannot solve NP problems quickly. Therefore ZK argument remains a very useful notion.

## 18.4.2   Zero-knowledge Proof

In a ZK *proof* protocol, the soundness property can be established without requiring $P$ or $\tilde{P}$ to be polynomially bounded.

Let us now see a ZK *proof* protocol. Proof of quadratic residuosity provides a good example for a ZK *proof* protocol. Such a protocol is again for a membership problem: $x \in \text{QR}_N$ for $N$ being an odd composite number.

### 18.4.2.1   ZK Proof of Quadratic Residuosity

Let $N$ be a large and odd composite integer which has at least two distinct odd prime factors. In §6.5 we have studied quadratic residues modulo an integer and learned the following number-theoretic facts:

**Fact 1**   Knowing the factorization of $N$, for any $x \in \mathrm{QR}_N$, a square root $y$ of $x$ modulo $N$, satisfying $y^2 \equiv x \pmod{N}$, can be efficiently extracted. This can be done using Alg 6.5.

**Fact 2**   For any $x \in \mathrm{QNR}_N$ (quadratic non-residue), in $\mathbb{Z}_N^*$ there exists no square root of $x$ (Step 1 of Alg 6.5 won't work).

**Fact 3**   If $x \in \mathrm{QNR}_N$, then $x \cdot y \in \mathrm{QR}_N$ implies $y \in \mathrm{QNR}_N$ (the reader can confirm this by examining all possible cases of Jacobi symbols of $x$, $y$ and $x \cdot y$).

Using these facts we can construct a perfect ZK *proof* protocol for Alice to *prove* to Bob that a number is a quadratic residue modulo an odd composite integer. This protocol is due to Goldwasser, Micali and Rackoff [128] and is specified in Prot 18.3.

Let us first analyze the soundness property for Prot 18.3.

### Soundness

Suppose $x \in \mathrm{QNR}_N$ (i.e., the protocol is run with Alice, a cheater). Let us find the soundness error probability $\delta$. Of course, we now consider Alice being computationally unbounded.

For Challenge $= 0$, Bob sees that Response is a square root of Commit, so Commit $\in \mathrm{QR}_N$.

For Challenge $= 1$, Bob sees that Response is a square root of Commit $x$, so Commit $x \in \mathrm{QR}_N$. By Fact 3, Bob further sees Commit $\in \mathrm{QNR}_N$.

So if $x \in \mathrm{QNR}_N$, then Bob sees Commit $\in \mathrm{QR}_N$ or Commit $\in \mathrm{QNR}_N$ alternatively depending on his random challenge bit being 0 or 1, respectively. Since Alice has sent Commit before Bob picks the random challenge bit, Alice must have correctly guessed Bob's challenge bit correctly. Clearly, we have $\delta = 1/2$ as the soundness error probability. Hence, Bob's verification passing $m$ times results in the soundness probability being $2^{-m}$.

The soundness property holds for an unbounded Alice since due to Fact 2, even unbounded, Alice cannot compute square root for $x \in \mathrm{QNR}_N$, and hence has to guess Bob's random challenge bit.

### Completeness and Perfect Zero-knowledge-ness

The completeness property is immediate from Fact 1.

---

**Protocol 18.3:** A Perfect Zero-knowledge Proof Protocol for Quadratic Residuosity

COMMON INPUT:
$N$: a large and odd composite integer which is not a power of a prime;
$x$: an element in $QR_N$.

Alice's PRIVATE INPUT:
$y \in \mathbb{Z}_N^*$: $y^2 \equiv x \pmod{N}$;

OUTPUT TO Bob: $x \in QR_N$.

Repeat the following steps $m$ times:

1. Alice picks $u \in_U QR_N$, computes $\mathsf{Commit} \leftarrow u^2 \pmod{N}$, and sends $\mathsf{Commit}$ to Bob;

2. Bob picks $\mathsf{Challenge} \in_U \{0, 1\}$, and sends it to Alice;

3. Alice computes $\mathsf{Response} \leftarrow \begin{cases} u & \text{if } \mathsf{Challenge} = 0 \\ u\,y \pmod{N} & \text{if } \mathsf{Challenge} = 1 \end{cases}$

   and sends $\mathsf{Response}$ to Bob;

4. Bob verifies:

   $\mathsf{Response}^2 \pmod{N} \equiv \begin{cases} \mathsf{Commit} & \text{for } \mathsf{Challenge} = 0 \\ \mathsf{Commit}\ x \pmod{N} & \text{for } \mathsf{Challenge} = 1 \end{cases}$

   if the verification fails, Bob rejects and aborts the protocol;

Bob accepts.

---

The perfect ZK property can be demonstrated by constructing an equator $\mathcal{EQ}$ which generates an equated proof transcript as follows:

For $i = 1, 2, \ldots, m$

1. $\mathcal{EQ}$ picks $\mathsf{Response}_i \in_U \mathbb{Z}_N^*$;

2. $\mathcal{EQ}$ picks $\mathsf{Challenge}_i \in_U \{0, 1\}$;

3. $\mathcal{EQ}$ sets $\mathsf{Commit}_i \leftarrow \begin{cases} \mathsf{Response}_i^2 \pmod{N} & \text{if } \mathsf{Challenge} = 0 \\ \mathsf{Response}_i^2/x \pmod{N} & \text{if } \mathsf{Challenge} = 1 \end{cases}$

It is easy to check that elements in this equated transcript have the same distributions as those in a proof transcript.

### 18.4.2.2   ZK Proof of Quadratic Non-residuosity

A protocol for ZK proof of quadratic non-residuosity can also be constructed using the idea in Prot 18.3. The basic idea is the following.

For common input $x \in \mathrm{QNR}_N$, Bob can challenge Alice at random using either Challenge $\leftarrow r^2 \pmod{N}$ or Challenge$' \leftarrow x\,r^2 \pmod{N}$ where $r$ is a random element in $\mathbb{Z}_N^*$. Clearly, Challenge $\in \mathrm{QR}_N$ and Alice can see this and answer YES. On the other hand, if $x$ is indeed in $\mathrm{QNR}_N$, then by Fact 3, Challenge$' \in \mathrm{QNR}_N$; also, Alice can see this and answer NO.

By repeatedly challenging Alice with so-constructed random elements either in $\mathrm{QR}_N$ or in $\mathrm{QNR}_N$, Bob can verify $x \in \mathrm{QNR}_N$ from Alice's consistently correct answers to his random challenges. The detailed formulation of this protocol can be found in [128].

ZK proofs of quadratic residuosity and non-residuosity have a good application for proving correct encryption of an arbitrary bit string where the encryption algorithm is Goldwasser-Micali probabilistic encryption (Alg 14.1). This application is useful for deriving the important theoretic result which we have discussed in §18.2.3.

# 18.5   Protocols with Two-sided-error

For all ZK (proof or argument) protocols studied so far, we have invariantly seen that their completeness probability expression (18.2.2) is always characterized by $\epsilon = 1$, and their soundness probability expression (18.2.3) is always characterized by $\delta > 0$. With $\epsilon = 1$, these protocols have perfect completeness, that is, if the prover does not cheat, then the verifier will always accept a proof. Using the terminology for error probability characterization for randomized algorithms which we have studied in §4.4, we can say that all these protocols have **one-sided-error** in the Monte Carlo subclass (i.e., in "always fast and probably correct" subclass, see §4.4.3). For such a protocol, a one-sided error may occur in prover's (Alice's) side, that is, Alice may cheat and try to "prove" $x \in L$ while in fact $x \notin L$, and Bob may be fooled to accept her "proof" (although the soundness error probability $\delta$ can be made to arbitrarily small by sequential independent repeating proofs).

Some ZK protocols can have verifier-side (Bob-side) errors too. That is, the completeness probability expression (18.2.2) is characterized by $\epsilon < 1$. Such protocols are said to have **two-sided errors,** or are in Atlantic City subclass (i.e., in "probably fast and probably correct" subclass, see §4.4.5). Let us now see one such protocol.

## 18.5.1    Zero-knowledge Proof of Two-prime Integers

A very useful application of the ZK proof of quadratic residuosity is to prove that an odd composite integer $N$ has exactly two prime factors, i.e., $N \in E_{2\_Prime}$ or is a valid RSA modulus.

In §4.7, the language $E_{2\_Prime}$ was called an ensemble. Any element in this language is an odd composite integer which has two distinct prime factors. In §4.7 we regarded this language to be indistinguishable from another ensemble (language) $E_{3\_Prime}$, which is the set of odd composite integers with three distinct prime factors.

Let Alice construct a large $N \in E_{2\_Prime}$ such that she knows the factorization (e.g., she construct it by multiplying two distinct odd primes together). She can *prove* to Bob in perfect ZK that $N \in E_{2\_Prime}$. Such a proof will make use of the three number-theoretic facts used by Prot 18.3 plus the following two additional facts:

**Fact 4**   If $N \in E_{2\_Prime}$, then precisely half the elements in

$$\mathrm{J}_N(1) = \{\, x \mid x \in \mathbb{Z}_N^*, \ \left(\frac{x}{n}\right) = 1 \,\}$$

are quadratic residues, i.e., $\#\mathrm{QR}_N = \dfrac{\#\mathrm{J}_N(1)}{2}$. This is because only half of these elements can have the positive Legendre symbol modulo both prime factors; the other half must have the negative Legendre symbol modulo both prime factors in order to have the positive Jacobi symbol.

**Fact 5**   If $N \notin E_{2\_Prime}$ and $N$ is not a prime or prime power, then at most a quarter elements in $\mathrm{J}_N(1)$ are quadratic residues, i.e., $\#\mathrm{QR}_N \leq \dfrac{\#\mathrm{J}_N(1)}{4}$. This is the generalization of Fact 4 to the cases of $N$ having 3 or more distinct prime factors. Remember, for $x$ to qualify a membership in $\mathrm{QR}_N$, it requires $x \pmod p \in \mathrm{QR}_p$ for each prime $p|N$.

In Fact 5, we require that $N$ is not a prime power. If $N$ is a prime power, i.e., $N = p^i$ for $p$ being prime and $i$ being an integer, then all elements in $\mathrm{J}_N(1)$ are quadratic residues. Fortunately, a prime power can be factored easily (review the hints in Ex 8.8 and Ex 8.9).

Prot 18.4 allows Alice to conduct a perfect ZK *proof* of membership in $E_{2\_Prime}$.

Let us now investigate security properties of Prot 18.4.

### 18.5.1.1   Security Properties

First of all, it is clear that the perfect ZK-ness of Prot 18.4 directly follows that of Prot 18.3. Below we only analyze the completeness and soundness properties.

---

**Protocol 18.4:** ZK Proof that $N$ Has Two Distinct Prime Factors

COMMON INPUT: a composite integer $N$;

Alice's Private Knowledge: the factorization of $N$;

OUTPUT TO Bob: $N \in E_{2\_\text{Prime}}$.

1. Bob checks that $N$ is not a prime or a prime power (e.g., applying Prime_Test against prime, and using the hint in Ex 8.8 to factor a prime power);

2. Bob picks a set Challenge of $m$ random numbers in $J_N(1)$, and sends Challenge to Alice;

3. Denote by $x_1$, $x_2$, ..., $x_k$ the all squares in Challenge; Alice proves to Bob that these $k$ elements are in $QR_N$ using Prot 18.3;

4. If $k > \lfloor \frac{3}{8}m \rfloor$ Bob accepts else he rejects.

   (* here, $k > \lfloor \frac{3}{8}m \rfloor$ is a "practical minority election criterion;" see §4.4.1.2 where we discussed the "majority election criterion" $k > \frac{1}{2}m$; this protocol cannot use that criterion simply because elements in $QR_N$ are not majority in $J_N(1)$; we will explain in §18.5.1.2 why we have chosen this "election criterion" *)

---

## Completeness

Consider that Alice has honestly constructed $N \in E_{2\_\text{Prime}}$. However, after a run of the protocol Bob may still reject. This is because it just happened that fewer than $\frac{3}{8}$ fractions of the random challenges picked by Bob were squares (bad luck for Alice!). This can occur when we have the completeness probability $\epsilon < 1$.

In the other protocols we have seen so far, the verifier will not tolerate any error, not even a single one in multiple rounds of repetition. Those protocols are all on-sided-error protocols: if the prover does not cheat, then the completeness probability satisfies $\epsilon = 1$ and therefore the verifier should of course not tolerate even a single error. Here in Prot 18.4, due to the fact that with $\epsilon = \frac{1}{2}$ (when Alice does not cheat, see Fact 4), Bob may happen to choose more than half non-residues, he should tolerate certain errors. However, if the number of errors exceeds a pre-fixed criterion, then Bob should consider that Alice is cheating and reject.

If Alice does not cheat but is rejected, we say an event BadLuckAlice occurs. Given the pre-fixed criterion for Bob to reach a decision, let us estimate the probability for BadLuckAlice. We have chosen $k > \lfloor \frac{3}{8}m \rfloor$ as the criterion, that is, if Bob sees the fraction of $\frac{3}{8}$ or more challenges being quadratic residues, he accepts, else he rejects. We will explain why we have chosen this criterion in §18.5.1.2.

After $m$ rounds of repetition, let us estimate $\epsilon(m)$. We consider the following equivalent form of the completeness probability bound which manifests the event BadLuckAlice more meaningfully:

$$\text{Prob}\,[\mathsf{BadLuckAlice}] = \text{Prob}\,[\text{Bob rejects} \mid N \in E_{2\_\text{Prime}}] < 1 - \epsilon(m).$$

Under the condition $m = \#\mathsf{Challenge} < \#\mathsf{J}_N(1)$, event BadLuckAlice is the sum of $m$ Bernoulli trials (see §3.5.2) of $k$ "successes" and $m - k$ "failures" for all cases of $k \leq \lfloor \frac{3}{8}m \rfloor$. Since Alice has constructed $N \in E_{2\_\text{Prime}}$, for Challenge containing random elements of $\mathsf{J}_N(1)$, in each Bernoulli trial the probabilities of "success" and "failure" are both $1/2$. Applying the binomial distribution function for "left tail" given in §3.5.2 (noticing to sum all possible cases of $k$ which offend Bob, i.e., all $k \leq \lfloor \frac{3}{8}m \rfloor$), we have

$$1 - \epsilon(m) = \text{Prob}\,[\mathsf{BadLuckAlice}] = \sum_{k=0}^{\lfloor \frac{3}{8}m \rfloor} \binom{m}{k} \left(\frac{1}{2}\right)^k \left(\frac{1}{2}\right)^{m-k} = \sum_{k=0}^{\lfloor \frac{3}{8}m \rfloor} \binom{m}{k} \left(\frac{1}{2}\right)^m.$$

This is a "left tail" of the binomial distribution function (see §3.5.2.1 for the meaning of a "left tail") because the point $\frac{3}{8}m$ is at the left of the central point $\frac{1}{2}m$.

To make BadLuckAlice negligibly small, we have to choose $m = 2000$ (reason to be provided in §18.5.1.2). This "left tail" is the following value

$$1 - \epsilon(2000) \approx 1.688 \cdot 10^{-29}.$$

Therefore, $\epsilon(2000)$ is an overwhelming probability. So if Alice does not cheat, Bob will accept with an overwhelming probability.

By the Law of Large Numbers (§3.5.3), the larger the number of challenges Bob picks, the larger the completeness probability value will be. By the way, if Bob picks $\#\mathsf{J}_N(1)$ challenges (though impractical), the completeness probability becomes 1, i.e., no Bob-side error (BadLuckAlice) can occur.

### Soundness

For the other side of error, let us suppose Alice has dishonestly constructed $N \notin E_{2\_\text{Prime}}$ (i.e., $N$ has more than two distinct prime factors). Still, Bob may accept Alice's "proof." This is because it just happens that more than $\frac{3}{8}$ fractions of the random challenges picked by Bob are quadratic residues (bad luck for Bob!).

Denote by BadLuckBob the conditional event of $N \notin E_{2\_\text{Prime}}$ while Bob accepting. For randomly chosen Challenge, we know from Fact 5, that now a Bernoulli trial has successful probability at most $\delta = \frac{1}{4}$ and failure probability at least $1 - \delta = \frac{3}{4}$. Applying the binomial distribution formula by summing all cases of $k > \left\lfloor \frac{3}{8}m \right\rfloor$ which cause Bob to accept, we obtain $\delta(m)$ (a "right tail" of the binomial distribution function)

$$\delta(m) = \text{Prob}\,[\mathsf{BadLuckBob}] = \sum_{\left\lceil \frac{3}{8}m \right\rceil}^{m} \binom{m}{k} \left(\frac{1}{4}\right)^k \left(\frac{3}{4}\right)^{m-k}.$$

For $m = 2000$, we have

$$\delta(2000) \approx 1.847 \cdot 10^{-35}.$$

It will be very foolish for Alice to try to cheat and expect not to be caught!

To this end we have completed our investigation on the ZK, completeness and soundness properties for Prot 18.4.

### 18.5.1.2   The Choice of the "Election Criterion"

When Alice does not cheat, with the completeness probability bound for one round satisfies $\epsilon = \frac{1}{2}$, i.e., exactly half the elements in $J_N(1)$ are quadratic residues, Prot 18.4 cannot use the "majority election criterion" given in §4.4.1.1 to enlarge the completeness probability. Our choice of the criterion being $\frac{3}{8}$ is the middle point between $\epsilon = \frac{1}{2}$ (Alice does not cheat) and $\delta = \frac{1}{4}$ (Alice cheats). This choice makes the two "bad luck" events roughly equally (im)probable.

This is a "minority election criterion." Thanks to the Law of Large Numbers (§3.5.3), as long as $\delta < \epsilon$, we can choose the middle point between them as the criterion and repeat multiple rounds $(m)$ to reduce $\delta(m)$ and enlarge $\epsilon(m)$. So a cheating Alice can be differentiated from an honest one, with a high confidence of the correct judgement, after repeating sufficiently many rounds.

In order for both "bad luck" events to be negligibly small, which is usually considered, by "rule of thumb," to be $2^{-100}$ (we have been sticking to this rule for all the protocols introduced so far in this chapter), we have to use 2000 as the number of repetition. If we reduce $m$ down from 2000 significantly, then the two error probability bounds will deteriorate drastically. For example, let $m = 100$ (which is usually considered an "acceptable" number of repetition, again according to our "rule of thumb"), then we will have $\epsilon(100) \approx 0.993$ (so BadLuckAlice occurs with probability $1 - \epsilon(100) \approx 0.007$) and $\delta(100) \approx 0.0052$ (probability for BadLuckAlice). These error probability bounds are far from satisfactory since the two "bad luck" events are too probable (i.e., the probabilities for both "bad luck" events are too significant).

In general, when $\epsilon$ and $\delta$ are close, two-sided-error protocols are not efficient.

Several authors have proposed more efficient, one-sided-error ($\epsilon = 1$) ZK protocols for showing $N$ having two prime factors, e.g., van de Graaf and Peralta [293],

Camenisch and Michels [64], Gennaro, Miccianicio and Rabin [122]. The protocol introduced here, which is based on a protocol proposed by Berger, Kannan and Peralta [33], is conceptually the simplest. The other important reason for us to have chosen to introduce this protocol is its two-sided-error feature which is a rare property in ZK protocols and hence we want the reader to gain some familiarity about it.

## 18.6  Round Efficiency

Let us now consider Question II listed in §18.1: how few interactions are needed for a prover to convince the verifier? This is a so-called **round efficiency** question. A round means a complete round cycle of message sending and receiving actions. Because many ZK (and IP) protocols generally involve Commit (a first move by $P$), Challenge (a move by $V$), Response (a second move by $P$), we often refer to such three moves as a round.

As we have seen that in general, a ZK protocol can achieve reduction of an error probability by repeating sequentially a plural number of rounds. For the case of completeness probability $\epsilon$ which bounds the probability in (18.2.2) from below, we consider $1 - \epsilon$ as an error probability bound from above. As in the case of soundness, such an error probability bound (bounded from above) should be as low as possible. In order to objectively measure round efficiency for a ZK protocol, we should consider error probabilities obtained by one single round. The lower an error probability is, the more efficient round efficiency the protocol has.

Roughly three different magnitudes of single-round error probabilities classify protocols to three different classes of round efficiencies.

**Logarithmic-round Protocols**  All ZK protocols we have studied so far, with the exception of Prot 18.4, have constant error probabilities in a single round, e.g., $1/2$ or $\log_2 \log_2 n$ (for $\log_2 n$ being a security parameter, such as in the case of Prot 18.1 or Schnorr's Identification Protocol, we equate $\log \log n$ to a constant). In order to reduce the error probability to a negligibly small quantity, i.e., being a quality bounded by $1/(\log n)^c$ for all constant $c$, a protocol with constant error probability must repeat $\log n$ rounds. Such a protocol is therefore called **logarithmic- (log-) round** protocol.

**Polynomial-round Protocols**  The round efficiency of a log-round protocol is in fact measured by a linear polynomial in the security parameter. Some ZK protocols have higher-order polynomials for their round-efficiency measures. A ZK protocol for an arbitrary NP language via general polynomial reduction to NPC problem (see §18.2.3) is a **polynomial-round (poly-round) protocol**.

Prot 18.4 is a poly-round protocol. First, it has a larger number of rounds due to its two-sided error property. Secondly, in each round, Prot 18.4 calls another log-round protocol (Prot 18.3).

**Constant-round (or single-round) Protocols**   If a ZK protocol can achieve a negligibly small error probability in a small constant rounds (or a single round), then there is no need to repeat running log-many rounds. Such a protocol is therefore called a **constant-round** (or a **single-round** ) protocol.

Much research effort has been focused on improving round efficiency for ZK protocols. Many results have been obtained. Let us now look at two such results for subgroup membership and discrete logarithm problems.

- In §18.6.1 we will derive a lower-bound round-efficiency result for ZK argument of subgroup membership for subgroups of $\mathbb{Z}_N^*$ with $N$ odd composite. This is a negative result in that the lower-bound is log-round, i.e., there exists no constant-round protocol for this membership proof.

- In §18.6.2 we will study a constant-round protocol for ZK proof of discrete logarithm equality for elements in finite field $\mathbb{F}_p$. This is a positive result and is a significant round-efficiency improvement from Schnorr's Identification Protocol (Prot 18.2).

## 18.6.1   Lower-bound Round Efficiency for Subgroup Membership

Let us reconsider again subgroup membership (argument) problem tackled by Prot 18.1. Now it is for the case that $f(x)$ is realized in §18.3.3.1; that is,

$$f(x) = y \equiv g^x \pmod{N}$$

where $N$ is a large odd composite number and $g \in \mathbb{Z}_N^*$ having a large multiplicative order. In this realization, we know

$$\{\, g^x \pmod{N} \mid x \in \phi(N)\,\} \subset \mathbb{Z}_N^*,$$

that is, the subset has fewer than $\phi(N)$ elements. This is because $\mathbb{Z}_N^*$ is non-cyclic.

Now, we also let the prover Alice know the factorization of $N$. (Recall that in §18.3.3, we did not allow Alice to know the factorization of $N$ and hence the variation of the protocol there was computational ZK.) Knowing the factorization of $N$ permits Alice to conduct *perfect* ZK for $y \in \langle g \rangle$.

Now we ask:

For $f(x) = g^x \pmod{N}$ with Alice knowing factorization of the composite integer $N$, can the round efficiency of Prot 18.1 be improved *via* enlarging the size of Bob's challenge as we did in Schnorr's Identification Protocol?

Recall that, e.g., in Schnorr's Identification Protocol (Prot 18.2), we made a slight enlargement on challenges: $\mathsf{Challenge} \in \{0, 1\}^{\log_2 \log_2 p}$. Consequently, the variant protocol achieves an improved performance: $\dfrac{m}{\log_2 \log_2 p}$ rounds suffices instead of $m$ rounds needed in Prot 18.1, while maintaining the soundness error probability unchanged.

Unfortunately, if Alice knows the factorization of $N$, then round-efficiency improvement using this challenge-enlargement method is no longer possible. The problem is not with the ZK property; it is with the soundness error probability. The protocol has the lower-bound soundness error probability $\delta = 1/2$, regardless how large challenge is used. With the constant and significant soundness error probability, the protocol has to be a log-round one. Galbraith, Mao and Paterson observe this fact [119] which we shall expose now.

To make the exposition explicit, let us investigate the soundness probability of a single-round three-move protocol which uses a large challenge (and hence as we have studied in §18.3.2, the protocol is honest-verifier ZK). As we shall see, the investigation result applies to any sizes of challenges larger than one bit.

Here we specify an honest-verifier zero-knowledge protocol named "Not To Be Used" (Prot 18.5) for showing subgroup membership where the subgroup is one of $\mathbb{Z}_N^*$. We must warn the reader that Prot 18.5 is not intended for any application use; we specify it only for the purpose of revealing a problem.

At first glance of Prot 18.5 it seems that because $\mathsf{Challenge}$ is large, Alice cannot guess it easily and therefore she has to follow the protocol instruction which will result in a soundness probability at the level of $\delta \approx 1/\phi(N)$. If this is true, then this protocol is indeed a single-round one. Unfortunately, this soundness probability estimate is incorrect. Example 18.4 demonstrates a cheating method.

**Example 18.4:** From now on, we use Al~ice since what she does in the following is dishonest.

Knowing the factorization of $N$, Al~ice can easily compute a non-trivial square root of 1, i.e., element $\xi \in \mathbb{Z}_N^*$ such that $\xi \neq \pm 1$ while $\xi^2 \equiv 1 \pmod{N}$. Square-root extraction can be done using Alg 6.5. She can choose $\xi$ such that $\xi \notin \langle g \rangle$.

Now, Al~ice computes the common input as

$$Y \leftarrow \xi g^z \pmod{N}.$$

Clearly, $Y \in \xi \langle g \rangle$, i.e., $Y$ is in the coset of $\langle g \rangle$. We explicitly notice that $Y \notin \langle g \rangle$ since $\xi \notin \langle g \rangle$ (see the properties of coset in the proof of Theorem 5.1, §5.2.1).

Instead of computing $\mathsf{Commit}$ by following the protocol instruction, Al~ice flips a fair coin $b \in_U \{0, 1\}$ as her guessing of the parity of Bob's challenge. She then computes $\mathsf{Commit}$ as follows:

$$\mathsf{Commit} \leftarrow \begin{cases} g^k \pmod{N} & \text{if } b = 0 \\ \xi g^k \pmod{N} & \text{if } b = 1 \end{cases} .$$

---

**Protocol 18.5:** "Not To Be Used"

COMMON INPUT $N$:     A large odd composite integer;

         $g, y$:   Two elements in $\mathbb{Z}_N^*$ satisfying
                  $g$ has a large order modulo $N$;
                  $y \equiv g^z \pmod{N}$

Alice's PRIVATE INPUT: Integer $z < \phi(N)$;

OUTPUT TO Bob: $y \in \langle g \rangle$, i.e., $y \equiv g^z \pmod{N}$ for some $z$.

1. Alice picks $k \in_U \mathbb{Z}_{\phi(N)}$ and computes $\mathsf{Commit} \leftarrow g^k \pmod{N}$; she sends $\mathsf{Commit}$ to Bob;

2. Bob picks uniformly random $\mathsf{Challenge} < N$ and sends it to Alice;

3. Alice computes $\mathsf{Response} \leftarrow k + z\,\mathsf{Challenge} \pmod{\phi(N)}$; she sends $\mathsf{Response}$ to Bob;

4. Bob accepts if $g^{\mathsf{Response}} \equiv \mathsf{Commit}\ y^{\mathsf{Challenge}} \pmod{N}$, or rejects otherwise.

---

In the remainder of the protocol Alice should proceed as instructed by the protocol specification.

Clearly, with $1/2$ odds Alice's guessing is correct. In the correct guessing of even $\mathsf{Challenge} = 2u$, Bob's verification step is:

$$g^{\mathsf{Response}} \equiv g^k g^{z2u} \equiv \mathsf{Commit}\ (\xi g)^{z2u} \equiv \mathsf{Commit}\ Y^{\mathsf{Challenge}} \pmod{N}$$

and hence Bob will accept. In the correct guessing of odd $\mathsf{Challenge} = 2u+1$, Bob's verification step is:

$$g^{\mathsf{Response}} \equiv g^k g^{z(2u+1)} \equiv \xi g^k (\xi g)^{z(2u+1)} \equiv \mathsf{Commit}\ Y^{\mathsf{Challenge}} \pmod{N}$$

and hence Bob will accept too.

Therefore, regardless of how large Bob's challenge is, we can only obtain $\delta = 1/2$ as the single-round soundness probability for Prot 18.5. That is why we have named this protocol "Not To Be Used." $\qquad\square$

Since Bob does not know the factorization of $N$, he cannot decide subgroup membership by himself alone (see Remark 18.1 and the discussion after for the difficulty). Hence there is no way, other then the soundness error probability $1/2$, for Bob to prevent Alice from cheating in the method given by Example 18.4. Enlarging the challenge size does not help at all!

We notice that the problem in Example 18.4 didn't show up in the (computational ZK) protocol in §18.3.3.2 where we also used a similar way to realize $f(x)$, i.e., $f(x) = a^x \pmod{N}$ with $N$ being an odd composite. Recall that that protocol uses bit challenges, and hence its soundness error probability is the same value $\delta = 1/2$. We also notice that Schnorr's Identification Protocol is immune to this problem because the group $\langle g \rangle$ in that protocol is of prime order $q$, which does not contain any element of order less than $q$ except for the identity element.

Using a non-trivial square root of 1 modulo $N$ provides Alice with the maximum probability value, $\delta = 1/2$, for a successful cheating. Using the trivial case $\xi = -1$ (the other trivial case $\xi = 1$ does not constitute an attack) seems to allow Bob to obtain a better conviction: either $Y$ or $-Y$ is in $\langle g \rangle$. However, because Alice knows the factorization of $N$ while Bob doesn't, she may also blind $g^k$ using other small-order multiplier, e.g., an order-3 one, which she can compute using the Chinese Remainder Theorem (Theorem 6.7 in §6.2.3, using CRT, Alice can compute elements of any order $d|\phi(N)$). Thus, the soundness error probability cannot be a negligible value. Prot 18.1 remains being the only version for showing (ZK argument) subgroup membership problem for the general setting of security parameters, which include the cases of subgroups of $\mathbb{Z}_N^*$.

To this end, we conclude that, in general, ZK subgroup membership is a log-round problem.

In an application of ZK protocol to be introduced in the next chapter we will need to show subgroup membership in $\mathbb{Z}_N^*$. However, in that application we cannot afford the cost of using a log-round protocol. There we will use a special setting for $N$ to get around of the problem.

## 18.6.2   Constant-round Proof for Discrete Logarithm

Schnorr's Identification Protocol (Prot 18.2) allows ZK argument of possession of the discrete logarithm of an element finite field $\mathbb{F}_p$. We have seen that it is a log-round protocol.

Now we show that for the same problem tackled by Schnorr's Identification Protocol, ZK proof with constant-round efficiency can be achieved. This is due to a protocol of Chaum [73]. Let us name that protocol **Chaum's ZK Dis-Log-EQ Proof Protocol**. It is for ZK proof of two elements having the same discrete logarithm value.

We shall introduce Chaum's ZK Dis-Log-EQ Proof Protocol using the security parameter setting which is the same as that for Schnorr's Identification Protocol. That is, let element $g \in \mathbb{F}_p$ with $p$ being an odd prime and $\mathrm{ord}_p(g) = q$ with $q$ also being an odd prime (hence $q|p - 1$). We denote $G = \langle g \rangle$.

Chaum's ZK Dis-Log-EQ Proof Protocol uses an additional element $h \in \langle g \rangle$ with $h \neq g$ and $h \neq 1$. Prot 18.6 specifies Chaum's protocol.

From the protocol specification we see that the protocol has a four message exchanges and it only needs to run once. We shall see in the soundness analysis that this single-round protocol achieves $\delta = 1/q$ as the soundness error probability. Hence, Chaum's ZK Proof of Dis-Log Protocol is extremely efficient.

Let us now investigate security properties of this protocol.

### 18.6.2.1   Security Properties of Chaum's ZK Proof of Dis-Log Protocol

#### Completeness

By direct observation of the protocol, it is straightforward to obtain $\epsilon = 1$ as the completeness probability. That is, if Alice has $z$ and follow the protocol instruction, Bob will always accept.

#### Soundness

We shall see that Chaum's ZK Dis-Log EQ Protocol is a proof protocol, that is, the prover Alice can be a computationally unbounded party. For this purpose, we will not put any restriction on Alice's computational resource in our analysis of the soundness property.

Suppose that Alice cheats. So the common input values $(p, q, g, h, X, Y)$ satisfy the following condition of discrete logarithm inequality:

$$X \equiv g^z \pmod{p} \quad \text{and} \quad Y \equiv h^{z'} \pmod{p} \quad \text{for some } z \not\equiv z' \pmod{q}. \qquad (18.6.1)$$

In order to let Bob accept her proof, i.e., let his verification in Step 5 pass, Alice must send to Bob, in Step 2 the value $\mathsf{Commit}_A^{(2)}$ satisfying

$$\mathsf{Commit}_A^{(2)} \equiv X^c X^a Y^b \pmod{p}. \qquad (18.6.2)$$

In other words, Alice, after having received $a$, $b$ from Bob, must decommit her committal value $c \in \mathbb{Z}_q$ which satisfies (18.6.2). With $a$, $b$ fixed by Bob in Step 1, and with $\mathsf{Commit}_A^{(1)}$, $\mathsf{Commit}_A^{(2)}$ fixed in Step 2, (18.6.2) says that $c \in \mathbb{Z}_q$ is also fixed in Step 2. In other words, Alice cannot change $c$ after she has sent out her commitments in Step 2.

With $c \in \mathbb{Z}_q$ fixed in Step 2, we have:

$$c \equiv \log_g \frac{\mathsf{Commit}_A^{(1)}}{g^a h^b} \pmod{q}, \qquad (18.6.3)$$

**Protocol 18.6:** Chaum's ZK Proof of Dis-Log-EQ Protocol

COMMON INPUT:

$p, q$: two primes satisfying $q|p - 1$;

(∗ typical size setting: $|p| = 1024$, $|q| = 160$ ∗)

$g, h$: $\mathrm{ord}_p(g) = \mathrm{ord}_p(h) = q$, $g \neq h$;

(∗ Bob checks: $g \neq 1, h \neq 1, g \neq h, g^q \equiv h^q \equiv 1 \pmod{p}$ ∗)

$X, Y$: $X = g^z \pmod{p}$, $X = h^z \pmod{p}$;

PRIVATE INPUT of Alice: $z \in \mathbb{Z}_q$;

OUTPUT TO Bob: Alice knows some $z \in \mathbb{Z}_q$ such that
$$X \equiv g^z \pmod{p} \text{ and } Y \equiv h^z \pmod{p}, \text{ or}$$
$$\log_g X \equiv \log_h Y \pmod{q}.$$

1. Bob picks $a, b \in_U \mathbb{Z}_q$ and computes $\mathsf{Commit}_B \leftarrow g^a h^b \pmod{p}$;

   he sends $\mathsf{Commit}_B$ to Alice;

   (∗ $\mathsf{Commit}_B$ is Bob's challenge ∗)

2. Alice picks $c \in_U \mathbb{Z}_q$; she computes

   $\mathsf{Commit}_A^{(1)} \leftarrow \mathsf{Commit}_B g^c \pmod{p}$,

   $\mathsf{Commit}_A^{(2)} \leftarrow (\mathsf{Commit}_A^{(1)})^z \pmod{p}$;

   she sends $\mathsf{Commit}_A^{(1)}$, $\mathsf{Commit}_A^{(2)}$ to Bob;

3. Bob discloses to Alice: $a, b$;

   (∗ Bob decommits his committals in order to show his correct construction of his challenge ∗)

4. Alice verifies whether $\mathsf{Commit}_B \equiv g^a h^b \pmod{p}$;

   if the equality holds, she discloses to Bob: $c$, otherwise, she aborts;

   (∗ Alice only decommits if Bob has properly constructed his challenge; Bob's correct construction of his challenge implies that he already knows $X^a Y^b \pmod{p}$ to be disclosed by Alice ∗)

5. Bob verifies

   $\mathsf{Commit}_A^{(1)} \equiv \mathsf{Commit}_B g^c \pmod{p}$;  $\mathsf{Commit}_A^{(2)} \equiv X^c X^a Y^b \pmod{p}$;

   if the equality holds, he accepts, otherwise, he rejects.

and from (18.6.2) we also have:

$$c \log_g X \equiv \log_g \frac{\mathsf{Commit}_A^{(2)}}{X^a Y^b} \pmod{q}. \tag{18.6.4}$$

Since $h \in \langle g \rangle$ (because $\mathrm{ord}_p(h) = q$, Bob can confirm this by checking $h \neq 1$ and $h^q \equiv 1 \pmod{p}$), we can write $h \equiv g^d \pmod{p}$ for some $d \in \mathbb{Z}_q, d \neq 0 \pmod{q}$. Consequently, (18.6.3) can be rewritten in the following equivalent form:

$$c - \log_g \mathsf{Commit}_A^{(1)} \equiv -a - bd \pmod{q}. \tag{18.6.5}$$

Analogously using (18.6.1), we can also rewrite (18.6.4) into:

$$c \log_g X - \log_g \mathsf{Commit}_A^{(2)} \equiv -az - bdz' \pmod{q}. \tag{18.6.6}$$

For $z \not\equiv z' \pmod{q}$, (18.6.5) and (18.6.6) forms the following linear congruence system:

$$\begin{pmatrix} c - \log_g \mathsf{Commit}_A^{(1)} \\ c \log_g X - \log_h \mathsf{Commit}_A^{(2)} \end{pmatrix} = \begin{pmatrix} -1 & -d \\ -z & -dz' \end{pmatrix} \begin{pmatrix} a \\ b \end{pmatrix} \pmod{q}.$$

The matrix in this linear congruence system is of the full rank ($rank = 2$). By a simple fact in linear algebra, this system has the unique pair of solution $(a, b) \in \mathbb{Z}_q \times \mathbb{Z}_q$. This solution pair satisfies Bob's construction of $\mathsf{Commit}_B$ in Step 1 and his verification in Step 5.

However, in Step 2 when Alice fixes $c \in \mathbb{Z}_q$, she only gets one equation (18.6.5). From that equation she has exactly $q$ distinct pairs of $(a, b)$. Each of these $q$ pairs satisfies (18.6.5), but only one of them also satisfies (18.6.6) which is Bob's verification in Step 5. Thus, even computationally unbounded, the probability for Alice to pinpoint the correct pair $(a, b)$ in Step 2 is precisely $1/q$.

To this end, we have not only obtained $1/q$ as the soundness error probability for a single-round run of Chaum's protocol, but also that the protocol provides a proof of the discrete logarithm equality (i.e., not an argument).

## Perfect Zero-knowledge-ness

Finally, let us investigate the ZK property for Prot 18.6.

The protocol is in fact perfect ZK. Let us construct an equator $\mathcal{EQ}$ to create a transcript which has the identical distribution to a proof transcript. For the common input tuple $(p, q, g, h, X, Y)$, $\mathcal{EQ}$ performs the following simple and efficient steps:

1. $\mathcal{EQ}$ picks $a, b \in_U \mathbb{Z}_q$ and computes $\mathsf{Commit}_B \leftarrow g^a h^b \pmod{p}$;

2. $\mathcal{EQ}$ picks $c \in_U \mathbb{Z}_q$; computes

$$\mathsf{Commit}_A^{(1)} \leftarrow \mathsf{Commit}_B g^c \pmod{p},$$

$$\mathsf{Commit}_A^{(2)} \leftarrow X^c X^a Y^b \pmod{p};$$

3. $\mathcal{EQ}$ outputs $\mathsf{Transcript} = \mathsf{Commit}_B, \mathsf{Commit}_A^{(1)}, \mathsf{Commit}_A^{(2)}, a, b, c.$

It is trivial to check that $\mathsf{Transcript}$ has the identical distribution as a proof transcript.

There is a different but more convincing way to manifest the perfect ZK-ness of Chaum's protocol. First, if Bob fools around by sending out an invalid challenge, i.e., $\mathsf{Commit}_B$ is not properly constructed, then he will receive nothing. Secondly, if Bob does send correctly constructed challenge using $(a, b) \in \mathbb{Z}_q \times \mathbb{Z}_q$, then he already knows, right in the beginning of Step 1, the value to be "disclosed" by Alice, which is $X^a Y^b \pmod{p}$. In both cases, Bob gets absolutely no new information about Alice's private input!

### 18.6.2.2   Discussions

- Chaum's ZK Dis-Log EQ Protocol can be used as an identification protocol. In this application, the pair $(g, X)$ can be a user's public key material which is certified by a key certification authority (CA, see §13.2).

- Computing $g^a h^b \pmod{p}$ and $X^c X^a Y^b \pmod{p}$ can use Alg 15.2 to achieve cost similar to computing single modulo exponentiation. So the cost for Alice and Bob is roughly three modulo exponentiation for each party. At this cost, the proof achieves a negligibly small error probability against Alice's cheating. In comparison, Schnorr's Identification Protocol will require Alice and Bob to compute $\log_2 p \approx 10$ (in case of $p \approx 2^{1024}$) modulo exponentiations in order to achieve similarly low error probability.

- The unrestricted computational resource for the prover makes the protocol usable in applications in which the prover is a powerful party, such as a government agency.

- Although the soundness proof is a strong one, it does not show that Alice necessarily knows the discrete logarithm value. All it has shown is that she has answered with a correct exponentiation. Maybe she has used somebody else as an exponentiation oracle. In the Schnorr's Identification Protocol, two correct answers, even if a prover obtains them from an oracle, form a **knowledge extractor** to extract the discrete logarithm value and this is the basis for forking lemma technique for proving the unforgeability of a triplet ElGamal signature (see §16.3.2). Here in Chaum's protocol, two correct answers do not form a knowledge extractor for the discrete logarithm value.

- Chaum proposes this protocol for an **undeniable signature scheme** [73] (also Chaum and Antwerpen [75]). An "undeniable signature scheme" provides a proof of authorship of a document using an interactive protocol in place of signature verification procedure in an ordinary signature scheme. Hence, it enables the signer to choose signature verifiers, and thereby protects the signer's right to the privacy of its signatures. This may be useful in certain applications where a publicly verifiable signature is not desirable. For example, a software vendor puts digital signatures on its products so that it can authenticate its products as genuine copies and virus free, but only wants paying customers to be able to verify the validity of these signatures. Using undeniable signatures the vendor can prevent a pirate from convincing others of the quality of the pirated copies of the software.

## 18.7   Non-interactive Zero-knowledge

We have seen that ZK protocols, as interactive protocols, generally require interactions. Although in the cases of single-round or constant round protocols (e.g., Chaum's ZK Proof of Dis-Log EQ Protocol) the number of interactions is small, the need for interaction means that both prover and verifier must be on-line at the same time. If a ZK proof (or argument) can be achieved without interaction, then a "mono-directional" communication means can be used. Such a communication means can have several advantages.

Consider an imaginary case of $P$, $V$ being mathematicians (a scenario imagined in [45]). The former may want to travel the world while discovering proofs for new mathematical theorems and may want to prove these new theorems to the latter in ZK. In this scenario, non-interactive proof is necessary because $P$ may have no fixed address and will move away before any mail can reach it. These two fancy users will appreciate non-interactive ZK proof.

In the beginning of Chapter 15 we have discussed a more realistic application of non-interactive ZK proof: constructing a provably secure public-key encryption scheme against the CCA2 attacker (although our purpose of introducing Chapter 15 is an advice against such an approach to secure encryption scheme). At any rate, a possibility for conducting a non-interactive ZK proof (or argument) is always a useful add-on feature.

Blum, Feldman and Micali propose a method for achieving **non-interactive ZK (NIZK)** if $P$ and $V$ share random challenge bits [45]. The shared random challenge bits may be served by a third party who is mutually trusted by $P$ and $V$ (such a mutually trusted random source is called a **random beacon** by Rabin [241], "randomness from the sky"). It is also possible that the two parties had generated them when they were together (e.g., before the fancy mathematician's departure for trotting the world).

In §18.3.2.2 we have introduced the Fiat-Shamir heuristic as a general method for constructing a non-interactive "proof of knowledge."[b] However, the non-interaction achieved using the Fiat-Shamir heuristic is at the cost of losing the ZK property: "proof in the dark" is turned to "in the open," i.e., becomes publicly verifiable.

Jakobsson, Sako and Impagliazzo devise an interesting technique which uses the Fiat-Shamir heuristic while maintaining the "proof in the dark" property [155]. They name their technique **designated verifier proofs**: if Alice conducts a proof for Bob to verify, then only Bob can be convinced of the validity of the proof. Anybody else will view the proof as either conducted by Alice, or simulated by Bob.

## 18.7.1  NIZK Achieved using Designation of Verifier

The NIZK technique of Jakobsson et al. is achieved by Alice constructing a non-interactive "proof of knowledge" from the Fiat-Shamir heuristic for the following logical expression:

"Alice's claim is true"  ∨  "Bob has simulated Alice's proof" .

Alice is able to construct a "proof" for this logical expression thanks to a primitive called **trapdoor commitment** (also called **simulatable commitment** by Brassard, Chaum and Crépeau [60]).

A trapdoor commitment is a special commitment which Alice constructs using a public key of Bob who is the designated verifier. Let us denote by

$$TC(w, r, y_B)$$

a trapdoor commitment which is constructed using Bob's public key $y_B$. In this commitment, $w$ is the committal value (committed by the principal who has constructed it) and $r$ is a random input. Property 18.1 specifies two important properties of $TC(w, r, y_B)$.

**Property 18.1: Trapdoor Commitment Properties**

i) *Without the private component of $y_B$, the commitment is binding, i.e., there exists no efficient algorithm for computing a pair of collision $w_1 \neq w_2$ such that $TC(w_1, r, y_B) = TC(w_2, r', y_B)$.*

ii) *Using the private component of $y_B$, it is easy to compute any number of pairs of collision.*

**Example 18.5: A Trapdoor Commitment Scheme** Let $(p, q, g)$ be the numbers in the common input of the Schnorr's Identification Protocol. Let $y_B = g^{x_B} \pmod{p}$ be Bob's public key where $x_b \in \mathbb{Z}_q$ be his private exponent.

---

[b]We will always use quoted form for the phrase "proof of knowledge" derived from the Fiat-Shamir heuristic because rigorously speaking, it is argument of knowledge, see §18.4.1.

If Alice wants to commit to value $w \in \mathbb{Z}_q$, she picks $r \in_U \mathbb{Z}_q$ and computes $\mathsf{TC}(w, r, y_B) \leftarrow g^w y_B^r \pmod{p}$. She can open (decommit) $\mathsf{TC}(w, r, y_B)$ by revealing the pair $(w, r)$. We now confirm that $\mathsf{TC}(w, r, y_B)$ satisfies the two properties of a trapdoor commitment.

Confirming TC Property (i): Without knowing Bob's private key $x_b$, $(w, r)$ is the only way for Alice to decommit. Suppose on the contrary that she also knows a different pair of decommitment values $(w', r')$ with $w' \neq w \pmod{q}$ (hence $r' \neq r \pmod{q}$). Then because

$$1 = g^{w-w'} y_B^{r-r'} \pmod{p}$$

we obtain

$$y_B \equiv g^{x_B} \equiv g^{\frac{w'-w}{r-r'}} \pmod{p}$$

i.e., Alice knows $x_B \equiv \dfrac{w' - w}{r - r'} \pmod{q}$. This contradicts the assumption that Alice does not know $x_B$.

Confirming TC Property (ii): Using $x_B$, Bob can pick $w_1, w_2, r_1 \in_U \mathbb{Z}_q$ with $w_1 \neq w_2 \pmod{q}$. Then he sets

$$r_2 \leftarrow \frac{w_1 - w_2 + r_1 x_B}{x_B}.$$

It is straightforward to check $\mathsf{TC}(w_1, r_1, y_B) = \mathsf{TC}(w_2, r_2, y_B)$.                                   $\square$

In §18.3.2.2 we have seen that a "proof of knowledge" obtained from the Fiat-Shamir heuristic is a triplet ($\mathsf{Commit}, \mathsf{Challenge}, \mathsf{Response}$) which is constructed by the prover Alice. In this triplet, $\mathsf{Commit}$ is a commitment in which Alice commits a value $k$ which she cannot change once committed.

In the NIZK scheme of Jakobsson et al., a proof is the following tuple

$$(w, r, \mathsf{Commit}, \mathsf{Challenge}, \mathsf{Response}). \tag{18.7.1}$$

Here the prefix pair $(w, r)$ is Alice's decommitment for $\mathsf{TC}(w, r, y_B)$. This added pair is for the purpose of allowing the designated verifier Bob to use his trapdoor information to find collisions. Bob's ability to find collisions will entitle him to simulate Alice's proof.

### Alice's Procedure to Construct Proof

Alice constructs the proof tuple in (18.7.1) as follows:

P.1  picking $w, r \in_U \mathbb{Z}_q$, computing $\mathsf{TC}(w, r, y_B) \leftarrow g^w y_b^r \pmod{p}$;

P.2  $\mathsf{Commit}$ is computed in the same way as that in the Fiat-Shamir heuristic: picking $k \in_U \mathbb{Z}_q$ and computing $\mathsf{Commit} \leftarrow g^k \pmod{p}$;

P.3 the generation of Challenge is usual: using a hash function (which may also take $M$ as an optional message):

Challenge $\leftarrow h(\mathsf{TC}(w, r, y_B) \parallel$ Commit $\parallel [M])$;

P.4 the computation of Response now also takes the committal $w$ as input:

Response $\leftarrow k + x_A(\mathsf{Challenge} + w) \pmod{q}$.

## Bob's Verification Procedure

Given the proof tuple in (18.7.1) (may be including the optional message $M$), Bob verifies using the following procedure

V.1 Challenge $\leftarrow h(\mathsf{TC}(w, r, y_B) \parallel$ Commit $\parallel [M])$;

V.2 check $g^{\mathsf{Response}} \overset{?}{\equiv}$ Commit $y_A^{\mathsf{Challenge}} y_A^w \pmod{p}$; accepts if checking passes, or rejects otherwise.

Now let us consider the security properties of this scheme.

### 18.7.1.1 Security Properties

#### Completeness

Alice's proof tuple in (18.7.1) is very similar to the case of (Commit, Challenge, Response) generated from the Fiat-Shamir heuristic. The only element which makes this "designated verifier proof" different from that obtained from the Fiat-Shamir heuristic is the additional value $y_A^w \pmod{p}$: this additional value is multiplied to the right-hand side expression in Bob's verification procedure (step V.2). Thus, the scheme has a straightforward completeness property.

#### Soundness

Viewed by the designated verifier Bob, the value $y_A^w \pmod{p}$ is fixed since $w$ in it is fixed in $\mathsf{TC}(w, r, y_B)$ and due to the TC property (i), Alice cannot change it, unless she knows Bob' private key $x_B$. Therefore, if Bob is sure that his private key $x_B$ is not known by Alice, then the multiplier $y_A^w \pmod{p}$ is a constant, and consequently, the triplet (Commit, Challenge, Response) is a Fiat-Shamir-heuristic based argument which is genuinely constructed by Alice. Thus, the soundness of this scheme is the same as that for an argument generated from the Fiat-Shamir heuristic. We remark that because the computational resource of Alice has to be polynomially bounded (to prevent her from inverting the hash function or Bob's public key), this scheme is an argument.

#### Perfect ZK-ness

Viewed by any other party, since Bob knows the trapdoor information $x_B$, the multiplier $y_A^w \pmod{p}$ appearing in the right-hand side of verification step (step V.2)

is no longer a fixed constant. Instead, it is can be any value free of manipulation by Bob. Indeed, because Bob can freely simulate $\mathsf{TC}(w, r, y_B)$, the proof tuple in (18.7.1) can be simulated perfectly. Let us now see the simulation.

## Bob's Simulation Procedure

Bob picks Response, $\alpha, \beta \in_U \mathbb{Z}_q$, and computes

S.1  $\mathsf{TC}(w, r, y_B) \leftarrow g^\alpha \pmod p$

S.2  $\mathsf{Commit} \leftarrow g^{\mathsf{Response}} y_A^{-\beta} \pmod p$

S.3  $\mathsf{Challenge} \leftarrow h(\mathsf{TC}(w, r, y_B) \parallel \mathsf{Commit} \parallel [M])$

S.4  $w \leftarrow \beta - \mathsf{Challenge} \pmod q$

S.5  $r \leftarrow (\alpha - w)/x_B \pmod q$

S.6  He outputs the tuple $(w, r, \mathsf{Commit}, \mathsf{Challenge}, \mathsf{Response})$ as the simulated proof.

We can confirm that this simulated proof is perfect.

First of all, due to step S.2, we have

$$g^{\mathsf{Response}} \equiv \mathsf{Commit}\ y_A^{\beta} \pmod p,$$

then via step S.3, the right-hand side becomes

$$\mathsf{Commit}\ y_A^{\beta} \equiv \mathsf{Commit}\ y_A^{w+\mathsf{Challenge}} \equiv \mathsf{Commit}\ y_A^{\mathsf{Challenge}} y_A^{w} \pmod p,$$

that is, we derive

$$g^{\mathsf{Response}} \equiv \mathsf{Commit}\ y_A^{\mathsf{Challenge}} y_A^{w} \pmod p$$

as desired, which agrees with the verification step V.2.

Secondly, from step S.5, we have

$$g^w y_B^r \equiv g^{w + r x_B} \equiv g^\alpha \pmod p.$$

Checking the construction of $\mathsf{TC}(w, r, y_B)$ in step S.1, the trapdoor commitment indeed has the correct construction.

Finally, it is easy to check that not only these values have the correct construction as shown, they also have the correct distributions as those generated by Alice. Therefore, Bob's simulation algorithm is an equating one. The perfect ZK-ness thus stands.

### 18.7.1.2  Applications

Jakobsson et al. envision interesting applications of their "designated verifier proofs" technique. One is an efficient alternative to "undeniable signatures" (see our discussions in §18.6.2.2 on "undeniable signatures"): the optional message $M$ in our description can be considered as a signature of Alice but is only verifiable by the designated verifier Bob. Consider the application of a software vendor authenticates the genuineness of its product; if the vendor Alice uses a "designated verifier proof" for the buyer Bob to verifier, then Bob cannot convince a third party of the genuineness of the copy he has bought since he could simulate a "designated verifier proof."

The other good application is electronic voting. A voting center, after receiving a voter Carol's vote, must send a receipt to Carol to convince her that her vote has been correctly counted. Here, it is very important for the center to convince Carol the correctness of center's proof, while an armed coercer, Malice, must be prevented from coercing Carol to vote the candidate of his choice. Now if the receipt is constructed using this "designated verifier proof," then Malice cannot check the correctness; clearly, Carol can simulate perfectly a receipt for the candidate of Malice's choice. This security service is called **receipt free electronic voting** which has been studied by Benaloh and Tuinstra [31].

# 18.8   Chapter Summary

In this chapter we have conducted a study on zero-knowledge protocols.

We began with introducing interactive proof systems in which we identify that IP protocols are closely related to the complexity class $\mathcal{NP}$ which we have studied in Chapter 4. This identification leads us to a better understanding of problems in $\mathcal{NP}$. After our study of Chapter 4 we know that for a language $L \in \mathcal{NP}$, question $I \overset{?}{\in} L$ is easy (hard) if an algorithm does (not) have an witness to work with. Now after our study of this chapter, we further know in a more intuitive way that the same decision problem is easy (hard) if a verifier does (not) have a prover to work together.

We then identified several notions of zero-knowledge-ness: perfect, honest-verifier, computational and statistical, differentiated notions of proof and argument, considered a protocol with two-sided-error error probability characterization, investigated the round-efficiency problem, and finally, studied non-interactive zero-knowledge protocols. In our introduction of each of these notions, we provided practical protocols for concrete exemplification. In this way of study, we hope that, zero-knowledge protocols, though considered as an advanced cryptographic topic, becomes accessible for readers who wish to develop information security systems which provide rather fancy services yet are practical.

Zero-knowledge protocols is an active research area in cryptography (and connecting it to theoretic computer science). For readers who intend to conduct a further study of the subject, this chapter serves an elementary introduction to the notions and concepts which are necessary for understanding, yet not introduced in, the advanced research papers.

## Exercises

18.1 Explain the following notions in ZK protocols:

    i) Common input.

    ii) Private input.

    iii) Random input.

    iv) Completeness.

    v) Soundness.

    vi) Proof transcript.

    vii) Cheating prover.

    viii) Dishonest verifier.

    ix) Equatability.

    x) Simulatability.

18.2 Differentiate the following notions:

    i) Perfect ZK.

    ii) Honest-verifier ZK.

    iii) Computational ZK.

    iv) Statistical ZK.

    v) ZK proof.

    vi) ZK argument.

    vii) Proof of knowledge.

18.3 The non-repudiation service provided by a digital signature means a proof of knowledge that a signer owns exclusively a private key (knowledge) which has enabled (s)he to issue the signature. What is the difference between this sense of proof of knowledge and that offered by a ZK protocol?

18.4 Can a perfect-ZK protocol be a ZK argument one? Can a computational-ZK protocol be a proof one?

18.5 In a ZK protocol, does a prover have to have a polynomially bounded computing power? Answer the same question for a verifier.

18.6 Why cannot Schnorr's Identification Protocol be a constant-round one?

18.7 Show the completeness property for Schnorr's Identification Protocol (Prot 18.2).

18.8 In the computational ZK protocol described in §18.3.3.2, we have discussed that Alice can choose her committal from the set $\mathbb{Z}_{N^{1+\alpha}}$ for any small and fixed $\alpha > 0$. Why?

18.9 Prove Fact 3 in §18.4.2.1.

18.10 Some ZK protocols use multiple rounds to reduce the (soundness) error probability. Usually, the verifier will only accept a proof if no any error is detected in all rounds. Can this "election criterion" be used for protocols with two-sided error?

18.11 Why cannot Prot 18.4 use the "majority election criterion?"

18.12 Why is a two-sided-error protocol not efficient, in particular when the behavior of an honest prover and that of a cheating one are similar in a single round of message exchange?

18.13 What is a constant-round (log-round, poly-round) protocol?

18.14 Can Prot 18.6 be simplified to an honest-verifier version with three moves only?

Hint: if Alice performs modulo exponentiation directly on Bob's challenge, then move 2, 3 and 4 can be compressed into a single message transmission.

18.15 What is the danger in the "honest-verifier" version of Prot 18.6 suggested in the preceding problem?

Hint: review the fourth bullet point discussed in §18.6.2.2.

18.16 What is a trapdoor commitment?

18.17 What are applications of a non-interactive ZK protocol?

# Chapter 19

# RETURNING TO "COIN FLIPPING OVER TELEPHONE"

The first cryptographic protocol of this book, "Coin Flipping Over Telephone" (Prot 1.1), is specified using a "magic function" $f$. Let us recap two properties of this function (Property 1.1):

I) For every integer $x$, it is easy to compute $f(x)$ from $x$ while given any value $f(x)$ it is *impossible* to find any information about a pre-image $x$, e.g., whether $x$ is an odd or even number.

II) It *impossible* to find a pair of integers $(x, y)$ satisfying $x \neq y$ and $f(x) = f(y)$.

So far, this "magic function" remains magic. No supporting evidence for the two uses of the word "impossible" has been provided, let alone the provision of a concrete realization of the function (and hence of Prot 1.1).

In fact, in §1.2.1 we did suggest a practical way to realize Prot 1.1: realizing the function $f$ using a practical hash function such as SHA-1. In the SHA-1 realization, for any integer $x$, the result $f(x)$ can be coded into 40 hexadecimal characters and so it is practical for Alice to read $f(x)$ to Bob over the phone. We have also mentioned that that realization is good enough for the two friends to decide a recreation venue.

However, there are plenty of cryptographic applications in which two untrusted communication partners need to use mutually trusted random numbers. Such applications will have much more serious security consequences than that of playing a lighthearted game. For example, a standard attacking technique which we have witnessed in numerous attacks throughout this book boils down to tricking a naive user into providing an oracle service in which the user performs a cryptographic operation on an innocent-looking "random" number. If a user knows with high confidence that a random number to be dealt with, whether or not is from an oracle service request, is a genuine one, then many such attacks will no longer work. Therefore, the genuine randomness and the knowledge that a random looking number is indeed random matter very much for cryptographic systems' security.

To see another reason behind the need of a trustworthy random source, let us recall the preceding chapter where we have seen that honest-verifier zero-knowledge protocols need mutually trusted random challenges. These random challenges should not be derived from a hash function. A dishonest verifier can attack an honest-verifier ZK protocol precisely because (s)he can use hash function to generate a "random" looking challenge (review §18.3.2.1). Therefore a realization of Prot 1.1 (a coin-flipping protocol for generating mutually trusted random numbers, not merely for deciding recreation venues) using a SHA-1 like practical hash function, as we suggested in Chapter 1, is certainly unsuitable for these applications.

Yet another reason behind the unsuitability for a coin-flipping protocol to use a practical hash function is the difficulty of conducting a precise security analysis. Such an analysis is necessary if the protocol is for serious applications.

The final protocol for this book is a concrete realization of the first protocol of the book. After our study through the book, we are now technically ready to provide a *good* realization for Prot 1.1. This realization is the famous "Coin-Flipping-by-Telephone" Protocol of Blum [44].

# 19.1   Blum's "Coin-Flipping-by-Telephone" Protocol

Blum's remote coin-flipping protocol is specified in Prot 19.1. The protocol runs in parallel, allowing two untrusted parties to agree on a mutually trusted random number of $m$-bit long. As in Prot 1.1, in Blum's protocol it is also the case that Alice flips a coin and Bob guesses the sides.

Blum's protocol uses a large composite integer $N = PQ$ where $P, Q$ are two large primes satisfying

$$P \equiv Q \equiv 3 \ (\mathrm{mod} \ 4).$$

After the publication of Blum's protocol [44], such integers are named **Blum integers**. Blum integers have many useful properties for cryptographic use. In §6.7 we have studied some number theory facts about Blum integers. Some of these facts will be useful here for us to analyze security properties of Blum's protocol.

Let us first provide a security analysis for Blum's remote coin-flipping protocol. After the security analysis, we shall measure the efficiency of the protocol.

**Protocol 19.1:** Blum's "Coin-Flipping-by-Telephone" Protocol

(∗ this protocol lets Alice and Bob agree on a string of mutually trusted random bits of length $m$; like in the case of Prot 1.1, Alice flips a coin and Bob guesses ∗)

CONVENTION

- Each party digitally signs each message sent to the other party.

- Each party aborts a run if any verification (including that for a digital signature) shows inconsistency.

1. Bob generates a large Blum integer $N = PQ$ and sends $N$ to Alice;

2. Alice picks $m$ random numbers: $x_1, x_2, \ldots, x_m \in_U \mathbb{Z}_N^*$; the values $\left(\dfrac{x_i}{N}\right)$ $(i = 1, 2, \ldots, m)$ are her coin-flipping results;

   she computes $y_1 \leftarrow x_1^2$, $y_2 \leftarrow x_2^2$, $\ldots$, $y_m \leftarrow x_m^2$ (mod $N$);

   she sends $y_1, y_2, \ldots, y_m$ to Bob;

3. Bob picks random signs $b_1, b_2, \ldots, b_m \in_U \{1, \text{-}1\}$ as his guesses on the signs of $\left(\dfrac{x_i}{N}\right)$ for $i = 1, 2, \ldots, m$;

   he sends these signs to Alice;

   (∗ Bob has finished his guessing of Alice's coin flipping ∗)

4. Alice reveals $x_1, x_2, \ldots, x_m$ to Bob;

   (∗ Alice has told Bob the correctness of his guessing ∗)

5. Bob verifies $y_i \equiv x_i^2$ (mod $N$) for $i = 1, 2, \ldots, m$;

   he reveals $P$, $Q$ to Alice;

6. Alice verifies $P \equiv Q \equiv 3$ (mod 4) and conducts primality test on $P$ and $Q$;

7. Both compute the agreed random bits as (for $i = 1, 2, \ldots, m$)

$$r_i \leftarrow \begin{cases} 1 & \text{if Bob's guessing is correct, i.e., } \left(\dfrac{x_i}{N}\right) = b_i \\ 0 & \text{otherwise} \end{cases}.$$

# 19.2  Security Analysis

In Blum's remote coin flipping protocol, Alice flips a coin and Bob guesses the sides. Therefore in the analysis of the protocol's security we need to measure the difficulties for these two parties to mount attacks in the following two possibilities:

**Alice's Cheating**

> Can Alice find a way to flip a coin and later reveal to Bob HEADS or TAILS as she wishes?

**Bob's Unfair Guessing Advantage**

> Can Bob's guessing advantage be different from $\frac{1}{2}$?

We are able to answer these two questions *quantitatively*. First, Alice's cheating is the problem for her to factor the Blum integer $N$. Secondly, Bob's guessing advantage is precisely $\frac{1}{2}$. These are now separately analyzed.

### Security Against Alice's Cheating

In order to cheat, Alice has to find a pair of collisions, i.e., two elements $z_1, z_2 \in \mathbb{Z}_N^*$ satisfying

- $z_1^2 \equiv z_2^2 \pmod{N}$, and

- $\left(\frac{z_1}{N}\right) \neq \left(\frac{z_2}{N}\right)$.

Suppose that Alice can indeed find such a pair of collisions. By Theorem 6.18.(i), we have $\left(\frac{-1}{N}\right) = 1$. This requires $z_1 \neq \pm z_2 \pmod{N}$, i.e., $0 < z_1 \pm z_2 < N$. Suppose on the contrary, e.g., $z_1 = -z_2 \pmod{N}$. We have

$$\left(\frac{z_1}{N}\right) = \left(\frac{-1}{N}\right)\left(\frac{z_2}{N}\right) = \left(\frac{z_2}{N}\right)$$

which contradicts to Alice's collision criterion $\left(\frac{z_1}{N}\right) \neq \left(\frac{z_2}{N}\right)$.

Now from

$$0 < z_1 + z_2 < N, \ \ 0 < |z_1 - z_2| < N$$

and

$$z_1^2 - z_2^2 = (z_1 + z_2)(z_1 - z_2) \equiv 0 \pmod{N}$$

we obtain (e.g.)

$$0 < \gcd(z_1 + z_2, N) < N.$$

This is, Alice has factored $N$.

To this end, we conclude that Alice's difficulty of finding a pair of collisions is precisely that of factoring $N$, a reputably hard problem. Here, again, we have conducted a "reduction-to-contradiction" security analysis. We are satisfied to use the difficulty of factorization as our quantitative measure for the difficulty of the second "impossible" in the description of the "magic function" properties. In practice, it is a well-known impossible problem, especially considering that Alice has to do the factoring job in real time.

Therefore, viewed by Alice, the function in Blum's protocol for sending coin-flipping commitment is indeed one-way, with confidence based on a "pedigree" problem.

### Bob's Guessing Advantage

We now show that Bob's guessing advantage is precisely $\frac{1}{2}$.

For the $i$-th coin flip, Alice sends to Bob $y_i \equiv x_i^2 \pmod{N}$. Bob's job is to guess the sign of $\left(\frac{x_i}{N}\right)$ after seeing $y_i$. By Theorem 6.18.(iii), $y_i$ has precise two square roots with the positive Jacobi symbol and precise two square roots with the negative one. Using Alg 6.5 Bob can compute each of these four square roots, but there is no way whatsoever for him to know which root Alice has chosen and so he has no way whatsoever to pinpoint the sign for Jacobi symbol of Alice's chosen root. For Bob, the function is precisely a 2-to-1 mapping. All he can do is a pure guess which has the correctness probability $\frac{1}{2}$ precisely.

This is our quantitative measure for the first "impossible" in the description the "magic function" properties. This impossibility is absolute!

## 19.3　Efficiency

Observing the protocol, we can measure the two parties' computational costs as follows.

### Alice's Cost

Alice's main cost amounts to those for (i) computing $m$ squarings, (ii) $m$ Jacobi symbols and (iii) conducting two primality tests. Squarings and evaluations of Jacobi symbols cost $O_B((\log N)^2)$. Primality tests costs $O_B(\log N)^3$. So if we consider $m = \log N$, the total costs for Alice is $C \cdot (\log N)^3$ where $C$ is a small constant. This estimate covers the cost for generating and verifying digital signatures. Speaking in ordinary words, the total computational cost for Alice is at the level of performing several RSA encryptions.

In communication bandwidth cost, Alice sends $2(\log N)^2$ bits (considering $m = \log N$).

### Bob's Cost

It is easy to see that Bob's computational cost is that of Alice's plus that for generating an RSA modulus. So speaking in ordinary words, Bob's computational cost is that of an RSA key generation plus performing several RSA encryptions. To express it formally, we can replace the constant $C$ in Alice's computational cost expression with $\log N$ to obtain Bob's computational cost expression: $O_B((\log N)^4)$.

Bob communication cost is much lower than that of Alice's since he only needs to send the modulus, $m$ random bits and the factor of the modulus, which amounts to $3 \log N$ (bits).

Clearly, the costs for both parties are suitable for practical applications.

## 19.4   Chapter Summary

Our quantitative measures on the performance and security for Blum's "Coin-Flipping-by-Telephone" Protocol identifies the following qualities for the protocol:

- Strong and measurable security

  We have seen from our security analysis in §19.2 that the eventual realization of the one-way function in the coin-flipping protocol is very strong in a *measurable* sense: one use of the word "impossible" is based on a one-way property from a "pedigree" problem: factorization and the other "impossible" is in the absolute sense: unconditional.

- Practical efficiency

  We have also seen from our performance analysis in §19.3 that the protocol allows two parties to agree on a string of mutually trusted random bits of length $m$ at the cost of performing several ordinary public-key cryptographic operations where the public-key cryptosystem uses $m$ as the security parameter. This efficiency is clearly suitable for practical applications.

- Based on practical and available primitives

  The protocol can use ordinary digital signature scheme, involves computing squaring, Jacobi symbols modulo a large integer and Monte-Carlo primality testing. These algorithms and operations are standard in most cryptographic algorithm libraries and are therefore widely available.

Thus, according to our criteria for good cryptographic algorithms, protocols and systems which we have listed in Chapter 1, Blum's "Coin-Flipping-by-Telephone" Protocol is indeed a good protocol.

# Chapter 20

# AFTERREMARK

Cryptography entered its modern era in the mid-1970s as the result of two events: publication of the US Data Encryption Standard and the discovery of public-key cryptography. The theoretic and practical importance of cryptography has since then been successfully stimulating proliferations of academic research advances and commercial application activities. To this day, modern cryptography has evolved to a vast area of study. With ceaseless emergence of new ideas and techniques, the area is still on its course of steady growth.

In this book, we have confined ourselves to the study of a chosen small but important part of modern cryptography. The selected part includes techniques, schemes, protocols and systems which either have been playing roles of the most common building blocks in the construction of information security systems (e.g., cryptographic primitives in Chapters 7—10 and basic authentication protocol constructions in Chapter 11), or have found the widest range of applications (e.g., real-world authentication systems in Chapter 12 and fit-for-application encryption and signature schemes in Chapters 15—16), or will likely to have a great potential and impact in building future and "fancy" applications of electronic business, commerce and services (e.g., identity-based schemes in Chapter 13 and zero-knowledge protocols in Chapter 18).

With focus, we are able to conduct a systematic and in-depth study of the selected techniques under several aspects which have importance not only for proper uses of the selected techniques in applications but also in further development of the methodologies for information security. These aspects are:

- Revelations of general weaknesses in "textbook" cryptographic schemes and protocols

- strengthening security notions to fit-for-application versions

- introduction to fit-for-application cryptographic schemes and protocols

- formal methodologies and techniques for security analysis, and

- exemplified formal establishment of strong security evidence for some schemes and protocols.

In addition, we have also conducted a study on theoretic foundations for modern cryptography, with which we intend to provide the reader with an introductory material to help her/his further exploration in the vast domain of modern cryptography.

# BIBLIOGRAPHY

[1] M. Abadi and R. Needham. Prudent engineering practice for cryptographic protocols. Technical Report DEC SRC Technical Report 125, Digital Equipment Corporation, November 1995.

[2] M. Abadi and P. Rogaway. Reconciling two views of cryptography (the computational soundness of formal encryption). *Journal of Cryptology*, 15(2):103–127, Spring 2002.

[3] M. Abadi and M.R. Tuttle. A semantics for a logic of authentication (extended abstract). In *Proceedings of Tenth Annual ACM Symposium on Principles of Distributed Computing*, pages 201–216, August 1991.

[4] M. Abdalla, M. Bellare, and P. Rogaway. DHAES: an encryption scheme based on the Diffie-Hellman problem. Submission to IEEE P1363: Asymmetric Encryption, 1998. Available at `grouper.ieee.org/groups/1363/P1363a/Encryption.html`.

[5] C. Abrams and A. Drobik. E-business opportunity index — the EU surges ahead. Research Note, Strategic Planning, SPA-10-7786, GartnerGroup RAS Services, 21, July 2000.

[6] C. Adams, P. Cain, D. Pinkas, and R. Zuccherato. Internet X.509 Public Key Infrastructure Time-Stamp Protocol (TSP). The Internet Engineering Task Force Request For Comments (IETF RFC) 3161, August 2001. Available at `www.ietf.org/rfc/rfc3161.txt`.

[7] C. Adams and S. Farrell. Internet X.509 Public Key Infrastructure Certificate Management Protocols. The Internet Engineering Task Force Request For Comments (IETF RFC) 2510, March 1999. Available at `www.ietf.org/rfc/rfc2510.txt`.

[8] M. Agrawal, N. Kayal, and N. Saxena. PRIMES is in P. Online News, August 2002. `www.cse.iitk.ac.in/users/manindra/primality.ps`.

[9] A.V. Aho, J.E. Hopcroft, and J.D. Ullman. *The Design and Analysis of Computer Algorithms.* Addison-Wesley Publishing Company, 1974.

[10] W. Aiello, S.M. Bellovin, M. Blaze, R. Canetti, J. Ioannidis, A.D. Keromytis, and O. Reingold. Efficient, DoS-resistant, secure key exchange for Internet Protocols. In B. Christianson et al., editor, *Proceedings of Security Protocols, Lecture Notes in Computer Science 2467*, pages 27–39. Springer-Verlag, 2002.

[11] W. Aiello, S.M. Bellovin, M. Blaze, R. Canetti, J. Ioannidis, A.D. Keromytis, and O. Reingold. Efficient, DoS-resistant, secure key exchange for Internet Protocols. In *Proceedings of ACM Conference on Computer and Communications Security (ACM-CCS'02)*, pages 48–58. ACM Press, November 2002.

[12] Alctel. Understanding the IPSec protocol suite. White Papers Archive, March 2000. Available at www.ind.alctel.com/library/whitepapers/wp_IPSec.pdf.

[13] W. Alexi, B. Chor, O. Goldreich, and C.P. Schnorr. RSA and Rabin functions: certain parts are as hard as the whole. *SIAM Journal of Computing*, 17(2):194–209, April 1988.

[14] R. Anderson. *Security Engineering: A Guide to Building Dependable Distributed Systems.* John Wiley & Sons, Inc., 2001.

[15] R. Anderson, E. Biham, and L. Knudsen. Serpent: A proposal for the advanced encryption standard. AES proposal: National Institute of Standards and Technology (NIST), 1998. Also available at www.cl.cam.ac.uk/~rja14/serpent.html.

[16] L. Babai. Talk presented at the 21st Annual Symposium on Foundation of Computer Science. San Juan, Puerto Rico, October 1979.

[17] R. Baldwin and R. Rivest. The RC5, RC5-CBC, RC5-CBC-Pad, and RC5-CTS algorithms. The Internet Engineering Task Force Request For Comments (IETF RFC) 2040, October 1996. Available at www.ietf.org/rfc/rfc2040.txt.

[18] N. Barić and B. Pfitzmann. Collision-free accumulatiors and fail-stop signature schemes without trees. In W. Fumy, editor, *Advances in Cryptology — Proceedings of EUROCRYPT'97, Lecture Notes in Computer Science 1233*, pages 480–494. Springer-Verlag, 1997.

[19] M. Bellare, R. Canetti, and H. Krawczyk. A modular approach to the design and analysis of authentication and key-exchange protocols. In *Proceedings of the 30th Annual Symposium on the Theory of Computing (STOC'98)*, pages 419–428. ACM Press, 1998.

[20] M. Bellare, A. Desai, D. Pointcheval, and P. Rogaway. Relations among nations of security for public-key encryption schemes. In H. Krawczyk, editor, *Advances in Cryptology — Proceedings of CRYPTO'98, Lecture Notes in Computer Science 1462*, pages 26–45. Springer-Verlag, 1998.

[21] M. Bellare and S. Micali. Non-interactive oblivious transfer and applications. In G. Brassard, editor, *Advances in Cryptology — Proceedings of CRYPTO'89, Lecture Notes in Computer Science 435*, pages 547–557. Springer-Verlag, 1990.

[22] M. Bellare, D. Pointcheval, and P. Rogaway. Authenticated key exchange secure against dictionary attacks. In B. Preneel, editor, *Advances in Cryptology — Proceedings of EUROCRYPT'00, Lecture Notes in Computer Science 1807*, pages 139–155. Springer-Verlag, 2000.

[23] M. Bellare and P. Rogaway. Random oracles are practical: a paradigm for designing efficient protocols. In *First ACM Conference on Computer and Communications Security*, pages 62–73, New York, 1993. ACM Press.

[24] M. Bellare and P. Rogaway. Entity authentication and key distribution. In D. Stinson, editor, *Advances in Cryptology — Proceedings of CRYPTO'93, Lecture Notes in Computer Science 773*, pages 232–249. Springer-Verlag, 1994.

[25] M. Bellare and P. Rogaway. Optimal asymmetric encryption. In A. de Santis, editor, *Advances in Cryptology — Proceedings of EUROCRYPT'94, Lecture Notes in Computer Science 950*, pages 92–111. Springer-Verlag, 1995.

[26] M. Bellare and P. Rogaway. Provably secure session key distribution — the three party case. In *Proceedings of 27th ACM Symposium on the Theory of Computing*, pages 57–66. ACM Press, 1995.

[27] M. Bellare and P. Rogaway. The exact security of digital signatures – How to sign with RSA and Rabin. In U. Maurer, editor, *Advances in Cryptology — Proceedings of EUROCRYPT'96, Lecture Notes in Computer Science 1070*, pages 399–416. Springer-Verlag, 1996.

[28] S.M. Bellovin. Problem areas for the IP security protocols. In *Proceedings of the Sixth Usenix UNIX Security Symposium*, pages 1–16, July 1996.

[29] S.M. Bellovin and M. Merritt. Limitations of the Kerberos authentication system. *ACM Computer Communication Review*, 20(5):119–132, 1990.

[30] S.M. Bellovin and M. Merritt. Encrypted key exchange: Password-based protocols secure against dictionary attacks. In *Proceedings of the 1992 IEEE Symposium on Research in Security and Privacy*, 1992.

[31] J.C. Benaloh and D. Tuinstra. Receipt-free secret-ballot elections. In *Proceedings of the 26th Annual Symposium on the Theory of Computing (STOC'94)*, pages 544–553, 1994.

[32] C. Bennett and G. Brassard. The dawn of a new era for quantum cryptography: the experimental prototype is working! *SIGACT News*, 20:78–82, Fall 1989.

[33] R. Berger, S. Kannan, and R. Peralta. A framework for the study of cryptographic protocols. In H.C. Williams, editor, *Advances in Cryptology — Proceedings of CRYPTO'85, Lecture Notes in Computer Science 218*, pages 87–103. Springer-Verlag, 1986.

[34] E. Biham and A. Shamir. Differential cryptanalysis of DES-like cryptosystems. *Journal of Cryptology*, 4:3–72, 1991.

[35] R. Bird, I. Gopal, A. Herzberg, P. Janson, S. Kutten, R. Molva, and M. Yung. Systematic design of two-party authentication protocols. In J. Feigenbaum, editor, *Advances in Cryptology — Proceedings of CRYPTO'91, Lecture Notes in Computer Science 576, Springer-Verlag*, pages 44–61, 1992.

[36] I. Blake, G. Seroussi, and N. Smart. *Elliptic Curves in Cryptography*. Cambridge University Press, 1999. London Mathematical Society Lecture Note Series 265.

[37] S. Blake-Wilson, D. Johnson, and A. Menezes. Key agreement protocols and their security analysis. In *Proceedings of the sixth IMA International Conference on Cryptography and Coding, Lecture Notes in Computer Science, 1355*, pages 30–45. Springer Verlag, 1997.

[38] S. Blake-Wilson and A. Menezes. Security proofs for entity authentication and authenticated key transport protocols emplying asymmetric techniques. In *Proceedings of 1997 Security Protocols Workshop, Lecture Notes in Computer Science 1361*, pages 137–158. Springer Verlag, 1998.

[39] S. Blake-Wilson and A. Menezes. Authenticated Diffie-Hellman key agreement protocols. In S. Tavares and H. Meijer, editors, *Proceedings of Selected Areas in Cryptography (SAC'98), Lecture Notes in Computer Science 1556*, pages 339–361. Springer Verlag, 1999.

[40] M. Blaze. Efficient, DoS-resistant, secure key exchange for Internet protocols (Transcript of Discussion). In B. Christianson et al., editor, *Proceedings of Security Protocols, Lecture Notes in Computer Science 2467*, pages 40–48. Springer-Verlag, 2002.

[41] M. Blaze, J. Feigenbaum, and J. Lacy. Distributed trust management. In *Proceedings 1996 IEEE Symposium on Security and Privacy*, pages 164–173. IEEE Computer Society Press, May 1996.

[42] D. Bleichenbacher. Generating ElGamal signature without knowing the secret key. In U. Maurer, editor, *Advances in Cryptology — Proceedings of EUROCRYPT'96, Lecture Notes in Computer Science 1070*, pages 10–18. Springer-Verlag, 1996.

[43] L. Blum, M. Blum, and M. Shub. A simple unpredictable pseudo-random number generator. *SIAM Journal of Computing*, 15(2):364–383, May 1986.

[44] M. Blum. Coin flipping by telephone: A protocol for solving impossible problems. In *Proceedings of the 24th IEEE Computer Conference*, pages 133–137, May 1981.

[45] M. Blum, P. Feldman, and S. Micali. Non-interactive zero-knowledge and its applications (extended abstract). In *Proceedings of the 20th Annual ACM Symposium on Theory of Computing*, pages 103–112, 1988.

[46] M. Blum and S. Goldwasser. An *efficient* probabilistic public-key encryption scheme which hides all partial information. In G.R. Blakley and D. Chaum, editors, *Advances in Cryptology — Proceedings of CRYPTO'84, Lecture Notes in Computer Science 196*, pages 289–299. Springer-Verlag, 1985.

[47] M. Blum and S. Micali. How to generate cryptographically strong sequences of pseudo-random bits. In *Proceedings of 23rd Annual IEEE Symposium on Foundations of Computer Science*, pages 112–117, 1982.

[48] D. Boneh. The decision Diffie-Hellman problem. In *Proceedings of 3rd Algorithmic Number Theory Symposium, Lecture Notes in Computer Science 1423*, pages 48–63. Springer-Verlag, 1997.

[49] D. Boneh. Twenty years of attacks on the RSA cryptosystem. *Notices of the AMS*, 46(2):203–213, February 1999.

[50] D. Boneh. Simplified OAEP for the RSA and Rabin functions. In J. Killian, editor, *Advances in Cryptology — Proceedings of CRYPTO'01, Lecture Notes in Computer Science 2139*, pages 275–291. Springer-Verlag, 2001.

[51] D. Boneh and G. Durfee. Cryptanalysis of RSA with private key $d$ less than $n^{0.292}$. In J. Stern, editor, *Advances in Cryptology — Proceedings of EURO-CRYPT'99, Lecture Notes in Computer Science 1592*, pages 1–11. Springer-Verlag, 1999.

[52] D. Boneh and M. Franklin. Identity based encryption from the Weil pairing. In J. Killian, editor, *Advances in Cryptology — Proceedings of CRYPTO'01, Lecture Notes in Computer Science 2139*, pages 213–229. Springer-Verlag, 2001.

[53] D. Boneh, A. Joux, and P.Q. Nguyen. Why textbook ElGamal and RSA encryption are insecure (extended abstract). In T. Okamoto, editor, *Advances in Cryptology — Proceedings of ASIACRYPT'00, Lecture Notes in Computer Science 1976*, pages 30–43. Springer-Verlag, 2000.

[54] A. Bosselaers, H. Dobbertin, and B. Preneel. The new cryptographic hash function RIPEMD-160. *Dr. Dobbs*, 22(1):24–28, January 1997.

[55] C. Boyd. Hidden assumptions in cryptographic protocols. *IEE Proceedings, Part E*, 137(6):433–436, November 1990.

[56] C. Boyd and W. Mao. On a limitations of BAN logic. In T. Helleseth, editor, *Advances in Cryptology — Proceedings of EUROCRYPT'93, Lecture Notes in Computer Science 765*, pages 240–247. Springer-Verlag, 1993.

[57] C. Boyd, W. Mao, and K. Paterson. Deniable authentication for Internet Protocols. In *International Workshop on Security Protocols, Lecture Notes in Computer Science (to appear)*, pages Pre–proceedings: 137–150. Springer-Verlag, April 2003. Sidney Sussex College, Cambridge, England.

[58] V. Boyko, P. MacKenzie, and S. Patel. Provably secure password-authenticated key exchange using Diffie-Hellman. In B. Preneel, editor, *Advances in Cryptology — Proceedings of EUROCRYPT'00, Lecture Notes in Computer Science 1807*, pages 156–171. Springer-Verlag, 2000.

[59] S. Brands. An efficient off-line electronic cash system based on the representati‹ problem. Technical Report CS-R9323, CWI Technical Report, 1993.

[60] G. Brassard, D. Chaum, and C. Crépeau. Minimum disclosure proofs of knowledge. *Journal of Computer and System Schiences*, 37(2):156–189, 1988.

[61] S.C. Brookes, C.A.R. Hoare, and A.W. Roscoe. A theory of communicating sequential processes. *Journal of the Association of Computing Machinery*, 31(7):560–599, 1984.

[62] M. Burrows, M. Abadi, and R. Needham. A logic of authentication. Technical Report SRC Technical Report 39, Digital Equipment Corporation, February 1989.

[63] C. Burwick, D. Coppersmith, E. D'Avignon, R. Gennaro, S. Halevi, C. Jutla, S.M. Matyas Jr., L. O'Connor, M. Peyravian, D. Safford, and N. Zunic. MARS - a candidate cipher for AES. AES proposal: National Institute of Standards and Technology (NIST), 1998. Also available at `www.research.ibm.com/security/mars.html`.

[64] J. Camenisch and M. Michels. Proving in zero-knowledge that a number is the product of two safe primes. In J. Stern, editor, *Advances in Cryptology — Proceedings of EUROCRYPT'99, Lecture Notes in Computer Science 1592*, pages 106–121. Springer-Verlag, 1999.

[65] R. Canetti, O. Goldreich, and S. Halevi. The random oracle methodology, revisited. In *Proceedings of the 30th Annual Symposium on the Theory of Computing (STOC'98)*, pages 209–218. ACM Press, 1998.

[66] R. Canetti, O. Goldreich, and S. Halevi. The random oracle methodology, revisited. A new version of [65], October 2002. Available at `xxx.lanl.gov/ps/cs.CR/0010019`.

[67] R. Canetti and H. Krawczyk. Analysis of key-exchange protocols and their use for building secure channels. In B. Pfitzmann, editor, *Advances in Cryptology — Proceedings of EUROCRYPT'01, Lecture Notes in Computer Science 2045*, pages 453–474. Springer-Verlag, 2001.

[68] R. Canetti and H. Krawczyk. Security analysis of IKE's signature-based key-exchange protocol. In M. Yung, editor, *Advances in Cryptology — Proceedings of CRYPTO'02, Lecture Notes in Computer Science 2442*, pages 143–161. Springer-Verlag, 2002. Also available at `eprint.iacr.org`.

[69] B. Canvel, A. Hiltgen, S. Vaudenay, and M. Vuagnoux. Password interception in a SSL/TLS channel. To appear in CRYPTO'03, March 2003. Available at `lasecwww.epfl.ch/memo_ssl.shtml`.

[70] U. Carlsen. Cryptographic protocol flaws: know your enermy. In *Proceedings of The Computer Security Foundations Workshop VII*, pages 192–200. IEEE Computer Society Press, 1994.

[71] S. Cavallar, B. Dodson, A.K. Lenstra, W. Lioen, P.L. Montgomery, B. Murphy, H.te Riele, K. Aardal, J. Gilchrist, G. Guillerm, P. Leyland, J. Marchand, F. Morain, A. Muffett, C. Putnam, C. Putnam, and P. Zimmermann. Factorization of a 512-bit RSA modulus. In B. Preneel, editor, *Advances in Cryptology — Proceedings of EUROCRYPT'00, Lecture Notes in Computer Science 1807*, pages 1–18. Springer-Verlag, 2000.

[72] D. Chaum. Demonstrating that a public predicate can be satisfied without revealing any information about how. In A.M. Odlyzko, editor, *Advances in Cryptology — Proceedings of CRYPTO'86, Lecture Notes in Computer Science 263*, pages 195–199. Springer-Verlag, 1987.

[73] D. Chaum. Zero-knowledge undeniable signatures (extended abstract). In I.B. Damgård, editor, *Advances in Cryptology — Proceedings of CRYPTO'90, Lecture Notes in Computer Science 473*, pages 458–464. Springer-Verlag, 1991.

[74] D. Chaum and T.P. Pedersen. Wallet databases with observers. In E.F. Brickell, editor, *Advances in Cryptology — Proceedings of CRYPTO'92, Lecture Notes in Computer Science 740*, pages 89–105. Springer-Verlag, 1993.

[75] D. Chaum and H. van Antwerpen. Undeniable signatures. In G. Brassard, editor, *Advances in Cryptology — Proceedings of CRYPTO'89, Lecture Notes in Computer Science 435*, pages 212–216. Springer-Verlag, 1990.

[76] B. Chor. *Two Issues in Public Key Cryptography, RSA Bit Security and a New Knapsack Type System*. MIT Press, 1985. An ACM Distinguished Dissertation.

[77] B. Chor and O. Goldreich. RSA/Rabin least significant bits are $\frac{1}{2} + \frac{1}{poly(\log N)}$ secure. In G.T. Blakley and D. Chaum, editors, *Advances in Cryptology — Proceedings of CRYPTO'84, Lecture Notes in Computer Science 196*, pages 303–313. Springer-Verlag, 1985.

[78] J. Clark and J. Jacob. A survey of authentication protocol literature: version 1.0. Online document, November 1997. Available at www.cs.york.ac.uk/jac/papers/drareview.ps.gz.

[79] C. Cocks. An identity-based public-key cryptosystem. In *Cryptography and Coding: 8th IMA International Conference, Lecture Notes in Computer Science 2260*, pages 360–363. Springer, December 2001.

[80] H. Cohen. *A Course in Computational Algebraic Number Theory*. Springer, 1996. Graduate Texts in Mathematics 138.

[81] S.A. Cook. The complexity of theorem-proving procedures. In *Proceedings of 3rd Annual ACM Symposium on Theory of Computing*, pages 151–158, 1971.

[82] D. Coppersmith. The Data Encryption Standard (DES) and its strength against attacks. *IBM Journal of Research and Development*, 38:243–250, 1994.

[83] D. Coppersmith. Finding a small root of a bivariate integer equation; factoring with high bits known. In U. Maurer, editor, *Advances in Cryptology — Proceedings of EUROCRYPT'96, Lecture Notes in Computer Science 1070*, pages 178–189. Springer-Verlag, 1996.

[84] J.S. Coron, M. Joye, D. Naccache, and P. Paillier. Universal padding schemes for RSA. In M. Yung, editor, *Advances in Cryptology — Proceedings of CRYPTO'02, Lecture Notes in Computer Science 2442*, pages 226–241. Springer-Verlag, 2002.

[85] R. Cramer and V. Shoup. A practical public key cryptosystem provably secure against adaptive chosen ciphertext attack. In H. Krawczyk, editor, *Advances in Cryptology — Proceedings of CRYPTO'98, Lecture Notes in Computer Science 1462*, pages 13–25. Springer-Verlag, 1998.

[86] R. Cramer and V. Shoup. Signature schemes based on the strong RSA assumption. In *Proceedings of 6th ACM Conference on Computer and Communication Security*. ACM Press, November 1999.

[87] J. Daemen and V. Rijmen. AES Proposal: Rijndael. AES proposal: National Institute of Standards and Technology (NIST), October 6 1998. Available at csrc.nist.gov/encryption/aes/.

[88] J. Daemen and V. Rijmen. *The Design of Rijndael: AES — the Advanced Encryption Standard*. Springer-Verlag, 2002. ISBN: 3540425802.

[89] I. Damgård. Towards practical public key systems secure against chosen ciphertext attacks. In J. Feigenbaum, editor, *Advances in Cryptology — Proceedings of CRYPTO'91, Lecture Notes in Computer Science 576*, pages 445–456. Springer-Verlag, 1992.

[90] D.W. Davies and W.L. Price. *Security for Computer Networks, An Introduction to Data Security in Teleprocessing and Electronic Funds Transfer (second edition)*. John Wiley & Sons, 1989.

[91] D. Davis and R. Swick. Workstation services and Kerberos authentication at Project Athena. Technical Memorandum TM-424, MIT Laboratory for Computer Science, February 1990.

[92] R.A. DeMillo, G.L. Davida, D.P. Dobkin, M.A. Harrison, and R.J. Lipton. *Applied Cryptology, Cryptographic Protocols, and Computer Security Models*, volume 29. Providence: American Mathematical Society, 1983. Proceedings of Symposia in Applied Mathematics.

[93] R.A. DeMillo and M.J. Merritt. Protocols for data security. *Computer*, 16(2):39–50, Febrary 1983.

[94] D. Denning. *Cryptography and Data Security*. Addison-Wesley Publishing Company, Inc., 1982.

[95] D.E. Denning and G.M. Sacco. Timestamps in key distribution protocols. *Communications of the ACM*, 24(8):533–536, August 1981.

[96] T. Dierks and C. Allen. The TLS Protocol, Version 1.0. Request for Comments: 2246, January 1999.

[97] W. Diffie. The first ten years of public key cryptology. In G.J. Simmons, editor, *Contemporary Cryptology, the Science of Information Integrity*, pages 135–175. IEEE Press, 1992.

[98] W. Diffie and M. Hellman. Multiuser cryptographic techniques. In *Proceedings of AFIPS 1976 NCC*, pages 109–112. AFIPS Press, Montvale, N.J., 1976.

[99] W. Diffie and M.E. Hellman. New directions in cryptography. *IEEE Trans. Info. Theory*, IT-22(6):644–654, 1976.

[100] W. Diffie, P.C. van Oorschot, and M. Wiener. Authentication and authenticated key exchanges. *Designs, Codes and Cryptography*, 2:107–125, 1992.

[101] D. Dolev, C. Dwork, and M. Naor. Non-malleable cryptography. In *Proceedings of 23rd Annual ACM Symposium on Theory of Computing*, pages 542–552, 1991. Journal version in *SIAM Journal on Computing*, vol 30, no. 2, 391–437, 2000.

[102] D. Dolev and A.C. Yao. On the security of public key protocols. In *Proceedings of IEEE 22nd Annual Symposium on Foundations of Computer Science*, pages 350–357, 1981.

[103] T. ElGamal. A public-key cryptosystem and a signature scheme based on discrete logarithms. *IEEE Transactions on Information Theory*, IT-31(4):469–472, July 1985.

[104] C. Ellison, B. Frantz, B. Lampson, R. Rivest, B. Thomas, and T. Ylonen. SPKI certificate theory. The Internet Engineering Task Force Request For Comments (IETF RFC) 2693, September 1999. Available at www.ietf.org/rfc/rfc2693.txt.

[105] eMarketer. Security online: Corporate & consumer protection, e-telligence for business. eMarketer Report, February 2003. Available at www.emarketer.com.

[106] A. Evans Jr., W. Kantrowitz, and E. Weiss. A user authentication scheme not requiring secrecy in the computer. *Communications of the ACM*, 17(8):437–442, 1974.

[107] U. Feige, A. Fiat, and A. Shamir. Zero-knowledge proofs of identity. *ACM Special Interest Group on Algorithms and Computation Theory (SIGACT)*, pages 210–217, 1987.

[108] H. Feistel. Cryptography and computer privacy. *Sci. Am.*, 228(5):15–23, May 1974.

[109] N. Ferguson and B. Schneier. A cryptographic evaluation of IPsec. Counterpane Labs, 2000. Available at www.counterpane.com/ipsec.pdf.

[110] A. Fiat and A. Shamir. How to prove yourself: practical solutions of identification and signature problems. In A.M. Odlyzko, editor, *Advances in Cryptology — Proceedings of CRYPTO'86, Lecture Notes in Computer Science 263*, pages 186–194. Springer-Verlag, 1987.

[111] Electronic Frontier Foundation. *Cracking DES: Secrets of Encryption Research, Wiretap Politics & Chip Design*. O'Reilly & Associates, May 1998. ISBN 1-56592-520-3.

[112] A.O. Freier, P. Karlton, and P.C. Kocher. The SSL Protocol, Version 3.0. INTERNET-DRAFT, draft-freier-ssl-version3-02.txt, November 1996.

[113] E. Fujisaki and T. Okamoto. Statistical zero knowledge protocols to prove modular polynomial relations. In B.S. Kaliski Jr., editor, *Advances in Cryptology — Proceedings of CRYPTO'97, Lecture Notes in Computer Science 1294*, pages 16–30. Springer-Verlag, 1997.

[114] E. Fujisaki and T. Okamoto. How to enhance the security of public-key encryption at minimum cost. In H. Imai and Y. Zheng, editors, *Public Key Cryptography — Proceedings of PKC'99, Lecture Notes in Computer Science 1560*, pages 53–68. Springer-Verlag, 1999.

[115] E. Fujisaki and T. Okamoto. Secure integration of asymmetric and symmetric encryption schemes. In M. Wiener, editor, *Advances in Cryptology — Proceedings of CRYPTO'99, Lecture Notes in Computer Science 1666*, pages 537–554. Springer-Verlag, 1999.

[116] E. Fujisaki, T. Okamoto, D. Pointcheval, and J. Stern. RSA-OAEP Is secure under the RSA assumption. In J. Killian, editor, *Advances in Cryptology — Proceedings of CRYPTO'01, Lecture Notes in Computer Science 2139*, pages 260–274. Springer-Verlag, 2001.

[117] K. Gaarder and E. Snekkenes. Applying a formal analysis technique to the CCITT X.509 strong two-way authentication protocol. *Journal of Cryptology*, 3(2):81–98, 1991.

[118] S. Galbraith. Supersingular curves in cryptography. In C. Boyd, editor, *Advances in Cryptology — Proceedings of ASIACRYPT'01, Lecture Notes in Computer Science 2248*, pages 495–513. Springer-Verlag, 2001.

[119] S.D. Galbraith, W. Mao, and K.G. Paterson. A cautionary note regarding cryptographic protocols based on composite integers. Technical Report HPL-2001-284, HP Laboratories, Bristol, November 2001.

[120] M.R. Garey and D.S. Johnson. *Computers and Intractability: A Guide to the Theory of NP-Completeness*. Freeman, San Francisco, 1979.

[121] C.F. Gauss. *Disquisitiones Arithmeticae*. Translated by A. Arthur and S.J. Clark, 1996, Yale University Press, New Haven, 1801.

[122] R. Gennaro, D. Miccianicio, and T. Rabin. An efficient non-interactive statistical zero-knowledge proof system for quasi-safe prime products. In *5th ACM Conference on Computer and Communications Security, Fairfax, Virginia*, 1998.

[123] M. Girault. An identity-based identification scheme based on discrete logarithms modulo a composite number. In I.B. Damgård, editor, *Advances in Cryptology — Proceedings of EUROCRYPT'90, Lecture Notes in Computer Science 473*, pages 481–486. Springer-Verlag, 1991.

[124] M. Girault. Self-certified public keys. In D.W. Davies, editor, *Advances in Cryptology — Proceedings of EUROCRYPT'91, Lecture Notes in Computer Science 547*, pages 490–497. Springer-Verlag, 1991.

[125] I. Goldberg and D. Wagner. Randomness and the Netscape browser, how secure is the World Wide Web? *Dr. Dobb's Journal*, pages 66–70, January 1996.

[126] O. Goldreich, S. Micali, and A. Wigderson. How to prove all NP statements in zero-knowledge and a methodology of cryptographic protocol design (extended abstract). In A.M. Odlyzko, editor, *Advances in Cryptology — Proceedings of CRYPTO'86, Lecture Notes in Computer Science 263*, pages 171–185. Springer-Verlag, 1987.

[127] S. Goldwasser and S. Micali. Probabilistic encryption. *Journal of Computer and System Sciences*, 28:270–299, 1984.

[128] S. Goldwasser, S. Micali, and C. Rackoff. The knowledge complexity of interactive proof-systems. In *Proceedings of 17th Ann. ACM Symp. on Theory of Computing*, pages 291–304, 1985. A journal version under the same title appears in: *SIAM Journal of Computing* vol. 18, pp. 186–208, 1989.

[129] S. Goldwasser, S. Micali, and R.L. Rivest. A digital signature scheme secure against adaptive chosen-message attacks. *SIAM Journal of Computing*, 17(2):281–308, 1988.

[130] S. Goldwasser, S. Micali, and P. Tong. Why and how to establish a private code on a public network. In *Proceedings of 23rd Annual IEEE Symposium on Foundations of Computer Science*, pages 134–144, 1982.

[131] D. Gollmann. *Computer Security*. John Wiley & Sons, Inc., 1999. ISBN: 0-471-97884-2.

[132] D. Gollmann. Authentication — myths and misconceptions. *Progress in Computer Science and Applied Logic*, 20:203–225, 2001. Birkhäuser Verlag Basel/Switzerland.

[133] L. Gong, R. Needham, and R. Yahalom. Reasoning about belief in cryptographic protocols. In *Proceedings of the 1990 IEEE Symposium on Research in Security and Privacy*, pages 234–248. IEEE Computer Society Press, 1990.

[134] F.T. Grampp and R.H. Morris. Unix operating system security. *AT&T Bell Laboratories Technical Journal*, 63(8):1649–1672, October 1984.

[135] C.G. Günther. An identity-based key-exchange protocol. In J.-J. Quisquater and J. Vanderwalle, editors, *Advances in Cryptology — Proceedings of EURO-CRYPT'89, Lecture Notes in Computer Science 434*, pages 29–37. Springer-Verlag, 1990.

[136] N.M. Haller. The S/KEY one-time password system. In *Proceedings of the Symposium on Network and Distributed System Security*, pages 151–157, 1994.

[137] D. Harkins and D. Carrel. The Internet key exchange protocol (IKE). The Internet Engineering Task Force Request For Comments (IETF RFC) 2409, November 1998. Available at www.ietf.org/rfc/rfc2409.txt.

[138] K.E.B. Hickman. The SSL Protocol. Online document, Feburary 1995. Available at www.netscape.com/eng/security/SSL_2.html.

[139] C.A.R. Hoare. Communicating sequential processes. *Communications of the ACM*, 21(8), 1978.

[140] C.A.R. Hoare. *Communicating Sequential Processes*. Prentice-Hall International, 1985. Series in Computer Science.

[141] P. Hoffman. Features of proposed successors to IKE. INTERNET-DRAFT, draft-ietf-ipsec-soi-features-01.txt, May 2002.

[142] R. Housley and P. Hoffman. Internet X.509 Public Key Infrastructure Operational Protocols: FTP and HTTP. The Internet Engineering Task Force Request For Comments (IETF RFC) 2585, August 2001. Available at www.ietf.org/rfc/rfc2585.txt.

[143] D. Hühnlein, M. Jakobsson, and D. Weber. Towards practical non-interactive public key cryptosystems using non-maximal imaginary quadratic orders. In *Prodeedings of Selected Areas of Cryptography — SAC 2000, Lecture Notes in Computer Science 2012*, pages 275–287. Springer-Verlag, 2000.

[144] ISO/IEC. Information Processing — Modes of operation for an $n$-bit block cipher algorithm. International Organization for Standardization and International Electro-technical Commission, 1991. 10116.

[145] ISO/IEC. Information Technology — Security Techniques — summary of voting on letter ballot No.6, Document SC27 N277, CD 9798-3.3 "Entity Authentication Mechanisms" — Part 3: Entity authentication mechanisms using a public key algorithm. International Organization for Standardization and International Electro-technical Commission, October 1991. ISO/IEC JTC 1/SC27 N313.

[146] ISO/IEC. Information Technology — Security Techniques — Entity Authentication Mechanisms — Part 2: Entity authentication using symmetric techniques. International Organization for Standardization and International Electro-technical Commission, 1992. ISO/IEC JTC 1/SC 27 N489 CD 9798-2, 1992-06-09.

[147] ISO/IEC. Information Technology — Security Techniques — Entity Authentication Mechanisms — Part 2: Entity authentication using symmetric techniques. International Organization for Standardization and International Electro-technical Commission, 1993. ISO/IEC JTC 1/SC 27 N739 DIS 9798-2, 1993-08-13.

[148] ISO/IEC. Information Technology — Security Techniques — Entity Authentication — Part 1: General. International Organization for Standardization and International Electro-technical Commission, 1996. ISO/IEC JTC 1/SC 27 DIS 9798-1: 1996 (E).

[149] ISO/IEC. Information Technology — Security Techniques — Entity Authentication — Part 2: Mechanisms using symmetric encipherment algorithms. International Organization for Standardization and International Electro-technical Commission, December 1998. ISO/IEC JTC 1/SC 27 N2145 FDIS 9798-2.

[150] ISO/IEC. Information Technology — Security Techniques — Entity Authentication — Part 3: Mechanisms using digital signature techniques. International Organization for Standardization and International Electro-technical Commission, October 1998. BS ISO/IEC 9798-3.

[151] ISO/IEC. Information Technology — Security Techniques — Entity Authentication — Part 4: Mechanisms using a cryptographic check function. International Organization for Standardization and International Electro-technical Commission, April 1999. ISO/IEC JTC 1/SC 27 N2289 FDIS 9798-4.

[152] ISO/IEC. Information technology — Security techniques — Digital signature schemes giving message recovery — Part 3: Discrete logarithm based mechanisms. International Organization for Standardization and International Electro-technical Commission, April 2000. ISO/IEC JTC 1/SC 27 9796-3.

[153] ISO/IEC. Information Technology — Security Techniques — Hash Functions — Part 3: Dedicated hash-functions. International Organization for Standardization and International Electro-technical Commission, November 2001. ISO/IEC JTC1, SC27, WG2, Document 1st CD 10118-3.

[154] ITU-T. Rec. X.509 (revised) the Directory — Authentication Framework, 1993. International Telecommunication Union, Geneva, Switzerland (equivalent to ISO/IEC 9594-8:1995.).

[155] M. Jakobsson, K. Sako, and R. Impagliazzo. Designated verifier proofs and their applications. In U. Maurer, editor, *Advances in Cryptology — Proceedings of EUROCRYPT'96, Lecture Notes in Computer Science 1070*, pages 143–154. Springer-Verlag, 1996.

[156] A. Joux. A one round protocol for tripartite Diffie-Hellman. In W. Bosma, editor, *Algorithmic Number Theory, IV-th Symposium (ANTS IV), Lecture Notes in Computer Science 1838*, pages 385–394. Springer-Verlag, 2000.

[157] A. Joux and K. Nguyen. Separating decision Diffie-Hellman from Diffie-Hellman in cryptographic groups. Cryptology ePrint Archive, 2001/003, 2001. Available at http:/eprint.iacr.org/.

[158] R. Kailar. Accountability in electronic commerce protocols. *IEEE Transactions on Sortware Engineering*, 22(5):313–328, May 1996.

[159] C. Kaufman. Comparison of IKEv2, JFK, and SOI requirements. The Internet Engineering Task Force: online document, April 2002. Available at www.ietf.org/proceedings/02mar/slides/ipsec-1/.

[160] C. Kaufman. Internet Key Exchange (IKEv2) Protocol. The Internet Engineering Task Force: INTERNET-DRAFT, draft-ietf-ipsec-ikev2-03.txt, October 2002. Available at www.ietf.org/internet-drafts/draft-ietf-ipsec-ikev2-03.txt.

[161] C. Kaufman, R. Perlman, and M. Speciner. *Network Security: Private Communication in a Public World, Second Edition*. Prentice-Hall PTR, 2002.

[162] R. Kemmerer, C. Meadows, and J. Millen. Three systems for cryptographic protocol analysis. *Journal of Cryptology*, 7(2):79–130, 1994.

[163] S. Kent and R. Atkinson. IP Authentication Header. The Internet Engineering Task Force Request For Comments (IETF RFC) 2402, November 1998. Available at www.ietf.org/rfc/rfc2402.txt.

[164] S. Kent and R. Atkinson. IP Encapsulating Security Payload (ESP). The Internet Engineering Task Force Request For Comments (IETF RFC) 2406, November 1998. Available at www.ietf.org/rfc/rfc2406.txt.

[165] S. Kent and R. Atkinson. Security Architecture for the Internet Protocol. The Internet Engineering Task Force Request For Comments (IETF RFC) 2401, November 1998. Available at www.ietf.org/rfc/rfc2401.txt.

[166] J. Klensin. Simple mail transfer protocol. The Internet Engineering Task Force Request For Comments (IETF RFC) 2821, April 2001. Available at www.ietf.org/rfc/rfc2821.txt.

[167] L.R. Knudsen. *Block Ciphers — Analysis, Design and Applications*. Århus University, 1994.

[168] N. Koblitz. Elliptic curve cryptosystems. *Math. Comp.*, 48(5):203–209, 1987.

[169] P.C. Kocher. Timing attacks on implementations of Diffie-Hellman, RSA, DSS, and other systems. In N. Koblitz, editor, *Advances in Cryptology — Proceedings of CRYPTO'96, Lecture Notes in Computer Science 1109*, pages 104–113. Springer-Verlag, 1996.

[170] J. Kohl and C. Neuman. The Kerberos network authentication service (v5). The Internet Engineering Task Force Request For Comments (IETF RFC) 1510, September 1993. Available at www.ietf.org/rfc/rfc1510.txt.

[171] L.M. Kohnfelder. *Towards a Practical Public-key Cryptosystem*. MIT B.S. Thesis, MIT Department of Electrical Engineering, May 1978.

[172] E. Kranakis. *Primality and Cryptography*. John Wiley & Sons, 1986. Wiley-Teubner Series in Computer Science.

[173] H. Krawczyk. SIGMA: the 'SIGn-and-MAc' approach to authenticated Diffie-Hellman protocols. Online document, 1996. Available at www.ee.technion.ac.il/~hugo/sigma.html.

[174] H. Krawczyk. SKEME: a versatile secure key exchange mechanism for Internet. In *Proceedings of Network and Distributed System Security Symposium (NDSS)*, pages 114–127. IEEE Computer Society Press, February 1996.

[175] L. Lamport. Constructing digital signatures from a one way function. SIR International, October 1979. Available at www.csl.sri.com/papers/676/.

[176] L. Lamport. Password authentication with insecure communication. *Communications of the ACM*, 24(11):770–772, 1981.

[177] A. Lenstra and E. Verheul. The XTR public key system. In M. Bellare, editor, *Advances in Cryptology — Proceedings of CRYPTO'00, Lecture Notes in Computer Science 1880*, pages 1–19. Springer-Verlag, 2000.

[178] W.J. LeVeque. *Fundamentals of Number Theorey.* Dover Publications, Inc., 1977.

[179] R. Lidl and H. Niederpeiter. *Finite Fields.* Cambridge University Press, 1997. Encyclopedia of Mathematics and its Applications 20.

[180] R.J. Lipton. How to cheat at mental poker. Technical Report, Comp. Sci., Dept. Univ. of Calif., Berkeley, Calif., August 1979. (This is an internal technical report; a simple description of the attack is available in page 174 of [92]).

[181] G. Lowe. Some new attacks upon security protocols. In *Proceedings of the 9th IEEE Computer Security Foundations Workshop*, pages 162–169. IEEE Computer Society Press, June 1994.

[182] G. Lowe. An attack on the Needham-Schroeder public-key authentication protocol. *Information Processing Letters*, 56(3):131–133, 1995.

[183] G. Lowe. Breaking and fixing the Needham-Schroeder public-key protocol using CSP and FDR. In *Procdings of TACAS, Lecture Notes in Computer Science 1055*, pages 147–166. Springer-Verlag, 1996.

[184] J. Malone-Lee and W. Mao. Two birds one stone: Signcryption using RSA. In M. Joye, editor, *Topics in Cryptology — the Cryptographers' Track, Proceedings of the RSA Conference 2003 (CT-RSA 2003), Lecture Notes in Computer Science 2612*, pages 210–224. Springer-Verlag, April 2003.

[185] W. Mao. An augmentation of BAN-like logics. In *Proceedings of Computer Security Foundations Workshop VIII*, pages 44–56. IEEE Computer Society Press, June 1995.

[186] W. Mao and C. Boyd. On the use of encryption in cryptographic protocols. In P.G. Farrell, editor, *Codes and Cyphers — Proceedings of 4th IMA Conference on Cryptography and Coding*, pages 251–262, December 1993. The Institute of Mathematics and Its Applications, 1995.

[187] W. Mao and C. Boyd. On the use of encryption in cryptographic protocols, February 1994. Distributed by International Organization for Standardization (ISO) and International Electro-technical Commission (IEC) JTC1, SC27, WG2, Document N262: "Papers on authentication and key management protocols based on symmetric techniques." This ISO document distributes the paper published in [186].

[188] W. Mao and C. Boyd. Methodical use of cryptographic transformations in authentication protocols. *IEE Proceedings, Comput. Digit. Tech.*, 142(4):272–278, July 1995.

[189] D. Maughan, M. Schertler, M. Schneider, and J. Turner. Internet security association and key management protocol (ISAKMP), version 10. INTERNET-DRAFT: draft-ietf-ipsec-isakmp-10.txt, November 1998. Also available at www.ietf.org/rfc/rfc2408.txt.

[190] U. Maurer. Protocols for secret key agreement by public discussion based on common information. In E.F. Brickell, editor, *Advances in Cryptology — Proceedings of CRYPTO'92, Lecture Notes in Computer Science 740*, pages 461–470. Springer-Verlag, 1993.

[191] U. Maurer. Secret key agreement by public discussion from common information. *IEEE Transactions on Information Theory*, IT-39:733–742, 1993.

[192] U. Maurer and S. Wolf. The relationship between breaking the Diffie-Hellman protocol and computing discrete logairhms. *SIAM Journal of Computing*, 28(5):1689–1721, 1999.

[193] U. Maurer and Y. Yacobi. Non-interactive public-key cryptography. In D.W. Davies, editor, *Advances in Cryptology — Proceedings of EUROCRYPT'91, Lecture Notes in Computer Science 547*, pages 498–507. Springer-Verlag, 1991.

[194] C. Meadows. Applying formal methods to the analysis of a key management protocol. *Journal of Computer Security*, 1(1):5–53, 1992.

[195] C. Meadows. Analyzing the Needham-Schroeder public key protocol: a comparison of two approaches. In E. Bertino et al, editor, *Proceedings of Computer Security, ESORICS'96, Lecture Notes in Computer Science 1146*, pages 351–364. Springer-Verlag, February 1996.

[196] C. Meadows. The NRL Protocol Analyzer: an overview. *Journal of Logic Programming*, 26(2):113–131, February 1996.

[197] C. Meadows. Analysis of the internet key exchange protocol using the NRL Protocol Analyzer. In *Proceedings of IEEE Symposium on Security and Privacy*, pages 216–231. IEEE Computer Society Press, May 1999.

[198] C. Meadows and P. Syverson. A formal specification of requirements for payment transactions in the SET protocol. In R. Hirschfeld, editor, *Proceedings of Financial Cryptography (FC'98), Lecture Notes in Computer Science 1465*, pages 122–140. Springer-Verlag, February 1998.

[199] A.J. Menezes, T. Okamoto, and S.A. Vanstone. Reducing elliptic curve logarithms to a finite field. *IEEE Trans. Info. Theory*, 39:1636–1646, 1983.

[200] A.J. Menezes, P.C. van Oorschot, and S.A. Vanstone. *Handbook of Applied Cryptography*. CRC Press, 1997.

[201] R.C. Merkle. Secure communications over insecure channels. *Communications of the ACM*, 21:294–299, 1978.

[202] R.C. Merkle and M.E. Hellman. Hiding information and signatures in trapdoor knapsacks. *IEEE Trans. on Info. Theory*, 24:525–530, 1978.

[203] S. Micali and R.L. Rivest. Micropayments revisited. In B. Preneel, editor, *Topics in Cryptology — the Cryptographers' Track, Proceedings of the RSA Conference 2002 (CT-RSA 2002), Lecture Notes in Computer Science 2271*, pages 149–163. Springer-Verlag, 2002.

[204] S.P. Miller, C. Neuman, J.I. Schiller, and J.H. Saltzer. Kerberos authentication and authorization system. Project Athena Technical Plan Section E.2.1, 1987.

[205] V. Miller. Use of elliptic curves in cryptography. In H.C. Williams, editor, *Advances in Cryptology — Proceedings of CRYPTO'85, Lecture Notes in Computer Science 218*, pages 417–426. Springer-Verlag, 1986.

[206] J.H. Moore. Protocol failures in cryptosystems. *Proceedings of the IEEE*, 76(5):594–601, 1988.

[207] J.H. Moore. Protocol failures in cryptosystems. In G.J. Simmons, editor, *Contemporary Cryptology, the Science of Information Integrity*, pages 541–558. IEEE Press, 1992.

[208] R. Morris and K. Thompson. Password security: a case history. *Communications of the ACM*, 22(5):594–597, 1979.

[209] M. Myers, R. Ankney, A. Malpani, S. Galperin, and C. Adams. X.509 Internet Public Key Infrastructure Online Certificate Status Protocol - OCSP. The Internet Engineering Task Force Request For Comments (IETF RFC) 2560, June 1999. Available at www.ietf.org/rfc/rfc2560.txt.

[210] M. Myers, X. Liu, J. Schaad, and J. Weinstein. Certificate Management Messages over CMS. The Internet Engineering Task Force Request For Comments (IETF RFC) 2797, April 2000. Available at www.ietf.org/rfc/rfc2797.txt.

[211] M. Naor and O. Reingold. Number theoretic constructions of efficient pseudo-random functions. In *Proceedings of FOCS'97*, pages 458–467, 1997.

[212] M. Naor and M. Yung. Public-key cryptosystems provably secure against chosen ciphertext attacks. In *Proceedings of 22nd ACM Symposium of Theory of Computing*, pages 427–437, 1990.

[213] NBS. Data Encryption Standard. U.S. Department of Commerce, FIPS Publication 46, Washington, D.C., January 1977. National Bureau of Standards.

[214] R. Needham and M. Schroeder. Authentication revisited. *Operating Systems Review*, 21:7, 1987.

[215] R.M. Needham and M.D. Schroeder. Using encryption for authentication in large networks of computers. *Communications of the ACM*, 21(12):993–999, 1978.

[216] B.C. Neuman and S.G. Stubblebine. A note on the use of timestamps as nonces. *ACM Operating Systems Review*, 27(2):10–14, April 1993.

[217] NIST. A Proposed Federal Information Processing Standard for Digital Signature Standard (DSS). Federal Register Announcement August 30, 1991. National Institute of Standards and Technology.

[218] NIST. Digital Signature Standard. Federal Information Processing Standards Publication 186, 1994. U.S. Department of Commerce/N.I.S.T.

[219] NIST. Secure Hash Standard. Federal Information Processing Standards Publication (FIPS PUB) 180-1, April 1995. U.S. Department of Commerce/N.I.S.T.

[220] NIST. Recommendation for block cipher modes of operation. NIST Special Publication 800-38A 2001 Edition, December 2001. U.S. Department of Commerce/N.I.S.T.

[221] NIST. Specification for the Advanced Encryption Standard (AES). Federal Information Processing Standards Publication (FIPS PUB) 197, November 2001. U.S. Department of Commerce/N.I.S.T.

[222] K. Nyberg and R. Rueppel. A new signature scheme based on the DSA giving message recovery. In *1st ACM Conference on Computer and Communications Security*, pages 58–61. ACM Press, 1993.

[223] A.M. Odlyzko. Discrete logarithms: the past and the future. *Designs, Codes and Cryptography*, 19:129–154, 2000.

[224] K. Ohta and T. Okamoto. On concrete security treatment of signatures derived from identification. In H. Krawczyk, editor, *Advances in Cryptology — Proceedings of CRYPTO'98, Lecture Notes in Computer Science 1462*, pages 345–370. Springer-Verlag, 1998.

[225] T. Okamoto and D. Pointcheval. REACT: rapid enhanced-security asymmetric cryptosystem transform. In D. Naccache, editor, *Topics in Cryptography, Cryptographers' Track, RSA Conference 2001 — Proceedings of CT-RSA'00, Lecture Notes in Computer Science 2020*, pages 159–175. Springer-Verlag, 2001.

[226] T. Okamoto and S. Uchiyama. A new public-key cryptosystem as secure as factoring. In K. Nyberg, editor, *Advances in Cryptology — Proceedings of EUROCRYPT'98, Lecture Notes in Computer Science 1403*, pages 308–318. Springer-Verlag, 1998.

[227] H. Orman. The Oakley key determination protocol, version 2. draft-ietf-ipsec-oakley-02.txt, 1996.

[228] D. Otway and O. Rees. Efficient and timely mutual authentication. *Operating Systems Review*, 21(1):8–10, 1987.

[229] Oxford. *Oxford Reference, Dictionary of Computing, Third Edition.* Oxford University Press, 1991.

[230] P. Paillier. Public-key cryptosystems based on composite degree residuosity classes. In J. Stern, editor, *Advances in Cryptology — Proceedings of EURO-CRYPT'99, Lecture Notes in Computer Science 1592*, pages 223–238. Springer-Verlag, 1999.

[231] J. Patarin and L. Goubin. Trapdoor one-way permutations and multivariate polynomials. In Y. Han, T. Okamoto, and S. Qing, editors, *Information and Communications Security — Proceedings of ICICS'97, Lecture Notes in Computer Science 1334*, pages 356–368. Springer-Verlag, 1997.

[232] PKCS. Public Key Cryptography Standards, PKCS#1 v2.1. RSA Cryptography Standard, Draft 2, 2001. Available at www.rsasecurity.com/rsalabs/pkcs/.

[233] S.C. Pohlig and M.E. Hellman. An improved algorithm for computing logarithms over $GF(p)$ and its cryptographic significance. *IEEE Transactions on Information Theory*, 24:106–110, 1978.

[234] D. Pointcheval. HD-RSA: hybrid dependent RSA, a new public-key encryption scheme. Submission to IEEE P1363: Asymmetric Encryption, 1999. Available at grouper.ieee.org/groups/1363/P1363a/Encryption.html.

[235] D. Pointcheval. Public-key cryptosystems based on composite degree residuosity classes. In J. Stern, editor, *Advances in Cryptology — Proceedings of EUROCRYPT'99, Lecture Notes in Computer Science 1592*, pages 239–254. Springer-Verlag, 1999.

[236] D. Pointcheval. Chosen-ciphertext security for any one-way cryptosystem. In H. Imai and Y. Zheng, editors, *Public Key Cryptography — Proceedings of PKC'00, Lecture Notes in Computer Science 1751*, pages 129–146. Springer-Verlag, 2000.

[237] D. Pointcheval and J. Stern. Security proofs for signature schemes. In U. Maurer, editor, *Advances in Cryptology — Proceedings of EUROCRYPT'96, Lecture Notes in Computer Science 1070*, pages 387–398. Springer-Verlag, 1996.

[238] D. Pointcheval and J. Stern. Security arguments for digital signatures and blind signatures. *Journal of Cryptology*, 13(3):361–396, 2000.

[239] J.M. Pollard. Theorems on factorization and primality testing. *Proceedings of the Cambridge Philosophical Society*, 76:521–528, 1974.

[240] J.M. Pollard. Monte Carlo method for index computation (mod $p$). *Mathematics of Computation*, 32(143):918–924, 1978.

[241] M. Rabin. Transaction protection by beacons. Technical Report Tech.Rep. 29-81, Aiken Computation Lab., Harvard University, Cambridge, MA, 1981.

[242] M.O. Rabin. Digitized signatures and public-key functions as intractible as factorization. Technical Report LCS/TR-212, MIT Laboratory for Computer Science, 1979.

[243] C. Rackoff and D. Simon. Non-interactive zero-knowledge proof of knowledge and chosen ciphertext attack. In J. Feigenbaum, editor, *Advances in Cryptology — Proceedings of CRYPTO'91, Lecture Notes in Computer Science 576*, pages 433–444. Springer-Verlag, 1992.

[244] R. Rivest and A. Shamir. PayWord and MicroMint: two simple micropayment schemes. *CryptoBytes, RSA Laboratories*, 2(1):7–11, Spring 1996.

[245] R.L. Rivest. The MD5 message-digest algorithm. Internet Request for Comments 1321, April 1992.

[246] R.L. Rivest. S-expressions. INTERNET-DRAFT, May 1997. Available at `theory.lcs.mit.edu/~rivest/sexp.txt`.

[247] R.L. Rivest and B. Lampson. SDSI - A simple distributed security infrastructure. Invited Speech at CRYPTO'96, August 1996. Available at `theory.lcs.mit.edu/~cis/sdsi.html`.

[248] R.L. Rivest, A. Shamir, and L. Adleman. A method for obtaining digital signatures and public-key cryptosystems. *Communications of the ACM*, 21(2):120–126, 1978.

[249] R. Sidney R.L. Rivest, M.J.B. Robshaw and Y.L. Yin. The RC6 Block Cipher, v1.1. AES proposal: National Institute of Standards and Technology (NIST), 1998. Available at `www.rsa.com/rsalabs/aes/`.

[250] A.W. Roscoe. Model checking CSP. In A.W. Roscoe, editor, *A Classical Mind: Essays in honour of C.A.R. Hoare*. Prentice-Hall, 1994.

[251] A.W. Roscoe. Modelling and verifying key-exchange protocols using CSP and FDR. In *Proceedings of Computer Security Foundations Workshop VIII*, pages 98–107. IEEE Computer Society Press, June 1995.

[252] P. Ryan and S. Schneider. *The Modelling and Analysis of Security Protocols: the CSP Approach*. Addison-Wesley, 2001.

[253] R. Sakai, K. Ohgishi, and M. Kasahara. Cryptosystems based on pairing. In *Proceedings of the 2000 Symposium on Cryptography and Information Security, Okinawa, Japan*, January 2000.

[254] T. Satoh and K. Araki. Fermat quotients and the polynomial time discrete log algorithm for anomalous elliptic curves. *Comm. Math. Univ. Sancti. Pauli*, 47:81–92, Spring 1998.

[255] S. Schneider. Security properties and CSP. In *Proceedings of the 1996 IEEE Symposium in Security and Privacy*, pages 174–187. IEEE Computer Society Press, 1996.

[256] B. Schneier. *Secrets and Lies*. John Wiley & Sons, 2001.

[257] B. Schneier, J. Kelsey, D. Whiting, D. Wagner, C. Hall, and N. Ferguson. Twofish: a 128-bit block cipher, AES proposal. AES proposal: National Institute of Standards and Technology (NIST), 1998. Available at `www.counterpane.com/twofish.html`.

[258] C.P. Schnorr. Efficient identification and signature for smart cards. In G. Brassard, editor, *Advances in Cryptology — Proceedings of CRYPTO'89, Lecture Notes in Computer Science 435*, pages 239–252. Springer-Verlag, 1990.

[259] C.P. Schnorr. Efficient signature generation for smart cards. *Journal of Cryptology*, 4(3):161–174, 1991.

[260] L.A. Semaev. Evaluation of discrete logarithms in a group of $p$-torsion points of an elliptic curve in characteristic $p$. *Math. Comp.*, 67(221):353–356, 1998.

[261] SET. Secure Electronic Transaction Specification, Version 1.0. Online document, May 1997. Available at `www.setco.org/`.

[262] A. Shamir. Identity-based cryptosystems and signature schemes. In G.T. Blakley and D. Chaum, editors, *Advances in Cryptology — Proceedings of CRYPTO'84, Lecture Notes in Computer Science 196*, pages 48–53. Springer-Verlag, 1985.

[263] A. Shamir, R. Rivest, and L. Adleman. Mental poker. In D. Klarner, editor, *The Mathematical Gardner*, pages 37–43, Boston, Mass, 1980. Prindle, Weber & Schmidt.

[264] C.E. Shannon. A mathematical theory of communication. *Bell Systems Technical Journal*, 27(3):379–423, July 1948.

[265] C.E. Shannon. A mathematical theory of communication. *Bell Systems Technical Journal*, 27:623–656, October 1948. Continued from July 1948 issue (i.e., [264]).

[266] C.E. Shannon. Communications theory of secrecy systems. *Bell Systems Technical Journal*, 28:656–715, October 1949.

[267] C.E. Shannon. Predilection and entropy of printed English. *Bell Systems Technical Journal*, 30:50–64, January 1951.

[268] R. Shirey. Internet Security Glossary. The Internet Engineering Task Force Request For Comments (IETF RFC) 2828, May 2000. Available at `www.ietf.org/rfc/rfc2828.txt`.

[269] P.W. Shor. Polynomial-time algorithm for prime factorization and discrete logarithms on a quantum computer. *SIAM Journal of Computing*, 26:1484–1509, 1997.

[270] P.W. Shor. Why haven't more quantum algorithms been found? *Journal of the ACM*, 50(1):87–90, January 2003.

[271] V. Shoup. Using hash functions as a hedge against chosen ciphertext attack. In B. Preneel, editor, *Advances in Cryptology — Proceedings of EUROCRYPT'00, Lecture Notes in Computer Science 1807*, pages 275–288. Springer-Verlag, 2000.

[272] V. Shoup. OAEP reconsidered. In J. Killian, editor, *Advances in Cryptology — Proceedings of CRYPTO'01, Lecture Notes in Computer Science 2139*, pages 239–259. Springer-Verlag, 2001.

[273] V. Shoup. A proposal for an ISO standard for public key encryption (version 2.1). Distributed by International Organization for Standardization (ISO) and International Electro-technical Commission (IEC) JTC1, SC27, WG2, December 2001. An earlier version appeared in ISO/IEC JTC 1/SC 27 N2765 "Editor's contribution on public key encryption" (February 2001).

[274] J.H. Silverman. *The Arithmetic of Elliptic Curves*. Sprinber-Verlag, 1986. Graduate Texts in Mathematics.

[275] R.D. Silverman. Fast generation of random, strong RSA primes. *CryptoBytes*, 3(1):9–13, 1997.

[276] G.J. Simmons. How to (selectively) broadcast a secret. In *Proceedings of the IEEE Symposium on Security and Privacy*, pages 108–113. IEEE Computer Society Press, 1985.

[277] G.J. Simmons. A survey of information authentication. In G.J. Simmons, editor, *Contemporary Cryptology, the Science of Information Integrity*, pages 379–419. IEEE Press, 1992.

[278] D. Simon. On the power of quantum computation. In *Proceedings of the 35th Annual IEEE Symposium on Foundations of Computer Science*, pages 116–123, 1994.

[279] S. Singh. *The Code Book*. Fourth Estate, 1999.

[280] N.P. Smart. The discrete logarithm problem on elliptic curves of trace one. *Journal of Cryptology*, 12:193–196, 1999.

[281] M.E. Smid and D.K. Branstad. The Data Encryption Standard, past and future. In G.J. Simmons, editor, *Contemporary Cryptology, the Science of Information Integrity*, pages 43–46. IEEE Press, 1992.

[282] D. Soldera. SEG - a provably secure variant of El-Gamal. Technical Report HPL-2001-149, Hewlett-Packard Laboratories, Bristol, June 2001.

[283] D. Soldera, J. Seberry, and C. Qu. The analysis of Zheng-Seberry scheme. In L. M. Batten and J. Seberry, editors, *7th Australian Conference in Information Security and Privacy — Proceedings of ACISP'02, Lecture Notes in Computer Science 2384*, pages 159–168. Springer-Verlag, 2002.

[284] R. Solovay and V. Strassen. A fast Monte-Carlo test for primality. *SIAM Journal of Computing*, 6(1):84–85, March 1977.

[285] M. Stadler. Publicly verifiable secret sharing. In U. Maurer, editor, *Advances in Cryptology — Proceedings of EUROCRYPT'96, Lecture Notes in Computer Science 1070*, pages 190–199. Springer-Verlag, 1996.

[286] D.R. Stinson. *Cryptography: Theory and Practice*. CRC Press, Inc., 1995.

[287] P. Syverson. On key distribution protocols for repeated authentication. *ACM Operating Systems Review*, 27(4):24–30, October 1993.

[288] P. Syverson and P.C. van Oorschot. On unifying some cryptographic protocol logics. In *Proceedings of 1994 IEEE Symposium on Security and Privacy*. IEEE Computer Society Press, 1994.

[289] H. Tanaka. A realization scheme for the identity-based cryptosystem. In C. Pomerance, editor, *Advances in Cryptology — Proceedings of CRYPTO'87, Lecture Notes in Computer Science 293*, pages 340–349. Springer-Verlag, 1988.

[290] G. Trudik. Message authentication with one-way functions. *Computer Communication Review*, 22:29–38, 1992.

[291] S. Tsuji and T. Itoh. An ID-based cryptosystem based on the discrete logarithm problem. *IEEE Journal on Selected Areas in Communication*, 7(4):467–473, 1989.

[292] W. Tuchman. Hellman presents no shortcut solutions to the DES. *IEEE Spectrum*, 16(7):40–41, 1979.

[293] G. van de Graaf and R. Peralta. A simple and secure way to show the validity of your public key. In C. Pomerance, editor, *Advances in Cryptology — Proceedings of CRYPTO'87, Lecture Notes in Computer Science 293*, pages 128–134. Springer-Verlag, 1988.

[294] P.C. van Oorschot. Extending cryptographic logics of belief to key agreement protocols (extended abstract). In *Proceedings of the First ACM Conference on Computer and Communications Security*, pages 232–243, 1993.

[295] V. Varadharajan, P. Allen, and S. Black. An analysis of the proxy problem in distributed systems. In *Proceedings of the 1991 IEEE Symposium on Security and Privacy*, pages 255–275, 1991.

[296] S. Vaudenay. Security flaws induced by CBC padding – Applications to SSL, IPSEC, WTLS .... In L.R. Knudsen, editor, *Advances in Cryptology — Proceedings of EUROCRYPT'02, Lecture Notes in Computer Science 2332*, pages 534–545. Springer-Verlag, 2002.

[297] U. Vazirani and V. Vazirani. Efficient and secure pseudo-random number generation (extended abstract). In G.T. Blakley and D. Chaum, editors, *Advances in Cryptology — Proceedings of CRYPTO'84, Lecture Notes in Computer Science 196*, pages 193–202. Springer-Verlag, 1985.

[298] E. R. Verheul. Evidence that XTR is more secure than supersingular elliptic curve cryptosystems. In B. Pfitzmann, editor, *Advances in Cryptology — Proceedings of EUROCRYPT'01, Lecture Notes in Computer Science 2045*, pages 195–210. Springer-Verlag, 2001.

[299] D. Wheeler. Transactions using bets. In M. Lomas, editor, *Security Protocols, Lecture Notes in Computer Science 1189*, pages 89–92. Springer-Verlag, 1996.

[300] M. Wiener. Cryptanalysis of short RSA secret exponents. *IEEE Transactions on Information Theory*, 36(3):553–558, 1990.

[301] M. Wiener. Efficient DES key search. Technical report, TR-244, School of Computer Science, Carleton University, Ottawa, May 1994.

[302] C.P. Williams and S.H. Clearwater. *Ultimate Zero and One*. Copernicus, Springer-Verlag New York, Inc., 2000.

[303] T.Y.C. Woo and S.S. Lam. Authentication for distributed systems. *Computer*, 25(1):39–52, January 1992.

[304] T.Y.C. Woo and S.S. Lam. A lesson on authentication protocol design. *Operating Systems Review*, 28(3):24–37, July 1994.

[305] A.C. Yao. Theory and applications of trapdoor functions (extended abstract). In *Proceedings of 23rd Annual IEEE Symposium on Foundations of Computer Science*, pages 80–91, 1982.

[306] T. Ylonen. The SSH (secure shell) remote login protocol. INTERNET-DRAFT, draft-ylonen-ssh-protocol-00.txt, September 1995.

[307] T. Ylonen. SSH authentication protocol. INTERNET-DRAFT, draft-ietf-userauth-16.txt, September 2002.

[308] T. Ylonen. SSH connection protocol. INTERNET-DRAFT, draft-ietf-connect-16.txt, September 2002.

[309] T. Ylonen. SSH protocol architecture. INTERNET-DRAFT, draft-ietf-architecture-13.txt, September 2002.

[310] T. Ylonen. SSH transport layer protocol. INTERNET-DRAFT, draft-ietf-transport-15.txt, September 2002.

[311] Y. Zheng. Digital signcryption or how to achieve cost(signature & encryption) cost(signature) + cost(encryption). In B.S. Kaliski Jr., editor, *Advances in Cryptology — Proceedings of CRYPTO'97, Lecture Notes in Computer Science 1294*, pages 165–179. Springer-Verlag, 1997.

[312] Y. Zheng and J. Seberry. Immunizing public key cryptosystems against chosen ciphertext attacks. *Special Issue on Secure Communications, IEEE Journal on Selected Areas on Communications*, 11(5):715–724, June 1993.

[313] Y. Zheng and J. Seberry. Practical approaches to attaining security against adaptively chosen ciphertext attacks (extended abstract). In E.F. Brickell, editor, *Advances in Cryptology — Proceedings of CRYPTO'92, Lecture Notes in Computer Science 740*, pages 291–304. Springer-Verlag, 1993.

[314] P.R. Zimmermann. *The Official PGP User's Guide*. MIT Press, Cambridge, Massachusetts, 1995. Second printing.

# SUBJECT INDEX

http://www.phptr.com/

Prentice Hall PTR   InformIT   InformIT Online Books   Financial Times Prentice Hall   ft.com   PTG Interactive   Reuters

TOMORROW'S SOLUTIONS FOR TODAY'S PROFESSIONALS

Prentice Hall **Professional Technical Reference**

| Browse | Book Series | What's New | User Groups | Alliances | Special Sales | Contact Us |

Search | Help | Home

Quick Search

**PTR Favorites**

Find a Bookstore

Book Series

Special Interests

Newsletters

Press Room

International

Best Sellers

Solutions Beyond the Book

Shopping Bag

*Keep Up to Date with*

# PH PTR Online

We strive to stay on the cutting edge of what's happening in professional computer science and engineering. Here's a bit of what you'll find when you stop by **www.phptr.com**:

**What's new at PHPTR?** We don't just publish books for the professional community, we're a part of it. Check out our convention schedule, keep up with your favorite authors, and get the latest reviews and press releases on topics of interest to you.

**Special interest areas** offering our latest books, book series, features of the month, related links, and other useful information to help you get the job done.

**User Groups** Prentice Hall Professional Technical Reference's User Group Program helps volunteer, not-for-profit user groups provide their members with training and information about cutting-edge technology.

**Companion Websites** Our Companion Websites provide valuable solutions beyond the book. Here you can download the source code, get updates and corrections, chat with other users and the author about the book, or discover links to other websites on this topic.

**Need to find a bookstore?** Chances are, there's a bookseller near you that carries a broad selection of PTR titles. Locate a Magnet bookstore near you at www.phptr.com.

**Subscribe today! Join PHPTR's monthly email newsletter!** Want to be kept up-to-date on your area of interest? Choose a targeted category on our website, and we'll keep you informed of the latest PHPTR products, author events, reviews and conferences in your interest area.

Visit our mailroom to subscribe today! **http://www.phptr.com/mail_lists**